Microsoft

Integrating PHP with Windows®

Arno Hollosi

Published with the authorization of Microsoft Corporation by:
O'Reilly Media, Inc.
1005 Gravenstein Highway North
Sebastopol, California 95472

ISBN: 978-0-7356-4791-6

1 2 3 4 5 6 7 8 9 M 6 5 4 3 2 1

Printed and bound in the United States of America.

Microsoft Press books are available through booksellers and distributors worldwide. If you need support related to this book, email Microsoft Press Book Support at mspinput@microsoft.com. Please tell us what you think of this book at http://www.microsoft.com/learning/booksurvey.

Acquisitions and Developmental Editor: Russell Jones
Production Editor: Holly Bauer
Editorial Production: Octal Publishing, Inc.
Technical Reviewer: Lars Dekenno
Copyeditor: Bob Russell
Indexer: Julie Hawks
Cover Design: Twist Creative • Seattle
Cover Composition: Karen Montgomery
Illustrator: Robert Romano
Author Photo: FH CAMPUS 02/Peter Melbinger

Contents at a Glance

Part IV **Exchange Server**

Table of Contents

Part II **SQL Server**

Part IV **Exchange Server**

What do you think of this book? We want to hear from you!

Microsoft is interested in hearing your feedback so we can continually improve our
books and learning resources for you. To participate in a brief online survey, please visit:

microsoft.com/learning/booksurvey

Introduction

PHP has changed the world: no other language has influenced and spurred web development so strongly. From simple home pages to social software and business applications to the largest global websites, PHP has played a leading role for years. Simultaneously, Microsoft and its Windows operating system has made computers available to all households. Along with Internet Information Services (IIS) for Windows Server, Microsoft SQL Server, Microsoft Active Directory, and Microsoft Exchange Server, it has created a solid and powerful platform for organizations and companies, as well. Microsoft recognizes the potential that lies in supporting PHP in its own products, and is now explicitly incorporating PHP into its development strategy, thus promoting interoperability with the Windows platform.

Thanks to the recent efforts by the Windows PHP team, including Pierre Joye, Ruslan Yakushev, and others, the combination of IIS and PHP is now faster, more stable, more secure, and easier to manage than ever. These efforts—FastCGI, WinCache, PHP Manager, new drivers for SQL Server, the integration with Microsoft's Web Platform Installer (Web PI), as well as development aids for Windows Azure, Virtual Earth, Webslices, Silverlight, and SQL Server (just to name a few)—make PHP development on Windows an enjoyable and productive experience.

Combined with the ever-improving interoperability of Microsoft's products, PHP is ready for just about every task in corporate environments. Whether you want to access Exchange Server through its SOAP web services, manage users in Active Directory with Lightweight Directory Access Protocol (LDAP), or use Windows credentials to provide seamless authentication of your users, PHP is up to the task.

In addition, Microsoft provides extensive developer documentation on its MSDN developer network and on TechNet, which leaves few common questions unanswered. Also, several of Microsoft's core PHP developers share valuable insights, tips, and tricks on their blogs.

If, like me, you have mostly been using PHP with Apache and MySQL, you should be excited about the functionality, stability, performance, and integrated security architecture of the Microsoft platform. This book shows you how to run your PHP applications effectively and securely with IIS and SQL Server, and how to access user data in Active Directory as well as the calendar and email data in Exchange Server.

Who Should Read This Book

This book exists to introduce PHP developers to Microsoft's web and database technologies. It is also especially useful for programmers developing applications that interface with Microsoft Active Directory or Microsoft Exchange Server.

After reading this book, you will have a deep understanding of how PHP interacts with IIS so that you can tweak your configuration for optimal security and performance. You will know how to access SQL Server, which authentication model is best suited for your needs, how to perform full-text searches, and how to interface with stored procedures. You will be able to access Active Directory to manage users and groups, or use it for authentication purposes. And finally, you will be able to use Exchange Web Services (EWS) to read and write emails, organize meetings, and manage your calendar.

Assumptions

This book assumes that you already have some experience in developing PHP applications and accessing relational database systems (for example, with Apache and MySQL). You should also be familiar with basic web concepts, such as the HTTP request/response cycle, and be familiar with the concepts of the relational database model, such as tables and rows, and have dabbled in SQL. In addition, this book assumes that you have a basic understanding of XML, because XML is used for configuration files and Exchange Server's SOAP web services.

Although this book describes the necessary steps to set up IIS, SQL Server, Active Directory, and Exchange Server, as well as the necessary steps to follow the given examples, it is not by any means a comprehensive description of these products. Therefore, you should have a minimal understanding of the purpose and function of these systems.

Who Should Not Read This Book

Not every book is aimed at every possible audience. If you have no prior experience with PHP or database systems, you might have a hard time following the explanations. Also, if you expect a complete introduction to Active Directory or Exchange Server, you might be disappointed—there's simply not enough room in a single book.

Organization of This Book

This book introduces you to programming IIS, SQL Server, Active Directory, and Exchange Server. In each section, you will learn how to set up your development environment, the basic architecture and inner workings of these systems, and how to implement common tasks in PHP. Example configurations and listings illustrate each point and help you to improve your understanding and achieve your goals. This book attempts to lower the entry barrier for programming these systems as well as to thoroughly prepare you for further exploration of Microsoft's ecosystem.

This book is divided into four sections that roughly correspond to the technologies discussed. Depending on your interest or prior knowledge, you can jump directly to any section. The four sections are:

- **Part I, "Internet Information Services (IIS)"**   This part discusses how PHP can be integrated into IIS and how IIS processes a request. You will gain a solid understanding of how to configure IIS and how it operates. This part is especially useful if you are switching to IIS from another web server. The chapters in this part discuss how to secure your PHP applications against attacks, how to use caching to dramatically increase the performance of your application, and how you can use URL Rewrite to create user-friendly URLs.

- **Part II, "SQL Server"**   This part shows how to interface PHP programs with SQL Server, or, to be more precise, SQL Server's database engine. You will learn how to create databases and tables and how to manage access rights. Because SQL Server uses a flavor of SQL called Transact-SQL (T-SQL), this part describes the T-SQL syntax and commands. Next you'll dive into using the native PHP driver for SQL Server, using it for tasks that range from reading the results of simple SQL *SELECT* statements to dealing with stored procedures and converting data types between SQL Server and PHP. This part also covers accessing SQL Server via PHP Data Objects (PDO), and the differences between PDO and the native driver. You'll also look at how to set up full-text search in the database, which is a common requirement of web applications.

- **Part III, "Active Directory"**   After introducing the general concepts of Active Directory, domains, and forests, this part explains the hierarchical data structure in detail, introducing important objects and attributes and visualizing them by way of a PHP LDAP browser that you'll develop as an example application. Other chapters in this part describe how you can search for and authenticate users and other principals by using LDAP, and how you can modify user attributes, manage their group memberships, create new users, and reset their passwords.

- **Part IV, "Exchange Server"** Accessing Exchange through its SOAP web service interface is the focus of this part. Each chapter focuses on one aspect, such as sending and reading email, searching for contacts in the address book, creating calendar entries, or accepting and denying meeting invitations. In each chapter, you'll also learn additional options and interface methods. This part contains valuable tips and tricks on how to coax PHP and Exchange to work together and helps you overcome the initial hurdles.

Conventions and Features in This Book

This book presents information using conventions designed to make the information readable and easy to follow.

- Each exercise consists of a series of tasks, presented as numbered steps (1, 2, and so on) listing each action that you must take to complete the exercise.

- Boxed elements with labels such as "Note" provide additional information or alternative methods for completing a step successfully.

- Text that you type (apart from code blocks) appears in bold type.

- A plus sign (+) between two key names means that you must press those keys at the same time. For example, "Press Alt+Tab" means that you hold down the Alt key while you press the Tab key.

- A vertical bar between two or more menu items (for example, File | Close) means that you should select the first menu or menu item, and then the next, and so on.

System Requirements

You will need the following hardware and software to complete the practice exercises in this book:

- Either Windows 7 or Windows Server 2008 R2. For Exchange Server, you need the 64-bit version of Windows Server 2008 R2.

- SQL Server 2008 R2 (Express Edition or higher), with SQL Server Management Studio (Express Edition or higher).

- Exchange Server 2010 (or 2010 SP1).

- A computer that has a reasonably fast processor (2 GHz recommended); a 64-bit processer for Exchange Server.

- 2 GB RAM for running IIS, SQL Server, and Active Directory in a development environment; another 4 GB RAM for Exchange Server.

- 3.5 GB of available hard disk space.

- An Internet connection to download software or chapter examples.

You will require Local Administrator rights for installation and configuration of the server systems; for Active Directory, you will require Domain Administrator rights.

Code Samples

Most of the chapters in this book include exercises that let you interactively try out new material learned in the main text. All sample projects, in both their pre-exercise and post-exercise formats, can be downloaded from the following page:

http://go.microsoft.com/FWLink/?Linkid=229620

Follow the instructions to download the PHP_sample_code.zip file.

Installing the Code Samples

Follow these steps to install the code samples on your computer so that you can use them with the exercises in this book.

1. Unzip the PHP_sample_code.zip file that you downloaded from the book's website (name a specific directory along with directions to create it, if necessary).

2. If prompted, review the displayed end-user license agreement. If you accept the terms, select the accept option, and then click Next.

> **Note** If the license agreement doesn't appear, you can access it from the same webpage from which you downloaded the PHP_sample_code.zip file.

Using the Code Samples

The folder created by extracting the zip file contains two subfolders.

- **Listings**   This folder contains all of the listings sorted by chapter, as they appear in the book. The listings are UTF-8 encoded, without a byte-order mark (BOM) at the beginning. The filename suffix indicates the content:
  - ***.php**   PHP script or PHP code snippet
  - ***.sql**   T-SQL script
  - ***.xml**   IIS configuration or EWS SOAP message
- **EWS**   This folder contains the modified WSDL definition of Exchange Web Services 2010 SP1. The modifications are necessary for PHP and Exchange to work together and are discussed in Chapters 19 to 23.

You should be able to use the provided examples as is, but sometimes you will need to adjust the configuration for your own development environment. When the book creates and adds to PHP files in a step-by-step fashion as part of an exercise (most notably the LDAP browser in Chapter 17, "Searching in Active Directory"), the listings also contain PHP files that incorporate all the edits.

Note that PHP files are referenced by other scripts without the chapter and listing number (just as they appear in the book). So you should either rename the files to be included or change the include/require statement accordingly. Also, many of the examples require the listings from Appendix A, "Example Scripts and Data," to be in the *include* path: either include this directory in the PHP *include* path or just copy the files into the directory, where the script you would like to run resides.

Acknowledgments

To write a book, authors need a supportive and motivating environment. At O'Reilly Media, I would like to thank my editor Russell Jones, along with Holly Bauer and Christie Rears, and Dianne Russell at Octal Publishing for their great help and teamwork; Brigitte Possin and Angela Walwick, for the skilled and seamless translation of the text from its original German to English; Christian Wenz, for his knowledgeable technical editing; Lars Denneko and Daniel Chapman, technical reviewers for the English translation; Manfred Steyer, for inciting me to write this book; Agnes Krispel, Julia Egger, and my colleagues at FH CAMPUS 02 for providing a comfortable and inspiring working environment; the teachers and mentors who have accompanied me on my journey; my long-time friends Doris "Donnerdackel" Leipold and Anton Huber; and my family, without whose support I can't imagine living my life. Dad, this one is for you.

Graz, September 2011

—Arno Hollosi

Errata & Book Support

We've made every effort to ensure the accuracy of this book and its companion content. Any errors that have been reported since this book was published are listed on our Microsoft Press site at oreilly.com:

http://go.microsoft.com/FWLink/?Linkid=229618

If you find an error that is not already listed, you can report it to us through the same page.

If you need additional support, email Microsoft Press Book Support at *mspinput@microsoft.com*.

Please note that product support for Microsoft software is not offered through the addresses above.

We Want to Hear from You

At Microsoft Press, your satisfaction is our top priority, and your feedback our most valuable asset. Please tell us what you think of this book at:

http://www.microsoft.com/learning/booksurvey

The survey is short, and we read every one of your comments and ideas. Thanks in advance for your input!

Stay in Touch

Let's keep the conversation going! We're on Twitter: *http://twitter.com/MicrosoftPress*.

Contacting the Author

PHP, Windows, and accompanying technologies are constantly being developed and improved. If you have ideas or remarks that you would like to share, or have had noteworthy experiences while programming Microsoft technologies with PHP, I would like to hear from you. Criticism is welcome, as well.

You can reach me by email at *ahollosi@xmp.net*. Additional information can be found on my website at *http://xmp.net/php/*.

Part I
Internet Information Services (IIS)

Chapter 1
Setting Up the Work Environment

This chapter describes how to set up your work environment, which consists of PHP and the Internet Information Services (IIS) web server. Initially, you will install only the essential components to keep resource use to a minimum and limit attack surfaces.

The examples in this book use the versions of the individual components that were current at the time of printing (October, 2011); these include PHP 5.3.8 and IIS 7 (version 7.5). The operating systems (OS) are Windows Server 2008 R2 SP1 and Windows 7 Ultimate SP1. The descriptions should (in slightly modified form) also work for other Windows OS versions.

IIS 6, although still widely used, is not covered in this book. The differences between IIS 6 and IIS 7 are significant. IIS 7 provides many new features that are especially pertinent to PHP programmers—and these features are not available in IIS 6. Furthermore, the configuration has been changed radically, so descriptions that apply to IIS 7 cannot be applied to IIS 6.

The following sections first describe the process to set up IIS 7, then PHP, and then the installation of PHP on IIS. You'll cover the installation with the help of the Windows Management Tools as well as how to set it up by using the command line. The latter is especially interesting for advanced users. Finally, you'll see how to perform the installation via the Microsoft Web Platform Installer, which automates many of the manual configuration steps.

Setting Up IIS

The current version of IIS has a modular design that ensures a fine granularity of selectable features that support a wide variety of usage scenarios. You only need to install the modules required for your particular usage scenario; thus, can use these features to customize IIS according to your requirements to save system resources. Furthermore, a server configured in this fashion provides a smaller attack surface, and therefore, improved security against attacks from the Internet.

You can install IIS in several different ways. The following sections explore the installation procedure using both Server Manager and via the command prompt. You can also install IIS via the command prompt on the Windows Server 2008 R2 Core edition.

The installation described here adds only the Common Gateway Interface (CGI) Role Service, which is required to run PHP with IIS. You can install other role services if you need them. Later chapters will indicate when you need to install additional features.

Installing IIS by Using the Server Manager

If you are using the Server Manager for installation, perform the following steps, which will start a wizard that takes you through the individual IIS installation steps.

1. Start the Server Manager by clicking the Start menu, and then clicking All Programs | Administrative Tools | Server Manager.

2. Select Roles | Add Roles.

   The Add Roles Wizard opens. Confirm the Before You Begin page by clicking Next.

3. On the Server Roles page, choose Web Server (IIS), and then click Next.

4. Click Next to confirm the Web Server (IIS) page.

5. On the Select Role Services page, select the Web Server (IIS) option. In the Application Development section, select the CGI check box (see Figure 1-1), and then click Next.

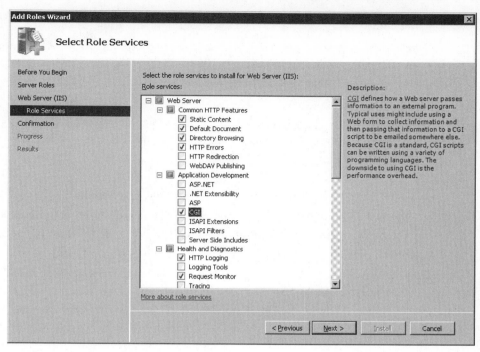

FIGURE 1-1 Adding the CGI role service to IIS.

6. Click Install to confirm your choices and begin the installation.

7. After the installation completes, click Close to complete the wizard.

You have now successfully installed IIS. You don't need to restart Windows. You can check whether the installation of IIS was successful by starting a web browser and opening the website *http://localhost/*. The default website with the welcome text will be displayed.

Installing from the Command Line

To install IIS from the command line, you need the pkgmgr.exe tool, which is a new command-line tool that ships with Windows Server 2008 for managing optional Windows features. It replaces the older sysocmgr.exe tool.

> **Important** You need administrator rights to perform this procedure. By default under Windows Server 2008, only the integrated administrator account has these rights. Other user accounts do not—even if they belong to the administrator group.

1. Open a command prompt window with administrator rights.

    You can find the command prompt in your Start menu by clicking All Programs | Accessories | Command Prompt, or you can launch it via the Start menu by typing **cmd** in the Search Programs And Files text field.

2. With the command prompt open, enter the following command to install the IIS Server Role and the CGI Role Service:

    ```
    pkgmgr /iu:IIS-WebServerRole;IIS-CGI
    ```

3. Ensure that the installation completed without errors by entering:

    ```
    echo %errorlevel%
    ```

You have now successfully installed IIS via the command prompt. You can check whether the installation of IIS was successful by starting a web browser and opening the website *http://localhost/.* You'll see the IIS default website containing some welcome text.

Setting Up PHP

After you have successfully installed IIS, you can install PHP and configure it for use with IIS. Again, you'll see how to configure PHP via the IIS Manager application as well as from the command line. Only experienced users should use the command-line version; typically you'd use it when there's no graphic interface (such as under Windows Server 2008 R2 Core edition) or when you want to automate the installation with a script.

Installing PHP

1. In Internet Explorer or another browser, open the website *http://windows.php.net/download/.*

2. Download the current PHP version 5.3.x (as of this book's printing, the latest version is 5.3.8) as a zip file. Choose the zip file from the VC9 x86 Non Thread Safe download section.

3. Create a C:\PHP folder, and then extract the zip file to that folder.

   You can actually unzip the files anywhere you like, but this book uses the folder C:\PHP, so following the examples will be easiest if your location folder matches this.

4. Copy the file C:\PHP\php.ini-development to C:\PHP\php.ini.

5. Open the file C:\PHP\php.ini with a text editor such as NotePad.

6. Look for the line that configures the *date.timezone*, and set the value to your local time zone, for example: **date.timezone = "America/Los_Angeles"**.

7. Set the option **cgi.force_redirect = 0**.

> **Note** You also set the option *fastcgi.impersonate=1*, but for now you can skip this option. It controls which account IIS uses to execute PHP code. You'll see more details later in Chapter 5, "Security," in the section "Identity and Access Rights."

8. To check whether your installation was successful, open a command prompt window, browse to the folder C:\PHP, and then run the command **php –c C:\PHP –info**. PHP will list all its settings and configuration data, as shown in Figure 1-2.

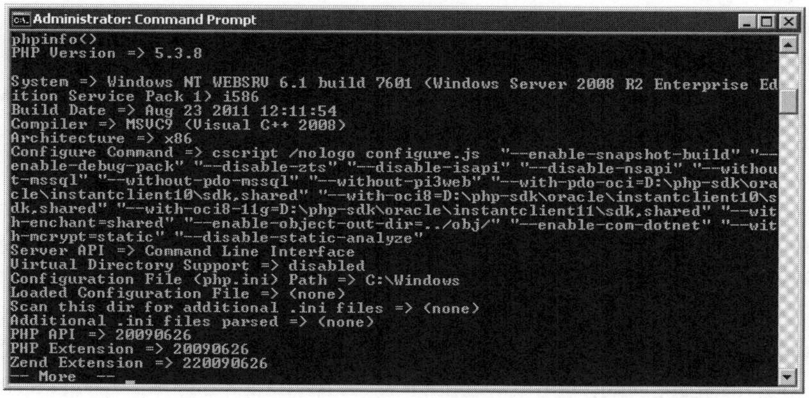

FIGURE 1-2 Output following the successful installation of PHP.

> **Important** If you receive an error message about an invalid side-by-side configuration, your system is missing the Visual C++ runtime component libraries that correspond to the PHP version. If that happens, download the Microsoft Visual C++ 2008 SP1 Redistributable Package (x86) from MSDN (you can find a link in the left bar on the PHP download page), and then install it on your system.

Available PHP Modules

Your PHP installation is now complete. The precompiled PHP installation files provided on *http://windows.php.net/* contain all the default PHP modules as well as some optional extensions. After installation, you can check the list of compiled modules by typing the command **php –m** at the command prompt in your C:\PHP folder.

You'll find additional modules that can be dynamically loaded when you launch PHP in the folder C:\PHP\ext. To activate these modules, you must configure PHP to load and activate them in the php.ini file.

> **Note** This book alerts you whenever you need to configure any of the dynamic modules to follow the examples.

Configuring PHP in IIS

Now that PHP is installed on your computer, you need to configure IIS to use PHP to process requested PHP pages. You configure PHP as a *handler* in IIS. Because of the modular structure of IIS, you can specify different programs (handlers) to process different types of content. The basic IIS installation sets up three handlers: the specific handlers for the HTTP methods, *OPTIONS* and *TRACE*, as well as the *StaticFile* handler, whose only task is to return an existing requested local file without changing it.

> **Note** Handlers are only a link in the IIS chain of commands for processing an incoming HTTP request. You will find a more detailed illustration of the complete chain in Chapter 2, "IIS Architecture."

By default, IIS simply uses the *StaticFile* handler to return requested files that have a .php extension. However, when you configure PHP as a handler, files with the extension .php are no longer delivered directly and unmodified, but are executed by the PHP Interpreter, and the result is sent back to the browser.

For now you'll perform only the minimal configuration required to run PHP programs. Chapter 3, "Configuring IIS," contains a more detailed description of other important configurations, particularly with regard to performance and security.

Configuring PHP by Using the IIS Manager

To configure PHP by using the IIS Manager, perform the following procedure:

1. Start the IIS Manager.

   You can do this via the Server Manager application by clicking Server Manager | Roles | Web Server (IIS) | Internet Information Services (IIS) Manager, or via the Windows Start menu by typing **inetmgr** in the Search Program And Files text box.

2. On the server level, open the Handler Mappings item, as shown in Figure 1-3.

FIGURE 1-3 Selecting the handler mappings in the IIS Manager.

3. In the right column, select the action Add Module Mapping.

4. Set the values to those shown in Figure 1-4.

   The request path should include all files with the PHP extension (*.php). Select FastCgiModule for the module, and php-cgi.exe for the executable file. You can choose any name you like.

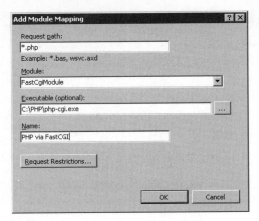

FIGURE 1-4 Module assignment of PHP in IIS.

5. Click the Request Restrictions button.

6. On the Mapping tab, select the Invoke Handler Only If Request Is Mapped To check box, and then select the File option.

7. On the Verbs tab, you can optionally set restrictions for the HTTP assignment methods (for example, restrict to the methods *HEAD*, *GET*, and *POST*).

8. Click OK to close the Request Restrictions dialog box.

9. Click OK to confirm your choices.

10. Click Yes to confirm the module mapping.

   This enables IIS to run PHP as a FastCGI application.

11. In the web server's root folder (C:\inetpub\wwwroot\), create the file phpinfo.php with the following content:

```
<?php phpinfo(); ?>
```

12. Start a web browser, and then browse to the address *http://localhost/phpinfo.php*.

   The response contains the phpinfo() information with the current PHP settings, as shown in Figure 1-5.

> **Important** If, instead of getting the phpinfo() page, you receive a server error "500—Internal server error," perform an error search as described in Chapter 8, "Error Messages and Error Search."

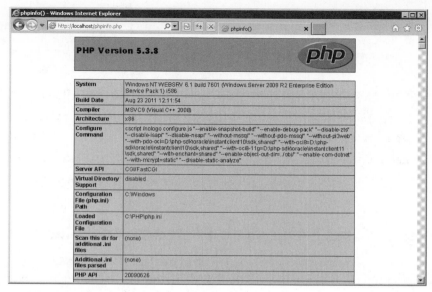

FIGURE 1-5 The phpinfo() output after successfully setting up PHP.

Configuring PHP from the Command Line

To configure IIS from the command line, you use the new IIS 7 command-line program *appcmd*, which is located in the C:\Windows\System32\inetsrv folder. By default, this folder is not in the Windows search path, so to launch the program, you must either browse to the folder and then open a command prompt, or enter the complete program path at the command prompt, or add the path to the *PATH* environment variable for your Windows installation. Here's the procedure to configure PHP from the command line:

1. Open a command prompt window with administrator rights.

2. Configure the FastCGI application pool by typing the following command:

   ```
   appcmd set config /section:system.webServer/fastCGI /+[fullPath='C:\PHP\php-cgi.exe']
   ```

3. To configure the handler assignment, run the following command:

   ```
   appcmd set config /section:system.webServer/handlers /+[name='PHP_via_FastCGI',
   modules='FastCgiModule',scriptProcessor='C:\PHP\php-cgi.exe',
   verb='*',path='*.php',resourceType='File']
   ```

> **Important** Due to space restrictions, the preceding command is shown on multiple lines. However, when you type the command, you must be sure to enter the configuration parameters on a single line.

4. In the web server's root folder (C:\inetpub\wwwroot\), create the file phpinfo.php with the following content:

```
<?php phpinfo(); ?>
```

5. Start a web browser, and then browse to the address *http://localhost/phpinfo.php*.

   You should see the phpinfo() page with the current PHP settings.

Installing by Using the Web Platform Installer

A simple alternative to the previously described methods for setting up your PHP and IIS work environment is to use the Microsoft Web Platform Installer (Web PI). Web PI bundles many of the manual steps you've just seen into a fully automatic installation. By installing the Windows Web App Gallery, Web PI also offers automatic installation of a number of other supported applications, such as the blog software WordPress, or the content management system Joomla!. Web PI is therefore perfectly suited for getting started with PHP under Windows, quickly and easily.

The following section describes how to install on a Windows 7 Ultimate SP1 OS. However, you can also use Web PI with Windows Vista, Windows XP SP2+, Windows Server 2003 SP1+, and Windows Server 2008. The steps are similar and should be easy to follow on these other systems.

Setting Up the Web PI

The Web PI is itself a program, so you need to install it first by performing the following steps.

1. Open the website *http://www.microsoft.com/web/downloads/platform.aspx*.

2. Download the Web PI and save the installation file wpilauncher_3_10.exe locally.

   The Web PI version used in this book is 3.0.

3. Run the installation file wpilauncher_3_10.exe.

   If you are not logged on as an administrator, confirm the User Account Control dialog by clicking Yes, to permit the installation to execute.

4. After a successful installation, you'll see the start window of the Web PI.

Setting Up IIS and PHP

With the Web PI configured, you can now set up the web server by performing the following:

1. Start the Web PI.

2. Click Products at the top. Add IIS 7 Recommended Configuration, IIS: CGI, and PHP Manager For IIS by clicking the respective Add buttons, as shown in Figure 1-6.

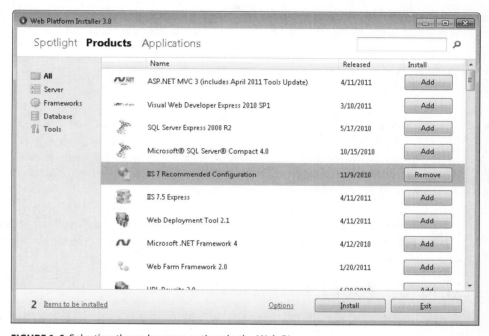

FIGURE 1-6 Selecting the web server options in the Web PI.

3. Click the Install button.

4. In the Web PI dialog box that appears, click the I Accept button.

   The Web PI now starts to download and install all the selected (and required) components—this process can take a few minutes.

5. When the installation is complete, click the Finish button.

6. Click the Exit button to close the Web PI.

7. Start a web browser, and then open the webpage *http://localhost/.*

   You should see the IIS welcome page.

Note Microsoft also provides a complete web development environment called WebMatrix. This is a very nice tool that is quick and easy to deploy, but it has limited configuration options. This is why we do not use WebMatrix for the examples in this book.

Checking Your PHP Installation

Just as with the other installation methods, it's a good idea to ensure that your PHP installation was successful by performing the following procedure:

1. In the web server's root folder (C:\inetpub\wwwroot\), create a file called phpinfo.php with the following content:

```
<?php phpinfo(); ?>
```

Note If you don't have sufficient rights to create a file in the root web folder, open Windows Explorer, select the folder C:\inetpub\wwwroot, and then from the context menu, select Properties | Security | Edit. In the ensuing dialog box, you can set the permissions appropriately for your user account.

2. Start a web browser, and then browse to the address *http://localhost/phpinfo.php*. The resulting webpage displays the phpinfo() information with the current PHP settings.

Backing Up Your Configuration

After successfully installing IIS and PHP, you should definitely back up the data of your server configuration. IIS stores configuration data in the C:\Windows\System32\inetsrv\config folder, in three files: applicationHost.config, administration.config, and redirection.config.

You can back up the entire folder manually, but alternatively, you can use the command line *appcmd* tool to create a backup copy of all essential configuration files by typing **appcmd add backup "MyBackup"**.

This command creates a backup copy of the current configuration in the folder C:\Windows\System32\inetsrv\backup\MyBackup.

Note In Windows 7, you need to run *appcmd* in a command prompt with administrator rights. Select Start | All Programs | Accessories | Command Prompt, right-click it, and then from the context menu, execute the command Run As Administrator.

You should create a backup copy of the current configuration after each modification, especially after you install new modules or components. By doing that, you can reset the configuration back to a defined state, if necessary.

A First Sample Application

After completing the IIS and PHP configurations as described in the preceding sections, you're ready to begin writing and using PHP applications. Before getting into more advanced configuration options in the next chapters, you can use the basic configuration you just completed to run your first sample application. This exercise serves to show that you can run and use PHP features such as forms and sessions as expected in the basic configuration.

This example creates a simple PHP application that guesses a random number between 1 and 100. Figure 1-7 shows the start page of the PHP application, and you can see the program code in Listing 1-1. When the session first starts, if no random number is set, the application generates one, and saves it in the session variable *$_SESSION['number']*. When a user enters a number (the variable *$_POST['guessed']*), the program compares it to the stored number to be guessed and display and appropriate message. The game ends when the user guesses the correct number. The program then calls the function *startGame()* to start a new game.

LISTING 1-1 A PHP example application to guess a number between 1 and 100.

```php
<?php session_start(); ?>
<html>
<head><title>Guessing Numbers</title></head>
<body>
<?php
/* Generate random number and return help text */
function startGame() {
    $_SESSION['number'] = rand(1, 100);
    echo "<p>Can you guess the number? It's between 1 and 100.</p>";
}

/* First Call? -> Start game */
if (!isset($_SESSION['number'])) {
    startGame();
}
/* Guess? */
elseif (isset($_POST['guessed']) && is_numeric($_POST['guessed'])) {
    if ($_SESSION['number'] == $_POST['guessed']) {
        echo "<p>Great! You guessed the correct number.</p>",
            "<p>Would you like to play again?</p>";
        startGame();
    } else elseif ($_SESSION['number'] < $_POST['guessed']) {
        echo "<p>Sorry, you're wrong! The number is smaller.<br />",
            "Try again.</p>";
    } else {
        echo "<p>Sorry, you're wrong! The number is larger.<br />",
            "Try again.</p>";
    }
}
```

```
/* Invalid or missing entry  */
else {
    echo "<p>Please enter a number.",
         "The number you are trying to guess is between 1 and 100.</p>";
}
?>
<form action="" method="post">
    <p>Number: <input name="guessed" /></p>
    <p><input type="submit" value="Guess number"></p>
</form>
</body>
</html>
```

FIGURE 1-7 The start page of the PHP sample application: guessing a number between 1 and 100.

Remote Access

By default, both Windows Server 2008 R2 and Windows 7 have an enabled Windows Firewall. Windows Firewall performs an important function, which is to protect and shield your computer from unwanted access: it blocks access by outside connections to services running on your computer or permits it, according to defined rules. For example, you might want to allow external users to connect to IIS—or you might want to prohibit such access. Either way, you specify such settings directly through Windows Firewall. While remote access might be a requirement when you deploy a program, you probably don't want to allow remote connections to your personal work environment.

Windows Firewall provides a set of predefined rules for IIS. You can control remote access (these steps apply to both Windows 7 and Windows Server 2008 R2) by using the following procedure:

1. Open the Windows Firewall settings by clicking Start | Control Panel | System And Security, and then select Windows Firewall | Allow A Program Or Feature Through Windows Firewall.

2. If the Change Settings button is enabled, click it; if it is not enabled, you'll need to get permission to change the settings.

3. To make IIS accessible or inaccessible from outside connections, enable or disable the World Wide Web Services (HTTP) option, as shown in Figure 1-8.

   When allowing remote access, you must also select whether you want to allow only computers belonging to the same domain, or allow access only via a private network, or allow general access (the Public column). (For this setting to work, your networks must be assigned to the appropriate profile.)

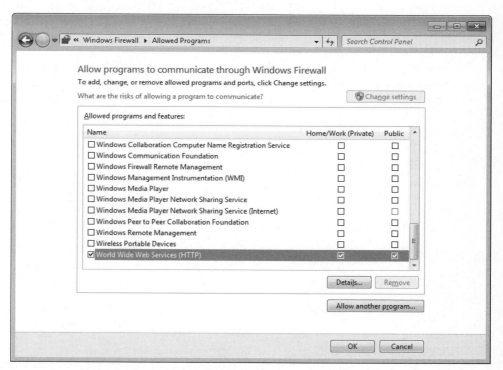

FIGURE 1-8 Enabling remote access to IIS under Windows 7.

4. Confirm your changes by clicking OK.

Summary

After setting up your work environment, you can take your first steps with PHP and IIS. The installation methods described in this chapter only set up the basic default components. IIS supports a large number of additional modules and functions, some of which you'll cover in subsequent chapters.

Of the three ways to set up PHP and IIS, using the Web PI is the simplest because it largely automates the process. Web PI is particularly well suited, for example, for setting up a quick default development environment so that you can get started easily. The other two setup options require more manual work, but support finer granularity and control over the installation.

Before discussing extended configuration options and additional modules, Chapter 2 provides an overview of IIS architecture and walks you through how an HTTP request executes internally.

Chapter 2
IIS Architecture

With the release of Internet Information Services (IIS) 7, Microsoft has improved the modularization of IIS architecture and improved security in many areas. If you are switching from other web servers, it's important to get an overview of how IIS processes a request, and how it assigns the request contents.

Just like other web servers, you can run several websites on the same server by using a single IIS instance. IIS uses three building blocks that on one hand simplify maintenance and operation, and on the other, support a tiered and granular configuration that enhances server security significantly. These three building blocks are *Site*, *Application*, and *Virtual Directory*. The description of these building blocks in the following sections cover the complete life cycle execution of an HTTP request, application pools, and FastCGI binding. Together, these should give you a solid overview of how IIS works, which will help you to plan and develop your PHP applications for IIS.

Sites

In IIS 7, a site is an area of the web server that has its own applications and virtual directories as well as its own bindings. Sites let you run several individual websites, which, for example, can be bound to different domain names, IP addresses, or ports by using a single IIS instance. Therefore, sites permit "virtual hosting" of websites.

> **Note** For Apache Administrators: Sites are comparable to the *<VirtualHost>* configuration directive, but IIS goes one step further—even the basic properties of the web server can be changed from site to site (for example, the available modules). You can find more details about IIS configuration in Chapter 3, "Configuring IIS."

Setting Up a New Site

You can set up sites by using the IIS Manager application or from the command line by using the *appcmd* tool.

Setting Up a Site by Using IIS Manager

To set up a new site in your configured work environment, perform the following steps:

1. Open IIS Manager.

2. In the Connections pane (on the left), select Sites, and then in the Actions pane (on the right), click Add Web Site.

    The Add Web Site dialog box opens, as shown in Figure 2-1.

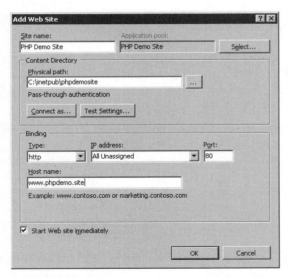

FIGURE 2-1 The Add Web Site dialog box with the values entered.

3. In the Site Name text box, enter the name of the site that you want to create.

    The name is not identical to the site's domain name, and you can name the site whatever you like; however, you should choose a meaningful name to make it easily recognizable for administration purposes later on.

4. Click the Connect As button.

    In the dialog box that opens, you can configure the user account that the site will use to access the files. You can find a detailed description of the path logon information in Chapter 5, "Security." If you deviate from the default setting—for example, by setting a special user account—it is recommended that you use the Test Settings button to check whether the specified user has access to the root folder.

5. In the Physical Path text box, enter the path of the folder that you want to use for the site.

    This folder is the root folder for the site. In the example, we're using C:\inetpub\phpdemosite as the root folder.

6. Enter the data for the binding.

    If you are setting up a site that should be accessible via HTTP on the default port 80, select http in the Type drop-down list, and then enter 80 in the Port text box. If your web server doesn't have several IP addresses, or if you don't want to bind the site to a specific IP address, then leave the IP address box set to the value All Unassigned.

7. In the Host Name text box, enter the domain name of the site. You can also leave it empty. This site then takes requests for all host names. You must ensure that for any given Type, IP address, and Port binding, no more than one site is defined without a host name (default site).

8. Select the Start Web Site Immediately check box, and then click OK to exit.

Your site has now been set up successfully. Figure 2-2 illustrates that you can now find the new site listed by going to the Connections pane, and then clicking Server Name | Sites. Here, you will find some brief information about the most important binding data, the root folder, and the state of the individual sites on the web server.

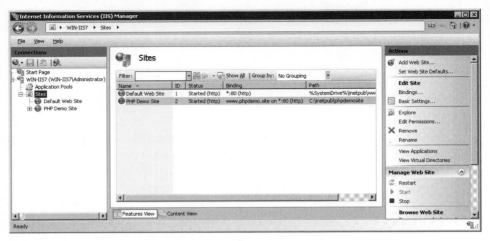

FIGURE 2-2 The list of the sites with information about state, binding, and path.

Setting Up a Site from the Command Line

You can use the command *appcmd* to set up a new site. This command requires parameters for the site name, the bindings, and the physical path if the root application of the site should be generated automatically. It is recommended that you create the root application at the same time.

The binding can be specified two ways:

- Similar to a URL, using the syntax *protocol://domain name:port number* (for example, http://www.phpdemo.site:80)

- As binding information, using the syntax *protocol/IP address:Port number:domain name*, (for example, http/*:80:www.phpdemo.site)

To set up the PHP Demo Site, as in the section "Setting up a Site by Using IIS Manager," enter the following command:

```
appcmd add site /name:"PHP Demo Site" /bindings:http/*:80:www.phpdemo.site
    /physicalPath:"C:\inetpub\phpdemosite"
```

> **Note** Unlike the IIS Manager setup method, setting up a site via the command line doesn't automatically generate its own application pool. You can find information on how to create an application pool and assign it to the site in the section "Application Pools," later in this chapter.

Testing Your New Site

Before you create a connection to your new site, you need to ensure that the domain name you have been using points correctly from your work environment to the web server. To do this, open the file C:\Windows\System32\drivers\etc\hosts in a text editor, and then enter the corresponding assignment. For example, if you used *www.phpdemo.site* as the domain name and are accessing the site from your local web server, you would enter the following, and then save the file:

`127.0.0.1 www.phpdemo.site`

> **Caution** If you are already calling the site http://www.phpdemo.site/, you will receive an HTTP error *403.14 – Forbidden*. This happens because no data exists in the specified root folder, and the site does not allow a folder list in the default configuration. Chapter 4, "Configuring PHP," provides more information about configuring the default document and permitting folder lists.

There are two ways to test your new site:

- To test HTML and graphics and site availability, copy the files iisstart.html and welcome .png from the folder C:\inetpub\wwwroot into the root folder (C:\inetpub\phpdemosite) of your new site. Then, open the site http://www.phpdemo.site/ in a browser. You should see the IIS welcome page displayed.

- To test PHP, create the file welcome.php in the root folder (C:\inetpub\phpdemosite) of your site by using the code shown in Listing 2-1.

  LISTING 2-1 The code for welcome.php.

```
<html>
<head><title>Welcome</title></head>
<body>
<h1>Welcome!</h1>
You are at:
<ul>
<?php
    echo "<li>Server: $_SERVER[SERVER_NAME]</li>";
    echo "<li>Port: $_SERVER[SERVER_PORT]</li>";
    echo "<li>Adresse: $_SERVER[LOCAL_ADDR]</li>";
    echo "<li>Protokoll: $_SERVER[SERVER_PROTOCOL]</li>";
    echo "<li>HTTPS: $_SERVER[HTTPS]</li>";
?>
</ul>
</body>
</html>
```

Browse to the *http://www.phpdemo.site/welcome.php*. Your output should look similar to that shown in Figure 2-3.

Note In IIS, you obtain the IP address of the server via the predefined PHP variable $_SERVER['LOCAL_ADDR'], and not via the more common variable $_SERVER['SERVER_ADDR']. Also, in IIS the variable $_SERVER['HTTPS'] is not empty when a request takes place via HTTP instead of HTTPS; instead, it contains the value *off*.

FIGURE 2-3 Output of welcome.php.

Adding Additional Bindings

Your site can have any number of bindings. This makes sense, for example, when you want to make a site accessible via the domain name www.example.com as well as under the name example.com (no *www*). However, during site setup, you can specify only one binding.

Adding Bindings by Using IIS Manager

You can use the IIS Manager application to add additional bindings by performing the following:

1. Open IIS Manager.

2. In the Connections pane, select the site that you want to configure.

3. In the Actions pane, click Edit Site | Bindings.

   The Site Bindings dialog box opens.

4. Click the Add button to open the Add Site Binding dialog box.

5. Enter the binding data according to your requirements; for example:

   - Type: http

   - IP address: All unassigned

   - Port: **80**

   - Host name: **phpdemo.site**

6. Click OK to confirm.

Now, when you click the Browse button, you can open a browser window with the corresponding URL.

> **Caution** If you are using new domain names, use the entry in your DNS server to ensure that the corresponding IP addresses point to the web server. Alternatively, you can insert the assignment into the file C:\Windows\System32\drivers\etc\hosts in your work environment, as described in the section "Testing Your New Site," earlier in this chapter.

7. To add further bindings, repeat the procedure from step 4. Otherwise, click Close to exit the dialog box.

Figure 2-4 shows two additional bindings added to the sample site for the domain name *phpdemo.site*, on ports 80 and 1234.

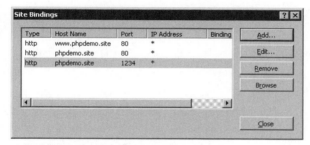

FIGURE 2-4 List of the site bindings.

If you now try browsing to welcome.php (Listing 2-1) by using the addresses of the new bindings, you will see that the PHP variables are set according to the binding data.

Adding Bindings from the Command Line

You can change the bindings of a site from the command line by using the *appcmd* tool. There is no unique command for adding or removing bindings. When making modifications, you must specify all of the bindings that you want the site to have. For example, to add the three bindings in the previous example, call *appcmd* as follows:

```
appcmd set site "PHP Demo Site"
    /bindings:http/*:80:www.phpdemo.site,http/*:80:phpdemo.site,http/*:1234:phpdemo.site
```

Managing the Website

IIS lets you start and stop individual sites at run time. This function is intended only for temporary site deactivation for maintenance purposes, so you don't need to shut down the web server itself.

Starting and Stopping a Website by Using IIS Manager

You can find the functions to start and shut down a site in IIS Manager. After you have selected a site in the Connections pane, you'll find the following options in the Actions pane in the Manage Web Site section:

- **Start**   Start a site that has been stopped.
- **End**   Stop a running site, making the site no longer available for requests.
- **Restart**   Stop a running site, and then restart it (cycle it). The site is temporarily unavailable. This process reloads all site configuration.

Starting and Stopping a Website from the Command Line

You can also list, start, and stop sites from the command line. Open a command prompt window with sufficient rights. To list all sites, enter the following command:

```
appcmd list sites
```

The output contains the name, the internal ID, the bindings, and the current state of the site. For example, the output for a configured PHP Demo Site would appear as follows:

```
SITE "Default Web Site" (id:1,bindings:http/*:80:,state:Started)
SITE "PHP Demo Site" (id:2,bindings:http/*:80:www.phpdemo.site,http/*:80:phpdemo.site,
                      http/*:1234:phpdemo.site,state:Started)
```

To stop a site, enter the following command:

```
appcmd stop site "Site name"
```

To start a site, enter:

```
appcmd start site "Name of Site"
```

The *appcmd* tool does not have a command equivalent to the IIS Manager Restart function. Instead, you need to stop the site and then start it again.

Applications

In IIS, an application is a collection of files grouped together. Usually, applications contain executable files and scripts. Each application has a virtual directory assigned to it, which is called the *root directory*. At least one application is assigned to each site, which is called the *root application*.

Applications are grouped into application pools. Doing so allows IIS to maintain a separation between execution environments; this improves isolation, which in turn increases both security and web server/application availability. When applications are programmed and configured properly, you can port them easily from one web server to another.

With IIS, it is possible for applications to use different PHP configurations across the web server or within a site. You can find more information about this in Chapter 3.

Paths and Folders

As just described, each application contains at least one virtual root directory. The root directory path is part of the application's URL. You can create a new application on any of several different layers:

- **Site**   Each site has at least one root application, which is generated automatically. Additional applications can be added.

- **Folder or virtual directory**   An application can also be set up in a virtual directory or folder. In this case, the path to the application is composed of the path to the folder or virtual directory and the path to the application. The physical application path (the assigned folder), however, can be selected independent of the virtual directory or folder.

- **Application**   Applications can also be nested. For URL paths and physical paths, the same rule applies as for folders and virtual directories.

The examples in Table 2-1 illustrate the connection between paths and folders. The sample application has the path myapp and the root folder (the physical path) C:\myapp. The application's root folder contains the file info.html. The physical path to info.html is independent of the folder of the parent element.

TABLE 2-1 Examples for the connections between application paths and folders

Element	Path	Folder	Path to info.html	Physical path
Site	/	C:\inetpub\wwwroot	/myapp/info.html	C:\myapp\info.html
Folder	/gallery	C:\inetpub\wwwroot\ gallery	/gallery/myapp/ info.html	C:\myapp\info.html
Virtual Directory	/apps/gallery	C:\app-gallery	/apps/gallery/myapp/ info.html	C:\myapp\info.html
Application	/phpapps	C:\phpapps	/phpapps/myapp/ info.html	C:\myapp\info.html

Setting Up a New Application

You can use IIS Manager to set up a new application, or you can do it from the command line.

Setting Up an Application by Using IIS Manager

To use IIS Manager to set up a new application, perform the following:

1. Start the IIS Manager.

2. In the Connections pane, right-click the site, folder, virtual directory, or existing application to which you want to add an application, and then from the context menu, select Add Application .

   The Add Application dialog box opens, as shown in Figure 2-5.

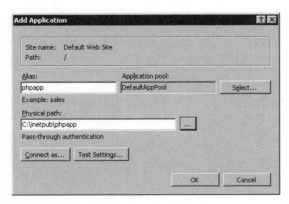

FIGURE 2-5 The Add Application dialog box.

3. In the Alias text box, enter the path to the application.

   This path becomes part of the URL.

4. The default Application Pool setting is the application pool of the parent element. If you want to change the application pool, click the Select button.

   In the dialog box that opens, select the desired application pool in the Application Pool drop-down list, and then click OK to confirm it.

5. Enter the desired physical path to the application.

6. Click OK to confirm your choices.

You have now created a new application and know how to assign an existing application pool.

Setting Up an Application from the Command Line

Using *appcmd add app*, you can create applications from the command line and add an application pool. The most important difference between setup via the command line and setup via IIS Manager is that when using the command line, you must specify the application path along with the paths of all parent elements. For example, to set up an application *myapp* in the virtual directory gallery, which is located directly below the site root, you need to specify the path /gallery/myapp as part of the *appcmd* command.

To expand on the example, you would enter the following command to set up the application the same way as in the preceding IIS Manager example:

```
appcmd add app /site.name:"Default Web Site" /path:/myapp /physicalPath:"C:\inetpub\phpapp"
```

You can also use *appcmd* to change the application pool. Again, you must specify the site name along with the path. For example, you would enter the following command to change the application pool for the application that you just created to the PHP Demo Site application pool:

```
appcmd set app "Default Web Site/myapp" /applicationPool:"PHP Demo Site"
```

Changing Application Settings

Use the following steps to change the settings of an existing application:

1. Start the IIS Manager.

2. In the Connections pane, select the application that you want to change.

3. In the Actions pane, select Basic Settings.

   The Edit Application dialog box opens.

4. Change the data by using the description in the previous section, "Setting Up a New Application."

You can also change the settings by using the command *appcmd set app*. The following commands let you establish which settings are possible:

```
appcmd set app /?
appcmd set app "Complete Application Path" /?
```

Note The process for changing the application pool is explained in the section "Setting Up an Application from the Command Line," earlier in this chapter.

Virtual Directories

A virtual directory is a pairing, or assignment, of a path to a folder of your choice. This makes the outwardly visible structure of your website independent of the actual folder structure on the web server.

As far as the configuration hierarchy is concerned, virtual directories can have only applications as a parent element. However, because you can choose the path assignment freely, virtual directories can appear anywhere in the path hierarchy, even as children of sites, folders, or other virtual directories. When you use IIS Manager as your management tool, it handles path conversions for you. But if you are using *appcmd*, you must take care of the conversions yourself.

Setting Up a Virtual Directory by Using IIS Manager

To set up a virtual directory by using IIS Manager, perform the following steps:

1. In the Connections pane of IIS Manager, right-click the element for which you want to set up the virtual directory (such as the site), and then from the context menu, select Add Virtual Directory.

   The Add Virtual Directory dialog box opens.

2. Enter the directory path into the Alias text box.

   The path you enter becomes part of the URL.

3. Enter the desired physical path of the directory.

4. Click OK to confirm your choices.

To view all the virtual directories of a site, select the site in the Connections pane, and then in the Actions pane, click View Virtual Directories. You can also edit directories from that location.

Setting Up a Virtual Directory from the Command Line

To set up a virtual directory from the command line, you again use the *appcmd* tool. As mentioned earlier, you need to specify the paths relative to the parent application.

To set up a virtual directory, run the following command:

```
appcmd add vdir /app.name:"PHP Demo Site/" /path:/tony /physicalPath:c:\inetpub\user\tony
```

Table 2-2 presents three examples of how IIS assembles the path of a virtual directory. The first example is a virtual directory located directly below the site's root application. The parent element of the second example is also the root application, but the virtual directory itself is set up one level further below. In this case, the user folder can exist in advance—but it doesn't have to. The /user folder can also be a different virtual directory. In the third example, /user is a standalone application, which is why it has a different path. If you are creating a virtual directory within an application, you must specify the path relative to that application.

TABLE 2-2 Examples for virtual directory paths

Application path	Relative directory path	Directory URL
PHP Demo Site/	/tony	http://phpdemo.site/tony
PHP Demo Site/	/user/tony	http://phpdemo.site/user/tony
PHP Demo Site/user/	/tony	http://phpdemo.site/user/tony

 Note You can use the command *appcmd list vdir* to display all virtual directories on the server.

HTTP Request Flow

IIS received a complete overhaul for version 7. The most important change is in improved modularization, resulting in a more economical use of resources, higher performance, the ability to customize your IIS installation to your own application's requirements, and last but not least, a smaller attack surface, which contributes to improved security.

In the following sections, you'll take a look at how IIS processes an HTTP request. After you understand the request sequence, you'll find it much easier to configure IIS and find configuration errors or server problems. This discussion is not complete; it focuses on only those points that PHP programmers would find beneficial.

IIS lets you embed modules and components that must either be programmed as managed .NET modules (for example, for use with ASP.NET) or written in C++. Creating managed modules in PHP that can be embedded into IIS is not currently possible.

Request Flow Overview

Figure 2-6 illustrates an overview of the request process, which includes the following steps:

1. The client—usually a web browser—generates an HTTP request and sends it to the server.

2. The HTTP protocol stack http.sys accepts the request. The protocol stack is part of the operating system's network subsystem and works in kernel mode, supporting rapid processing, especially for cached requests. The HTTP protocol stack passes the request to the Windows Process Activation Service (WAS), which queries the website configuration.

3. WAS determines the configuration data for the website by requesting it from the configuration file in memory applicationHost.config. The WWW Publishing Service receives this data. The configuration data contains, for example, information about which application pool should be used.

4. The WWW Publishing Service prepares the HTTP protocol stack for the answer from the application pool.

5. WAS starts the application process (w3wp.exe) for the selected application pool and transfers the request data.

6. The application process handles the request. If the request refers to a PHP script, the PHP program executable engages during this step. The result of this processing is returned to the HTTP protocol stack.

7. The HTTP protocol stack returns the completed, processed result to the web client as the response to the HTTP request from step 1. This completes the request process.

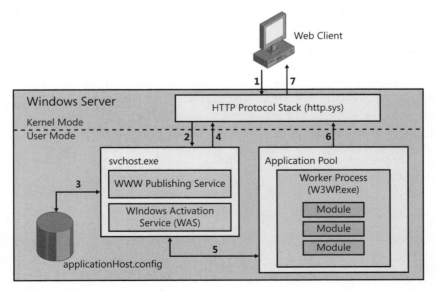

FIGURE 2-6 The HTTP request flow.

Application Process Flow

In the application process, an HTTP request is run through a number of steps, as shown in Figure 2-7. The individual steps and events are handled by system-integrated modules. As an example, Figure 2-7 shows the Anonymous Authentication, Static File, and Default Document modules. Other modules are, for example, responsible for the event log, or for querying and updating the cache.

If you want to call a managed module (usually written in .NET technology, such as ASP.NET), the managing module takes care of the necessary steps to instantiate and call the managed module.

The events that are important for PHP programs are *handler assignment* and *handler execution*.

The IIS selects the appropriate handler for the current request, based on configuration. For example, a request for a graphic or a simple HTML file would be passed to the module for static contents (*StaticFile*). Similarly, a request for an executable PHP program is passed to the *FastCGI* module, which then runs the PHP interpreter. The output (the result of running the PHP program) is returned to the application process, after which the remaining steps of the processing take place.

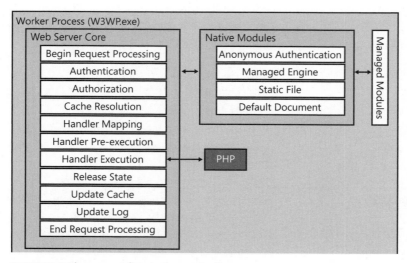

FIGURE 2-7 The request flow in the application process.

Modules

Because of the modularization of IIS, you can adjust the server to the exact requirements of your application. As described in the preceding section, the application process itself runs through a number of steps when handling an application request. To display a list of the enabled modules, perform the following steps:

1. Start IIS Manager.

2. In the Connections pane, select the corresponding server.

   The server Start Page opens.

3. From the Start Page, select the Modules feature.

4. If you have built your work environment by following the steps described in Chapter 1, "Setting Up the Work Environment," the list of active modules should correspond to the list in Table 2-3.

TABLE 2-3 System-internal modules that are installed by default

Module name	Module description
AnonymousAuthenticationModule	Generates the appropriate *HttpUser* object for anonymous authentication
CgiModule	Implements the Common Gateway Interface (CGI)
CustomErrorModule	Permits custom error messages and detailed IIS 7 error messages
DefaultDocumentModule	Redirects HTTP requests with a closing forward slash ("/") to a configurable default document
DirectoryListingModule	Permits displaying and searching folders
FastCgiModule	Provides the *FastCGI* functionality used by PHP
HttpCacheModule	Caches the HTTP answer; logic for Kernel mode cache with http.sys
HttpLoggingModule	Default logging of requests via http.sys
ProtocolSupportModule	Custom HTTP answer header and redirection header; HTTP verbs *TRACE* and *OPTIONS*; HTTP Keep Alive configuration
RequestFilteringModule	Security module that filters suspicious requests
StaticCompressionModule	Compresses static contents to save bandwidth
StaticFileModule	Sends static contents with the appropriate MIME data type, such as HTML, CSS, or graphic files

Application Pools

Requests are processed in applications, which IIS groups into application pools, as described earlier in the chapter. IIS manages these application pools, launches new application processes when request volume increases, and shuts down application processes to save resources when request volume diminishes.

Setting Up Application Pools by Using IIS Manager

The following procedure describes how to set up a new application pool:

1. Open IIS Manager.

2. In the Connections pane, select Application Pools.

3. In the Actions pane, click Add Application Pool.

4. In the dialog box that opens, enter the name for your new application pool into the Name text box.

   Microsoft recommends that you accept the default values for Pipeline Mode (Integrated) and the .NET Framework Version.

5. Click OK.

You have now created a new application pool that you can use for new applications.

Setting Up Application Pools from the Command Line

To set up an application pool from the command line, use the command *appcmd add apppool*, and then provide a name, as shown in the following command:

```
appcmd add apppool /name:"PhpApp"
```

To list all the existing application pools, use this command:

```
appcmd list apppool
```

To display the configured properties of an application pool, run one of the following two commands:

```
appcmd list apppool /config "PhpApp"
appcmd list apppool /text:* "PhpApp"
```

Application Pool Identity

Application pools also fulfill an important security function: they protect application processes from processes in other application pools. This way, applications are clearly separated at the process level as well. IIS generates a virtual account with a unique security identifier (SID) for each application pool. This virtual account is not a true user account; therefore, it is not listed among the local users. However, the virtual account contains the name of the application pool. For example, IIS AppPool\DefaultAppPool is the virtual account name for the default application pool.

For your applications, this architecture means that application processes (including the PHP FastCGI processes) execute in the context of the application pool identity. Therefore, you can grant file access rights for these accounts individually, which also helps shield PHP (and other) programs from each other at the data-access level.

Specifying Application Pool Identity by Using IIS Manager

You can specify which identity that you want to use to run an application pool. To specify the identity (the user) by using IIS Manager:

1. Open IIS Manager.

2. In the Connections pane, select Application Pools.

3. Select the application pool that you want to configure in the work environment, and then in the Actions pane, click Advanced Settings.

   The Advanced Settings dialog box opens, as shown in Figure 2-8.

4. In the Process Model section, click the [...] button to the right of Identity.

   Another Application Pool Identity dialog box opens.

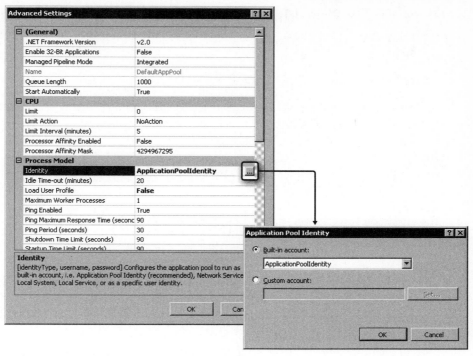

FIGURE 2-8 Specifying the identity of an application pool.

5. You can choose Built-In Account (from the drop-down list) or Custom Account.

   - If you choose a Built-In Account, you should use the ApplicationPoolIdentity option, because it causes every application pool to automatically use a different identity.

   - To choose a custom account, click the Specify button, and then enter the account name and password. The password is encrypted in the configuration automatically.

6. Click OK twice to close the dialog boxes.

Specifying Application Pool Identity from the Command Line

To specify the identity of an application pool from the command line, execute the following command:

```
appcmd set apppool PhpApp /processModel.identityType:ApplicationPoolIdentity
```

For the identity type, you can specify *ApplicationPoolIdentity*, *LocalSystem*, *LocalService*, *NetworkService*, or *SpecificUser*. To specify a custom account, you will also need to enter the user name and the password, as follows:

```
appcmd set apppool PhpApp
   /processModel.identityType:SpecificUser /processModel.userName:MyUserAccount
   /processModel.password:MyPassword
```

The password you enter is encrypted in the configuration automatically.

FastCGI

Using FastCGI for processing HTTP requests is an important new option in IIS 7. FastCGI provides a much higher level of performance than the older, still-common binding of PHP via CGI. Compared to binding PHP as an ISAPI module, FastCGI provides more stability and better configurability.

FastCGI vs. CGI

CGI is a standard that permits binding any desired program to a web server. The program that CGI calls runs as a standalone process. Figure 2-9 shows the process flow, which is described here:

1. The web client generates an HTTP request and sends it to the web server (IIS).

2. The web server processes the request. It starts the PHP interpreter in its own process and passes the HTTP request data (following the CGI standard) to PHP.

3. The PHP program calculates the result and returns the answer via CGI to the web server. The PHP program and the associated process then end.

4. The web server returns the PHP program's answer to the web client.

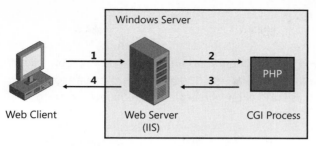

FIGURE 2-9 A PHP request flow with CGI.

The obvious disadvantage of CGI is that PHP must be restarted for each request. This kind of overhead devours resources and leads to significantly lower performance than you can achieve with FastCGI.

With FastCGI, the request flow looks similar to Figure 2-10, as described here:

1. The web client generates a request.

2. The web server processes the request and passes it to a free (not busy) PHP process in the application pool.

3. The PHP program generates a result and returns the answer to the web server. In FastCGI, however, the PHP process is not stopped; instead, it's freed for additional requests.

4. The web server returns the answer to the web client.

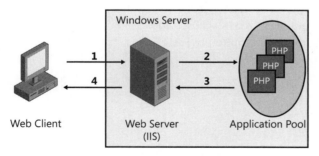

FIGURE 2-10 A PHP request flow with FastCGI.

The performance advantage of FastCGI, therefore, happens primarily because IIS can reuse the PHP process, avoiding the resource-intensive starting and ending process required by CGI. FastCGI preserves all the advantages of CGI, such as separation of web server processes and PHP. In addition, you can use the non-thread–safe version of PHP, because each PHP process handles only one request at a time. PHP thus saves work-intensive thread-safety checks, which in turn has a positive effect on performance.

FastCGI vs. ISAPI

Before FastCGI became available for IIS, binding PHP as an ISAPI extension was the only alternative to CGI. When PHP is configured as an ISAPI extension, it runs directly in the application process of the web server. That also dispenses with the need to start and stop PHP for each request, so PHP as ISAPI extension achieves a high level of performance and data throughput.

Unfortunately, because of its lack of separation from the web server, running PHP as an ISAPI extension also poses a disadvantage: both PHP and the web server use the same user account with the same access rights. Separating the two for security reasons is not possible. Furthermore, stability problems can arise: IIS can pass ISAPI extensions several requests, which should then be handled by that single process in a parallel fashion. Some PHP extensions, however, are not considered thread-safe, which is a requirement for parallel execution and handling of requests.

 Note This is one reason why PHP 5.3 no longer supports binding PHP as an ISAPI extension. PHP is only bound via FastCGI now.

Summary

This chapter provided a high-level overview of IIS architecture and functionality. You've seen information about sites, applications, and virtual directories, the process flow of an HTTP request, and the underlying reasons why IIS uses application pools mapped to individual applications. Together with the description of FastCGI and its advantages, you now have a solid foundation for a more in-depth discussion of the IIS and PHP configuration possibilities in the next two chapters.

Chapter 3
Configuring IIS

In Internet Information Services (IIS) 7, configuration has been freshly conceived from the bottom up. Instead of a centralized configuration, IIS 7 configuration is distributed over several files, depending on the structure of the websites and applications. The ubiquitous use of XML for the configuration file format is also new.

This chapter introduces IIS configuration in considerable detail, but a complete description is beyond the scope of this book. Instead, the focus here is on the general structure of IIS 7 configuration, and in particular, on the configuration of the essential building blocks (such as websites, applications, and virtual directories) that are of interest to PHP developers. The chapter also covers the configuration options for certain access paths with *location*.

The chapter closes with a discussion of how you can lock down parts of the configuration, thus permitting you to delegate IIS administration. Being able to lock the configuration is especially important for web hosts, or when system administrators want to grant restricted rights to allow others to administer their own applications.

Configuration Files

IIS saves configuration in plain text files. This simplifies copying, backing up, and editing the configuration: you can use common tools for the files when administering them.

There are several ways to read or edit the IIS configuration:

- Manually, with a text editor

- Using application programming interfaces (APIs) for native and managed programs

- Through tools such as Windows PowerShell or *appcmd*

- Through graphical interfaces, such as IIS Manager

IIS monitors all changes to configuration files; normally any configuration file changes become effective immediately, without requiring a computer reboot or server restart. This is a significant change when compared to previous IIS versions. The authoritative configuration sources are the configuration files themselves, not copies of the files in memory.

Global Configuration

The configuration of IIS is distributed over several files. This distribution has system-inherent causes, and at the same time brings certain advantages with it. The configuration files make up a hierarchy, at the top of which sit the global server-wide valid configurations. IIS recognizes two (or respectively three) global configuration files:

- **applicationHost.config** contains the IIS configuration (folder: C:\Windows\System32\inetsrv).

- **machine.config** contains the configuration of .NET Framework and ASP.NET (folder: C:\Windows\Microsoft.NET\Framework\[version number]\CONFIG).

- The **web.config** root file, located in the same folder, contains additional settings.

The distribution to these files takes place because IIS and Microsoft .NET are two different products with different product cycles.

Distributed Configuration

In addition to the global configuration files, there are distributed web.config configuration files. This distributed configuration orients itself along the physical layout of the websites, applications, virtual directories, and (physical) folders.

The configuration files constitute a hierarchy, as shown in Figure 3-1. At the top, there are the machine.config file and the root file web.config, followed by the file applicationHost.config. The settings for the following configuration files override or extend the settings of the previous files.

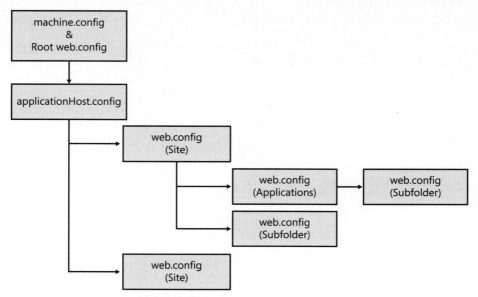

FIGURE 3-1 The hierarchy of the configuration files.

The global configuration is followed by the distributed configuration of the web.config files. These configurations impact only the websites, directories, and folders, in which they are saved (and their child elements). The configurations lower in the hierarchy override or extend the previous settings here, as well.

> **Note** For Apache administrators: the web.config files are comparable to the .htaccess files, whereas applicationHost.config corresponds to the file httpd.conf.

This structure permits PHP applications to supply the required settings themselves, together with a web.config file. Installing, moving, and copying of PHP applications becomes much easier and more comfortable than in the previous version of IIS.

Configuration Structure

The IIS configuration is grouped into sections; logically linked settings are defined and saved together in one section. A module represents a typical section grouping; each module has its own configuration section. The sections are closed within themselves, generally do not reference each other, and cannot be nested.

Sections and Section Groups

Sections are combined into section groups. The only task of section groups is to structure the configuration. They do not contain properties or settings themselves. Because section groups can be nested, a configuration hierarchy is created. Listing 3-1 shows the hierarchical structure of section groups and sections.

LISTING 3-1 Section groups and sections in the configuration.

```
<!-- Section group: Web server configuration -->
<system.webServer>
    <!-- Section: FastCGI configuration -->
    <fastCgi>
        <application fullPath="C:\PHP\php-cgi.exe" />
    </fastCgi>
    <!-- Section group: Trace configuration -->
    <tracing>
        <!-- Section: Trace configuration for request errors -->
        <traceFailedRequests />
        <!-- Section: Configuration of trace providers -->
        <traceProviderDefinitions>
            <add name="WWW Server" guid="{3a2a4e84-4c21-4981-ae10-3fda0d9b0f83}">
                <areas>
                    <clear />
                    <add name="StaticFile" value="16" />
                    <add name="FastCGI" value="4096" />
                </areas>
            </add>
        </traceProviderDefinitions>
    </tracing>
</system.webServer>
```

Elements and Configuration Listings

The sections contain the actual configuration settings in elements and attributes. The properties are saved in attributes, and the elements are for grouping. If there are several entries for a property that must be configured, configuration collections are used.

The element *system.webServer/tracing/traceProviderDefinitions/*areas in Listing 3-1 is an example for such a configuration collection. Configuration collections consist of three elements:

- **<add>** Adds a configuration entry. Each entry has an attribute for the name (name) and optional additional attributes for the values (for example, value).

- ■ **<remove>**   Entries can also be deleted. This way the configuration can be changed accordingly for certain server areas.

- ■ **<clear>**   Deletes all previously defined settings. This statement ensures that the subsequent local definition is the only valid definition for this configuration property.

Moving and Binding Sections

To maintain clarity, you can move sections and section groups into several different files. For example, this allows you to separate applicationHost.config into distinct files, which can be helpful during administration. IIS automatically recognizes configuration changes in external files. There is no need to restart the server.

To include the configuration files, you must specify the attribute *configSource*. Listing 3-2 shows you how to do this. Note that for the bound configuration file, you must start with the configuration element as the root.

LISTING 3-2 Binding an external configuration file.

applicationHost.config

```
<system.webServer>
    <defaultDocument configSource="defaultDoc.config" />
</system.webServer>
```

defaultDoc.config

```
<configuration>
    <system.webServer>
        <defaultDocument enabled="true" >
            <files>
                <add value="index.php" />
                <add value="index.html" />
            </files>
        </defaultDocument>
    </system.webServer>
</configuration>
```

The Configuration Editor

IIS Manager provides a configuration editor for working on the IIS configuration base. You need to know which configuration element you want to edit. For example, to configure the default document (see Listing 3-2), follow these steps:

1. In the Connections pane of the IIS Manager, browse to the desired element.

2. Open the Configuration Editor feature by double-clicking it.

3. Select the desired configuration element in the Section drop-down list box.

4. In the drop-down list box titled "From," select the configuration file to use.

You can then define and edit the *location* elements (see the section "Configuring Paths by using *location*," later in this chapter).

5. The properties of the element are displayed in the workspace, and you can change them by putting entries into the text boxes.

6. You can edit collections by using the button on the right, as shown in Figure 3-2.

You can create new entries by using Collection | Add, or edit the properties of existing entries in the Properties pane. Afterward, close the dialog box with the Close Window icon in the upper-right corner.

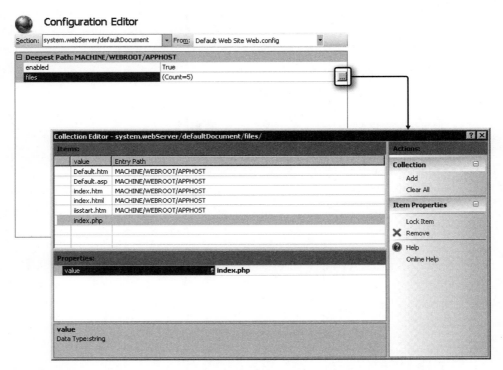

FIGURE 3-2 The Configuration Editor in the IIS Manager.

7. In the Actions pane, click Apply to apply your changes.

8. In the Actions pane, click Search Configuration to view and search the current configuration.

Schema and *configSections*

The XML configuration file content is based on a schema located in the folder C:\Windows\ System32\inetsrv\config\schema. The schema defines the syntax of the configuration's sections, elements, and attributes. In addition, the schema specifies default values for attributes, which is convenient because you don't need to specify all properties in a configuration file— it's sufficient to list the properties that deviate from the default values. This provides a clearer overview of the configuration files.

The applicationHost.config file contains a special section that serves as a point of registration for other sections and section groups: *configSections*. With *configSections*, other sections and section groups of IIS are registered at this location, as demonstrated in Listing 3-3.

LISTING 3-3 An excerpt for the *configSections* section.

```
<configSections>
    <sectionGroup name="system.webServer">
        <section name="defaultDocument" overrideModeDefault="Allow" />
        <section name="fastCgi" allowDefinition="AppHostOnly"
         overrideModeDefault="Deny" />
        <sectionGroup name="tracing">
            <section name="traceFailedRequests" overrideModeDefault="Allow" />
            <section name="traceProviderDefinitions" overrideModeDefault="Deny" />
        </sectionGroup>
    </sectionGroup>
</configSections>
```

Each IIS module has the correct schema for its configuration and an entry in the section configSections. This mechanism can also be used to extend the IIS configuration with settings and properties. For your own PHP applications, this configuration mechanism—compared to others such as simple .ini files—wouldn't necessarily be your first choice: to access the currently valid configuration of this path, you would either need to use Windows Management Instrumentation (WMI) or command-line tools such as *appcmd*.

Configuring Paths by Using *location*

IIS configuration is distributed into separate files: globally valid configuration resides in the files machine.config (and global, web.config) and applicationHost.config, whereas locally valid configuration for a path resides in web.config files in the folders assigned to the sites and applications.

Even though this distribution into local web.config files facilitates installing applications, it can't be applied to all application situations, for example, when two virtual directories that need to have different configurations point to the same folder, or if an administrator prefers to keep the complete application available in a single file for safety reasons.

In such cases, you can use the *location* statement, which lets you limit configurations to a certain path (the URL path, not the physical path). You specify *location* with the path attribute:

- **<location path=".">**   The current particular path.

- **<location path="PHP Demo Site/phpapp">**   The application path phpapp of the website PHP Demo Site.

- **<location path="PHP Demo Site/phpapp/wiki/index.php">**   Unlike web.config files, a location path can also reference individual files, such as index.php in our example.

If *location* is not specified in the applicationHost.config, but instead in a web.config file, the path specification is relative—in other words, the path must begin with the web.config location. Absolute path specifications are not permitted. With *location*, you can only modify paths below the web.config file's own *location* in the hierarchy.

Within *location*, you use the same sections and section groups as in the configuration files themselves (see Listing 3-4). For the relative path download, starting with the current path of the web.config file where this statement is located, the directory display is unlocked. Even though under normal circumstances download is most likely a subfolder of the web.config folder, that's not always the case; it could also be the path of a virtual directory, which means that the physical download folder could be located at a completely different position.

LISTING 3-4 A configuration statement with *location*.

```
<location path="download">
    <system.webServer>
        <directoryBrowse enabled="true" />
    </system.webServer>
</location>
```

Configuring by Using IIS Manager

With IIS Manager, you can edit location sections only by using the Configuration Editor. Other features always write into the appropriate web.config file. The status bar at the bottom of the open feature window shows you where the IIS Manager writes the configuration.

Here's how to configure individual files (the location entry is written into the web.config of the folder that contains the file):

1. In the Connections pane, select the directory that contains the file.

2. Click the Content View button at the bottom of the workspace.

3. Select the file that you want to configure, and then in the Actions pane, click Switch To Features View.

   You are now back in Features view, except for the selected file, as you can see in the Connections pane, or in the status bar of an open feature.

Configuring from the Command Line

Using the */commit* parameter, you can use the *appcmd* tool to create or update *location* elements. The */commit* parameter accepts the following values:

- **site**   Generates an entry in the web.config file of the website
- **app**   Generates an entry in the root folder of the application
- **appHost**   Generates an entry in applicationHost.config
- **<Path>**   Generates an entry in the specified path

You can generate Listing 3-4 as follows, assuming download is a subfolder of the application phpapp:

```
appcmd set config "Default Web Site/phpapp/download"
  -section:system.webServer/directoryBrowse /enabled:true /commit:app
```

Sites, Applications, and Directories

Configuring sites, applications, and virtual directories is an essential part of IIS administration. In the subsections that follow, you'll explore at the most important options. You can find a complete description in the online IIS documentation.

Sites, applications, and virtual directories are defined together in one section. Unlike other settings for features and modules, these must be defined in the file applicationHost.config, in the section group *system.applicationHost*, not the section group *system.webServer*.

Table 3-1 lists the most important sections of *system.applicationHost*. In addition to listeners and application pools, the sites are defined, which themselves also contain the applications and virtual directories.

TABLE 3-1 Section in the section group *system.applicationHost* (excerpt)

Section (element)	Description
applicationPools	Defines the application pools.
listenerAdapters	Defines the listener adapters being used, which bind to the Windows Process Activation Service (WAS)—for example, http.
log	Central setting for log creation.
sites	Defines the sites, applications, and virtual directories.
webLimits	Defines bandwidth and TCP/IP connection limits.

The default for all configuration sections of *system.applicationHost* is that settings can be specified only in the file applicationHost.config (*allowDefinition=AppHostOnly*) and that the configuration sections are locked (*overrideModeDefault=Deny*).

Listing 3-5 shows a configuration that defines two application pools and the directories for the log files.

LISTING 3-5 *system.applicationHost* configuration.

```
<system.applicationHost>
    <applicationPools>
        <add name="DefaultAppPool" autoStart="true" />
        <add name="PHP Demo Site" autoStart="true" />
    </applicationPools>
    <listenerAdapters>
        <add name="http" />
    </listenerAdapters>
    <log>
        <centralBinaryLogFile enabled="true"
                        directory="%SystemDrive%\inetpub\logs\LogFiles" />
        <centralW3CLogFile enabled="true"
                        directory="%SystemDrive%\inetpub\logs\LogFiles" />
    </log>
    <sites> [...] </sites>
    <webLimits />
</system.applicationHost>
```

Sites

Sites are defined in the *sites* section. The *site* configuration elements are listed in Table 3-2. You can define individual *sites* and set default values for application and virtual directories.

TABLE 3-2 The elements of the *sites* section

Element	Description
applicationDefaults	Defines default values for applications, such as the application pool that you want to use or the active logs.
site	Defines a single site (can be specified multiple times).
siteDefaults	Defines default values for sites; for example, the bindings, the log properties, or whether sites should start automatically.
virtualDirectoryDefaults	Defines default values for virtual directories; for example, whether web .config files are permitted in subfolders.

Defining a Single Site

You can define a website with the *site* configuration element. Its elements and attributes are listed in Table 3-3. Sites contain the required specifications for bindings and applications. You cannot define virtual directories on this level, because they must always be part of an application. Each site requires at least one application: the root application, which has the path "/".

TABLE 3-3 Configuration element <site> (excerpt)

Element	Attribute	Description
site		Defines a site
	id	Unique number of the site (the default website has the number 1)
	name	Name of the site; used for administration
	serverAutoStart	Specifies whether a site is started automatically (*true*, *false*)
site/application		Defines the applications of a site (can be defined multiple times)
site/bindings		Defines the bindings of a site
site/limits		Limits bandwidth as well as number and durations of connections

Listing 3-6 shows the definition of the default website directly after setting up the IIS: the site has a root application with the path "/" and a binding for the HTTP protocol to port 80.

LISTING 3-6 Configuration of the default website with root application and binding.

```
<site name="Default Web Site" id="1" serverAutoStart="true">
    <application path="/">
        <virtualDirectory path="/" physicalPath="%SystemDrive%\inetpub\wwwroot" />
    </application>
    <bindings>
        <binding protocol="http" bindingInformation="*:80:" />
    </bindings>
</site>
```

Bindings

A site can have multiple bindings. For each binding the protocol, host name, IP address, and port must be specified. Table 3-4 lists the configuration properties.

TABLE 3-4 Configuration element <bindings>

Element	Attribute	Description
bindings		Lists all bindings.
bindings/binding		Defines a single binding.
	bindingInformation	IP address, port, and host name separated by a colon; for example, *:80:phpdemo.site. You can use a placeholder for the IP address. The host name does not need to be specified (the binding applies to all host names).
	protocol	The protocol you are using, usually http or https.
bindings/clear		Deletes all inherited bindings and bindings set by default.

Applications

The purpose of an application is to assign virtual paths (URL paths) to application pools. Each site has at least one application: the root application, with the path "/". Table 3-5 lists the configuration properties for applications. Each application has at least one virtual directory: the root directory, which maps a virtual path to a physical path. Path specifications are relative, which means that the paths to the directories must be interpreted relative to the application path. Therefore, the root directory of an application always has the path "/".

TABLE 3-5 Configuration element <application>

Element	Attribute	Description
application		Defines an application
	applicationPool	The application pool you want to use
	enabledProtocols	Permitted protocols; usually http
	path	Application path
application/virtualDirectory		Assigned virtual directory
application/virtualDirectoryDefaults		Default values for virtual directories of the application

Even though applications can be logically nested, they are located next to each other in the configuration, as shown in Listing 3-7. The application /phpapp/wiki is part of the application /phpapp, but both definitions are located at the same level in the configuration file. The complete virtual path of the directory /data is /phpapp/wiki/data, because paths are relative to the applications.

LISTING 3-7 Configuration of applications and their virtual directories.

```
<application path="/" applicationPool="PHP Demo Site">
    <virtualDirectory path="/" physicalPath="C:\inetpub\phpdemosite" />
</application>
<application path="/phpapp" applicationPool="PhpApp">
    <virtualDirectory path="/" physicalPath="C:\inetpub\phpapp" />
</application>
<application path="/phpapp/wiki" applicationPool="PhpApp">
    <virtualDirectory path="/" physicalPath="C:\inetpub\phpwiki\scripts" />
    <virtualDirectory path="/data" physicalPath="C:\inetpub\phpwiki\data" />
</application>
```

Virtual Directories

Table 3-6 lists the configurable properties of virtual directories. You must specify the virtual and the physical path, because the core task of a virtual directory is to assign them to each other. If the web server accesses the directory with a special user account, you can also specify the user name and password.

TABLE 3-6 Attributes of the configuration element <virtualDirectory>

Attributes	Description
allowSubDirConfig	Specifies whether web.config should be taken into account in subfolders (*true*, *false*).
logonMethod	Specifies how IIS should be authenticated against the directory: *ClearText* (default value), *Interactive*, *Batch*, *Network*.
password	Optional password specification for authentication. The password should always be set via the IIS Manager or appcmd.exe, because this ensures that it is encrypted when it is inserted into the configuration file.
path	URL path of the virtual directory, relative to the parent elements.
physicalPath	Physical path of the assigned folder.
userName	Optional specification of the user name for authentication.

Locking the Configuration

For security reasons, you might want to ensure that certain configuration settings are not overridden or cancelled at other locations. This applies especially to central configurations of single modules, such as error handling or which modules are available for which websites. IIS 7 provides a highly granular mechanism for locking configuration settings. The default installation is set up in such a way that only the most essential settings can be rewritten on the lower hierarchy levels; yet another example of the continuous IIS security philosophy.

Locking with *configSections*

The section *configSections* serves as a registration point for other sections and section groups. You can define whether and how the definitions can be changed in lower hierarchy levels. You can use the following attributes:

- **overrideModeDefault**   Defines the default value for permitting configuration changes for this section or section group. *Allow* permits configuration changes, *Deny* prohibits them on lower configuration hierarchy levels. If the attribute is not specified, *Allow* is used by default.

- **allowDefinition**   Defines where in the configuration hierarchy changes are allowed if changing is enabled. If this attribute is not specified, changes are allowed everywhere. The following values can be set:

  - **MachineOnly**   The configuration can only be specified in machine.config.

  - **MachineToRootWeb**   In addition to *MachineOnly*, the configuration can also be changed in the root configuration file web.config of .NET Framework (same folder as machine.config).

  - **AppHostOnly**   The configuration may only be specified in applicationHost.config.

  - **MachineToApplication**   The configuration can (in addition to *MachineToRoot Web* and *AppHostOnly*) be changed in all root folders of IIS applications. This also includes configuration changes on the website level, because each website has a root application assigned to it.

  - **Everywhere**   The configuration can be changed everywhere, including in virtual directories and in all physical folders.

Locking and Unlocking with *location*

The settings in the section *configSections* specify the default values for changing and locking the configuration. With *location*, you can change these settings for individual paths.

Specifying Section Rights

In the *location* element, you can use the attribute *overrideMode* to specify for a path whether the configuration is locked or changes are allowed. The attribute can accept the following values:

- **Allow**   The listed sections permit configuration changes.

- **Deny**   The listed sections are locked, and therefore, prohibit configuration changes.

- **Inherit**   The configuration hierarchy is examined toward the top to determine whether changes are permitted. Ultimately, the values of the section *configSections* take effect. *Inherit* is the default value if the *overrideMode* attribute is not specified.

For example, Listing 3-8 prohibits changes to the module *defaultDocument* in *configSections* (*overrideModeDefault="Deny"*) in *applicationHost.config*. Because the *AllowDefinition* attribute is not set, changes (if allowed) could be made anywhere, such as in the web.config file of an application. Next, the globally valid settings for the module *defaultDocument* are defined in the section group *system.webServer*.

With *location*, you can enable the configuration to accept changes specifically for the path of the application phpapp. As you can see, you don't need to set new values directly with *location*. Unlocking the section to allow changes can also be achieved without any further specifications.

Because the configuration is no longer locked, you can specify new values for *defaultDocument* in the web.config file of the phpapp root folder.

LISTING 3-8 Changing the rights for the configurations of a certain path.

applicationHost.config

```
<configSections>
    <sectionGroup name="system.webServer">
        <section name="defaultDocument" overrideModeDefault="Deny" />
    </sectionGroup>
</configSections>
<system.webServer>
    <defaultDocument enabled="true">
        <files>
            <add value="index.html" />
            <add value="index.htm" />
        </files>
    </defaultDocument>
</system.webServer>
<location path="PHP Demo Site/phpapp" overrideMode="Allow">
    <system.webServer>
        <defaultDocument />
    </system.webServer>
</location>
```

web.config in the phpapp root folder

```
<defaultDocument enabled="true">
    <files>
        <clear />
        <add value="index.php" />
    </files>
</defaultDocument>
```

It also works the other way around: if a configuration section is never locked, but you would like to lock it for individual paths, you can lock the section with *overrideMode="Deny"* within a *location*. In this case, you should also specify properties and values within the location section. Otherwise, the general default values are used.

Specifying Rights for Individual Settings

By setting the *overrideMode* attribute, you can lock or unlock entire sections. Sometimes it can be useful to only lock or unlock individual settings for changes within a section. For this purpose, the IIS configuration provides you with five attributes:

- **lockAttributes**   Locks the specified attributes of the element.
- **lockAllAttributesExcept**   Locks all attributes of the element, except for the those listed.
- **lockElements**   Locks the specified child elements of the element that contains the definition.
- **lockAllElementsExcep**   Locks all child elements of the element, except for the those listed.
- **lockItem**   Locks the element that belongs to the attribute (useful for configuration collections).

These attributes can be set for all sections, whether they are located in applicationHost.config, web.config, or in a *location* section. With the exception of *lockItem*, all attributes accept as values individual names or comma-separated lists of names, while *lockItem* can have the value *true* or *false*.

Example: *lockAttributes*

Listing 3-9 shows how to lock individual attributes. The configuration in the example permits enabling and disabling directory contents, but the type of list cannot be changed: only size and file name extension are specified, but not the change date of the files.

LISTING 3-9 Locking individual attributes by using *lockAttributes*.

```
<location path="PHP Demo Site">
    <system.webServer>
        <directoryBrowse enabled="false" showFlags="Size,Extension"
                         lockAttributes="showFlags" />
    </system.webServer>
</location>
```

Example: *lockElements*

With *lockElements*, you can lock child elements, as shown in Listing 3-10. The default document for the application phpapp is set to index.php. The elements *remove* and *clear*, possible child elements of files, are locked. This locks their specification in subsequent configurations. In this example, the lock ensures that entries can be added to the configuration list, but no existing entries can be deleted.

LISTING 3-10 Locking individual child elements by using *lockElements*.

```
<location path="phpapp">
    <system.webServer>
        <defaultDocument enabled="true" >
            <files lockElements="remove,clear">
                <add value="index.php" />
            </files>
        </defaultDocument>
    </system.webServer>
</location>
```

Example: *lockItem*

The *lockItem* attribute is closely related to *lockElements*. While *lockElements* locks children of the current element, *lockItem* locks the current element itself. Listing 3-11 demonstrates this with another configuration. The entries for index.html and index.htm are locked and therefore cannot be deleted or altered. The entry index.php, however, can be deleted in the configuration hierarchy.

LISTING 3-11 Locking individual elements by using *lockItem*.

```
<system.webServer>
    <defaultDocument enabled="true" >
        <files>
            <add value="index.php" />
            <add value="index.html" lockItem="true" />
            <add value="index.htm" lockItem="true" />
        </files>
    </defaultDocument>
</system.webServer>
```

You can set the *lockItem* attribute for any desired element, even for sections.

Locking and Unlocking by Using *appcmd*

With *appcmd*, you can lock or unlock the configuration, but only on the level of the individual sections and not on the level of individual elements and attributes within the sections, as you can by direct editing of configuration files.

To do so, *appcmd* provides the following commands:

```
appcmd lock config "<PATH>" -section:<section>
appcmd unlock config "<PATH>" -section:<section>
```

<PATH> is the absolute (URL) path of a website, application, virtual directory, or physical folder, for example, *PHP Demo Site/phpapp/wiki*. If you leave out the path, the global server-wide configuration is targeted. *<section>* represents the section name such as *rewrite/ rewriteMaps* or *defaultDocument*.

Unfortunately, there is no command to retrieve the section status (locked or unlocked) for a certain path.

Locking and Unlocking by Using IIS Manager

You can also lock or unlock sections (not elements and attributes within sections) by using IIS Manager. Compared to *appcmd*, there is one additional restriction: you can access sections only globally or for a website. You cannot specify paths to applications or directories.

Locking and Unlocking Sections

To lock or unlock sections, perform the following steps:

1. In the Connections pane of the IIS Manager, select the web server.

2. In the area Home | Management, open the Feature Delegation module.

3. In the Feature Delegation workspace (which is now displayed), select a feature from the list.

4. In the Actions pane, in Set Feature Delegation, you can choose from among the following actions:

   - **Read/Write** Shares the features (corresponds to unlocking the section).
   - **Read Only** Locks the feature against changes.

- **Not Delegated**   Similar to the Read Only state. In addition, the feature is no longer displayed in the IIS Manager for users without administrator rights.

- **Reset To Inherited**   The configuration above the feature determines whether the feature is locked or unlocked.

5. The action is executed immediately. You can continue with other features or leave the pane.

Locking and Unlocking Features

You can lock or unlock features for individual websites from the same workspace:

1. In the Actions pane, click Custom Site Delegation.

2. The Custom Site Delegation workspace is displayed, as shown in Figure 3-3.

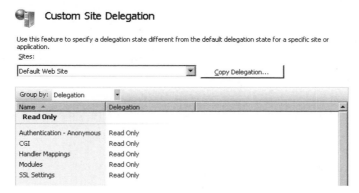

FIGURE 3-3 The Custom Site Delegation dialog box.

3. From the drop-down list, select the website that you want to configure.

4. Configuring the delegation of individual features is done in the same way as for server-wide configuration.

   You can delete the site-specific configurations in the Actions pane by clicking Reset All Delegation; the site takes over the server-wide configuration.

   Using the Copy Delegation button, you can transfer the delegation configuration of the current site to other sites.

5. In the Actions pane, click Default Delegation to return to the server-wide configuration.

Summary

The IIS configuration provides the appropriate kind of access for any administrator type: whether you are administering via the graphical interface of the IIS Manager, working from the command line, or editing the configuration files directly, the IIS configuration is always current and doesn't miss a step.

The ASP.NET-style distributed configuration with web.config files makes it easy for users coming from the other environments, such as an Apache web server, to orient themselves. Thanks to the XML structure, the purpose and scope of the specified settings is immediately obvious. No need to guess. Even unknown configuration sections can be assigned quickly, thanks to meaningful element names.

By providing the possibility to lock parts of the configuration, the IIS opens up new ways of delegating administrative tasks without compromising security: the locking option permits you to grant only the minimally-required rights.

Once you have read the description of the PHP configuration within IIS in the next chapter, you will know all the required methods and settings to run PHP applications efficiently and securely in IIS.

Chapter 4
Configuring PHP

This chapter discusses the configuration of PHP under Internet Information Services (IIS) in detail. You learn how to define time limits for request processing, how to specify index.php as the default document of a directory, and how to set up different PHP configurations and versions on the same server.

Not only can you configure PHP via the php.ini file, but you can also configure it via the Windows registration, with local .user.ini files, or through the IIS PHP Manager. As of IIS 7.5, FastCGI can also be configured in such a way that changes to the php.ini configuration file can be recognized automatically. In the following section, you will look at these configuration options in more detail.

Installing PHP Manager

IIS PHP Manager is a very useful tool to change PHP settings quickly and easily. If you have installed PHP with the Web Platform Installer (Web PI), PHP Manager is already available. To manually install it, perform the following:

1. Go to *http://phpmanager.codeplex.com/* and download the PHP Manager installer. Be sure that you download the proper version for your architecture (x64 versus x86).

2. Start the installer, and then click Next.

3. Agree to the license, and then click Next to start the installation.

4. Restart the IIS Manager.

5. In the Connections pane, select the server or a site, and then double-click the PHP Manager feature.

The PHP Manager screen appears, as shown in Figure 4-1.

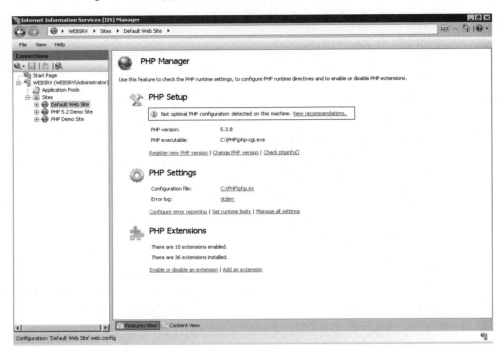

FIGURE 4-1 The PHP Manager start screen.

PHP Manager always changes PHP settings directly in php.ini; thus, any changes affect all sites using that PHP version. Also, PHP manager automatically adds handler mappings and default documents settings at the selected level chosen in the Connections pane of IIS Manager. Depending on your setup, you might need to manually adjust your settings afterward.

Important When using PHP Manager, you should always install additional PHP versions by using the Register New PHP Version function. If possible, you should install PHP Manager before you configure any PHP version in IIS. Otherwise, depending on your setup, PHP Manager might not recognize existing and configured PHP versions and (at least in 1.1.2) will not allow reregistering that PHP version.

Configuring PHP

PHP configuration can be specified at different locations and at different times. You can even adjust the PHP interpreter itself during compilation. Examples are the Suhosin Patch or the Hardening Patch of the Hardened PHP Project (*http://www.hardened-php.net/*). You can also change PHP configuration at runtime.

Some runtime settings must be specified (in php.ini) when starting PHP, and are therefore globally valid. Other settings can be changed at a later time, for example depending on the folder that contains the PHP script or even within the PHP script itself (with *ini_set()*). Table 4-1 shows you an overview of the four change modes of PHP settings.

TABLE 4-1 Change modes of PHP settings at runtime

Change mode	php.ini	.user.ini	Windows registration	PHP script
PHP_INI_ALL	Yes	Yes	Yes	Yes
PHP_INI_PERDIR	Yes	Yes	–	–
PHP_INI_USER	–	–	Yes	Yes
PHP_INI_SYSTEM	Yes	–	–	–

Before discussing the path-dependent configuration via php.ini, .user.ini, and Windows registration, you'll see how IIS can automatically apply configuration changes to php.ini.

Recognizing Configuration Changes

IIS automatically recognizes and implements changes to the IIS configuration. However, this is not the case for the PHP configuration; associated application pools must be restarted manually to reliably implement the configuration changes. As of IIS version 7.5 (Windows 7 and Windows Server 2008 R2), there is a feature that recognizes changes to the php.ini configuration file (or any other file you choose) and restarts PHP processes.

Caution Changes to files can only be recognized if this feature is supported by the file system. Files that are located on a network share are not supported.

Configuring by Using the IIS Manager

To configure the configuration monitoring feature, perform the following:

1. In the Connections pane of the IIS Manager, select the server, and then open the FastCGI Settings feature by double-clicking it.

2. From the list of FastCGI applications, select the desired PHP application, and then in the Actions pane, click Edit.

3. In the General section, in Monitor Changes To File, you can specify a file (for example, C:\PHP\php.ini). If this file is changed, the PHP processes are restarted, as shown in Figure 4-2.

FIGURE 4-2 Specifying a file to monitor for changes.

4. Click OK to close the dialog box.

From that point forward, changes to the php.ini configuration file are automatically implemented.

Configuring from the Command Line

To set up file monitoring with *appcmd*, use the following command:

```
appcmd set config /section:system.webServer/fastCgi
    /[fullPath='%PHP%\php-cgi.exe'].monitorChangesTo:"C:\PHP\php.ini"
```

Specify *%PHP%* in the *fullPath* parameter according to which FastCGI application you want to configure.

Configuring by Using PHP Manager

To set up file monitoring by using PHP Manager, perform the following:

1. In the Connections pane of the IIS Manager, select the server, and then open the PHP Manager feature by double-clicking it.

2. Click the View Recommendations link in the PHP Setup section.

3. Select the monitorChangesTo check box, and then click OK. (If this option is not available, monitoring is already activated.)

Path and Host-Dependent Configuration in php.ini

As of version 5.3, PHP gives you the option to specify configuration settings in the php.ini file, depending on the physical path of the PHP script or the host name. The configuration is quite simple; you just need to define a section in php.ini for the respective path or host, as follows:

- **[PATH=...]**   All subsequent settings apply only to this path. They are not applied to any subfolders.

- **[HOST=...]**   All subsequent settings apply only to this host name. PHP checks the *SERVER_NAME* variable to determine the host name. In IIS, *SERVER_NAME* is set to the host name in the URL (unlike in Apache).

The settings are applied to the defined host name or path up until the next *[HOST]* or *[PATH]* section. Other section statements, such as those in php.ini, have no effect. For this reason, these sections should always be placed at the end of the php.ini file.

Listing 4-1 shows a configuration. The *[PATH]* settings apply only to the respective folder, not to subfolders. The *[HOST]* setting applies to all PHP scripts independent of the physical path, if the request takes place via the specified host name. If a setting applies to both the *[PATH]* and the *[HOST]* setting, the *[PATH]* setting takes precedence.

LISTING 4-1 Path-dependent and host-dependent settings in php.ini.

```
[PATH=C:\inetpub\phpdemosite\wwwroot]
open_basedir = "C:\inetpub\phpdemosite"
[PATH=C:\inetpub\secondsite]
short_open_tags = On
[HOST=manfred.phpdemo.site]
memory_limit = 256M
```

IIS does not automatically recognize changes to the php.ini file (unless you configured the change monitoring). To implement the changes, the corresponding application pool must be restarted in this case.

PHP Manager does not yet support path or host-dependent configurations. All settings you make through PHP Manager's PHP Settings | Manage All Settings affect global settings only, and leave path or host-dependent settings untouched.

Configuring by Using .user.ini

As of PHP version 5.3, you can also configure PHP in individual configuration files directly in the folders—similar to web.config of IIS—if you are running PHP as FastCGI. These settings apply to the folder that contains the .user.ini file and to all subfolders.

The .user.ini files have the same structure as the standard php.ini file.

You can simply copy or move PHP configurations from a site or application to a different location. The .user.ini file is just copied along with the rest, and thus all settings are copied, as well.

> **Tip** With the configuration option *user_ini.filename*, you can choose a different name for the local configuration files. This can be helpful, because file names with a leading period are not common in Windows.

The settings you specify in .user.ini files can later be changed in the PHP script with *ini_set()*. If you make entries in the Windows registration as well as in the .user.ini file, the Windows registration takes precedence and prevents retroactive changes from the PHP script or .user.ini files.

> **Note** For Apache administrators: the .user.ini files correspond to the *php_value* and *php_flag* statements in an .htaccess file.

Also note the following two issues:

- For performance reasons, PHP saves .user.ini files in a cache. Changes to these files don't take effect immediately—only after the cache has expired (the default setting is five minutes, which you can edit via the *user_ini.cache_ttl* configuration setting). To allow a change to take effect earlier, you need to restart the corresponding IIS application pool.

- Searching for .user.ini files works only up to the root folder of the site (*DOCUMENT_ROOT*). In the current version of PHP, this means that .user.ini files in applications outside the site's root folder are valid only in the folder that contains the file itself. They are not valid for subfolders, which limits their use in such situations.

Configuring by Using the Windows Registry

PHP can read settings from the Windows Registry. You can restrict these setting to just physical paths. The registry key is *HKEY_LOCAL_MACHINE\SOFTWARE\PHP\Per Directory Values*.

> **Note** For 64-bit Windows, the registry key can also be *HKEY_LOCAL_MACHINE\SOFTWARE\Wow6432Node\PHP\Per Directory Values*. The Wow6432Node key is for 32-bit programs that run under 64-bit Windows.

Below this registry key the keys specify the path. For example, if you want to specify a setting only for the path C:\inetpub\phpdemosite\apps\phpapp1, you need to use the registry key *HKLM\SOFTWARE\PHP\Per Directory Values\c\inetpub\phpdemosite\apps\phpapp1*.

You need to specify the PHP setting as a string at the desired key. The setting name corresponds to the name in the php.ini configuration. If you enter the setting directly at the registry key *Per Directory Values*, the values are valid for all paths.

If you specify PHP settings in the Windows Registry, these settings can no longer be changed with *ini_set()* in the PHP script. Therefore, the settings are protected against changes. Depending on the circumstances under which you run your PHP application, this might be precisely what you want.

To specify settings in the Windows Registry, use the Registry Editor by following this procedure:

1. Start the Registry Editor by clicking Start | Run. Enter **regedit** as the program that you want to open.

2. In the left pane, browse to the appropriate registry key.

3. If the PHP key does not exist yet, create it by clicking New | Key in the context menu of the parent registry key. Do the same for the key *Per Directory Values* and any other keys for the physical path.

4. To enter a PHP setting, select the desired key, and then click Edit | New | String Value. Alternatively, you can use the same command from the context menu, as shown in Figure 4-3.

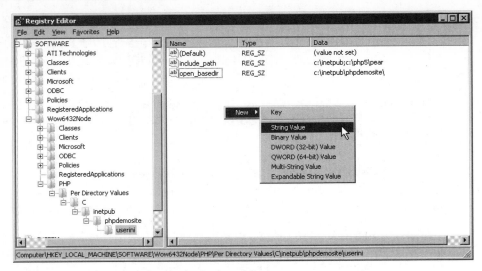

FIGURE 4-3 Editing PHP settings in the Registry Editor.

5. Click File, and then click Exit to close the Registry Editor.

 Note For Apache administrators: the settings in the Windows Registry correspond to the *php_admin_value* and *php_admin_flag* statements in the .htaccess file.

Configuring a FastCGI Application

Because PHP is executed in IIS via FastCGI, you can use various FastCGI applications and handler assignments to change any configuration options on any folder level—even those that can only be specified in php.ini.

To do so, you need to set up a new FastCGI application that loads an alternative configuration file as parameter (PHP command line parameter -*c*). You will read more about this in the section "Setting Up Different PHP Configurations," later in the chapter.

 Note PHP Manager does not support different FastCGI applications based on the same PHP version. Such configurations must be done manually.

Because the settings are specified directly in the php.ini file, and the handler assignment can be changed at any level (as long as the IIS configuration is not locked), you are free to change any PHP settings at any location on the server, on the site, or in the application. However, this advantage comes at the price of an increased consumption of resources (especially memory), because for each FastCGI application you set up, several PHP Interpreter instances are started. In addition, this kind of configuration can quickly become unclear: changes to PHP configurations that you want to apply globally must now be implemented in all php.ini files.

Nevertheless, being able to freely change all settings (even with the change mode *PHP_INI_SYSTEM*) cancels out these disadvantages in certain situations. Whether you prefer the configuration via FastCGI or the path-dependent configuration in the php.ini file is contingent upon the circumstances of your application scenario.

Specifying the Default Document

When requesting a folder, IIS gives you the option to display a document instead of the folder contents. This *default document* can be a simple HTML file or a PHP script. If you installed PHP with the Web PI or have registered PHP with the PHP Manager, the list of possible default document names already contains the name index.php; if you didn't, that file name is probably missing. However, the Web PI places index.php at the last position in the list (whereas PHP Manager places it at the first position). To increase performance, you might want to adjust the order in which IIS searches for default documents, or delete document names you are not using.

> **Note** With the IIS default installation, you can redefine the default document at any level. If your installation is different, you might first need to share the configuration accordingly.

For reasons of security and performance, it makes sense to only include the default document names in the list that you are actually using. You might also want to specify different default documents for different applications or folders.

Specifying the Default Document by Using the IIS Manager

The following procedure describes how to use the IIS Manager to specify the default documents for a directory:

1. Open the IIS Manager, and then in the Connections pane, select the element that you want to configure (site, application, directory, subfolder).

2. In the workspace, select the Default Document feature.

3. To add a new default document, in the Actions pane, click Add.

4. Enter the name of the default document into the dialog box, and then click OK.

   Figure 4-4 demonstrates that the local settings are entered at the top.

Default Document

Use this feature to specify the default file(s) to return when a client does not request a specific file. Set default documents in order of priority.

Name	Entry Type
index.php	Local
Default.htm	Inherited
Default.asp	Inherited
index.htm	Inherited
index.html	Inherited
iisstart.htm	Inherited

FIGURE 4-4 The Default Document feature workspace.

5. To remove default documents, select the document in the workspace, and then in the Actions pane, click Remove.

6. To change the order of the default documents, select the document that you want to move, and then in the Actions pane, click Move Up or Move Down.

 Caution If you are changing the order, all entries become local entries and inheritance is no longer in effect.

Specifying from the Command Line

To specify the standard documents from the command line, use the following commands:

- To list all default documents, run the following command:

  ```
  appcmd list config /section:defaultDocument <PATH>
  ```

- To add one default document, run the following command:

  ```
  appcmd set config /section:defaultDocument <PATH> /+files.[value='content.php']
  ```

- To remove a default document, run the following command:

  ```
  appcmd set config /section:defaultDocument <PATH> /-files.[value='iisstart.htm']
  ```

- To remove all default documents, run the following command:

  ```
  appcmd set config /section:defaultDocument <PATH> /~files
  ```

 Note In the preceding examples, *<PATH>* stands for the appropriate element; for example, "Default Web Site/phpapp/hamster" (the quotes are necessary because of the spaces). If you want to change the server-wide settings, just leave out *<PATH>*.

Defining Directly in the Configuration

To specify a default document in the configuration, either globally in applicationHost.config or distributed in the web.config files, specify the entries in the configuration section *system. webServer/defaultDocument*, as shown in Listing 4-2.

LISTING 4-2 Defining the default document in the XML configuration.

```
<defaultDocument enabled="true">
    <files>
        <add value="index.php" />
        <add value="index.html" />
    </files>
</defaultDocument>
```

If you apply the specifications in Listing 4-2 to a web.config file, those default documents that are inherited are not nullified. Use the configuration element *<clear />* to remove them.

> **Tip** To ensure that a default document is always at the top of the list—no matter if it has already been inherited in the configuration hierarchy—enter the following:
>
> ```
> <defaultDocument enabled="true">
>     <files>
>         <remove value="index.php" />
>         <add value="index.php" />
>     </files>
> </defaultDocument>
> ```
>
> Removing and adding the entry ensures that it is always first.

Request Limits

Using PHP with FastCGI means that the same PHP process is reused for multiple requests. The fact that PHP does not need to be restarted for each request increases performance. However, there is a possibility that stability can be compromised: if PHP or a PHP extension does not release all resources due to an error, those resources remain in use. In such cases, the server can eventually become unavailable because PHP is using all the resources.

To guard against this situation, both FastCGI and PHP provide the ability to automatically end processes after a certain number of requests. Doing so frees up any unreleased resources.

It's good practice to leave this automatic ending of processes to IIS—specifically, to the FastCGI module. The FastCGI module has more information than a single PHP process; it is therefore able to make better decisions. Also, FastCGI cannot always distinguish an automatically-ending PHP process from an error abort.

Two variables control process restarts: *instanceMaxRequests* on the FastCGI side, and *PHP_FCGI_MAX_REQUESTS* on the PHP side.

You should set the variables so that *instanceMaxRequests* is smaller than *PHP_FCGI_MAX_REQUESTS*. This ensures that FastCGI triggers the restart.

Configuring by Using the IIS Manager

The following is the procedure to specify the restart limit by using the IIS Manager:

1. In the Connections pane of the IIS Manager, select the server.

2. In the workspace, select the FastCGI Settings feature.

3. In the FastCGI Settings, select the PHP application that you want to configure, and then in the Actions pane, click Edit.

4. In the Edit FastCGI Application dialog box, enter the request limit for process restarts into the Instance MaxRequests text box. The recommended value is 10,000 requests.

5. Click the Collection button under Environment Variables.

    The EnvironmentVariables Collection Editor dialog box opens.

6. Click Add, and then in the Misc pane, in the Name text box, enter the value **PHP_FCGI_MAX_REQUESTS**. In the Value text box, type the number **10001**, as shown in Figure 4-5.

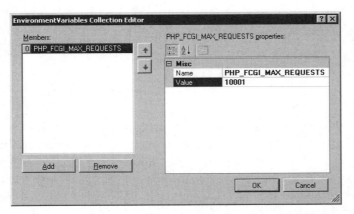

FIGURE 4-5 Configuration of the environment variable *PHP_FCGI_MAX_REQUESTS*.

7. Click OK to Close the open dialog boxes.

It's not necessary to restart the server or the application pool; IIS takes care of it automatically.

Configuring from the Command Line

To start the configuration from the command line, use *appcmd*, as follows:

1. Start a Command Prompt window with administrator rights.

2. To configure the FastCGI limit, run the following command:

```
appcmd set config /section:system.webServer/fastCgi
    /[fullPath='%PHP%\php- cgi.exe'].instanceMaxRequests:10000
```

3. To add the PHP limit, run the following command:

```
appcmd set config /section:system.webServer/fastCgi/+"[fullPath='%PHP%\php-
    cgi.exe'].environmentVariables.[name='PHP_FCGI_MAX_REQUESTS',value='10001']"
```

> **Note** *%PHP%* in the *fullPath* parameter stands for the FastCGI application that you want to configure.

Configuring Directly in the Configuration File

You can also set the parameters directly in the configuration file applicationHost.config, in the section *system.webServer/fastCGI*, as follows, and as shown in Listing 4-3:

- Specify the FastCGI limit as the value for the attribute *instanceMaxRequests* in the application configuration element.

- Specify the PHP environment variable in the *environmentVariables* collection.

LISTING 4-3 Setting the process restart limits in applicationHost.config.

```
<fastCgi>
    <application fullPath="C:\PHP\php-cgi.exe" instanceMaxRequests="10000">
        <environmentVariables>
            <environmentVariable name="PHP_FCGI_MAX_REQUESTS" value="10001" />
        </environmentVariables>
    </application>
</fastCgi>
```

Time Limits for Request Processing

It can take a long time to handle a request, depending on the data input and other parameters. A program error can also prevent a PHP program from ending. For such scenarios, you can limit the available processing time for a request.

IIS has three crucial time limits during request processing via PHP scripts: PHP limits, FastCGI limits, and limits by IIS itself. The IIS limit (*ConnectionTimeout*) is triggered only when a connection is inactive for a certain amount of time, but does not interfere with the processing of a running PHP script. Therefore, a running PHP script can only be prematurely ended when either the PHP time limit or the FastCGI time limit has been exceeded. The following is a description of these configuration limits.

PHP Limits

You can define two time limits in PHP:

- **max_execution_time**   Specifies the maximum script execution time in seconds
- **max_input_time**   Specifies the maximum time (in seconds) that is available for reading and evaluating input data (for example *$_POST*, *$_FILES*). This limit is especially important for large files and slow connections.

You can set both values in the PHP configuration, or you can use PHP Manager, which provides an interface for setting those limits (click PHP Manager | PHP Settings | Set Runtime Limits).

FastCGI Limits

FastCGI recognizes two time limits: the time a PHP application can use to process the request, and the time a request can wait before it's executed. The latter is crucial only during workload peaks: if more requests arrive than the number of PHP processes available to handle them, the requests are added to a waiting list, and are subsequently handled in sequence. If a request has been waiting too long for processing, it is removed from the waiting list and an error message is sent to the requesting client.

Configuring by Using the IIS Manager

To configure the time limits by using the IIS Manager, perform the following:

1. Open the FastCGI Settings feature of the desired server in the IIS Manager.

2. Select the FastCGI application that you want to configure from the list, and then in the Actions pane, click Edit.

   The Edit FastCGI Application dialog box opens.

3. In the Process Model section, in the Activity Timeout field, you can configure the time that the PHP script has for execution.

4. In the Request Timeout field, you can specify the time that a request can stay in the waiting list for execution.

5. Click OK to apply your entries.

Configuring from the Command Line

You can specify the activity timeout by using the following *appcmd* command:

```
appcmd set config /section:system.webServer/fastCgi
   /[fullPath='%PHP%\php-cgi.exe'].activityTimeout:90
```

To set the request timeout, use the following command:

```
appcmd set config /section:system.webServer/fastCgi
   /[fullPath='%PHP%\php-cgi.exe'].requestTimeout:90
```

Note *%PHP%* stands for the complete path to the PHP application that you want to configure.

Session Storage and Temporary Files

By default, PHP saves session data (accessible via *$_SESSION*) and temporary files in the directory C:\Windows\Temp. You can retrieve the folder PHP is currently using for session storage by using *session_save_path()*. The directory for temporary files, for example, those created during file upload, can be read with *sys_get_temp_dir()*.

You can change these folders by setting the configuration values *session.save_path* and *upload_tmp_dir* in php.ini to your preferred folders. Alternatively, you can set them in PHP Manager by using the command PHP Settings | Manage All Settings. In both cases, you must ensure that PHP has the necessary permissions for the folders.

To change permissions for folders, perform the following:

1. Right-click the folder in Windows Explorer, and then in the context menu, click Properties.

2. Browse to the Security tab, and then click Edit.

3. In the Permissions dialog box, click Add.

4. Enter **IIS_IUSRS** as the object name, and then click OK.

Note If the user is not recognized, ensure that the Search Path field in the dialog box contains the current computer, not the domain.

5. Select IIS_IUSRS in the list box, and then give it the additional right, Change.

6. Click OK to close the dialog box.

Restart the PHP application pool to apply the changed configuration. Now PHP uses the directories you specified for the session storage and for temporary files.

In Chapter 6, "Caching," you learn how to use the WinCache PHP extension as session memory.

Setting Up PHP Syntax Highlighting

With PHP, you can display the source code of a PHP file with colored syntax highlighting. You can accomplish this in two ways: by using a handler for all files with the extension .phps, or with the URL Rewrite module.

Configuring Syntax Highlighting by Using the IIS Manager

To set up the handler for PHP syntax highlighting via the IIS Manager, perform the following procedure:

1. Open the IIS Manager, and then in the Connections pane, select the server.

2. Select the Handler Mappings feature in the workspace.

3. In the Actions pane, click Add Module Mapping to start the assignment.

   The Add Module Mapping dialog box opens, as shown in Figure 4-6.

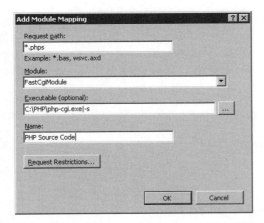

FIGURE 4-6 Adding a module assignment for PHP source code.

4. Enter the following data into the text boxes:

- Request Path: ***.phps**

- Module: **FastCgiModule**

- Executable (Optional): ***%PHP%\php-cgi.exe|-s***

  Be sure to separate the parameter from the program path with a pipe character
  (|) (not a space).

- Name: **PHP source code** (as desired)

5. Click the Request Restrictions button.

6. On the Mapping tab, select the check box, and then select the option File.

7. Browse to the Verbs tab, select the option One Of The Following Verbs, and then type
   GET, HEAD in the text box.

8. Click OK to close the Request Restrictions dialog box.

9. Confirm your entries by clicking OK.

10. Click Yes in response to the pop-up asking whether you want to set up a new FastCGI
    application.

Now, when you call up a file with the extension .phps, the PHP source code automatically
displays with colored syntax, as shown in Figure 4-7.

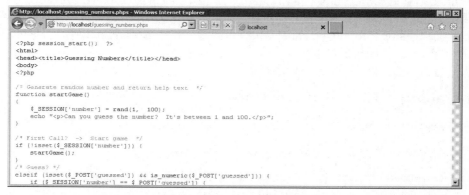

FIGURE 4-7 The source code of the number guessing example from Chapter 1, "Setting up the Work
Environment," displayed in color. In this illustration the colors are represented as shades of gray.

Caution Source code can provide hints about potential weak spots for attackers. Think care-
fully about which source code files you make accessible and which servers you want to allow to
display files that contain source code.

Configuring from the Command Line

You can also set up the syntax highlighting from the command line by using *appcmd*:

1. Start a Command Prompt Window with administrator rights.

2. To configure the FastCGI application pool, run the following command:

```
appcmd set config /section:system.webServer/fastCGI
    /+["fullPath='%PHP%\php-cgi.exe',arguments='-s'"]
```

3. To configure the handler assignment, run the following command:

```
appcmd set config /section:system.webServer/handlers
    /+["name='PHP_Quellcode',modules='FastCgiModule',
    scriptProcessor='%PHP%\php-cgi.exe|-s',verb='GET,HEAD',
    path='*.phps',resourceType='File'"]
```

Set the path to php-cgi.exe, according to the PHP installation that you want to configure.

Setting Up Different PHP Versions

PHP via FastCGI permits you to use different PHP versions on the same server—and even in the same site, if desired. This is possible because you can use different handler assignments for different paths.

In the following subsections, you will learn how to install PHP version 5.2, in addition to PHP version 5.3. You can apply the description to other PHP versions as well. This procedure leads you step-by-step through a manual installation, because installing different PHP versions with the Web PI is (currently) not possible.

Installing a New PHP Version

First, you need to install the new PHP version, as follows:

1. Open the website *http://windows.php.net/download/*.

2. Download the current PHP version, 5.2.x (at time of this book's printing: 5.2.17) as a zip archive. Select the VC6 x86 Non Thread Safe version.

3. Extract the zip file into a folder of your choosing. This book uses the folder C:\PHP_5_2.

4. Copy the file C:\PHP_5_2\php.ini-recommended to C:\PHP_5_2\php.ini.

5. Open the file C:\PHP_5_2\php.ini in an editor, and then set the following configuration options:

```
date.timezone = "Pacific/Auckland"
cgi.force_redirect = 0
```

Configuring by Using the PHP Manager

PHP Manager makes it very easy to configure the new PHP version:

1. Start the IIS Manager.

2. In the Connections pane, select the desired element.

3. Select the PHP Manager feature in the workspace, and then click PHP Setup | Register New PHP Version.

4. Provide the path to the php-cgi.exe executable in the dialog window, and then click OK.

That's it. PHP Manager creates the necessary FastCGI application and handler mappings. It also sets the newly configured PHP version as the default version of the element that you selected in the first step. Afterward, you can change the PHP versions on any level by going to the desired element in the Connections pane, starting PHP Manager, and then changing the version by clicking PHP Setup | Change PHP Version.

Although PHP Manager does not handle different FastCGI applications based on the same PHP version, it is easy to set up different PHP versions and assign them to sites, applications, or subfolders. Just keep in mind that all locations with the same PHP version share the same PHP configuration.

Configuring the Handler Assignment

If you do not use the PHP Manager, you need to configure the handler assignment yourself. The configuration can take place at your desired level (site, application, virtual directory, subfolder).

Configuring by Using IIS Manager

To specify the handler assignment by using IIS Manager, perform the following:

1. Open the IIS Manager.

2. In the Connections pane, select the desired element.

3. Select the Handler Mappings feature in the workspace.

4. If an assignment for *.php exists already, delete it by going to the Actions pane, and clicking Remove.

5. In the Actions pane, click Add Module Mapping to create a new assignment.

6. Enter the following values for the assignment into the text boxes:

   - Request Path: ***.php**
   - Module: **FastCGIModul**
   - Executable: **C:\PHP_5_2\php-cgi.exe**
   - Name: **PHP 5.2 via FastCGI**

7. Use the Request Restrictions button to limit the assignment, as desired.

8. Click OK to confirm your entries.

9. Click Yes in response to the pop-up asking whether you want to set up a new FastCGI application.

Configuring from the Command Line

To specify the handler mapping from the command line, run the following command:

```
appcmd set config /section:system.webServer/handlers <Path> /+[name='PHP_52_via_FastCGI',
    modules='FastCgiModule',scriptProcessor='C:\PHP_5_2\php- cgi.exe', verb='*',
    path='*.php',resourceType='File']
```

> **Note** *<Path>* stands for the (virtual) path to the element that you want to configure (for example PHP Demo Site/php52).

Configuring the FastCGI Application

Finally, you need to configure the FastCGI application—unless you used PHP Manager for the setup. It's important that you configure the path to the php.ini file. PHP offers different options for specifying the path. Here, you'll use the environment variable *PHPRC*.

Configuring by Using the IIS Manager

If you set up the handler assignment via the IIS Manager, FastCGI will already have been generated. All you need to do is set the environment variable as follows:

1. Open the IIS Manager, and then select the feature FastCGI Settings.

2. Select the appropriate FastCGI application, and then in the Actions pane, click Edit.

   The Edit FastCGI Application dialog box opens.

3. In the dialog box, click Environment Variables | Collection.

4. Click Add. In the right pane, in the Name text box, enter **PHPRC**; in the Value text box, enter the absolute physical path to the php.ini file (C:\PHP_5_2\php.ini), and then click OK.

5. Click OK to complete the configuration.

Configuring from the Command Line

To configure the FastCGI application from the command line, run the following commands:

1. To set up the application:

```
appcmd set config /section:system.webServer/fastCGI
    /+[fullPath='C:\PHP_5_2\php-cgi.exe']
```

2. To Specify the *PHPRC* environment variable:

```
appcmd set config /section:system.webServer/fastCgi
    /+"[fullPath='C:\PHP_5_2\php-cgi.exe'].environmentVariables.
    [name='PHPRC',value='C:\PHP_5_2\php-cgi.exe']"
```

Testing

To test the settings, you can either create and execute a file in the desired directory with the following content:

```
<?php phpinfo() ?>
```

Or, you can use the program from Listing 4-4.

LISTING 4-4 Using info.php to gather information about PHP version and the php.ini path.

```
<html>
<head><title>PHP Version</title></head>
<body>
<ul>
    <li><strong>PHP version:</strong> <?php echo phpversion(); ?></li>
    <li><strong>Path to php.ini:</strong>
        <?php
        $inipath = php_ini_loaded_file();
        echo empty($inipath) ? 'No php.ini loaded' : $inipath;
        ?>
    </li>
    <li><strong>Physical script path:</strong> <?php echo __FILE__ ?></li>
</ul>
</body>
</html>
```

Not only can you use two different PHP versions on one server or one site, you can even run the same PHP script with different PHP versions. To do this, you must be able to reach the script that you want to execute via two different URL paths that have two different handlers assigned to them, as follows:

1. Set up a path (application, virtual directory, or folder) for the first handler mapping for PHP version 5.3 (for example, /php53).

2. Set up a path for the second handler mapping for PHP version 5.2 (for example, /php52).

3. Set up a virtual directory in /php53 and in /php52 that both point to the folder containing the PHP scripts that you want to execute.

Because of the path, IIS recognizes which handler mapping should be selected, and therefore, which PHP version to execute. The virtual directories, however, point to the same folder. Listing 4-5 demonstrates how you can show the parallel execution. Figure 4-8 shows the result.

LISTING 4-5 Parallel script execution with different PHP versions.

```
<html>
<head><title>Two PHP versions on the same server</title></head>
<body>
    <h1>PHP 5.3</h1>
    <iframe src="php_5_3/php_x2/info.php" height="100" width="80%"></iframe>
    <h1>PHP 5.2</h1>
    <iframe src="php_5_2/php_x2/info.php" height="100" width="80%"></iframe>
</body>
</html>
```

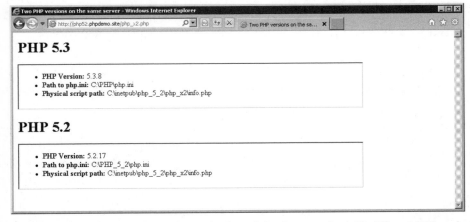

FIGURE 4-8 The window showing the result of parallel script execution with different PHP versions.

Setting Up Different PHP Configurations

Just as you can set up different PHP versions to run on the same server, you can also run different configurations on a server for a single PHP version.

IIS differentiates FastCGI applications for the handler assignment, based on two properties: the path of the executable file, and the passing parameters. If, as in this case, you are dealing with different applications for the same PHP version (the same executable file), the only way to differentiate the FastCGI applications from each other is to give PHP different parameters when calling them. Because you want to use different configurations, it makes sense to use the parameter -c for specifying the php.ini path.

> **Note** To use the path as the differentiator for different PHP configurations, follow the instructions in the preceding section, "Setting up Different PHP Versions."

1. Create an alternative php.ini configuration.

2. For the desired configuration element (site, application, and so on), remove the existing *.php handler assignment, if such an assignment exists.

3. Add a new handler assignment for the configuration element.

   Separate the parameters from the executable file with a pipe, for example: C:\PHP\php-cgi.exe|-c C:\PHP\alternative-php.ini.

4. Create the corresponding FastCGI application or let the IIS Manager generate it.

5. Check your configuration with a simple *phpinfo()* PHP script.

> **Note** PHP Manager currently does not support different configurations for the same PHP version. Therefore, such configurations must be set up manually.

Summary

You can configure PHP under IIS in a very flexible manner. In particular, path-dependent and hostname-dependent configuration facilitates the installation of different PHP applications on the same server. By configuring different PHP versions on the same server—or even the same site—you can migrate to new PHP versions gradually, application by application. This is a very helpful feature for installations with many applications, but thanks to FastCGI, you can implement it easily.

The next chapter discusses security aspects of the configuration and how PHP executes under IIS.

Chapter 5
Security

Due to its modular structure and integrated security philosophy, Internet Information Services (IIS) 7 is a very secure platform for running websites. IIS offers multiple features for securing PHP applications. One of the most important of these features is the ability to assign a specific user account to each application. This gives you the ability to clearly manage data access at file-system level by using access control lists (ACLs). The application must be structured accordingly, which is why you will see information about structuring your application first. Later in the chapter, you'll see tips on how to secure your PHP configurations as well as an in-depth discussion of identity and access rights for PHP processes. The Authentication, Authorization, and Request Filter features, along with the configuration of encrypted connections with HTTPS provide you with a good overview of the security features of IIS combined with PHP.

Structuring the Application

Because of the highly granular configuration of IIS, you can significantly increase the security of a PHP application by arranging the file and folder structure. The ability to configure IIS in such a way that PHP or other programs are only run in defined directories is the cornerstone of this approach.

A PHP application usually consists of the following parts:

- PHP scripts that can be called directly via a URL.

- PHP scripts that are included by other PHP scripts, but are not called directly them-selves—for example, third-party libraries or include files.

- Data files—for example, pictures, graphics, CSS files, or downloadable files.

- A writable, publicly-accessible zone for storing data permanently.

- A writable area for permanent files not publicly accessible via a URL—for example, to hold configuration files or log files.

- An area for temporary data storage—for example, to hold files while they are pro-cessed by a PHP script.

The properties of these areas can be divided into three dimensions:

- *Executable/Not executable* (Can PHP scripts be executed?)

- *Public/Private* (Can the area be accessed via a URL?)

- *Read-only/Read and write* (Do the access rights allow editing the area?)

Depending on which properties an area has, you can grant custom rights with the IIS config-uration. Figure 5-1 shows an example of a typical application structure, based on what you've learned thus far.

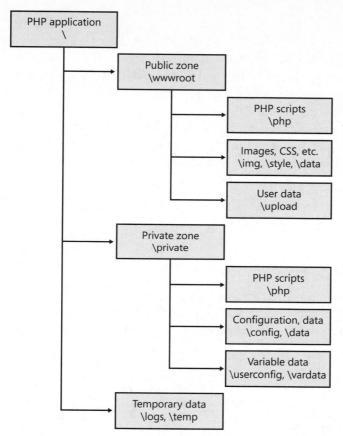

FIGURE 5-1 The folder structure of a PHP application.

From this point on, this chapter assumes that the PHP application has not been installed at the website level, but is instead configured as one of the website's multiple applications. You can then use the configuration and process information in the same fashion for a PHP application that is the root application of a website.

Root Folder or Virtual Directory

When installing a PHP application, you first need to determine whether you want to set up the application inside or outside of the website's physical root folder. Both approaches have advantages and disadvantages.

Setup in the Root Folder

Installing the application in the root folder gives you the advantage of keeping the physical path identical to the URL path. This simplifies website administration; however, there is a considerable disadvantage: by default, all files and folders within the root folder are accessible via a URL, which means that they are publicly accessible. For security reasons, you should not allow users to access the private zone of the application via a URL. Therefore, you need to configure IIS in such a way that requests for files in the private zone are rejected. To do so, you can use a request filter based on the URL, as described in the section "Request Filter," later in this chapter. You should also exclude any folders for temporary files.

Caution If you want to set up additional folders in the application, you need to check each time whether the new folder must be added to the filter.

Setup with a Virtual Directory

As an alternative to setting up the application in the root folder, you can embed the application by using a virtual directory. Figure 5-2 shows a possible folder structure: outside of the root folder of the site, an additional folder, \apps, is created that contains the individual applications.

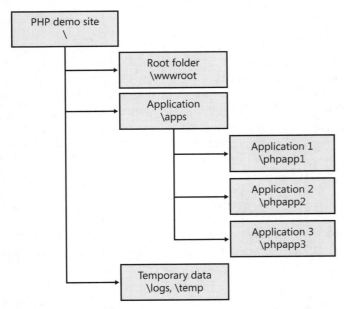

FIGURE 5-2 The folder structure for applications based on virtual directories.

You should set the physical path of the virtual directory to the public zone of the application right away, for example \apps\phpapp1\wwwroot. This also automatically excludes other application folders that you might create later from public access.

Specifying the Executable Files

Executable files are PHP scripts that are called by a URL and executed by the PHP Interpreter. This means that executable PHP scripts must meet two requirements: the file you are working with must be located in the public zone of the application, and IIS must have a handler assignment that executes these files via PHP.

> **Note** PHP scripts outside of an application's public zone are not directly executable via a URL request; therefore, they are not considered executable in this context.

Configuring the Handler Assignment

With IIS, you can change the handler assignment on all levels of the website, if the configuration has not been locked. To ensure that the configuration is secure, only the \php folder (or folders with executable PHP scripts) in the public zone should have a handler assignment for PHP. No other folder!

Configuring the Request Filter

Because the handler assignment is typically based on the file extension (*.php), you can also exclude access to PHP files outside of the \php folder with the request filter as an alternative to configuring the handler assignment. The advantage of this option is that the source code of the PHP files is not sent as a substitute, because general access is denied.

PHP Scripts in the Root Folder of the Public Zone

If PHP scripts are located directly in the root folder of the application's public zone, for example index.php, you have two options for separating executable folders from the others.

The first approach assumes that the PHP scripts in the public zone are always executable and you remove this right from the data folders (for example, \img, \data, \upload). The problem with this approach is that you must not forget to remove this directly from any folders you create later on.

The second approach prohibits the execution of PHP scripts in the public zone in general. You only configure the execution for the \php folder. You need to move any PHP scripts that are located in the root folder into the \php folder. You can then redirect or rewrite user requests by using *URL Rewrite* (see Chapter 7, "URL Rewrite").

> **Important** Ensure that PHP scripts cannot be executed in writable folders. An attacker who could execute his own PHP script on your server would have a much easier time than an attacker who didn't have this option.

PHP Configuration

PHP provides some configuration settings that impact the security of PHP applications. Among other things, these settings have an effect on which files allow PHP access, how to use variables, and which functions can be executed.

Table 5-1 contains general security-relevant configurations. It does not list settings for the PHP Safe Mode, because its security is deceptive and should instead be taken care of by using separate application pools. You should avoid escaping input data automatically, because this option does not sufficiently take into account the different encoding of input data and the various ways of escaping data for databases.

TABLE 5-1 General security settings

Configuration	Value	Description
allow_url_fopen	*Off*	Denies access to external resources on other servers (but not for special extensions such as cURL)
allow_url_include	*Off*	Prohibits embedding PHP scripts from external sources: if *allow_url_fopen* is set to *On*, this setting should be *Off*
default_charset	Character set	Specifies the default character set that is sent in the HTTP header *Content-Type* such as UTF-8
disable_classes	Class list	Lists PHP classes that must not be instantiated
disable_functions	Function list	Lists PHP functions that must not be executed; for example, *exec, dl, passthru, shell_exec, system, eval, popen, fsockopen, proc_open, proc_get_status, proc_nice, proc_terminate, show_source, stream_socket_server, symlink, link, lchgrp, lchown, chown, chgrp, posix_initgroups, posix_kill, posix_mkfifo, posix_mknod,* and *posix_setegid, posix_seteuid, posix_setgid, posix_setpgid, posix_setsid, posix_setuid*
enable_dl	*Off*	Prohibits dynamic reloading of extensions
expose_php	*Off*	Reduces the information that becomes visible from the outside via PHP
magic_quotes_gpc	*Off*	Prevents automatic escaping of input data
magic_quotes_runtime	*Off*	Prevents automatic escaping of data from external sources
open_basedir	Path	Limits data access to folders (and subfolders); the path should end with a back slash
register_globals	*Off*	Prevents input data from being registered as global variables

Table 5-2 lists settings for limiting resources. You should adjust the values according to the requirements of your application.

TABLE 5-2 Resource limits

Configuration	Value	Description
file_uploads	*Off*	Permits (*On*) or prohibits (*Off*) the uploading of files
max_execution_time	30	Maximum time in seconds that a PHP may take
max_input_time	60	Maximum time in seconds that it may take PHP to read the input data
memory_limit	16M	Maximum memory usage
post_max_size	8M	Maximum size of incoming HTTP POST data (including files to upload)
upload_max_filesize	2M	Maximum size of files to upload
upload_tmp_dir	Path	Temporary folder for uploaded files: should be located outside of *DOCUMENT_ROOT* and only accessible to PHP users

> **Tip** PHP Manager provides a special interface for setting most of the options in Table 5-2. For the desired PHP version, open PHP Manager from within IIS Manager, and then go to PHP Settings | Set Runtime Limits.

Table 5-3 contains the settings regarding error logs and error output. Unlike what you might expect, *display_errors=Off* only takes effect if *log_errors=On* and the file specified in *error_log* is writable. In production environments, the values should be set as shown, in development environments, errors can also be displayed directly.

TABLE 5-3 Error output and log

Configuration	Value	Description
display_errors	*Off*	Suppresses the error display
display_startup_errors	*Off*	Suppresses the error display on PHP start
error_log	Path to file	Log file that should be located outside of *DOCUMENT_ROOT*
error_reporting	*E_ALL*	Reports all errors (alternatively: *E_ALL|E_STRICT*)
log_errors	*On*	Logs the errors

> **Tip** PHP Manager provides two error reporting profiles appropriate for a development or production environment. Open PHP Manager for the desired PHP version, and then go to PHP Settings | Configure Error Reporting. There, you can select one of the two profiles and set the error log file.

Table 5-4 shows the settings for PHP session management. Session IDs in URLs should be prohibited, because they allow or facilitate attacks on sessions (session fixation, session hijacking).

TABLE 5-4 Configuration for the PHP session function

Configuration	Value	Description
session.cookie_httponly	On	Prevents session IDs from being read by using JavaScript
session.cookie_secure	On/Off	Set to On for HTTPS websites; otherwise, Off
session.hash_function	1	Use SHA-1 instead of MD5
session.save_path	Path	Set to a folder that is located outside of DOCUMENT_ROOT and can only be read by the executing PHP users
session.use_only_cookies	On	Prohibits the use of session IDs in URLs
session.use_trans_sid	Off	Prohibits the use of session IDs in URLs

User Authentication

Users can be authenticated in two different ways: either within the PHP application itself or via the authentication mechanisms of the HTTP protocol. Using the first method, the PHP application retrieves the user name and password—both are transferred as plain text—and checks the data against locally saved user data. If the check is successful, cookies or the PHP session function are used to assign an authenticated session ID to the user.

If authentication takes place via the HTTP protocol, IIS (instead of the PHP application) can take care of the user management and the authentication. Such an authentication not only protects PHP scripts, but also all resources within the order structure that you are using.

With HTTP and IIS, the user can be authenticated in three ways:

- **Basic authentication (Basic)**   The password is transferred as plain text.
- **Digest authentication (Digest)**   The password is transferred encrypted.
- **Windows Authentication (NTLM, Negotiate)**   Authentication takes place via the secure NT LAN Manager (NTLM) protocol and permits you to pass the Windows logon to the server, which allows for website single sign-on.

Which authentication method you want to use depends on the conditions in which you want to use it. The default authentication always works, but it should only be used for encrypted connections. The digest authentication works with many browsers, but does not function well with Mozilla Firefox. The Windows Authentication works with all modern browsers but is not supported by cell phones.

Installing the Required Role Services

Before you can use the additional authentication methods, you must install the necessary IIS role services.

Installing the Authentication Role Services by Using the Server Manager

To install the authentication role services by using the Server Manager, perform the following steps:

1. Open the Server Manager.

2. Click Roles, and then right-click Web Server (IIS). From the context menu, click Add Role Services.

3. In the Web Server section, in Security, select the Basic Authentication, Windows Authentication, and Digest Authentication options.

4. Click Next, and then click Install.

Installation via the Web Platform Installer

To install the authentication role services by using the Web Platform Installer (Web PI), perform the following steps:

1. Start the Web PI.

2. Click Products | Server, and then add the IIS: Basic Authentication, IIS: Windows Authentication, and IIS: Digest Authentication options.

3. Click Install, and then click I Accept.

You have now completed the installation and can configure the authentication method in IIS.

Setting Up User Authentication by Using IIS Manager

To set up user authentication by using the IIS Manger, perform the following steps:

1. In the Connections pane of IIS Manager, select the item that you would like to secure via authentication.

2. Open the Authentication feature by double-clicking it.

3. Select Anonymous Authentication, and then in the Actions pane, click Disable.

4. Select the type of authentication that you want, and then in the Actions pane, click Enable.

You can also enable several types:

- When using basic authentication, you can specify names for the application's authentication realm and default domain in the Actions pane by clicking Edit.

- When using Digest authentication, you can specify a name for the authentication realm.

- When using Windows authentication, you can enable extended security in the Actions pane by clicking Advanced Settings. This setting only makes sense for websites encrypted by using HTTPS. In this case, the option should be set to Accept.

Now you have enabled the user authentication for this site or directory.

Setting Up User Authentication from the Command Line

With *appcmd*, you can specify the authentication for a certain path. Use the following command to prevent anonymous authentication:

```
appcmd set config <PATH> /section:anonymousAuthentication /enabled:false
```

> **Note** If you receive an error message that the configuration section is locked, unlock it for the authentication sections, as described in Chapter 3, "Configuring IIS."

Use the following command to enable the default authentication:

```
appcmd set config <PATH>/section:basicAuthentication
    /enabled:true /realm:MyArea /defaultLogonDomain:"<Domain>"
```

Use the following command to enable the Digest authentication:

```
appcmd set config <PATH> /section:digestAuthentication /enabled:true /realm:MyArea
```

Use the following command to enable the Windows authentication:

```
appcmd set config <PATH> /section:windowsAuthentication
    /enabled:true /extendedProtection.tokenChecking:Allow
```

Windows Authentication and Host Names

If you are using Windows authentication and are using a server name that is not the same as the computer name in the URL, calling the page from your local computer that is running IIS will fail. This happens because Windows authentication also checks the computer name.

Note You can enter the server name via C:\Windows\System32\drivers\etc\hosts or in your local DNS-Server.

Local Authentication

To be able to use a different server name, do the following:

1. Click Start | Run, and the type **regedit** to start the Registry Editor.

2. Change the following two keys:

   - You can also turn off the name check during authentication: to do so, go to *HKEY_LOCAL_MACHINE\SYSTEM\CurrentControlSet\Control\Lsa*, and then create a new *DWORD* entry called **DisableLoopbackCheck**. Set its value to *1*.

   - Alternatively, you can add the desired domain name: go to *HKEY_LOCAL_MACHINE\SYSTEM\CurrentControlSet\Control\Lsa\MSV1_0*, create a new *multi-part string* entry named **BackConnectionHostNames**, and then enter the desired host names (one per line) there.

3. Close the Registry Editor and restart IIS.

Authentication Against Active Directory

During the authentication of domain users, the Windows authentication can also fail when the additional domain names are not known in Microsoft Active Directory. Use the command **setspn** to add names, as shown in the following:

```
setspn -A HTTP/<domain> <computer name>
Example: setstpn -A HTTP/www.phpdemo.site websrv
```

Use the following command to view the currently entered services:

```
setspn -L <computer name>
```

Retrieving the Authentication in PHP

In PHP, you can retrieve the user name via three different variables:

- *$_SERVER["LOGON_USER"]* contains the name of the assigned user account (possibly after a change of identity with an IIS authentication filter) that is used for the request.

- *$_SERVER["AUTH_USER"]* and *$_SERVER["REMOTE_USER"]* contain the (raw) user name exactly as it is retrieved from the HTTP headers.

Tip Normally, you should use *$_SERVER["LOGON_USER"]* to retrieve the current user.

Identity and Access Rights

For access rights to files and external data sources, such as SQL Server and Active Directory, it's important to understand with which identity and with which rights PHP is run. The rights depend on various settings in IIS and PHP.

The access rights or the identity of PHP scripts are the result of the following rules, which are applied one after the other. PHP takes the identity of the first rule that applies:

1. **fastcgi.impersonate=0**   Uses the identity of the IIS application pool, for example *IISAppPool\DefaultAppPool*.

2. **Path log-on information exists**   You can configure specific user accounts for IIS applications and virtual directories. PHP takes the identity of the configured user.

3. **Authenticated web user**   PHP takes the identity of the web user.

4. **Anonymous web user**   The IIS-internal anonymous user *NT AUTHORITY\IUSR* is applied.

> **Note** PHP only applies the identity of an authenticated web user if *fastcgi.impersonate=1* and there is no path logon information.

Next, you'll see how to define the identities of the application pool, the anonymous user, and the path logon information.

Identity of the Application Pool

You can define the application pool identity separately for each pool. By default, application pool identities (also custom accounts) are assigned dynamically to the group *IIS_IUSRS*. The security ID (SID) of the application pool's integrated account is also included in the process (for example, *IIS AppPool\DefaultAppPool*). You can always bind the access rights of files to the account of the application pool or to the group *IIS_IUSRS*.

To specify the application pool identity by using IIS Manager, perform the following steps:

1. In the IIS Manager, in the Connections pane, click Application Pool, and then from the drop-down list, select the desired application pool.

2. In the Actions pane, click Advanced Settings.

3. Select Process Model | Identity.

4. In the dialog box that opens, you can now choose from a list of integrated accounts or specify your own user.

5. Click OK to close the dialog boxes and apply the entries.

You can use *appcmd* to specify the application pool identity. For example, the following command denotes a specific user:

```
appcmd set apppool <Pool name> /processModel.identityType:SpecificUser
   /processModel.userName:manfred /processModel.password:top-secret
```

Path Logon Information

For applications and virtual directories, you can define a user who is employed by IIS, and therefore, also by PHP (assuming *fastcgi.impersonate=1*) to access the data.

To specify the path logon information by using IIS Manager, perform the following steps:

1. In the Connections pane of IIS Manager, select the site, the application, or the virtual directory.

2. In the Actions pane, click Basic Settings.

3. In the dialog box that opens, click Connect As.

4. In the new dialog box, you can either specify a certain user or select the application user (Pass-Through Authentication).

5. Click OK to confirm your entries.

You can also use *appcmd* to specify the path logon information. For example, use the following command to specify a virtual directory for a certain user:

```
appcmd set vdir <PATH> /userName:manfred /password:top-secret
```

Specifying the Identity of the Anonymous User

You can specify the identity of the anonymous user directly by using the authentication feature. To do so, perform the following steps:

1. In IIS Manager, open the authentication feature for the desired item.

2. In the work area, select Anonymous Authentication, and then in the Actions pane, click Edit.

3. In the dialog box that opens, you can now specify the user or use the application pool identity. The user IUSR does not need a password.

4. Click OK to complete your entry.

You can also use *appcmd* for this setting, for example:

```
appcmd set config <PATH> /section:anonymousAuthentication /userName:tony /password:top-secret
```

Securing the PHP Application

Based on the enabled identity, you can grant individual rights for PHP applications or files on the server. This makes it possible to separate the applications, based on file access rights (based on ACLs), which increases security tremendously.

> **Caution** When accessing other files (for example graphics), IIS has the same rights as PHP, if *fastcgi.impersonate=1*. To keep the rights consistent you should therefore always run PHP with the configuration *fastcgi.impersonate=1*.

To grant access to files and folders only to users who are permitted, perform the following steps:

1. In the Windows Explorer, select the file or folder, and then click the Properties command in the context menu.

2. On the Security tab, click Edit.

3. Click Add to add the desired user and specify the rights in the list box below.

   For PHP scripts and other files, the Read right is sufficient.

4. To remove inherited users from the rights (for example, the read access for the Users group), on the Security tab, click Advanced, and then click Change Permissions. Clear the Include Inheritable Permissions check box from this object's parent. In the dialog box that appears, click Add.

   Afterward, you can edit the access rights for the other principals or remove the principals completely.

To grant access from the command line, use the command *icacls* as shown here:

```
icacls auth.php /inheritance:d
icacls auth.php /grant "IIS AppPool\DefaultAppPool":R /remove "PREDEFINED\user"
icacls auth.php
```

The first two commands remove the rights inheritance and the rights of the Users group. In addition, the *DefaultAppPool* is assigned read/write permission for the file auth.php. Finally, the last line lists the current permissions for the auth.php file.

Authorization Rules

You can control access to sites and applications based on user authentication; for example, you can grant or deny access to specific groups or users by using authorization rules.

IIS provides two types of authorization rules: permission rules and rejection rules. The latter always take precedence. If a user or a group to which the user belongs is part of a rejection rule, access is always denied. You can create rule restrictions that apply only to individual HTTP verbs, which allows you to share sensitive areas for read access (*GET, HEAD*), but not for changes that typically take place with forms, via *POST*.

Installing the Required Role Services

You must install the necessary authorization IIS role service before you can start.

Installing Authorization Role Services by Using the Server Manager

To install the authorization role services by using the Server Manager, perform the following steps:

1. Open the Server Manager.
2. Click Roles, and then right-click Web Server (IIS). From the context menu, click Add Role Services.
3. In the Web Server/Security section, select the URL Authorization option.
4. Click Next, and then click Install.

Installation via the Web PI

To install the authorization role services by using the Web PI, perform the following steps:

1. Start the Web PI.
2. Click Products | Server, and then add the option IIS: URL Authorization.
3. Click Install, and then click I Accept.

You have now completed the installation and can configure authorization rules in IIS.

Defining the Rules by Using IIS Manager

You can also specify authorization rules via IIS Manager. To do so, perform the following steps:

1. In the Connections pane of IIS Manager, select the desired item.
2. Open the Authorization Rules feature by double-clicking it.
3. To set up a new permission rule, in the Actions pane, click Add Allow Rule. (For a new rejection rule, in the Actions pane, click Add Deny Rule.)

   The Add Allow Authorization Rule dialog box opens.

The rule can be applied to all users, all anonymous users, certain roles, user groups, or users (see Figure 5-3). You can restrict it to certain HTTP verbs (for example *POST*).

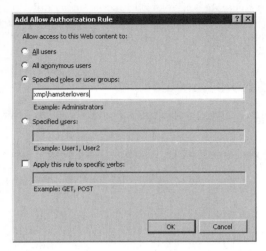

FIGURE 5-3 The Add Allow Authorization Rule dialog box, in which you can add an authorization permission rule.

4. Click OK to create the rule.

Defining the Rules from the Command Line

To manage authorization rules from the command line, use *appcmd* as follows:

- To add a permission rule for certain users:

```
appcmd set config <PATH> -section:security/authorization
    /+[accessType='Allow',users='doris,julia']
```

- To add a rejection rule for certain roles or groups:

```
appcmd et config <PATH> -section:security/authorization
    /+[accessType='Deny',roles='xmp\hamsterlovers']
```

- To set up a permission rule for all anonymous users for access with *HTTP GET*:

```
appcmd set config <PATH> -section:security/authorization
    /+[accessType='Allow',users='?',verbs='GET']
```

Note For authorization rules, use the following syntax:

- To represent all users: *users="*"*.
- To represent all anonymous users: *users="?"*.

Request Filter

IIS 7 provides a request filter feature that automatically filters and rejects unwanted requests. The request filter is called very early in the processing chain of an HTTP request so that it can prevent malicious or unwanted requests quickly and efficiently. This makes the request filter an effective tool for securing your PHP application.

If the filter denies a request, IIS returns an error message to the browser containing the status code *404*. The status subcode provides you more details about the reason for the filtration. If IIS is configured to display detailed error messages, the response includes the reason for the denial.

The request filter has eight different settings or functions:

- **General settings**   These settings handle request limits and coding of strings (see the section "Defining General Settings," later in this chapter).

- **Limits to the length of individual HTTP headers**   Defines size limit in bytes for specified headers.

- **Restrictions of permitted HTTP verbs**   Specifies which HTTP verbs are allowed or denied.

- **URL filtering**   If the beginning of a URL corresponds to a specified string, the URL can be marked as locked or allowed. If the URL is marked as allowed, no further URL filters will be run (*alwaysAllowedUrls*).

- **Query string filtering**   If the specified string is located anywhere in the query string, the request can be allowed or locked. If the query string is marked as allowed, no further URL filters will be run (*alwaysAllowedQueryStrings*).

- **File name extension allowing or filtering**   You can use this to prevent attacks on *.exe files (see the section "Filtering File Name Extensions," later in this chapter).

- **Hiding URL segments**   You can use this to prevent access to web.config.

- **Rule-based filtering**   Filters according to specified rules (see the section "Filtering with Rules," later in this chapter).

Next, you'll look at some selected request filter functions and their most important properties. For other functions and properties, for example, to exclude WebDAV from certain rules, you will be referred to the IIS documentation.

 Note The request filter is run after *URL Rewrite*. Therefore, all URL checks are performed for the rewritten URL. Be sure to keep that in mind when setting up rules.

Defining General Settings

The request filter provides a number of global settings, which impact all requests: request limits, character filter, and default behavior for HTTP verbs and file name extensions.

Request Limits

You can limit the request size by using three different settings:

- Content size (HTTP body), typically for a POST or PUT request
- Length of the URL
- Length of the query string

While the default values for URL and query string length should work for all applications, the content size default value of 30 MB might be too large for some applications and too small for others. If so, you need to adjust the setting.

Character Filter

The character filter parses the path of a URL for unwanted characters. Other parts of the URL, especially the query string, are not affected. The request filter provides two ways to filter for characters:

- **Prohibiting characters outside the US-ASCII range (00 to 7F hex)**   If you select this function, for example, you can no longer call URLs with umlaut characters (¨) in the file name. This function is disabled by default.

- **Prohibiting false or double-escaped characters**   This function is enabled by default and rejects requests with improperly escaped characters (for example, when special characters, such as <, >, #, ", and so on, are not escaped). Double-escaped characters are characters that have (intentionally or unintentionally) been masked multiple times with URL encoding. IIS filters out these requests, because in the past, hackers have used double-escaped characters to exploit gaps in application security.

> **Note** The filter for false or double-escaped characters also filters out a "+" (plus character) that is encoded as part of a URL path. In a query string, a plus character represents a space. For historical reasons, applications have also interpreted plus characters in a URL path as a space. However, this does not correspond to the HTTP standard. IIS 7 now filters out such URLs.

Best practice is to enable double-escaped character filtering. This should cause problems only if your application passes and processes parameters via a URL subpath (variable *PATH_INFO*). In this case, you should ensure that these parameters are coded correctly. In general, you should not allow the percent character (%) to be part of a parameter. Otherwise, you run the risk of unintentionally creating coding that is indistinguishable from a double-escaped character, which will be filtered out by the request filter.

> **Tip** To code the different parts of a URL path, use the PHP functions *rawurlencode()* and *rawurldecode()*, because they comply with the corresponding standards. For the query string, you should use *urlencode()* and *urldecode()*.

If your application produces or uses URLs that the filter rejects, you will need to either turn off the filter or rewrite your application. The latter makes more sense from a security standpoint.

URL Encoding

URL coding rules are specified by the Internet standards RFC 1738 and RFC 3986. Apart from how to structure a URL, these standards dictate that all characters, with the exception of alphanumeric characters and a few special characters, must be escaped. An escaped character is converted into a three-character string: the percent character followed by the hexadecimal value of the character.

As an example, the tilde character(~) is escaped as %7F.

Originally, characters outside of the US-ASCII character set (00 to 7F hex) had not been envisioned for use in URLs, which helps explain why URL paths and query strings are coded differently.

Coding the URL Path

Characters not in the US-ASCII character set—for example, German umlaut characters (¨)—are coded according to UTF-8 rules in the URL path. UTF-8 is a coding regulation for Unicode, which generates a variable number of bytes in the range 80 to FF hex for characters outside of the US-ASCII range. Characters based on Latin script, such as German characters with umlauts, are coded as two bytes. They're converted (escaped) into percent format according to the URL regulation.

For example, the umlaut character for A (Ä), whose Unicode code point is *U+00C4*, is coded as *C3* 84 hex in UTF-8. In a URL, the character would be escaped as %C3%84.

Coding the Query String

The coding of the query string varies depending on the conditions under which it is created. If a user enters the URL directly into a browser's address bar, the coding depends on the browser. If the query string contains only characters from the ISO-8859-1 character set (which contains the essential Central European special characters), ISO-8859-1 is used as the coding. The umlaut A (Ä) is coded as *%C4* in this case. However, if the query string also contains other characters, different browsers take different paths: some also use UTF-8 coding for the query string. Wherever possible, Internet Explorer substitutes equivalent characters from the Latin alphabet or substitutes a question mark.

If the query string is generated by the browser, for example, via a form on a page that uses the *GET* method, the query string coding will match the coding of the page. So if the HTML page is coded in UTF-8, the generated query string is also coded in UTF-8; if the HTML page is coded as ISO-8859-1, the browser generates a ISO-8859-1-coded query string.

PHP Coding

Unfortunately for programmers developing for an international audience, the core code in PHP is not Unicode-ready; it processes all input data as ISO-8859-1. To process Unicode characters, you need to use the multibyte string PHP extension or *iconv*.

In the rules, the search strings are checked against the original input data format. With query strings, the decoded format is checked as well. This ensures that unwanted strings can't be smuggled past the filters by using percent coding.

Specifying the Settings by Using IIS Manager

To define the general settings of the request filter, perform the following steps:

1. Open IIS Manager.

2. In the Connections pane, select the item that you want to configure.

3. In the work area, open the Request Filter feature by double-clicking it.

4. In the Actions pane, click Edit Feature Settings.

   The Edit Request Filtering Settings dialog box opens, as shown in Figure 5-4.

FIGURE 5-4 Editing the general settings of the request filter.

You can set the request limits in the text boxes of the Request Limits section.

5. To permit characters outside of the US-ASCII character set in the URL path, select the Allow High-Bit Characters check box.

6. To permit double-escaped characters in the URL path, select the Allow Double Escaping check box.

7. Click OK to close the dialog box.

Specifying the Settings from the Command Line

To change the general settings of the request filter from the command line, open a command prompt window with administrator rights, and then run the following *appcmd* commands:

- To specify the request-length limit, you need to set the attribute *maxAllowedContent Length*. Set the *maxUrl* attribute to control the maximum length of the URL, and the *maxQueryString* attribute to control the maximum length of the request string, as in the following example:

```
appcmd set config "<PATH>" /section:requestFiltering
   /requestLimits.maxAllowedContentLength:2500000 /requestLimits.maxUrl:4000
   /requestLimits.maxQueryString:1500
```

- To allow characters not in the US-ASCII character set in the URL path, run the following command:

```
appcmd set config "<PATH>" /section:requestFiltering /allowHighBitCharacters:true
```

- To allow double-escaped characters in the URL path:

```
appcmd set config "<PATH>" /section:requestFiltering /allowDoubleEscaping:true
```

- To turn off the extended check (against the decoded request string) when request strings are checked:

```
appcmd set config "<PATH>" /section:requestFiltering /unescapeQueryString:false
```

> **Note** *<PATH>* in the preceding examples represents the path to the server area that you want to configure, for example, *PHP Demo Site/phpapp*.

Filtering File Name Extensions

With the request filter, you can also selectively block requests that end with a certain file name extension. This filter can run in two modes:

- Prohibit all listed extensions (default setting).
- Allow only the listed extensions, prohibit all others.

Specifying the Settings by Using IIS Manager

To configure file name extensions by using IIS Manager, perform the following steps:

1. Start IIS Manager.
2. In the Connections pane, select the item that you want to configure.
3. In the work area, open the Request Filter feature by double-clicking it.
4. In the work area, click the File Name Extensions tab.
5. In the Actions pane, click Deny File Name Extension, enter into the text box the file name extension that you want to deny, and then click OK.
6. To set the behavior to denying all file name extensions that are not listed, in the Actions pane, click Edit Feature Settings, and then clear the Allow Unlisted File Name Extensions check box.

Specifying the Settings from the Command Line

To configure file name extensions from the command line, open a command prompt window with administrator rights, and then run the following commands:

- To add a file name extension (*false*: deny, *true*: allow):

```
appcmd set config "<PATH>" /section:requestfiltering
    /+fileExtensions.[fileextension='.exe',allowed='false']
```

- To remove a file name extension:

```
appcmd set config "<PATH>" /section:requestfiltering
    /-fileExtensions.[fileExtension='.exe']
```

- To specify whether unlisted file name extensions are allowed:

```
appcmd set config "<PATH>" /section:requestfiltering /fileExtensions.allowUnlisted:true
```

Filtering with Rules

As the last function of the request filter, you'll explore filtering with rules, an extremely powerful filter function. Filter rules can search for strings in URL paths, query strings, and HTTP headers. You can limit rules so that they apply only to specific file name extensions.

Setting up Filter Rules by Using IIS Manager

To set up a new filter rule by using IIS Manager, perform the following steps:

1. Start IIS Manager.

2. In the Connections pane, select the item that you want to configure.

3. In the work area, open the Request Filter feature by double-clicking it.

4. On the Rules tab, click Actions | Add Filtering Rule.

   The Add Filtering Rule dialog box opens, as shown in Figure 5-5.

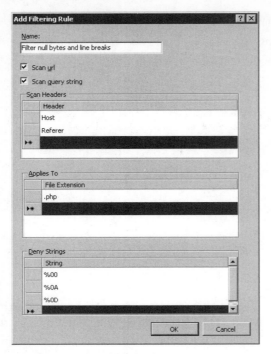

FIGURE 5-5 Adding filter rules.

5. Enter the desired values:

- In the Name text box, enter a name for the rule.

- If you want to search for a string in the URL path, select the Scan URL check box.

- If you want to search for a string in the query string, select the Scan Query String check box.

- If you also want to search for a string in the HTTP headers, enter the header you want to check in the Scan Headers section.

- If you want to limit the rule to certain file types, in the Applies To section, enter the file name extensions (including the dot) in the File Extension text box.

- Finally, enter the strings that you want to deny in the Deny Strings list box. The rule takes effect (and the request is denied) if one of the specified strings is found in the areas you want to check (URL path, query string, HTTP header).

6. Complete the dialog box by clicking OK to apply the rule.

Editing Filter Rules from the Command Line

To change filter rules from the command line, open a command prompt window with administrator rights, and then run the following commands:

- To set up a new rule:

```
appcmd set config "<PATH>" /section:requestfiltering
    /+"filteringRules.[name='directory change',scanUrl='true']"
```

- To add the HTTP headers that you want to check:

```
appcmd set config "<PATH>" /section:requestfiltering
    /+"filteringRules.[name='directory change'].scanHeaders.[requestHeader='Referer']"
```

- To limit the rule to certain file name extensions:

```
appcmd set config "<PATH>" /section:requestfiltering
    /+"filteringRules.[name='directory change'].appliesTo.[fileExtension='.php']"
```

- To specify a string that you want to check:

```
appcmd set config "<PATH>" /section:requestfiltering
    /+"filteringRules.[name='directory change'].denyStrings.[string='..']"
```

To delete strings, file name extensions, HTTP headers, or entire rules, use /– instead of /+ in the commands.

Encrypted Connections (HTTPS)

With HTTPS, you can perform an encrypted data transfer with the HTTP protocol, based on the TLS or SSL protocol. The encryption ensures that no attacker can monitor or manipulate the transferred data. If you transfer sensitive data, you should provide a secure, encrypted connection for your website via HTTPS.

For an HTTPS connection, you need a certificate for the web server. Client certificates for user authentication are optional. IIS Manager provides functions for all necessary setup steps, which are easy to use. In the following, you will learn how to set up a server certificate and an encrypted connection, how to request user certificates and how to use them for authentication, and how to query information via the encrypted connection in PHP.

Creating Keys and Certificates

IIS can manage several server certificates for different bindings and websites. IIS Manager provides functions for setting up three different certificates: self-signed certificates, certificates from the root certification authority of the Windows domain, and certificates for external certification authorities. This section only covers how to set up a domain certificate, but you can create the other types in the same fashion.

To set up a domain certificate, you must run Active Directory certificate services in the domain. Chapter 15, "Setting Up Active Directory," describes how to set up certificate services.

How to set up a domain certificate, perform the following steps:

1. In the Connections pane of IIS Manager, Select the server.

2. Open the Server Certificates feature by double-clicking it.

3. In the Actions pane, click Create Domain Certificate.

   The Create Domain Certificate dialog box opens.

4. Enter your company data.

   In the Common Name text box, you must enter the complete domain name of the secure website; for example, **www.phpdemo.site**. To generate a placeholder certificate that can be used for multiple child domain names, use the asterisk placeholder; for example, *.phpdemo.site.

5. Select the certification authority by clicking the Select button, and then enter any desired display name.

> **Note** If you are not able to select a certification authority, the Active Directory certificate services are either not enabled, your computer does not belong to the domain or the general structure in which these services are run, or the certificate authority is not among the server's Trusted Root Certification Authorities.

6. Click Finish to request the certificate and set up IIS.

You have now created and set up the certificate. In the next step, you can use the certificate for an encrypted connection.

Setting up an Encrypted Connection

To set up an encrypted connection, you need to add an HTTPS binding to a website. You can then specify whether using the encrypted binding is mandatory.

Setting up the Binding

To set up an HTTPS binding for a website, perform the following steps:

1. In the Connections pane of IIS Manager, select the website.

2. In the Actions pane, click Binding.

3. Click Add, and then enter the following values for the new binding:

   - Type: https

   - IP Address: **IP address of the binding** (optional)

   - Port: **443** (this is the default)

   - SSL Certificate: select the appropriate server certificate

   - Host Name: if you have selected a placeholder certificate, you can also enter the host name

> **Important** You can only use one certificate per IP address/port combination. You cannot use different certificates for different sites that have the same IP address and port. Only with a placeholder certificate can multiple sites share an HTTPS binding with the same IP address and port.

4. Click Close to exit the dialog box.

If you now call up the website with its HTTPS URL, an encrypted connection is established.

> **Note** If you call up the website from outside of the Windows domain, Internet Explorer will notify you that the server certificate is not valid because the root certificate of the Active Directory certification authority is not recognized outside of the domain.
>
> You can continue the connection (temporarily) and later add the root certificate of your certification authority to the certification storage of trusted root certification authorities, or classify only the server certificate itself as trusted (you can do this directly via the Certificate Error/View Certificates/Install Certificate dialog box right in the Address Bar in Internet Explorer).

You can find out how to add a binding by using *appcmd* from the command line in Chapter 2, "IIS Architecture," in the section "Adding Additional Bindings."

SSL Settings

Using the SSL Settings feature, you can predefine additional parameters for an encrypted connection. Specify the following settings in IIS Manager:

1. In the Connections pane of IIS Manager, select the website.

2. Open the SSL Settings feature by double-clicking it.

3. If you want to force the use of the encrypted connection, select the SSL Required option.

4. For user certificates, you can select one of the following three options: Ignore, Accept, or Required. The default setting (Accept) usually works best.

5. In the Actions pane, click Apply to complete your entries.

You can also use *appcmd* from the command line to force the use of client certificates and SSL:

```
appcmd set config <PATH> -section:security/access
   /sslFlags:"Ssl, SslNegotiateCert, SslRequireCert" /commit:apphost
```

When you open the website in a browser, you are now prompted to select a certificate, as shown in Figure 5-6.

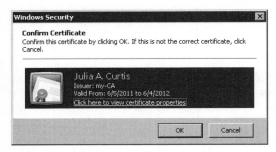

FIGURE 5-6 Use the Windows Security dialog box to select a user certificate.

Setting Up a User Certificate

With a user certificate, a server can identify itself to users, and users can authenticate themselves to the server. User certificates are not often employed for public servers. However, for intranet sites that can be reached from the outside, user certificates represent an interesting alternative to other authentication methods.

To issue a client certificate for a domain user, perform the following steps:

1. Click Start | Run, and then type **mmc** to open the Microsoft Management Console.

2. Add the snap-in Certificates by clicking File | Add/Remove Snap-in. Select My User Account as certificate type for the snap-in.

3. In the console root, select the item Certificates – Current User, right-click Personal, and then in the context menu, click All Tasks | Request New Certificate to start the Certificate Enrollment Wizard.

4. On the second page of the wizard, select the Active Directory Enrollment Policy, and then click Next.

5. Select the User option as certificate type, and then click Enroll.

6. After the certificate has been issued successfully, click finish to close the wizard.

7. You can view the completed certificate in the MMC by double-clicking Certificates – Current User | Personal | Certificates on the certificate in the list view.

Querying Information with PHP

In PHP, you can use different *$_SERVER* variables to retrieve information about the HTTPS connection, the server certificate, and the (optional) client certificate.

Table 5-5 shows the variables with example values for the HTTPS connection and the server certificate used. With *$_SERVER['HTTPS']=on*, you can check whether the PHP script has been called via an encrypted connection. With *$_SERVER['HTTPS_KEYSIZE']*, you can check the length (in bits) of the transport key. Requesting clients can negotiate different values.

TABLE 5-5 $_SERVER variables for retrieving connection and server certificate information

$_SERVER variable	Example value
HTTPS	On
HTTPS_KEYSIZE	128
HTTPS_SECRETKEYSIZE	1024
HTTPS_SERVER_ISSUER	DC=site, DC=xmp, CN=my-CA
HTTPS_SERVER_SUBJECT	C=AT, S=Styria, L=Graz, O=XMP, OU=HamsterClub, CN=*.phpdemo.site

If you are using a client certificate, you can use additional variables to query the certificate information; see Table 5-6. The user identity can be read into *$_SERVER['CERT_SUBJECT']*, and *$_SERVER['CERT_COOKIE']* contains a unique identifier for the certificate.

TABLE 5-6 $_SERVER variables for the client certificate

$_SERVER variable	Example value
CERT_COOKIE	1058a4ac31108e8dcebcee12ab2780da80777b77a7acfe5dc7ed7b308ebbccd3
CERT_FLAGS	1
CERT_ISSUER	DC=site, DC=xmp, CN=my-CA
CERT_SERIALNUMBER	1c-3f-a9-fb-00-00-00-00-00-0d
CERT_SUBJECT	DC=site, DC=xmp, OU=AdventureWorks, OU=Departments, OU=Engineering, CN=Julia A. Curtis, E=JuliaA.Curtis@xmp.site

Using this data, a PHP script can clearly identify and authenticate a user. When using client certificates, a separate authentication step is not really necessary.

Authentication with Client Certificates

Client certificates are useful for more than just setting up and authenticating encrypted connections: they can be used directly as an authentication method. In the following, you'll learn how to authenticate domain users. First you need to install the correct authentication feature.

Installing the Required Role Services

To install the IIS role service necessary for authentication with client certificates, perform the following steps:

1. Open the Server Manager.

2. Click Roles, and then right-click Web Server (IIS). From the context menu, click Add Role Services.

3. In the Web Server section, in Security, select the Client Certificate Mapping Authentication option.

> **Note** The other option, IIS Client Certificate Mapping Authentication, does not use Active Directory for the assignment. Instead, IIS itself manages a local assignment directly. You can find a description of this option on MSDN at *http://www.iis.net/ConfigReference/ system.webServer/security/authentication/iisClientCertificateMappingAuthentication.*

4. Click Next, and then click Install.

Alternatively, you can use the Web PI to install the necessary module, as follows:

1. Start the Web PI.

2. Click Products | Server, and then add the IIS: Client Certificate Mapping Authentication option.

3. Click Install, and then click I Accept.

You have now completed the installation and can configure the authentication method in IIS.

Activating the Client Certificate Assignment Authentication

You can enable the Client Certificate Assignment Authentication just like other authentication methods. Use the following *appcmd* command to enable this method (*/commit:apphost* is necessary to write the configuration into the applicationHost.config file):

```
appcmd set config <PATH> -section:clientCertificateMappingAuthentication /enabled:true
   /commit:apphost
```

> **Note** An error in IIS Manager currently prevents activation by using that method. Therefore, this section focuses on using *appcmd*.

If you are using a browser that has the correct client certificate installed for accessing the site, you will now be asked for the certificate. After selecting the certificate, you are automatically authenticated.

In PHP, you can then query the assigned user account; for example, with *$_SERVER['LOGON_USER']*. The variable *$_SERVER['AUTH_TYPE']* contains the value "SSL/PCT".

Other settings, such as the authorization rule, also apply now, depending on the logon.

Summary

The ability to assign various identities and access rights to different PHP applications, either with different application pools or via path logon information, is an essential building block for making websites secure. Using these tools, you can achieve sufficient application isolation to ensure that errors in an application will mostly have no impact on other applications. A secure PHP configuration also significantly reduces the attack surface. By taking advantage of user authentication, authorization rules, and the request filter options, you can implement a highly granular security scheme for PHP applications in IIS. If you also set up HTTPS connections, you can protect the data from unwanted access during transfer as well.

In the next chapter, you will learn how to increase the performance of your PHP application substantially by using various types of caching.

Chapter 6
Caching

Caching is an important technique for improving the performance of PHP applications and simultaneously reducing the amount of resources used on the server side.

Three caching options are available to you:

- With the HTTP headers, you can control whether and how long requesting clients or intermediate proxies can cache. The advantage of this option is that during later access, no new requests are sent to the server, and therefore, no server resources or bandwidth is required.

- With the Internet Information Services (IIS) Output Cache, frequently requested files are kept directly in the working memory and are issued upon request. Access to the file system is no longer necessary; PHP scripts and database access are no longer performed. The result is a correspondingly large increase in performance.

- The WinCache PHP Extension speeds up the execution of PHP scripts. WinCache caches the opcodes of the compiled PHP scripts and reduces execution time as well as the number of accesses to the file system.

You'll explore all three options in the sections that follow.

Caching in the Web

A webpage is composed of many individual elements: the HTML of the page itself, embedded graphics, formatting statements in Cascading Style Sheets (CSS) format, script files (such as JScript and JavaScript), and other active content (for example, Microsoft Silverlight and ActiveX). Each one of these files is transferred in its own HTTP request/reply cycle from the server to the client.

Even though HTML changes within a website from one page to the next, other embedded content stays the same—for example, the logo or CSS formatting statements. Many elements (including the HTML pages themselves) are relatively static. Their content seldom changes, or doesn't change at all. For a news portal, for example *http://msn.com/*, the start page might change quite frequently. However, the logo hardly ever changes, and it's likely that individual articles will not be rewritten.

Therefore, it makes sense to cache replies to HTTP requests locally on the client and thus save bandwidth and transfer time, to increase performance and improve the user experience. This becomes especially obvious when using the Back function of a web browser: If the previous page wasn't cached locally, it would need to be requested again by the server, which would result in a noticeable delay.

HTTP provides mechanisms and headers for caching, with which the server can control which contents may be cached, under which conditions, and for how long. For example, on *http://uk.msn.com/*, the logo can be cached for several months, individual articles for several minutes, but the start page only for the purposes of the Back function, otherwise it must be reloaded.

The HTTP protocol provides various techniques for caching, which target time, content changes, and conditions. In the following, you will look at them in more detail.

Caching for a Limited Time

HTTP provides two techniques to limit the caching duration: the *Expires* header and the *max-age* cache statement.

The *Expires* Header

To allow a resource to be cached for a certain amount of time, use the HTTP reply header *Expires*. The *Expires* header contains a specific time, after which cached content must no longer be used (neither by the browser nor by a proxy), but must be requested again from the source. Listing 6-1 shows this header in an HTTP reply.

LISTING 6-1 Using the *Expires* header to limit the caching duration.

```
HTTP/1.1 200 OK
Content-Type: image/jpeg
Date: Wed, 07 Sep 2011 07:31:07 GMT
Expires: Fri, 07 Sep 2012 07:25:03 GMT
```

The date format is specified in HTTP RFC; it must have the following format (the numbers in parentheses represent the number of required characters):

```
Day(3), date(2) month(3) year(4) time(8) GMT
```

You specify them using the Greenwich Mean Time (GMT) time zone.

> **Note** GMT in HTTP is identical to Coordinated Universal Time (UTC).

In PHP, this format can be generated by using the following statement:

```
$dateString = gmdate('D, d M Y H:i:s', $timeStamp) . ' GMT';
```

> **Note** The date/time you specify in the *Expires* header should not be more than a year in the future.

If you want to ensure that the content of pages that change frequently is always freshly requested, you should set the *Expires* header to the same date/time as the *Date* header:

```
Date: Wed, 07 Apr 2010 07:31:07 GMT Expires: Wed, 07 Apr 2010 07:31:07 GMT
```

> **Note** Many browsers also accept the value –1 in the *Expires* header. It also specifies that the resource must be requested again.

Max-Age Statement

The *Expire* header specifies an absolute point in time. With the *max-age* statement, however, you can set a relative time in the *Cache-Control* header. The *max-age* value is specified in seconds: the content can be cached for the specified number of seconds. For example, to allow the caching of a resource for two days, the header would look as shown Listing 6-2.

LISTING 6-2 The *max-age* statement is another way to limit the caching duration.

```
HTTP/1.1 200 OK
Content-Type: image/jpeg
Date: Wed, 07 Sep 2011 07:31:07 GMT
Cache-Control: max-age=172800
```

If both the *Expires* header and the *max-age* statement are used, the *max-age* statement takes precedence. To ensure that the content is always requested again, you need to set *max-age* to 0, as follows:

```
Cache-Control: max-age=0
```

Mutable Contents

HTTP provides two options to determine whether the content of a web resource has changed: a last-modified change date and an entity tag that denotes versions of a resource that are distinctly different.

Change Date

The change date is specified with the *Last-Modified* header. This way, clients can find out later whether the content of the resource has changed since the last time. If the content hasn't changed, the server responds with a corresponding message (HTTP code 304). This option does not prevent the HTTP request from the client to the server, but it reduces the amount of data that's transferred.

Listing 6-3 demonstrates what happens: the server replies to the first client request with the content of the resource and the header *Last-Modified*, which gives you the date of the latest change. If the client calls up the resource again at a later time, it also sends the header *If-Modified-Since*. This way, the PHP script can check whether the data has changed since. If not, an HTTP-304 reply is sent without supplying the resource content with it (see the Listing). The client retrieves the content from its cache. If the content has changed, it is transferred as usual with an HTTP-200 reply.

LISTING 6-3 Course of requests and replies when the *Last-Modified* header is specified.

First client request

```
GET /lastmodified.php HTTP/1.1
Host: phpdemo.site
```

Server reply

```
HTTP/1.1 200 OK
Last-Modified: Mon, 05 Sep 2011 07:31:07 GMT
Date: Wed, 07 Sep 2011 08:57:04 GMT
```

Second client request

```
GET /lastmodified.php HTTP/1.1
Host:phpdemo.site
If-Modified-Since: Mon, 05 Sep 2011 07:31:07 GMT
```

Server reply

```
HTTP/1.1 304 Not Modified
Date: Wed, 07 Sep 2011 08:57:13 GMT
```

The server or the PHP script must therefore evaluate the HTTP request header *If-Modified-Since* explicitly.

Entity Tag

It's not always possible to specify a change date; it simply might not be easy to find out what it is. For such situations, you can use the *ETag* header, which assigns an *Entity* tag to the content—a unique string for this version of the content—for example, a number or a hash value. It works the same as *Last-Modified*: If requests follow, the client sends an *If-None-Match* header, which is evaluated by the server or the PHP script.

Listing 6-4 shows both client requests. After the first request, the server replies with an *ETag* header: You must place the value between quotes, but you are free to choose any value you like. At the second client request (at a later time), it sends the *ETag* of the version in its cache as part of the header *If-None-Match*. The server or the PHP script can evaluate this information and answer either with an HTTP-304 code (if the content hasn't changed yet) or with an HTTP-200 code and the data of the new version.

LISTING 6-4 Course of requests and replies when the *ETag* header is specified.

```
First client request
GET /etag.php HTTP/1.1
Host: phpdemo.site

Server reply
HTTP/1.1 200 OK
ETag: "387060f9402aca1:5fff-35"
Date: Wed, 07 Sep 2011 08:57:04 GMT

Second client request
GET /etag.php HTTP/1.1
Host:phpdemo.site
If-None-Match: "387060f9402aca1:5fff-35"
```

> **Note** The *If-None-Match* header can also contain multiple comma-separated *ETag* values:
>
> ```
> If-None-Match: "387060f9402aca1:5fff-35", W/"3653412", "38:5fff:35aca1"
> ```

Entity tags can be classified as either strong or weak tags:

- *Strong tags* must differ from one other as soon as the resource version has changed by at least one byte.

- *Weak tags*, represented by the syntax *W/"..."*, should change only if the semantic meaning has changed.

For example, a strong tag for a visitor counter changes with each visitor, a weak tag might only change once a day, if the exact number of visitors is not important for the application. You should use strong tags whenever possible.

You can use *ETag* headers and *Last-Modified* headers together. If both the *If-None-Match* and *If-Modified-Since* headers are set in subsequent requests, the server should typically reply only with an HTTP-304 message when both conditions are met.

Caching Conditions

Using the *Cache-Control* HTTP header, you can set additional conditions for caching. Table 6-1 shows the most important *Cache-Control* statements. The *max-age* statement has already been introduced in the section *"Max-age* Statement," earlier in this chapter.

TABLE 6-1 Statements in the *Cache-Control* header

Statement	Description
max-age=seconds	Maximum age of the version in the cache, at which the client must request the content again from the server.
must-revalidate	The resource can be cached, but the client must contact the server before using it again, to check whether the resource has changed.
no-cache	The resource must never be cached, but instead must always be requested from the server.
no-store	The resource must not be cached or locally saved in a file (for example, in the Temporary Internet Files folder). This option is designed mainly for websites with sensitive content.
private	The resource can only be stored in a private cache for the individual user who has sent the request.
public	The resource can be stored in a cache, which is used for several users, typically a proxy cache. This is the default behavior when there is no authentication on the HTTP level.

You can combine and link statements in the header with commas, as demonstrated in the following:

```
Cache-Control: public, max-age=86400, must-revalidate
```

Different browsers interpret *no-cache* and *no-store* differently: for the Back and Forward functions, all browsers reload the page when *no-store* is specified. If *no-cache* is specified, the cached version is displayed, or (depending on the browser) the resource is reloaded.

Older browsers still have the (slightly repurposed) *Pragma* header:

```
Pragma: no-cache
```

You can use it to prohibit caching for these browsers.

Specifying the Headers with IIS

You can specify HTTP headers that have an impact on caching from PHP by using the *header()* method. For other contents, such as graphics, you can specify headers from IIS.

Entity tags (*ETag* headers) and *Last-Modified* headers are automatically added to content supplied via the *StaticFile* handler. For this type of content, IIS takes over management of the change headers by monitoring the file and adjusting both headers accordingly when there are changes.

You can specify other headers via IIS Manager or by using *appcmd*.

Specifying the Headers by Using IIS Manager

To set a cache time limit by using IIS Manager, perform the following steps:

1. Open IIS Manager.

2. In the Connections pane, select the desired site, application, or directory.

3. On the start page, open the HTTP Reply Response Headers module.

4. In the Actions pane, click Specify Set Common Headers.

   The Set Common HTTP Response Headers dialog box opens, as shown in Figure 6-1.

5. Select the Expire Web Content check box, and then choose one of three options:

   - **Immediately**   Content must not be cached (sets the header *Cache-Control* to *no-cache*)

   - **After**   Enter a duration for the caching (sets the header *Cache-Control* to *max-age=<value>*)

   - **At**   Specifies that content can only be cached up until a certain defined point in time (sets the reply header *Expires* to the desired time)

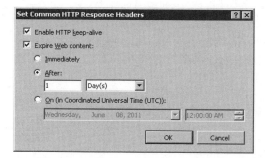

FIGURE 6-1 Specifying the HTTP reply header for expiring web content.

6. Click OK to apply the settings.

   You can specify additional headers, especially the *Cache-Control* header, in the same module by doing the following:

7. In the Actions pane, click Add.

8. In the dialog box that opens, enter the name of the HTTP header in the Name text box (for example, *Cache-Control*) and the desired header content in the Value text box (for example, *must-revalidate*, *public*).

9. Click OK to add the header for new requests.

> **Note** IIS automatically connects set *Cache-Control* statements of the Common Headers function to the manually added reply headers so that both can be used at the same time.

Specifying Headers from the Command Line

To set the desired headers from the command line, run the following commands by using *appcmd*:

- Prohibiting the caching of static content:

```
appcmd.exe set config "<PATH>"
-section:system.webServer/staticContent /clientCache.cacheControlMode:"DisableCache"
```

- Permitting the caching of static content for a certain amount of time (which is entered as *days.hours:minutes:seconds*):

```
appcmd.exe set config "<PATH>" -section:system.webServer/staticContent
/clientCache.cacheControlMode:"UserMaxAge" /clientCache.cacheControlMaxAge:"1.12:30:00"
```

- Permitting the caching of static content up to a defined point in time:

```
appcmd.exe set config "<PATH>"
-section:system.webServer/staticContent /clientCache.cacheControlMode:"UseExpires"
/clientCache.cacheControlMaxAge:"Thu, 07 Apr 2011 07:25:03 GMT"
```

To manage your own headers (no matter whether the content is supplied by the *StaticFile* handler), run the following *appcmd* commands:

- Adding a new header:

```
appcmd set config "<PATH>"-section:system.webServer/httpProtocol
/+customHeaders.[name='<Header Name>',value='<Header Value>']
```

- Removing a header:

```
appcmd set config "<PATH>"
-section:system.webServer/httpProtocol /-customHeaders.[name='<Header Name>']
```

Configuration Elements

Two different configuration elements are used to specify the cache settings directly in the configuration file: *staticContent/clientCache* and *httpProtocol/customHeaders*.

Table 6-2 shows the content caching attributes supplied via the *StaticFile* handler.

TABLE 6-2 Attributes for the *staticContent/clientCache* configuration element

Attribute	Description
cacheControlMaxAge	Specifies the allowed duration for the caching in the format *days .hours:minutes:seconds*—for example, *1.12:30:00;* only works in connection with *cacheControlMode=UseMaxAge*.
cacheControlMode	Specifies the mode for the cache: ■ *DisableCache* Caching is not allowed ■ *UseMaxAge* Caching is only allowed for the defined duration ■ *UseExpires* Caching is allowed up to the defined point in time
httpExpires	Specifies the date/time up to which caching is permitted—for example, *Thu, 07 Apr 2011 07:25:03 GMT;* only works in connection with *cacheControlMode=UseExpires*

Listing 6-5 shows how to set caching for a period of one day, 12 hours, and 30 minutes.

LISTING 6-5 Specifying the cache settings for static content.

```
<system.webServer>
  <staticContent>
    <clientCache cacheControlMode="UseMaxAge" cacheControlMaxAge="1.12:30:00" />
  </staticContent>
</system.webServer>
```

You can specify other headers with the help of the configuration collection *httpProtocol/ customHeaders*. Listing 6-6 shows how you can add the *Cache-Control* statement *must-revalidate*.

LISTING 6-6 Configuring the addition of reply headers.

```
<system.webServer>
  <httpProtocol>
    <customHeaders>
      <add name="Cache-Control" value="must-revalidate" />
    </customHeaders>
  </httpProtocol>
</system.webServer>
```

Output Cache

For faster HTTP request processing, IIS provides an output cache. Files and content in this cache are kept directly in the main storage. File access to the drives is not required. The output cache can also be used for PHP scripts and can thus increase performance significantly (because PHP execution and database access no longer take place).

IIS provides two options for configuring the output cache: User mode and Kernel mode. Caching in Kernel mode is extremely powerful, because the entire request is handled directly in the HTTP protocol stack (http.sys), and request data does not need to be passed on to the IIS modules in User mode. However, caching in Kernel mode has certain limits. Not all requests can be saved.

> **Note** You can find descriptions of the conditions that need to be met for the Kernel mode to work on *http://support.microsoft.com/kb/817445/* and *http://msdn.microsoft.com/en-us/library/aa364670%28VS.85%29.aspx.*

Logging the request errors also helps (see Chapter 8, "Error Messages and Error Search"), assuming the cache area feature is logged. You can find more information in the log entry under *HTTPSYS_CACHEABLE.*

Configuring by Using IIS Manager

To configure the output cache in IIS Manager, perform the following steps:

1. Start IIS Manager.

2. In the Connections pane, select the desired item.

3. On the item's start page, open the Output Caching module.

4. In the Actions pane, click Edit Feature Settings, ensure that the desired cache (kernel cache or user mode cache) is enabled, and then click OK.

> **Note** The maximum size of the HTTP replies and the cache size limit can only be set on the server level.

5. In the Actions pane, click Add.

   The Add Cache Rule dialog box opens, as shown in Figure 6-2.

6. Enter the file name extension for which you would like to enable caching. Select one of the two caching types, and then set the file cache monitoring for PHP scripts to At Time Intervals.

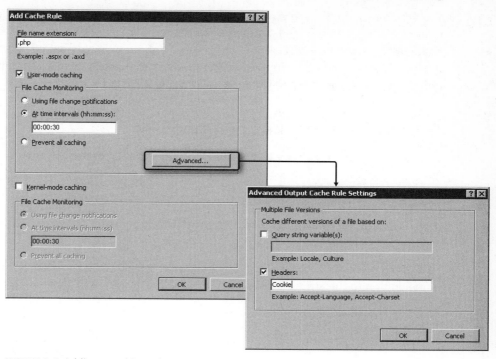

FIGURE 6-2 Adding a caching rule.

7. For caching in User mode, you can specify additional settings by clicking the Advanced button.

   For example, to make the caching dependent on the cookie content, select the Headers check box, and then enter Cookie into the corresponding text box. Click OK to apply the advanced settings.

8. Click OK to add the cache rule.

You have now enabled caching. You can check the function by writing a simple test script, such as that in Listing 6-7, and copy it to the corresponding location on your website. If you run the script a few times, you should see that the time does not change for 30 seconds.

LISTING 6-7 cachetest.php—a script for testing cache.

```
<html>
    <head><title>Cache Test</title></head>
    <body>
        <p>Time: <?php date('d.m.Y H:i:s'); ?></p>
    </body>
</html>
```

You can specify from which time forward IIS caches a file by using *frequentHitThreshold* (number of required hits) and *frequentHitTimePeriod* (time period in which the hits must happen) of the *system.webServer/ServerRuntime* configuration element. In IIS Manager, these values can only be set in the configurations editor (see Chapter 3, "Configuring IIS"). By default, two hits must happen within 10 seconds for a file to be saved.

Configuring from the Command Line

To enable caching in User mode, use the following *appcmd* command:

```
appcmd set config "<PATH>" -section:caching/+profiles.[extension='.php',
duration='00:00:30',policy='CacheForTimePeriod',varyByHeaders='Cookie']
```

If you want the file version to be dependent on the query string, you need to set the attribute *varyByQuerystring*.

To enable caching in Kernel mode, you need to set the attribute *kernelCachePolicy* instead of or in addition to the attribute policy.

To remove a cache rule, use *appcmd* as follows:

```
appcmd set config "<PATH>" -section:caching /-profiles.[extension='.php']
```

To control from what time forward a file should be cached, use the following command:

```
appcmd set config -section:system.webServer/ServerRuntime /frequentHitThreshold:5
/frequentHitTimePeriod:00:00:15
```

Both attributes can only be set server-wide, not for individual sites.

Once you have enabled the Kernel mode cache, you can use the command *netsh* to retrieve the current state of the cache, as shown in the following:

```
netsh http show cache
```

Configuration Elements

The cache is configured with the configuration collection caching/profiles. Table 6-3 shows the attributes for caching content.

TABLE 6-3 The attributes for the configuration collection caching/profiles

Attribute	Description
duration	Specifies the cache duration; works only with the *CacheForTimePeriod* policy
extension	File name extension
kernelCachePolicy	Type of the Kernel mode cache; same options as for the user mode cache
policy	Type of the User mode cache: ■ *CacheUntilChange* Cache until the file changes ■ *CacheForTimePeriod* Cache for a certain amount of time ■ *DontCache* Never cache
varyByHeaders	Specifies the parameters of the query strings that impact the caching (only for User mode cache)
varyByQueryString	Specifies the HTTP request headers that impact the caching (only for User mode cache)

Listing 6-8 shows how to permit caching for a period of 30 seconds.

LISTING 6-8 Configuration for the cache profile.

```
<system.webServer>
  <caching>
    <profiles>
      <add extension=".php" policy="CacheForTimePeriod" duration="00:00:30"
           varyByHeaders="Cookie" />
      <add extension=".png" kernelCachePolicy="CacheUntilChange" />
    <profiles>
  </caching>
</system.webServer>
```

The WinCache Extension for PHP

The WinCache extension for PHP does not target caching at HTTP level, but instead improves the performance when PHP scripts are executed. The extension provides the following functions:

■ **Opcode Cache**   PHP scripts are processed in two steps: the script is parsed and compiled into opcode statements, which are then run in the next step. The PHP opcodes of a script are cached in the opcode cache, and the compilation step is no longer needed for additional statements.

- **File Cache**   WinCache can also cache PHP script files to further reduce file access operations.

- **Session Handler**   PHP sessions let you save data (whose values are cached in a file by default) in the *$_SESSION* variable. WinCache provides a session handler that keeps this data in the main storage and thus makes slower file or database access unnecessary.

- **Cache for User Data**   The WinCache functions can also be addressed directly from the user script to save custom data in the cache and to address them from any PHP processes within the application pool.

The installation of WinCache and some of the functions are described in more detail in the following section.

Setting Up the WinCache Extension

You can either install the WinCache extension manually or with the help of the Web Platform Installer (Web PI).

 Note At the time of this book's printing, the current version of the WinCache extension and the version for PHP 5.3 required a manual installation.

Manually Installing the WinCache Extension

To manually install the WinCache extension, perform the following steps:

1. Download the current version of the extension's installation program that works for your PHP version (5.2 or 5.3) from *http://www.iis.net/expand/WinCacheForPhp*, and then save the file. This book uses and describes version 1.1 Beta 2 of the WinCache extension.

2. Start the installation program and confirm the licensing information by selecting Yes.

3. Select the directory into which you want to extract the files.

4. Go to the selected directory and copy the file php_wincache.dll into the PHP extension directory C:\PHP\ext.

5. Open the file php.ini (C:\PHP\php.ini) in a text editor, and then add the following line:

   ```
   extension = php_wincache.dll
   ```

6. Ensure that the extension directory in php.ini is set to *ext*, as shown in the following;

   ```
   extension_dir = "ext"
   ```

   If extension directory is not set this way, the extension will not be loaded.

7. Restart the corresponding IIS application pool.

8. Run a phpinfo() script.

You should see the WinCache extension, as shown in Figure 6-3.

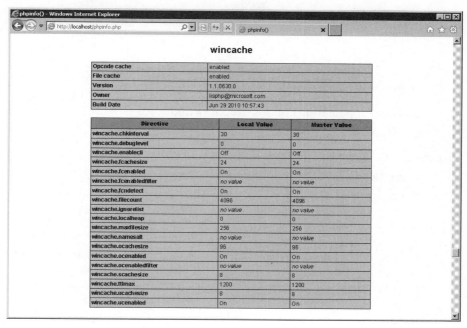

FIGURE 6-3 The WinCache extension for PHP.

Installing the WinCache Extension by Using the Web PI

To install the WinCache extension with the Web PI, perform the following steps:

1. Start the Microsoft Web PI with administrator rights.

2. Click Web Platform | Frameworks And Runtimes | Customize.

3. Select the Windows Cache Extension For PHP option, and then click the Install button.

> **Important** Ensure that the WinCache extension matches your PHP version. If it does not, you need to avoid manual installation.

4. Click the I Agree To Start The Installation button. After a successful installation, click the Finish button.

5. Click Exit to close the Web PI.

The PHP Opcode and File Cache

The PHP opcode cache and the file cache help you run PHP scripts faster because they minimize file access. This feature also minimizes the need for the compilation step during script execution, because the opcodes are cached.

Configuration

You can use configuration options to control both caches. Table 6-4 lists the most important properties.

TABLE 6-4 Configuration statements for the file cache and the opcode cache

Configuration options	Description
wincache.chkinterval	Specifies in seconds how long WinCache waits before checking whether a file has changed—the longer the interval, the fewer file accesses take place, but the longer it takes for file changes to take effect.
wincache.fcachesize, wincache.ocachesize	Maximum size of the file cache (f) and the opcode cache (o) in megabytes.
wincache.fcenabled, wincache.ocenabled	Turns the file cache (fc) or Opcode cache (oc) on (1) or off (0).
wincache.ignorelist	List of files (without path specification) that must not be cached (separated by a pipe).

As of version 1.1, WinCache detects changes to PHP files automatically. The check interval (*chkinterval*) has no impact in this case, unless the file system does not support change notifications (for example, a UNC share). In this case, WinCache checks these files at the specified interval.

 Note If necessary, you can use the function *wincache_refresh_if_changed()* to renew entries in the cache before the time specified in *wincache.chkinterval* has run out.

Status Information

The WinCache installation also includes a PHP script that can inform you about the current state of WinCache. To be able to use this script, perform the following steps:

1. Copy the file wincache.php from the installation directory into a directory on your website (for example, C:\inetpup\wwwroot\wincache\wincache.php).

2. Open the file with an editor, go to the section CONFIGURATION SETTINGS, and then enter a new password.

    If you have saved the script in an area that uses IIS authentication, enter the permitted users in the variable *$user_allowed*.

3. Save the file, and then open it in the browser.

    You are now receiving information about the current memory and cache status of WinCache, as shown in Figure 6-4.

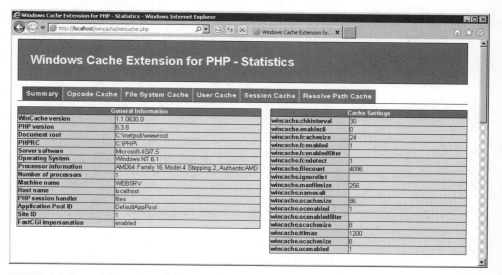

FIGURE 6-4 Status information of the WinCache extension for PHP.

Session Handler

As of version 1.1, WinCache provides a PHP session handler.

To use the WinCache session handler, perform the following steps:

1. Open the file php.ini (C:\PHP\php.ini).

2. Look for the line that contains the statement *session.save_handler*, and then replace it with:

```
session.save_handler = wincache
```

3. The session data is also saved in the Windows folder for temporary files. If you want to change the folder, set the configuration variable *session.save_path* to the desired folder path. Don't forget to grant the IIS application pool users (*IIS_IUSRS*) the required access rights to the folder.

4. Save the file and restart the associated IIS application pool.

PHP now uses WinCache to store the session data and keeps them in main storage memory for quick access.

You can specify the size of the available session cache together with the user cache by using the configuration option *wincache.ucachesize*. Its value is specified in megabytes.

User Cache

The user cache of the PHP WinCache extension has been available since version 1.1 of the extension. With it, you can save your own data in the cache. The data in the cache can be accessed from all PHP processes within the same application pool. Typically, it is used for saving global status information, global counters, or as cache for the result of frequent calculations or database operations.

You should use the cache for saving global data for the entire PHP application. The variable *$_SESSION* is better suited for user-related data.

> **Caution** When multiple PHP applications are using the same application pool, the PHP applications can access the data of the other applications in the user cache. This can pose a security risk.

Listing 6-9 shows a simple application of the user cache: a chat script that uses all of the following essential functions of the user cache:

- **wincache_ucache_clear()**   Deletes all entries in the user cache.
- **wincache_ucache_exists($key)**   Checks whether a certain entry exists.
- **wincache_ucache_add ($key, $value, $ttl)**   Adds a new entry, but only if it doesn't exist yet. *$ttl* specifies after how many seconds the entry must be deleted, *0* (the default) means that the value must not be deleted.
- **wincache_ucache_inc($key, $inc_by)**   Increases an entry by $inc_by or by *1*, if *$inc_by* is not specified. If an error occurs (for example, because the entry doesn't exist or is not a number), the function returns *false*.
- **wincache_ucache_get($key, &$success)**   Reads an entry and returns *false* if it doesn't exist. If you want to check *Boolean* variables for success, you can set the status in the optional variable *$success*.
- **wincache_ucache_set($key, $value, $ttl)**   Adds a new entry or overrides an existing entry. *$ttl* states the duration of the entry.

LISTING 6-9 wincache-chat.php—a short chat script with WinCache.

```
<html>
<head>
    <title>Chatroom</title>
</head>
<body>
<h1>Chatroom</h1>
<?php
if (isset($_POST['clear'])) {
    wincache_ucache_clear();
    echo '<p>Messages deleted, counter reset.</p>';
}
if (!wincache_ucache_exists('counter')) {
    wincache_ucache_add('counter', 0);
}
$cnt = wincache_ucache_inc('counter');
echo "$cnt page hits since the last restart.\n";
?>
<form action="" method="post">
    Message: <input name="msg" />
    <input type="submit" value="Send!" />
    <input type="submit" name="clear" value="Delete all" />
</form>
<hr />
<h2>The 5 latest messages</h2>
<p><?php
if (!wincache_ucache_exists('chat')) {
    wincache_ucache_add('chat', array());
}
$chat = wincache_ucache_get('chat');
if (isset($_POST['msg'])) {
    $chat[] = $_POST['msg'];
    if (count($chat) > 5) {
        array_shift($chat);
    }
    wincache_ucache_set('chat', $chat);
}
foreach (array_reverse($chat) as $msg) {
    echo htmlspecialchars($msg), "<br />\n";
}
?></p>
</body>
</html>
```

Figure 6-5 shows the chat script output after a few passes. The output is the same for all users. The value and content of the WinCache user cache are global.

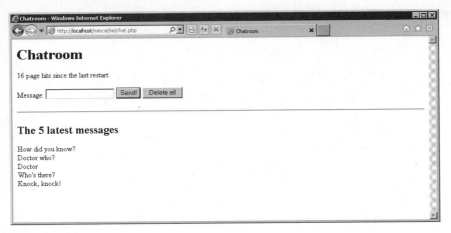

FIGURE 6-5 Chat script output.

Summary

With the techniques described in this chapter, you can increase the performance of your PHP applications significantly. Especially for popular pages, you should try to use all three options: caching based on HTTP headers, IIS output cache, and PHP caches such as WinCache.

You should pay special attention to the difference between anonymous and logged-in users: normally, anonymous users generate a lot more requests than logged-in users. Also, the pages for logged-in users are usually personalized; therefore, the IIS output caching for PHP scripts is not very efficient in this case. A simple differentiation between user types can be achieved via different URLs for the anonymous area and the area for logged-in users. You should already take this into account when you are designing your PHP application.

During configuration, it's helpful to set up files with different caching requirements (for example, graphics and style sheets) in their own folders and not mix them with PHP scripts.

In special cases, the caching can be configured at file level (with the *location* element; see Chapter 3) instead of on folder level. This might become necessary for index.php files.

Fine-tuning depends on your application and your users. Analyzing the log files can provide you with important information.

Chapter 7
URL Rewrite

URL Rewrite is an extremely useful and powerful tool for developing PHP applications: with it, you can assign the requested URL to any desired PHP script or other resource and thus override the mapping of the URL path to the physical path. PHP scripts can therefore be responsible for any URLs and process them. Starting with version 2.0, it's also possible to rewrite outgoing HTML and HTTP headers.

In this chapter, you will first learn the basics so that you understand the functionality behind URL Rewrite: URL paths, their parts and associated PHP variables, and how to evaluate rules. Then you will see how to create rules by using the IIS Manager. The patterns, conditions, and actions are discussed in detail. Finally, you will look at the XML configuration of the module, along with a few examples.

Setting Up URL Rewrite

You can use the Web Platform Installer (Web PI) to install the URL Rewrite module, or install the module manually by using an installation package.

Installing URL Rewrite Manually

To install the URL Rewrite module without the Web PI, perform the following steps:

1. Open the website *http://www.iis.net/expand/URLRewrite* and download the version (x86 or x64) of *URL Rewrite Module 2.0* that works for your system.

2. Run the downloaded installation file.

3. In the dialog box, select the check box to agree to the licensing conditions, and then click the Install button.

4. Exit the installation by clicking the Finish button.

   If you are asked to restart the server, do so.

You have now installed the module.

Installing URL Rewrite by Using the Web PI

To install the URL Rewrite module by using the Web PI, perform the following steps:

1. Start the Web PI as an administrator.

2. Click Products | Server.

3. Click to add URL Rewrite 2.0.

4. Click the Install button.

   The Web Platform Installation dialog box opens.

5. In the dialog box, click the I Agree button.

   The Web PI now starts the download and the installation.

6. After a successful installation, click the Finish button.

Predefined Variables

To understand the impact of redirecting and rewriting rules, let's first look at the predefined PHP variables that are important for the rewrite. Once you understand how the rules work, you will be better able to apply them yourself. The variables are based on three different sources: PHP, Internet Information Services (IIS), and the CGI specification.

Common Gateway Interface Variables

The *Common Gateway Interface* (CGI) is a specification (RFC 3875) that describes how external programs are called by a web server, and how request information is passed to these programs.

The important variables for rewriting are based on the URL of the HTTP request. A URL consists of several parts, as shown in Figure 7-1.

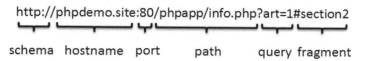

FIGURE 7-1 The structure of a URL.

The individual parts of a URL have the following meaning:

- The *schema* specifies the protocol that the application uses (for websites, either HTTP or HTTPS).

- The *host name* specifies the name of the server. Normally it is a fully qualified domain name, such as *www.bing.com* or *www.microsoft.com*.

- The *port number* is optional and specifies the TCP/IP port for the connection. For the HTTP protocol, port 80 is the default port; for the HTTPS protocol, it is port 443.

- The *path* identifies the requested resource within the server. In Figure 7-1, the path is */phpapp/info.php*. It contains a leading forward slash. URL paths behave like folder paths. By default, many web servers, including IIS, map the URL path to the physical folder path.

- The *query string* can be used for passing parameters—for example, search strings or actions that need to be performed. A query string may contain any number of parameters. In practice, however, it is limited to approximately 2,000 characters.

- The *document fragment* identifies a part within the document. It is only evaluated by the browser itself and is not transferred in the HTTP protocol. They are typically used as jump targets for headings or footnotes.

In the CGI specification, different variables are assigned to these parts of the URL, which can be queried in PHP with the global variable *$_SERVER*. CGI has one particularity which is different from the standard division of a URL: the path can be divided into two parts. Simply put, the path can be continued as desired behind the path for the script. The path after the script is passed to the script as a variable.

Table 7-1 shows all URL-based variables of the CGI specification. As a URL example, we are using *http://phpdemo.site:80/phpapp/info.php/sub/path?art=1*.

The PHP script (= the resource) is located in the root folder of the website at *phpapp\info.php*.

TABLE 7-1 CGI variables in $_SERVER, based on the URL of an HTTP request

CGI variable	Description	Example
PATH_INFO	Subpath, which is specified behind the script	/sub/path
PATH_TRANSLATED	Complete physical path of the script, including the subpath	%root folder% \phpapp\info.php\sub\path
QUERY_STRING	Query string of the URL	art=1
SCRIPT_NAME	URL path and name of the executed script	/phpapp/info.php
SERVER_NAME	Host name of the server, which is also contained in the host header of the HTTP request	phpdemo.site
SERVER_PORT	TCP/IP port number of the incoming HTTP request	80
SERVER_PROTOCOL	Protocol and version number	HTTP/1.1

Note If in your work environment the variables *PATH_INFO* and *PATH_TRANSLATED* don't contain the correct values, check whether the option *cgi.fix_pathinfo=1* is specified in php.ini.

CGI also defines a number of other variables. For example, all HTTP headers for the request are passed in the form of *HTTP_**, which means that the header *Content-Type* is passed as *HTTP_CONTENT_TYPE* or as a PHP variable in *$_SERVER['HTTP_CONTENT_TYPE']*. Information about the requesting client is also transferred according to the CGI specification; for example, the client's IP address is transferred as *REMOTE_ADDR* to the PHP script.

IIS and PHP Variables

IIS and PHP define several additional variables, which can be used for URL rewrites in HTTP requests. The variables give you information about the physical path of the script and the original URL of the request.

Table 7-2 lists the additional variables that are defined in the global variable *$_SERVER*. Our URL example is again *http://phpdemo.site:80/phpapp/info.php/sub/path?art=1*.

The PHP script is located in the root folder of the website *C:\inetpub\wwwroot* at *phpapp\info.php*.

The URL is rewritten internally.

TABLE 7-2 Relevant $_SERVER variables of an HTTP request

PHP variable	Description	Example
APPL_PHYSICAL_PATH (IIS only)	Physical path of the assigned IIS application of the PHP script.	C:\inetpub\wwwroot
DOCUMENT_ROOT	Root folder of the website.	C:\inetpub\wwwroot
HTTP_X_ORIGINAL_URL (IIS only)	If only the URL has been rewritten, this contains the original URL of the HTTP request.	/phpapp/info.php/sub/ path?art=1
HTTPS	Specifies whether this is an HTTPS request.	off
IIS_UrlRewriteModule (IIS only)	Specifies whether the URL Rewrite module is enabled.	1
IIS_WasUrlRewritten (IIS only)	If the URL has been rewritten, this variable is defined, otherwise not.	1
ORIG_PATH_INFO	If *PATH_INFO* is not set, *ORIG_PATH_INFO* can contain the path information. **Caution** This also contains the relative path of the script itself.	/phpapp/info.php/sub/path
PHP_SELF	Relative path of the script including the subpath.	/phpapp/info.php/sub/path
REQUEST_URI	URL of the HTTP request.	/phpapp/info.php/sub/ path?art=1
SCRIPT_FILENAME	Absolute physical path of the PHP script.	C:\inetpub\wwwroot\ phpapp\info.php
UNENCODED_URL (IIS only)	If the URL has been rewritten, this contains the original URL of the HTTP request, without decoding URL-coded characters.	/phpapp/info.php/sub/ path?art=1

> **Note** In contrast to Apache, *$_SERVER['HTTPS']* is not empty, but has the value *off* when the connection is encrypted. *PATH_INFO* and *ORIG_PATH_INFO* are always set correctly in IIS 7 with FastCGI and the php.ini setting *cgi.fix_pathinfo=1* (the default value).

In addition to the *$_SERVER* variables, there are two constants that provide further information about the current PHP script: __ *FILE*__ contains the complete physical path of the PHP file; __ *DIR*__ (as of PHP 5.3) contains the complete physical path of the folder in which the PHP file is located. One important difference is that the constants are dependent on the file in which they are located. Therefore, they are different for PHP files, which are included by the executed PHP script.

PHP also provides the global variable *$_ENV*, which contains environment variables. In the default installation of IIS, no environment variables are passed to PHP in *$_ENV*; instead, a lot of entries end up in *$_SERVER*.

Merging PHP Script

For you to better understand the impact of redirecting and rewriting rules, we are using the PHP script urlinfo.php from Listing 7-1. The *$_SERVER* variables are divided into three groups: specifications about the binding, the request URL, and the executing script. First, a *printServerVar()* function is defined, which returns the values of *$_SERVER* securely in a list.

LISTING 7-1 urlinfo.php—information about the HTTP request and the PHP script.

```
<!DOCTYPE html>
<html>
<head><title>Information about the HTTP Request</title></head>
<body>
<h1>Information about the HTTP Request</h1>
<h2>Binding specifications</h2>
<ul>
<?php
function printServerVar($text, $parameter) {
    echo "<li>$text ($parameter): ";
    if (isset($_SERVER[$parameter])) {
        echo '"', htmlspecialchars($_SERVER[$parameter]), '"';
    } else {
        echo '--not specified--';
    }
    echo "</li>\n";
}
printServerVar('Server name', 'SERVER_NAME');
printServerVar('Port', 'SERVER_PORT');
printServerVar('Protocol', 'SERVER_PROTOCOL');
printServerVar('Secure connection', 'HTTPS');
?>
</ul>
<h2>URL specifications</h2>
<ul>
<?php
printServerVar('Request URL', 'REQUEST_URI');
printServerVar('Query string', 'QUERY_STRING');
printServerVar('URL-Script path incl. subpath', 'PHP_SELF');
printServerVar('URL path of the script', 'SCRIPT_NAME');
printServerVar('Subpath', 'PATH_INFO');
printServerVar('Original path information', 'ORIG_PATH_INFO');
printServerVar('Did a URL rewrite take place?', 'IIS_WasUrlRewritten');
printServerVar('Original URL', 'HTTP_X_ORIGINAL_URL');
printServerVar('Unencoded URL', 'UNENCODED_URL');
?>
</ul>
<h2>Script specifications</h2>
<ul>
<?php
printServerVar('Root folder', 'DOCUMENT_ROOT');
printServerVar('Physical path of the IIS application', 'APPL_PHYSICAL_PATH');
printServerVar('Physical path of the script', 'SCRIPT_FILENAME');
```

```
printServerVar('Physical path incl. subpath', 'PATH_TRANSLATED');
echo '<li>__FILE__ constant: ', __FILE__, '</li>';
echo '<li>__DIR__ constant: ', __DIR__, '</li>';     // only as of PHP 5.3
?>
</ul>
</body>
</html>
```

Copy the file into the root folder of your website and call up the script in the browser. Figure 7-2 shows the output of urlinfo.php if it is contained in the root folder C:\inetpub\ wwwroot and is called with the URL *http://localhost/urlinfo.php/sub/path?article=1*.

FIGURE 7-2 The output of urlinfo.php.

Evaluating Rules

The URL Rewrite module is a rule-based system. The rewriting of URLs and other actions are triggered by defined rules. Each rule consists of three parts:

- The *pattern* against which the URL path is tested

- The *conditions* that must be met (in addition to the pattern)

- An *action*, which is performed upon the successful testing of the pattern and the conditions

For an incoming request, the rules are evaluated, one after the other, to check whether a rule applies. If a rule does apply, the action of that rule is executed. If there are further rules in the list, the process continues with the next rule.

Action Types

The module provides five different actions for rules:

- **Redirect**   Redirects to a different URL. The browser then loads the new page.
- **Rewrite**   Internally rewrites a URL to a different file. With this, the connection between URL and physical file layout can be lifted.
- **Custom Response**   Responds with an HTTP status code, which can be chosen freely.
- **Abort Request**   The server immediately disconnects without sending an appropriate HTTP reply.
- **None**   Nothing is done and no action is performed. The purpose of this action becomes apparent during the processing of rules. For example, it can be used to process subsequent rules, only conditionally.

Hierarchy and URL Paths

Rules can be defined on all levels: server, website, application, virtual directory, and subfolder. Server rules represent one category; all others are called distributed rules and they are processed differently:

- *Server rules* apply to the entire web server—for instance, to all websites. The rule patterns are applied to the complete and absolute URL path. These rules are applied before any others.
- *Distributed rules* are applied in sequence according to their hierarchy. Therefore, the rules of the parent element take precedence. The patterns are no longer evaluated against the complete URL path, but only against the relative URL path of the defining element. For example, if a virtual directory has the URL *http://phpdemo.site/phpapp/* and you define a rule for this directory, when calling *http://phpdemo.site/phpapp/demo/info.php*, only the path *demo/info.php* relative to the directory serves as input data for the pattern.

> **Important** Consequently, patterns should never begin with a forward slash when working with distributed rules.

Distributed rules are inherited downward. This means that the rules also apply to child elements. The reference point for the rule to extract the relative path does not change, however.

The reference point is always the element in which the rule has been defined. In practice, this means that the rules always behave as if they were run on the level of the defined element. The fact that inheritance takes place only becomes apparent when inherited rules are cancelled in child elements. In this case, the rule of the parent element is not applied for requests that fall into the scope of the child element.

The URL paths are also important for the actions of the redirect and rewrite rules: if you specify a relative path for the action of these two types, the path is relative to the element in which the rule is defined. Unlike with patterns, defining an absolute path (forward slash at the beginning) makes sense here: it allows you to rewrite or redirect virtual directories and subfolders application-wide. You can also redirect to complete URLs, not just relative and absolute URL paths. This means that you can redirect to other websites or foreign sites outside of the server.

Time of the Evaluation

The module's rules are applied very early in the request processing. Figure 7-3 shows this instance: the rules are already applied at the start of the request processing. This ensures that these rules impact all types of requests, no matter whether you are working with PHP scripts or graphic files.

The three action types *Redirect*, *Abort Request*, and *Custom Response* skip a large part of the processing pipeline. Only the action types *Rewrite* and *None* run completely through the requests, and thus through the pipeline.

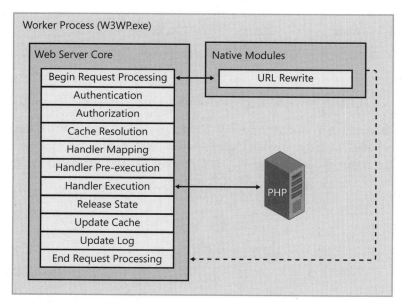

FIGURE 7-3 Processing of rules.

Setting Up Rules

Let's take a closer look at the individual rule types and how they are created. Later on, you will learn more details such as how to use conditions and regular expressions.

Setting Up Redirect Rules

A redirect is different from a rewrite of a URL: a redirect is known to and becomes effective from the outside, whereas a rewrite only influences the course of events within IIS itself. This means that the client (the web browser) is part of the redirect.

Flow

Figure 7-4 shows the request flow when a redirect rule is applied. Following that is a description of each step in the flow.

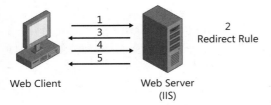

Web Client   Web Server
(IIS)

FIGURE 7-4 The course of events during a redirect of an HTTP request.

1. The web client sends a request to the web server.

2. The web server finds an applicable rule for the URL of the request.

3. The web server sends the status code for a redirect with a new URL to the client.

4. The client sends a new request with the URL from step 3.

5. The server replies with the requested page or resource (for example an image).

Table 7-3 shows possible HTTP status codes and what they mean. The most frequent status codes are 301 and 302. The latter is often used the wrong way, but has become generally accepted. With the status codes 303 and 307, HTTP/1.1 has defined alternatives to the status code 302.

TABLE 7-3 HTTP status codes for redirect

HTTP status code	Description
301 (permanent)	The request and all future requests must target the new URL. For example, 301 is used after a site has been reorganized permanently.
302 (found)	The request must target the new URL, but future requests must continue to use the old URL, because the redirect is only temporary. The HTTP method must not change for the new request (for example, *POST* must remain *POST*). In practice, browsers behave the same with 302 as with the status code 303.
303 (see other)	As of HTTP/1.1: the reply to the request is located at a different URL, but the request itself was processed correctly. The new URL must be requested with the *GET* method. Future requests must go to the original URL. 303 HTTP replies must not be cached. The idea behind 303 is that, for example, a form that is targeted with *POST* can redirect to different result pages after processing, depending on the content.
307 (temporary)	As of HTTP/1.1: the request must target a new URL, but future requests must continue to use the old URL, because the redirect is only temporary. The HTTP method must not change. The client can't assume that the request has already been processed.

Adding a Redirect Rule

To create a redirect rule and add it to the existing set of rules, perform the following steps:

1. Start the IIS Manager.

2. In the Connections pane, select the appropriate element; for example, Default Web Site.

3. In the Start Page pane, select the module URL Rewrite by double-clicking it.

4. In the Actions pane, select Add Rule(s).

    The Add Rule(s) dialog box opens.

5. Select the Blank Rule template.

6. The work area of the IIS Manager changes to the Edit Inbound Rule view, as shown in Figure 7-5.

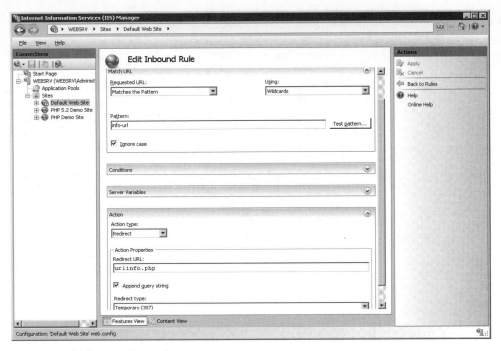

FIGURE 7-5 Adding a redirect rule.

7. In the Name text box of the rule, enter a unique name.

8. In the Using drop-down list, select Wildcards (Regular Expression will be covered later).

9. In the Pattern text box, enter the URL from which you want to redirect another URL.

   In the example, we are using info-url.

10. In the Action section, in the Actions Type drop-down list, select Redirect.

11. In the Action Properties subsection, in the Redirect URL text box, enter the URL to which you want to redirect.

   In the example, we are using urlinfo.php (the sample script from the section "Merging PHP Script," earlier in this chapter).

12. In the Redirect Type drop-down list, select Temporary (307).

13. In the Actions pane, click Apply to confirm your entries, and then click Back To Rules to return to the Rules view.

If you now call up the URL *http://localhost/info-url* in the browser, you are automatically redirected to the URL *http://localhost/urlinfo.php*. If the redirect is working, the new URL is displayed in the browser's address bar: the browser is included in the redirect. The redirect can also be checked in the IIS log file of the website. This file contains two entries that look as follows (the status code is the fourth number from the last):

```
2011-07-02 19:52:19 ::1 GET /info-url - 80 - ::1 Mozilla/4.0+(compatible;+MSIE+9.0;+Tride
nt/5.0) 307 0 0 0
2011-07-02 19:52:19 ::1 GET /urlinfo.php - 80 - ::1 Mozilla/4.0+(compatible;+MSIE+9.0;+Tride
nt/5.0) 200 0 0 15
```

> **Note** The IIS log files are located in the IIS root folder under C:\inetpub\logs\LogFiles\.

If you take a look at the result page of urlinfo.php after a redirect, you will notice that there is no difference between a direct call via *http://localhost/urlinfo.php* and a redirected call via *http://localhost/info-url*. The reason for this is the redirect flow: the browser generates a standalone second request with the URL *http://localhost/urlinfo.php*. This request is a regular *HTTP-GET* request and is indistinguishable from a direct (manual) URL request.

Setting Up Rewrite Rules

A rewrite rule permits you to rewrite the request URL internally within the server (server-internal) and replace it with another URL. This allows you to design the mapping of URL paths to physical file paths as you wish. For example, rewrite rules are used for Blog software to generate readable URLs (*pretty URLs*) for the individual Blog entries.

Flow

Rewrite rules are applied very early on in the request processing—like all rules of the URL Rewrite module—and impact all resources, PHP scripts, and image files. The rewrite happens exclusively internally within the server for the request processing. From the outside, on the client page, the rewrite is not noticeable.

While any further processing is aborted when redirect rules are applied, the processing continues when rewrite rules are applied. The subsequent rules are evaluated and applied. If the action of the rule has been enabled, the subsequent rules use the action URL for pattern tests, but not for the original URL of the request. Therefore, it is possible that a URL is rewritten multiple times before the request processing continues. You can use an option to prohibit the processing of subsequent rules, and control exactly which rules can be applied and when.

Adding a Rewrite Rule

To create a rewrite rule, perform the following steps:

1. In the IIS Manager of the desired element, select Start Page | URL Rewrite | Add Rule(s); for example, the Default Web Site.

   The Add Rule(s) dialog box opens.

2. Select the Blank Rule template. The center pane of the IIS Manager changes to the Edit Rules view.

3. In the Name text box of the rule, enter a unique name.

4. Fill in the Match URL fields according to your requirements.

> **Note** The pattern syntax is explained in the section "Pattern," later in the chapter.

5. In the Action section, in the Actions Type drop-down list, select Redirect.

6. Enter the new URL (the rewrite target) into Action Properties.

   If you want to retain the query string of the original request, leave the check box Append Query String selected.

   If you want to end rule processing, select the Stop Processing Of Subsequent Rules check box.

7. In the Actions pane, click Apply to confirm your entries, and then click Back To Rules to return to the Rules view.

For example, if you enter **other-url/*** (type: Wildcards) as a pattern during rule creation and **urlinfo.php/{R:1}** as the URL that you want to rewrite, you will see the following output of the script urlinfo.php when calling the URL *http://localhost/other-url/test/path*:

URL specifications

```
Request URL (REQUEST_URI): "/other-url/test/path"
Query string (QUERY_STRING): ""
URL Script path incl. subpath (PHP_SELF): "/urlinfo.php/test/path"
URL path of the script (SCRIPT_NAME): "/urlinfo.php"
Subpath (PATH_INFO): "/test/path"
Original path information (ORIG_PATH_INFO): "/urlinfo.php/test/path"
Did the rewrite take place? (IIS_WasUrlRewritten): "1"
Original URL (HTTP_X_ORIGINAL_URL): "/other-url/test/path"
Unencoded URL (UNENCODED_URL): "/other-url/test/path"
```

Script specifications

```
Root folder (DOCUMENT_ROOT): "C:\inetpub\wwwroot"
Physical path of the IIS application (APPL_PHYSICAL_PATH): "C:\inetpub\wwwroot\"
Physical path of the script (SCRIPT_FILENAME): "C:\inetpub\wwwroot\urlinfo.php"
Physical path including subpath (PATH_TRANSLATED): "C:\inetpub\wwwroot\urlinfo.php\test\path"
__FILE__ constant: C:\inetpub\wwwroot\urlinfo.php
__DIR__ constant: C:\inetpub\wwwroot
```

The script specifications show that the request has been rewritten internally to the PHP script urlinfo.php. The variables *PHP_SELF* and *SCRIPT_NAME* reflect the same. You can only read the path of the original request from the variables *REQUEST_URI* and the IIS-specific *HTTP_X_ORIGINAL_URL* and *UNENCODED_URL*.

> **Tip** PHP programs that must recognize the request URL should use the variable *REQUEST_URI*. This ensures that the program can be used across platforms.

Additional Action Types

You can set up rules with other action types the same way as the redirect and rewrite rules. Only the Action section is different.

Customizing a Reply

The *Custom Response* action type permits you to send any desired HTTP status codes and substatus codes. To set up a rule with such an action, simply do the same as when setting up other rules:

1. For the new rule you want to create, in the Action section, in the Action Type drop-down list, select the Custom Response.

2. Enter the HTTP status code (for example 403) and the IIS-specific substatus code into the corresponding text boxes. In the Reason text box, you can enter a plain text description of the status code. The reason is transferred in the status line of the HTTP reply.

3. In the Error Description text box, you can enter a more detailed description. This box can be used for debugging.

4. In the Actions pane, click Apply to Confirm your entries.

If you use the browser to call up a URL to which this rule applies, you will receive an error message that corresponds to your entries, as shown in Figure 7-6. For known status codes, IIS returns an HTML page with a user-friendly error message.

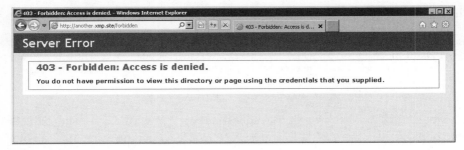

FIGURE 7-6 Defined error message for a rule with custom reply.

The *Abort Request* Action Type

The *Abort Request* action type ends a request as quickly as possible. No HTTP reply is returned to the requesting client. IIS does not generate a log entry for such aborted requests. You should therefore think twice before using an *Abort Request* action. It makes sense to use it when you know that there are unwanted or malicious requests or if the server is overrun with too many requests (such as during a Denial-of-Service attack). You can protect your resources by cancelling requests immediately.

You can't add further options to the Action section for this rule.

The *None* Action Type

As the name suggests, the *None* action type does not perform an action. Based on the pattern and the conditions of the *None* rule, the processing of the subsequent rules can be canceled.

The Action section of the rule only contains a single check box: Stop Processing Of Subsequent Rules. If you don't want the subsequent rules to be applied, select this check box.

Setting Up Rules with Templates

So far, we have used the Blank Rule template when setting up rules. URL Rewrite also offers two templates to simplify rewriting and canceling requests.

User-Friendly URL

Rewrite rules are mainly used for creating user-friendly URLs. A user-friendly URL generally uses no query string, and the individual parts of the URL are separated with forward slashes. The template for creating user-friendly URLs does this for you. It takes care of the formulation of the rewrite rule.

1. In the IIS Manager, click URL Rewrite | Add rule(s).

   The Add Rule(s) dialog box opens.

2. Select the User-Friendly URL template.

   The Add Rules To Enable User-Friendly URLs Wizard opens.

3. In the first text box, enter an example for a URL that you want to rewrite.

4. In the drop-down list, you can choose among various suggestions for user-friendly URLs.

5. In the Rewrite Rule Definition section, you can see the suggested URL pattern and the replacement URL.

6. If you want to make the user-friendly URLs the canonical URLs of your application, you can select the Create Corresponding Redirect Rule check box to create a redirect rule that redirects clients from internal to user-friendly URLs. If you select the Create Corresponding Outbound Rewrite Rule check box, then an outbound rule will be added that replaces all occurrences of internal URLs in the response HTML with their corresponding user-friendly URLs.

7. Click OK to close the wizard. The corresponding rules with the name *RewriteUser FriendlyURLn*, *RedirectUserFriendlyURLn*, and *OutboundRewriteUserFriendlyURLn* are generated (depending on what you chose in step 6).

The rules are now displayed in the rule list like regular rules. From there, they can be edited, renamed, disabled, or deleted.

Blocking Requests

To use the template for creating request blockings, perform the following steps:

1. In the IIS Manager, click URL Rewrite | Add rule(s).

   The Add Rule(s) dialog box opens.

2. Select the Request Blocking template.

   The Add Request Blocking Rule Wizard opens, as shown in Figure 7-7.

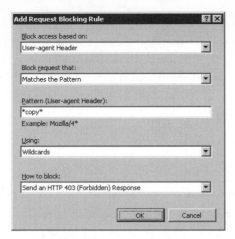

FIGURE 7-7 The template for creating a request blocking.

You can block the requests based on different request data: URL path, User-agent HTTP header, IP address, query string, reference (*Referer* HTTP header), or host header.

3. Enter the rule pattern into the Pattern text box. You can specify the pattern syntax in the Using drop down list.

4. In the How To Block drop-down list, you can enter the type of reply; you can choose between custom replies with the status codes 401, 403, and 404, or abort the request.

5. Click OK to close the dialog box; the corresponding rule with the name *RequestBlockingRuleN* is created.

You can now view, edit, disable, or delete the generated rule just as with all other rules in the rule list.

Rewrite Maps

If you need to define rules for many different URLs, it makes sense to use rewrite maps. A rewrite map is a number of name-value pairs. It is used for replacing a name with the corresponding value. The names are usually URL paths that you want to rewrite or redirect to other URLs. Rewrite maps, however, are not limited to URL paths.

Creating a Rewrite Map

To create a rewrite map, perform the following steps:

1. Start the IIS Manager.

2. In the Connections pane, select the element (for example, the Default Web Site).

3. Click URL Rewrite

4. In the Actions pane, click View Rewrite Maps.

5. In the URL Rewrite Maps pane, a list of existing maps is displayed.

6. In the Actions pane, click Add Rewrite Map.

   The Add Rewrite Maps dialog box opens.

7. Enter the name of the map into the text box and confirm your entry with OK. The work area Edit Rewrite Map is displayed.

8. In the Actions pane, click Add Mapping Entry.

   The Add Mapping dialog box opens.

9. Fill in the Original Value and New Value text boxes according to your requirements, and then click OK to close the dialog.

> **Caution** Neither the original value nor the new value allows placeholders or back references. Maps simply replace one string with another.

You have now set up a rewrite map and an entry.

A rewrite map also permits you to specify a default value, if none of the map entries apply. You should be very careful with default values, because they might lead to unintentional rewrites when using the maps. To set the default value, perform the following:

1. In the Actions pane, click Edit Rewrite Maps to open the work area of the selected rewrite map.

2. In the Actions pane, click Edit Map Settings.

   The Edit Rewrite Map dialog box opens.

3. Enter the desired default value into the text box, and then click OK to confirm.

> **Note** Rewrite maps are inherited. However, they cannot be extended by additional entries, and individual entries cannot be deleted from them. Even though the user interface suggests this, what actually happens is that the old rewrite map is deleted on the level where the change takes place, and a new map is generated with the content of the old one.
>
> If you change the original map that is higher in the hierarchy, these changes do not take effect lower in the hierarchy.
>
> However, since the changed rewrite map has the same name as the original one, inherited rules are applied to the changed rewrite map.

Creating an Associated Rule

Rewrite maps by themselves do not cause a request rewrite. The maps must first be entered into the rules. Rewrite maps can be used within a condition or in the action properties. They cannot be used in patterns.

IIS provides a rule wizard for creating a rule:

1. Select URL Rewrite.

2. In the Actions pane, click Add Rule(s).

3. Select the Rule With Rewrite Map rule template, and then click OK to confirm.

    The Add Rule With Rewrite Map Wizard opens.

4. Select The Rule Action drop-down list, choose whether you want to create a rewrite or a redirect rule.

5. Select the rewrite map from the second drop-down list, and then click OK to confirm.

You have now created a rule with the desired action and rewrite map.

> **Caution** The rule you created is using the rewrite map in a condition for which the server variable *REQUEST_URI* is used as condition entry. Unlike the paths in the rule patterns, *REQUEST_URI* always begins with a slash and also contains the query string. The original values of the map entries must therefore also begin with a slash and take the query string into account.

Rules in Detail

Rules consist of patterns, conditions, and actions. In the following subsections, you will find more detailed descriptions of these components.

Patterns

Rules are only applied when your URL follows certain patterns and when the conditions work for these patterns, as well. IIS recognizes three different syntaxes for patterns: exact match, simple wildcards, and regular expressions.

Wildcards

Wildcards represent a simple syntax for rule patterns, but can still cover a variety of typical application situations. The placeholder syntax has only one special character, the asterisk "*".

The * character is a placeholder for any number of any characters. This means that neither the type nor the number of the characters is limited. The asterisk can even represent zero characters. A back reference is created for the content of the placeholder.

Table 7-4 presents a few examples. In the notes, back references are represented as *{R:x}* according to IIS syntax. The null back reference *{R:0}* always represents the entire content of the search pattern if there is a hit, such as when it is identical to the input data.

TABLE 7-4 Examples for the placeholder syntax of search patterns

Pattern	Input data	Applies	Notes
a*c	abc	Yes	{R:0}=abc, {R:1}=b.
a*c	a/b/d-e/c	Yes	{R:0}=a/bde/c, {R:1}=/b/d-e/; the placeholder can contain special characters such as slashes .
a*c	a/b/d-e/c/d	No	The input data must always completely match the search pattern: Here the "/d" at the end prevents a hit.
ab/*/cd/*	ab/12/cd/cd	Yes	{R:0}=ab/12/cd/cd, {R:1}=12, {R:2}=cd; a search pattern can contain several placeholders.

Regular Expressions

Regular expressions are much more powerful than placeholders. They permit a very granular and exact definition of the search pattern. However, with this power comes more complexity.

Regular expressions recognize the following control characters that have special meanings:

. ( ) [ ] * + ? { } \ | ^ $

If you prefer not to use these characters as control characters, you need to escape them with a backslash. For example, to test for a point (period) in the pattern, you need to write "\." in the pattern.

One important difference to the placeholder syntax is that the search pattern of regular expressions does not need to match the entire input data, but only a certain string within the input data. Therefore, it is possible that the input data has other characters before and/or after the search pattern. You should keep this in mind, because otherwise the search pattern might capture many more URLs than you had intended.

Table 7-5 lists all control characters and their meaning. All other characters can be used without any restrictions. Back references in the form of *{R:x}* are generated with parentheses, *{R:0}* contains the entire matching search pattern.

Regular expressions make for a powerful tool, but it can easily lead to mistakes due to its complexity. To support you, IIS provides a tool for testing regular expressions, which makes working with them much easier.

TABLE 7-5 Control characters in regular expressions

Control character	Description
.	The period stands for one character of your choice (only one, never several).
[ ]	Defines a group of characters; for example, [ADE] stands for A, D, or E, but not for the string ADE. You can use the – (hypen character) to specify a range in alphanumerical order; for example, [A-Z] stands for all letters from A to Z.
[^]	If the caret is in front, the square bracket defines a group of characters that contains all characters with the exception of the specified character. For example, [^3-8] means all characters except for the numbers 3 to 8.
|	The pipe represents an or-relation. For example, abc|def applies to either the string abc or the string def.
^	Defines the beginning of the input data without representing the first character. For example, the pattern ^be applies to beat or best, but not to strobe or lobe.
$	Defines the end of the input data without representing the last character. For example, the pattern er$ applies to better or longer but not to verb or erase.
( )	The parentheses serve to group and to generate a back reference.
(?:)	Parentheses with a leading question mark and colon are also used for grouping, but do not generate a back reference.
*	The preceding expression may appear any amount of time, or not at all. For example, A* means zero or any amount of As, and AB* means one A followed by zero or multiple Bs. With the help of grouping, the strings can be repeated. The pattern (AB)*, therefore, means any number of the string AB such as ABABAB.
+	The preceding expression may appear any amount of time, but at least once. For example, [AB]+ means any sequence of the characters A and B, but at least one.
?	The preceding expression may appear once or not at all.
{ }	The preceding expression appears a certain amount of times. {4} means that the expression appears exactly four times, {2,4} means that the expression appears two to four times, {2,} means that the expression appears at least twice.
*?, +?, ??	If the quantifiers *, +, and ? are followed by a question mark, it means that the search algorithm is not greedy and ends after the first possible hit. For example, if the input data is ABBBC, the back references for the search pattern A(B+)(B*)C are set as follows: {R:1}=BBB, {R:2}=empty. But the back references for the search pattern A(B+?)(B*)C (not greedy) are set as follows: {R:1}=B, {R:2}=BB, because now the search is stopped in the first group after the shortest hit.
(?=), (?!)	Look-Ahead: (?=) means that the hit must be followed by this group. Thus, (?!) means that the hit must not be followed by this group. For example, the pattern BCD(?=EF) applies to the string ABCDEFG, because EF follows BCD. Because the Look-Ahead expression itself is no longer part of the hit, the zeroth back reference (the entire hit) is {R:0}=BCD.

Control character	Description
\	The backslash is used for escaping control characters, but also defines additional standalone control characters
\u0000	\u defines a character by its Unicode value in hexadecimal syntax. For example, \u0041 stands for A.
\x00	\x defines a character by its ISO-8859-1 value in hexadecimal syntax. For example, \xdc stands for Ü.
\b, \B	\b stands for a word boundary without being a character of the word boundary itself. A word boundary is always created when a word character (letter, number or underscore) meets a non-word character. \B stands for a spot which is not a word boundary. \B itself does not represent a character.
\d, \D	\d stands for the numbers 0 to 9; \D stands for all character except for the numbers 0 to 9.
\s, \S	\s stands for all kinds of space characters; \S stands for all characters that are not space characters.
\w, \W	\w stands for word character and corresponds to the group of characters that contains all letters, numbers, and the underscore. \W stands for all characters, except for word characters.

Testing Patterns

IIS provides a comfortable function for testing patterns:

1. In the IIS Manager, open the URL Rewrite module, and then create a rule by using the Add Rule(s) dialog box, or select a rule, and then in the Actions pane, click Edit.

2. In the Edit Rule pane, select the corresponding pattern type in the Using drop-down list, and then click the Test Pattern button.

    The Test Pattern dialog box opens.

3. In the Pattern text box, enter the pattern that you want to test. In the Input Data To Test text box, enter the URL path that you want to test with the pattern, and then click Test.

    The Test Results pane shows whether the entered URL path corresponds to the pattern. If so, the list of generated back references is displayed, as well.

4. Repeat the tests with different entry data, until you are satisfied with the accuracy of your pattern, and then click Close to exit the dialog box.

    If you have changed the pattern configuration, you will be asked whether you want to keep the changes. Answer with Yes or No to return to the Edit Rule pane.

Conditions

With the rule patterns you have learned so far, you can only test the URL path. Other parts of the URL or the HTTP headers can't be queried via the Pattern text box. To test for patterns in this HTTP request data, you need to use the rule conditions.

In addition to matching the pattern of the URL path, the condition also must be met so that the action of a rule can be performed. Conditions consist of three parts: condition input, condition type, and (depending on the type) condition pattern.

The *condition input* specifies which data will be used as input data for the test or the pattern. You can use the CGI and IIS variables from the section "Predefined Variables," earlier in the chapter, as input data. Examples for such variables are *QUERY_STRING* for the query string, *SERVER_NAME* for the host name of the server, and *HTTP_USER_AGENT* for the *User-Agent* HTTP header.

IIS provides six different *condition types*. Apart from the pattern tests, there are types that test whether the target of a request is a file or a directory. In addition to these three positive tests, there are equivalent negative tests: the request target is not a file, not a directory, or the entry data doesn't correspond to the condition pattern.

Adding and Editing Conditions

To add conditions to a rule, perform the following steps:

1. In the IIS Manager, open the rule you want to edit in the URL Rewrite module.

2. Click the Conditions section to expand it.

3. In the Logical Grouping drop-down list, choose whether you want all conditions to be met before the action of the rule is triggered, or whether it's enough if one condition is met.

4. Click Add to add a new condition.

    The Add Condition dialog box opens, as shown in Figure 7-8.

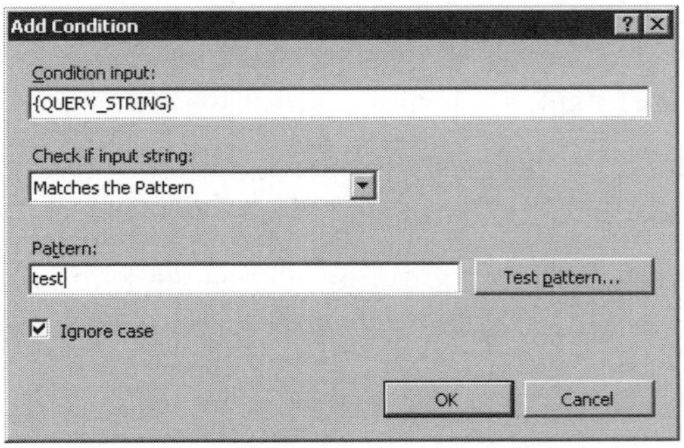

FIGURE 7-8 Adding a condition to a rule.

5. Enter the input data that you want to test into the Condition Input text box.

   Server variables are written in curly brackets. Even though it's possible to use multiple variables at the same time, you should use only one server variable per condition to retain a better overview. You can also use back references and rewrite maps (see also the section "Actions," which follows this section).

6. Specify the condition type in the Check If Input String drop-down list.

   Note that file or directory-related tests only make sense when input data that makes up the physical path are checked. If that is not the case, you should only perform pattern tests.

7. If you are performing pattern tests, enter the pattern into the Pattern text box. By using the Test Pattern button, you can check various entry data against the pattern, as described in the section "Testing Patterns," earlier in the chapter.

8. Click OK to close the dialog box.

9. To add more conditions, in the Conditions section, click the Add button.

10. In the Actions pane, click Apply to finish the rule edit.

Back References

Just like patterns for URL paths, conditions can also generate back references. These back references can be addressed in the following conditions or action properties of the rule as *{C:0}*, *{C:1}* ... *{C:n}*.

By default, the *{C:n}* variables receive the back references of the condition that was applied last. You can no longer access the back references of other previous conditions. As of version 2.0 of URL Rewrite, you can enable the *trackAllCaptures* option by selecting the Track Capture Groups Across Conditions check box. When enabled, the capture groups are sequentially numbered. For example, if you have two rules, each one with two capture groups, then the groups of the first rule are numbered *{C:0}* and *{C:1}*, whereas the groups of the second rule are numbered *{C:2}* and *{C:3}*.

In both modes, the order of conditions is important. You can sort the conditions when editing rules and put them into the desired order.

Actions

A rule's actions define how to continue the request processing. As you already learned in the section "Setting Up Rules," earlier in the chapter, URL Rewrite provides five different action types: *Redirect*, *Rewrite*, *Custom Response*, *Abort*, and *None* (no action). You can use variables and functions in the action properties.

Variables   You can use different variables for the action properties, especially the URL specifications of the *Redirect* and *Rewrite* action types:

- Server variables, for example *{QUERY_STRING}*, *{SERVER_NAME}*
- Back references from the pattern of the rule *{R:0}*, *{R:1}*, ... *{R:n}*
- Back references from conditions *{C:0}*, *{C:1}*, ... *{C:n}*
- Redirect maps, using *{Name of map:entry value}*; for example, when you want to use the variable *{REQUEST_URI}* as input data for the map *My_Map*: *{My_Map:{REQUEST_URI}}*

> **Note**   These variables can also be used for the condition entry of the data against which the condition pattern tests.

Functions   In addition to the variables, you can also use functions in the action properties. The URL Rewrite module defines three functions:

- **ToLower**   The uppercase letters of the entry data are converted into lowercase letters.
- **UrlEncode**   Entries are URL-encoded. Special characters or characters prohibited in URLs are escaped according to the URL specification.
- **UrlDecode**   The opposite of *UrlEncode*.

You again use curly brackets, for example *{ToLower:House}* to return the string "house." You can also specify other variables as parameters; for example, *{UrlEncode:search. php?string={R:1}}*.

> **Note**   These functions can also be used for condition entries. The function *UrlDecode* should only be used in this context, because it can lead to undesirable results in the action properties (prohibited characters in the URL path).

Setting Server Variables and HTTP Headers

In addition to the actions taken, when pattern and conditions match, URL Rewrite also provides a function to set server variables and HTTP headers for the incoming request. Both can be specified in the Server Variables section when editing a rule.

You can choose any name for the server variable—even replace well-known server variables. HTTP headers must use the same HTTP_* naming scheme as in PHP. For example, to set the HTTP header *Referer*, you would set the variable *HTTP_REFERER*.

IIS has a built-in precautionary measure: before a rule is allowed to set variables, you must name the variables that rules are allowed to set or change, as follows:

1. In the Connections pane, select the desired element, and then open the URL Rewrite feature.

2. In the Actions pane, click View Server Variables.

3. To add a new variable, again, in the Actions pane, click Add, enter the variable name in the dialog box, and then click OK.

Next, you can add these server variables and values to rules, by adding them in the Server Variables section of the Edit Inbound Rule pane. Figure 7-9 shows how to set the HTTP *Referer* header to the client's remote address if the header is missing. Be sure that the Replace The Existing Value check box is cleared, because you do not want to overwrite an existing header.

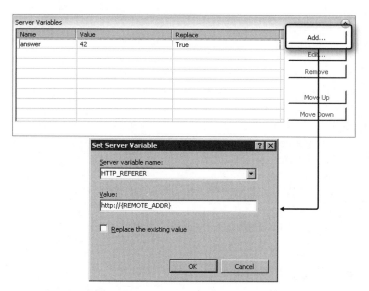

FIGURE 7-9 Modifying an HTTP header with an inbound rewrite rule.

Server variables and headers are set in the *$_SERVER* global variable of PHP. If you set the variable answer as shown in the variable list in Figure 7-9, you could access it with *$_SERVER['answer']* from PHP.

Note that adding or changing inbound headers and server variables only makes sense if you use a *Rewrite* or *None* action, unless you have deployed special IIS custom modules. Setting headers or variables within a *None* action allows you to augment incoming requests, without a rewrite taking place. You could also use this to distinguish different cases in later rules, by testing for those headers or variables in the rule's conditions.

Outbound Rules

With URL Rewrite, you can also rewrite outgoing responses; you can again set HTTP headers and server variables, but you can also change the content of the response. Rewriting responses can be useful if you would like to change links or add a notice to all pages. The basic structure of outbound rules is the same as for inbound rules. However, because IIS must parse the content, outbound rules can affect performance. This is why IIS has several additional mechanisms to minimize the performance impact: pre-conditions, tag filters, and caching. The caching method is only available through XML configuration and will be discussed there.

Pre-Conditions

Pre-conditions are checked before the rule is processed any further. The most common usage of these conditions is checking whether the response has the right content type. To this end, URL Rewrite provides one predefined condition called *ResponseIsHtml1*, which checks whether the content type of the response starts with *text/html*. To create your own pre-conditions, perform the following steps:

1. In the Connections pane, select the desired element, and then open the URL Rewrite feature.

2. In the Actions pane, click Outbound Rules | View Preconditions.

3. Again, in the Actions pane, click Add.

   The Add Precondition dialog box opens.

4. In the dialog box, set the name of the pre-condition collection, and then click Add to add a new condition.

5. In the Add Condition dialog box, specify the Condition Input for the pattern.

   Here, HTTP headers must be prefixed with "RESPONSE_". For example, to specify the *Cache-Control* header, you would write *{RESPONSE_CACHE_CONTROL}*.

6. Enter the pattern and whether the pattern should or should not match for the pre-condition to be true, and then click OK.

7. You can either add additional conditions by using Add or save the pre-condition collection by clicking OK.

Tag Filters

To improve the performance of pattern matching, you can and should use tag filters. Tag filters specify to which attributes of HTML elements the pattern should be applied—for example, only to the *src* attribute of the *Img* element. Tag filters only allow the definition of attributes, not that of the content of elements. It is still a useful concept, because usually you are using outbound rules to rewrite URLs, which are stored in HTML attributes.

URL Rewrite provides predefined tag filters for the elements *A*, *Area*, *Base*, *Form*, *Frame*, *Head*, *IFrame*, *Img*, *Input*, *Link*, and *Script*. To define your own tag filter, perform the following:

1. In the Connections pane, select the desired element, and then open the URL Rewrite feature.

2. In the Actions pane, click Outbound Rules | View Custom Tags.

3. Again, in the Actions pane, click Add Group.

   The New Custom Tags Collection dialog box opens, as shown in Figure 7-10.

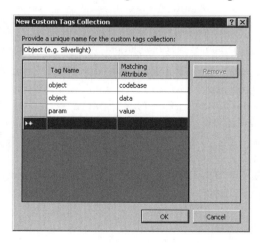

FIGURE 7-10 Creating a custom tag filter collection for outbound rewrite rules.

4. In the dialog box, enter a name for the tag collection, and then enter element and attribute names.

5. Click OK to create the tag filter collection.

Creating an Outbound Rule

The outbound rule itself is created similarly to inbound rules:

1. In the Connections pane, select the desired element, and then open the URL Rewrite feature.

2. In the Actions pane, click Add Rule(s).

3. Select Outbound Rules | Blank Rule, and then click OK.

4. In the Edit Outbound Rule pane, define the name of the rule in the associated text box.

5. Select a pre-condition that should be checked.

   If you are rewriting the content of the response, you should always use a pre-condition that checks the content type of the response.

6. Select the Matching Scope: either Response or Server Variable.

   With the option Server Variable, you can again add or modify outgoing HTTP headers or set variables for custom IIS modules later in the process chain. HTTP headers use the prefix "RESPONSE_"; (for example, *RESPONSE_COOKIE)*. The following steps assume that you have selected Response as the matching scope.

7. If you are going to match against attribute values, select a set of tag filters from the Match Content Within drop-down list; otherwise, leave this option empty.

8. Define the matching pattern, its syntax, and the case-sensitivity according to your needs.

   Optionally, you can define additional conditions, just like with inbound rules.

9. Finally, you specify the action. Two action types are available: *Rewrite* and *None*. Again, *None* only makes sense if you are using it to stop processing of subsequent requests. The value you can specify for the *Rewrite* action type is the value that is replaced for the matching pattern; for example, for the matching attribute value.

10. In the Actions pane, click Apply to create the rule.

For example, if you would like to rewrite all links to the login URL of applications from *http://insecure.xmp.site/application/login* to *https://secure.xmp.site/application/login*, you would use the following settings:

- Pre-Condition: **ResponseIsHtml1**
- Matching Scope: *Response*, matching content within *A*, *Form*
- Using the Wildcards syntax, the pattern would be **http://insecure.xmp.site/*/login**
- Action type: *Rewrite* with Value **https://secure.xmp.site/{R:1}/login**

XML Configuration

Like all other configuration settings, URL Rewrite rules are mapped to the IIS XML configuration files. In the following, you will find an overview of the most important settings.

The rules are entered into the *system.webServer* section of the configuration files (for example, web.config). Listing 7-2 shows a rule example that allows an http://php.net/-type search.

LISTING 7-2 A configuration example.

```
<system.webServer>
    <rewrite>
        <rules>
            <rule name="Automatic search" stopProcessing="true">
                <match url="^(\w+)$" />
                <conditions>
                    <add input="{SERVER_NAME}" pattern="^phpdemo\.site$" />
                </conditions>
                <action type="Rewrite" url="/search.php?search={R:1}" />
            </rule>
        </rules>
    </rewrite>
</system.webServer>
```

URL Rewrite

Table 7-6 lists the configuration elements of the URL Rewrite module. The global server rules can only be specified in applicationHost.config.

TABLE 7-6 Configuration element <rewrite>

Element	Description
rewrite	Definitions of the URL Rewrite module
rewrite/allowedServerVariables	Definition of server variables and HTTP headers that can be added or modified
rewrite/globalRules	Global rules (valid server-wide)
rewrite/outboundRules	Definition of distributed outbound rules
rewrite/providers	Custom rewrite providers written in .NET
rewrite/rewriteMaps	Rewrite maps
rewrite/rules	Distributed rules

Allowed Server Variables

To specify the server variables and HTTP headers that can be modified by URL Rewrite, you use the *<allowedServerVariables>* configuration collection element. Table 7-7 describes the elements.

TABLE 7-7 Configuration elements for <allowedServerVariables>

Element	Description
add	Adds a variable that can be modified by subsequent rewrite rules. The variable is specified with the name attribute, for example: *<add name="is_webbot" />*.
clear	Deletes all previously defined variables. Used to clear any inherited values. *<clear />* has no attributes and not content.
remove	Deletes the variable that is specified with the name attribute, for example: *<remove name="HTTP_REFERER" />*.

Rules

Like the global rules, the distributed rules are configured as shown in Table 7-8. While it is good practice to begin the definition of the global rules with a *<clear>* statement, using *<remove>* in a global context makes no sense.

TABLE 7-8 Configuration elements for <rules> and <globalRules>

Element	Description
clear	Deletes all previously defined rules on this hierarchy level, including inherited rules. Normally put at the beginning of *<rules>* when the inherited rules should not be used for this section. *<clear />* has no attributes and no content.
remove	Deletes the rule that is specified with the name attribute. This is used to delete individual inherited rules; for example, *<remove name="searchRule" />*.
rule	Definition of a rule.

The definition of an individual rule consists of three sections: pattern, conditions, and action (as shown in Table 7-9). Each rule receives a unique name. This makes it possible to remove the rule from deeper within the hierarchy by using <remove>. The rule order is important: a URL can be rewritten multiple times by different rules, unless the processing of subsequent rules is stopped due to the action type (for example *Abort*) or because of the *stopProcessing* property.

TABLE 7-9 Configuration element <rule>

Element	Attribute	Description
rule		Definition of a rule
	enabled	Specifies whether the rule is enabled (*true*) or disabled (*false*)
	name	Unique name of the rule
	patternSyntax	Syntax to be used for placeholders in the pattern and the conditions: regular expressions (*ECMAScript*), simple placeholders (*Wildcard*), or exact match (*ExactMatch*)
	stopProcessing	Specifies whether to stop the processing of the subsequent rule if the rule applies (*false*, *true*)
rule/match		Definition of the pattern of a rule
	negate	Specifies whether an action is triggered when a pattern matches (*false*) or does not match (*true*)
	ignoreCase	Specifies whether the case of letters (*upper/lower*) is ignored
	url	Pattern against which the URL path is tested
rule/conditions		Definition of the conditions of a rule
	logicalGrouping	Specifies whether all conditions must be met (*MatchAll*) or at least one (*MatchAny*)
	trackAllCaptures	If *true*, then URL Rewrite tracks capture groups across all conditions; if *false*, then only the capture groups of the last condition are used for *{C:x}*
rule/conditions/add		Definition of an individual condition
rule/serverVariables/set		Set server variables and HTTP headers
rule/action		Definition of the action of a rule
	type	Defines the action type: *Redirect* *Rewrite* *CustomResponse* *AbortRequest* *None*: No action

Conditions

The conditions of a rule are defined in the configuration element *<add>* within the element *<conditions>*. Table 7-10 shows which attributes can be used with the individual conditions.

TABLE 7-10 Attributes for the <add> conditions of a rule

Attribute	Description
ignoreCase	Only for *pattern* type: specifies whether the case of letters (*upper/lower*) is ignored.
input	The condition entry defines which data should be checked for the condition.
matchType	Defines the type of test: testing against a pattern (*pattern*, default), testing whether an object is a file (*isFile*), testing whether an object is a folder (*isDirectory*).
negate	Specifies whether the condition is fulfilled if there is a match (*false*) or no match (*true*).
pattern	Only for *pattern* type: specifies the pattern you want to check.

Server Variables and HTTP Headers

Changes to server variables are specified in the element *<set>* within the element *<server-Variables>*. Table 7-11 lists the attributes of the *<set>* element.

TABLE 7-11 Attributes for setting server variables using <set>

Attribute	Description
name	Server variable to change. Inbound HTTP headers have the prefix "HTTP_", outbound HTTP headers have the prefix "RESPONSE_".
replace	Specifies whether an existing variable/header should be replaced. If *false*, then existing variables and headers are left untouched.
value	Value to be set in the variable or header.

Actions

You can specify various attributes with the *<action>* configuration element for the five different action types. Table 7-12 lists the attributes for a redirect rule, Table 7-13 presents the attributes of a rewrite rule, and Table 7-14 gives the attributes for a custom reply.

There are no additional attributes for the action types *Abort* and *No Action*.

TABLE 7-12 Attributes for the *redirect* action type

Attribute	Description
appendQueryString	Defines whether the query string should be appended to the target URL (true, false).
redirectType	Specifies the HTTP status code that should be sent. Can be a number or text. Possible values: *301, Permanent*; *302, Found*; *303, See other*; *307, Temporary*.
url	Target URL to which you want to redirect. Can be an absolute URL.

TABLE 7-13 Attributes for the *rewrite* action type

Attribute	Description
appendQueryString	Defines whether the query string should be appended to the target URL
url	Target URL to which you want to rewrite (see also the section "Actions," earlier in the chapter)

TABLE 7-14 Attributes for the *custom reply* action type

Attribute	Description
statusCode	HTTP status code of the reply
statusDescription	Single-line description of the status code that is sent in headers with the HTTP reply
statusReason	Reason for reply
subStatusCode	Substatus code—only used within IIS

Rewrite Maps

Rewrite maps are defined in the section *<rewriteMaps>*. Table 7-15 shows that in addition to defining a single rewrite map, you can also delete individual or all defined maps.

TABLE 7-15 Configuration element <rewriteMaps>

Element	Description
rewriteMaps	Rewrites maps
rewriteMaps/clear	Deletes all previously defined rewrite maps, including the inherited rewrite maps
rewriteMaps/remove	Removes a single, named rewrite map (for example, *<remove name="rewriteMap1" />*)
rewriteMaps/rewriteMap	Defines an individual rewrite map

The configuration options for a single rewrite map are listed in Table 7-16. You can define the name and default value for the map as well as the name/value pairings for the individual map entries.

TABLE 7-16 Configuration element <rewriteMap>

Element	Attribute	Description
rewriteMap		Defines the rewrite map
	name	Name of the rewrite map
	defaultValue	Default value if none of the map entries applies
	ignoreCase	Specifies whether to ignore the letter case (*upper/lower*)
rewriteMap/add		Defines an entry
	key	Original value (*key, name*)
	value	New value

Outbound Rules

Outbound rules are specified in the configuration element *<outboundRules>*. Table 7-17 shows its elements. The *rewriteBeforeCache* attribute allows caching of the rewritten response, which can drastically increase performance, especially if no tag filters are applied and the complete response is used for the pattern matching. You should not enable caching if you use HTTP chunked transfer encoding.

TABLE 7-17 Configuration element <outboundRules>

Element	Attribute	Description
outboundRules		
	rewriteBeforeCache	If *true*, the result of the rewriting will be cached, if IIS caching is enabled (see Chapter 6, "Caching")
outboundRules/customTags		Definition of custom tag filters
outboundRules/preConditions		Definition of pre-conditions
outboundRules/rule		Outbound rules

Custom tag filter groups can be defined with the configuration collection *<customTags>*. The tag filter group is itself a configuration collection. Table 7-18 presents the details.

TABLE 7-18 Configuration elements for <customTags>

Element	Description
clear	Deletes all previously defined and inherited definitions.
remove	Deletes the filter group that is specified with the name attribute, for example: *<remove name="Object tags" />*.
tags	Definition of tag filter group, name is given in the name attribute. This is a configuration collection.
tags/clear	Deletes all previously defined tags.
tags/remove	Deletes the tag that is specified by the name/attribute pair, for example: *<remove name="param" attribute="value" />*.
tags/tag	Adds a tag filter. The element name is given in the *name* attribute and the attribute's name is given in attribute. For example, *<tag name="object" attribute="codebase" />*.

Preconditions are defined in the configuration collection *<preConditions>*. Apart from the standard *<clear/>* and *<remove/>* elements, the collection defines preconditions with the *<precondition>* element, as shown in Table 7-19.

TABLE 7-19 Configuration elements for <preConditions/preCondition>

Element	Attribute	Description
preCondition		
	name	Name of the pre-condition group
	logicalGrouping	*MatchAll*, if all conditions must be fulfilled, *MatchAny*, if at least one condition must be satisfied
	patternSyntax	Either regular expression syntax (*ECMAScript*, default value), wildcard matching (*Wildcard*), or an exact match (*ExactMatch*)
preCondition/add		Definition of a single pre-condition inside the group
	ignoreCase	Specifies whether the pattern matching is case-sensitive (*true*) or not (*false*)
	input	Input data to match against
	negate	If *true*, condition is satisfied, if pattern does not match
	pattern	Definition of the match pattern

Single Outbound Rule

A single outbound rule is defined with the configuration element *<rule>* inside of *<outboundRules>*. The basic structure is the same as with inbound rules. Table 7-20 provides the details. The attribute *occurrences* is useful to increase performance, especially when the full response body is checked: *occurrences* defines the number of matches, after which the rewriting stops. If you use the rewrite rule only to modify a single element, setting *occurences="1"* can increase performance.

TABLE 7-20 Configuration Element <rule>

Element	Attribute	Description
rule		Definition of a rule.
	enabled	Specifies whether the rule is enabled (*true*) or disabled (*false*).
	name	Unique name of the rule.
	patternSyntax	Syntax to be used for placeholders in the pattern and the conditions: regular expressions (*ECMAScript*), simple placeholders (*Wildcard*), or an exact match (*ExactMatch*).
	preCondition	Name of the pre-condition group that should be checked, before the rule match is executed.
	stopProcessing	Specifies whether to stop the processing of the subsequent rule if the rule applies (*false*, *true*).
rule/match		Definition of the pattern of a rule.
	customTags	Name of custom tag filter group that should be used. Is only applied if *CustomTags* flag is set in *filterByTags*.
	filterByTags	A bit array defining which tag filters should be applied. Values: *None* (0), *A* (1), *Area* (2), *Base* (4), *Form* (8), *Frame* (16), *Head* (32), *IFrame* (64), *Img* (128), *Input* (256), *Link* (512), *Script* (1024), *CustomTags* (32768).
	ignoreCase	Specifies whether the case of letters (upper/lower) is ignored.
	negate	Specifies whether an action is triggered when a pattern matches (*false*) or does not match (*true*).
	occurrences	Specifies the maximum number of matches, after which pattern matching stops. Useful for increasing performance in certain cases.
	pattern	Pattern against which the specified content is tested.
	serverVariable	Specifies the server variable or HTTP response header to be added or modified. This cannot be combined with rewriting the response body; that is, this attribute cannot be combined with *customTags*, *filterByTags*, and *occurrences*.

Element	Attribute	Description
rule/conditions		Definition of the conditions of a rule. Same as for inbound rules. See Table 7-10.
rule/action		Definition of the action of a rule.
	replace	Specifies whether an existing server variable or header should be replaced (*true*, *false*). Only affects matching of server variables.
	type	Defines the action type, can be one of *Rewrite* or *None*.
	value	Value to be inserted in place of the match.

Examples

In the following subsections, you will find a few typical examples for URL Rewrite: user-friendly URLs, multilingual pages, preventing the embedding of graphics on foreign pages, canonical host names and user directories, and redirecting HTTPS. Together, these examples should give you a good overview of the functions of URL Rewrite.

User-Friendly URLs

With user-friendly URLs, you can redirect all kinds of different URLs to a single PHP script. Such a redirect is desirable for Blog software and PHP Framework. Listing 7-3 shows how a simple rule might look: it writes all URLs of the type *http://phpdemo.site/2011-08-12/Hamsters-and-other-pets* to the urlinfo.php PHP script in the form *http://phpdemo.site/urlinfo.php?date=2011-08-12&title=Hamsters-and-other-pets*.

Because you might be able to retrieve graphics or other resources in the same folder, you need to define two bindings that prohibit a rewrite if folders or files with this URL exist.

LISTING 7-3 Setting a rule for a user-friendly URL.

```
<rule name="RewriteUserFriendlyURL1" stopProcessing="true">
    <match url="^([A/]+)/(.*)" />
    <conditions>
        <add input="{REQUEST_FILENAME}" matchType="IsFile" negate="true" />
        <add input="{REQUEST_FILENAME}" matchType="IsDirectory" negate="true" />
    </conditions>
    <action type="Rewrite" url="urlinfo.php?date={R:1}&amp;title={R:2}" />
</rule>
```

Canonical Host Name

The binding of a website frequently contains multiple host names. A typical example is a binding that contains the server name with and without the *www* prefix. You can take advantage of a redirect rule to redirect the user and especially browsers to the preferred syntax. For HTTP status code, you should use 301 (permanent redirect) to send subsequent requests directly to the new address.

Listing 7-4 shows how such a rule might look. It uses a condition to query the server name and another to query the port. For example, if you don't just want to redirect from *www .phpdemo.site* to *phpdemo.site*, but from all host names of the binding to the canonical host name, you should test whether the host name is unequal to the canonical name (as shown in the rule).

LISTING 7-4 Setting a rule for a canonical host name.

```
<rule name="Canonical host name" patternSyntax="Wildcard" stopProcessing="true">
    <match url="*" />
    <conditions>
        <add input="{SERVER_NAME}" negate="true" pattern="phpdemo.site" />
        <add input="{SERVER_PORT}" negate="true" pattern="80" />
    </conditions>
    <action type="Redirect" url="http://phpdemo.site/{R:1}" redirectType="Permanent" />
</rule>
```

Important In the form as shown in the preceding example, this rule can only be inserted at website level, because the action URL appends the back reference directly to the host name. For the back reference to contain the complete URL path, the rule must be applied at website level (see the section "Hierarchy and URL Paths," earlier in the chapter).

Multilingual Pages

Websites that offer their contents in multiple languages usually use different URLs for their different language versions. For example, English content can be accessed at *http://php-demo.site/en/*, German content at *http://phpdemo.site/de/*, and Hungarian content at *http://phpdemo.site/hu/*. Browsers send their preferred language as part of the HTTP header *Accept-Language*.

Listing 7-5 shows how the header can be evaluated to redirect the user automatically to the matching language.

In the conditions, the rule *has_language* first tests whether a language version is already being accessed (directory with two letters) and then whether the *Accept-Language* header has been set. If both conditions apply, the rewrite map *language_map* is used to select the correct subfolder (*value*) for the language (*key*). If no language applies, an automatic redirect to the English version takes place (*defaultValue*)

The rule *has_no_language* is only applied when the first rule is not applied. In this case, an automatic redirect to the English version takes place.

LISTING 7-5 Setting rules for redirecting to a matching browser language.

```
<rewrite>
  <rules>
    <rule name="has_language">
      <match url=".*" />
      <conditions>
        <add input="{REQUEST_URI}" negate="true" pattern="^/../" />
        <add input="{HTTP_ACCEPT_LANGUAGE}" pattern="^(..)" />
      </conditions>
      <action type="Redirect" url="{language_map:{C:1}}/{R:0}" redirectType="Found" />
    </rule>
    <rule name="has_no_language">
      <match url=".*" />
        <add input="{REQUEST_URI}" negate="true" pattern="^/../" />
      </conditions>
      <action type="Redirect" url="/en/{R:0}" redirectType="Found" />
    </rule>
  </rules>
  <rewriteMaps>
    <rewriteMap name="language_map" defaultValue="en">
      <add key="en" value="en" />
      <add key="de" value="de" />
      <add key="hu" value="hu" />
    </rewriteMap>
  </rewriteMaps>
</rewrite>
```

Canonical User Directories

To set up personal websites on a server for multiple users, you can use one of two common URL formats: the syntax with tilde, and child domains. In some cases, the physical layout of the user directories is the same: inside a folder, each user has his own subfolder, which contains the personal user directory.

Listing 7-6 shows the syntax with tilde using a URL rewrite. In addition, you can add the path /user via a virtual directory to any desired location on the server drives.

LISTING 7-6 Setting a rule for canonical user directory URLs by using the tilde.

```
<rule name="User directories with tilde">
    <match url="^~(.+?)/(.*)" />
    <action type="Rewrite" url="user/{R:1}/{R:2}" />
</rule>
```

Listing 7-7 shows how to convert user directories with child domains. It's important that all entries for the child domains resolve to the IP address of the server and that the IIS website has bindings for these domains. Compared to the previous codes sample, this one contains three changes:

- The first rule prevents the rewritten URL */user* from being called directly. This is necessary, because otherwise the contents belonging to other users could be called in foreign user domains. This rule must be placed before the second rule; if it isn't, all requests are aborted.

- The user directory selection now takes place via a condition, because the host name itself cannot be queried in the search pattern of the rule.

- The condition pattern grabs the first letter of the name and uses it to introduce an additional subfolder. This can be helpful, if you want a lot of users to have a personal directory on the server. You can then use virtual directories to distribute these subfolders to various drives, for example.

LISTING 7-7 Setting rules for canonical user directories, based on child domains.

```
<rule name="Prohibiting the binding of foreign user directories" stopProcessing="true">
    <match url="^user\b" />
    <action type="CustomResponse" statusCode="403" />
</rule>
<rule name="User directories with child domains">
    <match url=".*" />
    <conditions>
        <add input="{SERVER_NAME}" pattern="^(.)(.+?)\.phpdemo\.site$" />
    </conditions>
    <action type="Rewrite" url="user/{C:1}/{C:1}{C:2}/{R:0}" />
</rule>
```

Note IIS 7 doesn't yet support placeholders for child domains in the bindings. You only have two ways to transfer domain-based user directories: either each domain is entered into the bindings of the website, or the website you are editing is the default website that has a standard binding without host name. If you are using the standard binding, you should add another rule that blocks all requests with unknown main domains, for security reasons.

For PHP programs, some *$_SERVER* variables change depending on whether the user directories were converted with a tilde or with child domains:

```
With tilde: http://phpdemo.site/~tony/urlinfo.php
Server name (SERVER_NAME): "phpdemo.site"
URL of the request (REQUEST_URI): "/~tony/urlinfo.php"
URL path of the script (SCRIPT_NAME): "/user/tony/urlinfo.php"
Root folder (DOCUMENT_ROOT): "C:\inetpub\phpdemosite"
Physical path of the script (SCRIPT_FILENAME): "C:\inetpub\user\tony\urlinfo.php"

With child domains: http://tony.phpdemo.site/urlinfo.php
Server name (SERVER_NAME): "tony.phpdemo.site"
URL of the request (REQUEST_URI): "/urlinfo.php"
URL path of the script (SCRIPT_NAME): "/user/t/tony/urlinfo.php"
Root folder (DOCUMENT_ROOT): "C:\inetpub\phpdemosite"
Physical path of the script (SCRIPT_FILENAME): "C:\inetpub\user\t\tony\urlinfo.php"
```

In our example, the user folders are located in C:\inetpub\user and the domain phpdemo.site is used. The virtual directory /user is located outside the root folder of the website.

Preventing the Embedding of Graphics on Foreign Sites

With HTML, you can embed and display graphics from different sources—for example, different servers. Even though this function can be very useful (for instance, in advertising), it permits the embedding of graphics on foreign sites without your permission.

With the rule in Listing 7-8, you can prevent *hotlinking* (the embedding of graphics on foreign sites). The rule takes advantage of the *Referer* HTTP header. Most browsers send this header to show which page embeds the graphic.

The search pattern is a regular expression that checks if the URL path ends in *.jpg*, *.gif*, or *.png*. Additionally, two conditions are specified, which both need to be met: the reference must come from your own site or must be empty, otherwise the action (blocking the request with status code 403) is executed. Checking for an empty reference is necessary, because certain firewalls and antivirus programs filter out this header to secure your privacy.

LISTING 7-8 Setting the rule for preventing the embedding of images on foreign sites.

```
<rule name="Preventing hotlinking" stopProcessing="true">
    <match url=".*\.(jpg|gif|png)$" />
    <conditions>
        <add input="{HTTP_REFERER}" pattern="^http://phpdemo\.site/" negate="true" />
        <add input="{HTTP_REFERER}" pattern="^$" negate="true" />
    </conditions>
    <action type="CustomResponse" statusCode="403" />
</rule>
```

Instead of blocking the request, you can also rewrite the URL to a standard image, which might, for example, contain the note that the embedding of your graphics is prohibited.

Redirecting to HTTPS

If you want to ensure that your users are using an HTTPS-encrypted connection for certain sections of your website, you can use the rule in Listing 7-9. The rule is set up in the directory *secure-area*.

LISTING 7-9 Forcing an HTTPS connection.

```
<rule name="enforce-https" patternSyntax="Wildcard" stopProcessing="true">
    <match url="*" />
    <conditions>
        <add input="{HTTPS}" pattern="off" />
    </conditions>
    <action type="Redirect" url="https://phpdemo.site/secure-area/{R:0}"
            redirectType="Permanent" />
</rule>
```

Adding a Notice to Each Page

Listing 7-10 shows how you can add HTML content to each response, for example, to display a notice. As the notice should only be inserted once, we limit the number of matches by setting *occurrences="1"*.

LISTING 7-10 Adding a notice to each page.

```
<rule name="notice" preCondition="ResponseIsHtml1" patternSyntax="ExactMatch">
    <match pattern="&lt;body>" occurrences="1" />
    <action type="Rewrite" value="&lt;body>&lt;div class=&quot;notice&quot;>
    The content of this page is deprecated.&lt;/div>" />
</rule>
```

You can use this method to add other HTML content, as well. For example, you could add code for incorporating website statistics tools. In that case, you should insert the content at the end of the body element (match against *</body>*) for a better user experience.

Converting from Apache *mod_rewrite*

URL Rewrite provides a helpful function for converting rules of the Apache module *mod_rewrite*. Many software packages supply you with finished *mod_rewrite* rules. URL Rewrite during import helps you speed up the conversion.

Caution The architecture of Apache is different from the one of IIS. Therefore, not all *mod_rewrite* rules can be ported to IIS.

To convert *mod_rewrite* rules into URL Rewrite rules, perform the following procedure:

1. In the IIS Manger, in the Connections pane, select the desired element, and then open the URL Rewrite module.

2. In the Actions pane, click Import rules.

3. Either select the file with the Apache rules (Configuration file), and then click Import, or copy the files into the Rewrite Rules text box.

   The structure view of the URL Rewrite rule is displayed in the Converted Rules section, as shown in Figure 7-11. Successfully converted rules are highlighted in green; errors are highlighted in red.

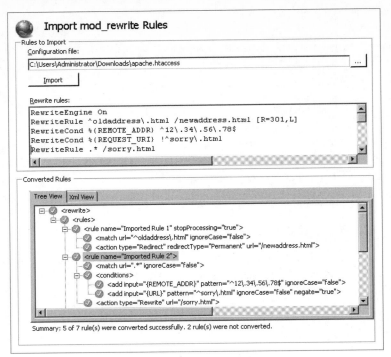

FIGURE 7-11 Importing Apache *mod_rewrite* rules into URL Rewrite.

If you are clicking a node in the Tree View, the corresponding Apache rewrite rule is also highlighted. Likewise, you can highlight a statement in the Apache rewrite rules and the corresponding nodes in the Tree View are highlighted.

4. You can rename a rule from the context menu of a node in the Tree View.

5. In the XML View tab, the generated XML of the URL Rewrite rule configuration is displayed.

6. In the Actions pane, click Apply to apply the generated rules to IIS.

    If there are errors, you need to remove them first by deleting or changing the corresponding Apache *mod_rewrite* statements.

7. In the Actions pane, click Back To Rules to return to the URL Rewrite work area, in which you can continue to edit the generated rules.

Afterward, you should test the rules with a few requests to ensure that the rules work as expected. Even though the Import function usually works without errors, you need to understand both rule systems in order to handle more complex expressions.

Summary

URL Rewrite leaves nothing to be desired with its rule-based system. To work with URL Rewrite, it is necessary, however, to completely understand how the evaluation of rules works, especially which part of the URL is checked and when. In this chapter, you learned more about evaluating rules, the patterns and conditions of a rule, and the executable actions. You can use the examples and the sample script urlinfo.php as an aid when developing your own rules.

In the next chapter, you will learn about error messages and error logs as well as IIS tracing. A trace can provide you with valuable insights, even with errors in URL Rewrite rules, because it shows exactly which rules have been activated and which input and output data they had.

Chapter 8
Error Messages and Error Search

Errors occur in applications and in the configuration during development and production. Error messages and warnings give you valuable insight during error search. With the trace option, Internet Information Services (IIS) provides information about each step of the request processing. It helps you to locate errors quickly and resolve them.

In this chapter, you will learn about tracing as well as how to handle PHP error messages. You will receive advice on how to search for problems in IIS and PHP.

Detailed Error Messages

By default, IIS error messages are replaced by standard error messages, instead of sending them unchanged to the user. This is done for security reasons: error messages might contain sensitive information that could supply a potential attacker with valuable information about the structure of your system.

However, detailed error messages are important during the development stage. In the subsections that follow, you will learn how to display detailed error messages.

 Caution For production systems, detailed error messages should be disabled for reasons of security. The configuration you see in this chapter is intended for development environments only.

Disabling Friendly Error Messages in Internet Explorer

Internet Explorer displays its own short error messages, which explain to users in simple words what happened and give possible ways of resolving the error, as shown in Figure 8-1.

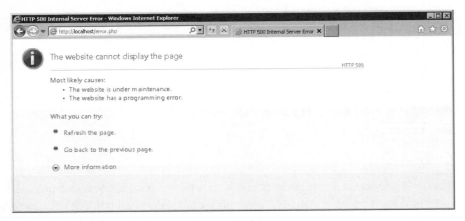

FIGURE 8-1 Friendly error message in Internet Explorer.

For developers, these error messages are cumbersome because they don't reveal the actual cause of the problem; thus, you'll want to disable them.

To disable friendly error messages in Internet Explorer, perform the following procedure:

1. Start Internet Explorer.

2. Click the Tools icon (the cogwheel in the upper-right corner), and then select Internet Options.

   The Internet Options dialog box opens.

3. Click the Advanced tab.

4. In the Browsing section, clear the check box for Show Friendly HTTP Error Messages.

5. Click OK.

Enabling Detailed Error Messages

IIS replaces error messages that originate from PHP scripts or other error sources with custom error pages. In a production environment, this is a useful measure that helps keep your system secure, because error messages might contain sensitive information. Figure 8-2 shows a custom error message that was caused by a syntax error in a PHP script.

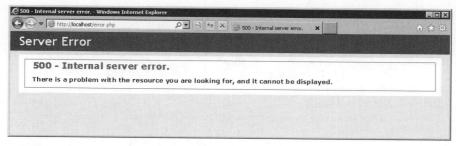

FIGURE 8-2 Custom IIS error message for a PHP script error.

IIS also provides detailed error messages or can send the PHP errors directly to the browser. By default, this only works from your local computer. If you establish access from a different computer, you will only receive the custom error messages.

The following procedure shows how to enable detailed error messages for all access locations:

1. Start IIS Manager.

2. In the Connections pane, select the desired element (normally a site or an application).

3. Open the Error Pages feature by double-clicking it.

4. In the Actions pane, click the Edit Feature Settings link.

5. In the Error Responses section of the dialog box, select the Detailed Errors option to enable the detailed error messages for all requests.

6. Click OK to close the dialog box.

You will now either receive error messages from the PHP script directly or get detailed information if the error occurred in the IIS processing chain, as shown in Figure 8-3.

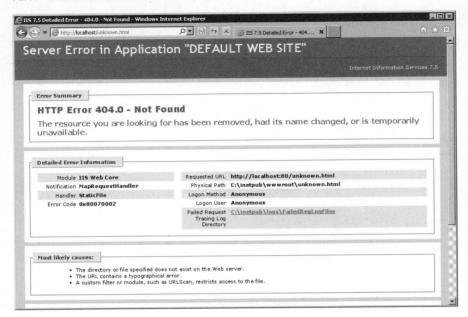

FIGURE 8-3 A detailed IIS error message.

PHP Error Output

In PHP, you can use configuration options to control whether error messages should be passed on to the client or logged in a file. Table 8-1 lists these options.

TABLE 8-1 Configuration options for PHP error messages

Configuration option	Description
display_errors	Specifies whether an error is displayed (*On/stderr*) or not (*Off*).
display_startup_errors	Specifies whether errors caused during PHP startup should be displayed (*On*) or not (*Off*).
error_log	Specifies the error log file.
error_reporting	Specifies which errors are displayed. All messages are displayed with *E_ALL	E_STRICT*. Only warnings and errors are displayed with *E_ALL & ~E_NOTICE*.
log_errors	Specifies whether errors should be logged to a file (*On*) or not (*Off*).

Caution If *log_errors=On*, you also need to specify a file with the option *error_log*; otherwise, the error messages output to *STDERR*; therefore, they are visible to clients. The same is true if the file specified in *error_log* cannot be written to, because the executing user (for example, the user of the application pool) does not have the required write permissions. In both cases, PHP ignores the setting *display_errors*.

To display PHP errors during development, perform the following procedure:

1. Open the php.ini file (C:\PHP\php.ini) in an editor.

2. Add the following configuration options or edit the existing ones:

    ```
    display_errors = On
    display_startup_erros = On
    error_reporting = E_ALL | E_STRICT
    ```

3. If you also want to log the errors in a file, add the following options:

    ```
    log_errors = On
    error_log = "C:\inetpub\logs\php-error.log"
    ```

4. Save the php.ini file.

5. Start the corresponding IIS application pools again.

You should check the settings with phpinfo() or a PHP script that generates an error.

> **Note** If *display_errors=On*, errors are written directly into HTML and the HTTP status code 200 (OK) is sent.

Alternatively, you can set the level of error reporting by using PHP Manager:

1. Start IIS Manager.

2. In the Connections pane, select an element with the desired PHP version.

3. Double-click the PHP Manager feature in the workspace, and then click PHP Settings | Configure Error Reporting.

4. Choose the Development Machine profile, and then in the Actions pane, click apply to save your choice.

The selected error reporting profile sets *display_errors=On*, *display_startup_errors=On*, *log_errors=On*, and *error_reporting to E_ALL|E_STRICT*.

Tracing

With tracing, you can keep a detailed log of each step and module in IIS that's called to process requests. The possibility to make the logging dependent on certain conditions, such as the execution duration or the HTTP status code, makes it ideal for error search or monitoring in a production environment.

Installing the Tracing Role Service

You can either install the Tracing module by using the Server Manager or by using the Web Platform Installer (Web PI).

To set up the tracing role service by using the Server Manager, perform the following steps:

1. Start the Server Manager.
2. Select Roles, and then click the Web Server (IIS). In the Role Services section, click Add Role Services.
3. Select the Web Server, click Health and Diagnostics, and then select the Tracing check box.
4. Click Next, and then click Install to start the installation.
5. After a successful installation, restart IIS Manager to see the new feature.

Alternatively, you can set up the tracing role service by using the Web PI:

1. Start the Web PI.
2. Click Products | Server, and then add IIS: Tracing.
3. Click Install, and then click I Accept to start the installation.
4. After a successful installation, restart IIS Manager.

> **Note** If you have installed the URL Rewrite feature before installing the trace, it's possible that you can't enable the trace for URL Rewrite. In this case, you need to repair the URL Rewrite installation.
>
> To do so, open the Control Panel, and then select Programs | Uninstall A Program. In the program list, select the URL Rewrite module, and then click the Repair button.

You have now added the trace role service to IIS and are ready to use it. To do so, you need to enable tracing.

Enabling a Trace

You first need to enable tracing for the desired website, before you can configure and use it.

Enabling Tracing by Using IIS Manager

To enable tracing by using IIS Manager, perform the following steps:

1. Start IIS Manager.
2. In the Connections pane, select the desired website.

3. In the Actions pane, click Manage Web Site | Configure, and then click the Failed Request Tracing link.

4. In the dialog box, select the Enable check box.

5. Change the folder for the log files, if you don't want to use the suggested folder.

6. Click OK to confirm your entries.

Enabling Tracing from the Command LIne

You can use *appcmd* to enable the trace from the command line, as follows:

```
appcmd configure trace "<Sitename>" /enablesite
```

To disable the trace from the command line, use the following command:

```
appcmd configure trace "<Sitename>" /disablesite
```

Configuring Logging Rules

Once you have enabled tracing for a website, you can define individual logging rules.

Defining Logging Rules by Using IIS Manager

The following procedure lists the steps for defining tracing rules:

1. Start IIS Manager.

2. In the Connections pane, select the desired element.

3. Open the Failed Request Tracing Rules feature.

4. In the Actions pane, click the Add link.

5. In the wizard, select the Custom For PHP Programs option, and then enter ***.php** into the corresponding text box.

6. In this step, you can specify conditions for the trace:

   - **Status code**   Specifies which status codes are logged; for example, 400–599.

   - **Time taken**   Specifies that requests can be logged only if they exceed the defined time period.

   - **Event severity**   Specifies which kind of request is logged.

7. In this step, you specify what information is logged:

- **Providers**   For logging PHP scripts, the option WWW Server is sufficient.

- **Verbosity**   Specifies whether only severe errors or general information is logged. For error search, set the severity level to *Verbose* or *Information*.

- **Areas**   Specifies which IIS features log information. Select the desired areas.

8. Click the Finish button to set up the rule.

Configuring from the Command Line

To configure trace rules from the command line, run the command *appcmd configure trace*, as shown in the following example:

```
appcmd configure trace "Default Web Site/phpapp" /enable /path:*.php
   /areas:"WWW Server/Security,Cache,FastCGI,Rewrite" /statuscodes:400-599
   /timeTaken:00:00:10 /verbosity:Warning
```

To delete trace rules, run the *appcmd configure trace* command, as shown here:

```
appcmd configure trace "Default Web Site/phpapp" /disable /path:*.php
```

Trace Entries

Now, when the web server receives requests that match the request conditions for one of the defined trace rules, the server creates an entry in the log folder (by default C:\inetpub\logs\ FailedReqLogFiles). You can open these files directly in Internet Explorer.

In the browser, you can use the Request Summary, Request Details, and Compact View tabs to retrieve details and information about the request. Figure 8-4 shows the compact view of a trace entry.

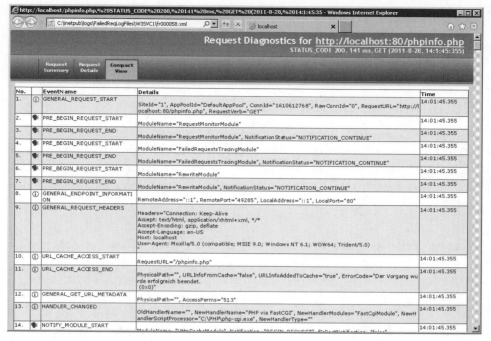

FIGURE 8-4 Compact view of a logged trace entry.

A trace entry consists of a number of events that inform you about the individual steps of the request processing. The beginning and the end of the individual processing steps are usually indicated with _START and _END events. The events GENERAL_REQUEST_START and GENERAL_REQUEST_HEADERS give you information about the request itself. The web server reply appears in the events GENERAL_RESPONSE_HEADERS and GENERAL_RESPONSE_ENTITY_BUFFER.

You can use the *appcmd list traces* command to search for entries, as shown in the following examples:

```
appcmd list traces /site.name:"Default Web Site" appcmd list traces /verb:POST /statuscode:500
appcmd list traces /url:http://localhost/error.php /timetaken:"$>1000"
```

PHP Error Messages

PHP error messages can be added to the trace, and the mechanism can also be used for logging PHP internal processes.

Outputting to *STDERR*

For IIS to recognize PHP errors as such, the errors must be issued to the standard error output *STDERR()*. With *display_errors=On*, the errors are written only into HTML, and the server returns HTTP status code 200. With *display_errors=stderr*, the errors are written to *STDERR*, and the server returns HTTP status code 500. For filtering during the trace, this would be desirable.

> **Note** Unfortunately, due to an error in PHP 5.3.6, *display_errors=stderr* does not lead to the desired result; instead, you need to set *log_errors=On* and *error_log=stderr*.

Figure 8-5 shows a sample output in a trace entry.

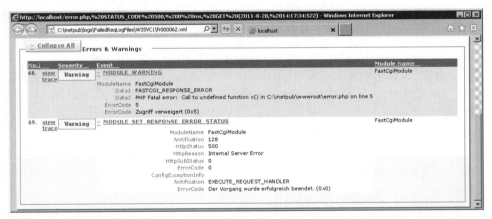

FIGURE 8-5 A PHP error that was passed to IIS via *STDERR*.

PHP Messages in the Trace

As of version 7.5, IIS provides the option of writing your own information or error messages into the trace entry. The message must start with *IIS_TRACE_*:* and end with *:IIS_TRACE_END* for the trace to handle it correctly. Listing 8-1 shows how you can write info, warning, and error message events into the trace entry.

LISTING 8-1 Writing PHP messages into the trace.

```php
<?php
echo 'Writing messages into the trace';
error_log('IIS_TRACE_INFO: PHP info event :IIS_TRACE_END');
error_log('IIS_TRACE_WARNING: PHP warning event :IIS_TRACE_END');
error_log('IIS_TRACE_ERROR: PHP error event :IIS_TRACE_END');
?>
```

Figure 8-6 shows the resulting events in the trace entry.

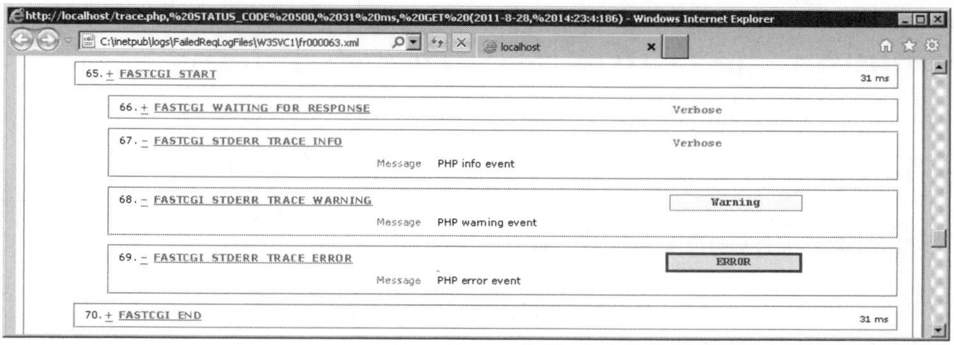

FIGURE 8-6 Message entries in the trace entry (detail view).

FastCGI and *STDERR*

When information is written to *STDERR*, the *FastCGI* module suppresses any other output by default. However, if you would like to use *error_log()* for logging, that's not a desirable behavior. As of IIS 7.5, the *FastCGI* module provides an appropriate configuration option:

1. Start IIS Manager.

2. In the Connections pane, select the server.

3. Open the FastCGI Settings feature by double-clicking it.

4. Select the desired FastCGI application from the list, and then in the Actions pane, click Edit.

5. Set the General/Standard option error mode to the value *IgnoreAndReturn200*. The possible values are:

   - ***ReturnStdErrIn500***   Only the text that was written to *STDERR* is returned.

   - ***ReturnGeneric500***   A generic error message is returned.

- *IgnoreAndReturn200*   The output to *STDERR* is ignored and the content of the website is returned.

- *TerminateProcess*   The associated IIS process is ended and a generic error message is returned.

6. Click OK to apply your settings.

Using this configuration option, you can ensure that PHP errors and outputs from *error_log()* display in the trace. At the same time, you can receive an HTML output, with an HTTP status code of 200.

Determining the Causes of Server Problems

If you have problems reaching the web server after installation or after changing configuration, you can use the steps that follow to find the cause of the problem.

The Server Can't Be Reached

When you can't reach the web server, you need to check your work environment and your settings:

- Ensure that the host name that you're using is found, that it resolves to the correct IP address, and that there is a network connection. You can use the *ping* command in the command line:

```
ping www.phpdemo.site
```

- Ensure that IIS and the websites have been started and that there is an active binding for the desired domain name, port, and IP address.

- When you select the Sites element in the Connections pane of IIS Manager, a list of sites is displayed that shows if they have been started.

- The command line *net start* command shows you whether the WWW Publishing Service is running, and *appcmd list sites* shows you the status of the individual sites.

- Check the Windows Event Viewer for possible errors. To do so, start the Server Manager, and then click Diagnostics | Event Viewer | Windows Protocols | System. Look for results that have *WAS* as their source. Also check Diagnostics | Event Viewer | Custom Views | Server Roles | Web Server (IIS) for possible events.

- Check whether the website is accessible from your local computer running IIS by starting Internet Explorer on that computer and browsing to the URL *http://localhost/.* If you can access the website locally, either the Windows Firewall is prohibiting incoming connections, or no website has an adequate binding for incoming requests.

- Check whether the application pools belonging to the website have been started:

  - In IIS Manager, in the Connections pane, select the Application Pools element, and then check the status of the application pools displayed in the list.

  - From the command line, you can view the application pools and their status with *appcmd list apppools*.

PHP Scripts are not Executing

If you can browse to simple HTML files or graphics and load them successfully, but PHP scripts are not executing, you can check the following settings:

Examine your PHP installation by running the correct *php-cgi.exe* command in the command line; for example, *C:\PHP\php-cgi.exe –i* (or *–v*). You can also run one of your PHP scripts, such as *C:\PHP\php-cgi.exe path\to\example.php*. Make sure that there are no warnings and that the expected php.ini file is loaded. A PHP extension might pose a problem (for example, a missing Dynamic Link Library).

Check your FastCGI settings by opening IIS Manager, and then in the Connections pane, selecting the server. Open the FastCGI Settings feature, and check whether the path of the FastCGI-PHP application is correct.

You can also control the settings by using *appcmd*, as follows:

```
appcmd.exe list config /section:fastcgi /text:*
```

Ensure that you have assigned the PHP FastCGI applications for the desired site via a handler:

In IIS Manager, in the Connections pane, select the server. Open the Handler Mappings feature by double-clicking it. Check whether an active handler mapping exists for *.php.

You can also control the settings by using *appcmd*, as follows:

```
appcmd.exe list config /section:handlers /text:* | find /i "php"
```

> **Important** Ensure that the PHP handler mapping is located in the list before the *StaticFile* handler. Otherwise, the PHP script is treated as a text file. Also, other handlers whose path specification could include PHP scripts (Path=*) can only be listed behind the PHP handler (unless they refer to special HTTP verbs, such as *OPTIONSVerbHandler* and *TRACEVerbHandler*).

Also examine the settings of the handler assignment. The specified conditions might restrict the assignment too much.

Enable tracing and evaluate the associated entries: does a module cause an error? Is FastCGI being called?

Summary

In this chapter, you explored how to set up and use IIS tracing and how IIS handles PHP error messages. By redirecting a trace through output to *STDERR*, PHP error messages and applications can take advantage of an interesting and useful way of logging, which also works well for a production environment.

This concludes the description of PHP with IIS. IIS 7.5 with FastCGI is a big step forward for PHP applications: not only have speed and the stability been improved significantly, PHP applications can now also access numerous IIS features and take advantage of the modular and secure architecture of IIS.

Next you will be introduced to Microsoft SQL Server, including installation, streaming of binary data directly from the database, full-text search, and important functions and features.

Part II
SQL Server

Chapter 9
Setting Up SQL Server

Microsoft SQL Server has developed into a well-engineered, feature-rich, and scalable data platform. SQL Server consists of four components or services:

- The *database module* saves and processes rational data in tables. You can access it with Transact-SQL (T-SQL) statements. T-SQL is an extension or dialect of the SQL standard. The database module supports transactions, replications, and high-availability features.

- *Integration Services* is a data integration platform that transforms and integrates data from various data sources. It is used for extract, transform, load (ETL), and Data Warehouse solutions.

- The *Analysis Services* are used for parsing large amounts of data. Online Analytical Processing (OLAP), Business Intelligence, and Data Mining applications can be realized by using the Analysis Services.

- The *Reporting Services* provide a platform for creating reports from a number of different data sources and their server-based administration. There are many different formatting options for the reports, and the reports can be accessed via web services.

In this book, we only address the function of the relational database module of SQL Server 2008. In the following chapters, you will learn how to set up databases and tables and how to manipulate data. You will be introduced to the features of the new SQL Server PHP extension and the concepts for user administration and naming of objects in SQL Server.

Installing SQL Server

As of this printing (October, 2011), SQL Server 2008 R2 SP1 is the current version of SQL Server, and it can be installed in just a few steps, as long as the necessary requirements are met:

- For operating systems, you can use Windows Server 2003 SP2 or Windows Server 2008 or 2008 R2 for the Enterprise version. For the Standard version or for Express, Windows XP as of SP3, Windows Vista, or Windows 7 are sufficient.

- You need at least 512 MB of main memory; however, 2 GB are recommended.

- SQL Server is available as 32-bit and 64-bit systems; a current processor with a clock rate of at least 2 GHz is recommended.

In the following, you will learn how to install on a Windows Server 2008 R2, how to install SQL Server Express on Windows 7, and how to install the SQL Server driver for PHP.

Configuring SQL Server

To install SQL Server 2008 R2 SP1 on Windows Server 2008 R2, you should first install Microsoft .NET Framework.

Installing .NET Framework

SQL Server 2008 R2 requires .NET Framework, version 3.5. Under Windows Server 2008 R2, you first need to set up the Framework and the corresponding role services, as described in the following procedure:

1. Open the Server Manager.

2. Select Features (on the left). Then in the central pane, click Add Features.

   The wizard for adding features opens.

3. Select the .NET Framework 3.5.1 Features option. In the new dialog box, confirm the addition of the required role services.

4. Click the Next button three times to confirm your specifications.

   You should be on the Confirm Installation Selection wizard page.

5. Click Install to start the installation.

6. After a successful installation, close the wizard by clicking on the Close button.

You have now installed .NET Framework 3.5. Now it's time to install SQL Server.

Installing SQL Server 2008 R2 SP1

To install SQL Server, perform the following steps:

1. Start the setup file from the installation media.

   If the correct version of the Windows Installer is not yet installed on your computer, it will be installed for you. Following that, you can continue with the setup.

   You can use Planning/System Configuration Checker to determine if your system fulfills all necessary requirements for installing SQL Server.

2. To start the setup, select Installation | New Installation or Add Features To An Existing Installation.

3. The setup checks the installation conditions. Continue by clicking OK.

4. Enter the product key or select one of the free options (SQL Server Express, evaluation) and agree to the license agreement by selecting the check box.

5. Click Install to install the support files. Click Next to continue.

> **Note** If you receive a warning regarding the firewall configuration while checking the setup support rules again, you can ignore them for now. But don't forget to configure the firewall if you want SQL Server to be available for external clients.

6. On the Setup Role page, select SQL Server Feature Installation, and then click Next.

7. On the Feature Selection page, choose the desired features.

   You should definitely select Database Engine Services and Management Tools (Basic and Complete) as well as Client Tools Connectivity, as shown in Figure 9-1. In this step, you can also specify the feature directories.

   Click Next to confirm your selection.

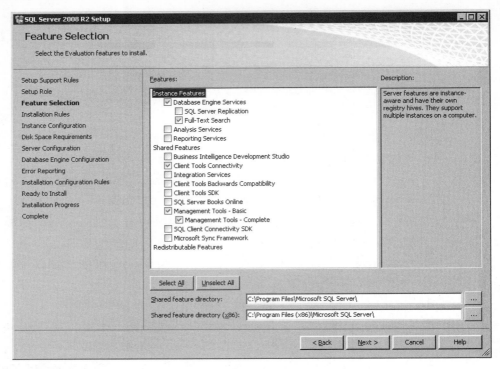

FIGURE 9-1 Selecting the SQL Server features.

 Note You can install additional features at a later time by running the installation program again. It is therefore not necessary to install all features immediately.

8. On the Instance Configuration page, you can give the SQL Server instance a name of your choosing by using the Named Instance option (the default name is the name of the computer).

   If this is the first instance on the server, you should keep the Default Instance option.

9. Click Next to confirm your settings.

   The wizard now checks the required memory for the installation.

10. On the Server Configuration page, specify the user accounts for the individual services.

    For an installation in a development environment, you can specify the account *NT-AUTHORITY/NETWORK SERVICE* for all services. In a production environment, for security reasons, you should follow the recommendation to set up separate accounts for the services. You can still change the account assignment after the installation. You should also start the SQL Server Browser automatically (by selecting the option in the drop-down list), as shown in Figure 9-2.

Click Next to confirm your entries.

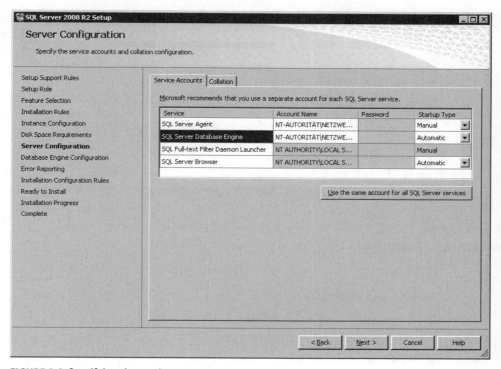

FIGURE 9-2 Specifying the service accounts.

11. On the Database Engine Configuration page, in the Authentication Mode section,
    select the Mixed Mode option.

    This setting is important and essential for PHP programs, which usually work with their
    own database account. You then need to specify the password for the database admin-
    istrator account (sa). In addition, you can grant other user accounts SQL Server
    administrator rights.

> **Note** It is not necessary for the Windows administrator to take over the role of an
> SQL Server administrator. In most production environments, these two roles are strictly
> separated.

12. Click Next to confirm the next steps, and then on the Ready To Install page, start the
    installation by clicking Install.

13. After the installation has completed successfully, click Close to end the Setup wizard.

SQL Server 2008 R2 SP1 is now installed. Next, you should install the SQL Server driver for PHP.

Installing SQL Server Express

For most purposes and for the functions introduced in this book, the Express edition of SQL Server is sufficient. SQL Server Express is well suited for developing PHP applications in your own working environment. You have three options for installing Express:

- From SQL Server 2008 R2 installation media
- With a standalone SQL Server Express installation package
- With the Web Platform Installer (SQL Server Express 2008 SP1)

The first option corresponds to the installation described in the section "Installing SQL Server 2008 R2 SP1," earlier in the chapter. Simply specify the desired SQL Server Express version in step 4, instead of the *product key*. The other two options are described in the following subsections.

Manual Installation

For the manual installation, you can choose between different installation packages:

- **Express**   Installs only the database, no additional tools or functions.
- **Express with Administration Tools**   Includes the database as well as the graphical user interface SQL Server Management Studio Express.
- **Express with Advanced Services**   The same as Express with Administration Tools, but also includes modules for full-text search and powerful report functions.

Download the corresponding installation package from *http://www.microsoft.com/download/ en/details.aspx?id=26729* for the installation. If you want to use full-text search, you should install Express with Advanced Services; otherwise, Express with Administration tools.

The installation steps are practically identical to those in the section "Installing SQL Server 2008 R2 SP1," earlier in the chapter. Figure 9-3 shows the basic functions necessary for the examples in this book.

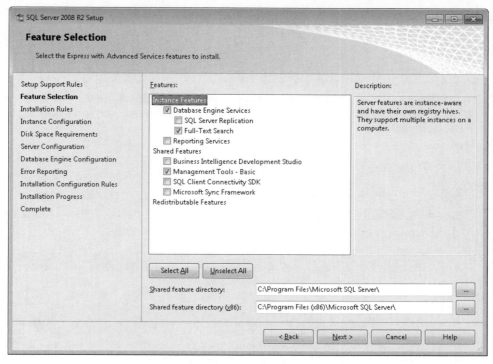

FIGURE 9-3 Selecting features during the SQL Server Express installation.

Tip If you run into any problems with your installation (for example, errors during the creation of an XML document or errors with an object reference), try the following:

- Verify that you have the correct version of .NET Framework (3.5.1) installed on your computer.

- Uninstall old versions of SQL Server (including old versions of the SQL Server native client libraries) and try installing again.

- If the object reference is missing, enable SQL Client Connectivity SDK (shown in Figure 9-3) during installation.

- In certain cases, it might be helpful to set up a new administrator account (user with administrator rights and without spaces in the name) and to install SQL Server via this account.

Installing with the Web Platform Installer

Using the Web Platform Installer (Web PI), you can install SQL Server Express 2008 R2 in a few simple steps:

> **Important** The version install with the Web PI does not contain the additional modules for the full-text search or report functions. If you need these functions, you must install SQL Server Express manually.

1. Start the Web PI with administrator rights.

2. Go to Products | Database.

3. Add the features SQL Server Express 2008 R2 and SQL Server 2008 R2 Management Studio Express, as shown in Figure 9-4, and then click Install.

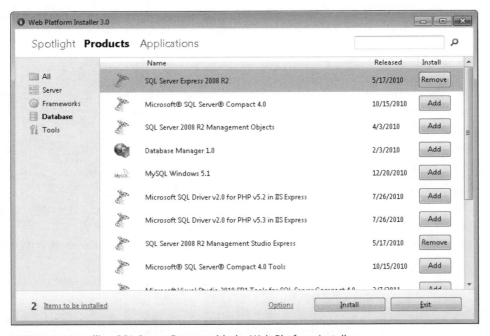

FIGURE 9-4 Installing SQL Server Express with the Web Platform Installer.

4. In the new dialog box, select Mixed Mode Authentication, and then enter a password for the SQL Server administrator (*sa*).

5. Click Next to start the installation.

You have now successfully installed SQL Server Express. If you run into problems during installation, you can try the tips from the previous section, "Manual Installation." If you have a previous version of Microsoft Visual Studio or SQL Server installed, you also might want to have a look at *http://support.microsoft.com/kb/956139*.

Installing the SQL Server PHP Extension

PHP provides two extensions for SQL Server

- **mssql**   This is the original PHP extension that is available for many platforms.
- **sqlsrv**   This is a newly developed PHP extension, which is only available for Windows operating systems developed and maintained by Microsoft.

This book uses the sqlsrv PHP extension. It offers support for Windows authentication, transactions, bound parameters, and data streaming. You can set up the extension manually or by using the Web PI.

 Note You can find current information from the developer team concerning the sqlsrv PHP extension on the SQL Server Driver for PHP Team Blog at *http://blogs.msdn.com/b/sqlphp/*.

Manual Installation

The sqlsrv PHP extension requires the Microsoft SQL Server Native Client libraries to be installed on the computer that runs PHP. To install this library, if it is not installed yet, perform the following steps:

1. Go to the MSDN website *http://msdn.microsoft.com/library/cc296170.aspx*.
2. Download the native client that fits your version and computer architecture. (There are links at the end of the first list.)
3. Start the installation program *sqlncli.msi*.
4. On the Feature Selection page, it's sufficient to select Client Components.
5. You might need to restart your computer after a successful installation.

You have now fulfilled the requirements for installing the extension and can set up the sqlsrv PHP extension:

1. Download the installation package from the Microsoft website at *http://www.microsoft .com/download/en/details.aspx?id=20098*.

2. Create a folder where you want to extract the driver data, for example C:\Program Files\Microsoft SQL Server Driver for PHP.

3. Start the installation file *SQLSRV20.exe*.

4. Select the folder for the files that you need to extract, and then click OK to confirm it.

5. Go to the installation folder and select the appropriate driver version:

   - For PHP 5.3, non-thread safe, Visual C++ 9.0: *php_sqlsrv_53_nts_vc9.dll*

   - For PHP 5.2, non-thread safe, Visual C++ 6.0: *php_sqlsrv_52_nts_vc6.dll*

6. If you want to enable PHP Data Objects (PDO) support as well, then additionally select the appropriate PDO driver versions:

   - For PHP 5.3, non-thread safe, Visual C++ 9.0: *php_pdo_sqlsrv_53_nts_vc9.dll*

   - For PHP 5.2, non-thread safe, Visual C++ 6.0: *php_pdo_sqlsrv_52_nts_vc6.dll*

7. Copy the selected drivers to the PHP extension folder to C:\PHP\ext.

8. Open the php.ini configuration file and enter the following lines (depending on your driver version) to load the SQL Server extension in PHP:

```
extension_dir = "ext"
extension = php_sqlsrv_53_nts_vc9.dll
; if you would like to enable PDO as well:
extension = php_pdo_sqlsrv_53_nts_vc9.dll
```

9. Restart Internet Information Services (IIS) or at least the PHP application pools so that PHP will apply the configuration changes.

10. Alternatively, you can use the PHP Manager to enable the extensions through its screen PHP Extensions | Enable or Disable an Extension.

11. Call up the phpinfo.php script. You can now see the sqlsrv section for the SQL Server driver, as shown in Figure 9-5.

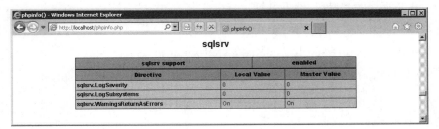

FIGURE 9-5 phpinfo() after a successful installation of the SQL Server driver.

Installing by Using the Web PI

If you are working with Microsoft's WebMatrix environment, you can also use the Web PI to install the SQL Server driver by performing the following steps:

1. Start the Web PI with administrator rights.

2. Add the option Products | Database | Microsoft SQL Server Driver v2.0 for PHP v5.3 in IIS Express, and then click Install.

3. Agree to the license agreement to start the installation.

You have now completed the installation. You can check whether the driver has been embedded correctly by using phpinfo().

SQL Server Tools

You will normally use two tools when working with SQL Server: Microsoft SQL Server Management Studio and the command-line program *sqlcmd*. The Management Studio provides a graphical user interface for many of the SQL Server functions, whereas *sqlcmd* only allows for entering T-SQL commands.

SQL Server Management Studio

The SQL Server Management Studio (SSMS) provides a graphical user interface for many administrative tasks with which database administrators are constantly confronted. In addition, SSMS can generate and display the correct T-SQL statement for most tasks. This makes SSMS the ideal tool for learning the SQL dialect, step by step. SSMS is also available for SQL Server Express (see the section "Installing SQL Server Express," earlier in the chapter).

When starting SSMS, you are asked to log on to SQL Server. You should do so from the same computer on which SQL Server is installed immediately after installing SQL Server, because remote access to SQL Server is not yet shared. Log on to the server with an SQL Server administrator account. After a successful logon, SSMS is started, as shown in Figure 9-6.

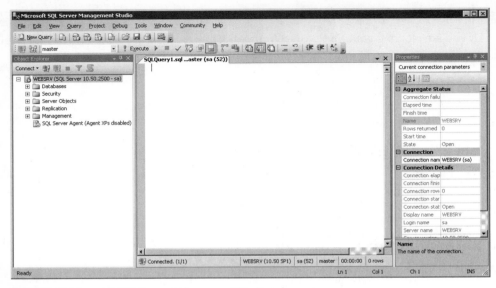

FIGURE 9-6 Microsoft SQL Server Management Studio.

By default, the interface is divided into four sections:

- The menu and the toolbar on the upper margin
- Object Explorer on the left
- A work area in the center
- The Properties pane on the right

In Object Explorer, you can select the desired elements (for example tables, databases, or logons) for editing.

The following procedure shows how to execute T-SQL commands in SSMS:

1. In the toolbar, click New Query.

   A new query window opens in the work pane.

2. In the drop-down list in the toolbar, make a selection below the database for the query (in Figure 9-6, master is selected).

3. Enter the T-SQL command into the query window, and then run the command by clicking the Execute button on the lowermost tool bar.

If you make changes to the structure of SQL Server or create new elements, it is possible that Object Explorer might not update accordingly. If this is the case, click the Update icon, as shown in Figure 9-7.

FIGURE 9-7 Manually updating Object Explorer.

The *sqlcmd* Command-Line Tool

sqlcmd is a command-line tool with which you can connect to an SQL Server instance and send T-SQL statements. If you want to use your local computer to connect with the current user, the following call is sufficient (the *–d* parameter specifies the database):

```
sqlcmd –d AdventureWorksLT2008
```

To connect with an instance on another computer or to use another user name, call up *sqlcmd* as follows:

```
sqlcmd –S server_name –U user_name
```

> **Note** The user specified with *-U* must be an SQL Server user account, not a Windows or domain user account.

If *sqlcmd* has been started, you can use *:help* to retrieve some commands. *sqlcmd* can be ended with *exit* or *quit*.

The T-SQL Batch

SQL Server processes T-SQL statements by batch. Multiple statements are combined in one batch, compiled together in an execution plan, and then processed step by step. The end of a batch is marked with the statement *GO*.

This is why *sqlcmd* does not execute statements until it reaches the *GO* statement.

> **Note** It's good practice to perform changes to the data model in its own batch and separate them from data access.

Configuring for Remote Access

By default, SQL Server is configured to only allow access from the local computer. If SQL Server and IIS are installed on two different computers in your work area or production environment, you need to configure and share remote access.

Two steps are necessary: first, end points that can receive connections need to be configured in SQL Server. Second, you need to share the necessary ports in the Windows Firewall to make it possible to connect from the outside.

Enabling the TCP/IP Protocol

To allow for remote access via TCP/IP, you first need to ensure that SQL Server permits statements via this protocol. To do so, start the Configuration Manager by clicking Start | All Programs | Microsoft SQL Server 2008 R2 | Configuration Tools | SQL Server Configuration Manager, and then select SQL Server Network Configuration | Protocols (for the desired instance) in the left pane. Make sure that the TCP/IP protocol is enabled for the selected instance. If you first need to enable the protocol, you must restart the associated SQL Server service. Then, go to the SQL Server Services in the left pane and select the Restart command in the context menu of the SQL Server (Instance) service.

SQL Server can now receive client requests via TCP/IP. Next, you need to check the firewall settings and allow access from the outside.

Enabling TCP/IP for Selected Networks Only

If the computer has multiple IP addresses, for example, because it possesses several network adapters, you can also configure SQL Server in such a way that the services are only permitted for certain local IP addresses.

For this purpose, go to the SQL Server Configuration Manager | SQL Server Network Configuration | Protocols and call up the properties of the TCP/IP protocol from the context menu. On the Protocol tab, set the Listen All option to No, and then on the IP Addresses tab, set the Enabled option to Yes for the desired addresses, as shown in Figure 9-8.

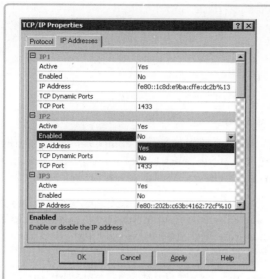

FIGURE 9-8 Enabling the TCP/IP protocol for individual local IP addresses.

By doing this, you can minimize the attack surface of SQL Server and prohibit access to certain local IP addresses completely.

Sharing Access in the Windows Firewall

By default, the Windows Firewall blocks all access to running services from the outside. With this, Microsoft consistently employs good security practice by blocking all services and only making them available selectively, if necessary. For remote access to SQL Server, you therefore need to first enter the appropriate rules into the Windows Firewall:

1. Start the Firewall configuration:

    - Using Windows Server 2008 R2: click Start | Administrative Tools | Windows Firewall With Advanced Security

    - Using Windows 7: click Start | Control Panel | System And Security | Windows Firewall | Advanced Settings

2. Select Inbound Rules in the navigation pane, and then in the Actions pane, click New Rule.

3. In the New Inbound Rule Wizard, select the Port option, and then click Next to confirm.

4. Select the TCP option, and then in the Specific Local Ports text box, enter **1433**.

   The TCP port 1433 is the default port for the first instance of SQL Server.

5. Select the Allow The Connection option.

6. On the Profile page, you should be as restrictive as possible: if remote access is only possible from a domain network, select the check box of this profile. If you only access it from networks which are marked as private, only select this check box.

   These settings assume that your networks are assigned to the corresponding profile. The Public option permits access from any computer. In this case, you should ensure (for example, by using an external firewall) that access is only permitted from authorized computers.

7. Give the rule a name (for example, **SQL Server Database Default Instance**), and then click Finish to complete the setup.

8. If you also want to permit access to the SQL Server browser service, repeat steps 2 to 6, and in step 4 share the UDP port 1434.

> **Tip** To further limit the attack surface, you can edit the rule properties after you have set them up. Select the rule in the rule list and call up Properties from the context menu. For example, you can restrict the remote access in the dialog box to a defined IP range or require that access is only permitted for authorized users (assumes an IPsec-authenticated connection).

After performing these configuration steps, you can access SQL Server from the permitted computers or networks. To use the Windows authentication, however, you first need to enter and authorize the users in SQL Server. You can find a description in Chapter 14, "Users and Permissions," but you can already log on with the *sa* account via the SQL Server Authentication method.

Installing the Sample Database

Microsoft provides a sample database for SQL Server called *AdventureWorks*. This database contains data and tables for you to try out various different application situations. *AdventureWorks* is available for every version of SQL Server and in many different formats. You can find a complete overview and download options on Codeplex at *http:// msftdbprodsamples.codeplex.com/*.

For our purposes, the version *AdventureWorksLT* (*Light*) is sufficient: it contains 12 tables, a schema, and takes up only about 7 MB, which makes it quick to install. You can find more information about this version at *http://msftdbprodsamples.codeplex.com/wikipage?title= AWLTDocs*.

To install the sample database, perform the following procedure:

1. Open the webpage *http://msftdbprodsamples.codeplex.com/releases/view/37109* (sample database version SQL Server 2008 SR4).

2. Download SQL2008.AdventureWorksLT2008_Only_Database.zip.

3. Unpack the Zip file in a folder of your choice; for example, C:\Data\AdventureWorks or the SQL Server default folder for database files C:\Program Files\Microsoft SQL Server\ MSSQL10.MSSQLSERVER\MSSQL\DATA.

4. Make sure that the extracted files have the proper access permissions and are writeable by the database principal.

5. Start SSMS, and then connect to the database.

6. In Object Explorer, right-click Databases, and then in the context menu, click the Attach command.

   The Attach Databases dialog box opens, as shown in Figure 9-9.

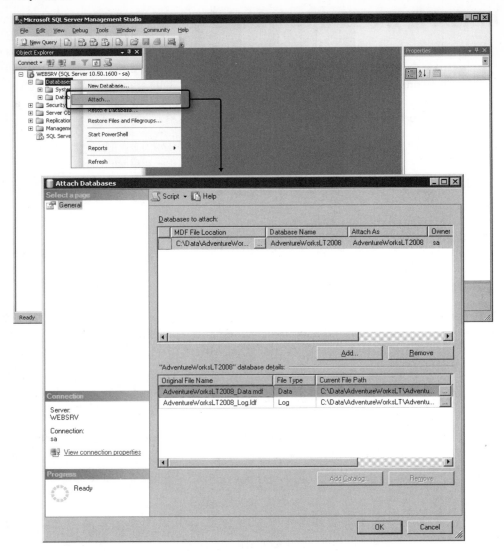

FIGURE 9-9 Appending the sample database *AdventureWorks*.

7. In the dialog box, click Add, and then select the file AdventureWorksLT2008_Data.mdf. Click OK to confirm it.

8. Click OK to finish attaching.

In Object Explorer, you will now see the newly appended sample database *AdventureWorksLT2008* under Databases.

9. In Object Explorer, right-click the *AdventureWorksLT2008* database, and then in the context menu, open the Properties.

The Database Properties dialog box opens.

10. In the dialog box, go to the Files section, and then specify the owner of the database in the Owner text box. (You can also use the button to the right of the text box to find existing users.)

11. Click OK to complete the dialog box.

To bind the sample database by using the command line, in step 5, start the command-line tool *sqlcmd* instead of SSMS, and then enter the following commands to append the database (paths according to your installation path) and specify the database user (for example, the administrator):

```
sp_attach_db AdventureWorksLT2008,
'C:\Data\AdventureWorks\AdventureWorksLT2008_Data.mdf',
'C:\Data\AdventureWorks\AdventureWorksLT2008_Log.ldf'
GO
ALTER AUTHORIZATION ON DATABASE::AdventureWorksLT2008 TO [WEBSRV\Administrator]
GO
```

You have now appended the sample database and assigned the required rights. The database can now be used.

Migrating MySQL Databases

Microsoft provides SQL Server Migration Assistant for MySQL (SSMA) for migrating MySQL databases to SQL Server. The SSMA takes care of the migration of the database schema and the data itself.

 Note The Migration Assistant for MySQL (SSMA) was developed for MySQL 5.1. Older versions of MySQL might pose problems.

Installing the Migration Assistant

The installation of SSMA is divided into three steps: installation of the MySQL Open Database Connectivity (ODBC) driver, installation of SSMA, and registration of SSMA. The SSMA may be installed on any computer, which means it does not necessarily need to be installed on the same computer as SQL Server.

Installing the MySQL ODBC Driver

The MySQL ODBC driver is used for connecting to the MySQL database. To install it, perform the following steps:

1. Go to *http://dev.mysql.com/downloads/* and download the appropriate Connector/ODBC for your work environment.

2. Start the installation program. In the second step, Setup Type, select the option Typical.

3. Click Next, and then click Install to install the driver.

4. Click Finish to complete the successful installation.

Installing the SSMA

The SSMA for MySQL is currently at version 5.1. To install the SSMA, perform the following procedure:

1. Download the SSMA from *http://www.microsoft.com/download/en/detailsaspx?displaylang=en&id=26712.*

2. Unpack the Zip file and start the SSMA For MySQL 5.1 installation program.

3. In the Choose Setup Type dialog box, click the Typical button, and then start the installation by clicking Install.

4. Start the SSMA For MySQL 5.1 Extension Pack installation program.

5. Again, choose the Typical setup type and proceed with the installation.

6. Choose the database instance and the connection parameters.

7. Choose a password for the extension pack database.

   If you don't want to remember too many passwords, it's acceptable to reuse the password from the user performing the migration.

8. Click Next to install the utilities database on your instance.

9. Click Exit to finish the installation.

Registering the SSMA

When you start the SSMA for the first time, you are asked for a license:

1. In the License Management dialog box, open the License Registration Page link.

2. Log on with your Windows Live ID or register a new Windows Live ID.

3. Enter the required data for the license registration, and then click Finish.

4. Save the created license file mysql-ssma.license in the SSMA default directory %user%\AppData\Roaming\Microsoft SQL Server Migration Assistant.

5. In the SSMA dialog box, click Refresh License.

You have now successfully installed and registered the SSMA and can start with the migration.

Migrating a MySQL Database

To migrate a MySQL database to SQL Server, perform the following procedure:

1. Start a new migration project by clicking File | New Project

   The New Project dialog box opens.

2. In the dialog box, give the project a name, optionally change the project location, and then click OK.

3. Click Connect To MySql, enter the connection data, and then click Connect.

   If you are connecting to a remote server, ensure that no firewall is blocking access and that MySQL allows remote connections.

4. Ensure that SQL Server Agent service is running. Either check with the SQL Server Configuration Manager or start the service by clicking Windows Start | Administrative Tools | Services.

5. Click Connect To SQL Server, enter the connection data and a database, and then click Connect. The database can still be changed later.

6. Select the database that you want to migrate in the MySql Metadata Explorer.

7. On the Schema Mapping tab, you can select the target database and schema in SQL Server by clicking Modify.

8. On the Type Mapping tab, you can specify the data type conversion properties for the entire database, or separately for individual tables.

9. Click Convert Schema to perform the database conversion.

   Initially it is not yet saved in SQL Server, so the conversion can take place without risk. Possible errors are displayed as shown in Figure 9-10. If the Convert Schema button is disabled, ensure that you have actually selected the database item in the MySql Metadata Explorer, not just selected the check box of the item.

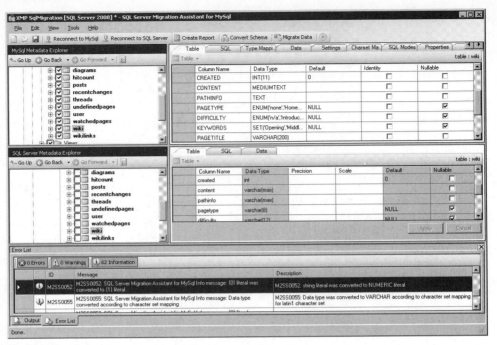

FIGURE 9-10 SQL Server Migration Assistant for MySQL.

10. Tables with conversion problems are marked with a red X. You have the following options for resolving conversion errors:

   - For *NULL* values, you can enable or disable the *Nullable* option of the column in the SQL Server table.

   - In MySQL, you can customize the database schema and perform the conversion again.

   - You can save the conversion script from the SQL Server Metadata Explorer with the context menu command Save As Script, edit it manually, and then run it in SQL Server.

   - You can exclude the object that has the error from the conversion in the Metadata Explorer.

11. If you were able to perform the conversion without errors or have resolved the errors, you can apply the schema within the SQL Server Metadata Explorer by using the context menu command Synchronize With Database.

12. Select the check boxes of the database (or the desired tables) for the data migration in the MySql Metadata Explorer, and then click the Migrate Data button.

13. Specify the connection data to MySQL and SQL Server again.

The migration is started and finishes with a Data Migration Report. Errors during data migration are most likely due to schema problems. Resolve the database schema and run the migration for the failed tables again.

You have now migrated a MySQL database to SQL Server in just a few steps.

Summary

In this chapter, you learned about the installation of SQL Server and the associated PHP extension. If you want to access the database from a different computer, you need to configure this remote access separately, because for security reasons it is not part of the default installation.

With the SQL Server Migration Assistant, you can migrate databases from MySQL to SQL Server quickly and easily. The sample database *AdventureWorksLT* that you set up will be used as the basis for data in the next chapters. Alternatively, instead of the smaller *LT* version, you can also install the complete *AdventureWorks* sample database.

In the next chapter, you will learn how databases, tables, keys, and indexes are created.

Chapter 10
Databases and Tables

Relational database management systems (RDBMS), such as Microsoft SQL Server, save data in a structured format. In this chapter, you will learn about the elements of this structure: databases, schemas, tables, and (column) data types.

Databases

In SQL Server, as in other RDBMS, data is saved in databases. A database contains not only the data itself in the form of datasets in tables, but also metadata for efficient data management. Each database has its own storage location.

Apart from the custom databases, an SQL Server instance also contains system databases that are necessary for running SQL Server. In the section that follows, we introduce these system databases and show you how to set up and delete databases and how to create a database snapshot.

System Databases

SQL Server uses four system databases, which are necessary for its correct operation. They contain important configuration data:

- **master** The *master* database contains all the information necessary for running SQL Server. It contains information about other databases, access data, account information, security settings, and configurations that are valid server-wide. SQL Server cannot be run without the master database. You should therefore back it up regularly.

- **model**   The *model* database serves as a template for creating new databases. Properties and objects from this database are applied to the newly created database. This way every new database automatically receives a basic configuration.

- **msdb**   In the *msdb* database, the SQL Server agent saves information about tasks that need to be executed periodically as well as their schedules. This database is also used by SQL Server Integration Services (SSIS) for storing configuration data.

- **tempdb**   As the name indicates, the *tempdb* contains only temporary data. It is used for storing temporary tables. SQL Server also uses it for caching data during sorting or aggregating.

There is one more system database, the *distribution* database, which only exists when the SQL Server uses the replication of databases to other instances.

Database Structure

An SQL Server database is saved to three different file types:

- **Primary data files (extension .mdf)**   Contain all information about the database and possibly the data itself.

- **Secondary data files (extension .ndf)**   Contain all data that is not stored in the primary file. A database can contain as many secondary files as desired, but does not need to have any if all of the data is contained in the primary file.

- **Transaction log files (extension .ldf)**   Contain information about the transactions in the database and are used to recover a correct and consistent database state after a disruption. Each database contains at least one log file.

Data and logs are never mixed, and each file is mapped to a single database. To facilitate management, SQL Server groups data files into file groups. Log files are never part of a file group.

SQL Server recognizes two file group types:

- **PRIMARY**   The standard file group that contains system databases and—unless specified otherwise during database setup—the newly created databases.

- **FILEGROUP**   Custom file groups that are created with the keyword *FILEGROUP*.

During database design, you can take advantage of the option to distribute data to individual files in order to distribute them to different drives and thus optimize performance and resource consumption. The distribution can take place at database, table, or index level, and can be used for partitioning tables or indexes themselves.

To take a look at a PRIMARY files group, go to the Windows Explorer and open the root folder of your database:

```
C:\Program Files\Microsoft SQL Server\<Name of instance>\MSSQL\DATA
```

In the folder, you will find the primary file for each system database and an associated transaction log file.

Setting Up Databases

To set up new databases, use the *CREATE DATABASE* command, as follows:

```
CREATE DATABASE database_name
    [ ON
        { [ PRIMARY ] [ <filespec> [ ,...n ]
                [ , <filegroup> [ ,...n ] ] ]
    [ LOG ON { <filespec> [ ,...n ] } ] } }
    ]
    [ COLLATE collation_name ]
    [ WITH <external_access_option> ]
[;]
```

With the *COLLATE* option, you can specify the default sort order to be used within the database, which you'll learn more about in the section "Sorting and Code Page," later in the chapter.

Specifying Files and File Groups

With *CREATE DATABASE*, you can further define the storage location and the storage type of databases, as follows:

```
<filespec> ::=
{
(
   NAME = logical_file_name ,
      FILENAME = { 'os_file_name' | 'filestream_path' }
      [ , SIZE = size [ KB | MB | GB | TB ] ]
      [ , MAXSIZE = { max_size [ KB | MB | GB | TB ] | UNLIMITED } ]
      [ , FILEGROWTH = growth_increment [ KB | MB | GB | TB | % ] ]
   ) [ ,...n ]
}
<filegroup> ::=
{
FILEGROUP filegroup_name [ CONTAINS FILESTREAM ] [ DEFAULT ]
   <filespec> [ ,...n ]
}
```

For the files, you can specify the initial size, the maximum size, and the step width for incremental file growth. If no size is specified, the number represents megabytes (MB). The differentiation into a logical file name (*logic_file_name*) and a physical file name (*os_file_name*) simplifies file handling.

Examples

The following three examples demonstrate how you can set up new databases.

Database with Default Settings

To create a first database with the default settings, run the following command:

```
CREATE DATABASE test_db;
```

If you now update Object Explorer in the SQL Server Management Studio (SSMS), you will see your new database with the name *test_db*.

Database with Alternative Sort Order

To set up a database that sorts in a case-sensitive, but accent-insensitive manner, run the following command:

```
CREATE DATABASE test_db COLLATE Latin1_General_CS_AI;
```

You can take a look at the database properties in the SSMS. The sort uses the default alphabet and language (Latin1_General) and is case sensitive (suffix CS) and ignores accents (suffix AI).

> **Tip** To see an overview of all available sort orders, run the following command:
>
> ```
> SELECT * FROM fn_helpcollations()
> ```

Database with File Groups

The final example, which is presented in Listing 10-1, shows you how to specify files and file groups in a database:

LISTING 10-1 Creating a database and specifying files and file groups.

```
CREATE DATABASE test_groups
ON PRIMARY
( NAME = tg_prim,
    FILENAME = 'C:\data\tg.mdf',
    SIZE = 15, MAXSIZE = 40, FILEGROWTH = 5MB ),
```

```
FILEGROUP TG_UserData1
( NAME = TG_BD1_dat,
    FILENAME = 'D:\data\tg_bd1_1.ndf',
    SIZE = 1GB, MAXSIZE = UNLIMITED, FILEGROWTH = 10% ),
FILEGROUP TG_UserData2
( NAME = TG_BD2_1_dat,
    FILENAME = 'E:\data\tg_bd2_1.ndf',
    SIZE = 100, MAXSIZE = 4GB, FILEGROWTH = 200 ),
( NAME = TG_BD2_2_dat,
    FILENAME = 'E:\data\tg_bd2_2.ndf',
    SIZE = 100, MAXSIZE = 2GB, FILEGROWTH = 100 )
LOG ON
( NAME = TG1_log,
    FILENAME = 'F:\transactions\tg1.ldf',
    SIZE = 10MB, MAXSIZE = 50MB, FILEGROWTH = 10MB ),
( NAME = TG2_log,
    FILENAME = 'G:\transactions\tg2.ldf',
    SIZE = 15MB, MAXSIZE = 75MB, FILEGROWTH = 15MB )
```

This command creates the following files and file groups:

- The primary file tg_prim in the *PRIMARY* filegroup. As you can see, the files of a file group don't need to be located in the same directory. (By default, the *PRIMARY* file group is located in the root folder of the server.)

- The file group *TG_UserData1* with the file TG_UD1_dat, which is created with a size of 1 GB and can grow in 10 percent increments, without restriction.

- The file group *TG_UserData2* with the two files TG_UD2_1_dat and TG_UD2_2_dat, both of them on the same drive (not required).

- Two transaction log files on different drives.

Setting Up a Database with SSMS

To create databases with the SSMS user interface, perform the following steps:

1. Connect to SQL Server by using SSMS.

2. In Object Explorer, right-click Databases, and then from the context menu, select New Database.

3. Enter the name of the database into the Database Name text box.

4. You can use the Add button to add files for the database in the Database Files table field. Figure 10-1 shows the example from the previous section, "Database with File Groups." Sizes are specified in megabytes.

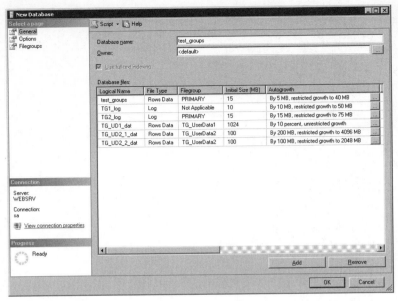

FIGURE 10-1 Setting up a new database with SQL Server Management Studio.

5. You can add file groups either with the File groups page or ad hoc when creating a new file by selecting the option <new file group> in the drop-down list.

6. On the Options page, you can specify further database properties; for example, the sort order.

7. If you have specified your settings according to your requirements, you can create the database by clicking OK. If you click the Script button beforehand, you can also write the Transact-SQL (T-SQL) script into a query window and study the generated T-SQL script.

Deleting a Database

To delete a database, use the *DROP DATABASE* command, as shown in the following:

```
DROP DATABASE { database_name | database_snapshot_name } [ ,...n ] [;]
```

With this command, you can delete one or multiple databases and database snapshots. When a database is deleted, the associated files on the drives are deleted as well. Therefore, be careful when performing a deletion, because you might permanently lose data.

Run the following command to delete the sample database:

```
DROP DATABASE test_db;
```

Deleting a database can fail for the following reasons:

- The user does not have the required right (*CONTROL*).

- The database is currently being used. While a database is in use, it cannot be deleted. You can use the *ALTER DATABASE* command to force that only one user is active in the database. This user can then delete the database:

  ```
  ALTER DATABASE database_name SET SINGLE_USER WITH ROLLBACK IMMEDIATE;
  ```

  The deletion takes place via a connection whose database context is the database you want to delete. In this case, you can use the command *USE* to change the context; for example, by changing to the *master* system database:

  ```
  USE master;
  ```

- There are still snapshots of the database. In this case, you need to delete the snapshots first.

  To delete a database by using SSMS, select the database in Object Explorer, click Edit, and then click Delete. In the Delete Object dialog box, confirm the deletion by clicking OK.

Creating a Snapshot

With SQL Server, you can create a snapshot of a database. A snapshot is a read-only view of the database as it looks at the moment the snapshot is taken. A snapshot can be used to create manual evaluations or reports with the SQL Server Reporting Services, without blocking database use or setting a database back to an earlier point in time. You can create a database snapshot with the *CREATE DATABASE* command, as in the following:

```
CREATE DATABASE database_snapshot_name
   ON  (
      NAME = logical_file_name,
      FILENAME = 'os_file_name'
   ) [ ,...n ]
   AS SNAPSHOT OF source_database_name
[;]
```

When creating a snapshot, you need to specify a file for each data file of the database (primary and secondary files, but not transaction log files). All necessary information is copied to these files to create the snapshot.

The *logical_file_name* becomes the logical name of the database file. The *os_file_name* specifies the physical file (including path) into which the database file is copied.

Example

The following example illustrates how this works:

1. Create a test database, and then create a test table in the database:

```
CREATE DATABASE test_db;
GO
USE test_db;
CREATE TABLE test (id int IDENTITY(1,1) PRIMARY KEY, value int);
```

2. Insert some values into the table:

```
INSERT INTO test VALUES (12), (13), (14);
```

3. Output the values in the table:

```
SELECT * FROM test;
```

4. Create a snapshot of the test database. For each data file of the database, you need to specify its own file for the snapshot. The logical name is the name that this file has in the database:

```
CREATE DATABASE test_snapshot
    ON (
        NAME=test_db, FILENAME='C:\Data\test_snapshot.snap'
    )
    AS SNAPSHOT OF test_db;
```

5. You can now use the snapshot like a regular database, with the restriction that the snapshot is read-only. In SSMS, you can find the snapshots in Object Explorer by clicking Databases | Database Snapshots, as shown in Figure 10-2.

FIGURE 10-2 Database snapshot in Object Explorer.

6. Insert a few new values into the table of the *test_db* database, and then check the result:

```
USE test_db;
INSERT INTO test VALUES (15), (16), (17);
SELECT * FROM test;
```

7. Now compare the result to the snapshot. The snapshot retains the old data status (at the time of the snapshot creation):

```
USE test_snapshot;
SELECT * FROM test;
```

Restoring the Database

A database can be restored to its state at the time of the snapshot creation. This reverts all changes to the database and its content that were made up to the point when the snapshot was created. To do so, use the *RESTORE* command, as shown in the following:

```
RESTORE DATABASE database_name
FROM DATABASE_SNAPSHOT = database_snapshot_name
```

Restoring only works if the database has exactly one snapshot; otherwise, you receive an error. If there are multiple snapshots, you need to delete them first.

You check this function with the test database and the test snapshot:

1. Restore the database to its state at the time of the snapshot:

```
USE master;
RESTORE DATABASE test_db
FROM DATABASE_SNAPSHOT = 'test_snapshot';
```

2. Check whether the changes were actually reverted:

```
USE test_db;
SELECT * FROM test;
```

 Note To restore a database to the time of the snapshot, the same basic conditions apply as those for deleting a database (presented earlier in the section "Deleting a Database"): no other users may use the database, and the database context of the connection must be different.

Snapshots are no substitute for a regular database backup. But they can be a valuable tool during development.

Deleting a Snapshot

Use the *DROP DATABASE* command to delete a snapshot:

```
DROP DATABASE database_snapshot_name [ ,...n ] [;]
```

Run the following commands to delete the created test snapshot and the test database:

```
USE master;
DROP DATABASE test_snapshot;
DROP DATABASE test_db;
```

Data Types

SQL Server provides several varied data types for saving data: numbers, strings, binary files, date and time, and unique identifiers. When selecting the correct data type, you should take into consideration not only the type of the data that you want to save, but also the amount of memory this data type requires, possible operations, and how efficiently the most frequent queries of your application can be implemented.

Numeric Data Types

SQL Server provides data types for integers, for numbers with a defined number of decimal places, and for floating-point numbers. For each class of number, there are multiple types that differ in value range and storage size.

Table 10-1 presents a list of integer types, from *bigint* with its value range of 64 bits, down to *bit*, which is of course, a single bit. With the exception of *tinyint* and *bit*, all types are signed.

TABLE 10-1 Data types for integers

Data type	Size	Value range
bigint	8 bytes	-2^{63} to 2^{63}-1 (approximately $-9*10^{18}$ to $9*10^{18}$)
bit	1 bit	0 or 1
int	4 bytes	-2^{31} to $2^{31}-1$ (approximately $-2*10^9$ to $2*10^9$)
smallint	2 bytes	-2^{15} to $2^{15}-1$ (-32768 to 32767)
tinyint	1 byte	0 to 2^8-1 (0 to 255)

Table 10-2 lists data types with a fixed number of decimal places and floating-point numbers. For the type *decimal*, you can specify the number of places altogether and the decimal places behind the point; for example, the definition of decimal(10,3) is a type with a maximum of 10 places, seven before the point and three behind it.

Floating-point numbers are used for calculations with a large range of values. The type *float* is more precise than *real*, but it requires twice as much memory. Calculating with floating-point numbers can lead to rounding errors. When running queries, you should therefore never test for an exact match, but rather whether two numbers are only a small interval apart.

TABLE 10-2 Numeric data types and floating-point numbers

Data type	Size	Description
decimal(p,s) numeric(p,s)	5–17 bytes	Numeric type with up to 38 places. The size depends on the number of places. The first parameter specifies the total number of places; the second, the number of decimal places.
float(n)	4 or 8 bytes	Floating-point number with a variable mantissa of up to 53 bits. The parameter *n* specifies the number of bits in the mantissa. Value range $-1.79*10^{308}$ to $-2.23*10^{-308}$, 0 and $2.23*10^{-308}$ to $1.79*10^{308}$.
money	8 bytes	Four decimal places. Value range of approx. $-9*10^{11}$ to $9*10^{11}$.
smallmoney	4 bytes	Four decimal places. Value range of -214748.3648 to $+214748.3647$.
real	4 bytes	Floating-point number with a mantissa of 24 bits. Value range of $-3.4*10^{38}$ to $-1.18*10^{-38}$, 0 and $1.18*10^{-38}$ to $3.4*10^{38}$.

Strings and Binary Data

SQL Server differentiates between two kinds of strings: strings based on Unicode and strings based on the character set of a defined code page. Data types for binary data are related to strings. The data types of these three classes are listed in Table 10-3.

TABLE 10-3 Strings and binary data

Data type	Size	Description
char(n)	max. 8000 bytes	String with fixed length, 1 byte per character
varchar(n)	max. 8000 bytes	String with variable length, 1 byte per character
varchar(max) text	max. $2*10^9$ bytes	String with variable length, 1 byte per character; *varchar(max)* should be used instead of *text* (obsolete)
nchar(n)	max. 4000 characters	Unicode string with fixed length, 2 bytes per character
nvarchar(n)	max. 4000 characters	Unicode string with variable length, 2 bytes per character
nvarchar(max) ntext	max. 10^9 characters	Unicode string with variable length, 2 bytes per character; *nvarchar(max)* should be used instead of *ntext* (obsolete)
binary(n)	max. 8000 bytes	Binary data with fixed length
varbinary(n)	max. 8000 bytes	Binary data with variable length
varbinary(max) image	max. $2*10^9$ bytes (2 GB)	Binary data with variable length; *varbinary(max)* should be used instead of *image* (obsolete)

To differentiate between the basic types—Unicode and code pages—for string literals, SQL Server uses different syntax for each:

- **Unicode**   Precede the string with *N*; for example, N'Doris laughing and dancing'.

- **Code page**   Without special escaping; for example, 'Doris laughing and dancing'.

   If there is an apostrophe within a string, you must escape it by placing another apostrophe before it; thus, 'Tony's beard' becomes 'Tony''s beard'.

Sorting and Code Page

The sorting of string data type depends on the value of the individual characters as well as the language, culture, and context. SQL Server supports many internationally common sort orders. You can retrieve a list of all sort orders by using the following command:

```
SELECT * FROM fn_helpcollations()
```

The name of the sort order already contains hints regarding the sorting. The name itself provides information about the language and context, the mapped code page, and which characteristics need to be taken into consideration for the sorting. Table 10-4 lists suffixes for sort characteristics.

TABLE 10-4 Suffixes for sort orders

Characteristic	Suffix for *considers*	Suffix for *does not consider*
Accents	AS	AI
Binary sort	BIN BIN2	(no suffix)
Case sensitive	CS	CI
Kana (Japanese characters)	KS	(no suffix)
Coding (width of 1 or 2 bytes)	WS	(no suffix)

If the string is not a Unicode string, the specified sort order determines the code page of the character set.

The sort order can be specified at server, database, table, column, and expression level, and the most specific definition is used (for example, column sort instead of database sort). For the definition, the T-SQL attribute *COLLATE* is used, as shown here:

```
COLLATE { <collation_name> | database_default }
<collation_name> :: =
    { Windows_collation_name } | { SQL_collation_name }
```

The following is an example for creating a table:

```
CREATE TABLE test_table (
    id int PRIMARY KEY,
    English varchar(50) COLLATE Latin1_General_100_CI_AI,
    Hungarian nvarchar(10) COLLATE Hungarian_100_CS_AS
);
```

Dates and Times

Table 10-5 provides an overview of the different SQL Server data types that you can use for saving the date and time. If you want to specify both date and time, you should use the data type *datetime2(n)*; otherwise, use the types *date* or *time(n)*.

TABLE 10-5 Data types for saving date and time

Data type	Size	Description
date	3 bytes	Date from 0001-01-01 until 9999-12-31.
datetime	8 bytes	Date and time from 1753-01-01 until 9999-12-31, accurate to 3.33 milliseconds.
datetime2(n)	6–8 bytes	Date and time from 0001-01-01 until 9999-12-31. The parameter specifies the number of places for split seconds (max. 7 places; corresponds to 100 ns).
datetimeoffset(n)	8–10 bytes	Same as datetime2. In addition, a time zone can be specified.
smalldatetime	4 bytes	Date and time from 1900-01-01 until 2079-06-06, accurate to 1 minute.
time(n)	3–5 bytes	Time from 00:00:00 until 23:59:59. The parameter specifies the number of places for split seconds (max. 7 places; corresponds to an accuracy of 100 ns).

Other Data Types

SQL Server offers additional data types, some of which are listed in Table 10-6. The data type *rowversion* (or the obsolete synonym *timestamp*) can be used to perform a sort according to the latest change in the table.

TABLE 10-6 Various additional data types

Data type	Size	Description
hierarchyid	Up to 892 bytes	Efficient data type for saving hierarchical relations
rowversion timestamp	8 bytes	Database-wide unique number that is updated with each change
uniqueidentifier	16 bytes	A global unique identifier (GUID)
xml	max. 2×10^9 bytes (2 GB)	Data type with variable length for saving XML data

Schemas and Object Names

In SQL Server, each object has a unique name. Schemas combine these objects into groups for easier administration. On the schema level, you can also assign access rights. This makes schemas in SQL Server an important grouping level. A complete object name always contains the name of the schema.

Object Names

Object names have a hierarchical structure and are composed of four parts separated by a period, as follows:

```
<SQL server instance> . <Database> . <Schema> . <Object>
```

With the exception of the object name, all parts are optional. If the instance is not specified, the instance of the current connection is used. If the database specification is missing, the database context of the connection is used. If the schema is missing, the default schema is used.

The default schema of a database is *dbo* (database owner). If no schema is specified in the object names, this schema is used. Alternatively, you can map your own default schema to each user for each database. If it is specified, it is used as long the objects have no schema specified.

If the object name contains spaces or represents a T-SQL keyword, you can put it into square brackets, as demonstrated here:

```
Invalid: SELECT Where AS Specification of location FROM tempdb.My DB.My Table
Correct: SELECT [Where] AS [Specification of location] FROM tempdb.[My DB].[My Table]
Alternative: SELECT [Where] AS 'Specification of location' FROM [tempdb].[My DB].[My Table]
```

Creating Schemas

Use the *CREATE SCHEMA* command to create a schema, as shown in the following:

```
CREATE SCHEMA schema_name
   [ AUTHORIZATION owner_name ]
   [ <schema_element> [ ...n ] ]
[;]
```

In addition to the schema name, you can also specify the owner (user or role), and while creating the schema, you can also create tables and other objects within it. The simplest example for creating a schema is as follows:

```
CREATE SCHEMA testschema
GO
```

In this case, the owner of the schema is the user who is creating it.

In SSMS, you can find schemas in Object Explorer under Databases | <database> | Security | Schemas. You can create a new schema by going to the context menu and clicking New Schema. In the dialog box that opens, you only need to fill in the Schema Name text box. The rights specifications are optional. Confirm your entries and create the schema by clicking OK.

Deleting Schemas

Use the *DROP SCHEMA* command to delete a schema:

```
DROP SCHEMA schema_name
```

To delete a schema in SSMS, in Object Explorer, in the Security section, click Schemas, and then right-click the schema of the associated database. In the context menu that opens, click Delete to open the Delete Object dialog box. Confirm your entries by clicking OK.

> **Note** A schema can only be deleted if it does not contain objects. Therefore, you first need to delete all objects in the namespace of the schema.

Tables

Tables represent the basic structure for saving data in relational databases. They consist of rows and columns. Rows represent a data set, and columns specify the data types that are saved for a data set. Data manipulation in databases always means creating a data set in a table (adding a row), removing a data set (deleting a row), or changing a data set (changing the column values for the row).

Creating Tables

Tables are created in the database by using the *CREATE TABLE* statement. With SQL Server, you can specify the data type for the columns and a number of other options, as demonstrated in the following:

```
CREATE TABLE
    [ database_name . [ schema_name ] . | schema_name . ] table_name
    ( { <column_definition> | <computed_column_definition>
        | <column_set_definition> | [ <table_constraint> ] [ ,...n ] ) }
    [ ON { partition_scheme_name ( partition_column_name ) | filegroup
        | "default" } ]
    [ { TEXTIMAGE_ON { filegroup | "default" } ]
    [ FILESTREAM_ON { partition_scheme_name | filegroup
        | "default" } ]
    [ WITH ( <table_option> [ ,...n ] ) ]
[ ; ]
```

The command consists of the following parts:

- Definition of the table name
- Definition of the columns, their types, and their restrictions
- Memory location of the table or the table partition
- Memory location of the "large" data types *varchar(max)*, *nvarchar(max)*, *varbinary(max)*, and *xml*
- Memory location of the *FILESTREAM* data types (large binary files that are located outside the database but are managed by the database)
- Additional table options

You will only learn about the most important options here: column definitions and constraints. You can find a complete documentation of the *CREATE TABLE* statement on MSDN at *http://msdn.microsoft.com/en-us/library/ms174979.aspx*. Using these options, database administrators can perform a very granular data distribution to different file groups and drives in order to optimize system stability and performance at table level.

Defining Columns

To define a column, you need to specify its name, column type, and other optional specifications and constraints, as shown in Listing 10-2:

LISTING 10-2 Creating a table.

```
CREATE TABLE users (
    id int NOT NULL IDENTITY(1,1),
    name varchar(60) COLLATE Latin1_General_100_CI_AI NOT NULL,
    email varchar(80),
    description nvarchar(MAX) DEFAULT 'No description available',
    registered smalldatetime DEFAULT CURRENT_TIMESTAMP
);
```

The example creates a table called *users* with five columns: id, name, email, description, and registered. The additional constraints and specifications used are listed in Table 10-7. The list also represents the most important specifications for columns.

TABLE 10-7 Optional specifications and constraints for the column definition

Restriction	Description
COLLATE name	Specifies a sort order for this column.
DEFAULT	Specifies a default value for the column, which is used if this column is not specified with the *INSERT* command.
IDENTITY(start, inc)	Generates consecutive numbers for all rows that are inserted. The numbers begin with *start* and are increased by *inc*. Only one *IDENTITY* column per table is permitted. The column is normally used as primary key.
NULL / NOT NULL	Specifies whether NULL values are permitted in the column.

Tip To retrieve the value of the automatically inserted *IDENTITY* number after an *INSERT* or *UPDATE* operation, you can either query the variable *@@IDENTITY* or call the function *SCOPE_IDENTITY()*, which is restricted to the current scope (for example, stored procedure or batch). To retrieve the latest *IDENTITY* value of a table independently of an operation, you can use *IDENT_CURRENT()*, as shown in the following:

```
SELECT @@IDENTITY AS [IDENTITY];
SELECT SCOPE_IDENTITY() AS [SCOPE_IDENTITY];
SELECT IDENT_CURRENT('SalesLT.Person') AS [IDENT_CURRENT];
```

You can find out how to specify primary keys, indexes, and foreign keys in the section "Keys and Indexes," later in the chapter.

Creating Tables by Using SSMS

With SSMS, you can comfortably create tables by using the graphical user interface. To do so, perform the following steps:

1. Open SSMS, and then connect to SQL Server.

2. In Object Explorer, select the Databases, select the desired database, and then click Tables. In the context menu that appears, select New Table.

3. In the central pane, enter the column names and their types, as shown in Figure 10-3.

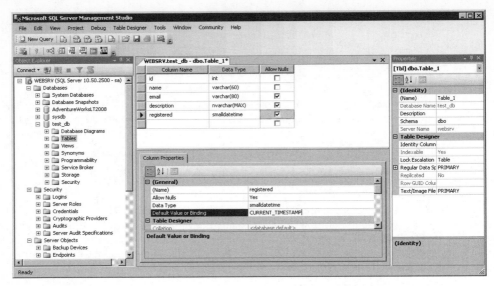

FIGURE 10-3 Creating a table by using SSMS.

4. You can enter the following additional column specifications in the Column Properties tab:

   - **DEFAULT**   General/Default Value or Binding
   - **COLLATE**   Table Designer/Collation
   - **IDENTITY**   Table Designer/Identity Specification, including Identity Seed and Identity Increment

5. In the Properties pane on the left, enter the table name into the text box (Identity)/ (Name).

   If you want to map the table to a certain schema, in the Properties pane, in the (Identity) section, change the Schema text box accordingly.

6. Create the table by clicking the Save icon in the toolbar.

   If you have skipped step 5, a dialog box opens, prompting you to enter the table name. Enter a name, and then confirm it by clicking OK.

You have now created a new table. If you want to make changes to a table, select it in Object Explorer, and then select Design in the context menu.

Deleting Tables

Tables can be deleted by using the *DROP TABLE* command, as shown in the following:

```
DROP TABLE table_name [ ,...n ]
```

A table can only be deleted if it is not currently in use and no other objects (such as foreign keys) are referring to it. Otherwise, the references or referencing objects must be deleted prior to deleting the table.

You can delete a table in SSMS by selecting it in Object Explorer and selecting Delete in the context menu. Confirm the Delete Object dialog box that opens by clicking OK.

Keys and Indexes

In relational databases, table keys are used to identify data records and for linking data records from multiple tables: primary keys for identification, and foreign keys for linking data. Indexes allow fast access to data records (rows) with certain properties (column values).

Primary Keys

One of the principles of relational data modeling is that the rows of a table (data records) must be uniquely identifiable. The column (or columns) used to differentiate between data records is called the primary key of the table. It is good practice to keep the primary key to only one column; for example, of the type *int* with the property *IDENTITY*.

Defining the Primary Key When Creating a Table

SQL Server supports primary keys from any number of columns. In a T-SQL expression, the specification can take place directly in the associated column if the primary key consists of only one column, as shown in Listing 10-3:

LISTING 10-3 Defining a primary key consisting of one column.

```
CREATE TABLE users (
    id int IDENTITY(1,1) PRIMARY KEY,
    name nchar(10)
)
```

If the primary key consists of two or more columns, it is placed at the end of the column definition, as illustrated in Listing 10-4:

LISTING 10-4 Defining a primary key consisting of two columns.

```
CREATE TABLE bill (
    bill_date date,
    bill_num int,
    amount money,
    PRIMARY KEY (bill_date, bill_num)
)
```

SQL Server automatically generates an index for the primary key. Therefore, access with the primary key in the *WHERE* clause is especially efficient.

The primary key represents a *CONSTRAINT*. If the primary key is set up as shown in the two examples, a name is automatically created for the corresponding constraint (pattern: *PK   table_name__ID*). If you want to give the primary key a name for later use, you need to name the corresponding constraint, as demonstrated in Listing 10-5:

LISTING 10-5 Defining a named primary key consisting of two columns.

```
CREATE TABLE bill (
    bill_date date,
    bill_num int,
    amount money,
    CONSTRAINT PK_bill PRIMARY KEY (bill_date, bill_num)
)
```

Changing the Primary Key

For existing tables, you can also add or remove the primary key later on by using the *ALTER TABLE* command. Changing the key takes place in two steps: first, the old key needs to be removed, and then the new key is created. For the changes, the name of the constraint is used.

For example, to change the primary key from our billing table in Listing 10-5, run the following commands:

```
ALTER TABLE bill DROP CONSTRAINT PK_bill;
ALTER TABLE bill ADD CONSTRAINT PK_bill PRIMARY KEY (bill_num);
```

Tip If you don't know the name of the key, run one of the following two commands:

```
SELECT * FROM sys.key_constraints
```

```
SELECT constraint_schema, constraint_name, constraint_type
FROM INFORMATION_SCHEMA.TABLE_CONSTRAINTS WHERE table_name='<table name>'
```

Alternatively, in SSMS, in Object Explorer, select the table, and then look under Keys.

Defining the Primary Key by Using SSMS

SSMS also provides functions for defining or changing the primary key, which are easy to use. You can add, change, or delete the primary key in the Design view of the table:

1. Open SSMS, and then connect to the database.

2. In Object Explorer, select the table that you want to edit, and then in the context menu, click Design.

   If you want to create a new table, go to Databases | *<database>* | Table, and then in the context menu, click New Table.

3. Select the columns in the work area that you want to use as primary key.

   Click the Set Primary Key icon in the toolbar, as shown in Figure 10-4 (the highlighted icon on the left). The columns will be marked with a key symbol.

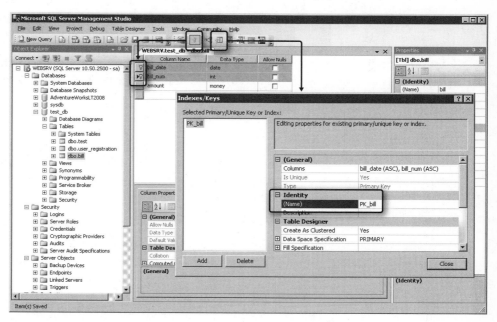

FIGURE 10-4 Using SSMS for primary key management.

4. To give the primary key a defined name, click the Manage Indexes And Keys icon (the highlighted icon on the right; see Figure 10-4).

5. In the dialog box that opens, select the key on the left.

   You can then define the name of the key constraint on the right, in the Name text box, in the (Identity) section. You can also define the fields belonging to the key by specifying the columns (and their sorting) in the Columns text box in the (General) section.

6. Click the Save icon in the toolbar.

7. You can now find the primary key that you created in Object Explorer under Key of the table. The associated index can be found under Indexes.

Foreign Keys

A good database design means that the same data does not appear multiple times within the database. If data exists twice or multiple times, it's called a redundancy, and that can lead to complications when data is modified. Inconsistent data stock can only be prevented with some extra work in the application.

For example, a client's email address should only appear in the client table, but not in the client transactions table. Should the client change his email address, you only need to update it in the client table and nowhere else. When reading a client transaction, the email address can then be merged with the updated address from the client table (*JOIN* of tables).

To set up this relationship between table entries, you need to enter the primary key of one table in another table as a reference. This is called a foreign key. For example, the primary key of the client table is entered into the client transactions table, where it becomes a foreign key.

Defining Foreign Keys

SQL Server supports foreign keys and actions based on foreign keys (for example, cascading). Foreign keys are also defined with a constraint, as shown in the following:

```
[ CONSTRAINT constraint_name ]
{ [ FOREIGN KEY ] | FOREIGN KEY ( column [ ,...n ] ) }
   REFERENCES [ schema_name . ] referenced_table_name [ ( ref_column ) ]
   [ ON DELETE { NO ACTION | CASCADE | SET NULL | SET DEFAULT } ]
   [ ON UPDATE { NO ACTION | CASCADE | SET NULL | SET DEFAULT } ]
   [ NOT FOR REPLICATION ]
```

If you define a foreign key directly in the corresponding column, the keyword *FOREIGN KEY* is not necessary. If you define it afterward, you need to specify the keyword *FOREIGN KEY* as well as the columns in question.

This syntax is also valid for changing foreign keys with *ALTER TABLE*.

Listing 10-6 uses two tables to show you how to specify a foreign key directly while defining the associated column:

LISTING 10-6 Defining the foreign key directly with the associated column.

```
CREATE TABLE users (
    id int IDENTITY PRIMARY KEY,
    name nchar(10),
    email varchar(80)
)

CREATE TABLE bill (
    bill_num int PRIMARY KEY,
    bill_date date,
    amount money,
    user_id int NULL
    CONSTRAINT FK_bill_users
        FOREIGN KEY REFERENCES users (id)
        ON DELETE NO ACTION
        ON UPDATE CASCADE
)
```

Actions Based on Foreign Keys

If the data in the referenced table (*user* in Listing 10-6) is changed, it's possible that the foreign keys in the table *bill* don't match anymore. This can happen due to the deletion of rows from the referenced table (*DELETE*) or changes to the primary key (*UPDATE*). In both cases, referencial integrity is at risk. SQL Server therefore permits you to specify four different actions for reacting to these changes:

- **SET NULL**   If the referenced entry is deleted or its primary key changed, the foreign key is set to *NULL*. In this case, the foreign key columns must not be defined as *NOT NULL*.

- **SET DEFAULT**   Similar to *SET NULL*, but instead of *NULL*, the defined default value of the foreign key columns is set.

- **NO ACTION**   SQL Server cancels the original modification in the referenced table with an error message. It is not possible to make a change as long as rows with foreign keys refer to the entry that you want to change in the referenced table.

- **CASCADE**   The modification is applied to the current table as well: if the primary key has changed, the foreign key values are adjusted as necessary. If the row in the referenced table was deleted, all corresponding rows are deleted from the current table. Therefore, think twice before using *ON DELETE CASCADE*.

Defining Foreign Keys by Using SSMS

Foreign keys can also be defined via SSMS by performing the following steps:

1. Open SSMS, and then connect to the database.

2. In Object Explorer, select the table into which you want to enter the foreign key constraints, and then in the context menu, go to Design.

3. Click the Relationships icon in the toolbar above, or go to Relationships in the context menu of the work area.

   The Foreign Key Relationships dialog box opens.

4. Click the Add button.

5. Select the entry Tables And Columns Specification, and then click the button on the right.

   The Tables and Columns dialog box opens, as shown in Figure 10-5.

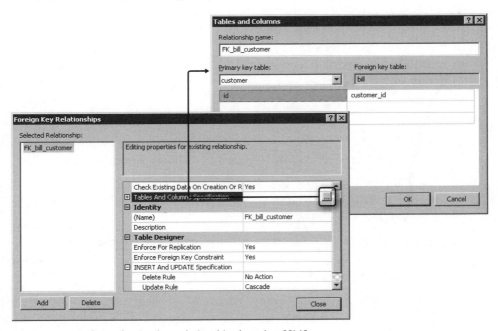

FIGURE 10-5 Defining foreign key relationships by using SSMS.

6. Select the primary key table from the drop-down list, and then select the columns that you want to use in both tables. Click OK to confirm your entries.

7. In the Foreign Key Relationships dialog box, in the Table Designer section, under INSERT And UPDATE Specification, you can define the actions that you want to take place when there is a change to the primary key table (Update Rule is *ON UPDATE*, Delete Rule is *ON DELETE*).

8. After you have performed the necessary changes, close the dialog box by clicking Close, and then click Save in the toolbar above.

Indexes

If your program frequently searches a certain column (normally in a *WHERE* clause but sometimes also as part of a *JOIN* or *GROUP BY*), you can increase the database's performance by setting up an index for this column (or columns). If a column has an index, the database no longer has to search the entire table for a certain value. This improvement in performance, however, requires an additional management effort: the database must update the index with each change. This disadvantage usually does not pose a problem with database query patterns, which normally occur in web applications (there are many more queries than changes). Nevertheless, you should not set up indexes without taking the disadvantages into consideration.

Creating an Index

An index can be created for a table or a *VIEW* by using the *CREATE INDEX* command, as shown in the following:

```
CREATE [ UNIQUE ] [ CLUSTERED | NONCLUSTERED ] INDEX index_name
   ON <object> ( column [ ASC | DESC ] [ ,...n ] )
```

The specifications include the type of index, the name, and which columns you want to include in the index. You can include columns into several indexes simultaneously. The command has a few other options that are used (among other things) for performance optimization. You can read a complete documentation of the command on MSDN at *http://technet .microsoft.com/en-us/library/ms188783.aspx*.

The clauses have the following meanings:

- **UNIQUE**   Specifies whether the values collected by the index must be unique.

- **CLUSTERED**   Specifies that the index (also) defines the physical sorting of the table. This is why there can be only one *CLUSTERED* index per table. The index connected to the primary key is set up as *CLUSTERED* by default.

- **NONCLUSTERED**   The index is created in an area outside of the table and contains a sorted list of references to the table. This is the default setting for indexes. You can create 999 *NONCLUSTERED* indexes per table.

Listing 10-7 shows how to create two indexes for the table from Listing 10-6. Both indexes are *NONCLUSTERED*.

LISTING 10-7 Creating two indexes.

```
CREATE UNIQUE INDEX IX_users_email
ON users (email)

CREATE INDEX IX_bill_date
ON bill (bill_date, user_id)
```

> **Tip** To speed up your most frequent queries even further, you might want to create a so-called *covering index*, which contains all columns retrieved by the query. If SQL Server is able to retrieve all columns from the index itself, it does not need to look up the data in the table, which gives a tremendous performance boost, as fewer disk operations are required. The drawback is that such indexes tend to take a substantial amount of space and make inserts and updates expensive. But for your most frequent queries, this trade-off might well be worth it.

Indexes are created implicitly for columns that are defined as *UNIQUE* or *PRIMARY KEY*. In Listing 10-8, a *CLUSTERED* index is created for the column *id* and a *UNIQUE NON-CLUSTERED* index is created for the column *email*:

LISTING 10-8 A table with two implicitly defined indexes.

```
CREATE TABLE users (
    id int IDENTITY PRIMARY KEY,
    name nchar(10),
    email varchar(80) UNIQUE
)
```

Creating an Index by Using SSMS

To use SSMS to create an index, perform the following steps:

1. Start SMSS, and then connect to the database.

2. In Object Explorer, select the table for which you want to create an index, and then in the context menu, click the New Index command.

   The New Index dialog box opens, as shown in Figure 10-6.

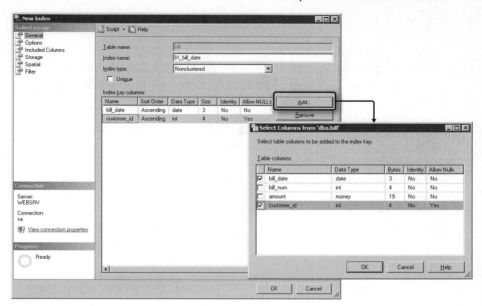

FIGURE 10-6 Creating a new index by using SSMS.

3. Enter a name into the Index Name text box. If you want the index to be *UNIQUE*, select the Unique check box.

4. To add the columns that you want to index, click Add.

   The Select Columns dialog box opens.

5. Select the columns that you want to index, and then click OK.

6. Finish your entries, and then click OK to create the index.

You have now created the index. It should be automatically displayed in Object Explorer. If it is not, you need to update the view.

Deleting an Index

You can use the *DROP INDEX* command to delete an index, as shown here:

```
DROP INDEX index_name [ ON <object> ]
```

To delete an index by using SSMS, perform the following steps:

1. In Object Explorer, select the table for which the index was created.

2. In Object Explorer, open Indexes of the table.

3. Select the index that you want to delete, and then in the context menu, click Delete. Click OK to confirm the dialog box.

Summary

Data is set up structurally in relational database systems: individual properties of an object are grouped into data records, which are saved in a table. Schemas are used to combine tables (and other objects) into logical units. Schemas (and the objects they include) are saved in databases.

In this chapter, you were introduced to the creation of databases, schemas, and tables and learned about the most important data types for table columns and the naming of objects in databases. Then you learned how to define indexes as well as primary and foreign keys for efficient access, and how to link data records.

In the next chapter, you will learn how to insert data records into tables, how to delete and change them, how to read data from databases, and how to join data records from different tables.

Chapter 11
Working with SQL Server

When working with data in Microsoft SQL Server, four Transact-SQL (T-SQL) statements are most commonly used: *SELECT* (for selecting data records), *INSERT* (for inserting data records), *UPDATE* (for updating data records), and *DELETE* (for deleting data records). In this chapter, you will be introduced to these statements and a few additional features, such as *common table expressions*.

 Note For the examples in this chapter, you will be using the sample database *AdventureWorks LT2008* that you installed in Chapter 9, "Setting Up SQL Server." You can find a database diagram of the sample database in Appendix A, "Example Scripts and Data," which gives you an overview of all tables and table relationships.

Querying Data (*SELECT*)

Querying data from a database by using the *SELECT* command is the most frequent action performed on databases. The *SELECT* command offers a large number of options and functions. You will learn about the most important ones in the following sections and subsections.

The basic structure of a *SELECT* command looks like this:

```
[ WITH <common_table_expression> ]
SELECT select_list [ FROM table ]
[ WHERE search_conditions ]
[ GROUP BY grouping ] [ HAVING search_condition ]
[ ORDER BY sorting ]
```

Simple *SELECT* Expressions

To select data from a table, you need to specify at least the name of the table and the columns that you want to query. Listing 11-1 shows such a *SELECT* command. The columns you want to select must be separated by a comma, and the table name must follow the keyword *FROM*:

LISTING 11-1 Simple *SELECT* query of the table *SalesLT.SalesOrderHeader*.

```
SELECT SalesOrderID, ShipDate, SubTotal, TotalDue
FROM SalesLT.SalesOrderHeader;
GO

SalesOrderID ShipDate                  SubTotal   TotalDue
------------ -----------------------   ---------- ----------
71774        2004-06-08 00:00:00.000     880.3484   972.7850
71776        2004-06-08 00:00:00.000      78.8100    87.0851
71780        2004-06-08 00:00:00.000   38418.6895 42452.6519
...
```

If you want to select all columns of a table, you can use the placeholder "*" (asterisk) character, as shown here:

```
SELECT * FROM SalesLT.SalesOrderHeader
```

You can also add calculations to your column specification, as shown in Listing 11-2. By using the options keyword *AS*, you can rename the columns in the result. In the example, the calculated column receives the name *SurchargePercent*.

LISTING 11-2 *SELECT* with calculation in the selected columns.

```
SELECT SalesOrderID, SubTotal, (TotalDue-SubTotal)/SubTotal*100 AS SurchargePercent
FROM SalesLT.SalesOrderHeader;
GO

SalesOrderID SubTotal              SurchargePercent
------------ --------------------- ---------------------
71774        880.3484              10.5000
71776        78.8100               10.5000
71780        38418.6895            10.5000
...
```

Constraining Queries by Using *WHERE*

If you don't want to retrieve all the rows of a table, but only those that have a certain prop-erty, you can specify these constraints by using the *WHERE* clause. Listing 11-3 shows a query that selects only the rows whose *LastName* column contains the text "brown" and whose *CustomerID* column value is less than 1000.

> **Note** Because the default sorting order is not case-sensitive, even though we are searching for **b**rown, the columns with **B**rown are found. See the section "Sorting and Code Page," in Chapter 10, "Databases and Tables," for information on how to change the sort order.

LISTING 11-3 Constraining a query by using a *WHERE* clause.

```
SELECT FirstName, LastName, EmailAddress
FROM SalesLT.Customer
WHERE LastName='brown' and CustomerID < 1000;
GO


FirstName  LastName  EmailAddress
---------- --------- ----------------------------
Robert     Brown     robert5@adventure-works.com
Jo         Brown     jo2@adventure-works.com
Steven     Brown     steven1@adventure-works.com
```

The *WHERE* clause may contain complex conditions, calculations, and additional *SELECT* queries. This is described in the section "Subqueries," later in the chapter.

Grouping Query Data (*GROUP BY, HAVING*)

The *GROUP BY* clause is used to combine the query results into groups. Groups are necessary if you want to determine the number of entries per group or, for example, if you want to add up the values of a column by using the group.

The most important aggregate functions for grouping are:

- **count(*)**   Counts the entries in the group.
- **sum(expression)**   Adds up the specified expression using the group.
- **min(expression), max(expression)**   Determines the minimum or maximum of the expression in the group.

Listing 11-4 shows a grouping. The table *SalesOrderDetail* contains information about the orders individual invoice items. To group the invoice items according to the corresponding invoice, *GROUP BY SalesOrderID* is used. The aggregate columns *OrderCount, SumLineTotal*, and *MaxQty* specify the values for the data grouped by *SalesOrderID*. The keyword *HAVING* is used to select those groups that have five or more entries.

LISTING 11-4 Grouped result output.

```
SELECT SalesOrderID, count(*) AS OrderCount, sum(LineTotal) as SumLineTotal,
max(OrderQty) AS MaxQty
FROM SalesLT.SalesOrderDetail
WHERE UnitPriceDiscount > 0
GROUP BY SalesOrderID HAVING count(*) >= 5;
GO

SalesOrderID OrderCount SumLineTotal     MaxQty
------------ ---------- ---------------- ------
71780        5              1016.982000     6
71783        8             33533.591986    25
71784        5             21935.704314    23
71797        6              1978.089418    23
71902        5               949.183200     5
71936        5              1370.538024    14
```

The difference between *WHERE* and *HAVING* is the moment at which the respective conditions are applied. With *WHERE*, the rows are filtered *before* the grouping. Of the 542 rows in *SalesOrderDetail*, 43 rows meet the condition in Listing 11-4. These 43 rows are then grouped by *SalesOrderID*. The result is 13 groups (= different *SalesOrderID*). With the inclusion of *HAVING*, these 13 rows become subject to another condition *after* the grouping; as a result, 6 rows remain.

This is why the *WHERE* clause must not contain any aggregate functions, and no columns must be selected that are calculated with aggregate functions. The *HAVING* clause, on the other hand, may only contain columns that are either the basis for a group (in Listing 11-4 the column *SalesOrderID*) or are calculated with aggregate functions.

Sorting (*ORDER BY*)

The *ORDER BY* clause is used to sort a *SELECT* query. It specifies the columns by which you want to sort. If multiple columns are specified, the data is sorted by the first column. If there are identical entries, they are sorted by the second column, and so on. The keywords *ASC* and *DESC* after the column names specify whether the sort order is ascending (*ASC*) or descending (*DESC*).

Caution If you don't specify *ORDER BY*, you should assume that the column output will be random; that is, in an order that you can't predict. Even though in practice the rows are usually returned in the order in which they were inserted or according to the primary key, you shouldn't count on it.

In Listing 11-5, the output is sorted in descending order by the *City* column, and for matching entries, ascending by the *AddressLine1* column.

LISTING 11-5 Sorting the result of a *SELECT* query.

```
SELECT City, PostalCode, AddressLine1
FROM SalesLT.Address
ORDER BY City DESC, AddressLine1;
GO

City        PostalCode   AddressLine1
---------   -----------  -------------------------
Zeeland     49464        855 East Main Avenue
York        Y024 1GF     308-3250 Casting Road
York        Y03 4TN      7 Pioneer Business Park
Woolston    WA1 4SY      Warrington Ldc Unit 25/2
...
```

Queries with Multiple Tables

So far, you have only been introduced to *SELECT* expressions, which query data from a single table. One of the strengths of relational databases, however, the ability to link multiple tables during a query.

Joining Tables (*JOIN*)

With the T-SQL *JOIN* expression, you can link two or more tables. There are different kinds of *JOIN* expressions:

- **INNER JOIN**   Tables are linked by using common columns with comparison operators. Only those rows are returned for which both tables have the correct value. *INNER JOIN* expressions are the most frequently used *JOIN* expressions.

- **OUTER JOIN**   If you want to join tables, and one of the tables does not contain the right kind of values for the other table, but you still want to output all rows, you need to use an *OUTER JOIN*. The missing values will be filled with *NULL*. There are three kinds of *OUTER JOIN* expressions: *LEFT [OUTER] JOIN*, *RIGHT [OUTER] JOIN*, and *FULL [OUTER] JOIN*. With *LEFT JOIN*, all rows of the left table are returned and the missing values of the right table are replaced by *NULL*. With *RIGHT JOIN*, all rows of the right table are returned and the missing values of the left table are replaced by *NULL*. With *FULL JOIN*, all rows of both tables are returned and the missing values of both tables are replaced with *NULL*.

- **CROSS JOIN**   A Cartesian product of two tables is created: every row of the first table is linked to every single row of the second table. Accordingly, the result can become quite big!

JOIN expressions have a similar structure:

```
FROM left_table <join_type> right_table
ON join_condition
```

The condition is located in its own *ON* clause. For *INNER JOIN* expressions, the conditions may be located directly in the *WHERE* clause. Columns must be uniquely mapped to the tables: either the column names only appear in a table or the table name is specified with the column name. You can rename the tables within a *SELECT* by using *AS* and save yourself a lot of typing.

Listing 11-6 shows a typical *INNER JOIN*. To retrieve the name and category of products, you need to link the tables *SalesLT.Product* and *SalesLT.ProductCategory* via the primary key of the category.

LISTING 11-6 An *INNER JOIN* of two tables.

```
SELECT p.ProductID, p.Name, pc.ProductCategoryID, pc.Name
FROM SalesLT.Product AS p JOIN SalesLT.ProductCategory AS pc
ON p.ProductCategoryID = pc.ProductCategoryID;
GO

ProductID  Name                      ProductCategoryID Name
---------- ------------------------- ----------------- ------------
680        HL Road Frame - Black, 58 18                Road Frames
706        HL Road Frame - Red, 58   18                Road Frames
707        Sport-100 Helmet, Red     35                Helmets
708        Sport-100 Helmet, Black   35                Helmets
709        Mountain Bike Socks, M    27                Socks
...
```

Listing 11-7 shows a *LEFT OUTER JOIN*. We are looking for the correct description (*SalesLT.ProductModelProductDescription*) of the product models (*SalesLT.ProductModel*). The result must show all product models. With an *INNER JOIN*, only the models with a description would be listed. As the Listing shows, the model *Rear Brakes* has no description: the values are filled in with *NULL*.

LISTING 11-7 *LEFT OUTER JOIN* of two tables.

```
SELECT Name AS ModelName, Culture, ProductDescriptionID
FROM SalesLT.ProductModel AS pm LEFT JOIN SalesLT.ProductModelProductDescription AS pd
ON pm.ProductModelID = pd.ProductModelID
WHERE pm.Name like 'Rear%';
GO
```

```
Model  Name           Culture  ProductDescriptionID
-----  -------------  -------  --------------------
Rear   Brakes         NULL     NULL
Rear   Derailleur     en       2005
Rear   Derailleur     ar       2006
...
```

You can also use *JOIN* to link tables to themselves or to more than two tables in one query. Listing 11-8 shows that to link the address info (*SalesLT.Address*) with the customer data (*SalesLT.Customer*), the table *SalesLT.CustomerAddress* must be included because it is the link between the two tables. You can picture the *JOIN* process as taking place in two steps: in the first step the tables *SalesLT.Customer* and *SalesLT.CustomerAddress* are linked; in the second step the resulting table is linked to *SalesLT.Address*. Because *INNER JOIN* is used, the result only lists customers who have a new address.

LISTING 11-8 *JOIN* of three tables.

```
SELECT c.CustomerID, c.FirstName, c.LastName, a.City, a.PostalCode
FROM SalesLT.Customer AS c
JOIN SalesLT.CustomerAddress AS ca ON c.CustomerID = ca.CustomerID
JOIN SalesLT.Address AS a ON a.AddressID = ca.AddressID;
GO

CustomerID  FirstName   LastName      City          PostalCode
----------  ----------  ------------  ------------  ----------
29485       Catherine   Abel          Van Nuys      91411
29486       Kim         Abercrombie   Branch        55056
29489       Frances     Adams         Modesto       95354
...
```

Subqueries

A subquery nests *SELECT* queries inside another *SELECT* query. Usually a query is used to find values, and the columns are checked for those values (keywords *IN, ANY, ALL*).

Listing 11-9 shows a nested *SELECT* query that finds all product categories belonging to sub-category 3. The outer *SELECT* query finds all products that belong to these categories (link with *IN*). Subqueries of this kind can frequently be converted into the corresponding *JOIN* queries.

LISTING 11-9 An example of a Subquery.

```
SELECT ProductID, Name
FROM SalesLT.Product
WHERE ProductCategoryID IN
    ( SELECT ProductCategoryID
      FROM SalesLT.ProductCategory
      WHERE ParentProductCategoryID = 3
    );
GO


ProductID   Name
----------- ----------------------------
709         Mountain Bike Socks, M
710         Mountain Bike Socks, L
712         AWC Logo Cap
...
```

A nested *SELECT* query may also depend on the outer query. Listing 11-10 shows such a situation. The inner query refers to the outer *SELECT* query (check for identical entries with *sod.SalesOrderID*) in the *WHERE* clause. The inner query determines the maximum of *OrderQty* for each row of the outer query. To determine the name of the most frequently used product, a *JOIN* with the tables *SalesLT.SalesOrderDetail* and *SalesLT.Product* is made.

LISTING 11-10 A dependent *SELECT* subquery.

```
SELECT soh.SalesOrderID, soh.TotalDue,
       p.Name, sod.LineTotal, sod.LineTotal/soh.SubTotal*100 AS PercentOfSubTotal
FROM SalesLT.SalesOrderHeader AS soh
JOIN SalesLT.SalesOrderDetail AS sod ON sod.SalesOrderID = soh.SalesOrderID
JOIN SalesLT.Product AS p ON p.ProductID = sod.ProductID
WHERE sod.OrderQty =
    ( SELECT max(sod2.OrderQty)
      FROM SalesLT.SalesOrderDetail as sod2
      WHERE sod2.SalesOrderID = sod.SalesOrderID
    );
GO


SalesOrderID  TotalDue     Name                            LineTotal   PercentOfSubTotal
------------- ------------ ------------------------------- ----------  -----------------
71774           972,7850  ML Road Frame-W - Yellow, 48    356.8980    40.5405
71774           972,7850  ML Road Frame-W - Yellow, 38    356.8980    40.5405
71776            87,0851  Rear Brakes                      63.9000    81.0810
71780         42452,6519  Women's Mountain Shorts, L      293.9580     0.7651
...
```

Common Table Expressions (*WITH*)

SQL Server provides a practical and powerful feature for SQL queries: the *common table expressions* (CTE). CTEs can be used to create temporary views and tables. They are defined by using the keyword *WITH* before the *SELECT* query itself.

Simple Expressions

Listing 11-11 shows an application with only one original table. A temporary view/table is defined by using the keyword *WITH* which lists the sum of the orders by *SalesOrderID*. In the *SELECT* expression, the generated table can be accessed just like a regular table. It is not necessary to specify a schema, because the table is only defined in the context of this query.

LISTING 11-11 Defining a common table expression by using *WITH*.

```
WITH OrderQtys (SalesOrderID, SumOrderQty) AS (
    SELECT SalesOrderID, sum(OrderQty)
    FROM SalesLT.SalesOrderDetail
    GROUP BY SalesOrderID
)
SELECT avg(SumOrderQty) AS AvgSumOrderQty FROM OrderQtys;
GO


AvgSumOrderQty
--------------
65
```

Listing 11-12 shows how the query from Listing 11-10 might look with a CTE. By using *WITH*, the view *ProductDetail* is generated, which merges all the required data from the three tables *SalesLT.SalesOrderHeader*, *SalesLT.SalesOrderDetail*, and *SalesLT.Product*. The actual *SELECT* query then only selects those rows whose *OrderQty* corresponds to the maximum that is specified in the subquery.

LISTING 11-12 A CTE with multiple tables.

```
WITH ProductDetail (SalesOrderID, TotalDue, Name,
                    LineTotal, PercentOfSubTotal, OrderQty) AS (
    SELECT soh.SalesOrderID, soh.TotalDue, p.Name, sod.LineTotal,
           sod.LineTotal/soh.SubTotal*100, sod.OrderQty
    FROM SalesLT.SalesOrderHeader AS soh
    JOIN SalesLT.SalesOrderDetail AS sod ON sod.SalesOrderID = soh.SalesOrderID
    JOIN SalesLT.Product AS p ON p.ProductID = sod.ProductID
)
```

```
SELECT SalesOrderID, TotalDue, Name, LineTotal, PercentOfSubTotal,
FROM ProductDetail AS pd
WHERE pd.OrderQty =
    ( SELECT max(pd2.OrderQty)
      FROM ProductDetail AS pd2
      WHERE pd2.SalesOrderID = pd.SalesOrderID
    );
GO
```

Recursive Expressions

A special feature of CTEs is that they can be used recursively. This means that the table expression can reference itself in the expression definition.

In Listing 11-13, all product categories belonging to the products with the *ProductID* 706 and 707 must be returned. The product categories are organized in hierarchical order and contain a reference to the parent category (*ParentProductCategoryID*). The definition of the CTE *ProductInfo* is composed of two parts:

- **Starting expression**   The first *SELECT* initializes *ProductInfo* with the desired values from *SalesLT.Product*.

- **Recursive expression**   Extends the dataset (*UNION ALL*) with the rows of the immediate parent category (*JOIN* with selection of *ParentProductCategoryID*).

The definition is iterated through repeatedly until no more new rows are added to the CTE. This means that beginning with a product category, each iteration adds the next parent category until the entire category hierarchy has been added all the way to the root.

The *SELECT* expression then selects the rows for the products 706 and 707, and adds the category name by using a *JOIN*. In the result, you can see that both products are part of a two-level category hierarchy.

LISTING 11-13 A recursively defined CTE.

```
WITH ProductInfo (ProductID, ProductName, CategoryID) AS (
    SELECT ProductID, Name, ProductCategoryID
    FROM SalesLT.Product
    UNION ALL -- recrusive table extension
    SELECT ProductID, ProductName, ParentProductCategoryID
    FROM ProductInfo
    JOIN SalesLT.ProductCategory ON CategoryID = ProductCategoryID
)
```

```
SELECT ProductID, ProductName, CategoryID, Name
FROM ProductInfo
JOIN SalesLT.ProductCategory ON CategoryID = ProductCategoryID
WHERE ProductID=706 or ProductID=707
ORDER BY ProductID, CategoryID;
GO
```

```
ProductID   ProductName                   CategoryID  Name
----------  ------------------------      ----------  -----------
706         HL Road Frame - Red, 58       2           Components
706         HL Road Frame - Red, 58       18          Road Frames
707         Sport-100 Helmet, Red         4           Accessories
707         Sport-100 Helmet, Red         35          Helmets
```

Tip Change the table *SalesLT.ProductCategory* as follows (the changes don't have any effect on the examples later on in this chapter.):

`UPDATE SalesLT.ProductCategory SET ParentProductCategoryID=23 WHERE ProductCategoryID=35`

Then run the query from Listing 11-13 again and compare the results: product 707 is now part of a three-level hierarchy.

Paging Through Data

A frequent requirement in web applications is to show tables with many entries in page views. The lists are usually restricted to 10, 20, 50, or 100 entries, and the user can click links to page forward or backward through the data.

TOP()

To limit the result of a *SELECT* query to a certain number of rows, you can use the function *TOP()*, as shown in Listing 11-14.

LISTING 11-14 Using *TOP()* to limit the number of lines in the result.

```
SELECT TOP(5) ProductID, Name
FROM SalesLT.Product
ORDER BY ProductID;
GO

ProductID   Name
----------- -------------------------
680         HL Road Frame - Black, 58
706         HL Road Frame - Red, 58
707         Sport-100 Helmet, Red
708         Sport-100 Helmet, Black
709         Mountain Bike Socks, M
```

For the next five entries, the PHP application remembers the highest *ProductID* and can retrieve the next five entries by constraining the query with *WHERE ProductID > 709*.

When using this option, you need to take some detours to find the previous five entries in the current result list: the sort order must be reversed and then set correctly in the PHP application. With a CTE, you can do the same directly in SQL Server, as shown in Listing 11-15. The table expression *Product* selects the five previous entries beginning at a certain position (in the listing, *ProductID=910*). Then they are put into the desired sort order.

LISTING 11-15 Paging backward by using *TOP()* and a CTE.

```
WITH Product (ProductID, Name) AS (
    SELECT TOP(5) ProductID, Name
    FROM SalesLT.Product
    WHERE ProductID < 910
    ORDER BY ProductID DESC
)
SELECT *
FROM Product
ORDER BY ProductID;
GO

ProductID   Name
----------- --------------------------------
905         ML Mountain Frame-W - Silver, 42
906         ML Mountain Frame-W - Silver, 46
907         Rear Brakes
908         LL Mountain Seat/Saddle
909         ML Mountain Seat/Saddle
```

ROW_NUMBER()

Using the function *ROW_NUMBER()* is a more flexible method for paging through data. It assigns a unique sequential number to each row in the result. In addition, the numbering can also be used for sorting.

Listing 11-16 shows how you can use *ROW_NUMBER()* to list products page by page, which are sorted by list price. In the table expression *Product*, the row number is defined by the sort, by descending list price. In the *SELECT* expression, the rows 21 to 25 are selected. Restricting them by using the defined column *RowNum* is easier than using *TOP()*, because paging forward or backward can use the same query.

LISTING 11-16 Paging through data by using *ROW_NUMBER()*.

```
WITH Product (ProductID, Name, ListPrice, RowNum) AS (
    SELECT ProductID, Name, ListPrice,
            ROW_NUMBER() OVER (ORDER BY ListPrice DESC)
    FROM SalesLT.Product
)
SELECT *
FROM Product
WHERE RowNum BETWEEN 21 AND 25;
GO


ProductID   Name                        ListPrice   RowNum
----------- --------------------------- ----------- ------
795         Road-250 Black, 52          2443.3500   20
796         Road-250 Black, 58          2443.3500   21
954         Touring-1000 Yellow, 46     2384.0700   22
955         Touring-1000 Yellow, 50     2384.0700   23
956         Touring-1000 Yellow, 54     2384.0700   24
```

Tip The upcoming SQL Server 2011 provides the following new syntax for paging data:

```
SELECT (column list) FROM (table) WHERE (expression)
ORDER BY (sort order)
OFFSET (amount) ROWS
FETCH NEXT (amount) ROWS ONLY
```

With *OFFSET*, you can specify how many rows should be skipped. With *FETCH*, you specify how many rows should be fetched. The amount given can either be a number or an expression. For details, take a look at the documentation on MSDN at *http://msdn.microsoft.com/en-us/library/ms188385%28v=SQL.110%29.aspx*.

Manipulating Data

T-SQL provides three basic operations for changing data: inserting new data with *INSERT*, changing or updating data with *UPDATE*, and deleting data with *DELETE*. In the following, you will find a brief description of these operations. You will also learn how you can manipulate data by using SQL Server Management Studio (SSMS).

The *INSERT* Command

The T-SQL *INSERT* command is used to insert data into a table. In its simplified form, it has the following syntax:

```
INSERT [ INTO ] <object>
{
  [ ( column_list ) ]
  [ <OUTPUT Clause> ]
   { VALUES ( { DEFAULT | NULL | expression } [ ,...n ] ) [ ,...n ]
     | DEFAULT VALUES }
}
[; ]
```

For example, to insert new product categories into the *AdventureWorks* database, run the command from Listing 11-17. The columns are specified in the second line. If you fill all columns in table order, you don't need to specify them. Because in the listing the column *ProductCategoryID* is not explicitly filled, as the category number is generated and assigned automatically (column type *IDENTITY*), the columns must be specified. The keyword *VALUES* is followed by the rows to insert. If columns have default values, the default value can be set explicitly by using *DEFAULT*, as you can see in the second line.

LISTING 11-17 Inserting new product categories by using *INSERT*.

```
INSERT INTO SalesLT.ProductCategory
( ParentProductCategoryID, Name, rowguid, ModifiedDate )
VALUES
( 37, N'Rear Lights', newid(), CURRENT_TIMESTAMP ),
( 37, N'Front Lights', DEFAULT, DEFAULT );
```

Default Values

If you don't specify any columns during the insert operation, they are automatically filled with default values. Because the default values for the columns *rowguid* and *ModifiedDate* correspond exactly to the values inserted in Listing 11-17, the simplified version of the *INSERT* command could have been written as follows:

```
INSERT INTO SalesLT.ProductCategory ( ParentProductCategoryID, Name ) VALUES
( 37, N'Rear Lights' ),
( 37, N'Front Lights' );
```

If default values are defined for all columns and you want to insert a row with only default values, you can use the following statement:

```
INSERT INTO myTable DEFAULT VALUES;
```

The *OUTPUT* Clause

You can use the *OUTPUT* clause to retrieve the rows that you just inserted. This function is especially useful if you want to ensure that the default values you are using are immediately available for further processing. In Listing 11-18, the *OUTPUT* clause is used to retrieve the category number, GUID, and date. The columns you want to output need the prefix *INSERTED*, because they come from the automatically-generated table *inserted*.

LISTING 11-18 Output of inserted values with the *OUTPUT* clause.

```
INSERT INTO SalesLT.ProductCategory ( ParentProductCategoryID, Name )
OUTPUT INSERTED.ProductCategoryID, INSERTED.rowguid, INSERTED.ModifiedDate
VALUES
( 37, N'Rear Lights' ),
( 37, N'Front Lights' );
GO

ProductCategoryID rowguid                              ModifiedDate
----------------- ------------------------------------ -----------------------
42                0E0492E9-ADB6-4597-A697-A6104002DD0E 2011-09-20 13:25:54.650
43                1FAEFCB7-C279-42BB-ACBD-933D360937EC 2011-09-20 13:25:54.650
```

Inserting by Using SSMS

To insert a table by using SSMS, perform the following procedure:

1. In the SSMS Object Explorer, right-click the desired table, and then in the context menu, click Edit Top 200 Rows.

2. In the work area, scroll to the last row, and then enter the column values.

    Figure 11-1 shows the entries for Rear Lights and Front Lights. As soon as you finish your entries by clicking Enter (or if you move to a different field by clicking it or pressing the Tab key), the currently edited row is added to the database. The red marking lets you know that view is not correct, due to the automatic insertion of default values.

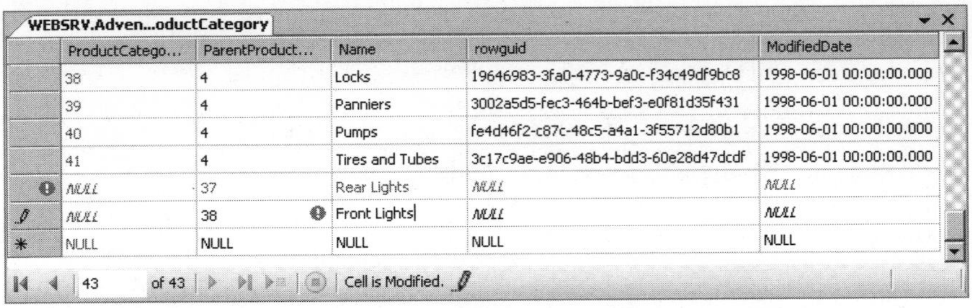

FIGURE 11-1 Inserting new rows by using SQL Server Management Studio.

3. To see the current values, click the Run SQL icon (the red exclamation mark) in the toolbar.

The *UPDATE* Command

The T-SQL *UPDATE* command is used to change existing datasets:

```
UPDATE <object>
SET { column_name = { expression | DEFAULT | NULL }
| column_name { += | -= | *= | /= | %= | &= | ^= | |= } expression
} [ ,...n ]
[ <OUTPUT Clause> ]
[ FROM{ <table_source> } [ ,...n ] ] [ WHERE { <search_condition> } ]
[ ; ]
```

Listing 11-19 shows a typical situation. The address in a *SalesLT.Address* entry is changed. The first line specifies the table, the second line the columns that you want to change, and the third uses a *WHERE* clause to limit the corresponding rows.

> **Caution** Without a *WHERE* clause, all rows of a table are affected by *UPDATE*, but you usually only want to change entries in defined rows.

LISTING 11-19 Changing a dataset by using *UPDATE*.

```
UPDATE SalesLT.Address
SET AddressLine1=N'The Farm', AddressLine2=N'Hamster Road 6'
WHERE AddressID=660;
GO
```

You can use the *OUTPUT* keyword to output the data of the specified rows.

Specifying Which Rows to Change

The *WHERE* clause for specifying the rows you want to change can be used just like the *WHERE* clause for querying data with *SELECT*. You can also link multiple tables to select the rows that you want to change by using *FROM* in the command. *UPDATE* can also be used with CTEs (*WITH*).

Listing 11-20 shows how *FROM* is used with multiple tables. With *JOIN*, all rows in *SalesLT* *.Product* are selected that are part of the parent category 3 (*Clothing*). In these rows, the list price is incremented by 10% (*ListPrice *= 1.1*).

LISTING 11-20 Using multiple tables (*FROM*) for specifying the rows that need to be changed.

```
UPDATE SalesLT.Product
SET ListPrice *= 1.1
FROM SalesLT.Product AS p
JOIN SalesLT.ProductCategory AS pc ON p.ProductCategoryID = pc.ProductCategoryID
WHERE pc.ParentProductCategoryID = 3;
GO
```

The *OUTPUT* clause

The *OUTPUT* clause can be used to return the changed values before and after the *UPDATE* command. The automatically-generated *INSERTED* table contains the new values after the changes, and the *DELETED* table contains the original values before the changes.

In Listing 11-21, a CTE (*WITH*) is used in addition to the *OUTPUT* clause. The table expression *ProductSellDate* is a join of *SalesLT.Product* and *SalesLT.ProductCategory*. It contains the product number, the sale end date, and the parent product category. In the *UPDATE* expression, the *ProductID* and the *EndDate* (=*SalesLT.Product.SellEndDate*) before and after the change are returned with the *OUTPUT* clause.

LISTING 11-21 Returning changed values by using *OUTPUT*.

```
WITH ProductSellDate (ProductID, EndDate, ParentCategory) AS (
    SELECT p.ProductID, p.SellEndDate, pc.ParentProductCategoryID
    FROM SalesLT.Product AS p
    JOIN SalesLT.ProductCategory AS pc ON p.ProductCategoryID = pc.ProductCategoryID
)
UPDATE ProductSellDate
SET EndDate=CURRENT_TIMESTAMP
OUTPUT INSERTED.ProductID, DELETED.EndDate AS EndDateBefore,
       INSERTED.EndDate AS EndDateAfter
WHERE ParentCategory=4;
GO

ProductID   EndDateBefore           EndDateAfter
----------- ----------------------- -----------------------
707         NULL                    2011-07-20 18:24:58.450
708         NULL                    2011-07-20 18:24:58.450
711         NULL                    2011-07-20 18:24:58.450
842         2003-06-30 00:00:00.000 2011-07-20 18:24:58.450
843         2003-06-30 00:00:00.000 2011-07-20 18:24:58.450
```

Changing Values by Using SSMS

To change values in tables by using SSMS, perform the following procedure:

1. In the SSMS Object Explorer, right-click the desired table, and then in the context menu, click Edit Top 200 Rows.

2. In the work area, scroll to the desired row. Click the column that you want to change and enter the new value.

   You can press the Tab key to move to the next column. Press the Enter key to save the changes to the row in the database.

3. If the row is not located in the range of the 200 displayed rows, you can change the range in two ways (see step 1 in Figure 11-2).

   - Show the criteria by clicking the Show Criteria Pane icon

   - Show the SQL query by clicking the Show SQL Pane icon

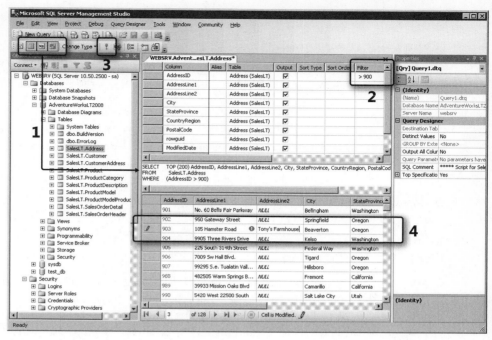

FIGURE 11-2 Changing the editing area in SSMS.

4. Enter the criteria for the editing area (step 2 in Figure 11-2), and then click the Run SQL icon (step 3).

5. You can now change columns as usual in the result pane by clicking them and adding them to the database by pressing the Enter key (step 4 in Figure 11-2).

The *DELETE* Command

The T-SQL *DELETE* command is used to delete data from a table. *DELETE* has a syntax similar to *UPDATE*:

```
DELETE [ FROM ] <object> [ <OUTPUT Clause> ]
[ FROM <table_source> [ ,...n ] ]
[ WHERE <search_condition> ]
[; ]
```

Listing 11-22 shows how to use the *DELETE* command to delete a customer from the table *SalesLT.Customer*.

LISTING 11-22 Deleting a dataset by using *DELETE*.

```
DELETE FROM SalesLT.Customer
WHERE CustomerID = 474;
GO
```

> **Caution**   Once datasets are deleted, they are gone for good. They can only be restored if you
> have performed a database backup beforehand (or partially via transaction logs with special
> tools). You cannot directly undo the action.

During a delete operation, you can specify multiple tables by using the *FROM* clause (as with
UPDATE) or define CTEs by using *WITH*.

Errors During Deletion

The deletion of rows can fail due to constraints (for example, foreign keys in a different table).
In this case, the dependent rows in the other tables must be deleted beforehand or the reference to the row that you want to delete must be removed (by setting it to *NULL* or another
valid value). Foreign keys offer three options for automatic deletion: *SET NULL*, *SET DEFAULT*,
and *CASCADE* (see the section "Foreign Keys," in Chapter 10, "Databases and Tables").

Listing 11-23 shows how deleting can fail due to a foreign key relationship: a customer
(*CustomerID=29906*) cannot be deleted because there is an associated address, as the
SELECT command shows. When trying to delete the data record, an error message is
displayed.

LISTING 11-23 The deletion of a dataset fails due to a foreign key relationship.

```
SELECT CustomerID, AddressID FROM SalesLT.CustomerAddress WHERE CustomerID=29906;
GO

CustomerID  AddressID
----------- -----------
29906       600
(1 rows affected)

DELETE FROM SalesLT.Customer WHERE CustomerID = 29906;
GO

Msg 547, Level 16, State 0, Line 1
The DELETE statement conflicted with the REFERENCE constraint "FK_CustomerAddress_
Customer_CustomerID". The conflict occurred in database "AdventureWorksLT2008", table
"SalesLT.CustomerAddress", column 'CustomerID'.
The statement has been terminated.
```

If you choose the foreign key relationship in such a way that, for example, during deletion linked data records are also deleted, no error occurs. Listing 11-24 shows the old foreign key being deleted by using *ALTER TABLE* and the new one created exactly the same way, but instead using *ON DELETE CASCADE*.

> **Note** If you specify *WITH NOCHECK*, the constraint for existing rows is not checked. The newly created foreign key relationship is identical to the old one. This saves resources, because existing rows no longer need to be checked. Newly inserted or changed rows are not affected.

If you now delete the customer from the table *SalesLT.Customer*, the entry in the table *SalesLT.CustomerAddress* is also deleted.

LISTING 11-24 Cascading deletion of datasets.

```
ALTER TABLE SalesLT.CustomerAddress
DROP CONSTRAINT [FK_CustomerAddress_Customer_CustomerID];

ALTER TABLE SalesLT.CustomerAddress
WITH NOCHECK ADD CONSTRAINT [FK_CustomerAddress_Customer_CustomerID]
FOREIGN KEY (CustomerID)
REFERENCES SalesLT.Customer (CustomerID)
ON DELETE CASCADE;
GO

DELETE FROM SalesLT.Customer WHERE CustomerID = 29906;
GO
```

Deleting All Rows of a Table

If you don't specify a *WHERE* clause when deleting a table, all rows are deleted. To completely delete all rows, you can use the *TRUNCATE TABLE* command:

```
TRUNCATE TABLE table_name;
```

The advantage of the *TRUNCATE* command is that it is more efficient and uses fewer resources than the *DELETE* command. The counter for *IDENTITY* columns is reset to the start value (or 1).

Deleting by Using SSMS

With SSMS, you can delete datasets from a table, as long as they are not subject to a constraint, or referenced by a foreign key. To delete datasets, perform the following procedure:

1. Start SSMS.

2. In Object Explorer, right-click the desired table, and then in the context menu, click Edit Top 200 Rows.

3. Select the rows that you want to delete by clicking them (or using Ctrl+click) in the gray area to the left of the rows.

4. In the Edit menu, click Delete. Click Yes to confirm the dialog box (see Figure 11-3).

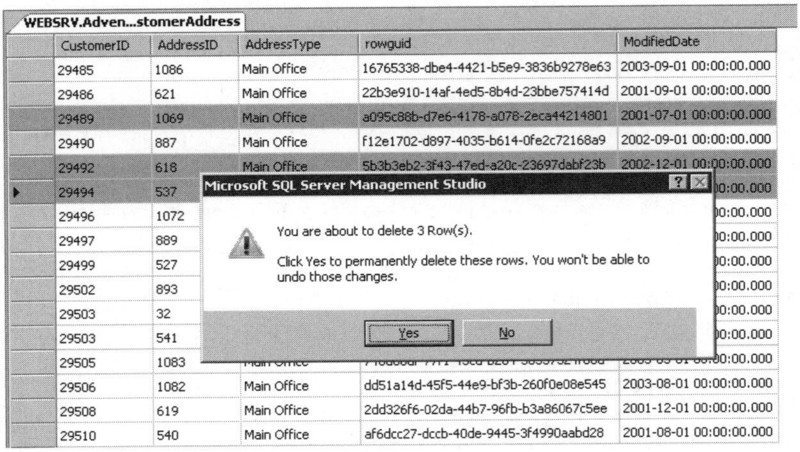

FIGURE 11-3 Deleting rows by using SSMS.

If the rows you want to delete are not displayed in the result pane, you can define the criteria according to the sections "Changing Values by Using SSMS," earlier in the chapter, to achieve the desired row selection in the result pane.

Querying Metadata

When working with databases and tables, you frequently need information about data types as well as the types, names, number of table columns, and other information about the database schema. SQL Server provides two possibilities to retrieve these metadata: via pre-defined T-SQL procedures, and via querying the tables of the information schema.

Listing Databases

You can use the *sp_databases* procedure to retrieve a list of all databases of the SQL Server instance, including their size, as shown in the following:

```
EXECUTE sp_databases;
GO

DATABASE_NAME           DATABASE_SIZE  REMARKS
----------------------  -------------  -------
AdventureWorksLT2008    9016           NULL
master                  5376           NULL
model                   3072           NULL
msdb                    18752          NULL
tempdb                  8704           NULL
```

The size of the current database can also be queried by using *sp_spaceused*. You can retrieve more information about databases, such as the exact status and owners, by using the command *sp_helpdb*:

```
EXECUTE sp_helpdb;
GO

name                  db_size owner                  dbid created
--------------------- ------- ---------------------- ---- -----------
AdventureWorksLT2008  8.80 MB WEBSRV\Administrator    9   Jun 14 2011
...
status
---------------------------------------------------------------------------------
Status=ONLINE, Updateability=READ_WRITE, UserAccess=MULTI_USER, Recovery=SIMPLE,
Version=655, Collation=SQL_Latin1_General_CP1_CI_AS, SQLSortOrder=52, IsAnsiNullsEnabled,
IsAnsiPaddingEnabled, IsAnsiWarningsEnabled, IsArithmeticAbortEnabled,
IsAutoCreateStatistics, IsAutoUpdateStatistics, IsFullTextEnabled, IsNullConcat,
IsQuotedIdentifiersEnabled
...
```

Alternatively, you can retrieve names and status of databases from the *sysdatabases* table:

```
SELECT name, status, status2 FROM master..sysdatabases;
GO
```

Listing Tables

You can use the *sp_tables* procedure to list all tables in a database:

```
EXECUTE sp_tables;
GO

TABLE_QUALIFIER       TABLE_OWNER TABLE_NAME       TABLE_TYPE REMARKS
--------------------- ----------- ---------------- ---------- -------
AdventureWorksLT2008  SalesLT     Address          TABLE      NULL
AdventureWorksLT2008  SalesLT     Customer         TABLE      NULL
AdventureWorksLT2008  SalesLT     CustomerAddress  TABLE      NULL
...
```

The list with *sp_tables*, however, contains all system tables and views as well. If you want to display only the custom tables, you can use the following *SELECT* query:

```
SELECT name, crdate, USER_NAME(uid) AS username FROM sysobjects WHERE type='U';
GO
```

Alternatively, you can fall back on the information schema:

```
SELECT * FROM INFORMATION_SCHEMA.TABLES;
GO
```

TABLE_CATALOG	TABLE_SCHEMA	TABLE_NAME	TABLE_TYPE
AdventureWorksLT2008	dbo	BuildVersion	BASE TABLE
AdventureWorksLT2008	SalesLT	Address	BASE TABLE
AdventureWorksLT2008	SalesLT	Customer	BASE TABLE
...			

Retrieving Table Information

Detailed information about tables can be retrieved by using the *sp_help* procedure. For example:

```
EXECUTE sp_help [SalesLT.Product];
GO
```

The output is distributed into several result lists:

- Specifications about table owner and creation date
- Description of the columns
- Use of *IDENTITY* and *GUID*
- File groups used by the table
- Indexes
- Constraints (*CONSTRAINT*)
- References of foreign keys and views

You can retrieve the size of tables by using *sp_spaceused*, as demonstrated in the following:

```
EXECUTE sp_spaceused [SalesLT.SalesOrderHeader];
GO
```

name	rows	reserved	data	index_size	unused
SalesOrderHeader	32	64 KB	8 KB	56 KB	0 KB

Listing the Columns of a Table

To list the columns of a table, you can run the command *sp_help*, as illustrated here:

```
EXECUTE sp_help [SalesLT.Product];
GO
```

An alternative procedure is *sp_columns*:

```
EXECUTE sp_columns @table_name='Product', @table_owner='SalesLT';
GO
```

sp_help and *sp_columns* provide very comprehensive information. To only list the column names of a table, you can use the following *SELECT* command:

```
SELECT name FROM syscolumns WHERE id=OBJECT_ID('SalesLT.Product');
GO
```

Alternatively, you can fall back on the information schema:

```
SELECT COLUMN_NAME, DATA_TYPE, COLUMN_DEFAULT, IS_NULLABLE
FROM INFORMATION_SCHEMA.COLUMNS
WHERE TABLE_NAME=N'Address' AND TABLE_SCHEMA=N'SalesLT';
GO
```

Listing Constraints

You can use the *sp_helpconstraint* command to display all constraints of a table:

```
EXECUTE sp_helpconstraint [SalesLT.Product]; GO
```

The command returns three result lists:

- Name of the object
- Constraints (*UNIQUE, CHECK, PRIMARY KEY*, and *FOREIGN KEY*, among others)
- Foreign keys which reference this table

Alternatively, you can query the information schema for constraints:

```
SELECT CONSTRAINT_NAME, CONSTRAINT_TYPE
FROM INFORMATION_SCHEMA.TABLE_CONSTRAINTS
WHERE TABLE_SCHEMA=N'SalesLT' AND TABLE_NAME=N'CustomerAddress';
GO
```

Listing Keys and Indexes

To list the primary key columns in a table, you can use the *sp_pkeys* procedure:

```
EXECUTE sp_pkeys @table_owner='SalesLT', @table_name='Product';
GO
```

```
TABLE_QUALIFIER       TABLE_OWNER TABLE_NAME COLUMN_NAME KEY_SEQ PK_NAME
--------------------- ----------- ---------- ----------- ------- --------------------
AdventureWorksLT2008 SalesLT      Product    ProductID   1       PK_Product_ProductID
```

You can also use the *sp_fkeys* procedure for listing foreign keys:

```
EXECUTE sp_fkeys @fktable_owner='SalesLT', @fktable_name='Product';
GO
```

You can also retrieve information about the keys from the information schema:

```
SELECT CONSTRAINT_SCHEMA, CONSTRAINT_NAME, COLUMN_NAME
FROM INFORMATION_SCHEMA.KEY_COLUMN_USAGE
WHERE TABLE_SCHEMA=N'SalesLT' AND TABLE_NAME=N'Product';
GO
```

The *sp_helpindex* procedure lists indexes in a table, including the indexes belonging to keys:

```
EXECUTE sp_helpindex [SalesLT.Product];
GO
```

```
index_name                 index_description                                           index_keys
-------------------------- ----------------------------------------------------------- --------------
AK_Product_Name            nonclustered, unique, unique key located on PRIMARY          Name
AK_Product_ProductNumber   nonclustered, unique, unique key located on PRIMARY          ProductNumber
AK_Product_rowguid         nonclustered, unique, unique key located on PRIMARY          rowguid
PK_Product_ProductID       clustered, unique, primary key located on PRIMARY            ProductID
```

Summary

In this chapter, you were introduced to the four basic T-SQL statements for data manipulation and data query: *SELECT, INSERT, UPDATE,* and *DELETE*. You also learned about advanced features, such as the CTEs, paging through data, and the *OUTPUT* clause. For querying metadata of the database schema, you learned how to access information such as foreign keys, table definitions, and memory requirements of databases by using stored procedures and system tables.

Chapter 12, "PHP and SQL Server," builds upon this chapter and the statements, functions, and features described in Chapter 10, and will teach you about SQL Server programming with PHP. You will learn how to build a database connection, how to start database queries, and how to convert data types between PHP and SQL Server.

Chapter 12
PHP and SQL Server

In this chapter, you will learn how to access data in Microsoft SQL Server from PHP. We will describe how the basic functions of an SQL Server PHP extension are processed, how your choice of the user who connects to the database affects the connection pooling, and how you can prevent SQL injection with parameterized statements. You will also learn how the conversion of different data types between PHP and SQL Server functions. Starting with version 2.0, the SQL Server extension also supports PHP Data Objects (PDO). We will discuss PDO toward the end of the chapter, but first we have a look at the native applications programming interface (API), because it provides a richer and more powerful set of options and commands.

Approach and Process

Accessing SQL Server from PHP always follows the same process: open the database connection, send a Transact-SQL (T-SQL) statement, read and retrieve results, and finally, close the database connection again. We'll be using a sample program to describe this process and the required functions.

Preparations

To be able to run the sample program successfully, you must have the SQL Server PHP extension and the *AdventureWorksLT2008* sample database installed on your computer (see Chapter 9, "Setting Up SQL Server").

You also need a valid logon for the sample database. In the example, the logon is done by the current Windows user of the PHP application. The various authentication methods are described in the section "Authentication," later in this chapter. Chapter 14, "Users and Permissions," shows you how to set up users and logons in SQL Server and grant rights.

If the database is not located on the computer that runs the PHP script, you also need to ensure that you have set up remote access to SQL Server and that it works properly (see Chapter 9).

The Sample Program

Listing 12-1 shows the sample program product_list.php. This program contains all the essential steps for using SQL Server from PHP:

- Opening the database connection
- Sending a T-SQL command; retrieving the reply
- Closing the database connection

The section "An Overview of the Individual Steps," later in the chapter, describes the functionality of the individual program steps in more detail. You can find the PHP script we are using (utils.php) in the section "Supporting Script," also later in the chapter.

LISTING 12-1 product_list.php—listing the Adventure Works products.

```
<!DOCTYPE html>
<html>
<head>
    <title>Adventure Works : Products</title>
    <style type="text/css">
        th { font-size: 110%; border-bottom: 2px solid black; }
        td { padding: 3px; border-bottom: 1px solid #aaa }
    </style>
</head>
<body>
<h1>Adventure Works : Products</h1>
<table>
<?php
require './utils.php';
// Connect via Windows authentication
$server = '(local)';
$connectionInfo = array('Database' => 'AdventureWorksLT2008',
                        'CharacterSet' => 'UTF-8');
$db = sqlsrv_connect($server, $connectionInfo);
if ($db === false) {
    exitWithSQLError('Database connection failed');
}
```

```php
// Select products by name, list price, and category
$query = "SELECT p.ProductID, p.Name AS ProductName, p.ListPrice,
                 pc.Name AS CategoryName
          FROM SalesLT.Product AS p
          JOIN SalesLT.ProductCategory AS pc
          ON p.ProductCategoryID = pc.ProductCategoryID
          ORDER BY p.Name";
// Run query
$qresult = sqlsrv_query($db, $query);
if ($qresult === false) {
    exitWithSQLError('Query of product data failed.');
}
echo '<tr><th>ID</th><th>Product</th><th>Category</th><th>List price</th></tr>';
// Retrieve individual rows from the result
while ($row = sqlsrv_fetch_array($qresult)) {
    echo '<tr><td>', htmlspecialchars($row['ProductID']),
         '</td><td>', htmlspecialchars($row['ProductName']),
         '</td><td>', htmlspecialchars($row['CategoryName']),
         '</td><td>', htmlspecialchars($row['ListPrice']),
         "</td></tr>\n";
}
// null == no further rows, false == error
if ($row === false) {
    exitWithSQLError('Retrieving product data entry failed.');
}
// Release statement resource and close connection
sqlsrv_free_stmt($qresult);
sqlsrv_close($db);
?>
</table>
</body>
</html>
```

Figure 12-1 shows the output of product_list.php. The products, their identification numbers, names, categories, and list prices are returned as a sorted list.

Note If you receive an error message from SQL Server, verify that you meet all the requirements for the PHP/SQL Server binding. Missing rights frequently cause errors.

ID	Product	Category	List price
879	All-Purpose Bike Stand	Bike Stands	159.0000
712	AWC Logo Cap	Caps	8.9900
877	Bike Wash - Dissolver	Cleaners	7.9500
843	Cable Lock	Locks	25.0000
952	Chain	Chains	20.2400
866	Classic Vest, L	Vests	63.5000
865	Classic Vest, M	Vests	63.5000
864	Classic Vest, S	Vests	63.5000
878	Fender Set - Mountain	Fenders	21.9800
948	Front Brakes	Brakes	106.5000
945	Front Derailleur	Derailleurs	91.4900
863	Full-Finger Gloves, L	Gloves	37.9900

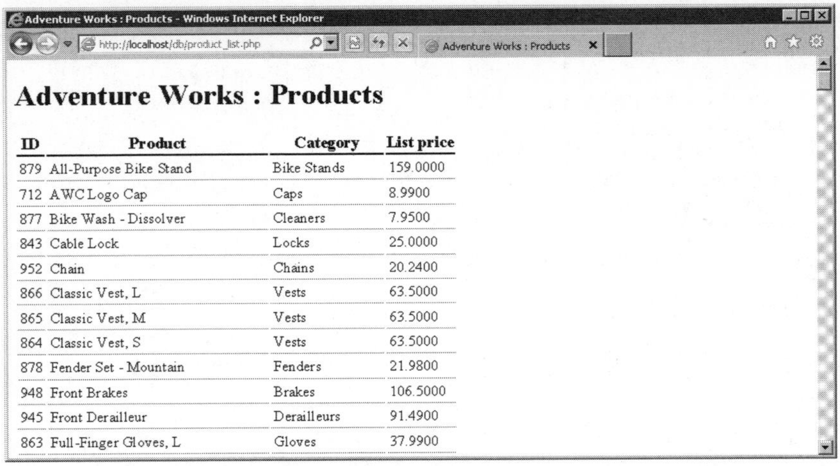

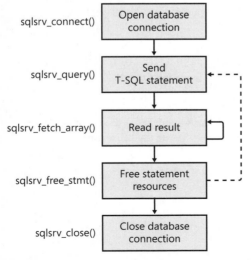

FIGURE 12-1 The Adventure Works product output with product_list.php.

An Overview of the Individual Steps

Let's take a look at the individual steps of the sample program from Listing 12-1 in a bit more detail. Each PHP program that reads or writes data from SQL Server basically goes through the steps shown in Figure 12-2. First, the database connection is opened. Next, one or several commands are sent to SQL Server via this connection; the result is evaluated and returned. Finally, the database connection is closed again.

FIGURE 12-2 Steps of a typical database query process.

Opening the Database Connection

The first step is to establish a connection to the SQL Server database. The connection is made by using the *sqlsrv_connect()* function. This function has two parameters: the name of the server to which you want to connect, and the connection parameters; most important is the database that you want to select as database context of the connection.

In the sample program from Listing 12-1, a connection to the local running SQL Server is established and the *AdventureWorksLT2008* database is selected:

```
// Connect using Windows authentication
$server = '(local)';
$connectionInfo = array('Database' => 'AdventureWorksLT2008', 'CharacterSet' => 'UTF-8');
$db = sqlsrv_connect($server, $connectionInfo);
```

If, as in this case, no user name or password is passed along with the connection parameter, PHP authenticates itself with the current Windows user of the PHP application pool (for example, *IIS AppPool\DefaultAppPool*). The benefit of this is that no passwords need to be saved in the PHP scripts.

Sending the Query

In the next step, the *sqlsrv_query()* function sends the query to the database. This function has two parameters in this case: the database connection (*$db*) to use and the T-SQL command (*$query*) that is sent to the database:

```
// Select products by name, list price, and category
$query = "SELECT p.ProductID, p.Name AS ProductName, p.ListPrice,
                 pc.Name as CategoryName
          FROM SalesLT.Product AS p
          JOIN SalesLT.ProductCategory AS pc ON p.ProductCategoryID = pc.ProductCategoryID
          ORDER BY p.Name";
// Run query
$qresult = sqlsrv_query($db, $query);
```

The *SELECT* query retrieves the information via a *JOIN* of the tables *SalesLT.Product* and *SalesLT.ProductCategory*.

As the result of the *sqlsrv_query()* call, a statement resource object is returned (saved in *$qresult*). It can now be used to fetch the results of the *SELECT* query.

Retrieving the Result

After the T-SQL command has been sent to the database, the rows of the *SELECT* result can be read by using the returned statement structure (*$qresult*) with *sqlsrv_fetch_array()*. *sqlsrv_fetch_array()* generates an associated array in which the names correspond to the column names of the *SELECT* statement:

```
// Read individual rows from the result
while ($row = sqlsrv_fetch_array($qresult)) {
    echo '<tr><td>', htmlspecialchars($row['ProductID']),
        '</td><td>', htmlspecialchars($row['ProductName']),
        '</td><td>', htmlspecialchars($row['CategoryName']),
        '</td><td>', htmlspecialchars($row['ListPrice']),
        "</td></tr>\n";
}
```

If no further rows are available, *sqlsrv_fetch_array()* returns *null* as a result, and the *while* loop is ended.

> **Caution** If an error occurs, *sqlsrv_fetch_array()* returns the *Boolean* value *false*. To be able to differentiate between an error and the end of a result list, you can check the identity with *$row === false*. Other tests, such as *!$row* or *empty($row)* don't allow a differentiation.

Freeing the Result Resource and Closing the Database Connection

After the data has been retrieved, you should free the statement resources belonging to the query. Unless you have activated the multiple active result sets (MARS) option (see the section "Connection Options," later in the chapter), a SQL Server connection can handle only one active query at a time. Therefore, before you issue the next query, you must ensure that either all results from the previous query are read or that you close the query result set by using *sqlsrv_free_stmt()*.

Finally, you should close the database connection before ending the script.

In SQL Server, you use *sqlsrv_free_stmt()* for freeing the statement resource and *sqlsrv_close()* for closing the database connection, as shown here:

```
// Free result list and close connection
sqlsrv_free_stmt($qresult);
sqlsrv_close($db);
```

Supporting Script

The sample program also embeds the utility script utils.php from Listing 12-2, which contains the support function *exitWithSQLError()* for returning error messages. The function is called when errors occur during the communication with SQL Server.

LISTING 12-2 utils.php—supporting functions for error handling and data output.

```php
<?php
/**
 * End program, return SQL Server error message
 * @param string $txt Description of the error context
 */
function exitWithSQLError($txt) {
    $errors = sqlsrv_errors();
    echo '<h1>Database error</h1>';
    echo "<p>Error: $txt</p>";
    foreach ($errors as $error) {
        echo '<p><b>SQL-Status:</b> ', htmlspecialchars($error['SQLSTATE']), '<br />',
            '<b>Code:</b> ', htmlspecialchars($error['code']), '<br />',
            '<b>Message</b>: ',
            // Error messages are transferred in ISO-8859-1 format
            htmlspecialchars(iconv('ISO-8859-1', 'UTF-8', $error['message'])),
            '</p>';
    }
    echo '<p>Program ended with errors.</p>';
    exit;
}
?>
```

As Listing 12-2 shows, error information can be retrieved with the function *sqlsrv_errors()*. It returns an array with status, code, and text description of the errors that occurred.

Database Connections

Establishing a connection to SQL Server is the first step to sending queries and statements to the database. The connections are made by using the *sqlsrv_connect()* function. This function has two parameters: the server name or the instance to which you want to connect, and the specifications of the connection properties.

Server Names

SQL Server allows you to establish a connection in various ways. The three most important are:

- **Shared memory**   The default connection when SQL Server and PHP are running on the same server. Shared memory is usually the most efficient way to connect.
- **TCP/IP**   A connection to a certain port is established via the network.
- **Named pipe**   A type of inter-process communication via pipes with a defined name.

When setting up a connection, you can use the first parameter not only to specify the server and the instance, but also the type of connection. The generic form of a server name is:

```
[ <Protocol>: ] <Server name> [ ,<Port> ]
```

The following abbreviations are used as protocol identifiers:

- **lpc** for shared memory connections
- **tcp** for TCP/IP connections
- **np** for named pipes connections

Table 12-1 shows a few examples of server names for different types of connections.

> **Important**   Connections to SQL Server are only possible when corresponding end points are configured (see Chapter 9). External access is only possible if it is not blocked by the Windows Firewall or external firewalls.

TABLE 12-1 Examples for server names, depending on the connection type

Connection type	Example	Description
Named pipes	np:\\.\pipe\sql\query	Connects to the default instance on the local computer
	np:\\db.xmp.site\pipe\ MSSQL$AdvWorks\sql\query	Connects to the instance *AdvWorks* on the server *db.xmp.site* using the default pipe
	np:\\db.xmp.site\pipe\php\app	Connects to the default instance on the server *db.xmp.site* via the pipe *php/app*
Shared memory	lpc:localhost	Connects to the default instance on the local server
	lpc:webhost.local\AdvWorks	Connects to the instance *AdvWorks* on the server *webhost.local,* which must be equal to the local server
	(local)	Connects to the default instance on the local server

Connection type	Example	Description
TCP/IP	tcp:localhost	Connects to the default instance on the local server
	tcp:db.xmp.site,2566	Connects to the default instance on the server *db.xmp.site* on port 2566
	tcp:10.12.24.48	Connects to the default instance on the server with the IP address 10.12.24.48 via the default port (1443)

Authentication

If configured correctly, SQL Server allows two different types of connection authentication:

- **Windows authentication**   The Windows user account that is run by the PHP program is also used as SQL Server login. The logon information of the process is reused.

- **SQL Server authentication**   A user who is (exclusively) set up for SQL Server is used for logon. User name and password must be specified for the connection.

Both methods have advantages and disadvantages. An advantage of the Windows authentication is that you can use it to centralize the entire user management, which aids general administration and the implementation of rights. Additionally, the PHP script does not require passwords in this case. Windows authentication is recommended when working with intranet applications.

SQL Server user accounts can be especially powerful if you are working with publicly accessible web applications that are consumed mainly by anonymous access or have self-registered accounts that are managed in the PHP application: a few SQL Server accounts serve as roles for various types of web users or for separating different areas of the PHP application.

Windows Authentication

Windows authentication is the default option for connecting to SQL Server. You don't need to specify additional parameters. To establish a connection to the default instance of the locally running SQL Server by using Windows authentication, use *sqlsrv_connect()* as follows:

```
$db = sqlsrv_connect('');
```

The empty string stands for the default instance on your local computer. Alternatives are *(local)*, "." (point), *(localhost)* or *localhost*. Because no other parameters were specified, the database context is set to the user's default database, or to the system database *master*, if the user has not specified a default database. You can specify the database you want to use with parameters:

```
$db = sqlsrv_connect('.', array ('Database' => 'AdventureWorksLT2008'));
```

The Windows user who is used for authentication against SQL Server depends on the configuration of IIS and PHP, as described in Chapter 5, "Security":

- **fastcgi.impersonate=0** If the identity transfer of the application user is turned off, the user of the IIS application pool; for example, IIS *AppPool\DefaultAppPool* is used.

- **fastcgi.impersonate=1, anonymous web user** The anonymous user *NT-AUTHORITY\ IUSR* of IIS is used.

- **fastcgi.impersonate=1, authenticated web user** The identity of the PHP web user is applied, and with this user account, the authentication with SQL Server is performed.

- **fastcgi.impersonate=1, path log-on information** The path credentials defined for the IIS application or virtual directory are used for authentication against SQL Server.

Depending on your situation, you need to set the rights in SQL Server.

> **Tip** After a successful authentication, you can use the following statement to find out the current user of the database connection and the selected database:
>
> ```
> SELECT SYSTEM_USER AS CurrentUser, DB_NAME() AS CurrentDatabase
> ```

SQL Server Authentication

The SQL Server authentication is independent of the Windows user who is running PHP: user name and password are directly specified when establishing the connection with *sqlsrv_ connect()*, as shown in Listing 12-3. The user name is passed on with the connection parameter *UID*, and the password with the parameter *PWD*.

LISTING 12-3 Building a connection with SQL Server authentication.

```
// Connect via SQL Server authentication
$server = '(local)';
$connectionInfo = array('UID' => 'Tony',           // SQL Server user name
                        'PWD' => 'top-secret',   // Password
                        'Database' => 'AdventureWorksLT2008',
                        'CharacterSet' => 'UTF-8');
$db = sqlsrv_connect($server, $connectionInfo);
```

The obvious disadvantage is that the password is contained in the PHP script as plain text, and that users cannot be centrally administered (for example, via Microsoft Active Directory). The advantages of this authentication method are the separation of database user and executing PHP user as well as the simple way of switching between different SQL Server users within the same PHP application.

SQL Server authentication (or using database users instead of operating system users) is the most common authentication method for PHP applications.

Connection Pooling

Connection pooling means reusing existing database connections. To establish a connection and authenticate, it can mean a lot more work when compared to the execution of a T-SQL statement. Connection pooling helps you perform database queries by reusing already authenticated connections. It is not necessary to establish the connection again.

By default, connection pooling is enabled for the SQL Server PHP driver: if there is already a connection in the pool that you are trying to reestablish with *sqlsrv_connect()*, it is applied, and the connection status is reset. *sqlsrv_close()* does not close the connection completely; instead, it returns the connection to the connection pool.

> **Caution** Because connections are being reused, you should not use T-SQL statements or SQL Server procedures to make changes to the basic settings of the connections themselves. This would apply the changes to any subsequent use of the connection, which could lead to unwanted consequences. You should also avoid using application roles (with *sp_setapprole()*).

Fragmenting

Connection pooling does not immediately close a connection. Rather, it is first returned to the pool and only closed after a defined period of inactivity. Whether a connection can be reused or a new connection is established (possibly in a new pool) depends on the parameters of *sqlsrv_connect()*.

If the user or database is different, a new connection in a new pool is created. This is something you should be aware of when designing web applications.

If a web application has many different authenticated users, and the users are also used for the communication with SQL via Windows authentication, a connection pool is generated for each user. If the number of simultaneously active users rises, this leads to fragmentation of the connection pools and might have an impact on performance.

If this is the case, you should modify the design of your PHP application to accommodate very few (role-independent) database users so that it can be used for all web users. You can do so by:

- Switching to SQL Server authentication.
- Using Windows authentication to configure PHP by using *fastcgi.impersonate=0*.
- Defining a fixed user for the application with IIS path credentials.

In general, in your PHP script, database connections should be opened as late as possible and closed as early as possible to save resources.

Connection Options

When establishing a connection with *sqlsrv_connect()*, you can use the parameter *Connection Pooling* to specify whether you want to use connection pooling (*true*) or not (*false*). By default, connection pooling is used. Listing 12-4 shows how to prevent connection pooling for an open connection. If this is the case, *sqlsrv_close()* closes the connection immediately. There is no return to a pool and no time-delayed closing.

LISTING 12-4 Establishing a connection without connection pooling.

```
// Connect via Windows Authentication without connection pooling
$server = '(local)';
$connectionInfo = array('ConnectionPooling' => false,
                        'Database' => 'AdventureWorksLT2008',
                        'CharacterSet' => 'UTF-8');
$db = sqlsrv_connect($server, $connectionInfo);
```

More Connection Options

SQL Server provides many more connection options that can be set in the *$connectionInfo* parameter array, when calling *sqlsrv_connect()*. Table 12-2 gives an overview of the most important options not discussed so far.

TABLE 12-2 Additional connection options

Option	Description
CharacterSet	Defines the character set. Possible values are *SQLSRV_ENC_BINARY* for binary encoding, *SQLSRV_ENC_CHAR* for using the current code page active on the server (this is the default), and *UTF-8*.
Encrypt	Specifies whether the connection to SQL Server should be encrypted (*1*) or unencrypted (*0*). Only useful if PHP and SQL Server are not on the same server. Bear in mind that encryption might have an impact on performance.
Failover_Partner	If you have configured a failover server, you can specify it with this option and the driver will switch transparently in case of an error.
LoginTimeout	Specifies the number of seconds, before failing the logon attempt.
MultipleActiveResultSets	Enable (*1*) or disable (*0*) MARS. MARS can be used to execute queries on a connection that has an open active result set. If disabled, you either need to cancel or free the previous result statement or finish fetching all results, before starting a new query.
ReturnDatesAsStrings	Specifies whether to return SQL date types as strings (*1*) or as objects (*0*). For a more comprehensive discussion, see the section "Data Types," later in this chapter.

Option	Description
TraceOn *TraceFile*	If *TraceOn=1*, ODBC tracing is enabled and written into *TraceFile*. With the additional options *WSID* and *APP*, you can set the computer and application name for tracing.
TransactionIsolation	Defines the transaction isolation level. See Chapter 13, "Advanced Database Functions," for a discussion of the different levels.
TrustServerCertificate	Specifies whether a self-signed server certificate should be trusted (*1*) or rejected (*0*).

Database Queries

SQL Server provides you with different possibilities for creating database queries from PHP and retrieving results. In the following subsection, you will be introduced to parameterized statements that permit a secure transfer of parameters to the T-SQL statement, and you will learn about prepared statements that allow for an efficient execution of multiple statements. You will also be introduced to two additional methods for retrieving results: retrieving datasets as objects, and retrieving individual columns of the datasets.

> **Note** The following examples use two different scripts that you can find in Appendix A, "Example Scripts and Data":
>
> - **DatabaseConnection.php**   Opens and closes the database connection and returns SQL Server error messages.
>
> - **HTMLPage.php**   Creates an HTML page and securely outputs data as HTML.

Parameterizing Statements

Web application security is mainly based on the correct use of user input data. The filtering and masking of this data is essential if you don't want to jeopardize your application or your users. Unfiltered data can lead to an SQL injection. Apart from filters, the parameterized statements offer a solution to this problem.

SQL Injection

SQL injection—the malicious insertion and execution of SQL statements—is a common problem in web applications. The reason for it is missing validation and masking of user-dependent input data. Listing 12-5 shows a program snippet of a typical situation.

LISTING 12-5 Program with errors, which permits SQL injection.

```
$productID = $_GET['id'];
$query = "SELECT Name, Color FROM SalesLT.Product WHERE ProductID=$productID";
$stmt = sqlsrv_query($db, $query)
```

The program expects a number (the product number), as input value. The problem is that $GET['id']$ can contain any kind of string, for example:

```
-1 UNION SELECT CompanyName, EmailAddress FROM SalesLT.Customer;
```

If the PHP program is executed, *$query* has the following content:

```
SELECT Name, Color FROM SalesLT.Product
WHERE ProductID=-1 UNION SELECT CompanyName, EmailAddress FROM SalesLT.Customer;
```

The combined statement represents a valid query, but instead of the product name and color, the company name and the customer's email address are returned.

SQL injection can also be used to insert values (for example, users with increased rights), to change values, to delete rows or tables, to call procedures, and much more. SQL injection represents a serious threat to web applications.

Filtering and Masking Data

Your first approach is to filter for dangerous characters or to mask the transfer to SQL Server. Table 12-3 gives you an overview of the most important characters typically used for SQL injection. If at all possible, these characters should not be permitted.

TABLE 12-3 Dangerous characters and strings used for SQL injection

Character	Meaning
; (semi-colon)	Separates a T-SQL statement from the next statement
' (apostrophe)	Delimits strings
--	Indicates a comment (valid until the end of the line)
/* and */	Delimits comments

Possible number filters, such as for *ProductID*, can look as follows:

```
// Variant 1: cast to integer
$productID = (int)$_GET['id'];
// Variant 2: filter out anything that is not a number
$productID = preg_replace('/[^0-9]/', '', $_GET['id']);
// Variant 3: use filter_input function of PHP
$productID = filter_input(INPUT_GET, 'id', FILTER_SANITIZE_NUMBER_INT);
```

If you want to pass strings as input data—for instance, to look for a product by name—you should keep the filter as tight as possible. For example, if only letters and spaces are allowed, you could use the following function:

```
mb_regex_encoding('UTF-8');
if (!mb_check_encoding($_GET['product'], 'UTF-8')) {
    die('Character coding with errors at input value.');
}
$name = mb_ereg_replace('[^[:alpha:] ]', '', $_GET['product']);
```

> **Caution** If you are working with Unicode input data (as in the examples in this book), you should only use multi-byte string functions (*mb_**). PCRE functions (*preg_**) and other simple character operations can yield false results or destroy the string coding.

If you want to allow the apostrophe, you need to double it, as shown here:

```
$name = mb_ereg_replace("[^[:alpha:]' ]", '', $_GET['product']);
$name = mb_ereg_replace("'", "''", $name);
```

You can now use *$name* for T-SQL queries.

> **Important** Security against SQL injection and related security weaknesses can only be guaranteed if you use the same character coding for the entire processing chain (HTML, PHP, SQL Server). Otherwise, the different interpretations of data during transfer can lead to security problems. Therefore, in this book, we use only UTF-8.

Parameterizing Statements

SQL Server provides the simple alternative of parameterized queries to ensure that data is masked correctly. *sqlsrv_query()* can take additional parameters when called, as displayed in the following:

```
sqlsrv_query($DBConnection, $T-SQL [,$parameter [,$options]])
```

$parameter is an array of values that are added to the T-SQL statement instead of question marks. *$options* specify additional query options such as a time limit for processing the query. For example, to query the number of a certain product, use the *sqlsrv_query()* as follows:

```
sqlsrv_query($db, 'SELECT ProductID FROM SalesLT.Products WHERE Name=?', array($name));
```

The question mark in *Name=?* is replaced with the value of *$name*. *sqlsrv_query()* and ensures that the value is passed in such a way that no SQL injection can take place.

The advantage of parameterized queries is that the SQL Server PHP driver automatically selects the correct coding for the database connection to insert the value into the SQL statement, and it can take care of the masking according to the data type.

Sample Program

Listing 12-6 and Listing 12-7 show the sample program for a product name search. It uses a parameterized query and removes unwanted characters from the entry data.

> **Note**   The search_products.php file (Listing 12-6) takes care of input and output.

An *HTMLPage* object is created and a form inserted into the page.

If a search term has been entered, the input data is cleaned up with *sanitizeName()*, as described in the section "Filtering and Masking Data," earlier in the chapter.

After *getProductsByName()* has retrieved the data from the database, the results are inserted as a table into the HTML script and the HTML page is returned.

> **Note**   The PHP extension for the multi-byte functions (*mb_**) is not enabled in the default installation of PHP. To enable the extension, either use the PHP Manger or insert *extension=php_mbstring.dll* into php.ini, and then restart the associated IIS application pools.

LISTING 12-6 search_products.php—a product name search.

```php
<?php
namespace net\xmp\phpbook;

require './DatabaseConnection.php';
require './HTMLPage.php';
require './search_products_db.php';

$html = new HTMLPage('AdventureWorks : Product Search');
$form = <<<EOF
<form action="" method="get">
Product name: <input name="product" />
<input type="submit" value="Search" />
</form><br />
EOF;
$html->addHTML($form);
if (isset($_GET['product'])) {
    $name = sanitizeName($_GET['product']);
    $products = getProductsByName($name);
    if ($products) {
        $html->addTable($products);
```

```
        } else {
            $html->addElement('p', 'No products found.');
        }
    }
}
$html->printPage();
exit;

/**
 * Check string for correct coding and filter out forbidden characters
 */
function sanitizeName($txt) {
    if (!mb_check_encoding($txt, 'UTF-8')) {
        die('Character coding with errors at input value.');
    }
    mb_regex_encoding('UTF-8');
    return mb_ereg_replace("[^-[:alnum:]', ]", '', $txt);
}
?>
```

 Note The file search_products_db.php (Listing 12-7) contains the functions for the database query.

At first, a *DatbaseConnection* object is created and the database connection is opened.

The SQL statement is parameterized; in the *WHERE* clause, *$query* contains the placeholder (question mark), which is replaced by the parameters (*$params*, only one value).

Next, *sqlsrv_fetch_array()* retrieves the data and to writes it into an array for HTML output.

Finally, *sqlsrv_free_stmt()* frees the resource of the query and the database connection is closed.

LISTING 12-7 search_products_db.php—database function for the name search.

```php
<?php
namespace net\xmp\phpbook;

/**
 * Query of all products whose name starts with $name.
 * @return array Data for the HTML table
 */
function getProductsByName($name) {
    $db = new DatabaseConnection();
    $db->connect();
    // Select products by name and list price
    $query = 'SELECT ProductID, Name, ListPrice
            FROM SalesLT.Product WHERE Name LIKE ?
            ORDER BY Name';
    $params = array($name . '%');
```

```
    // Run query
    $stmt = sqlsrv_query($db->handle, $query, $params);
    if ($stmt === false) {
        $db->exitWithError('Product data query failed.');
    }
    if (!sqlsrv_has_rows($stmt)) {
        return false; // No hits in the database (empty result)
    }
    // Retrieve individual rows from the result
    $table = array(array('ID', 'Product', 'List Price'));
    while ($row = sqlsrv_fetch_array($stmt)) {
        $table[] = array($row['ProductID'], $row['Name'],
            $row['ListPrice']);
    }
    // null == no more rows, false == Error
    if ($row === false) {
        $db->exitWithError('Retrieving product data entry failed.');
    }
    sqlsrv_free_stmt($stmt);
    $db->close();
    return $table;
}
?>
```

> **Tip** Using the *sqlsrv_has_rows()* function, you can query whether result rows exist. In Listing 12-7, the function is used to determine whether there were any hits for the search term.

As an alternative, you can use the *sqlsrv_num_rows()* function, which returns the number of rows in the result. However, this function cannot be used with the default cursor type of SQL Server queries.

Figure 12-3 shows the result of the product search for "Men's".

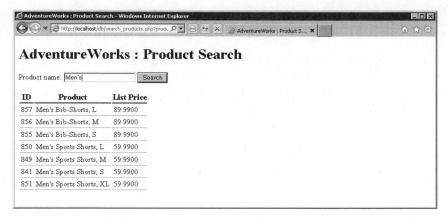

FIGURE 12-3 Result of the product name search when using a parameterized T-SQL statement.

Retrieving Results

After SQL Server has received a request, the statement resource is returned, from which the results can be retrieved. So far, you have been using *sqlsrv_fetch_array()* to retrieve results. In the next sections, you will learn about two other methods: retrieving results as objects, and retrieving individual object fields.

Retrieving as Object

To retrieve the result rows of a T-SQL query as an object, use the *sqlsrv_fetch_object()* function. You can also use this function to specify a class that you want to instantiate for the result object.

Listing 12-8 shows a program snippet (without error handling). The properties of the generated object have the names of the selected field of the *SELECT* expression.

LISTING 12-8 Querying data by using the *sqlsrv_fetch_object()* function.

```
$stmt = sqlsrv_query($db, 'SELECT DISTINCT TOP(10) FirstName, LastName, EmailAddress
                    FROM SalesLT.Customer ORDER BY LastName, FirstName');
while ($obj = sqlsrv_fetch_object($stmt)) {
    printf("<li>%s %s &lt;%s&gt;</li>\n", htmlspecialchars($obj->FirstName),
           htmlspecialchars($obj->LastName), htmlspecialchars($obj->EmailAddress));
}
sqlsrv_free_stmt($stmt);
```

In case of an error, *sqlsrv_fetch_object()* returns false (just like *sqlsrv_fetch_array()*), and when there are no more result rows, it returns the value *null*.

Result columns must have a name so that they can be assigned as object properties. Columns without names lead to a warning or an error. Calculated columns, such as *count(*)*, *max(ListPrice)*, and *SubTotal+TaxAmt* must be assigned an alias so that they can be set as object properties, such as *count(*) AS amount*.

> **Important** The column names are case-sensitive; therefore, the object property names are used exactly as specified in the T-SQL statement. If you use a different case later on, you are accessing undefined object properties.

To instantiate a result object in a certain class, you need to specify an additional parameter, as shown in Listing 12-9.

LISTING 12-9 Instantiating a certain class by using the *sqlsrv_fetch_object()* function.

```
class Customer
{
    function printData() {
        printf("<li>%s %s &lt;%s&gt;</li>\n", htmlspecialchars($obj->FirstName),
                htmlspecialchars($obj->LastName), htmlspecialchars($obj->EmailAddress));
    }
}
$stmt = sqlsrv_query($db, 'SELECT DISTINCT TOP(10) FirstName, LastName, EmailAddress
                        FROM SalesLT.Customer ORDER BY LastName, FirstName');
while ($obj = sqlsrv_fetch_object($stmt, 'Customer')) {
    $obj->printData();
}
sqlsrv_free_stmt($stmt);
```

If the class is located in a PHP 5.3 namespace, you must specify the complete class name. For example, if the class *Customer* is located in the namespace *net\xmp\phpbook*, it would look as follows:

```
$obj = sqlsrv_fetch_object($stmt, 'net\\xmp\\phpbook\\Customer');
```

If the constructor of a class requires parameters, you can add them to *sqlsrv_fetch_object()* as an array, for example:

```
$obj = sqlsrv_fetch_object($stmt, 'Customer', array($param1, $param2, $param3));
```

Retrieving Individual Fields

You can use a combination of the two functions, *sqlsrv_fetch()* and *sqlsrv_get_field()*, to retrieve individual fields. *sqlsrv_fetch()* retrieves a result row; *sqlsrv_get_field()* can then read the individual columns.

In Listing 12-10, *sqlsrv_fetch($stmt)* retrieves the next result row after the T-SQL statement has been sent. If the row reads successfully, the function returns *true*; if there are errors, it returns *false*, and if there are no further rows, it returns the value *null*. You use *sqlsrv_get_field()* to read the individual columns. You must access the columns with an index, because column names cannot be used.

LISTING 12-10 Retrieving results by using the functions *sqlsrv_fetch()* and *sqlsrv_get_field()*.

```
$stmt = sqlsrv_query($db, 'SELECT DISTINCT TOP(10) FirstName, LastName, EmailAddress
                          FROM SalesLT.Customer ORDER BY LastName, FirstName');
while (sqlsrv_fetch($stmt)) {
    printf("<li>%s %s %s</li>\n", sqlsrv_get_field($stmt, 0),
                                  sqlsrv_get_field($stmt, 1),
                                  sqlsrv_get_field($stmt, 2));
}
sqlsrv_free_stmt($stmt);
```

It depends on your personal programming style whether you prefer to use *sqlsrv_fetch_array()* or *sqlsrv_fetch_object()*. The combination of *sqlsrv_fetch()* and *sqlsrv_get_field()*, however, has two important distinguishing features. First, only the very column that is being requested is loaded into PHP's process memory, whereas *sqlsrv_fetch_array()* and *sqlsrv_fetch_object()* transfer the entire row into the PHP process memory. This can have an impact when working with large columns (*nvarchar(MAX)*, *varbinary(MAX)*). The second feature is that you can specify the PHP type of the column you want to read, and—again important for large columns—read the column as stream. You can read more about this in the section "Data Types," later in the chapter

Prepared Statements

If a T-SQL statement is run multiple times in a PHP program, you can use prepared statements to simplify programming and increase performance. For prepared statements, *sqlsrv_query()* is divided into two steps:

- **sqlsrv_prepare()**   Analyzes the T-SQL statement and prepares it for execution. The statement does not yet contain parameters.

- **sqlsrv_execute()**   Adds the parameters and runs the statement. This step can happen multiple times (each time with new data). Because there is no analysis and no execution preparation, the performance is increased and the resource consumption decreased.

The small sample application that follows shows you how to program with prepared statements. The binding of parameters is especially important. With a prepared T-SQL statement, the sample application updates the order quantity and the discount for individual products on an invoice. You can find the associated data in the table *SalesLT.SalesOrderDetail*.

Listing 12-11 contains the database class, the constructor, and a method called *getByHeader()*, which is used for listing the content before and after the update. *getByHeader()* follows a structure with which you are already familiar: execute a parameterized T-SQL statement by using *sqlsrv_query()*, read the result rows with *sqlsrv_fetch_array()*, and finally, free the statement resource with *sqlsrv_free_stmt()*.

The *prepare()* method prepares the T-SQL statement by using *sqlsrv_prepare()*. At first glance, it looks like a parameterized statement, as the placeholders in T-SQL indicate. However, it is essential that the parameters are bound as references (*&$...*) and not as values (*$...*). This applies all later changes of the variables to the locations where references were used.

The *update()* method then runs *sqlsrv_execute()*. The parameters are not set directly with *sqlsrv_execute()*. Instead, the current values of the bound variables are automatically applied when the T-SQL statement is executed.

The *free()* method finally frees the used statement resource.

> **Tip** With the *sqlsrv_rows_affected()* function, you can determine the number of affected rows for *UPDATE*, *INSERT*, and *DELETE* operations. If no rows were changed, the function returns 0. If there is no information (for example, after a *SELECT*), the function returns -1, and if there is an error, it returns *false*.

LISTING 12-11 update_salesorder_db.php—a database class for updating order data with prepared T-SQL statements.

```php
<?php
namespace net\xmp\phpbook;

class UpdateOrders
{
    protected $db;
    protected $stmt;
    // Variables bound to statement
    protected $sql_qty, $sql_discount, $sql_id;

    /**
     * Constructor sets database connection
     */
    function __construct($db) {
        $this->db = $db;
    }
```

```php
/**
 * Read relevant data from the table and write it to HTML array.
 * @param int $id Number of SalesOrder
 */
function getByHeader($id) {
    $query = 'SELECT SalesOrderDetailID, OrderQty, UnitPriceDiscount
            FROM SalesLT.SalesOrderDetail WHERE SalesOrderID = ?';
    $params = array($id);
    $stmt = sqlsrv_query($this->db->handle, $query, $params);
    if ($stmt === false) {
        $this->db->exitWithError('Data query has failed.');
    }
    // Read individual result rows
    $table = array(array('ID', 'Amount', 'Discount'));
    while ($row = sqlsrv_fetch_array($stmt)) {
        $table[] = array($row['SalesOrderDetailID'], $row['OrderQty'],
                    $row['UnitPriceDiscount']);
    }
    if ($row === false) {
        $this->db->exitWithError('Retrieving data has failed.');
    }
    sqlsrv_free_stmt($stmt);
    return $table;
}


/**
 * Prepare update statement.
 */
function prepare() {
    $query = 'UPDATE SalesLT.SalesOrderDetail
            SET OrderQty = ?, UnitPriceDiscount = ?
            WHERE SalesOrderDetailID = ?';
    // Parameters must be used as references (&$...)n.
    // This way all later changes to the variables are
    // applied to the prepared T-SQL statement
    $params = array(&$this->sql_qty, &$this->sql_discount, &$this->sql_id);
    // Prepare statement
    $this->stmt = sqlsrv_prepare($this->db->handle, $query, $params);
    if ($this->stmt === false) {
        $this->db->exitWithError("Statement preparation failed.");
    }
}


/**
 * Run prepared statement.
 * The updated values are passed as parameters.
 */
```

```
        function update($id, $qty, $discount) {
            // Variable update is applied to T-SQL statement,
            // because the variables are bound as references.
            $this->sql_id = $id;
            $this->sql_qty = $qty;
            $this->sql_discount = $discount;
            if (sqlsrv_execute($this->stmt) === false) {
                $this->db->exitWithError('Update failed.');
            }
        }
    }

    function free() {
        sqlsrv_free_stmt($this->stmt);
    }
}
?>
```

Listing 12-12 contains the required framework for running the update:

- The new updated values are hard-coded in the script. In an actual application, they would be set with the input data (*$_GET, $_POST*).

- Next, the database connection is opened, the *UpdateOrders* class is instantiated, and the table values are read before the update (*getByHeader()*) and displayed (*$html->addTable()*).

- The multiple execution of the prepared statement takes place as follows: the statement is prepared with *prepare()*, *update()* is used in a loop for all datasets, and then finally, the statement is released with *free()*. Here, you can see how prepared statements can simplify programming.

As a final demonstration, the updated table data is read again (*getByHeader()*) and displayed.

LISTING 12-12 update_salesorder.php—updating order data with prepared T-SQL statements.

```
<?php
namespace net\xmp\phpbook;
require './DatabaseConnection.php';
require './HTMLPage.php';
require './update_salesorder_db.php';

// Firmly defined for demonstration purposes
$updateOrderHeader = 71915;
$updateOrders = array(array(113089, 6, 0.10), array(113090, 1, 0.0),
                      array(113091, 10, 0.20), array(113093, 3, 0.035));
$html = new HTMLPage('AdventureWorks : Order Amount and Discount Correction');
$db = new DatabaseConnection();
$db->connect();
$orders = new UpdateOrders($db);
```

```
// Read and display data before update
$before = $orders->getByHeader($updateOrderHeader);
$html->addHTML('<div style="position:absolute;top:4em">');
$html->addElement('h2', 'Before Update');
$html->addTable($before);

// Prepare query and run multiple times
$orders->prepare();
foreach ($updateOrders as $order) {
    list($id, $qty, $discount) = $order;
    $orders->update($id, $qty, $discount);
}
$orders->free();

// Read and display data after update
$after = $orders->getByHeader($updateOrderHeader);
$html->addHTML('</div><div style="position:absolute;top:4em;left:15em">');
$html->addElement('h2', 'After update');
$html->addTable($after);
$html->addHTML('</div>');
$db->close();
$html->printPage();
?>
```

Figure 12-4 shows the result of one iteration: the changes were applied as appropriate.

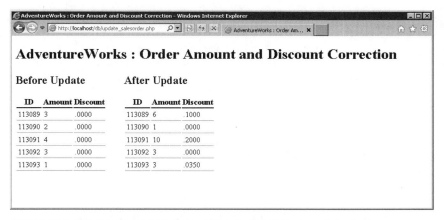

FIGURE 12-4 The sample program for updating order amounts and discounts.

Data Types

SQL Server and PHP have their own data types. When data is transferred, those data types need to be converted accordingly. Frequently, strings or numbers are used for this purpose: for example, a PHP floating-point number becomes a string (between apostrophes) in a T-SQL statement, but in SQL Server it becomes a *smallmoney* type. When data is converted in such a way, the conversion is implicit, which means that SQL Server and PHP use the default conversions.

Converting from PHP to SQL Server

The default conversion of data types can be controlled with parameterized statements for which explicit data types are specified. In Listing 12-13, the parameters *$sellEnd* and *$maxPrice* are converted into the SQL Server data types *datetime* and *money*. In *$params*, an array is passed (instead of individual variables), whose last entry is the desired SQL Server data type.

LISTING 12-13 Specifying SQL Server data types for a parameterized query.

```
$query = 'SELECT ProductID, Name
          FROM SalesLT.Product
          WHERE ProductCategoryID = ? AND SellEndDate >= ? AND ListPrice <= ?';
$categoryID = 6;
$sellEnd = '2003-01-01';
$maxPrice = 799.90;
$params = array($categoryID,
                array($sellEnd, null, null, SQLSRV_SQLTYPE_DATETIME),
                array($maxPrice, null, null, SQLSRV_SQLTYPE_MONEY));
$stmt = sqlsrv_query($db, $query, $params);
```

You can find the complete list of constants, *SQLSRV_SQLTYPE_**, in the documentation of the SQL Server PHP driver. The rule of thumb is to append the data type name in capital letters; for example, the constant *SQLSRV_SQLTYPE_DATETIMEOFFSET* names the SQL Server type *datetimeoffset*.

Converting from SQL Server to PHP

The other way around, you can specify the desired PHP data types of the result rows when querying with *sqlsrv_get_field()*. In Listing 12-14, the desired PHP data type is specified as the third parameter of *sqlsrv_get_field()*.

LISTING 12-14 Specifying the PHP data type when querying with *sqlsrv_get_field()*.

```
$query = 'SELECT ProductID, Weight, ListPrice, SellEndDate
          FROM SalesLT.Product';
$stmt = sqlsrv_query($db, $query);
while (sqlsrv_fetch($stmt)) {
    echo sqlsrv_get_field($stmt, 0, SQLSRV_PHPTYPE_INT), ' ',
         sqlsrv_get_field($stmt, 1, SQLSRV_PHPTYPE_FLOAT), ' ',
         sqlsrv_get_field($stmt, 2, SQLSRV_PHPTYPE_FLOAT), ' ',
         sqlsrv_get_field($stmt, 3, SQLSRV_PHPTYPE_STRING(SQLSRV_ENC_CHAR)), "\n";
}
```

Table 12-4 lists possible PHP data types. A direct conversion to *Boolean* or arrays and objects is not possible, but the objects can be instantiated by using *sqlsrv_fetch_object()*.

TABLE 12-4 PHP data types into which you can convert

PHP data type	Constant	Notes
DateTime	*SQLSRV_PHPTYPE_DATETIME*	By default, date types are converted into PHP *DateTime*.
Float	*SQLSRV_PHPTYPE_FLOAT*	Works for all number types with decimal places.
Integer	*SQLSRV_PHPTYPE_INT*	Only integer SQL Server data types can be converted into *Integer*. An automatic conversion of *money* to *Integer* is not possible, for example.
Stream *String*	*SQLSRV_PHPTYPE_STREAM()* *SQLSRV_PHPTYPE_STRING()*	A coding must be specified as parameter: ■ *SQLSRV_ENC_BINARY:* data is passed on without being processed. ■ *SQLSRV_ENC_CHAR:* data is converted according to the current 8-bit Windows character set; unconvertible characters are replaced by question marks. ■ *UTF-8:* data is passed on coded in UTF-8.

A frequent source of errors—especially for developers coming from other databases—is the fact that by default the SQL Server PHP driver returns the date and time types as a *DateTime* PHP data type and not as a string. As Listing 12-14 shows, you can use *sqlsrv_get_field()* to convert the data type explicitly to *string*. Alternatively, you can specify directly when you are establishing a connection that data types must be returned as *string*:

```
$serverName = "(local)";
$connectionInfo = array('Database' => 'AdventureWorksLT2008',
                        'ReturnDatesAsStrings' => true);
$db = sqlsrv_connect($serverName, $connectionInfo);
```

Streams

The SQL Server PHP driver offers you the possibility to treat data as streams. This is especially interesting for binary data types (*binary*, *varbinary*) and large data volume (for example, with *varchar(MAX)*).

Retrieving Data as Stream

If data is retrieved by using *sqlsrv_get_field()*, the named types are always returned as stream by default. An essential advantage is that not all of the data must be kept in PHP's memory, but can be read and returned in snippets via the stream.

We will illustrate this process by using the example for product search from the section "Parameterizing Statements," earlier in the chapter. The product search is extended with thumbnail photos of the products.

Listing 12-15 shows the associated script for reading and displaying the pictures. After opening the database connection, the column *ThumbNailPhoto* of *SalesLT.Products* is queried. The column has the type *varbinary(MAX)* and is used as stream by default. Therefore, *$stream* can be returned directly with the function *fpassthru()*.

LISTING 12-15 get_image.php—reading the picture from the database as stream and displaying it.

```php
<?php
namespace net\xmp\phpbook;
require './DatabaseConnection.php';
require './HTMLPage.php';

// Establish database connection
$db = new DatabaseConnection();
$db->connect();

// Query picture for product
$query = 'SELECT ThumbNailPhoto FROM SalesLT.Product WHERE ProductID = ?';
$params = array((int) $_GET['id']);
$stmt = sqlsrv_query($db->handle, $query, $params);
if (!sqlsrv_fetch($stmt)) {
    $db->exitWithError('The query of the photo has failed.');
}
// varbinary() is returned as stream with direct output
$stream = sqlsrv_get_field($stmt, 0);
header('Content-type: image/gif');
fpassthru($stream);
// Free statement; close database
sqlsrv_free_stmt($stmt);
$db->close();
```

Note Ensure that your editor does not insert any UTF-8 coding (*byte order mark* [BOM]) at the beginning of your PHP script; otherwise, *header()* won't work or the additional bytes will make the graphic format unreadable.

Because space characters at the end of the file might also cause problems, the ending PHP *tag ?>* was left out. This is a common and valid practice in such cases.

If you don't want the image to be returned as stream, but instead as a string, you need to specify the coding directly:

```
// varbinary() is returned as a string
$img = sqlsrv_get_field($stmt, 0, SQLSRV_PHPTYPE_STRING(SQLSRV_ENC_BINARY));
header('Content-type: image/gif');
echo $img;
```

The file get_image.php from Listing 12-15 only provides the image display. If you want to include the image display into the search result, you need to modify Listing 12-6. Listing 12-16 shows the changed script *search_products_img.php*. The table now also embeds *<img>* items whose source is the PHP script from Listing 12-15.

LISTING 12-16 search_products_img.php—a product search with images.

```
<?php
namespace net\xmp\phpbook;
require './DatabaseConnection.php';
require './HTMLPage.php';
require './search_products_db.php';

$html = new HTMLPage('AdventureWorks : Product Search');
$form = <<<EOF
<form action="" method="get">
Product name: <input name="product" />
<input type="submit" value="Search" />
</form><br />
EOF;
$html->addHTML($form);
if (isset($_GET['product'])) {
    $name = sanitizeName($_GET['product']);
    $products = getProductsByName($name);
    if ($products) {
        addImageColumn($products);
        $html->addTable($products, array(false, false, false, true));
    } else {
        $html->addElement('p', 'No products found.');
    }
}
```

```
$html->printPage();
exit;

function sanitizeName($txt) { ... } // Same as before

/**
 * Adds a column with a product photo to the table
 */
function addImageColumn(&$products) {
    $products[0][] = 'Photo ';
    for ($i = 1; $i < count($products); $i++) {
        $products[$i][] = '<img src="get_image.php?id='
                        . $products[$i][0]
                        . '" alt="Product photo" />';
    }
}
?>
```

Figure 12-5 shows the result: in the fourth column, the product pictures from the column *ThumbNailPhoto* are displayed.

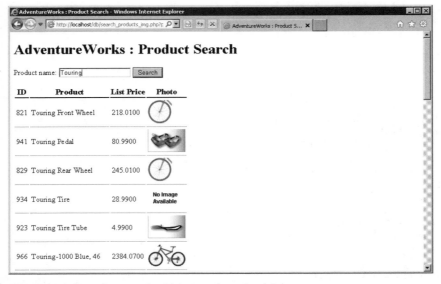

FIGURE 12-5 A product search with images from the database.

Inserting Data as Stream

Streams can be used for more than just reading data from the database. You can also use them when inserting data into the database. In this case, an open stream is passed for parameterized queries.

Listing 12-17 demonstrates how you can use streams to insert a picture into the database. The handler for the open file is transferred in the variable *$params*. Because the database connection has been opened as UTF-8, it is recommended that you specify the data type (binary, no recoding necessary) for *$params*. This ensures a correct data transfer.

LISTING 12-17 upload_product_img.php—inserting an image via stream into a database.

```php
<?php
namespace net\xmp\phpbook;
require './DatabaseConnection.php';
require './HTMLPage.php';

$html = new HTMLPage('AdventureWorks : Upload Product Photo');
$form = <<<'EOF'
<form action="" enctype="multipart/form-data" method="post">
ProductID: <input name="productID" /><br />
File: <input type="file" name="productPhoto" /><br />
<input type="submit" value="Upload" />
</form><br />
EOF;
$html->addHTML($form);

if (isset($_POST['productID'])) {
    // Connect to database
    $db = new DatabaseConnection();
    $db->connect();
    // Prepare query
    $query = 'UPDATE SalesLT.Product
            SET ThumbNailPhoto = ?, ThumbnailPhotoFileName = ?
            WHERE ProductID = ?';
    $id = (int) $_POST['productID'];
    $filename = filter_var($_FILES['productPhoto']['name'],
                        FILTER_SANITIZE_STRING, FILTER_FLAG_STRIP_LOW);
    // Open file
    $file = fopen($_FILES['productPhoto']['tmp_name'], 'rb');
    // Set coding and data type
    $params = array(array($file, null, SQLSRV_PHPTYPE_STREAM(SQLSRV_ENC_BINARY),
                            SQLSRV_SQLTYPE_VARBINARY('MAX')),
                $filename, $id);
    $stmt = sqlsrv_query($db->handle, $query, $params);
    // Close file
    fclose($file);
    if ($stmt === false) {
        $db->exitWithError('Phote updoad failed.');
    }
    if (sqlsrv_rows_affected($stmt) != 1) {
        $db->exitWithError('Did you specify the wrong ID?');
    }
    $html->addElement('p', 'Upload successful.');
    // Close database connection
    sqlsrv_free_stmt($stmt);
    $db->close();
}
$html->printPage();
?>
```

PDO and SQL Server

Starting with version 2.0 of the Microsoft Drivers for PHP for SQL Server, PDO support has been added. PDO provides a consistent object-oriented interface for accessing databases from different vendors. PDO has gained popularity with PHP frameworks because it provides a lightweight data-access abstraction layer. Complete coverage of PDO is beyond the scope of this book; therefore, we will focus our discussion on the most important differences between the native driver and PDO, and special features of the SQL Server PDO driver. The following discussion assumes that you already have some precursory knowledge of PDO.

PDO Database Access Lifecycle

Similar to the native driver, the typical database access lifecycle comprises opening the connection, sending the query or queries, reading the results, freeing result sets if necessary, and then eventually closing the connection. Listing 12-18 shows the relevant parts of Listing 12-1 rewritten with PDO.

LISTING 12-18 Querying data with PDO.

```php
try {
    $dbh = new PDO( "sqlsrv:server=(local); Database=AdventureWorksLT2008", "", "");
    $dbh->setAttribute( PDO::ATTR_ERRMODE, PDO::ERRMODE_EXCEPTION );
    // Select products by name, list price, and category
    $query = "SELECT p.ProductID, p.Name AS ProductName, p.ListPrice,
                    pc.Name AS CategoryName
            FROM SalesLT.Product AS p
            JOIN SalesLT.ProductCategory AS pc
            ON p.ProductCategoryID = pc.ProductCategoryID
            ORDER BY p.Name";
    // Run query
    $stmt = $dbh->query($query);
    // Retrieve individual rows from the result
    while ($row = $stmt->fetch(PDO::FETCH_ASSOC)) {
        // ... output $row in desired format ...
    }

    // Release resources and close connection
    $stmt->closeCursor(); // alternatively, you could use $stmt = null;
    $dbh->close();
}
catch(Exception $e) {
    die( print_r($e->getMessage()) );
}
```

Connecting to SQL Server

PDO opens a connection to the database when you create a new PDO object. The constructor takes three arguments: the data source name (DSN), username, and password.

The DSN string is comprised of the prefix "sqlsrv:" followed by the specification of the server and connection attributes, typically the database. The SQL Server driver additionally supports the connection options given in Table 12-2, earlier in the chapter, except for *CharacterSet*, *ReturnDateAsString* (PDO always returns dates as strings), and *UID* and *PWD* (they are passed as parameters to the constructor). A typical call to the constructor would look this:

```
$dbh = new PDO('sqlsrv:server=(local); Database=AdventureWorksLT2008', 'sqluser',
'confidential');
```

If you specify username and password, then SQL Server authentication mode is used. If you would like to use the active Windows user for connecting, just leave username and password empty:

```
$dbh = new PDO( "sqlsrv:server=(local); Database=AdventureWorksLT2008");
```

The same benefits and drawbacks of SQL Server authentication versus Windows authentication discussed in section "Database Connections," earlier in the chapter, also apply to PDO.

Direct Queries and Prepared Statements

Apart from the direct execution of queries with *PDO::query()*, prepared statements can be executed with *PDO::prepare()* and *PDOStatement::execute()*. Prepared statements improve performance if you execute the same query multiple times, and prevent SQL injection security problems, because parameters are automatically masked as necessary. Listing 12-19 shows how values and parameters are bound to the statement with *PDOStatement::bindParam()* and *PDOStatement::bindValue()*. The third parameter is optional and specifies the preferred data type. By default, PDO::PARAM_STR is used. The bound variables are evaluated when *PDOStatement()::execute()* is called. Therefore, we can change these variables in a loop and get new query results each time.

LISTING 12-19 Binding parameters and values with prepared statements.

```
$search = array('Brown' => 1000, 'Miller' => 500, 'Lee' => 600);
$stmt = $dbh->prepare("SELECT EmailAddress FROM SalesLT.Customer "
                . "WHERE LastName = ? AND CustomerID < ? AND EmailAddress LIKE ?");
$stmt->bindParam(1, $name, PDO::PARAM_STR);
$stmt->bindParam(2, $maxId, PDO::PARAM_INT);
$stmt->bindValue(3, '%@adventure-works.com');
foreach ($search as $name => $maxId) {
    $stmt->execute();
    while ($addr = $stmt->fetchColumn(0)) {
        echo "<p>$name: $addr\n";
    }
}
```

Internally, the SQL Server PDO driver always executes queries in a prepared query context, even queries run with *PDO::query()*. If you do not execute a query multiple times, this might actually have a slight performance impact. In this case, you can use the attribute *PDO::SQLSRV_ATTR_DIRECT_QUERY* to disable the use of prepared statements, as shown in the following:

```
$dbh->setAttribute(PDO::SQLSRV_ATTR_DIRECT_QUERY, true);
```

The preceding statement disables prepared statements for the connection, even for *prepare()/ execute()*, too. You can also use this attribute to get the equivalent of parameterized queries. Listing 12-20 gives an example. An alternative to setting the attribute on the connection level, is to pass it to *PDO::prepare()*, as shown in the listing.

LISTING 12-20 Parameterized query using *PDO::SQLSRV_ATTR_DIRECT_QUERY*.

```
$stmt = $dbh->prepare("SELECT EmailAddress FROM SalesLT.Customer WHERE LastName = ?",
                    array(PDO::SQLSRV_ATTR_DIRECT_QUERY => true));
$stmt->bindValue(1, 'Brown');
$stmt->execute();
```

Enabling the direct query mode also enables the use of temporary tables across multiple queries and the setting of database options. Listing 12-21 shows a complete example of how to set the language of the connection. The result is shown in Figure 12-6.

LISTING 12-21 Setting the database language option by using *PDO::SQLSRV_ATTR_DIRECT_QUERY*.

```php
<?php
require './HTMLPage.php';
$page = new \net\xmp\phpbook\HTMLPage('PDO Direct Query Example');
$page->addElement('p', 'Name of the current month in different languages.');

$dbh = new PDO("sqlsrv:server=(local)");
$dbh->setAttribute(PDO::SQLSRV_ATTR_DIRECT_QUERY, true);
$stmt = $dbh->query('SET LANGUAGE Greek');
$stmt = $dbh->query("SELECT DATENAME(month, CURRENT_TIMESTAMP)");
$page->addElement('p', 'Greek: ' . $stmt->fetchColumn(0));
$stmt = $dbh->query('SET LANGUAGE Finnish');
$stmt = $dbh->query("SELECT DATENAME(month, CURRENT_TIMESTAMP)");
$page->addElement('p', 'Finnish: ' . $stmt->fetchColumn(0));
$stmt = $dbh->query("SET LANGUAGE 'Traditional Chinese'");
$stmt = $dbh->query("SELECT DATENAME(month, CURRENT_TIMESTAMP)");
$page->addElement('p', 'Traditional Chinese: ' . $stmt->fetchColumn(0));
$page->printPage();
?>
```

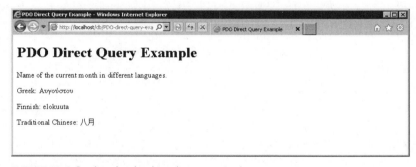

FIGURE 12-6 Setting the database language option.

Retrieving Results

PDO offers several different methods to retrieve your results, such as an associative array or object. Table 12-5 provides an overview of the most commonly used fetch modes. You can either set the mode directly, when calling *PDOStatement::fetch()* like this:

```
$result = $pdo_stmt->fetch(PDO::FETCH_OBJ);
```

Or you can set the fetch mode for the statement by using *setFetchMode()* and later on call *fetch()* without parameters, as shown here:

```
$pdo_stmt->setFetchMode(PDO::FETCH_INTO, $myObj);
$pdo_stmt->fetch(); // result columns are set as properties in $myObj
```

TABLE 12-5 The most commonly used fetch modes in PDO

Mode	Description
PDO::FETCH_ASSOC	Returns an associative array indexed by column names. If two columns have the same name, only one value is returned. Note that all columns have to have names—use column aliases if needed.
PDO::FETCH_BOTH	Returns combined array of *PDO::FETCH_ASSOC* and *PDO::FETCH_NUM*. This is the default mode.
PDO::FETCH_BOUND	Does not return the results, but instead writes them to the PHP variables previously bound with *PDOStatement::bindColumn($var)*.
PDO::FETCH_CLASS	Returns the results as properties of a newly instantiated object of the named class. Mode has to be set with *PDOStatement::setFetchMode (PDO::FETCH_CLASS, $classname, $constr_args_array)*. The arguments for the class constructor are optional. This is equivalent to using *PDOStatement::fetchObject($classname, $constr_args_array)*.
PDO::FETCH_COLUMN	Returns the single column specified by the additional argument. Mode has to be set with *PDOStatement::setFetchMode(PDO::FETCH_COLUMN, $num)*. This is equivalent to using *PDOStatement::fetchColumn($num)*.
PDO::FETCH_INTO	Returns the results as properties set in an existing object. Mode has to be set with *PDOStatement::setFetchMode(PDO::FETCH_INTO, $object)*.
PDO::FETCH_LAZY	Similar to *PDO::FETCH_OBJ*, but an instance of the *PDORow* class is returned and its properties are only populated when accessed. This can be a good choice, if the result is comprised of many columns.
PDO::FETCH_NAMED	Same as *PDO::FETCH_ASSOC*, but if two or more columns have the same name, the array entry contains an array of all values.
PDO::FETCH_NUM	Returns an array index by column number. Columns do not necessarily have to have names.
PDO::FETCH_OBJ	Returns the results as properties of a newly instantiated object of the *stdClass* class. Equivalent to using *PDOStatement::fetchObject()*.

If you know that you are going to process all result rows and that the complete result set fits into memory, you can use *PDOStatement::fetchAll()* instead of *fetch()*. Combined with *PDO::FETCH_COLUMN*, this is especially useful if you construct selection lists from database tables. By providing the special *PDO::FETCH_GROUP* flag, you can group the result by the specified column. For example, to get a list of all supported languages of SQL Server and their IDs, you would write:

```
$stmt = $dbh->query("SELECT msglangid, name FROM master.sys.syslanguages");
$res = $stmt->fetchAll(PDO::FETCH_COLUMN|PDO::FETCH_GROUP);
```

The result would be an array that looks similar to the following (output from *var_dump()*):

```
array(32) {
  [1033]=> array(2) { [0]=> string(10) "us_english"
                      [1]=> string(7) "British" }
  [1031]=> array(1) { [0]=> string(7) "Deutsch" }
  [1036]=> array(1) { [0]=> string(9) "Français" }
  [1041]=> array(1) { [0]=> string(9) "日本語" }
...
}
```

Data Types and Streams

Compared to the granularity with which you can control conversion between the different PHP and SQL Server data types using the SQLSRV driver, the PDO driver is somewhat limited. Table 12-6 shows the supported parameter types. Any type not listed is automatically treated as string data type. An important implication (compared to SQLSRV) is that PDO handles date and time types as strings.

TABLE 12-6 Parameter data types in PDO

Parameter data type	Description
PDO::PARAM_BOOL	*Boolean* data type
PDO::PARAM_INT	Generic SQL *integer* data type
PDO::PARAM_LOB	*Large Object* data type, used for streaming
PDO::PARAM_NULL	SQL *NULL* data type
PDO::PARAM_STR	SQL *char()*, *nchar()*, *varchar()*, *nvarchar()* datatype. Fallback for all other types.

When binding a parameter *PDOStatement::bindParam()* or a column of an output result set by using *PDOStatement::bindColumn()*, you can specify the data type. Both statements also provide the possibility to set the parameter encoding. Table 12-7 shows the four different possible values for parameter encoding. The encoding can also be set connection wide by using *PDO::setAttribute()*, or query wide by using *PDOStatement::setAttribute()* or as parameter to *PDO::prepare()*.

TABLE 12-7 Encoding types in PDO

Encoding type	Description
PDO::SQLSRV_ENCODING_BINARY	No encoding takes place, raw byte stream.
PDO::SQLSRV_ENCODING_DEFAULT	Either the connections encoding or if specified during connection, the system encoding.
PDO::SQLSRV_ENCODING_SYSTEM	8-Bit encoding according to the code page of the Windows system. Data may be transcoded during transmission. Characters that are out of range (for example, multi-byte characters) are replaced by a question mark.
PDO::SQLSRV_ENCODING_UTF8	Default encoding: all character data is handled as UTF-8.

Listing 12-22 shows how to read an image from the database and display it. This is the PDO version of Listing 12-15. For the output column, both parameter type and encoding are specified. There is one important distinction to how the SQLSRV driver handles this: the value returned is not a stream, but just a string. This is why at the end the resulting variable is just output with *echo*. Note that this behavior is not as defined in the PDO documentation, which would also suggest that a stream handle is returned. Oddly enough, in the reverse direction—that is when uploading a file to the database—the PDO driver expects a file stream handle, just as described in the PDO documentation.

LISTING 12-22 Displaying an image directly from the database using PDO.

```php
<?php
try {
    // Establish database connection
    $dbh = new PDO( "sqlsrv:server=(local); Database=AdventureWorksLT2008");
    $dbh->setAttribute(PDO::ATTR_ERRMODE, PDO::ERRMODE_EXCEPTION);

    // Query picture for product
    $query = 'SELECT ThumbNailPhoto FROM SalesLT.Product WHERE ProductID=:prodId';
    $stmt = $dbh->prepare($query);
    $stmt->bindValue('prodId', $_GET['id'], PDO::PARAM_INT);
    $stmt->execute();
    $stmt->bindColumn(1, $blob, PDO::PARAM_LOB, 0, PDO::SQLSRV_ENCODING_BINARY);
    $stmt->fetch(PDO::FETCH_BOUND);
}
catch(Exception $e) {
    die( print_r($e->getMessage()) );
}

header('Content-type: image/gif');
echo $blob;
```

Summary

Working with the SQL Server PHP extension is easy for PHP programmers: the basic functions for structuring a connection as well as sending T-SQL statements and reading the data are similar to other database PHP extensions.

The possibility to instantiate proper classes while reading results simplifies the mapping between application logic with PHP objects and the database. The granular control of the data types you want to use on the PHP and SQL Server side is a helpful feature during the development of applications.

As with other database-specific drivers, however, its use makes the later support of other database systems more difficult. With version 2.0 of *SQLSRV* the driver supports *PHP Data Objects* (PDO), which allows for a transparent access to SQL Server and other databases. The PDO driver's robust and feature rich implementation, especially the possibility of executing direct queries that preserve context, make it an ideal choice for application developers. But if you need to handle corner cases, need more control, or output large database objects as streams, the native driver still is your first choice.

In the following chapter, you will learn more about advanced SQL Server features, among them the full-text search, stored procedures, and triggers.

Chapter 13
Advanced Database Functions

Today, a web application without generic search function is no longer imaginable. In addition to the navigation features, users also expect to be able to take advantage of the website search to quickly find the content in which they're interested. With the full text search, Microsoft SQL Server provides the tool to search and find data saved in a database. SQL Server is also ideal for international websites because it supports more than 50 languages.

This chapter also describes transactions and the programming of databases using stored procedures, custom functions, and triggers. The transfer of the data logic of a PHP application into the database not only increases the performance and security but also the quality and accuracy of the data.

Full-Text Search

You can use the full-text indexes of SQL Server to search for text. A full-text index is a data structure optimized for text queries to search for words in a fast and efficient way. To use the full-text search, perform the following steps:

1. **Create a full-text catalog**   The catalog is the structure in which the full text indexes are created.

2. **Create the full-text index within the catalog**   The index is created for specific table columns.

3. **Search the full-text index**   SQL Server offers four different methods to search the index.

The methods using SQL Server Management Studio (SSMS) as well as Transact-SQL (T-SQL) statements are described below.

Installing the Module

If your SQL Server installation doesn't include the full-text search module, perform the following steps to install it:

1. Start the SQL Server setup from the installation media.

2. Select Installation | New SQL Server Stand-Alone Installation.

 Warning The installation support files must have been installed successfully before continuing with the rest of this procedure.

3. Select the Add Features To An Existing Instance Of SQL Server 2008 R2 option as installation type, and then click Next.

4. In the Instance Features section, under Database Engine Services, select the Full-Text Search check box, and then click Next. In the Ready To Install dialog box, click Install.

5. When the installation is complete, click Close to exit setup.

The full-text module is now installed; you might need to restart SQL Server.

Language Selection

The full-text search in SQL Server 2008 R2 supports about 50 languages. The selected language impacts the recognition of word boundaries, words, and root words, as well as the stop words and the thesaurus (if applicable). Therefore, it is important to select the appropriate language for indexing while creating a full-text index.

You can find a list of all supported languages in the *sys.fulltext_languages* system table:

```
select * from sys.fulltext_languages;
```

If you don't specify a language, SQL Server uses the default setting, which you can query by using the following statement:

```
SELECT sc.value_in_use, fl.name FROM sys.configurations AS sc
JOIN sys.fulltext_languages AS fl ON sc.value=fl.lcid
WHERE sc.name=N'default full-text language';
```

Creating the Catalog and the Index by Using SSMS

The following sections describe how to create the catalog and the index by using SSMS to perform a full-text search.

Creating the Catalog

To create a full-text catalog, perform the following steps:

1. In Object Explorer, click Storage, and then right-click Full Text Catalogs. In the context menu that opens, click New Full-Text Catalog.

2. Enter the name of the full-text catalog in the text box and optionally select an owner for the catalog.

3. Select the accent sensitivity option that meets your requirements.

4. Click OK to confirm your settings.

Creating the Index

To create a full-text index by using SSMS, perform the following steps:

1. In Object Explorer, right-click the desired table. In the context menu that opens, select Full-Text Index, and then click Define Full-Text Index.

   The Full-Text Indexing Wizard opens.

2. On the second page of the wizard, select the associated index used to map the full-text search results to the corresponding table rows. It is best practice to select the primary table key. Click Next to confirm.

3. On the Select Table Columns page, select the columns for the full-text index.

   For each column, specify the Language For Word Breaker, and for a binary or varbinary() column, select the Type Column, which is required so that SQL Server can recognize the data type of the column.

4. On the Change Tracking page, you can specify whether table changes are applied to the full-text index manually or automatically.

   Unless you have special requirements, it is OK to enable automatic change tracking.

5. Assign the full-text catalog or create a new catalog and specify a stop list with words that should be excluded from the index.

   For larger indexes, you can configure the times at which the index is filled on the Population Schedules page.

6. Verify your settings. Click Finish to create the index.

Creating the Catalog and the Index by Using T-SQL

The following sections describe how to create the catalog and the index by using T-SQL statements.

Creating the Catalog

To create the full-text catalog, run the *CREATE FULLTEXT CATALOG* command:

```
CREATE FULLTEXT CATALOG catalog_name
    [ WITH ACCENT_SENSITIVITY = {ON|OFF} ]
    [ AS DEFAULT ]
    [ AUTHORIZATION owner_name ]
```

The *ACCENT_SENSITIVITY* option indicates if letters with accents are incorporated or the basic form of a letter is used. A full-text catalog groups indexes but doesn't use disk space. For example, to create a full-text catalog for the *AdventureWorksLT2008* database, run the following command:

```
USE AdventureWorksLT2008
CREATE FULLTEXT CATALOG FT_Products
GO
```

Creating the Index

After the catalog is created, run the *CREATE FULLTEXT INDEX* command to create a full-text index in this catalog:

```
CREATE FULLTEXT INDEX ON table_name
    [ ( { column_name [ TYPE COLUMN column_name ] [ LANGUAGE language_term ]
        } [ ,...n] ) ] KEY INDEX index_name
    [ ON <catalog_filegroup_option> ]
    [ WITH [ ( ] <with_option> [ ,...n] [ ) ] ]
[;]
<with_option> ::= {
    CHANGE_TRACKING [ = ] { MANUAL | AUTO | OFF [, NO POPULATION ] }
    | STOPLIST [ = ] { OFF | SYSTEM | stoplist_name } }
```

Each table can only have one full-text index, but the index can have several columns. A full-text index requires a unique index (*KEY INDEX*) to map the full-text search results to table rows. In addition to the full-text catalog, you can specify a *FILEGROUP* by using the *ON* keyword if the full-text index is saved in a different location. With *CHANGE_TRACKING*, you specify when table changes are applied to the full-text index.

To create a full-text index for the Description column in the *SalesLT.ProductDescription* table, run the following command:

```
CREATE FULLTEXT INDEX ON SalesLT.ProductDescription
  ( Description LANGUAGE 0 )
  KEY INDEX PK_ProductDescription_ProductDescriptionID ON FT_Products
  WITH CHANGE_TRACKING AUTO, STOPLIST SYSTEM
GO
```

In this command, the language is set to *LANGUAGE 0* (neutral) because the table contains descriptions in different languages. For example, the locale ID (*LCID*) for German is 1031, for English UK, 2057, and for English US, 1033.

Search with Full-Text Index

SQL Server offers two methods for the search with a full-text index: the exact search with operators and weights (*CONTAINS*), and the free text search (*FREETEXT*), which can be specified within a *WHERE* clause (*CONTAINS/FREETEXT*) or return a temporary table for *JOIN* (*CONTAINSTABLE/FREETEXTTABLE*).

Exact Search (*CONTAINS/CONTAINSTABLE*)

The exact search queries words precisely as indicated in the search clause. Listing 13-1 shows how to search for the word "aerodynamic" in a product description. This search finds only the entries containing the exact word.

LISTING 13-1 Full-text search for the word "aerodynamic" with *CONTAINS*.

```
SELECT ProductDescriptionID, Description
FROM SalesLT.ProductDescription
WHERE CONTAINS(Description, N'lightweight')
GO


ProductDescriptionID Description
-------------------- --------------------------------------------------------------
375                  Cross-train, race, or just socialize on a sleek, aerodynamic
                     bike. Advanced seat technology provides comfort all day.
376                  Cross-train, race, or just socialize on a sleek, aerodynamic
                     bike designed for a woman. Advanced seat technology provides
                     comfort all day.
```

You can use the results returned by *CONTAINSTABLE()* as a temporary table. Listing 13-2 shows that this table consists of two columns: the value of the key that is used to find the row in the table (in this example, *SalesLT.ProductDescription*), and a relative priority to sort the result list.

LISTING 13-2 The result of the search with *CONTAINSTABLE*.

```
SELECT * FROM CONTAINSTABLE (SalesLT.ProductDescription, Description, N'road')
GO

KEY  RANK
---- ----
   8   32
  64   32
 170   48
...
(13 rows affected)
```

Listing 13-3 shows how to sort a search with *CONTAINSTABLE*. The temporary table with the search results is linked with the other tables by *JOIN*. This example shows why a key index is required for the table entries when defining a full text index.

LISTING 13-3 Full text search for the word "road" with *CONTAINSTABLE*.

```
SELECT p.ProductID, p.Name, pd.Description
FROM SalesLT.Product AS p
JOIN SalesLT.ProductModelProductDescription AS pmpd
    ON pmpd.ProductModelID = p.ProductModelID
JOIN SalesLT.ProductDescription AS pd
    ON pd.ProductDescriptionID = pmpd.ProductDescriptionID
JOIN CONTAINSTABLE (SalesLT.ProductDescription, Description, N'road') AS ft
    ON ft.[KEY] = pd.ProductDescriptionID
WHERE pmpd.Culture = N'en'
ORDER BY ft.[RANK] DESC
GO

ProductID Name                  Description
--------- --------------------- ------------------------------------------------
808       LL Mountain Handlebars All-purpose bar for on or off-road
818       LL Road Front Wheel    Replacement road front wheel for entry-level cyclist
803       ML Fork                Composite road fork with an aluminum steerer tube
...
(25 rows affected)
```

CONTAINS/CONTAINSTABLE doesn't only search for single words. Table 13-1 lists an overview of the search expressions.

TABLE 13-1 Search expressions for the full-text search with CONTAINS

Search expression	Description
word	Searches for the specified word.
"text phrase"	Searches for a phrase that appears in the exact order in the text.
wor* / "text phra*"	The * placeholder searches for words (or phrases) beginning with certain letters.
phrase1 *AND* phrase2 phrase1 *AND NOT* phrase2 phrase1 *OR* phrase2	Boolean operators to link search expressions.
FORMSOF (INFLECTIONAL, word) *FORMSOF (THESAURUS*, word*)*	Searches for word forms (for example, plural) or similar words. **Tip** Note the index language and verify that the thesaurus exists.
word1 *NEAR* word2 word1 ~ word2	Searches for words close in the text, which need not necessarily be consecutive words.
ISABOUT (phrase1 WEIGHT (n), phrase2 *WEIGHT (m))*	Weighting of search expressions.

Free-Text Search (*FREETEXT/FREETEXTTABLE*)

You pass the searched text to the free-text search with *FREETEXT*. *FREETEXT* searches for corresponding entries in the full-text index. The search considers word forms and the thesaurus and phrases are automatically weighted.

Listing 13-4 shows an example in which the search criteria are based on the text "entry level mountain bike" and the search returns the five best results.

LISTING 13-4 Free-text full-text search with *FREETEXTTABLE*.

```
SELECT pd.ProductDescriptionID, pd.Description
FROM SalesLT.ProductDescription AS pd
JOIN FREETEXTTABLE(SalesLT.ProductDescription, Description,
                N'entry level mountain bike', 5) AS ft
    ON ft.[KEY] = pd.ProductDescriptionID
GO


ProductDescriptionID Description
-------------------- --------------------------------------------------------
  686                Replacement mountain wheel for entry-level rider.
  867                Replacement rear mountain wheel for entry-level rider.
  1981               Replacement mountain wheel for entry-level rider.
  689                Replacement road front wheel for entry-level cyclist.
  703                Unique shape reduces fatigue for entry level riders.
(5 rows affected)
```

> **Tip** The fourth parameter of *CONTAINSTABLE/FREETEXTTABLE* specifies how many search re-
> sults are returned. If this parameter is set, the results are automatically sorted by relevance. In
> Listing 13-4, the five best results are returned.

Transactions

An important characteristic of relational database systems is that database operations are
atomic and isolated—that is to say, the operations don't interact. These separate operations
are called transactions. SQL Server also supports transactions. By default, each T-SQL statement is a separate transaction (auto commit mode).

T-SQL Transactions

You can combine several T-SQL statements in a single transaction. For this purpose, SQL
Server offers the following commands:

- **BEGIN TRANSACTION**   Starts a transaction

- **COMMIT TRANSACTION**   Completes a transaction and saves changes in the
  database

- **ROLLBACK TRANSACTION**   Completes a transaction and discards all changes

- **SAVE TRANSACTION**   Saves the current transaction status; future rollback commands
  discard changes up to this point

Transactions can be named and nested. If transactions are nested, a *ROLLBACK* rolls back
all transactions. It is not possible to only roll back an inner transaction. Listing 13-5 shows
the functionality of transactions based on a temporary table (if the table name starts with
a pound sign [hash], the corresponding table is automatically saved as a temporary table).
SELECT returns the values 1, 2, 3, and 6 because 4, 5, and 7 were rolled back.

LISTING 13-5 T-SQL transactions based on a temporary table.

```
CREATE TABLE #testTable (number int); -- Create temporary table
GO
BEGIN TRANSACTION;                     -- Starts the first transaction
INSERT INTO #testTable VALUES (1);
BEGIN TRANSACTION T_Two;               -- Starts the second nested transaction
INSERT INTO #testTable VALUES (2);
COMMIT TRANSACTION T_Two;              -- Note that T_Two can still be rolled
INSERT INTO #testTable VALUES (3);     -- back together with first transaction
SAVE TRANSACTION Protection_point;     -- Defining a protection point
```

```
INSERT INTO #testTable VALUES (4);
INSERT INTO #testTable VALUES (5);
ROLLBACK TRAN Protection_point;        -- Roll back up to the protection point
INSERT INTO #testTable VALUES (6);
COMMIT TRANSACTION;                     -- Complete the first transaction
BEGIN TRAN                             -- Starts the third transaction
INSERT INTO #testTable VALUES (7);
ROLLBACK TRAN;                          -- Roll back the third transaction
SELECT * FROM #testTable;               -- Returns the values 1,2,3,6
GO
DROP TABLE #testTable;
GO
```

Transaction Isolation Levels

Transactions not only ensure the atomicity of the executed statements in the transaction (either all or none are applied), but also isolate changes from other concurrent users (this is the "I" of the ACID model). Isolation comes at a price: other users might be locked out until the current transaction has completed. Without isolation, concurrent transactions might run into one of the following issues:

- **Dirty reads**   A transaction might read data written by another, yet uncommitted transaction. If the latter rolls back its changes, the former transaction is left with dirty data.

- **Non-repeatable reads**   If a transaction reads the same data twice, another transaction might change the data in between. Reading the same data thus renders two different results.

- **Phantom reads**   Closely related to non-repeatable reads, phantom reads occur when another transaction inserts or deletes data records. If this happens between two reads of the same range, then so-called phantom rows seem to appear and disappear.

- **Lost updates**   This happens, when two concurrent transactions that are unaware of each other consecutively update the same record. The update of the first transaction might be lost.

SQL Server provides five different isolation levels, each with its distinct advantages and disadvantages. You should choose the isolation level suitable for your application needs:

- **READ UNCOMMITTED**   This level offers no isolation between transactions. Every one of the aforementioned problems mentioned above can occur. It is the fastest of all levels, as transactions do not block each other, and lock contention cannot occur.

- **READ COMMITTED**   This is the default isolation level. It prevents dirty reads of uncommitted data, but not phantom and non-repeatable reads, as transactions that are committed can change data between two reads.

- **REPEATABLE READ**   As the name suggests, this ensures repeatable reads. In addition to the restrictions of the read-committed level, other transactions are forbidden to modify records the current transaction has read, until it finishes. To ensure this, SQL Server uses shared locks. If your application has a high transaction volume, this could pose performance problems. Phantom reads are still possible, as newly inserted records by other transactions are not affected by the locking mechanism.

- **SNAPSHOT**   This isolation level protects against all four problems, because it makes a snapshot of all data requested by the transaction. Thus, each statement has the same consistent view, from start until the end of the transaction, unaffected by other transactions. Under the hood, SQL Server uses row-level versioning for this level. Again this is resource intensive, so performance is not as good as for the first two levels, but it operates without locks, so lock contention does not occur. However, a transaction can fail if another transaction modified the same data at the same time. This approach is sometimes called *optimistic concurrency control*.

- **SERIALIZEABLE**   This level also protects against all four problems, but uses range locks to prevent phantom reads (see the Note that follows). It employs a pessimistic approach to concurrency control. Range locks can cover quite a lot of records, so depending on circumstances, this isolation level has very low performance and lock contention, possibly even deadlocks, occur.

> **Note** Craig Freedman wrote a good explanation regarding the difference between the *SNAPSHOT* and *SERIALIZEABLE* isolation levels on his SQL Server blog, which you can access at *http://blogs.msdn.com/b/craigfr/archive/2007/05/16/serializable-vs-snapshot-isolation-level.aspx*.

The transaction level is set by using the T-SQL command:

```
SET TRANSACTION ISOLATION LEVEL ( isolation level ) [ ; ]
```

The transaction isolation level should be set before the transactions starts. Within certain limits, it is possible to change the isolation level within a transaction. Go to MSDN for a more in-depth discussion of the various levels at *http://msdn.microsoft.com/en-us/library/ms173763.aspx*.

PHP Transactions

T-SQL transactions should only be used for stored procedures. In PHP, you should use the functions of the PHP SQL Server extension, because the extension needs to know the transaction status to ensure the correct behavior. The following functions are available:

- **sqlsrv_begin_transaction()**   Starts a transaction.

- **sqlsrv_commit()**   Completes a transaction and saves changes.

- **sqlsrv_rollback()**   Completes a transaction and discards changes.

There is no equivalent to *SAVE TRANSACTION* because PHP and transactions cannot be nested. Listing 13-6 shows the effect of transactions: The values 1, 2, and 5 are returned because the values 3 and 4 are inserted into a transaction that is rolled back.

LISTING 13-6 PHP transactions based on a temporary table.

```
sqlsrv_query($db, "CREATE TABLE #testTable (number int);");
sqlsrv_begin_transaction($db);
  sqlsrv_query($db, "INSERT INTO #testTable VALUES (1);");
  sqlsrv_query($db, "INSERT INTO #testTable VALUES (2);");
sqlsrv_commit($db);
sqlsrv_begin_transaction($db);
  sqlsrv_query($db, "INSERT INTO #testTable VALUES (3);");
  sqlsrv_query($db, "INSERT INTO #testTable VALUES (4);");
sqlsrv_rollback($db);
sqlsrv_query($db, "INSERT INTO #testTable VALUES (5);");
$stmt = sqlsrv_query($db, "SELECT * FROM #testTable;");
while ($o = sqlsrv_fetch_object($stmt)) {
    echo $o->number, '<br />';
}
sqlsrv_free_stmt($stmt);
```

If you would like to specify the transaction isolation level, you specify it as the connection attribute *TransactionIsolation* when connecting to SQL Server. There, you can use one of the following self-explanatory constants:

- *SQLSRV_TXN_READ_UNCOMMITTED*

- *SQLSRV_TXN_READ_COMMITTED*

- *SQLSRV_TXN_REPEATABLE_READ*

- *SQLSRV_TXN_SNAPSHOT*

- *SQLSRV_TXN_SERIALIZABLE*

Here is an example of setting the isolation level to *REPEATABLE READ*:

```
$connectionInfo = array(
    'Database' => 'AdventureWorksLT2008',
    'CharacterSet' => 'UTF-8',
    'TransactionIsolation' => SQLSRV_TXN_REPEATABLE_READ
);
$dbh = sqlsrv_connect('(local)', $connectionInfo);
```

Transactions Using PHP Data Objects

If you are using PHP Data Objects (PDO), then you can use the following functions for SQL transactions:

- **PDO::beginTransaction()**   Starts a transaction.
- **PDO::commit()**   Completes a transaction and saves any changes made.
- **PDO::rollBack()**   Completes a transaction and discard changes.

Listing 13-7 shows how you would use PDO transactions in your programs. Again the result is 1, 2, and 5, just as in Listing 13-6, because the other values are rolled back.

LISTING 13-7 PHP transactions with PDO.

```
try {
    $dbh->exec("CREATE TABLE #testTable (number int);");
    $dbh->beginTransaction();
    $dbh->exec("INSERT INTO #testTable VALUES (1);");
    $dbh->exec("INSERT INTO #testTable VALUES (2);");
    $dbh->commit();
    $dbh->beginTransaction();
    $dbh->exec("INSERT INTO #testTable VALUES (3);");
    $dbh->exec("INSERT INTO #testTable VALUES (4);");
    $dbh->rollBack();
    $dbh->exec("INSERT INTO #testTable VALUES (5);");
    foreach ($dbh->query("SELECT * FROM #testTable;") AS $row) {
        echo $row['number'], '<br />';
    }
    $dbh = null;
} catch (Exception $e) {
    echo "Failed: " . $e->getMessage();
}
```

To specify the transaction isolation level, you add the *TransactionIsolation* keyword to the connection string. The same predefined constants are used, just as with the native driver, but this time inside the PDO class; thus, they are named *PDO::SQLSRV_TXN_**:

```
$dbh = new PDO('sqlsrv:server=(local); Database=AdventureWorksLT2008;' .
        'TransactionIsolation=' . PDO::SQLSRV_TXN_READ_UNCOMMITTED, "", "");
```

Both PHP SQL Server extensions, *sqlsrv* and PDO, will automatically roll back any open transactions at the end of the script. This ensures that the database is left in a consistent state if the PHP script exits unexpectedly. Note that you actually should ensure that the begin transaction commands succeeds; otherwise, SQL Server will remain in auto commit mode.

Stored Procedures

With stored procedures, you can program SQL Server with T-SQL statements. T-SQL statements correspond to a T-SQL batch with input and output variables. Stored procedures are powerful tools for optimizing the performance, comfort, and the security of databases. The following sections describe variables, control structures, and procedures. Unlike custom functions, procedures can change the data in tables as well as the database structure. Chapter 14, "Users and Permissions," explains the permissions of stored procedures in more detail.

Variables

In T-SQL, variables are defined by using the *DECLARE* statement and specified and changed with the *SET* statement. Listing 13-8 shows an example.

LISTING 13-8 Declaring and calculating variables.

```
DECLARE @a int = 3;
DECLARE @b int;
SET @b = @a + 2;
PRINT @b;
PRINT 'A:' + CAST(@a AS varchar) + ', B:' + CAST(@b AS varchar);
GO

5
A:3, B:5
```

> **Note** The *CAST* statements for the second *PRINT* are required because the plus operator adds strings as well as numbers, and the addition would take priority.

Variables are only valid within a function, a procedure, or a T-SQL batch. The following example causes an error because the *PRINT* statement is outside of the batch:

```
DECLARE @a int = 3;
GO
PRINT @a;
```

Valid data types for variables are all data types that can be used for table columns (see Chapter 10, "Databases and Tables"), except *varchar(max)*, *nvarchar(max)*, and *varbinary(max)*. Variables can also contain tables, as is demonstrated in Listing 13-9.

LISTING 13-9 Defining a variable containing a table.

```
DECLARE @friends TABLE (name nvarchar(30));
INSERT INTO @friends VALUES (N'Doris'), (N'Tony'), (N'Julia');
SELECT name FROM @friends;
GO


name
----
Doris
Tony
Julia
```

Defining Procedures

To define a procedure, use the *CREATE PROCEDURE* (short *CREATE PROC*) statement. Listing 13-10 shows an example procedure, followed by an explanation of the steps. The procedure is created in the *AdventureWorksLT* database.

LISTING 13-10 Defining a stored procedure.

```
IF OBJECT_ID('SalesLT.getProducts', N'P') IS NOT NULL
   DROP PROC SalesLT.getProducts;
GO
CREATE PROC SalesLT.getProducts
   @category nvarchar(50),
   @color nvarchar(15) = N'Blue'
AS
   SELECT p.ProductId, p.Name
   FROM SalesLT.Product AS p JOIN SalesLT.ProductCategory AS pc
   ON p.ProductCategoryID = pc.ProductCategoryID
   WHERE p.Color=@color AND pc.Name=@category;
GO
```

The example consists of three sections. *OBJECT_ID()* checks if the procedure exists. If it does, the procedure is deleted with *DROP PROCEDURE*.

```
IF OBJECT_ID('SalesLT.getProducts', N'P') IS NOT NULL DROP PROC SalesLT.getProducts;
GO
```

The next section defines the procedure and the parameters. The procedure is in the *SalesLT* schema, has the name *getProducts*, and expects the two parameters: *@category* and *@color*.

@color has a default value (*N'Blue'*) and doesn't need to be specified.

```
CREATE PROC SalesLT.getProducts
   @category nvarchar(50),
   @color nvarchar(15) = N'Blue'
```

The third section contains the procedure body starting with the keyword *AS*. This includes the T-SQL statements that should run when the procedure is called. The procedure can be understood as a T-SQL batch that accepts parameters and (optional) returns results. The batch in the example consists of a single *SELECT* statement, and the *WHERE* clause checks for parameters:

```
AS
    SELECT p.ProductId, p.Name
    FROM SalesLT.Product AS p JOIN SalesLT.ProductCategory AS pc
    ON p.ProductCategoryID = pc.ProductCategoryID
    WHERE p.Color=@color AND pc.Name=@category;
GO
```

Calling Procedures

Stored procedures are called by using *EXECUTE* (short *EXEC*), and the parameters are passed during the call, as shown in the following example:

```
EXECUTE SalesLT.getProducts @category=N'Helmets', @color=N'Red';
GO

ProductId Name
--------- --------------------
707       Sport-100 Helmet, Red
```

You don't need to enter the parameter names if the parameters are specified in the same order as defined in the procedure:

```
EXECUTE SalesLT.getProducts N'Helmets', N'Red';
```

To call a procedure, the user must have *EXECUTE* permission (see Chapter 14).

Output Parameters and Return Values

Stored procedures can return values in output parameters or a return value with the *RETURN* statement. The return value should not be used to pass data; use it instead to pass status codes.

Listing 13-11 shows an example. In the listing, the *getLowestPrice* procedure returns the lowest product price in a category in the *@lowestPrice* output parameter marked with the keyword *OUTPUT*. The *RETURN* statement at the end of the procedure returns the value *0* if *@lowestPrice=NULL*; otherwise, it returns a value of *1*.

LISTING 13-11 A stored procedure with output parameter and return value.

```
IF OBJECT_ID('SalesLT.getLowestPrice', 'P') IS NOT NULL
  DROP PROC SalesLT.getLowestPrice;
GO
CREATE PROC SalesLT.getLowestPrice
  @category nvarchar(50),
  @lowestPrice money OUTPUT
AS
SET @lowestPrice = (
  SELECT MIN(p.ListPrice) FROM SalesLT.Product AS p
  JOIN SalesLT.ProductCategory AS pc ON p.ProductCategoryID = pc.ProductCategoryID
  WHERE pc.Name=@category);
RETURN ISNULL(@lowestPrice,0) / ISNULL(@lowestPrice,1);
GO
```

Listing 13-12 shows how the procedure is called. In this example, the return value is saved in @*status* and the @*lowestPrice* output parameter is saved in the @*lp* variable. The output parameter must also have the keyword *OUTPUT* (short *OUT*) when called.

LISTING 13-12 Calling a procedure with output parameter and return value.

```
DECLARE @lp money;
DECLARE @status bit;
EXEC @status = SalesLT.getProducts2 @category=N'Helmets', @lowestPrice=@lp OUT;
SELECT @status, @lp;
```

Control Structures

T-SQL provides known control structures for procedures: queries with *IF/ELSE* and *CASE* queries as well as loops with *WHILE,* which can be controlled with *BREAK* and *CONTINUE.* Because control structures always refer to a statement, you can define statement blocks with *BEGIN* and *END*.

Listing 13-13 shows how to use structures based on the *getCreditPrice* procedure. The procedure calculates the product price for a credit purchase. This example also shows how to use comments: single-line comments begin with two hyphens "--", and multiline comments are enclosed in /* ... */.

LISTING 13-13 A procedure with T-SQL control structures.

```
/* getCreditPrice:
 * Calculates the product price for a credit purchase
 */
CREATE PROC SalesLT.getCreditPrice
  @id int,                           -- SalesLT.Product.ProductId
  @rate real,                        -- Monthly interest rate
  @months int = 12,                  -- Number of months
  @listPrice money OUTPUT,
  @price money OUTPUT
AS
  DECLARE @fee money;                -- Definition of a local variable for fees
  SET @price = (
    SELECT ListPrice FROM SalesLT.Product
    WHERE ProductID = @id);
  SET @listPrice = @price;
  SET @fee = CASE                    -- Fees depend on product price
    WHEN @price < 10.0 THEN 0.50
    WHEN @price < 50.0 THEN 1.00
    ELSE                   2.00
  END;
  IF (@months >= 24) BEGIN           -- If credit period is over 2 years, the fee
doubles
    SET @fee *= 2;
  END
  WHILE (@months > 0) BEGIN          -- Calculating the interest and compound interest
    SET @price = @price * (1+@rate);
    SET @months -= 1;
  END
  SET @price += @fee;
GO
```

Note If you use the *CASE* statement to check for equivalency, the syntax is simpler because the variable is located next to the keyword *CASE*, as demonstrated in the following:

```
SET @fee = CASE @color          -- Fees depend on product color
  WHEN 'Blue'   THEN 0.50
  WHEN 'Red'    THEN 1.00
  ELSE               2.00
END;
```

Calls from PHP

In PHP, stored procedures are called by using the *sqlsrv_query()* function. To call the procedure in Listing 13-10, enter the following command:

```
$stmt = sqlsrv_query($db, "EXEC SalesLT.getProducts N'Helmets'");
while ($obj = sqlsrv_fetch_object($stmt)) {
    ...
}
sqlsrv_free_stmt($stmt);
```

Using prepared statements, you can easily access output parameters of stored procedures. When binding parameters to a prepared statement, you can indicate the parameter direction as follows:

- **SQLSRV_PARAM_IN**   Defines an input parameter.
- **SQLSRV_PARAM_INOUT**   Defines a bidirectional parameter, used for input and output.
- **SQLSRV_PARAM_OUT**   Defines an output parameter.

To set these options, you pass the PHP variable inside an array to *sqlsrv_prepare()*:

```
array(&$phpvar [, $param_direction [, $phpType [, $sqlType]]])
```

You should always pass PHP variables by reference (*&$phpvar*) instead of by value (*$phpvar*). Also, ensure that the variable is not *NULL* if you use it as bidirectional or output parameter. An error might occur otherwise.

Listing 13-14 shows how to execute the *SalesLT.getCreditPrice* stored procedure from Listing 13-13. The variables *$listPrice* and *$creditPrice* are used as output parameters. Note that the *sqlsrv* driver infers the data type from the current value of the variable. Because *SalesLT.get CreditPrice* returns money values, you should use the PHP *float* data type. There are two ways to ensure this: one is to state the PHP data type explicitly with *SQLSRV_PHPTYPE_FLOAT* as is done with *$listPrice*. The other (less secure) way is to have the PHP variable hold a float value when it is bound to the statement, as is done with *$creditPrice*=0.0.

LISTING 13-14 Retrieving output parameters in PHP.

```
$listPrice = 0;
$creditPrice = 0.0;
$stmt = sqlsrv_prepare($db, "EXECUTE SalesLT.getCreditPrice ?, ?, ?, ?, ?;",
    array(
        711, 0.01, 24,     // first three parameters
        array(&$listPrice, SQLSRV_PARAM_OUT, SQLSRV_PHPTYPE_FLOAT),
        array(&$creditPrice, SQLSRV_PARAM_OUT)
    )
);
sqlsrv_execute($stmt);
sqlsrv_free_stmt($stmt);
echo "List price: $listPrice<br />";
echo "Price for credit purchase: $creditPrice <br />";
```

Calling Stored Procedures from PDO

Using PDO, it is possible to call stored procedures with output parameters, as well. You should keep in mind though that PDO does not support as many data types as the native SQL Server driver. PDO does not provide pure output parameters but only input or bidirectional parameters.

Bidirectional parameters are indicated with the option *PDO::PARAM_INPUT_OUTPUT*. There is one important caveat when using bidirectional parameters with PDO: you need to define the maximum result size (in bytes) while binding the parameter. If the result is larger, the query will return an error.

Listing 13-15 shows how to call the stored procedure *SalesLT.getCreditPrice* from Listing 13-13. Both *$listPrice* and *$creditPrice* are bound as bidirectional parameters with a maximum result size of 20 bytes. Other than the native SQL Server driver, PDO does not require you to pass PHP variables by reference, as you can see in the *bindParam()* calls. As PDO does not provide any special money or float type, we have to define the data type as string (*PDO::PARAM_STR*). Note that PDO rounds the money type to two decimal places. If you require all four decimal places of the money SQL data type, then you need to use a decimal SQL data type for the parameters of your stored procedure, instead.

LISTING 13-15 Retrieving output parameters with PDO.

```php
try {
    $stmt = $dbh->prepare("EXECUTE SalesLT.getCreditPrice ?, ?, ?, ?, ?;");
    $stmt->bindValue(1, 711);
    $stmt->bindValue(2, 0.01);
    $stmt->bindValue(3, 24);
    $listPrice = 0;
    $creditPrice = 0;
    $stmt->bindParam(4, $listPrice, PDO::PARAM_STR|PDO::PARAM_INPUT_OUTPUT, 20);
    $stmt->bindParam(5, $creditPrice, PDO::PARAM_STR|PDO::PARAM_INPUT_OUTPUT, 20);
    $stmt->execute();
    echo "List price: $listPrice<br />";
    echo "Price for credit purchase: $creditPrice <br />";
}
catch(Exception $e) {
    die( print_r($e->getMessage()) );
}
```

Custom Functions

You create custom functions by using *CREATE FUNCTION*. Functions are similar to stored procedures; however, custom functions are limited because you can't use them to change data and the function must not have any side effects. For example, you cannot call the *NEWID* or *RAND* functions. But you can use functions in queries and other T-SQL statements.

Scalar Functions

The return value of a scalar function is a basic data type, such as *int*, *datetime*, or *nchar*, but not *timestamp*, *cursor*, or *table*. Listing 13-16 shows an example function. Like PHP functions, the parameters are enclosed in parentheses, the return value is defined with *RETURNS* and the function body is encapsulated within a *BEGIN/END* block.

LISTING 13-16 A custom function to calculate the gross margin in percent.

```sql
IF OBJECT_ID('SalesLT.margin') IS NOT NULL
  DROP FUNCTION SalesLT.margin;
GO
CREATE FUNCTION SalesLT.margin (@cost money, @listprice money)
RETURNS float
BEGIN
  RETURN (@listprice/@cost)-1;
END
GO
```

The function can be called within a *SELECT* statement:

```
SELECT ProductID, Name FROM SalesLT.Product
WHERE SalesLT.margin(StandardCost, ListPrice) < 0.30;
```

Table-Valued Functions

Table-valued functions return a table as return value. You could use the results in the *FROM* section of a *SELECT* statement. There are two types of table-valued functions: inline functions and multistatement functions.

Inline Table-Valued Functions

An inline table-valued function is basically an encapsulated *SELECT* statement (see Listing 13-17). The return data type is *RETURNS TABLE*.

LISTING 13-17 Defining an inline table-valued function.

```
CREATE FUNCTION SalesLT.TopSalesPersons(@persons)
RETURNS TABLE
RETURN (
  SELECT TOP (@persons) c.SalesPerson FROM SalesLT.Customer AS c
  JOIN SalesLT.SalesOrderHeader AS soh ON c.CustomerID=soh.CustomerID
  GROUP BY c.SalesPerson
  ORDER BY SUM(soh.SubTotal) DESC
);
```

To view all regions with customers of the top three sellers, you would run the following statement using the *TopSalesPersons(3)* function as table in *JOIN*, as shown in Listing 13-18.

LISTING 13-18 Calling an inline table function.

```
SELECT DISTINCT a.StateProvince, a.CountryRegion
FROM SalesLT.Address AS a
JOIN SalesLT.CustomerAddress AS ca ON a.AddressID=ca.AddressID
JOIN SalesLT.Customer AS c ON ca.CustomerID=c.CustomerID
JOIN SalesLT.Top3SalesPersons(3) AS t3sp ON c.SalesPerson=t3sp.SalesPerson;
```

Multi-Statement Table-Valued Functions

A multi-statement table-valued function creates the table within a variable and returns this variable. Listing 13-19 shows an example function. In the example, the function in Listing 13-17 and the query in Listing 13-18 are combined to define the *RegionsOfTopSalesPersons()* function to return the regions in which the customers of the best sellers reside.

LISTING 13-19 A multi-statement table-valued function.

```
CREATE FUNCTION SalesLT.RegionsOfTopSalesPersons (@persons int)
RETURNS @Regions TABLE (StateProvince nvarchar(50),
                        CountryRegion nvarchar(50))
BEGIN
  DECLARE @TopSalesPersons TABLE (SalesPerson nvarchar(256));
  INSERT INTO @TopSalesPersons
    SELECT TOP (@persons) c.SalesPerson FROM SalesLT.Customer AS c
    JOIN SalesLT.SalesOrderHeader AS soh ON c.CustomerID=soh.CustomerID
    GROUP BY c.SalesPerson ORDER BY SUM(soh.SubTotal) DESC;
  INSERT INTO @Regions
    SELECT DISTINCT a.StateProvince, a.CountryRegion FROM SalesLT.Address AS a
    JOIN SalesLT.CustomerAddress AS ca ON a.AddressID=ca.AddressID
    JOIN SalesLT.Customer AS c ON ca.CustomerID=c.CustomerID
    JOIN @TopSalesPersons AS t3sp ON c.SalesPerson=t3sp.SalesPerson;
  RETURN;
END;
```

Triggers

Triggers are useful tools to ensure the consistency of data or to execute T-SQL statements based on events. Triggers can be initiated if tables are accessed or the data model is changed. The most common trigger types responding to table data (*UPDATE*, *INSERT*, *DELETE*) are described below.

Creating a Trigger

Listing 13-20 shows how to create a trigger by using *CREATE TRIGGER*. The syntax is similar to the syntax for stored procedures.

LISTING 13-20 Creating a trigger.

```
IF OBJECT_ID('SalesLT.CorrectDates','TR') IS NOT NULL
  DROP TRIGGER SalesLT.CorrectDates;
GO
CREATE TRIGGER SalesLT.CorrectDates ON SalesLT.SalesOrderDetail
FOR INSERT, UPDATE
AS
  IF EXISTS (SELECT * FROM inserted AS i
                      JOIN SalesLT.Product AS p ON i.ProductID = p.ProductID
                    WHERE p.SellEndDate < getdate())
  BEGIN
    RAISERROR ('Product no longer available.', 16, 1);
    ROLLBACK TRANSACTION;
  RETURN
END;
GO
```

You can define several triggers for a table even if they are initiated by the same action. Let's have a closer look at each step in Listing 13-20.

Detailed Explanation

First you check if the trigger already exists. If yes, the trigger is deleted. Afterward, you define the trigger:

```
CREATE TRIGGER SalesLT.CorrectDates ON SalesLT.SalesOrderDetail
```

Triggers are linked to table actions. Therefore, the table is specified after the *ON* keyword. Next, you specify the actions that initiate the trigger:

```
FOR INSERT, UPDATE
```

In this case, the *INSERT* and *UPDATE* statements initiate the trigger. The trigger is not initiated by the *DELETE* statement. You can also use the *AFTER* keyword instead of *FOR*.

You can also execute a trigger instead of the action: instead of *FOR*, use the *INSTEAD OF* keyword. For each triggering action, only one alternative trigger is allowed. These triggers are usually used for views.

Afterward, you define the body:

```
AS
    IF EXISTS (SELECT * FROM inserted AS i
                    JOIN SalesLT.Product AS p ON i.ProductID = p.ProductID
                    WHERE p.SellEndDate < getdate())
```

Within a trigger, two tables are available: *inserted* and *deleted*. The *inserted* table contains the rows to be added or the rows after a change made by *UPDATE*. The *deleted* table contains the deleted rows or the rows before a change was made by *UPDATE*. The condition checks if a product is included in the order that is no longer available *(p.SellEndDate < getdate())*.

> **Note** The *inserted* and *deleted* tables might be empty if the *UPDATE* function doesn't change any rows, because the *WHERE* clause is too restrictive.

Next follows the action executed if the product is no longer available:

```
    BEGIN
        RAISEERROR ('Product no longer available.', 16, 1);
        ROLLBACK TRANSACTION;
    RETURN
END;
```

RAISEERROR generates an error message and *ROLLBACK TRANSACTION* discards the changes.

Initiating the Trigger

For example, if a new line is added to *SalesOrderDetail*, SQL Server calls the trigger and causes an error:

```
INSERT INTO SalesLT.SalesOrderDetail (SalesOrderID, OrderQty, ProductID, UnitPrice)
      VALUES (71774, 3, 709, 9.50);
GO

Msg 50000, Level 16, State 1, Procedure CorrectDates, Line 8
Product no longer available
Msg 3609, Level 16, State 1, Line 1
The transaction ended in the trigger. The batch has been aborted.
```

Summary

This chapter introduced the full-text search, transactions, and programming in T-SQL. The full-text search in PHP applications is useful to search descriptions, comments, pages, titles and other content. The combination of several columns in an index allows a combined search in a single query.

With transactions, you can combine several T-SQL statements into an atomic execution unit to save all changes or to roll back all changes. You should use transactions if a PHP application function changes several tables at once. If a change causes an error, you can reset the tables by using *sqlsrv_rollback()* or its PDO equivalent.

Stored procedures, custom functions, and triggers are useful tools to perform data-intensive tasks directly in the database without the detour through the PHP application. By transferring part of the program logic into the database, you can also ensure the consistency and accuracy of the data. The next chapter explains how stored procedures can increase the database security.

Chapter 14
Users and Permissions

Data security in Microsoft SQL Server is controlled through users and roles (so-called principals). The users and roles are granted rights for server objects. Each time data is written, read, or executed (stored procedures), the required rights of the principal are verified. The principal can access data only if he has the required permission. The following sections describe principals, rights, and objects.

SQL Server Principals

SQL Server principals are divided into the following classes:

- **Authentication type** Either a Windows user (or group) or a SQL Server user account. The authentication with asymmetric keys or certificates is also possible.

- **Principal level** You can create principals on the server level or database level.

- **Role or login** A login is an authenticated user or group. Roles are internal SQL Server groups. SQL Server provides predefined roles on the database or server level.

Usually, you create a user login on the server level, assign a database user to this login, and then assign the user roles with the required access rights to database elements. The next sections describe the SQL Server principals in this order.

Server Principals

You define server principals on the SQL Server level. Server principals can be assigned rights for all databases. In SQL Server, a user principal is called login. The two login types are described below in the following subsections.

Login Types

The login types of server principals are based on Windows users and SQL Server users.

From a database administrator's point of view, Windows users and groups are preferred to SQL Server users. Password policies and other management functions are managed outside the database. The use of Windows groups saves the database administrator a lot of work. If users leave or join the organization or take on a different position, the security structure of the database is maintained because the group members change but not the group itself. With that said, SQL Server users offer the advantage that they are independent from Windows users and ideal for application-oriented logons which are typical for public websites.

Server Roles

Table 14-1 lists the nine available predefined server roles. Logins can be members of these roles, but you cannot create your own server roles. Server roles are primarily intended for the management of SQL Server. Each user is assigned the *public* role (default role). Therefore, you should only grant the *public* role access if you want all users to be able to access the server.

TABLE 14-1 Server roles in SQL Server

Server role	Description of the rights
bulkadmin	Add data to the database with *BULK INSERT*
dbcreator	Create, change, delete, and restore databases
diskadmin	Manage the data files of SQL Server
processadmin	Stop, cancel, or restart SQL Server processes
public	Default role for all users, only minimum rights
securityadmin	Manage access rights, reset passwords
serveradmin	Change the server configuration and restart or shut down servers
setupadmin	Add or remove connected servers
sysadmin	Full access, has all rights

Database Principals

Database principals are only valid for the database in which they are defined. There are also roles on the database level. On this level, you can define your own roles.

Database Users

To grant access to database objects for server principals, you need to create a user for this login in the database. A database user represents the login within the database that is assigned permissions for database elements.

You can also create database users without assigned server login. A user without login is typically used to access elements as this user (*EXECUTE AS*). The combination of login, server role, (database) user, and database role allows more flexibility in the design of security concepts. Usually, users without login are used only by applications.

Database Roles

You can assign roles to users on the database level. A role consists of database users, and you can assign permissions for elements to a role. It is best practice to not grant users permissions directly but to instead assign roles to users and permissions to roles. If users change, only their role assignments change, and you don't need to modify the permissions.

Table 14-2 lists the predefined database roles. The roles *db_datareader* and *db_datawriter* are commonly used roles to grant users access to the elements in the database. The roles *db_denydatareader* and *db_denydatawriter* deny access, even if a user has equivalent access rights somewhere else. In the SQL Server security concept, a restraint always has priority over a permission.

TABLE 14-2 Predefined database roles in SQL Server

Database role	Description of the rights
db_accessadmin	Add or remove database users
db_backupoperator	Backup databases without access to the database content
db_datareader	Read (*SELECT*) the data in all (custom) tables
db_datawriter	Write (*INSERT, UPDATE, DELETE*) data in all (custom) tables
db_ddladmin	Run DDL commands (data definition language)—for example, *CREATE TABLE, ALTER TABLE, DROP TABLE, CREATE INDEX*
db_denydatareader	Deny read rights (*SELECT*) for all table data
db_denydatawriter	Deny write rights for all table data
db_owner	All rights for all database elements and permission to delete the database (*DROP DATABASE*)
db_securityadmin	Manage roles and permissions

Contrary to roles on the server level, you can define your own database roles to ensure a granular security concept.

Creating SQL Server Principals

The following sections explain how to create logins on the server level by using SQL Server Management Studio (SSMS) or Transact-SQL (T-SQL) statements and how to assign new users to these logins on the database level. The assignment of permissions is described in the section "Objects and Permissions," later in the chapter.

Creating Logins

The first step is to create a login to grant access to SQL Server. Depending on whether the login is a SQL Server user or a Windows user, the passwords are managed by SQL Server.

Creating Logins by Using SSMS

To create a new login on the server level by using SSMS, perform the following steps:

1. Start SSMS, and then connect to the desired server instance.

2. In Object Explorer, select the desired server, click Security, and then right-click Logins. In the context menu that opens, select New Login.

   The Login - New dialog box opens, as shown in Figure 14-1.

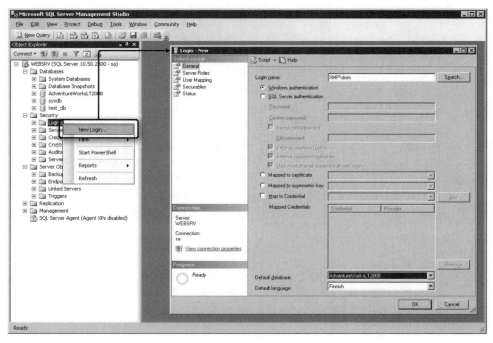

FIGURE 14-1 Creating a new login on the server level.

3. Activate the desired Windows authentication for Windows users or groups, or the SQL Server authentication.

4. Enter the user name in the Login Name text box, and then click Search to search for that name on the server (or in the Windows domain).

> **Note** You cannot add Internet Information Services (IIS) application pool users by clicking Search; you must enter them into the Login name text box manually. When the users are found, they are added erroneously into the text box. The default user of the standard IIS application pool is *IIS AppPool\DefaultAppPool*.

5. For an SQL Server login, enter the password in the text box, and then select the check boxes next to the password properties that you want to enable.

6. Use the drop-down lists to specify the default database and the default language.

7. To assign the login to a server role, select the check box for the desired roles on the Server Roles page.

   Unless the login is used for administration purposes, you should not assign additional roles here.

8. Click OK to create the login. The login is created on the server level.

Creating Logins by Using T-SQL

To create a new login on the server level by using T-SQL- Data Definition Language (DDL), run the *CREATE LOGIN* command.

To create the login for a Windows user, run the following command:

```
CREATE LOGIN loginName FROM WINDOWS
WITH [ DEFAULT_DATABASE = database | DEFAULT_LANGUAGE = language [ ,... ] ]
```

To create a login for the default user of the standard IIS application pool, run the following command:

```
CREATE LOGIN [IIS AppPool\DefaultAppPool] FROM WINDOWS
CREATE LOGIN is also used to create a SQL Server user:
CREATE LOGIN loginName
WITH PASSWORD = 'password' [ HASHED ] [ MUST_CHANGE ]
[ , { SID = sid
    | DEFAULT_DATABASE = database
    | DEFAULT_LANGUAGE = language
    | CHECK_EXPIRATION = { ON | OFF}
    | CHECK_POLICY = { ON | OFF}
    | CREDENTIAL = credential_name
    } [ ,... ] ]
```

CHECK_POLICY ensures that the password complies with the Windows password policies on the computer running SQL Server. CHECK_EXPIRATION indicates that the login is locked after several failed attempts, and MUST_CHANGE forces the user to change his password at the first login.

To create a login for the user *doris* with a password complying with the local password policy, run the following command:

```
CREATE LOGIN [doris] WITH PASSWORD 'hamster lover' MUST_CHANGE, CHECK_POLICY_ON
GO
```

To assign server roles to a login, use the *sp_addsrvrolemember* procedure:

```
EXEC master..sp_addsrvrolemember @loginame = N'doris', @rolename = N'dbcreator'
GO
```

To remove a server role, use the *sp_dropsrvrolemember* procedure:

```
EXEC master..sp_dropsrvrolemember @loginame = N'doris', @rolename = N'dbcreator'
GO
```

Creating Users

After you create the logins on the server level, you need to create the users on data-base level. The following sections describe how to create users by using SSMS or T-SQL statements.

Creating Users by Using SSMS

To create a new database user by using SSMS, perform the following steps:

1. Start SSMS, and then connect to the server.

2. In Object Explorer, select the desired database, click Security, and then right-click Users. In the context menu that opens, select New User.

    The Database User - New dialog box opens, as illustrated in Figure 14-2.

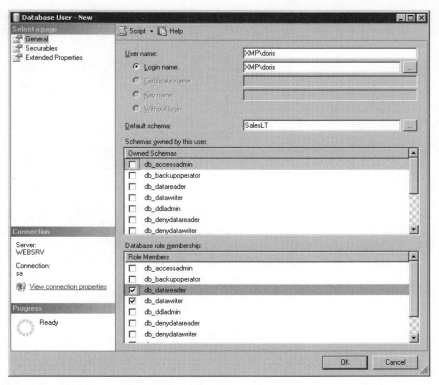

FIGURE 14-2 Creating a new database user via SSMS.

3. Select the login names that you want to assign on the server level, and then click the [...] button located at the right of the text box to search for logins.

4. Enter the user name in the User name text box.

You can enter any user name but it is best practice to use the same name for the database user and the login.

5. You can assign a default schema to the user in the appropriate text box. Click the button to the right of the text box to search the database for schemas.

The default schema is used if a database element is used without schema name.

6. In the Database Role Membership pane, you can assign database roles to the user by selecting the appropriate check boxes.

7. Click OK to create the user.

You also can create database users by using SSMS and assigning a login directly in the login properties:

1. In Object Explorer, select the desired server, click Security, and then right-click Logins. In the context menu that opens, click Properties.

   The Login Properties dialog box opens.

2. Select User Mapping.

3. In the login table, you can assign a user and a default schema to each database. In the bottom section, specify the database role memberships for the database user, as demonstrated in Figure 14-3.

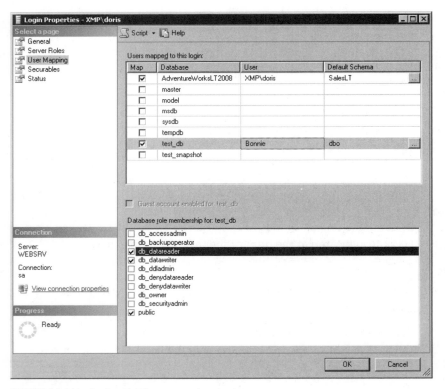

FIGURE 14-3 Assigning database users to a login.

4. Click OK to confirm your settings. If the assigned database users don't exist, they are created automatically and assigned to the desired database roles.

Creating Users by Using T-SQL

To create a database user via T-SQL-DDL, run the *CREATE USER* command, as follows:

```
CREATE USER user_name
    [ { FOR | FROM } LOGIN login_name | WITHOUT LOGIN ]
    [ WITH DEFAULT_SCHEMA = schema_name ]
```

You must run the command within the database context. To create the user doris in the *AdventureWorksLT2008* database, for the XMP\doris login, run the following command:

```
USE AdventureWorksLT2008
CREATE USER [doris] FOR LOGIN [XMP\doris] WITH DEFAULT_SCHEMA=[SalesLT]
GO
```

To assign database roles to a user use the *sp_addrolemember* procedure:

```
USE AdventureWorksLT2008
EXEC sp_addrolemember N'db_datareader', N'doris'
EXEC sp_addrolemember N'db_datawriter', N'doris'
GO
```

To remove an assigned role, use the *sp_droprolemember* procedure:

```
USE AdventureWorksLT2008
EXEC sp_droprolemember N'db_datawriter', N'doris'
GO
```

Creating Database Roles

You can define your own roles on the database level and assign members and rights to these roles. Because roles can have other roles as members, you can create a role hierarchy for your permission concept. If you use more than one application user and pass several user logins for the PHP application to SQL Server, you should use roles with permissions to reduce the administration effort.

Creating Database Roles by Using SSMS

To create a new database role by using SSMS, perform the following steps:

1. In Object Explorer, select the desired database, click Security | Roles, and then right-click Database roles. In the context menu that opens, click New Database Role.

   The Database Role - New dialog box opens.

2. In the dialog box, enter the role name of the database role, and then in the Owner text box, select a user (see Figure 14-4). Click the [...] button to the right of the text box to search for database users.

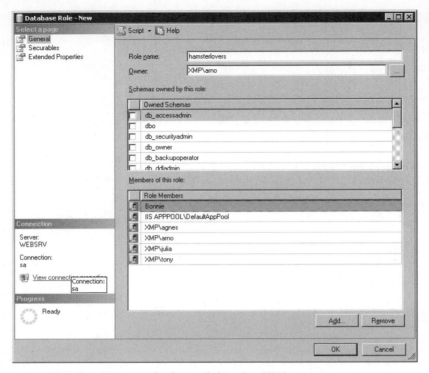

FIGURE 14-4 Creating a new database role by using SSMS.

3. Click the Add button to add members (users or other database roles) to the role.

4. Click OK to create the database role.

Creating Database Roles by Using T-SQL

In T-SQL, you can create database roles by using the *CREATE ROLE* command:

```
CREATE ROLE role_name [ AUTHORIZATION owner_name ]
```

To create the *CallCenterRep* role in the *AdventureWorksLT2008* database, run the following command:

```
USE AdventureWorksLT2008
CREATE ROLE CallCenterRep
GO
```

Members are added by using the *sp_addrolemember* procedure *sp_droprolemember* to remove them:

```
USE AdventureWorksLT2008
EXEC sp_addrolemember N'CallCenterRep', N'Bonnie'
EXEC sp_droprolemember N'CallCenterRep', N'XMP\tony'
GO
```

Objects and Permissions

Objects are the core SQL Server elements for which permissions are granted. Each object has an owner with full control over the object. The database owner *dbo* is the default owner of database objects. For other users to access objects, these users are granted object-specific permissions. The permissions are divided into read, write, and manage rights for objects. For web applications, the read and write permissions for object data are important.

You can assign permissions not only to users but also to database roles. It is best practice to not grant users permissions directly and to keep the user management and the permission structure separated.

> **Note** The objects in databases always belong to a schema. Since SQL Server 2005, schemas are user independent: a schema has an owner and includes objects defined independently from users. The naming of objects—for example, tables—independent from the table owner simplifies the management of users and permissions.

Permissions

Table 14-3 lists the permissions you can grant in SQL Server. Depending on the object type, not all permissions might be relevant; for example, only stored procedures have executions rights but not tables. As shown in the table, the permissions are granular, especially for tables and views. Almost all T-SQL statements have their own permission.

TABLE 14-3 Common permissions for objects

Permission	Description
UPDATE	Change the data in a table or view
ALTER	Change and delete objects
EXECUTE	Execute stored procedures
SELECT	Select data in tables or views
TAKE OWNERSHIP	Take over ownership of an object
VIEW DEFINITION	Display the definition of an object—for example, a stored procedure or a table
INSERT	Add data to a table
IMPERSONATE	Impersonate another user
DELETE	Delete data from a table or view
CONTROL	Full control over an object
REFERENCES	Query to control foreign key restrictions

These permissions can be granted (*GRANT*), denied (*DENY*), or granted with the authorization to pass the permission to other principals (*GRANT WITH GRANT OPTION*).

Effective Permissions

The effective permission for an object is calculated from the rights of all roles assigned to the user and the user rights for this object and all parent objects. For example, to retrieve data from the *SalesLT.Customer* table with *SELECT*, the user julia needs one of the following permissions:

- julia has select permission for the *SalesLT.Customer* table

- julia has select permission for the *SalesLT* schema

- The *CallCenterRep* database role of which julia is a member has select permission for the *SalesLT* schema

- julia is a member of the predefined *db_datareader database* role

If the user or one of their roles is explicitly denied permission, that user cannot access the object. *DENY* always has priority over the permissions granted with *GRANT*.

Ownership Chains

If data objects have the same owner and are processed consecutively in a command, the permission is checked in a different way; if the calling and the called object have the same owner, the permissions are not checked.

Figure 14-5 shows an example in which the Procedure P in a database accesses View V. View V combines data of Tables T1 and T2. If Tony has permission to call Procedure P, his permissions for View V are not checked because P and V have the same owner (Doris). If the View retrieves the data from Table T1, Tony's permissions are not checked because V and T1 have the same owner. This is different for Table T2: V and T2 have different owners (Doris, Julia), so Tony's access permission for T2 is checked.

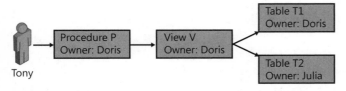

FIGURE 14-5 Linking permissions based on ownership chains.

Because the permissions are chained together based on the owner, Tony might not be able to directly access Table T1 and View V, but he can run the procedure P because he has execute permission for P. Tony needs access rights only for Table T2. Ownership chains, therefore, provide a powerful tool in restricting access to certain data. See the section "Stored Procedures," later in the chapter, for more on this topic.

Permissions can be linked based on the owner only for *SELECT*, *INSERT*, *UPDATE*, and *DELETE*.

> **Note** The objects must be called as shown in Figure 14-5; that is, they must be called with a stored procedure, a trigger, or a view. A simple *JOIN* statement doesn't trigger the ownership chain mechanism.

Managing Permissions by Using SSMS

There are two ways to use SSMS to grant permissions for security-enabled elements (usually database objects and databases): define the permission for the object entry, or for the user or login.

Defining Permissions Through Objects

To specify the permissions through the object, perform the following steps:

1. In Object Explorer, right-click the desired object (for example, a table), and then from the context menu that appears, select Properties.

2. In the dialog box that appears, select the Permissions page.

3. Click the Search button (step 1 in Figure 14-6), and then in the dialog box that opens, click Browse (step 2). You can select the users and roles in a list including all users and database roles. Click OK to confirm your selection.

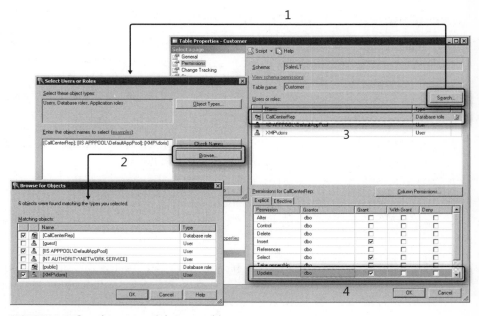

FIGURE 14-6 Granting access rights to a table.

4. Select the principal granting rights (step 3 in Figure 14-6), and then grant the required permissions (step 4).

5. Click OK to confirm your settings.

> **Note** Figure 14-6 illustrates that you can define table permissions by column. Click the Column Permissions button on the right to grant rights for the selected columns.

Defining Permissions Through Principals

You also can assign permissions directly through database users or roles by performing the following steps:

1. In Object Explorer, right-click the user or the database role, and then from the context menu, select Properties.

2. In the dialog box that appears, click the Securables page.

3. Click the Search button to select the desired objects. Click OK to confirm your selection.

4. In the Securables list, select the desired object, and then assign the permissions in the bottom pane in the Explicit tab. Repeat these steps for all objects for which you want to grant permissions.

5. Click OK to confirm your settings.

Managing Permissions by Using T-SQL

To manage permissions with T-SQL, you can use the commands *GRANT, DENY,* and *REVOKE*. *GRANT* grants permissions, *DENY* denies permissions, and *REVOKE* revokes the permissions assigned with *GRANT* or *DENY*.

Granting Permissions (*GRANT*)

With *GRANT*, you can grant permissions for all SQL Server securables. The syntax to grant permissions for database objects or schemas is as follows:

```
GRANT <permission> [ ,...n ] ON
    { [ OBJECT :: ][ schema_name ]. object_name [ ( column [ ,...n ] ) ]
    | SCHEMA :: schema_name }
    TO <database_principal> [ ,...n ]
    [ WITH GRANT OPTION ]
```

Table 14-3 lists the names of the permissions. You can also use the (obsolete) *ALL* keyword to specify the permissions required to edit data. *ALL* includes the table permissions *DELETE, INSERT, REFERENCES, SELECT,* and *UPDATE*.

WITH GRANT OPTION grants the user (or the role) the right to pass these rights on to others.

To grant the *CallCenterRep* role read permission for all tables in the *SalesLT* schema as well as write permission for the tables *SalesLT.Customer, SalesLT.CustomerAddress,* and *SalesLT .Address,* run the following command:

```
USE AdventureWorksLT2008
GRANT SELECT ON SCHEMA::SalesLT TO CallCenterRep
GRANT SELECT,UPDATE,DELETE,INSERT ON OBJECT::SalesLT.Customer TO CallCenterRep
GRANT SELECT,UPDATE,DELETE,INSERT ON SalesLT.CustomerAddress TO CallCenterRep GRANT
SELECT,UPDATE,DELETE,INSERT ON SalesLT.Address TO CallCenterRep
GO
```

Explicitly Denying Rights (*DENY*)

With *DENY,* you can explicitly deny permissions. The syntax is similar to the *GRANT* statement:

```
DENY <permission> [ ,...n ] ON
    { [ OBJECT :: ][ schema_name ]. object_name [ ( column [ ,...n ] ) ]
    | SCHEMA :: schema_name }
    TO <database_principal> [ ,...n ]
    [ CASCADE ]
```

The *CASCADE* option indicates that the restraint not only applies to the specified principal but also for all users and roles authorized by this principal.

To deny the user XMP\tony the right to delete or change the data in the tables of the *SalesLT* schema as well as the right to change the *dbo.ErrorLog* table, run the following command:

```
USE AdventureWorksLT2008
DENY DELETE,UPDATE ON SCHEMA::SalesLT TO [XMP\tony]
DENY INSERT,UPDATE,DELETE ON OBJECT::dbo.ErrorLog TO [XMP\tony]
GO
```

Revoking Permissions (*REVOKE*)

Use the T-SQL *REVOKE* statement to revoke or delete permissions. The syntax is similar to the *DENY* statement:

```
REVOKE [ GRANT OPTION FOR ] <permission> [ ,...n ] ON
    { [ OBJECT :: ][ schema_name ]. object_name [ ( column [ ,...n ] ) ]
    | SCHEMA :: schema_name }
    { FROM | TO } <database_principal> [ ,...n ]
    [ CASCADE ]
```

If you specify the *GRANT OPTION FOR* keyword, the permission is not revoked but only the right to grant other principals the permission. *CASCADE* revokes the permission not only for the specified principal but for all users and roles granted this permission by that principal.

To revoke the permissions that are granted in the sections "Granting Permissions (*GRANT*)," and "Explicitly Denying Rights (*DENY*)," run the following command:

```
USE AdventureWorksLT2008
REVOKE SELECT ON SCHEMA::SalesLT TO CallCenterRep
REVOKE SELECT,UPDATE,DELETE,INSERT ON OBJECT::SalesLT.Customer TO CallCenterRep
REVOKE SELECT,UPDATE,DELETE,INSERT ON SalesLT.CustomerAddress TO CallCenterRep
REVOKE SELECT,UPDATE,DELETE,INSERT ON SalesLT.Address TO CallCenterRep
REVOKE DELETE,UPDATE ON SCHEMA::SalesLT TO [XMP\tony]
REVOKE INSERT,UPDATE,DELETE ON OBJECT::dbo.ErrorLog TO [XMP\tony]
GO
```

Stored Procedures

Stored procedures can also be used to improve security. You can grant users the right to run procedures but deny other permissions.

Security Through Permissions

The table *AccessLog* in Listing 14-1 shows how stored procedures can improve the security of a database. This table is used to log access attempts. You want to save the user name, time of the last access, and the number of access attempts in a table. However, you want to ensure that the users don't enter wrong data or manipulate the data. Therefore, you deny the public role (all users) the *INSERT*, *UPDATE*, and *DELETE* permissions.

LISTING 14-1 Creating the *AccessLog* table.

```
CREATE TABLE xmp.AccessLog (
  Username nvarchar(256) NOT NULL DEFAULT user_name() PRIMARY KEY,
  LastAccess datetime NOT NULL DEFAULT getdate(),
  AccessCount int NOT NULL DEFAULT 1
);
GO
DENY INSERT, UPDATE, DELETE ON xmp.AccessLog TO public
GO
```

Listing 14-2 shows the associated stored *logAccess* procedure. In this example, the procedure increases the access value by 1 and sets the current time (*getdate()* function) as the last access date for the current user (*user_name()* function). If *UPDATE* fails because no entry for the user exists (*@@ROWCOUNT* contains the number of the affected lines in the last statement), a new line is added, instead. The *public* role is granted the right to execute the procedure.

LISTING 14-2 A stored procedure to add a log entry.

```
CREATE PROC xmp.logAccess AS
  UPDATE xmp.AccessLog SET AccessCount=AccessCount+1, LastAccess=getdate()
        WHERE Username=user_name();
  IF @@ROWCOUNT != 1 BEGIN
    INSERT INTO xmp.AccessLog DEFAULT VALUES;
  END;
GO
GRANT EXECUTE ON xmp.logAccess TO public
GO
```

All users can now log their access attempts by calling the procedure (*EXEC xmp.logAccess;*); for example, they can manipulate the data in the specified way. However, the users cannot manipulate or delete data in any way.

You can also limit the read access to certain entries (see Listing 14-3). Again, *public* is granted the right to run the procedure but cannot retrieve the table content.

LISTING 14-3 A stored procedure and access rights for restricted read permissions.

```
CREATE PROC xmp.getAccessLog AS
  SELECT AccessCount, LastAccess
  FROM xmp.AccessLog
  WHERE Username=user_name();
GO
GRANT EXECUTE ON xmp.getAccessLog TO public;
DENY SELECT ON xmp.AccessLog TO public;
GO
```

Note You can also use custom functions to create this permission concept; however, functions cannot change data, they can only retrieve it. Functions also don't have execute permission (*EXECUTE*). The select permission (*SELECT*) indicates if a table function can be used.

If the *public* role includes all users, why can the users run *INSERT*, *UPDATE*, and *SELECT* within the procedure, but not as a T-SQL statement? The answer is because the permissions are linked, as described in the section "Ownership Chains."

Execute as User

SQL Server allows users to impersonate other users. You control the impersonation for the active connection by using the *EXECUTE AS* and *REVERT* statements. Because of the connection pooling in PHP applications, you should use this function with caution. Stored procedures can also be executed as another user. This is an interesting method for PHP applications; it is introduced in the following section.

Defining the User

While creating a procedure, you can specify the user to execute the procedure. The following options are available:

- **EXECUTE AS CALLER**   The stored procedure is executed as calling user (default behavior).
- **EXECUTE AS OWNER**   The stored procedure is executed with the user account of the owner of the procedure.
- **EXECUTE AS *'user name'***   The stored procedure is executed as the specified user.
- **EXECUTE AS SELF**   A simpler form of *EXECUTE AS 'user name'*. The user is the user defining or changing the procedure.

Listing 14-4 shows how the user running a procedure *WITH EXECUTE AS* is specified.

LISTING 14-4 A procedure executed as another user.

```
CREATE PROC runAsJulia
WITH EXECUTE AS 'Julia'
AS
  SELECT user_name() AS DatabaseUser;
GO
```

When the user Doris calls this procedure with *EXEC runAsJulia,* the result is Julia, because the procedure runs as the user *Julia.*

Required Permissions

Sometimes the impersonation requires special permissions. Listing 14-4 illustrates that Doris only needs execute permission for the *runAsJulia* procedure.

If Julia creates the *runAsJulia* procedure, she doesn't need any other permissions, except for creating the procedure (*CREATE PROCEDURE*).

If Tony were to create the procedure, he would need the right to impersonate Julia:

```
GRANT IMPERSONATE ON USER::julia TO tony
```

No special permissions are required for *EXECUTE AS CALLER* and *EXECUTE AS SELF*. Usually *EXECUTE AS OWNER* doesn't require special permissions either, because most of the time a procedure is created and owned by the same user.

Summary

This chapter explained how to create logins, users, and roles in SQL Server and how to assign permissions for database objects. With stored procedures and ownership chains or impersonation, you can design a granular security concept based on the minimum permissions required.

Important decisions you need to make when designing your PHP application and the permission structure are:

- Under which account does PHP run? (See Chapter 5, "Security.")

- Should you pass the executing PHP/Windows user or should the application use SQL Server logins? (See Chapter 12, "PHP and SQL Server.") In the latter case, should you use a SQL Server login for the PHP application or should you manage users in SQL Server?

- How can you divide tables into useful schemas?

- Who should own the tables and other objects? How can you apply PHP application roles to database roles and users?

- Where can you improve data access security with stored procedures?

There is no universal policy, although usually for PHP applications, developers choose SQL Server logins over Windows logins. In this case, analyze your PHP application to determine if you can create different database roles for the application roles (for example, for anonymous users, authenticated users, and application administrators).

This concludes the topics for SQL Server. In the next part, you will look at Microsoft Active Directory.

Part III

Active Directory

Chapter 15
Setting Up Active Directory

Microsoft Active Directory is a directory service that you can use to save and manage users, groups, printers, and network device data. Active Directory is the central information source for users and objects in an organization and plays an essential role for the authentication of users and permissions.

This chapter explains the installation of the Active Directory Domain Services (AD DS) and how to create users, groups, computers, and organizational units from the management interface.

It also describes the installation of the Active Directory Certificate Services, which you can use to run your own certificate authority. In this book, we use certificates of this service to protect the connections between PHP, Active Directory, and Microsoft Exchange Server.

Overview

System-critical data for users, computers, and other entries are saved in Active Directory. This can include account names, passwords and access rights, as well as general information—for example, the office number of a user.

Unlike a database (for example, Microsoft SQL Server), Active Directory is designed to manage static information that is retrieved on a regular basis. The underlying data model isn't relational, and the entries in the directory are organized hierarchically. Active Directory is optimized for replicating data between servers, and there is no master to handle the data.

Domains

Entries in Active Directory are combined in domains, and the directory service to save data in the domain is called a *domain controller*. A domain defines its own namespace. All entries in a domain have a common root name to avoid conflicts between different domains. The root names of domains follow the Internet-standard Domain Name System (DNS); contoso.com, sales.en-ca.adventureworks, or xmp.site are examples of valid domain names.

Using Active Directory, you can manage several domains and create trust relationships between different domains; for example, a user in domain A can log on to a computer in domain B. If you combine domains in this way, you create a *forest* of domains. The term forest is used because of the hierarchic structure of the directory entries, which are also called directory trees.

A domain forest serves as security and trust boundary: programs and services within the forest trust each other but services outside the forest are not trusted by default. Figure 15-1 shows a graphic representation of a forest. The arrows between the domains illustrate trust relationships. Users in the domain support.adventure.works can use a printer in the domain region.contoso.com but not the printer in the domain other.domain, because other.domain doesn't belong to the forest; therefore, it resides outside the trust boundary.

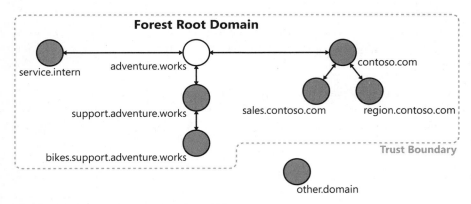

FIGURE 15-1 Active Directory domains and forest.

The first domain generated in a forest is the forest root domain, which performs necessary management tasks in the forest. Other than that, the root domain isn't particularly special from the users' point of view.

You should keep the number of domains in an organization as low as possible; as the number of domains increase, so too does the management effort. Because of the hierarchical structure of the directory entries, delegated management is possible within a domain instead of within different domains.

Domain controllers can include a global catalog to improve the replication and scalability. In a global catalog, not only are the entries from within its own domain saved, but all entries from all domains are saved, as well. This means that not all domain controllers have to be contacted to search the forest; in most cases, searching the global catalog is sufficient.

Entries

The entries in Active Directory are hierarchically sorted and can have parent and child entries. Entries include three different types of information:

- **Name and identity of the entry**   Each entry has a unique name, which you can use to search and retrieve entries.

- **Attribute**   The entry information is saved in attributes and is subject to defined syntax and structure rules to simplify the usage in programs. The set of all these rules is called a scheme.

- **Metadata**   Each entry has metadata such as the access rights to entries.

> **Note**   The access rights to entries are independent of the rights of the objects to which these entries apply. For example, a user cannot change the entry for a computer in Active Directory, but he can change data on the computer, change its local settings, and so on.

Because of the capability to organize entries hierarchically and the granular access rights, you can structure and manage the directory according to the requirements and structure of your organization.

The entries of all domains and the associated attributes within a forest are subject to the same syntax and structure rules; in other words, they use the same scheme. The scheme also determines which attributes are replicated in the global catalog. To ensure that the global catalog doesn't use too much storage, only the attributes needed for frequent searches are copied.

Installing Active Directory

Because Active Directory is very extensive, you need to plan the domain structure and forest, and consider the basic requirements and parameters. A detailed description is beyond the scope of this book.

The installation described is mainly used to create a suitable environment for PHP development. For this reason, a separate domain is created in a new forest, independent of other domains and forests. Because the main focus is on reading and editing the domain objects, the replication, the global catalog, and the forest are also not explained in detail.

Preparation

Together with the Active Directory Domain Services, a DNS server is installed on the domain controller to resolve the domain names for computers and other network devices. Even though installation of the DNS server is optional, it is recommended because it simplifies the handling of device names and addresses.

A DNS server should have a static IP address that is registered with the network adapters of the devices in the domain. Therefore, you should assign at least one static IP address to the computer on which the DNS server is installed. If the computer has several network adapters, select the adapter connected to the network that contains the computers and devices in the future domain.

You only need one static IP address because not all network adapters require static addresses. Depending on your network, a static IP address for IPv4 but not for IPv6 (or vice versa) might also be sufficient.

Do not begin the installation until you have assigned at least one static IP address, because it might be necessary to reboot the computer to apply the changes.

> **Important** If the computer was installed with a pre-configured image, ensure that the computer (the domain controller) has a unique security ID (SID). Depending on the image software, this might not be the case. Identical SIDs can cause problems at a later time. You can query the SID of your computers by using PsGetSID, which is available at *http://technet.microsoft.com/en-us/sysinternals/bb897417.aspx*.

Installing the Role

To install the Active Directory server role, perform the following steps:

1. Start the Server Manager, and then select Roles | Add Roles.

   The Add Roles Wizard starts up.

2. On the Server Roles page, select the Active Directory Domain Services option.

   If the required Microsoft .NET Framework feature is not installed, the dialog box illustrated in Figure 15-2 appears, and you are prompted to add this feature. Click Add Required Features to confirm.

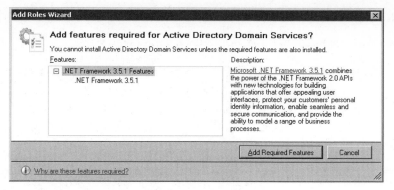

FIGURE 15-2 Adding the .NET Framework 3.5.1 Features.

3. Click Next twice to confirm, and then click Install to start the installation.

After the installation finishes successfully (see Figure 15-3), click Close to exit the wizard.

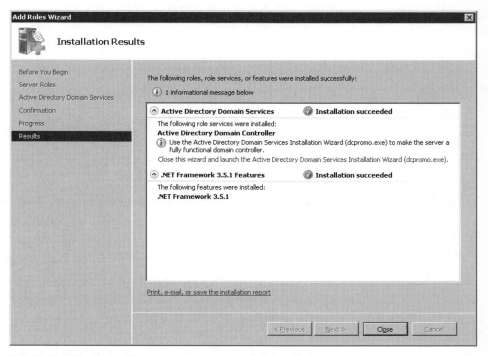

FIGURE 15-3 The Active Directory role was successfully installed.

Installing the Domain Services

To continue the installation of the AD DS, launch dcpromo.exe:

1. In the Server Manager, click Roles | Active Directory Domain Services.

   A message is displayed stating that the domain services are not active because first you need to perform the installation with the Active Directory Domain Services Installation Wizard (dcpromo.exe). Click the link to start the installation with dcpromo.exe (see Figure 15-4).

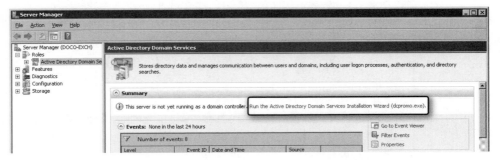

FIGURE 15-4 Installing the Active Directory Domain Services with dcpromo.exe.

   The Active Directory Domain Services Installation Wizard opens.

2. On the Choose A Deployment Configuration page, select the Create A New Domain In A New Forest option.

3. On the Name The Forest Root Domain page, enter the fully-qualified domain name (FQDN) in the text box.

   The FQDN should consist of at least two levels: contoso.com or development.internal. In this book, we use xmp.site as domain.

4. On the Set Forrest Functional Level page, use the drop-down box to select the operating system versions with which your domain controller needs to be compatible.

   If you don't need to consider older versions because you configure the controller only for your development environment, you can select the newest version (Windows Server 2008 R2) for the functional level of the forest.

> **Tip** If you select Windows Server 2008 R2 as the functional level for the forest, you can (later) activate the recycle bin feature to simplify the recovery of deleted users and other objects.

5. On the Additional Domain Controller Options page, select the DNS Server option.

This allows you to manage and assign computer names within the domain by using your domain controller and to resolve the computer names with DNS.

6. If you still have dynamic IP addresses, the dialog box shown in Figure 15-5 appears. If you have assigned static IP addresses to a network adapter for the internal network, you can ignore the warning and select Yes.

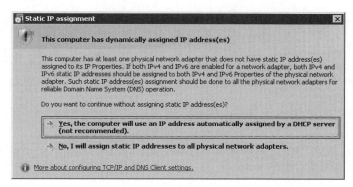

FIGURE 15-5 A warning message about dynamic IP addresses.

7. When no parent authorizing zone is found, a dialog box with a corresponding message appears. This usually happens if you create a root domain without a parent zone (for example, development.internal or xmp.site) or the automatic integration with the existing DNS infrastructure is not possible. In this case, you must perform the integration or delegation manually. Select Yes to continue.

8. On the Location For Database, Log Files, And SYSVOL page, specify the folder in which to save the Active Directory data.

If there are no special requirements for the location, you can keep the standard settings.

9. Enter the administrator password for the recovery mode. This administrator password is different from the password for the administrator account.

> **Tip** Because this password is only required for rarely occurring recoveries, the chances are good that you'll forget it. However, you need the password to perform a recovery. In case of an emergency, you would need to reinstall Active Directory, which can result in data loss. For this reason you should note the password and keep it at a safe place.

10. After the Summary page, click Finish to start the installation.

11. When the installation completes successfully, you need to reboot the server.

The AD DS are available upon reboot. The next steps involve adding computers to the domain and creating users within this domain.

First Steps

Chapter 16 "LDAP Basics," introduces the programming and information model of Active Directory. But before you get there, this section provides a short overview of the important entry types and shows you how to edit entry types with the AD DS snap-in for the Microsoft Management Console (MMC). The first steps are not intended to explain the entire administration of Active Directory; rather, they're designed to serve as a general guideline.

Active Directory Domain Services

To perform administration tasks for users and computers, use the MMC snap-in *Active Directory Users and Computers*.

1. Start the snap-in by clicking Start | Administrative Tools | Active Directory Users And Computers.

   You can also open the Management Console and add the snap-in by clicking File, and then clicking Add/Remove Snap-In.

   The left navigation pane lists the Active Directory hierarchy and the right navigation pane lists the content of the actual containers, as shown in Figure 15-6.

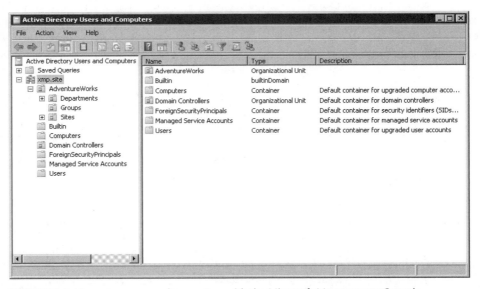

FIGURE 15-6 Managing users and computers with the Microsoft Management Console.

2. The existing (visible) hierarchy includes:

   • **Builtin**   Predefined known groups with standard permissions for different tasks in Windows and the domain.

- **Computers**   All computers in the domain.
- **Domain Controllers**   These computers are domain controllers in the current domain.
- **ForeignSecurityPrincipals**   Users and other security principals from a trusted domain outside the forest.
- **Managed Service Accounts**   Principals for services automatically managed by Active Directory.
- **Users**   Standard container for users and groups.

It is good practice to create your own organizational units for users and groups as well as computers. You can use organizational units to structure and separate the principals according to the requirements of your organization. You can also then use group policies to manage the principals.

Among other things, group policies are used to define and manage access rights, approved applications, standard folders, and entries in the Windows registry for a group of entries. Group policies are inherited in the directory hierarchy and can override and supplement each other. They are an important administration tool for domain administrators.

Organizational Units

In Active Directory, organizational units serve as containers for entries. They are the most important building blocks for the directory hierarchy (see Figure 15-7). Organizational units are not part of a group and don't have their own security principals. However, you can apply group policies to organizational units to manipulate child entries.

FIGURE 15-7 Organizational units hierarchy.

Creating an Organizational Unit

To create a new organizational unit, perform the following steps:

1. In the navigation pane of the MMC, select the container in which you want to create the organizational unit.

2. In the Action menu, select New, and then click the Organizational Unit command.

3. In the dialog box that opens, enter the name for the organizational unit.

    To protect the container against inadvertent deletion, select the appropriate check box.

4. Click OK to confirm your settings and create the organizational unit.

Defining Additional Properties

To assign additional informative properties to organizational units, perform the following steps:

1. In the navigation pane of the MMC, select the organizational unit.

2. In the Action menu, click the Properties command.

    A dialog box opens, in which you can enter a description of the organizational unit and an address (see Figure 15-8).

3. On the Managed By tab, you can delegate the administration of an organizational unit and its child elements to other users.

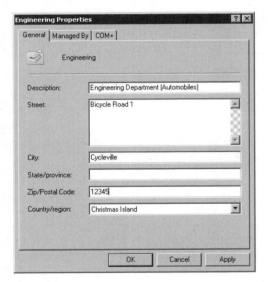

FIGURE 15-8 The properties dialog box for an organizational unit.

4. Click OK to confirm your settings.

Deleting an Organizational Unit

To delete an organizational unit, select it in the navigation pane of the MMC. On the menu bar, click Action, and then click Delete. The organizational unit is deleted when you confirm the security question.

> **Caution** If the organizational unit has child entries, those entries are also deleted. Therefore, you should be certain that it is OK for any child entries to be deleted before you perform this action.

If an organizational unit is protected against accidental deletion, do the following:

1. In the MMC, in the View menu, click Advanced Features.

2. In the navigation pane, select the organizational unit that you want to delete, and then in the Action menu, click Properties.

3. On the Object tab, clear the Protect Object From Accidental Deletion check box, and then click OK.

4. In the Action menu, click Delete.

5. Confirm the security questions to delete the organizational unit.

Users

Users are primary security principals that represent programs and services or users who want to use computers or services. You can create, change, and delete users in the same way that you create, change, and delete organizational units.

Creating a User

You can create users almost everywhere in the directory hierarchy by performing the following steps.

1. In the navigation pane of the MMC, select the container in which you want to create the user.

2. In the Action menu, select New, and then click the User command.

   The New Object - User dialog box opens, as illustrated in Figure 15-9.

3. Enter the names and user logon names (the name to log on to services and computers) in the associated fields.

   The User Logon Name must be unique to the domain, and the pre-Windows 2000 name should be identical with the User logon Name. Click Next.

Note For Windows versions prior to Windows 2000, user names cannot exceed 20 characters.

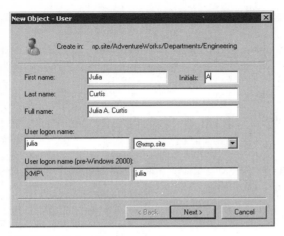

FIGURE 15-9 Creating a new user.

4. Enter a password for the user, enable or disable the password options as necessary, and then click Next.

5. Click Finish to create the user.

Changing the User Properties

To change the user properties, select the user in the list pane of the MMC, and then in the Action menu, click Properties. Figure 15-10 illustrates that there are many ways to specify additional information (for example, address, phone number, organization) or to change system-relevant data (on the Account tab) and to manage group memberships (the Member Of tab).

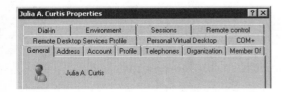

FIGURE 15-10 The array of tabs in the user's Properties dialog box.

Deleting a User

To delete a user, select the user in the list pane of the MMC. In the Action menu, click Delete, and then click Yes to confirm the security question.

Use caution when deleting a user because this action cannot always be undone. The re-creation of a user with the same name and logon name is not always possible. Users are differentiated by their SIDs, but a new user with the same name has a different SID; therefore, the new user will be treated as an independent user.

> **Tip** In Windows Server 2008 R2, a recycle bin feature was introduced in Active Directory to make it easier to restore deleted objects. For more information about the Active Directory recycle bin, go to *http://technet.microsoft.com/en-us/library/dd392261%28WS.10%29.aspx*.

Groups

Groups are independent security principals. They can be the destination of permissions for file access or logons to services and computers. Groups have other principals (users, groups, computers) as members which inherit their permissions. Because groups can be members of groups, you can create a group hierarchy that is different from the hierarchy of the Active Directory entries. While a group hierarchy is a permission hierarchy, the directory hierarchy in Active Directory is primarily an administration and organization hierarchy. In addition, principals can be members of any number of groups, whereas an entry in Active Directory only has one parent entry.

Creating a Group

Groups vary in type and scope. If a group has the type *Distribution*, it isn't a security principal but only serves for grouping its members—for example, for an email distributor in Exchange. A group with the type *Security* is a principal that can be assigned access rights and other permissions.

The group scope determines the members and permissions of a group. Universal groups differ from global groups insofar that they can have members from all domains of the forest and can be assigned rights in all domains. Global groups can contain only members of their own domain, can be only a group member in other domains, and may be assigned rights only in their own domain. Groups of scope *Domain Local* can have members from all domains within the forest but can be assigned rights only within their own domain.

Global groups are often the best choice because they ensure the balance between the functionality and replication effort across domains.

To create a new group, perform the following steps:

1. In the navigation or list pane of the MMC, select the container in which you want to create the group. In the Actions menu, select New, and then click Group.

   The New Object - Group dialog box opens, as shown in Figure 15-11.

2. Enter the name of the group in the text box (the pre-Windows 2000 name should be the same). Select the desired options in the Group Scope and the Group Type areas.

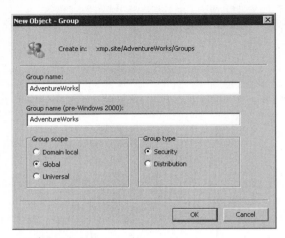

FIGURE 15-11 Creating a new group.

3. Click OK to create the group.

Setting Members and Memberships

To manage the members and memberships of a group, in the MMC, in the Action menu, click Properties, and then in the Properties dialog box, perform the following steps.

1. Click the Members tab.

2. To add new members to the group, click Add (see Figure 15-12).

3. In the dialog box that opens, you can enter the names of the users (or of other objects) in the text box.

   Click the Check Names button to find and assign users. You can limit the search path by clicking the Locations button to select the locations to be searched.

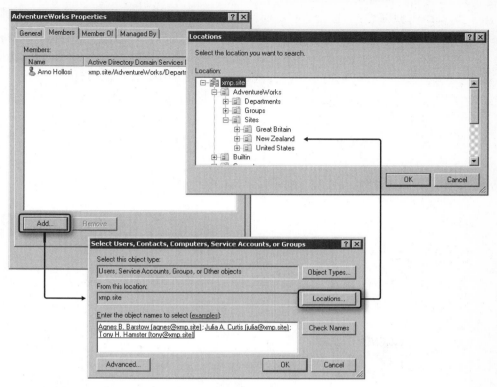

FIGURE 15-12 Managing the members of a group.

4. Click the Advanced button to search for users.

   In the dialog box that opens, you can click the Columns button to set the properties. Click Find Now to start the search. The list field below the Find Now field shows the search results that you can use to select a user.

5. After you've entered the users (or other objects), click OK to add the users to the group. Click OK to close the Properties dialog box.

You can use the Member Of tab in the same way to specify the membership of the group.

Computer

Computers joining the domain also have entries in Active Directory that identify them to other computers and users as a domain member. To enter a computer in the domain, perform the following procedure:

1. On the computer that you want to enter, open the Control Panel via the Windows Start button.

2. In the Control Panel, select System And Security | System.

   The System Properties dialog box opens.

3. Click the Change Settings link, as illustrated in Figure 15-13.

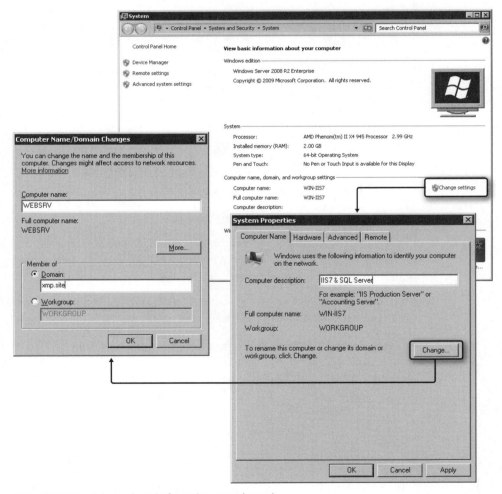

FIGURE 15-13 Joining a domain from the control panel.

4. On the Computer Name tab, click the Change button.

5. In the dialog box that appears, select the Member Of Domain option, and then enter the name of the domain in the text box. Click OK to confirm.

6. In another dialog box, you are prompted to enter the user name and password of an authorized domain user (usually the domain administrator).

   A message should appear informing you that the computer was successfully added to the domain.

7. Reboot your computer to apply the changes.

At the same time, an entry for the computer is created in the Active Directory container Computer. In the MMC snap-in, you can drag this entry into another container.

Setting Up Active Directory Certificate Services

Using Active Directory Certificate Services (AD CS), you can run your own certification authority to issue certificates. Certificates are used to assign the identities of users, services, or computers to a cryptographic key pair used to encrypt HTTP or Lightweight Directory Access Protocol (LDAP) connections. Certificates are also used to identify and authenticate the communication partner (usually the server).

You can obtain certificates from different providers or run your own certification authority by using AD CS. Development environments are best suited for running your own certification authority. The installation of a certification authority is described in the following procedure list. For a production environment, you should consider the advantages and disadvantages of running your own certification authority and whether sufficient knowledge about Public Key Infrastructure (PKI) tasks and processes should be available in your organization.

To install AD CS, perform the following steps:

1. Start the Server Manager, and then in the Action menu, click Add Roles.

   The Add Roles Wizard starts up.

2. On the Server Roles page in the wizard, select the Active Directory Certificate Services option.

Caution Remember that after the installation is complete, you cannot change the name and the domain settings of the computer. For this reason, you should install the certificate services on a single computer that is already configured with the required properties.

3. On the Role Services page, select the Certification Authority option.

   Even though the Certification Authority Web Enrollment option provides a comfortable web user interface, it requires that Internet Information Services (IIS) be installed. This book assumes that you don't want to install IIS on the certificate services computer; therefore, don't select the Certification Authority Web Enrollment option.

4. On the Setup Type page, you can choose the Enterprise or Standalone option.

   If you mainly issue certificates for users in your own domain, you should select the Enterprise option. In this case, the required proof of identity can take place based on the user credentials to simplify the process of issuing certificates. In this book, we select the Enterprise option.

5. On the CA Type page, select the Root CA option.

6. Select the Create A New Private Key if you don't already have a key pair prepared that you want to use.

7. Set the cryptographic parameters for the key pair and the certificate (see Figure 15-14). You can use the standard settings (RSA, 2048 Bit, SHA-1 hash algorithm).

> **Note** The alternative algorithms—elliptic curves (elliptic curve cryptography, ECC) or SHA-256/SHA-512—offer better performance and security but are not as widely used and could cause interoperability problems at a later time. If you know the application of the certificates, you can use alternative settings. The security provided by 2048-Bit RSA with SHA-1 is sufficient for issuing certificates.

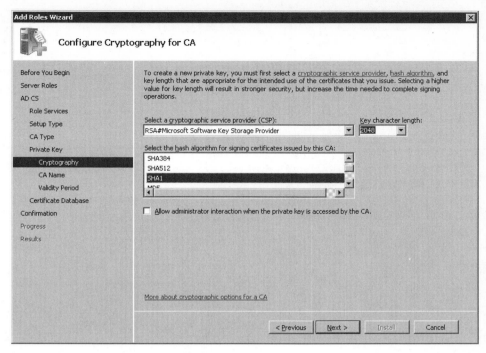

FIGURE 15-14 Setting the cryptographic parameters.

8. Give the certification authority a name.

The name should be descriptive and can contain spaces and other characters. The suffix should match the Active Directory domain name context. In this book, the full name *CN=my-CA,DC=xmp,DC=site* is used.

9. Select the validity period for the root certificate, and then click Next. (After the root certificate expires, you need to issue a new root certificate.)

10. On the Certificate Database page, you can specify the location for the certificate database and the log files. Click Next to confirm.

11. Before the installation starts, the selected configuration is shown again, as illustrated in Figure 15-15. Click the Install button to start the installation.

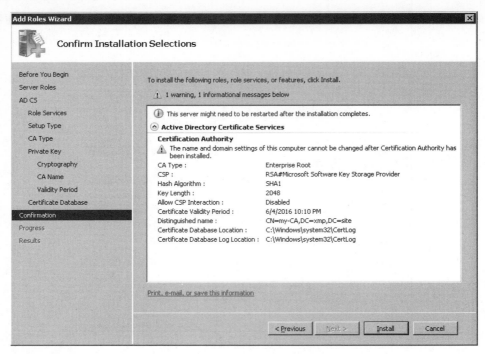

FIGURE 15-15 Configuration overview before the certificate services are installed.

12. When the installation is finished, click Close to exit the wizard.

The AD CS are now installed.

To check if the root certificate from the certification authority is published in Active Directory, run the following command at the command prompt:

```
certutil -viewstore "ldap:///CN=my-CA,CN=Certification Authorities,CN=Public Key
Services,CN=Services,CN=Configuration,DC=xmp,DC=site?cACertificate?base?objectClass=
certificationAuthority"
```

Replace *CN=my-CA and DC=xmp,DC=site* with the name of your certificate authority.

Working with Certificates

Similar to directory services, you can organize certification authorities hierarchically. A root certification authority confirms the identity of a child certification authority, which in turn confirms the identity of a service or user. The identity is confirmed based on certificates. Therefore, at least two certificates need to be checked for each authentication operation: the user or service certificate to determine the identity of a service or user, and the certificate of the root certification authority to ensure the correct (known or trusted) certification authority issued the user certificate.

In the following subsection, you learn how to issue a certificate for the AD DS and how to export the root certificate of the certificate authority (for example, to configure a known and trusted root certificate from the certification authority) in a PHP application.

Issuing a Certificate for Active Directory

If you want to establish an encrypted LDAP connection to Active Directory (perhaps to change a password), the AD DS need a certificate.

Issuing a Certificate

Using the MMC, you can issue a certificate for Active Directory and import the certificate easily and quickly. The following description assumes that the domain controller and the certificate services run on the same computer. If this is not the case for your installation, you must select these when choosing the connection.

To issue the certificate for AD DS, perform the following steps:

1. In the MMC, in the File menu, select Add/Remove Snap-In, and then click Add to add the Certificates Snap-in.

2. In the dialog box that opens, select the Computer Account option, and then click Next.

3. Select the Local Computer option, click Finish, and then click OK.

4. In the Console Root, select the Certificates (Local Computer) node, and then in the context menu, select All Tasks | Automatically Enroll And Retrieve Certificates.

5. On the information page of the Register Certificate dialog box, click Next. On the Request Certificates page, select the Domain Controller enrollment policy. If the enrollment policy for the domain controller isn't available, select the Show All Templates check box, and then select the domain controller template.

6. Click Enroll to create the certificate and to install it on the computer.

   There is no need to perform other tasks, such as authenticating or providing proof of identity, because the certification authority has the type Enterprise; thus the authentication occurs automatically.

7. Click Finish to close the dialog box.

 Note On the Server Manager page Roles/Active Directory Domain Services, an event (level: Information) should appear in the list confirming the availability of an encrypted connection along with the message "LDAP over Secure Sockets Layer (SSL) is now available."

Checking the Encrypted LDAP Access

To check if the encrypted access to LDAP works, you can use the LDP tool, which is further explained in Chapter 16.

1. In the Windows Start menu, enter **LDP** in the Search Programs And Files text box to start LDP.

2. In the Connection menu, click Connect. Enter **localhost** in the Server text box, and then click OK.

3. In the Connection menu, click Bind, and then select the Encrypt Traffic After Bind check box (see Figure 15-16). Click OK, and then check in the results if the encryption option is set, as demonstrated in the following:

```
0 = ldap_set_option(ld, LDAP_OPT_ENCRYPT, 1)
res = ldap_bind_s(ld, NULL, &NtAuthIdentity, NEGOTIATE (1158)); // v.3
{NtAuthIdentity: User='NULL'; Pwd=<unavailable>; domain = 'NULL'}
Authenticated as: 'XMP\Administrator'.
```

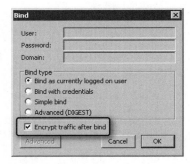

FIGURE 15-16 Encrypting the connection by using LDP.

> **Note** Encrypting the traffic at the point of binding (LDAP protocol element Start TLS) is preferred to a generic connection over SSL (on port 636 instead of port 389).

Exporting the Root Certificate

The root certificate of the certification authority is distributed automatically as a trusted certificate to all domain computers through Active Directory. For this reason, you can perform the following steps directly on a domain computer. To export the root certificate of the certification authority, perform the following steps:

1. In the MMC, in the File menu, click Add/Remove Snap-In to add the Certificates snap-in.

2. In the dialog box that appears, select Computer Account, and then click Local Computer.

3. In the Console Root, select Certificates | Trusted Root Certification Authorities | Certificates. In the list area, right-click your own certification authority, and then in the context menu that appears, select All Tasks | Export (see Figure 15-17).

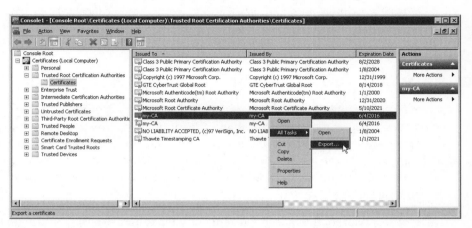

FIGURE 15-17 Exporting the root certificate from your own certification authority.

4. In the Certificate Export Wizard, select the Base-64 Encoded X.509 (CER) format.

5. Select a location, and then click Finish to export the certificate.

The root certificate of your certification authority is now successfully exported. Among other things, you need the root certificate to configure the PHP LDAP extension (see Chapter 16) and for accessing the Exchange server web services, if you use a certificate issued by your AD CS for the encrypted connection.

Exporting Other Certificates

To export the certificates of other services, perform the same steps you used to export the root certificate. However, instead of Trusted Root Certification Authorities in the Management Console, navigate to Personal | Certificates, and then right-click the desired certificate. In the context menu that appears, select the All Tasks | Export option to export the certificate.

If you cannot find the certificate you are looking for, export the certificate directly from the certificate authority by performing the following steps:

1. Start the Management interface by clicking Start | Administrative Tools | Certification Authority.

2. Browse to Certification Authority | *<name>* | Issued Certificates.

3. Double-click the desired certificate.

4. In the Certificate dialog box, click the Details tab.

5. Click Copy To File to start the Certificate Export Wizard.

6. Select the Base-64 Encoded X.509 (CER) format.

7. Select a location, and then click Finish to export the certificate. The export operation is completed, and you can use the certificate file.

Summary

Active Directory is an important pillar of the IT infrastructure, especially for enterprises and companies. It allows the centralized management of users, groups, and computers, as well as delegating administrative tasks and creating a tree across all domains. Because of its granular permission model, the hierarchically-structured inheritance of group policies and the identity management features, Active Directory is an important building block in the security strategy in an organization.

The short overview of the most important entry types in Active Directory and how to create these entries gives you some information of the directory structure. The next chapter explains this and the LDAP interface, which allows access to Active Directory, in more detail.

Chapter 16
LDAP Basics

There are two ways to work with Microsoft Active Directory by using PHP: Active Directory Service Interface (ADSI) and Lightweight Directory Access Protocol (LDAP). ADSI is an interface specified by Microsoft, which, despite its name, can be used for other directory services than Active Directory. ADSI is controlled by PHP through Component Object Model (COM) objects.

LDAP is the most common and platform-independent interface for directory services. LDAP provides extensive interoperability between programs, platforms, and directory services. In this book, Active Directory is used through LDAP because LDAP is widely available and can be easily implemented in Active Directory.

The structure of LDAP directories is explained in the following sections in more detail. The structure described applies to the entries within a domain or the entries in a forest for the LDAP scheme. Two tools are installed with the Active Directory Domain Services (AD DS), which are also explained because they are useful for developing LDAP PHP programs.

LDAP Basics

LDAP is a protocol for querying and writing entries in directory services. It has its origin in the X.500 specification family developed by the International Telecommunication Union (ITU) in the 1980s. LDAP was developed as a lightweight, alternative protocol based on TCP/IP to access directory services data. Since then, LDAP has become the standard protocol for interoperable access to directory services.

Hierarchical Structure

An LDAP directory consists of entries that are hierarchically sorted in a tree structure. Each entry has a distinguished name (DN) and consists of named attributes with one or more values. A DN is made up of the local part of the name (Relative Distinguished Name [RDN]) and parts of the parent entries (similar to a full path of a file).

Figure 16-1 shows part of a LDAP tree in Active Directory. Next to the entries is the attribute that is part of the RDN. For example, the RDN for the entry Tony equals *CN=Tony H. Hamster*. The DN consists of all RDNs for the preceding entries: *CN=Tony H. Hamster,CN=Users,DC=xmp, DC=site*.

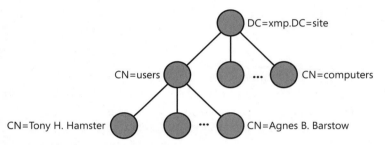

FIGURE 16-1 LDAP tree with the RDNs of the entries.

Listing 16-1 shows the attributes of an entry with the DN CN=WEBSRV,CN=Computers,DC=xmp, DC=site for a computer in the Active Directory domain. Notice that some attributes have several values such as the *objectClass* or *servicePrincipalName* attributes.

LISTING 16-1 Selected attributes of the Active Directory entry for the computer websrv.xmp.site.

```
Dn: CN=WEBSRV,CN=Computers,DC=xmp,DC=site;
cn: WEBSRV;
dNSHostName: WEBSRV.xmp.site;
objectCategory: CN=Computer,CN=Schema,CN=Configuration,DC=xmp,DC=site;
objectClass (5): top; person; organizationalPerson; user; computer;
operatingSystem: Windows Server 2008 R2 Enterprise;
operatingSystemVersion: 6.1 (7600);
primaryGroupID: 515 = ( GROUP_RID_COMPUTERS );
servicePrincipalName (11): MSSQLSvc/WEBSRV.xmp.site:1433; MSSQLSvc/WEBSRV.xmp.site;
WSMAN/WEBSRV; WSMAN/WEBSRV.xmp.site; HTTP/auth.phpdemo.site; TERMSRV/WEBSRV; TERMSRV/
WEBSRV.xmp.site; RestrictedKrbHost/WEBSRV; HOST/WEBSRV; RestrictedKrbHost/WEBSRV.xmp.
site; HOST/WEBSRV.xmp.site;
userAccountControl: 0x1000 = ( WORKSTATION_TRUST_ACCOUNT );
whenChanged: 7/13/2011 8:39:42 AM W. Europe Daylight Time;
whenCreated: 6/4/2011 10:07:55 PM W. Europe Daylight Time;
```

Active Directory defines several structure rules to ensure the integrity of the directory. Entries can only have certain types of parent entries; for example, user accounts cannot be included in the program data (*CN=program data*).

Classes and Inheritance

LDAP not only sorts entries hierarchically, it also defines what entry types are allowed in a directory, the attributes for these entries, and the valid values for the attributes. These entry types are called *classes*.

Classes can be derived from each other and inherit their definitions. Figure 16-2 shows part of the class hierarchy in Active Directory. At the beginning of the hierarchy is always the top class. This class defines four attributes each entry must have and more than 100 optional attributes. Each class extends the preceding class by additional mandatory and optional attributes. This way, more than 370 attributes can be defined for computer entries.

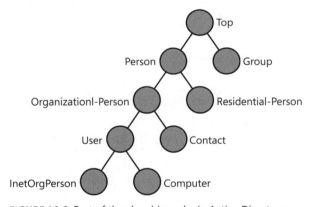

FIGURE 16-2 Part of the class hierarchy in Active Directory.

Protocol Elements

Similar to HTTP, the LDAP protocol consists of a series of requests and responses. The LDAP client establishes a connection to the server and is authenticated (also called *Directory System Agent* or DSA). One or more requests are sent subsequently. However, it is not necessary to wait for the answers before new requests are sent. The server can respond to the requests in random order, because each request can take a different amount of time. The server can also send messages without a request, such as when the connection is closed because of a timeout.

LDAP provides operations for querying and changing entries and attributes. These operations are listed in Table 16-1. The PHP LDAP extension provides a function for each of them.

TABLE 16-1 LDAP Operations

LDAP operation	Description
abandon	Cancels the previous request
add, delete, modify	Adds, deletes, or changes an entry
bind	Authenticates the client (at this point, the connection is already open)
compare	Verifies if an entry has an attribute with a certain value
extended operation	Generic method to define more operations
modify DN	Changes the DN and thus moves the entry in the tree
search	Searches for entries and returns the results
start TLS	Encrypts the connection with LDAP version 3
unbind	Closes the connection

Utilities

Active Directory includes several utilities with which you can access the directory data directly. Two of these utilities are LDP and ADSI Edit. LDP works well for testing LDAP queries and ADSI Edit is a user-friendly data editor for Active Directory. You can find additional tools in the Server Manager by clicking Roles | Active Directory Domain Services.

Both LDP and ADSI Edit are installed with the AD DS and are therefore only available on the domain controller. To use these programs on other computers, you must install them on those computers by following these instructions:

- **Windows Server 2008 R2**   Start the Server Manager, select Features | Add Features, and then install the Remote Server Administration Tools | Role Administration Tools/AD DS and AD LDS Tools

- **Windows 7**   Install the remote server administration tools for Windows 7. The tools and installation instructions can be found on the Microsoft website at *http://www .microsoft.com/download/en/details.aspx?displaylang=en&id=7887.*

Caution Both programs work directly with the data in Active Directory. If you have the required permissions, all changes are applied directly and immediately even if they are made to system-critical entries. There is no Undo function. Therefore, you should proceed with caution.

LDP

LDP is mostly an LDAP browser, even though it provides functions for editing entries and managing access permissions to LDAP objects. With LDP, you can perform single steps (queries or attribute changes) on the same technical level with the PHP programming. For this reason, LDP is a very useful developer tool.

Working with LDP

To work with LDP, perform the following procedure:

1. To start LDP, click the Windows Start button, and then in the Search Programs And Files text box, enter **LDP**.

2. In the Connection menu, click Connect. In the Server text box, enter the server name, and then click OK. Enter **localhost** to access the local server.

3. In the Connection menu, click Bind. You can use the Bind As Currently Logged On User setting or specify a different user. Click OK to confirm.

    In the result window, you should see the message "Authenticated as: *<user>*".

> **Note** If the connection or logon fails in step 3, try to establish a connection without encryption (clear the Encrypt Traffic After Bind option). If you access Active Directory from another computer, ensure that a network connection to the Active Directory server is active and port 389 is not blocked by a firewall. Also, in the Server Manager, verify if the AD DS are started and running without problems.

4. To use the tree navigation, in the View menu, click Tree.

    In the dialog box that opens, enter the basic DN for your domain (for example, **DC=xmp,DC=site**) or another known DN. You can also select a DN in the drop-down list or leave the text field empty.

5. When you click OK, the tree navigation displays in the left pane (see Figure 16-3). Double-click an entry to open its child entries. You can also double-click to display the attributes of an entry.

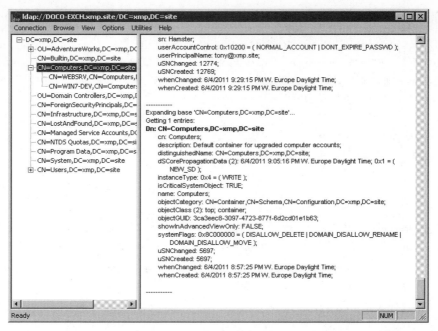

FIGURE 16-3 LDP tree navigation displays in the left pane and result messages display in the right pane.

Searching by Using LDP

To start an LDAP search, in the Browse menu, click Search. In the dialog box that opens, you can specify the following settings (also see Figure 16-4):

- **Base DN**   The first entry where the directory search starts.

- **Filter**   LDAP filter to search for objects (see the section "LDAP Filter," later in the chapter).

- **Area**   Select the Subtree option to search all entries below the basic entry. Select One Level to search only the direct child entries of the basic entry. Select Base to only search for the base entry.

- **Attributes**   Specify the desired attributes. If you enter an * (asterisk), all attributes of an entry are listed.

FIGURE 16-4 The LDP Search dialog box.

Click Run to start the search. The right pane of the LDP window contains status messages and the results.

Changing Entries by Using LDP

The Browse menu also contains commands that you can use to change entries and attributes.

- **Add Child**   Creates a new entry.
- **Delete**   Deletes an entry.
- **Modify**   Deletes, adds, or changes a single entry attribute.
- **Modify DN**   Changes the DN of an entry and moves the entry in the directory tree.

For all commands, you must enter the DN of the object that you want to edit. However, changes are not as easily performed as with ADSI Edit. But LDP can be useful to find errors because LDP uses the LDAP interface in the same way PHP does, and the user can be selected while the bind operation is performed.

> **Note** Active Directory supports changes through LDAP only for encrypted connections.

ADSI Edit

ADSI Edit is a snap-in for the Microsoft Management Console (MMC). You can use the editor to change, add, and delete entries in Active Directory. Similar to LDP, ADSI Edit provides instant access to the data model on which Active Directory is based.

Working with ADSI Edit

Perform the following steps to work with ADSI Edit:

1. To start the editor, click the Windows Start button, and then in the Search Programs And Files text box, Enter **ADSI Edit**. You can also add the editor in the MMC by clicking the File menu, and then clicking Add/Remove Snap-In.

2. In the Action menu, click Connect To.

   The Connection Settings dialog box opens, as shown in Figure 16-5. In this dialog box, you can set the connection parameters. Click the Advanced button to log on as a different user. You can enter a DN as connection point or select one of the predefined name contexts. Typically, you would use the Default naming context option. Click OK to confirm.

FIGURE 16-5 Connection settings for ADSI Edit.

3. In the left navigation pane, you can browse in the directory tree (see Figure 16-6). Simply select an entry to display its child entries in the list pane in the center.

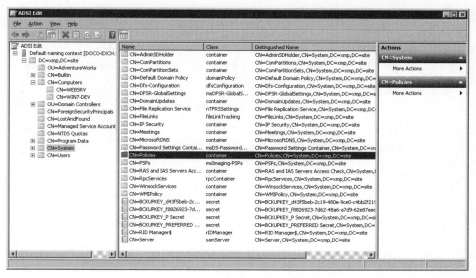

FIGURE 16-6 Browsing the directory tree in the ADSI Edit window.

4. To check the attributes of an entry, right-click the entry, and then in the context menu that appears, click Properties.

   A dialog box opens that lists the attributes.

5. To edit an attribute, double-click it (or select it, and then click Edit).

   In the dialog box that opens, you can change the value or click the Clear button to delete the attribute.

6. To add a new attribute to the entry, in the Properties dialog box, click Filter and clear the Show Only Attributes That Have Values check box.

   The listing shows all possible entry attributes. You can now click Edit to set the value for an attribute.

7. On the Security tab, you can change the access rights to this Active Directory entry. The access rights apply to the entry in Active Directory, not to the referenced object itself (for example, a group or a computer).

Creating New Entries

To create a new entry, perform the following steps:

1. Right-click the parent entry, and then in the context menu that appears, select New | Object.

2. In the dialog box that opens, select the desired object class (entry type).

3. The next pages prompt you to enter the mandatory fields for the entry such as the common name (CN).

4. On the last page, click the More Attributes button to define more attributes.

5. Click Finish to save the entry in Active Directory.

The Action menu and the context menu for the entry contain more editing functions, which are described here.

- **Move**   Moves the entry to another location in the directory structure.
- **Rename**   Changes the RDN of the entry.
- **Delete**   Deletes the entry and possibly all child entries.

Configuring the PHP LDAP Extension

PHP provides an extension for LDAP with which you can work with LDAP-compatible directories. The extension has functions for all LDAP protocol operations.

Activating the LDAP Extension

The LDAP extension is precompiled but not integrated. To activate the LDAP extension, perform the following steps:

1. Open the php.ini file in an editor (default path C:\PHP\php.ini).

2. Add the following line and save the file:

   ```
   extension=php_ldap.dll
   ```

3. Restart the associated Internet Information Services (IIS) application pool by using *appcmd*, as follows:

   ```
   appcmd recycle apppool "DefaultAppPool"
   ```

4. Call phpinfo.php to check the configuration.

   You should see the ldap section depicted in Figure 16-7.

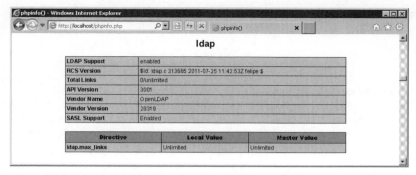

FIGURE 16-7 Output of the PHP LDAP extension with phpinfo().

You can also enable the PHP LDAP extension through the PHP Manager:

1. Start the IIS Manager, and then in the Connections pane, select the server or desired site.

2. Go to the PHP Manager by double-clicking its icon.

3. Click PHP Extensions | Enable Or Disable An Extension.

4. Select php_ldap.dll from the list, and then in the Actions pane, click Enable.

   PHP Manager automatically restarts the associated application pool, so the extension should be immediately available.

Communication Process

To establish communication with an LDAP server, you must perform the following:

- Establish the connection by using *ldap_connect()*.

- Set the optional connection parameters by using *ldap_set_option()*.

- Authenticate the connection via *ldap_bind()*.

- Submit the specified LDAP operations.

- Close the connection by using *ldap_unbind()*.

The *ldap_** functions return *false* if an error occurs and another value if the command was successful.

 Note If an error occurs, the *ldap_** functions also generate a warning. In a production environment, you should redirect these warnings into a log file (see Chapter 8, "Error Messages and Error Search"). Otherwise, IIS might prevent the page from displaying (depending on the configuration).

To establish and authenticate the connection in the sample applications, a separate *LDAPConnection* class is created that takes care of these standard steps and the output of error messages.

> **Caution** Because Windows PHP binaries don't support the LDAP Simple Authentication and Security Layer (SASL) authentication, the user name and the password are submitted to Active Directory in clear text. For security reasons, even in a secure network, passwords should not be sent in clear text. Therefore, it is recommended to encrypt the connection, which is explained in the section "Establishing an Encrypted Connection," later in the chapter.

Supporting Script

The supporting LDAPConnection.php script in Listing 16-2 is used to open and close the connection and to return error messages. The *LDAPConnection* class provides the following methods and properties:

- **$handle**   The LDAP connection resource.

- **connect()**   Establishes the connection to the LDAP server. *ldap_connect()* initializes the connection resource, *ldap_set_option()* sets the LDAP protocol version 3, and *ldap_bind()* opens and authenticates the connection. If you want to use a secure connection, encrypt the connection by using *ldap_start_tls()*. You should use the full principal name as user name.

- **close()**   Closes the connection with *ldap_unbind()*.

- **exitWithError()**   Returns the error code with *ldap_errno()* and the error message with *ldap_error()*, and then terminates the connection process.

LISTING 16-2 The *LDAPConnection* class for LDAP connections.

```php
<?php
namespace net\xmp\phpbook;
require_once './HTMLPage.php';

class LDAPConnection {

    public $handle = null;

    /**
     * Connect with LDAP directory.
     *
     * @param string $server Name of the LDAP server
     * @param string $username User name
     * @param string $password Password
     * @param boolean $secure Specifies if a connection is encrypted with TLS
```

```
    */
    function connect($server, $userName, $password, $secure=false) {
        $this->handle = ldap_connect($server);
        ldap_set_option($this->handle, LDAP_OPT_PROTOCOL_VERSION, 3);
        ldap_set_option($this->handle, LDAP_OPT_REFERRALS, 0);
        if ($secure) {
            if (!ldap_start_tls($this->handle)) {
                $this->exitWithError('TLS start failed');
            }
        }
        if (!ldap_bind($this->handle, $userName, $password)) {
            $this->exitWithError('Binding of LDAP connection failed');
        }
    }

    /**
     * Close connection to LDAP directory.
     */
    function close() {
        if ($this->handle) {
            ldap_unbind($this->handle);
            $this->handle = null;
        }
    }

    /**
     * Exit program, show error message from LDAP directory
     * @param string $txt Description of the error context
     */
    function exitWithError($txt) {
        $html = new HTMLPage('LDAP error');
        $html->addElement('p', $txt);
        $table = array(array('Number', 'Message'),
                       array(ldap_errno($this->handle), ldap_error($this->handle)));
        $html->addTable($table);
        $html->printPage();
        $this->close();
        exit;
    }
}
?>
```

Establishing an Encrypted Connection

To create an encrypted connection to Active Directory from PHP, you need to configure the LDAP extension. In *OpenLDAP* (an open source LDAP implementation on which the PHP LDAP extension is based), you have to define the root certificate of the certification authority as trusted. The following instructions assume that you already issued a certificate for Active Directory (see Chapter 15, "Setting Up Active Directory").

Configuring PHP and *OpenLDAP*

For *OpenLDAP*, the basic library of the PHP LDAP extension, to trust the certificates from LDAP servers, the root certificate from the associated certification authority must be included in the *OpenLDAP* configuration. To do so, perform the following steps:

1. Create the directory C:\openldap\sysconf.

2. In this directory, save the ldap.conf file with the following text:

```
TLS_CACERT C:\openldap\sysconf\rootcertificate.cer
TLS_REQCERT demand
```

3. Give the base-64 encoded X.509 root certificate of the certification authority the name **rootcertificate.cer** and copy it to C:\openldap\sysconf.

4. Restart the IIS application pool associated with the LDAP application.

The configuration is now complete and will be applied. Next, you should test the connection.

Testing the Encrypted LDAP Connection

Create the test_ldap_tls.php file shown in Listing 16-3, and then call the file from the command line or IIS. If you see the success message, the connection encrypted with the LDAP protocol element *Start TLS* works.

LISTING 16-3 test_ldap_tls.php—testing the encrypted LDAP connection.

```php
<?php
namespace net\xmp\phpbook;
require './LDAPConnection.php';

// Optionally enable debugging for LDAP
// ldap_set_option(NULL, LDAP_OPT_DEBUG_LEVEL, 7);

// Open secure connection
$ad = new LDAPConnection();
$ad->connect('doco-exch.xmp.site', 'arno@xmp.site', 'confidential', true);
// This point is only reached if the connection works
echo 'LDAP with START_TLS works.';
// Close connection
$ad->close();
?>
```

The secure connection is started by using the PHP function *ldap_start_tls($ldapLink)*. If the certificate from Active Directory is not issued by a trusted certificate authority (root certificate in C:\openldap\sysconf\), the function returns *false*.

Note If you enable LDAP debugging in the script, the debug output is written to *stderr*, but not caught in IIS and therefore not displayed on the HTML page. Thus you should start PHP from the command line when debugging.

Verifying the Connection Certificate

Use *TLS_REQCERT* in C:\openldap\sysconf\ldap.conf to determine the behavior of PHP/OpenLDAP if the certificate for the encrypted connection doesn't match. Alternative configuration options for *TLS_REQCERT* are:

- **never** Ensures that a certificate is never requested from the server.

- **allow** Requests the server certificate. Even when the server doesn't have a certificate or the associated root certificate isn't configured, the connection is resumed.

- **try** Requests the server certificate. Even when the server doesn't have a certificate, the connection is resumed. If the server has a certificate that was issued by an unknown certificate authority, the connection is terminated.

- **demand** Requests the server certificate and the connection is only resumed if a valid certificate is available.

For security reasons, you should select *demand* for *TLS_REQCERT*.

Authenticating Users

Active Directory plays a vital role in authenticating domain users. You can use the *ldap_bind()* authentication method to check user names and passwords. Depending on whether *ldap_bind()* returns a success or error message, the credentials you enter are correct and the authentication is successful or the credentials are wrong and the authentication fails. If the authentication fails, you should check the error code (*49: Invalid credentials*), because the LDAP connection can also fail for other reasons.

Listing 16-4 shows how the *authenticate()* function could look: when *ldap_bind()* returns *false*, error code 49 is checked, and the corresponding value is returned.

LISTING 16-4 Authenticating a user through LDAP.

```php
<?php
namespace net\xmp\phpbook;

// Exception class
class LDAPException extends Exception { }

/**
 * Authenticating a user in Active Directory
 * @param string $server Name of the server
 * @param string $username User name
 * @param string $password Password
 * @param boolean $secure Specifies if the connection is encrypted
 * @return boolean True if successful, false if not successful
 * @throws LDAPConnectionException
 */
function authenticate($server, $username, $password, $secure=true) {
    $handle = ldap_connect($server);
    if ($secure) {
        if (!ldap_start_tls($handle)) {
            throw new LDAPException('LDAP connection error');
        }
    }
    if (!ldap_bind($handle, $username, $password)) {
        $code = ldap_errno($handle);
        ldap_unbind($handle);
        if ($code != 49) {
            throw new LDAPException('LDAP connection error');
        }
        return false;
    }
    ldap_unbind($handle);
    return true;
}
```

Important If possible the connection should be encrypted with *ldap_start_tls()*; otherwise, the user name and password are sent to Active Directory in clear text.

ldap_bind() and *ldap_start_tls()* generate a warning if an error occurs. For this reason error messages should be redirected into a log file when working in a production environment (see the PHP configuration options in Chapter 8).

Querying Entries

Searching for entries in the LDAP directory is a basic function. PHP provides different functions to search or query entries. These functions are the *ldap_read()*, *ldap_list()*, and *ldap_search()*. Three parameters are passed to all three functions: a DN, a filter string, and several attributes. The difference between the functions is the hierarchical directory structure.

- **ldap_read()**   Only reads the entry identified by the DN.

- **ldap_list()**   Searches all direct children of the entry identified by the DN.

- **ldap_search()**   Searches the whole tree (child and descendant entries) of the entry identified by the DN, including the entry itself.

The filter string that is passed contains the actual search criteria. This is explained in more detail in the section "LDAP Filter," later in the chapter. You must always specify a filter string, because in LDAP an empty filter is not allowed.

The attribute list contains the attributes that are to be returned in the search result. For efficiency reasons, not all attributes of an entry should be retrieved but only the required attributes.

Sample Program: Searching for Domain Users

Listing 16-5 shows how a search for domain users in Active Directory with LDAP can look. First, the connection to Active Directory is established. Because only read access is required, you can specify any domain user, as all users in the domain have read access to the entries in the directory.

> **Important** Enter the user name in the user@domain format shown in the listing, or else the authentication might fail.

User entries typically are located under the entry Users of the domain—for example, *CN=Users,DC=xmp,DC=site*.

The defined filter searches for new users and excludes system users.

Only the attributes *name*, *userPrinicpalName*, and *sAMAccountName* should be retrieved. The names are not case sensitive.

After the search with *ldap_search()* is completed, *ldap_get_entries()* retrieves the results. The required attributes can be retrieved as associated array and the DN of the entry can always be queried with the index dn. The names of attributes in the array are always lowercase.

> **Caution** Entries also contain optional attributes. If an entry doesn't have an attribute, the index in the associated result array is also not set. Because it cannot be assumed that attributes exist, you should check by using *isset()* or *empty()* if the array contains the entry that you're looking for.

Because an attribute can have several values, *ldap_get_entries()* returns the values as an array. If the first value is required, it must be accessed with *[0]*.

Afterward, the memory for the search result is released by using *ldap_free_result()* and the connection is closed. The explicit release of the memory is not mandatory because the memory is freed up after the PHP script is completed. However, if a script runs several queries that are returning extensive results, you should release the memory from time to time.

LISTING 16-5 ldap_search_ad.php—searching for domain users.

```php
<?php
namespace net\xmp\phpbook;
require './HTMLPage.php';
require './LDAPConnection.php';
$html = new HTMLPage('LDAP User Search');

// Connect
$ad = new LDAPConnection();
$ad->connect('doco-exch.xmp.site', 'arno@xmp.site', 'confidential');
// Query Users
$baseDN = "CN=users,DC=xmp,DC=site";
// Filter looks for user objects with the userPrincipalName attribute
$filter = "(&(objectcategory=Person)(userPrincipalName=*))";
// Definition of the attributes to retrieve
$attributes = array('name', 'userPrincipalName', 'sAMAccountName');
// Start search
$qresult = ldap_search($ad->handle, $baseDN, $filter, $attributes);
if (!$qresult) {
    $ad->exitWithError('LDAP search failed.');
}
// Retrieve entries ...
$entries = ldap_get_entries($ad->handle, $qresult);
if (!$entries) {
    $ad->exitWithError('Reading of LDAP failed.');
```

```
    }
    // ... and write in table
    $table = array(array('Name', 'Principal', 'DN', 'Account Name'));
    for ($i = 0; $i < $entries['count']; $i++) {
        $table[] = array($entries[$i]['name'][0], $entries[$i]['userprincipalname'][0],
                         $entries[$i]['dn'], $entries[$i]['samaccountname'][0]);
    }
    $html->addTable($table);

    // Share result, close connection
    ldap_free_result($qresult);
    $ad->close();
    $html->printPage();
    ?>
```

Figure 16-8 shows the result of a query. System users such as administrators or guests are not displayed because they are excluded by the filter.

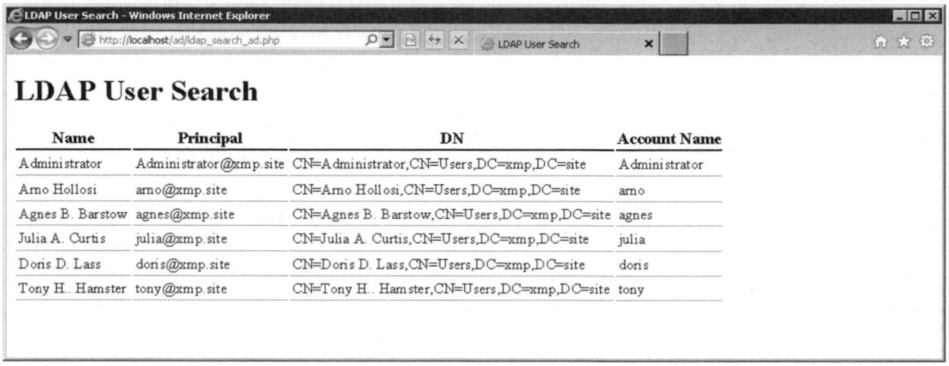

FIGURE 16-8 Searching for domain users by using ldap_search_ad.php.

LDAP Filter

An LDAP search is always designated by two parameters: the position in the tree at which the search begins, and the values that the attributes must have to ensure that the associated entries are not excluded. The definition of the LDAP filter is based on attribute values and the *Boolean* logic to link expressions.

An LDAP filter consists of two basic building blocks: a filter expression, and linked filter expressions.

```
filter := '(' { <operator> filter [ ,...n ] | filter expression } ')'
filter expression := { <attribute> <comparator> <value>
   | <attribute> ':' <comparison rule> ':=' <value> }
```

Operators

Table 16-2 lists the valid operators, comparators, and comparison rules for LDAP filters. Comparison rules are specified with standardized object identifiers (OID). If an attribute has several values, at least one value must meet the defined conditions. Note that not all attribute types support all comparators; for example, only the identity of the *objectClass* attribute can be checked.

TABLE 16-2 Operators and comparators for LDAP filters

Type	Expression	Description
Operator	&	*AND* operator: all filters must apply.
	|	*OR* operator: only one filter must apply.
	!	*NOT* operator: the filter must not apply.
Comparison operator	=	The attribute value equals the specified value.
	~=	The attribute value is about the same as the specified value.
	>=	The attribute value is greater or equal to the specified value.
	<=	The attribute value is less or equal to the specified value.
	= ...*...	The asterisk is a placeholder for any character in the specified value and can only be used with the equal operator.
Comparison rule	1.2.840.113556.1.4.803	Bit-by-bit *AND* operator: only true if all set bits of the specified value are also set for the attribute value.
	1.2.840.113556.1.4.804	Bit-by-bit *OR* operator: only true if at least one set bit is also set for the attribute value.
	1.2.840.113556.1.4.1941	Only for the comparison of attributes containing a DN. Verifies not only the current entry but also all referenced entries recursively.

Escape (Masking) Characters

To use special characters for a filter string value, you need to replace them with an escape sequence. Table 16-3 lists the escape sequences for characters that need to be replaced.

TABLE 16-3 Escape sequences for LDAP filter strings

Character	Escape sequence
(	\28
)	\29
*	\2a
/	\2f
\	\5c
NUL (00$_{hex}$)	\00

Examples

The filter syntax is shown in the following few examples.

To find an entry with the CN Doris:

`(cn=Doris)`

It's also no problem if the attribute value contains spaces:

`(cn=Doris D. Lass)`

To find all entries beginning with "A", use a placeholder, as shown here:

`(cn=A*)`

To find entries with an operating system version less than or equal to 5 (*operatingSystem Version*) or to search for entries created before January 1st 2011 (*whenCreated*), the two filter expressions are linked with *OR*, as demonstrated in the following:

`(|(operatingSystemVersion<=5)(whenCreated<=20110101000000.0Z))`

More complex combinations are also possible:

`(&(|(objectClass=User)(objectClass=Computer))(!(mail=*xmp.site)))`

This filter searches for user or computer entries not containing an email address (mail attribute) that ends with xmp.site.

> **Caution** This also excludes all entries without a mail attribute because it cannot be determined if they meet the condition.

To check if an attribute exists, the value is specified as "*", shown below:

```
(mail=*)
```

This filter returns all entries with a mail attribute. The following filter returns all entries without a mail attribute:

```
(!(mail=*))
```

Because in LDAP a filter string must be specified, you need a filter that doesn't filter but lets all entries pass through:

```
(objectClass=*)
```

Since each entry is derived from the top class for which the *objectClass* attribute is mandatory, all entries are found because each entry has an *objectClass* attribute.

The attribute type is important for comparison operations: placeholders and comparators (<=, >=, ~=) can only be used for attributes containing strings. *objectClass* and other attributes, for example *memberOf* for group memberships, aren't strings—even though they are displayed in clear text—and cannot be filtered with these comparators. For example, the following filters never return a result:

```
(objectClass=Pers*)
(objectClass<=Z)
```

The syntax for comparison rules appears as follows:

```
(&(objectClass=User)(userAccountControl:1.2.840.113556.1.4.804:=18))
```

This filter finds all user entries that are locked (*LOCKOUT=16*) or deactivated (*ACCOUNTDISABLE=2*).

Iterating Through Search Results

ldap_get_entries() returns all search results as array (see Listing 16-5). An alternative is to incrementally retrieve the attributes and results.

Incremental Entry Queries

The functions *ldap_first_entry()* and *ldap_next_entry()* retrieve entries incrementally. To retrieve the attributes of an entry, use *ldap_get_attributes()*.

Listing 16-6 demonstrates how these functions are used. After the search with *ldap_search()* is completed, *ldap_first_entry()* retrieves the first entry returned in the search results. In the loop, *ldap_get_attributes()* retrieves the attributes of the current entry. To get the next entry, call *ldap_next_entry()*, which returns the next entry or *false* if no more entries exist.

LISTING 16-6 The entries of a search result are retrieved incrementally.

```
$result = ldap_search($ldapLink, $baseDN, $filter, $attributes);
if (!$result) {
    // Error occurred
}
$entry = ldap_first_entry($ldapLink, $result);
if (!$entry) {
    // Error occurred
}
do {
    $attr = ldap_get_attributes($ldapLink, $entry);
    if (!$attr) {
        // Error occurred
    }
    // ...
} while ($entry = ldap_next_entry($ldapLink, $entry));
ldap_free_result($result);
```

Caution   Unlike *ldap_get_entries()*, the names of attributes for *ldap_get_attributes()* are not low-ercase, but the capitalization rules are identical with the corresponding rules in Active Directory.

Incremental Attribute Queries

Like entries, attributes can also be retrieved incrementally. For this purpose, the *ldap_first_attribute()* and *ldap_next_attribute()* functions are used to iterate through the attributes of an entry. These functions return the name of the next attribute as a string. (Again, the capitalization rules are the same as in Active Directory.) You can retrieve the values for a certain attribute as an array with *ldap_get_values()*. Listing 16-7 shows how these functions are used.

LISTING 16-7 The attributes of an entry in the search result are incrementally retrieved.

```
// $ldapLink, $entry are set according to the query.
// $entry point to an entry in the search result
$attr = ldap_first_attribute($ldapLink, $entry);
if (!$attr) {
    // Error occurred
}
do {
    $values = ldap_get_values($ldapLink, $entry, $attr);
    if (!$values) {
        // Error occurred
    }
    // ...
} while ($attr = ldap_next_attribute($ldapLink, $entry));
// ...
```

You can use *ldap_get_values()* without *ldap_first_attribute()/ldap_next_attribute()*. To retrieve binaries, use the *ldap_get_values_len()* function.

> **Note** At least for the platforms and program versions described in this book, you can use *ldap_get_values()*, *ldap_get_attributes()*, and *ldap_get_entries()* to query binaries such as the GUID and SID of a user.

Summary

Filters and the DN are the foundation for interactions with Active Directory through the LDAP interface: the data model hierarchy is reflected in the hierarchic syntax of the DN and the filters allow specific queries based on entry attributes. You can use the PHP functions for connecting to Active Directory and retrieving entries explained in this chapter to query all required information about users, groups, organizational units, and computers.

The next chapter explains the differences between these entries as well as the corresponding syntax and structure rules. The PHP LDAP sample browser developed in the next chapter is useful for application development because it allows you to quickly browse between linked objects and entries and attributes.

Chapter 17
Searching in Active Directory

This chapter explains the schema of Microsoft Active Directory in more detail as well as the structure of the directory information tree (DIT) and the important object types (user, groups, and organizational units). In this chapter, you create a PHP Lightweight Directory Access Protocol (LDAP) browser that you can use to search and view data in Active Directory. The browser also includes several useful routines that you can use with Active Directory to convert a Security ID (SID) to a string, convert a Global Unique Identifier (GUID), and to convert PHP and Windows timestamps.

The PHP LDAP Browser

In this chapter, the PHP LDAP Browser (PLB) serves as a sample program. This browser provides a simple extensible search interface and converts binary data to a readable format for attributes. The following sections describe the most important PLB components: the user interface, the class for formatting LDAP entries, and the structure of search definitions and type information.

Main Program and User Interface

The main program of the PLB controls the activities and the user interaction. The program is divided up and presented in Listings 17-1 to 17-5, which make up the complete PHP script.

Entry Form

Listing 17-1 shows the structure of the entry form. The page is created by using the *HTMLPage* class (for more information, see Appendix A, "Example Scripts and Data"). The options in the drop-down list are dynamically composed of the existing search definitions (*$objectClasses* from browse_ldap_types.php). At the end, the routine checks if both input parameters (*$_GET['type']* and *$_GET['name']*) are set. If not, the form is displayed and the script is finished. The type variable specifies which search is performed, and the name variable specifies a parameter for the search filter.

LISTING 17-1 browse_ldap.php—the entry form.

```php
<?php
namespace net\xmp\phpbook;

require './HTMLPage.php';
require './LDAPConnection.php';
require './LDAPEntryFormatter.php';
require './browse_ldap_types.php';
require './AD_util.php';

$html = new HTMLPage('LDAP Browser');
$form = <<<EOF
<form action="" method="get">
Name: <input name="name" />
<select name="type">
EOF;
foreach ($objectClasses as $name => $config) {
    $form .= sprintf('<option value="%s">%s</option>', htmlspecialchars($name),
            htmlspecialchars($config['name']));
}
$form .= <<<EOF
</select>
<input type="submit" value="search" />
</form><br />
EOF;
$html->addHTML($form);
// Check if parameters exist
if (!isset($_GET['name']) || !isset($_GET['type'])) {
    $html->printPage();
    exit;
}
```

LDAP Search

In the next step, you create and authenticate the LDAP connection by using the *LDAP Connection* class (for more information, see Chapter 16, "LDAP Basics"), as shown in Listing 17-2. Depending on the search type you use, one of the following two PHP functions is used:

- **Search for distinguished name (DN) with ldap_read()**   Because each DN is unique, only a single entry is found in Active Directory. *ldap_read()* retrieves only the specified entry instead of searching the entire directory. Because you must specify a filter with LDAP, you can use (*objectClass=**) as a filter that applies to all objects.

- **General search with ldap_search()**   The other queries always start at the basic DN and search the entire underlying directory tree. The filter and basic DN come from the search definitions in *$objectClasses* in *browse_ldap_types.php*.

LISTING 17-2 browse_ldap.php—creating the connection and sending the query.

```
// Establish connection
$ad = new LDAPConnection();
$ad->connect('doco-exch.xmp.site', 'arno@xmp.site', 'confidential');
// Filter parameters
if (!isset($objectClasses[$_GET['type']])) {
    $ad->exitWithError('Invalid entry type!');
}
$class = $objectClasses[$_GET['type']];
// Two different search types: Search for object DN ...
if (isset($_GET['getDN'])) {
    $result = ldap_read($ad->handle, $_GET['name'], '(objectClass=*)',
$class['attributes']);
}
// ... or search for baseDN with filter
else {
    $name = preg_replace($class['filterchars'], '', $_GET['name']);
    $filter = sprintf($class['filter'], $name);
    $result = ldap_search($ad->handle, $class['baseDN'], $filter,
$class['attributes']);
}
if (!$result) {
    $ad->exitWithError('LDAP search failed.');
}
```

Evaluating the Search Results

After the search is complete, the result is evaluated and displayed (see Listing 17-3). The *ldap_count_entries()* function returns the number of search results. The *listSingleEntry()* and *listEntries()* functions process the search results. Afterward, the search results are released by using *ldap_free_result()* and the connection is closed.

LISTING 17-3 browse_ldap.php—the search results are evaluated and returned.

```php
// The displayed information depends on the number of hits
$cnt = ldap_count_entries($ad->handle, $result);
if (!$cnt) {
    $html->addElement('p', 'No matches found.');
} elseif ($cnt == 1) {
    list($heading, $table) = listSingleEntry($ad, $result, $_GET['type']);
    $html->addElement('h2', $heading);
    $html->addTable($table, array(true, true));
} else {
    $list = listEntries($ad, $result, $_GET['type']);
    $html->addElement('h2', 'Search result');
    $html->addList($list, true);
}
// Free result buffer, close connection
ldap_free_result($result);
$ad->close();
$html->printPage();
```

Viewing the Results

To prepare the result output, you use two different functions, depending on whether you want to display the information for a single result or a result list.

Listing 17-4 shows the search results displayed by the *listEntries()* function. The *ldap_get_entries()* function returns all results in a single array. Because the object classes of the entries are unknown, only the DN of the search results is displayed. The DN of an entry in the array is retrieved by using *$entries[$i]['dn']*. For the generated link, the *getDN=1* parameter is set to use the corresponding search.

LISTING 17-4 browse_ldap.php—lists more search results.

```php
/**
 * Returns several search hits and displays them
 */
function listEntries($ad, $result, $class) {
    $entries = ldap_get_entries($ad->handle, $result);
    if (!$entries) {
        $ad->exitWithError('Reading the LDAP search results failed.');
    }
    $list = array();
    for ($i = 0; $i < $entries['count']; $i++) {
        $list[] = '<a href="browse_ldap.php?name=' . rawurlencode($entries[$i]['dn'])
                . '&amp;type=' . rawurlencode($class)
                . '&amp;getDN=1">' . htmlspecialchars($entries[$i]['dn']) . '</a>';
    }
    return $list;
}
```

Listing 17-5 shows the *listSingleEntry()* function that displays the details of an entry. Since the case sensitivity for the attributes should be maintained, *ldap_first_entry()* and *ldap_get_attributes()* are used instead of *ldap_get_entries()*. The *ldap_get_dn()* function returns the DN of the entry. The *LDAPEntryFormatter* class formats the output.

LISTING 17-5 browse_ldap.php—returns a single hit.

```php
/**
 * Reads a single search hit and formats it for viewing
 */
function listSingleEntry($ad, $result, $class) {
    $entry = ldap_first_entry($ad->handle, $result);
    if (!$entry) {
        $ad->exitWithError('Reading the LDAP entry failed.');
    }
    $attr = ldap_get_attributes($ad->handle, $entry);
    $ef = new LDAPEntryFormatter($attr, $class, 'browse_ldap.php');
    $table = $ef->getAttributes();
    $title = $class . ': ' . ldap_get_dn($ad->handle, $entry);
    return array($title, $table);
}
?>
```

Formatting an LDAP Entry

The *LDAPEntryFormatter* class together with *HTMLPage* formats and processes the output (Listing 17-6). The type and attributes of the entry are passed to the constructor.

LISTING 17-6 *LDAPEntryFormatter*—this class generates a detailed view of the LDAP entries.

```php
<?php
namespace net\xmp\phpbook;

class LDAPEntryFormatter {

    protected $attr;
    protected $type;
    protected $url;

    function __construct($attributes, $type, $url) {
        $this->attr = $attributes;
        $this->type = $type;
        $this->url = $url;
    }

    function getAttributes() { ... }
    function getValue($name, $link) { ... }
    function link($value, $link) { ... }
}
?>
```

Listing 17-7 shows the *LDAPEntryFormatter->getAttributes()* method. This method generates an array that can be passed to *HTMLPage->addTable()*. The entry attributes are processed step by step in a loop and converted with a conversion routine in AD_util.php, if an entry exists in *$attributeConversion (from browse_ldap_types.php)*.

LISTING 17-7 *LDAPEntryFormatter->getAttributes()*—iterating through attributes.

```
/**
 * Returns the attributes of the LDAP entry
 * in an array compatible with HTMLPage->addTable()
 */
function getAttributes() {
    global $attributeConvertion;

    $table = array(array('attribute', 'value'));
    for ($i = 0; $i < $this->attr['count']; $i++) {
        $attr = $this->attr[$i];
        $link = isset($attributeConvertion[$attr]) ? $attributeConvertion[$attr] :
false;
        $table[] = array($this->link($attr, 'attributeSchema'),
                         $this->getValue($attr, $link));
    }
    return $table;
}
```

The *LDAPEntryFormatter->getValue()* method handles the list of attribute values and aggregates the values in a single string (Listing 17-8).

LISTING 17-8 *LDAPEntryFormatter->getValue()*—returns the attribute values.

```
/**
 * Returns the linked and converted values of an attribute
 */
function getValue($name, $link=false) {
    if (!($cnt = $this->attr[$name]['count'])) {
        return '(empty)';
    }
    if ($cnt == 1) {
        return $this->link($this->attr[$name][0], $link);
    }
    $val = "($cnt) ";
    for ($i = 0; $i < $cnt; $i++) {
        $val .= $this->link($this->attr[$name][$i], $link) . '; ';
    }
    return $val;
}
```

The *LDAPEntryFormatter->link()* method in Listing 17-9 links and converts the attributes: if *$link* is set, the routine checks if a conversion function with the same name exists (in the namespace *net\xmp\phpbook*). If the function exists, it is called; otherwise, a link for the entry type is generated.

LISTING 17-9 The *LDAPEntryFormatter->link()* method—linking and converting values.

```
/**
 * Links a single attribute value
 */
function link($value, $link=false) {
    $txt = htmlspecialchars($value);
    // No information -> clear text
    if ($link === false) {
        return $txt;
    }
    // Does the conversion function exist?
    elseif (function_exists('net\\xmp\\phpbook\\' . $link)) {
        $func = 'net\\xmp\\phpbook\\' . $link;
        return htmlspecialchars($func($value));
    }
    // Otherwise it is an object class
    else {
        $getdn = '';
        if (substr($link, 0, 3) === 'DN-') {
            $link = substr($link, 3);
            $getdn = '&amp;getDN=1';
        }
        return "<a href='" . $this->url . '?name=' . rawurlencode($value)
            . "&amp;type=$link$getdn'>$txt</a>";
    }
}
```

Type Information and Search Definitions

The file browse_ldap_types.php contains the definitions for the LDAP object classes and searches (see Listing 17-10). The two main arrays are:

- **$objectClasses**   An associative array that contains the following entries for each entry type or for each search:
    - **name**   The text for the drop-down list.
    - **baseDN**   Basic DN for the directory tree search.
    - **filter**   LDAP filter string, %s is a placeholder for user entries.

- **attributes** An array of the attributes to be listed; an empty array means that all attributes are listed.

- **filterchars** A regular expression to filter out unwanted characters in the user input.

- **$attributeConvertion** An associative array that displays attribute names for function names or entry types. In the first case, the function converting the attributes is called; in the latter case, the entry is linked accordingly.

LISTING 17-10 browse_ldap_types.php—type information and search definitions.

```php
<?php
namespace net\xmp\phpbook;

$rootDN = 'DC=xmp,DC=site';

/**
 * Definition for search operations and object classes
 */
$objectClasses = array(
    // ...
);

// Sets the default values
foreach ($objectClasses as &$oc) {
    if (isset($oc['base'])) {    // Copies from another definition
        foreach ($objectClasses[$oc['base']] as $name => $val) {
            if (!isset($oc[$name])) {
                $oc[$name] = $val;
            }
        }
    }
    if (!isset($oc['filterchars'])) {
        $oc['filterchars'] = "/[^-_ a-z0-9*.']/i";
    }
}

/**
 * Linking and converting attributes
 */
$attributeConvertion = array(
    // ...
);
?>
```

Conversion Functions

The conversion functions for attribute values are saved in the file AD_util.php. Listing 17-11 uses the *dec2hex()* function to convert a decimal number to a hexadecimal number.

LISTING 17-11 AD_util.php—conversion functions.

```php
<?php
namespace net\xmp\phpbook;

/**
 * Converts a number to the hexadecimal format.
 * @param int $dec Number
 */
function dec2hex($dec) {
    return '0x' . dechex($dec);
}
?>
```

The Directory Information Tree and Naming Contexts

The directory information tree (DIT) of a directory service (for example, Active Directory) is the sum of all information saved in the directory: not only do the data objects belong to the DIT but so does the schema. A DIT is divided into several naming contexts. The referenced objects belong to different partitions of the DIT.

The DIT (the directory structure) in Active Directory is divided into at least three different naming contexts. Some naming contexts are specific to a domain and others are uniform for an Active Directory forest. The naming contexts are:

- **Domain context**   For example, *DC=xmp,DC=site*: in this context the domain objects—for example, computer, user, groups, and so on—are saved. You usually work in this naming context. The Active Directory forest can include many domain contexts.

- **Configuration context**   For example, *CN=Configuration,DC=xmp,DC=site*: the configuration context includes information to the Active Directory forest, such as the domains in the forest and the domain controllers and services in the domains.

- **Schema context**   For example, *CN=Schema,CN=Configuration,DC=xmp,DC=site*: the schema contains the definition of all object and attribute classes as well as the structure and content rules for the directory tree. Entries and attributes in Active Directory can only be created and changed according to the specified rules.

■ **Optional application contexts**   For example, *DC=DomainDnsZones,DC=xmp,DC=site*: applications in Active Directory, such as the Active Directory DNS service, have their own naming contexts. These application contexts save application information but no user accounts or other principals.

An LDAP search can only be performed in one naming context at a time, and an overall search is not possible. When searching in Active Directory, the first step is the selection of the appropriate naming context using the basic DN.

> **Important**   Although the DN of the naming context suggests that the schema is included in the configuration and the domain includes the schema and the configuration, this is not the case. A naming context is always autonomous.

Active Directory Schema

The Active Directory schema is extensive: it consists of more than 200 object classes and more than 1,200 attribute definitions with about 30 different syntaxes for values. The most important properties of the schema are described in the following subsections.

> **Note**   For a complete description of the Active Directory schema, see the MSDN website at *http://msdn.microsoft.com/en-us/library/ms675085.aspx*.

The Active Directory schema is saved in the schema naming context of the DIT (usually the basic *DN CN=Schema,CN=Configuration,DC=...,DC=...*). The schema naming context doesn't have a deep hierarchy. The object and attribute classes important for the schema exist one level below the basic DN.

Object Classes

Object classes define content and structure rules for entries: for example, which attributes are mandatory or optional, and what object class has to be the parent object in the directory tree? Listing 17-12 shows the entry of the top object class that serves as base for all other object classes in Active Directory.

LISTING 17-12 Attributes of the top object class.

```
Dn: CN=Top,CN=Schema,CN=Configuration,DC=xmp,DC=site
cn: Top;
defaultHidingValue: TRUE;
defaultObjectCategory: CN=Top,CN=Schema,CN=Configuration,DC=xmp,DC=site;
distinguishedName: CN=Top,CN=Schema,CN=Configuration,DC=xmp,DC=site;
instanceType: 0x4 = ( WRITE );
lDAPDisplayName: top;
mayContain (4): msSFU30PosixMemberOf; msDFSR-ComputerReferenceBL; [ ... ]
name: Top;
objectCategory: CN=Class-Schema,CN=Schema,CN=Configuration,DC=xmp,DC=site;
objectClass (2): top; classSchema;
objectClassCategory: 2 = ( ABSTRACT );
objectGUID: db474ff7-44d0-486c-988f-6cab04cd9be8;
schemaIDGUID: bf967ab7-0de6-11d0-a285-00aa003049e2;
subClassOf: top;
systemFlags: 0x10 = ( SCHEMA_BASE_OBJECT );
systemMayContain (104): description; createTimeStamp; cn; [ ... ]
systemMustContain (4): objectClass; objectCategory; nTSecurityDescriptor;
instanceType;
systemOnly: TRUE;
systemPossSuperiors: lostAndFound;
whenChanged: 2/11/2009 6:37:20 PM W. Europe Daylight Time;
whenCreated: 2/11/2009 6:37:20 PM W. Europe Daylight Time;
```

Attributes of Object Classes

Table 17-1 lists interesting attributes for object class entries in the schema. These attributes help you to arrange the classes and to get an overview of the valid attributes.

TABLE 17-1 Attributes of the object class description (classSchema)

Attribute	Description
adminDescription	Includes a short description of the object class (not for all classes).
auxiliaryClass, systemAuxiliaryClass	List of additional classes whose attributes are also used.
defaultHidingValue	If *TRUE* the object of this class is not displayed in the Microsoft Management Console (MMC) and in other programs by default.
defaultObjectCategory	DN of the *objectCategory* attribute for entries of this class.
lDAPDisplayName	Name of the class used for LDAP queries.
mayContain, systemMayContain	List of the optional class attributes.
mustContain, systemMustContain	List of the mandatory class attributes.
name	Name and relative distinguished name (RDN) of the object class.
objectClassCategory	Object class category (see Table 17-2).

Attribute	Description
possibleInferiors	Automatically generated list of the classes that can have children of an object of this class. (read-only structure rule)
possSuperiors, systemPossSuperiors	List of the classes that need a parent object of this class (structure rule).
subClassOf	Class hierarchy: specifies from which classes attributes are inherited.
systemOnly	If *TRUE* the generated object can only be changed by Active Directory.

Not all classes are associated with class categories. Only structure classes can instantiate objects directly in the directory. Table 17-2 lists an overview of the class categories. With only a few exceptions, the object classes in Active Directory are structure classes.

TABLE 17-2 Object class categories

Name	Value	Description
88	0	Classes existing before class categories were introduced. Example: *person, country*.
Abstract	2	*Abstract* object classes cannot be directly instantiated and are only used for the inheritance hierarchy. Examples: *top, domain*.
Auxiliary	3	*Auxiliary* classes can pass their attributes to abstract and structure classes but cannot be instantiated. Examples: *mailRecipient, securityPrincipal*.
Structural	1	*Structural* category classes are concrete classes allowing instantiation of the object in the directory. Example: *user, group*.

PLB: Finding and Viewing Object Classes

To use the PLB to search and view object classes, you need to extend the definitions in browse_ldap_types.php, as shown in Listing 17-13. The *Schema: Object Class* option is added to the LDAP search. You can use this to search for classes by LDAP name. Figure 17-1 shows an example search for the *User* class.

LISTING 17-13 browse_ldap_types.php—object class extension.

```
$objectClasses = array(
    // ...
    'classSchema' => array(
        'name' => 'Schema: Object Class',
        'baseDN' => "CN=Schema,CN=Configuration,$rootDN",
        'filter' => '(&(lDAPDisplayName=%s)(objectClass=classSchema))',
        'attributes' => array(
```

```
                'name', 'lDAPDisplayName', 'subClassOf', 'defaultObjectCategory',
                'objectCategory', 'systemPossSuperiors', 'possSuperiors',
                'auxiliaryClass', 'systemAuxiliaryClass', 'mustContain',
                'systemMustContain', 'mayContain', 'systemMayContain',
                'systemOnly', 'possibleInferiors', 'defaultHidingValue',
                'adminDescription')
    ),
);

$attributeConvertion = array(
    // ...
    'subClassOf' => 'classSchema',
    'possSuperiors' => 'classSchema',
    'systemPossSuperiors' => 'classSchema',
    'possibleInferiors' => 'classSchema',
    'auxiliaryClass' => 'classSchema',
    'systemAuxiliaryClass' => 'classSchema',
    'mustContain' => 'attributeSchema',
    'systemMustContain' => 'attributeSchema',
    'mayContain' => 'attributeSchema',
    'systemMayContain' => 'attributeSchema',
);
```

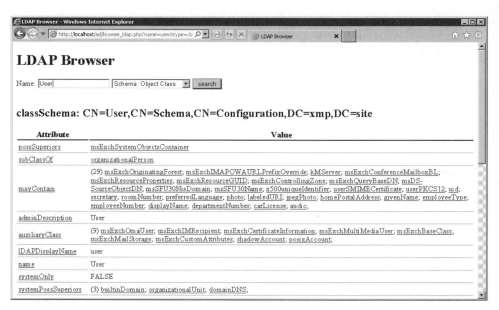

FIGURE 17-1   PLB—a detailed view of the *User* object class.

Object Classes vs. Object Categories

Each entry in Active Directory has two attributes to provide information to an object class: *objectClass* and *objectCategory*. The difference between the two attributes is that *objectClass* contains the object identifier (OID) of all classes, whereas *objectCategory* only contains a DN (usually of the most specific class). For this reason, the *objectClass* attribute includes about four to five values, and the *objectCategory* attribute has only a single value.

If you want to select object types as specific as possible for the search, you should look for *objectCategory* in the LDAP filter. For example, the *User* class has the following attribute values:

```
objectClass (4): top; person; organizationalPerson; user;
objectCategory: CN=Person,CN=Schema,CN=Configuration,DC=xmp,DC=site;
```

If you use an LDAP filter with (*objectClass=user*), you find not only users but also computers, because they are a subclass of the *User* class:

```
objectClass (4): top; person; organizationalPerson; user; computer;
objectCategory: CN=Computer,CN=Schema,CN=Configuration,DC=xmp,DC=site;
```

> **Note** Active Directory simplifies the search with *objectClass* and *objectCategory* because in addition to being able to find an OID (*objectClass*) or a DN (*objectCategory*), it also inserts the *LDAPDisplayName* of the class as value into the filter. Active Directory searches the schema and replaces *LDAPDisplayName* with the corresponding OID or DN (from *defaultObjectCategory*).
>
> For example, if you specify (*objectCategory=computer*) in the filter, Active Directory will search for (*objectCategory=CN=Computer,CN=Schema,CN=Configuration,DC=xmp,DC=site*).

Attribute Classes

Attribute classes define the attributes of entries. If the attribute can have one or more values, what is the syntax for the attribute value? Listing 17-14 shows selected definitions of the *userPrincipalName* attribute class that includes the full account name of a user.

LISTING 17-14 Attributes of the *userPrincipalName* attribute class.

```
Dn: CN=User-Principal-Name,CN=Schema,CN=Configuration,DC=xmp,DC=site
attributeID: 1.2.840.113556.1.4.656;
attributeSecurityGUID: e48d0154-bcf8-11d1-8702-00c04fb96050;
attributeSyntax: 2.5.5.12 = ( UNICODE );
cn: User-Principal-Name;
distinguishedName: CN=User-Principal-Name,CN=Schema,CN=Configuration,DC=xmp,DC=site;
instanceType: 0x4 = ( WRITE );
isMemberOfPartialAttributeSet: TRUE;
isSingleValued: TRUE;
lDAPDisplayName: userPrincipalName;
```

```
name: User-Principal-Name;
objectCategory: CN=Attribute-Schema,CN=Schema,CN=Configuration,DC=xmp,DC=site;
objectClass (2): top; attributeSchema;
objectGUID: 32fc1ed7-466e-40e6-a989-881ec2b5cc1f;
oMSyntax: 64 = ( UNICODE_STRING );
rangeUpper: 1024;
schemaFlagsEx: 1;
schemaIDGUID: 28630ebb-41d5-11d1-a9c1-0000f80367c1;
searchFlags: 0x1 = ( INDEX );
showInAdvancedViewOnly: TRUE;
systemFlags: 0x12 = ( ATTR_REQ_PARTIAL_SET_MEMBER | SCHEMA_BASE_OBJECT );
systemOnly: FALSE;
whenChanged: 2/11/2009 6:37:17 PM W. Europe Daylight Time;
whenCreated: 2/11/2009 6:37:17 PM W. Europe Daylight Time;
```

Attributes of Attribute Classes

Table 17-3 lists interesting attributes for attribute class entries in the schema. These details help to retrieve important information to the attribute, such as the number of values and the syntax for the values.

TABLE 17-3 Attributes of the attribute class description (classSchema)

Attribute	Description
adminDescription	Includes a short description of the attribute class (not for all classes).
attributeSyntax, oMSyntax	Syntax for the attribute values; for example, if it is a DN, an OID, a number or a string. oMSyntax specifies the sub types.
isMemberOfPartialAttributeSet	If TRUE the attribute is part of the global catalog.
isSingleValued	Specifies if the attribute can have only one value (TRUE) or any number of values (FALSE).
lDAPDisplayName	Name of the class used for LDAP queries.
name	Name and RDN of the attribute class.
searchFlags	Bitmask for search settings. If (searchFlags & 1)==1, the attribute values are indexed to enable a fast search. If (searchFlags & 4)==4, the attribute is included in Ambiguous Name Resolution (ANR).
systemFlags	Bitmask for settings. If (systemFlags & 2)==2, the attribute is part of the global catalog.
systemOnly	The attribute can only be set while the associated entry is generated. Afterward, only Active Directory can change the attribute.

PLB: Finding and Viewing Attribute Classes

To use the PLB to search and view attribute classes, you need to extend the definitions in browse_ldap_types.php as shown in Listing 17-15. The option "Schema: Attribute Class" is added to the search. You can use this to look up attributes by their LDAP name.

LISTING 17-15 browse_ldap_types.php—attribute class extension.

```php
$objectClasses = array(
    // ...
    'attributeSchema' => array(
        'name' => 'Schema: Attribute Class',
        'baseDN' => "CN=Schema,CN=Configuration,$rootDN",
        'filter' => '(&(lDAPDisplayName=%s)(objectClass=attributeSchema))',
        'attributes' => array(
            'name', 'lDAPDisplayName', 'objectCategory', 'isSingleValued',
            'attributeID', 'attributeSyntax', 'oMSyntax', 'systemOnly',
            'isMemberOfPartialAttributeSet','systemFlags', 'searchFlags',
            'adminDescription')
    ),
);
```

Attribute Syntax

The syntax of an attribute specifies which syntax rules apply to the attribute values, how these values are saved, and how a comparison in an LDAP filter works.

The syntax is controlled by two attributes of the associated attribute class: *attributeSyntax* (main type) and *oMSyntax* (sub type).

Table 17-4 shows the main syntax variations in Active Directory.

Including the sub types, there are about 30 different syntax variations in Active Directory.

The general rule is that in an LDAP filter, only the equal comparator (=) can be used, unless the value is a number or a string.

TABLE 17-4 Attribute syntax of active directory

Name	OID	Description
Distinguished Name (DN)	2.5.5.1	A DN for another object in Active Directory. If the referenced object is moved or renamed, the attribute is automatically updated. In a filter, you always need to enter the complete DN. Placeholders and comparators (<=, >=, ~=) are not allowed.
OID	2.5.5.2	String containing an OID. In a filter, you always have to enter the complete OID. Only the equal comparator (=) is allowed.
Case sensitive string	2.5.5.3	The string is case sensitive (seldom used syntax).

Name	OID	Description
Case insensitive string	2.5.5.4	The string is not case sensitive and uses the Teletex character set.
Printable string, IA5 String	2.5.5.5	String with a character set similar to US-ASCII.
Numeric string	2.5.5.6	String only containing numbers (seldom used syntax), not the same as the integer syntax.
DN with octet string, OR name	2.5.5.7	Contains the DN and binary data. The DN is updated automatically (seldom used syntax).
Boolean	2.5.5.8	*Boolean* value similar to *TRUE* or *FALSE* in filters.
Integer, Enumeration	2.5.5.9	Integers and special enumeration types which can also be used as integer.
Octet string	2.5.5.10	Binary data.
Time string	2.5.5.11	Time in Coordinated Universal Time (UTC), often used for the *whenCreated* attribute.
Case insensitive Unicode string	2.5.5.12	A case insensitive Unicode string and the most commonly used string syntax in Active Directory.
OSI Presentation address	2.5.5.13	Presentation address for the OSI layer model (seldom used).
DN with Unicode string	2.5.5.14	Contains the DN and a string. The DN is updated automatically (seldom used syntax).
NT security descriptor	2.5.5.15	NT security definition.
Large integer Interval	2.5.5.16	64-bit integer or time interval (the accuracy depends on the attribute).
SID string	2.5.5.17	Security ID (SID).

To display the description in the PLB, add the *oidInfo()* function to the AD_util.php file (Listing 17-16).

LISTING 17-16 AD_util.php/oidInfo()—additional information for OID.

```
/**
 * Returns additional information for known OIDs (Object Identifier).
 * @param string $oid OID as string
 */
function oidInfo($oid) {
    static $info = array(
        '2.5.5.1' => 'Distinguished Name (DN)',
        '2.5.5.2' => 'OID',
        '2.5.5.3' => 'Case sensitive string',
        '2.5.5.4' => 'Case insensitive string',
        '2.5.5.5' => 'Printable string / IA5 String',
        '2.5.5.6' => 'Numeric string',
        '2.5.5.7' => 'DN with octet string / OR name',
        '2.5.5.8' => 'Boolean',
        '2.5.5.9' => 'Integer / Enumeration',
        '2.5.5.10' => 'Octet string',
```

```
        '2.5.5.11' => 'Time string (UTC)',
        '2.5.5.12' => 'Unicode string',
        '2.5.5.13' => 'OSI presentation address',
        '2.5.5.14' => 'DN with Unicode string',
        '2.5.5.15' => 'NT security descriptor',
        '2.5.5.16' => 'Large integer / Interval',
        '2.5.5.17' => 'SID',
    );
    return empty($info[$oid]) ? $oid : "$oid ($info[$oid])";
}
```

You also have to assign the conversion routine in *$attributeConvertion* (Listing 17-17).

LISTING 17-17 browse_ldap_types.php—linking with *oidInfo()*.

```
$attributeConvertion = array( ...
    // attributeSchema
    'attributeSyntax' => 'oidInfo',
    ...
);
```

Figure 17-2 shows how *oidInfo()* is used to add additional information to the attribute syntax of an attribute class.

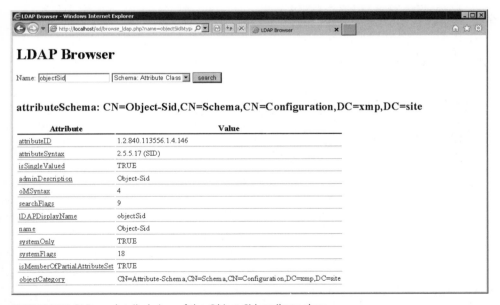

FIGURE 17-2 PLB—a detailed view of the *Object-Sid* attribute class.

Domain Objects

For the most part, PHP web applications use objects in the domain naming context to manage users with the *Group* and *Organizational Unit* object classes. In the following subsections, three entry types and their attributes are explained in more detail and the PLB is extended with searches and definitions for these objects classes.

General Attributes for Domain Objects

All objects are derived from the top object class. This class already has more than 100 attributes, four of which are mandatory (*objectClass*, *objectCategory*, *nTSecurityDescriptor*, and *instanceType*). Table 17-5 lists several attributes.

TABLE 17-5 Attributes that can be used for all objects

Attribute	Description
cn	Common name of the object.
description	Description of the object.
displayName	Display name of the object in programs. For example, the complete name of user objects consisting of first name, middle initial, and last name.
distinguishedName	DN of the object; Active Directory automatically adds the DN as attribute to objects.
instanceType	Contains status information as bitmask. The value *4* indicates that the object can be changed.
isCriticalSystemObject	If *TRUE* the entry is replicated on other domain controllers in the domain.
name	RDN of the object.
nTSecurityDescriptor	NT security definition.
objectCategory	DN of the object category.
objectClass	Object class of the entry. The attribute contains all object classes in the inheritance hierarchy.
objectGUID	GUID of the object.
systemFlags	Bitmask for native flags.
whenChanged	Time the object was last changed.
whenCreated	Time the object was created.

PLB: General Search for Domain Objects

To use the PLB to search for any objects in the domain naming context, the user can define the filter string. Instead of only one attribute, all attributes of the object are displayed. Listing 17-18 shows the required extensions that you need to add to browse_ldap_types.php.

LISTING 17-18 browse_ldap_types.php—general object search.

```php
$objectClasses = array(
    // ...
    'object' => array(
        'name' => 'Definable Filter',
        'baseDN' => $rootDN,
        'filter' => '%s',
        'filterchars' => '/\x00/',
        'attributes' => array()
    ),
);

$attributeConvertion = array(
    // ...
    'objectCategory' => 'DN-classSchema',
    'objectClass' => 'classSchema',
    'objectGUID' => 'guid2str',
    'systemFlags' => 'dec2hex',
    'instanceType' => 'dec2hex',
);
```

PLB: Converting the Object GUID

The object GUID is a binary LDAP string and needs to be converted to the corresponding text format. Listing 17-19 shows the conversion of a GUID into a text string (*guid2str()* function) and vice versa (*str2guid()* function).

LISTING 17-19 AD_util.php—conversion functions for GUIDs.

```php
/**
 * Converts the binary GUID to a string
 * @param string $guid binary GUID
 */
function guid2str($guid) {
    $last = substr(bin2hex($guid), 20);
    $x = unpack('Vhead/v2mid/nmid3', $guid);
    return sprintf("%08x-%04x-%04x-%04x-%s", $x['head'], $x['mid1'],
                                             $x['mid2'], $x['mid3'], $last);
}

/**
 * Converts the string to a binary GUID
 * @param string $guidstr GUID as string
 */
function str2guid($guidstr) {
    $v = explode('-', $guidstr);
    return pack('VvvnH*', hexdec($v[0]), hexdec($v[1]), hexdec($v[2]),
                          hexdec($v[3]), $v[4]);
}
```

Users

Active Directory contains user account entries from the *Person* object category and the *User* object class that are derived from the *Top*, *Person*, and *OrganizationalPerson* object classes. User attributes can be divided into four groups: personal information (name, organization), contact information (email, web, phone, address), user account, and system specific information. The attributes for the first three groups are explained in more detail in the sections that follow.

Personal Information

Personal information includes the name, a general description, and information about the company that the user works for. Table 17-6 lists these attributes.

TABLE 17-6 Organization name and information

Attribute	Description
company	Name of the company
department	Name of the department
description	General description field
displayName	Display name (first name, middle initial, and last name)
givenName	First name
initials	Middle initial
name (cn)	RDN of the object, usually the same as *displayName*
sn	Last name
title	Position within an organization

Contact Information

Contact information includes electronic data such as email addresses, websites, and phone numbers, as well as postal addresses. Table 17-7 lists the contact information. The *wWWHomePage* and *telephoneNumber* attributes can be found in the Properties dialog box of a user in the MMC, on the General tab; the other phone numbers are located on the Phone Numbers tab.

TABLE 17-7 Email address, web addresses, and phone numbers

Attribute	Description
facsimileTelephoneNumber	Fax number
homePhone	Private phone number
mail	Email address
mobile	Cell phone number
telephoneNumber	Primary phone number
url	Additional website address
wWWHomePage	Primary website

Table 17-8 shows the attributes for a postal address. The postal address is divided into the usual address fields (street, postal code, location, state, country).

TABLE 17-8 Postal address

Attribute	Description
c, co, countryCode	Country/region: *c* is the two-letter code (for example, AT), *co* is the full name (for example, Austria), *countryCode* is the country code (for example, 40)
l	Location
postalCode	ZIP (or postal) code
postOfficeBox	PO box
st	State
streetAddress	Street

User Account Information

Table 17-9 shows several attributes for a user account including logon name, account state, and the time different user activities were performed.

TABLE 17-9 User account information

Attribute	Description
accountExpires	Date on which the account is deactivated
badPasswordTime	Time of the last failed logon
badPwdCount	Number of failed logon attempts
lastLogoff	Time of the last logout
lastLogon, lastLogonTimestamp	Time of the last successful logon on the queried domain controller (*lastLogon*) or of the last successful logon on the domain (*lastLogonTimestamp*)
memberOf	DN of the groups the account is a (direct) member of
objectSid	SID in binary format
sAMAccountName	Logon name with domain
userAccountControl	Bitmask for the account state.
userPassword	Password for the user account (write-only)
userPrincipalName	Domain logon name in name@domain syntax

PLB: Searching for Users

To use the PLB to look up user objects, add the entries in Listing 17-20 to browse_ldap_types .php. The default setting lists only a few account attributes but no other data such as the email address or postal address. To view all attributes of a user object, replace the attributes array with an empty array.

LISTING 17-20 browse_ldap_types.php—searching for user objects.

```
$objectClasses = array(
    // ...
    'user' => array(
        'name' => 'User',
        'baseDN' => $rootDN,
        'filter' => '(&(objectClass=User)(objectCategory=Person)(name=%s))',
        'attributes' => array(
            'name', 'displayName', 'userPrincipalName', 'memberOf', 'lastLogon',
            'userAccountControl', 'accountExpires', 'objectCategory',
            'objectClass', 'objectGUID', 'objectSid')
    ),
);

$attributeConvertion = array(
    // ...
    'lastLogon' => 'winStamp2str',
    'lastLogonTimestamp' => 'winStamp2str',
    'badPasswordTime' => 'winStamp2str',
    'userAccountControl' => 'accountControl2str',
    'accountExpires' => 'winStamp2str',
    'objectSid' => 'sid2str',
    'memberOf' => 'DN-group',
);
```

Figure 17-3 shows a detailed view of a user object in PLB if all conversions in *$attribute Conversion* (Listing 17-20) are performed by user attributes.

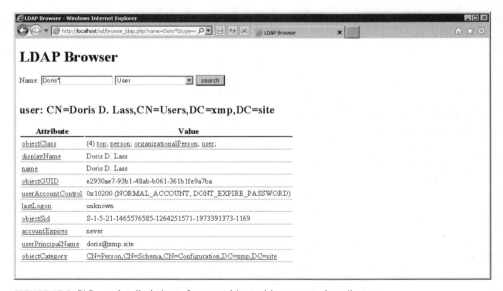

FIGURE 17-3 PLB—a detailed view of a user object with converted attributes.

PLB: SID Conversion

The SID is passed as binary data and needs to be converted to a string. Listing 17-21 shows the conversion of a SID into a text string (*sid2str()* function) and vice versa (*str2sid()* function).

LISTING 17-21 AD_util.php—a SID is converted to a string and vice versa.

```
/**
 * Converts the binary SID to a string
 * @param string $sid binary SID
 */
function sid2str($sid) {
    $v = unpack('Crev/Ccnt/Sx/Nauth/V*sub', $sid);
    $str = "S-$v[rev]-$v[auth]";
    for ($i = 1; $i <= $v['cnt']; $i++) {
        $str .= '-' . $v["sub$i"];
    }
    return $str;
}

/**
 * Converts the string to a binary SID
 * @param string $sidstr SID as string
 */
function str2sid($sidstr) {
    $v = explode('-', $sidstr);
    $cnt = count($v) - 3;
    $sid = pack('CCSN', $v[1], $cnt, 0, $v[2]);
    for ($i = 0; $i < $cnt; $i++) {
        $sid .= pack('V', $v[$i + 3]);
    }
    return $sid;
}
```

PLB: Converting a Windows Timestamp in PHP

Windows timestamps used in Active Directory have a higher resolution (100 nanoseconds instead of 1 second) and an earlier zero point (1601 instead of 1970) than PHP timestamps. Listing 17-22 shows the conversion of a timestamp. Because PHP integers are 32-bit numbers but the Windows timestamp has 64 bits, the subtraction or addition is performed by using the BCMath maths library included in the Windows version of PHP.

LISTING 17-22 AD_util.php—converting a Windows timestamp.

```php
/**
 * Converts the Windows timestamp to a string
 * @param string $stamp Windows timestamp
 */
function winStamp2str($stamp) {
    if (!$stamp) {
        return 'unknown';
    } elseif ($stamp == '9223372036854775807') {
        return 'never';
    }
    $stamp = substr($stamp, 0, -7);          // 100ns -> s
    $stamp = bcsub($stamp, '11644473600');   // 1601 -> 1970
    return date('Y-m-d H:i:s O', $stamp);
}


/**
 * Converts the Unix time (time()) to a Windows timestamp
 * @param int $stamp Unix time (seconds since 1970)
 */
function time2winStamp($stamp) {
    if (!$stamp) {
        return '0';
    } elseif ($stamp == 0xffffffff) {
        return '9223372036854775807';
    }
    $stamp = bcadd($stamp, '11644473600');   // 1970 -> 1601
    return $stamp . '0000000';               // s -> 100ns
}
```

PLB: Viewing the Account State

The *userAccountControl* attribute of a user entry contains important information regarding the type and status of the user account. This attribute is a bitmask, and the bits depend on the status. Listing 17-23 shows a function returning additional information for some interesting flags.

LISTING 17-23 AD_util.php—information for the *userAccountControl* attribute.

```php
/**
 * Returns additional information for UserAccountControl.
 * @param int $ac Value of UserAccountControl
 */
function accountControl2str($ac) {
    // List of a few flags, not complete
    static $flags = array(
        'ACCOUNTDISABLE' => 0x0002,
        'LOCKOUT' => 0x0010,
        'PASSWD_NOTREQD' => 0x0020,
        'PASSWD_CANT_CHANGE' => 0x0040,
        'NORMAL_ACCOUNT' => 0x0200,
        'INTERDOMAIN_TRUST_ACCOUNT' => 0x0800,
        'WORKSTATION_TRUST_ACCOUNT' => 0x1000,
        'SERVER_TRUST_ACCOUNT' => 0x2000,
        'DONT_EXPIRE_PASSWORD' => 0x10000,
        'PASSWORD_EXPIRED' => 0x800000);
    $info = array();
    foreach ($flags as $name => $value) {
        if ($ac & $value) {
            $info[] = $name;
        }
    }
    return dec2hex($ac) . ' (' . join(', ', $info) . ')';
}
```

Groups

Groups (*Group* object class) combine other objects (such as users) to process these objects simultaneously. There are two types of groups: security groups and distribution groups. You can grant security groups permissions to access files and websites. Distribution groups cannot have access rights, because they are mainly used to create email distribution lists in Active Directory.

Because groups can contain other groups as members, you can create a group hierarchy. Unlike organizational units, the group hierarchy is expressed by the *member* and *memberOf* attributes rather than in the structural hierarchy of the directory.

Table 17-10 shows the important attributes for a group.

TABLE 17-10 Attributes of groups in Active Directory

Attribute	Description
cn, name	Name of the group (the name is the RDN)
description	General description
groupType	Bitmask:
	80000000_{hex} set: security group (*SECURITY_ENABLED*), otherwise distribution group (for email)
	02_{hex} set: global group scope (*ACCOUNT_GROUP*)
	04_{hex} set: local group scope (*RESOURCE_GROUP*)
	08_{hex} set: universal group scope (*UNIVERSAL_GROUP*)
mail	email address of the distribution group
member	DN of the (direct) members of the group
memberOf	DN of the groups the group is a (direct) member of
objectSid	SID in binary format
sAMAccountName	Group name (pre-Windows 2000), can differ from *cn/name*

PLB: Searching for Groups

To use the PLB to look up groups, add the entries in Listing 17-24 to browse_ldap_types.php.

LISTING 17-24 browse_ldap_types.php—searching for group objects.

```php
$objectClasses = array(
    // ...
    'group' => array(
        'name' => 'Group',
        'baseDN' => $rootDN,
        'filter' => '(&(objectCategory=Group)(name=%s))',
        'attributes' => array(
            'name', 'sAMAccountName', 'member', 'memberOf', 'objectCategory',
            'objectClass', 'groupType', 'objectGUID', 'objectSid', 'mail')
    ),
);

$attributeConvertion = array(
    // ...
    'member' => 'DN-object',
    'groupType' => 'groupType2Str',
);
```

PLB: Viewing the Group Type

The *groupType* attribute contains important information to the group type. The function in Listing 17-25 adds additional attribute information to the PLB, based on the properties in Table 17-10.

LISTING 17-25 AD_util.php—information to the group type.

```php
/**
 * Returns additional information for groupType.
 * @param int $type Value of the groupType attribute
 */
function groupType2str($type) {
    static $flags = array(
        'SECURITY_ENABLED' => 0x80000000,
        'ACCOUNT_GROUP' => 0x02,
        'RESOURCE_GROUP' => 0x04,
        'UNIVERSAL_GROUP' => 0x08,
    );
    $info = array();
    foreach ($flags as $name => $value) {
        if ($type & $value) {
            $info[] = $name;
        }
    }
    return dec2hex($type) . ' (' . join(', ', $info) . ')';
}
```

Organizational Units

Organizational units (*OrganizationalUnit* class) are generic structural elements in Active Directory. Unlike groups, organizational units create a hierarchy in the directory tree. The name of the organizational unit becomes a part of the DN of all underlying entries (DN name part *ou*).

Organizational units together with organizations (*Organization* object class) and countries (*Country* object class) form the classic X.500 hierarchy of directory services. In Active Directory, organizational units become more important: they can be the target of group policies. Therefore, they can be of particular importance for the administration and security configuration.

Table 17-11 lists several attributes for an organizational unit. The most important attribute is *ou* because it determines the name of the organizational unit and appears in the DN of all entries under an organizational unit.

TABLE 17-11 Attributes of an organizational unit

Attribute	Description
Description	General description.
ou, name	Name of the organizational unit (the name is the RDN).
street, postOfficeBox, postalCode, l, st, c, co, countryCode	Same postal address as in Table 17-8, but the attribute for the street is *street* not *streetAddress*.

To use the PLB to look up organization units, add the entries in Listing 17-26 to browse_ldap_ types.php. Figure 17-4 shows the result of an organizational unit search.

LISTING 17-26 browse_ldap_types.php—searching for organizational units.

```
$objectClasses = array(
    // ...
    'organizationalUnit' => array(
        'name' => 'Organizational Unit',
        'baseDN' => $rootDN,
        'filter' => '(&(objectClass=organizationalUnit)(ou=%s))',
        'attributes' => array(
            'ou', 'name', 'description', 'objectCategory',
            'objectClass', 'objectGUID')
    ),
);
```

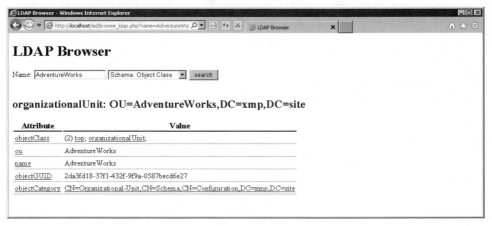

FIGURE 17-4 Detailed view of an organizational unit.

Concrete Search Examples

This section includes several concrete search examples especially for users and groups and the ANR that combines the most important attributes.

Add the appropriate entries to browse_ldap_types.php to use these examples in the PHP LDAP browser.

Schema

A search in the schema should always start at the basic *DN CN=Schema,CN=Configuration, DC=...,DC=...*. Because the hierarchy is flat (all attribute and object classes are one level below), use *ldap_list()* instead of *ldap_search()*.

You can configure a schema search for the PLB as follows:

```
$objectClasses = array(
    // ...
    '<typ_name>' => array(
        'name' => '<description>',
        'filter' => '<filter>',
        'base' => '< classSchema | attributeSchema >',
    ),
);
```

Set the base parameter according to the expected results (attribute or object classes). If you use the base parameter, you don't need to specify the attribute list and the basic DN.

Attributes

Object classes specify which attributes an object can or must have through the *mayContain* and *mustContain* attributes and the associated system pendants. A search has to be performed conversely.

Search   Find all object classes that must have a certain attribute:

```
(&(objectCategory=classSchema)(|(mustContain=%s)(systemMustContain=%s)))
```

Explanation   Because the desired attribute can be specified in *mustContain* or *system MustContain*, the *OR* operator is used. The *objectCategory* is not essential because only object classes have the associated attributes.

Search   Find all object classes that can have a certain attribute:

```
(&(objectCategory=classSchema)
    (|(mayContain=%s)(systemMayContain=%s)(mustContain=%s)(systemMustContain=%s)))
```

Explanation   This format is identical to the previous search but uses the *mayContain* and *systemMayContain* attributes.

> **Note** Both queries find only the object classes for which the attribute is set. Because of the inheritance, other object classes can also use this attribute. An LDAP search including these classes is not possible.

Search   Find all possible attributes for a certain object:

```
ldap_read($ldaplink, $objectDN, '(objectClass=*)', array('allowedAttributes'));
```

Explanation   Active Directory allows this search with the calculated *allowedAttributes* attribute. The search is not performed in the schema but for the desired (domain) object, as shown in the example search with *ldap_read()*.

Search   Find all attributes that can be set for a certain object:

```
ldap_read($ldaplink, $objectDN, '(objectClass=*)', array('allowedAttributesEffective'));
```

Explanation   Unlike *allowedAttributes*, *allowedAttributesEffective* lists only writeable attributes. For example, user entries can have 350 attributes. The domain administrator can set or change 285 of these attributes, and more than 50 attributes can be set or changed by the user. Users without special permission cannot change the attributes.

Search   Find all attributes that are part of the global catalog:

```
(&(objectCategory=attributeSchema)
   (|(isMemberOfPartialAttributeSet=TRUE)(systemFlags:1.2.840.113556.1.4.804:=2)))
```

Explanation   Attributes are saved in the global catalog if the *isMemberOfPartialAttributeSet* attribute is set or the flag in the *systemFlags* attribute has the value *2*.

Search   Find all attributes that are calculated automatically:

```
(&(objectCategory=attributeSchema)(systemFlags:1.2.840.113556.1.4.804:=4))
```

Explanation   Some attributes are not saved in the directory but instead are automatically calculated from other attributes. An example is *allowedAttributes*. Don't confuse calculated attributes with automatically-set attributes (for example, *lastLogonTimestamp*) whose values are saved in Active Directory.

Object Classes

For object classes, the structure rules (what object can have another object as parent or child) can be directly retrieved with the *possSuperiors*, *systemPossSuperiors*, and *possibleInferiors* attributes. For the inheritance hierarchy, the *subClassOf* attribute specifies from what class the current object class is derived. Otherwise, a search is necessary.

Search   Find all object classes that are derived directly from an object class:

```
(&(objectCategory=classSchema)(subClassOf=%s))
```

Explanation   Even though directly derived classes are easy to find, there is no appropriate pendant to list all derived classes in the hierarchy. The only way is to search the tree recursively (the recursive operator 1.2.840.113556.1.4.1941 cannot be used, because the *objectClass* isn't a DN but an OID).

Search   Find all abstract (=2) or auxiliary (=3) or 88 classes (=0):

```
(objectClassCategory=%s)
```

ANR

With ANR, Active Directory offers a simple method to quickly search the most important name fields. This includes the *name*, *sn*, *displayName*, *givenName*, and *sAMAccountName* attributes.

A search with ambiguous name resolution is started with the virtual *anr* filter attribute, as shown here:

```
(anr=Tony Hamster)
```

The search in ANR attributes is performed as follows:

- A prefix search with *Tony Hamster** is performed in all attributes.
- For the first name and last name (*givenName*, *sn*), the search term is broken up at the space, and the following additional search is performed:

```
(|(&(givenName=Tony*)(sn=Hamster*))(&(givenName=Hamster*)(sn=Tony*)))
```

You can create simple and efficient search filters by using the virtual *anr* filter attribute.

To find all attributes that are part of the ANR, use the following filter:

```
(&(objectCategory=attributeSchema)(searchFlags:1.2.840.113556.1.4.803:=5))
```

This filter uses the bitwise *AND* operator and checks the *searchFlags* attribute to determine if the attribute has an index (*1*) and is part of the ANR attributes (*4*). In Windows Server 2008 R2, the following attributes are included in ANR: *name, sn, displayName, givenName, sAMAccountName, legacyExchangeDN, physicalDelivery-OfficeName, proxyAddresses, msDS-AdditionalSamAccountName, msDS-PhoneticCompanyName, msDS-PhoneticDepartment, msDS-PhoneticDisplayName, msDS-PhoneticFirstName, msDS-PhoneticLastName.*

Users

User entries in Active Directory are always queried in the domain naming context (*DC=xmp,DC=site*).

You can configure a user search for the PLB as follows:

```
$objectClasses = array(
    // ...
    '<typ_name>' => array(
        'name' => '<description>',
        'filter' => '<filter>',
        'base' => 'user',
    ),
);
```

Search   Find users created before a certain date:

```
(&(objectCategory=Person)(objectClass=user)(whenCreated<=%s))
```

Explanation   Active Directory sets the *whenCreated* attribute automatically when the user entry is specified. The syntax for the used timestamp is *YYYYMMDDhhmmss.0Z (Y=year, M=month, D=day, h=hour, m=minute, s=second, Z=UTC time zone)*.

Search   Find users changed after a certain date:

```
(&(objectCategory=Person)(objectClass=user)(whenChanged>=%s))
```

Explanation   Active Directory sets the *whenChanged* attribute automatically when the user entry is changed. The syntax for the timestamp is identical to *whenCreated*.

Search   Find users or computers not requiring a password or with a password that never expires:

```
(&(objectClass=user)(userAccountControl:1.2.840.113556.1.4.804:=65568))
```

Explanation   The filter uses the bitwise *OR* operator to look for two indicators in the *user AccountControl* attribute: If passwords are not necessary (*32*) or if passwords never expire (*65536*). This search also finds computers because they are derived from the object class user.

> **Note** The numbers in LDAP filters always must be decimal. The hexadecimal values of flags need to be converted.

Search   Find users with locked or deactivated accounts:

```
(&(objectCategory=Person)(objectClass=user)(userAccountControl:1.2.840.113556.1.4.804:=18))
```

Explanation   The filter uses the bitwise *OR* operator to look for a locked (*16*) or deactivated (*2*) user account.

Search   Find all users who have not logged on since a certain time:

```
(&(objectCategory=Person)(objectClass=user)(lastLogonTimestamp<=%s))
```

Explanation   The *lastLogonTimestamp* attribute is set automatically. However, a Windows timestamp must be used for the time. You can use the *time2winStamp()* function in Listing 17-22 to convert a PHP *time()* timestamp to a Windows timestamp.

> **Note**   The *lastLogon* attribute also saves the time of the last logon, but unlike *lastLogonTimestamp,* it is not replicated to other domain controllers in the domain.

Search   Find all users who have never logged on:

```
(&(objectCategory=Person)(objectClass=user)(!(lastLogonTimestamp=*)))
```

or

```
(&(objectCategory=Person)(objectClass=user)(lastLogon=0))
```

Explanation   If a user never logged on, the value for the *lastLogon* attribute is *0* or the *lastLogonTimestamp* attribute is not set. If you create a corresponding entry in browse_ldap_types.php, the result looks similar to that in Figure 17-5.

FIGURE 17-5   PLB—a list of all users who have never logged on.

Groups

Groups in Active Directory are always queried in the domain naming context (*DC=xmp,DC=site*).

You can configure a user search for the PLB as follows:

```
$objectClasses = array(
    // ...
    '<typ_name>' => array(
        'name' => '<description>',
        'filter' => '<filter>',
        'base' => 'group',
    ),
);
```

Search   Find all distribution groups:

```
(&(objectCategory=Group)(!(groupType:1.2.840.113556.1.4.803:=2147483648)))
```

Explanation   The bitwise operator checks if the security group bit $(80000000_{hex}=2147483648)$ is set. If the bit is not set, it is a distribution group.

Membership Through *member/memberOf*

You can query group memberships with the *member* and *memberOf* attributes.

Search   Find groups without members:

```
(&(objectCategory=Group)(!(member=*)))
```

Explanation   The member attribute contains the members of a group. *member=** checks whether the attribute exists; *(!(member=*))* checks whether the attribute doesn't exist (there are no group members).

Search   Find all groups containing a certain member:

```
(&(objectCategory=Group)(member:1.2.840.113556.1.4.1941:=%s))
```

Explanation   To look up the groups of which the user is a direct member, you can query the member attribute. If you want to find all groups, including the groups the user is only an indirect member through other groups (group hierarchy), you need to search the directory tree recursively. The specified recursion operator performs this task. The operator checks the values of the member attribute and tracks the corresponding objects recursively. If the required user object is found in the member attribute, the groups in the search path are returned. However, the recursion operator works only for attributes with a DN. The search parameter (*%s*) also must be the full DN of the user—for example, *CN=Agnes B. Barstow,OU =Technology,OU=AdventureWorks,DC=xmp,DC=site*.

> **Tip**   For efficiency reasons, the basic DN shouldn't be the domain context but the parent entry of the wanted groups.

Search Find all members of a group:

```
(&(objectCategory=Person)(memberOf:1.2.840.113556.1.4.1941:=%s))
```

Explanation You can also search for all members, including indirect members, by using the recursion operator for the *memberOf* attribute. You must specify the full DN of the group as parameter. Together with *objectCategory=Person,* the result is limited to users. Computers or other groups are not displayed. To look up all members of any type, exclude this part of the filter.

```
(memberOf:1.2.840.113556.1.4.1941:=%s)
```

> **Tip** For efficiency reasons the basic DN shouldn't be the domain context but the parent entry of the wanted members.

Search Determine if users are members of a group:

```
$r = ldap_read($ldapLink, $userDN, "(memberOf:1.2.840.113556.1.4.1941:=$groupDN)");
if (ldap_count_entries($ldapLink, $r)) {
    // The user is a member
}
```

Explanation This search is identical with the search already described. But for efficiency reasons, the basic DN is set for the user, and only the user is retrieved with *ldap_read()* instead of searching the whole subtree with *ldap_search()*. If the search returns a result, the user (*$userDN*) is a member of the group (*$groupDN*).

Membership Through *primaryGroupID*

The group membership can also be indicated through the *primaryGroupID* attribute. For example, system groups such as domain users and domain computers use this method for group membership. For this reason, groups can have many members and exceed the maximum number of attribute values.

The *primaryGroupID* attribute for members is set to the Relative Identifier (RID) of the group. The RID is the last number of the SID:

```
User SID: S-1-5-21-1465576585-1264251571-1973391373-1108
Domain RID: S-1-5-21-1465576585-1264251571-1973391373
User RID: 1108
```

The domain RID is identical for all objects within a domain. Membership through the *primary GroupID* is only possible within the same domain. Armed with this knowledge, you should be able to write search queries (in the interest of clarity, error handling is skipped).

Search   Listing 17-27 demonstrates how to find all members with a group as primary group.

LISTING 17-27 Find all members with a group as primary group.

```
// Retrieving the group SID
$result = ldap_read($ldapLink, $groupDN, '(objectSid=*)', array('objectSid'));
$entry = ldap_first_entry($ldapLink, $result);
$attr = ldap_get_attributes($ldapLink, $entry);
// Retrieving the RID
$sid = sid2str($attr['objectSid'][0]);
preg_match('/(\d+)$/', $sid, $match);
$rid = $match[1];
// Find all members
$result = ldap_search($ldapLink, $baseDN, '(primaryGroupID=$rid)', $attributeList);
```

Explanation   First, the SID of the specified group is retrieved. If the SID is already known, the first steps can be skipped. The *sid2str()* function in Listing 17-21 converts the SID to a string and the RID is identified by using *preg_match()*. With this information, you can perform a normal LDAP search. You can set the filter and the basic DN to meet your requirements.

Search   Listing 17-28 shows how to find the primary group of an entry:

LISTING 17-28 Searching for the primary group of an object.

```
// Retrieving the SID and primaryGroupID of the entry ($entryDN)
$result = ldap_read($ldapLink, $entryDN,
                    '(objectSid=*)', array('objectSid','primaryGroupID'));
$entry = ldap_first_entry($ldapLink, $result);
$attr = ldap_get_attributes($ldapLink, $entry);
$sid = sid2str($attr['objectSid'][0]);
$pgid = $attr['primaryGroupID'][0];
// Retrieving the SID of the group
$grSidStr = preg_replace('/\d+$/', $pgid, $sid);
// Prepare for LDAP search filter
$grSid = str2sid($grSidStr);
$searchsid = preg_replace('/(..)/', '\\\\$1', bin2hex($grSid));
// Search for group
$result = ldap_search($ldapLink, $baseDN, "(objectSid=$searchsid)", $attributeList);
```

Explanation   First the SID and the *primaryGroupID* of the entry are retrieved. With *preg_replace()*, this becomes the full SID of the wanted group. To use the SID in the LDAP filter, you must convert it to the binary format by using the *str2sid()* function presented in Listing 17-21. Because the binary data can contain invalid characters, simply mask the entire SID (*$searchsid*). With the SID masked, you can perform a normal LDAP search.

Summary

Active Directory provides an extensive schema to save user, group, and principal information. This chapter introduced object and attribute classes as well as naming contexts and the syntax for attributes. The description of users, groups, and organizational units, as well as the introduced conversion functions should give you a sound basis to develop your own Active Directory applications. The next chapter explains how to write data in Active Directory.

Chapter 18
Writing in Active Directory

This chapter explains how to change, create, and delete entries and entry attributes. With this knowledge, you can handle the normal events occurring in an organization, such as employees joining or leaving the company, name changes, reorganizations, promotions, address changes, or the replacement of computers and printers. However, the user who owns the Lightweight Directory Access Protocol (LDAP) connection must have the necessary permissions.

Preparation

Before you use a PHP application to make changes, in Microsoft Active Directory, you must grant the PHP user the necessary permissions, unless the user should only be able to change his own entries. If you write code, you should also activate the server-side error logging. You also need to make some changes to the sample scripts if you want to use the examples in this chapter to write your own code.

Access Rights

While authenticated users are able to read (almost) all objects in Active Directory, only certain users have permissions to change these objects. The write access to Active Directory objects has far-reaching consequences: in Active Directory, the rights for all principals are managed in a single domain; therefore, full write permissions amount to the permission of a domain administrator.

For this reason, users can change only the attributes of their own entries; they cannot change the object attributes of other users or object owners.

Administrator Groups

The installation of Active Directory creates several administrator groups with different access rights, which are described in the following:

- **Account operators**   Create, change, or delete users, groups, and computers.
- **Administrators**   Full access to all objects in the domain. Members of this group are, for example, the Domain Admins and Enterprise Admins groups.
- **Print operators**   Create, change, or delete printers.
- **Domain administrators**   Full access to all objects in the domain.
- **Enterprise administrators**   Full access to all objects in the Active Directory forest.

To grant a PHP user write access, you can add that user to one of the preceding groups (for example, to the account operators group). Alternatively, you can grant access rights directly to an entry.

Changing the Access Rights to an Entry

To grant a PHP user (or a defined group) rights to only a certain entry or section of the Active Directory hierarchy, use the access control list (ACL) for that entry. Here's the process to change access rights:

1. Click the Windows Start button, select Administrative Tools, and then start ADSI Edit or start the Microsoft Management Console (MMC) with the Active Directory Users And Computers snap-in.

2. In the MMC, in the View menu, click Advanced Features.

3. Browse to the entry that you want to edit, right-click it, and then in the context menu that appears, click Properties.

4. On the Security tab, click Add to add a user or a group. Select the principal in the dialog box, and then click OK.

5. In the Permissions list box, select the write or full access rights for the entry.

6. To grant granular rights or to ensure that the rights are inherited by all child objects, click Advanced.

   The Advanced Security Settings dialog box opens, as shown in Figure 18-1.

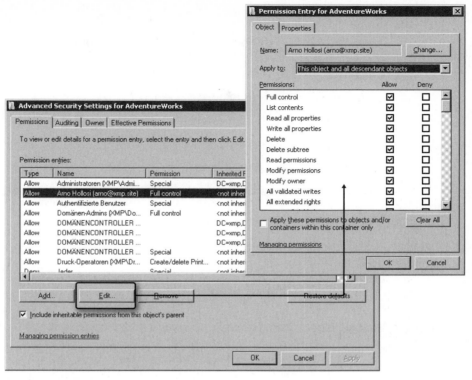

FIGURE 18-1 Editing the access rights for Active Directory objects.

7. Select the entry for the user to be added, and then click Edit.

The Permission Entry dialog box opens, in which you can grant granular permissions.

8. In the Apply To drop-down box, select the objects for which you want to grant rights:
only for the current object or for the selected (or all) child objects.

9. Click OK to close all dialog boxes and to apply the changes.

> **Note** Only grant the essential rights (such as the ability to write all properties) that are required
> by your application. Normally you shouldn't grant full access.

Error Logging

The messages returned by *ldap_errno()* and *ldap_error()* are sometimes not sufficient to identify the cause of an error. In this case, you can activate error logging in Active Directory by
performing the procedure that follows.

1. Click the Windows Start button, and then in the Search Programs And Files text box,
enter **regedit**.

2. In the registry editor, browse to *HKEY_LOCAL_MACHINE\SYSTEM\CurrentControlSet\Services\NTDS\Diagnostic*.

3. Enter one of the following values for 16 LDAP Interface Events:

- **0 (None)**   The default setting logs only critical events and errors

- **1 (Minimal)**   Also logs important events

- **2 (Basic)**   Logs important events and warnings

- **3 (Extensive)**   Logs the steps to be followed to complete a request

- **4 (Verbose)**   Even more information

- **5 (Internal)**   Logs all events, sometimes with additional information

To search for errors, level 3 is usually sufficient.

To review the events, open the event viewer (click Start | Administrative Tools | Event Viewer), and then select Event Viewer | Custom Views | Server Roles | Active Directory Domain Services. As illustrated in Figure 18-2, the viewer contains a list of recent events and a short, detailed description of the event (General tab and Details tab, respectively).

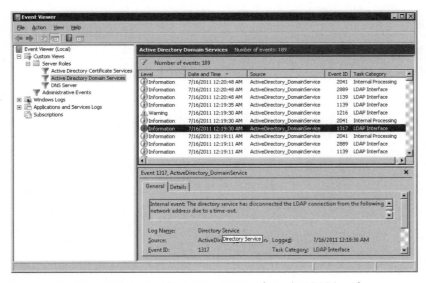

FIGURE 18-2 An event viewer with an error message from the LDAP interface.

Supporting Scripts

The examples in this chapter use supporting scripts to ensure a concise output. Functions are also added to existing scripts, the *LDAPConnection* class, and the AD_util.php file.

Main Program

The general program (modify_ldap.php) for the examples in this chapter is shown in Listing 18-1. The program includes the example scripts that make the changes in Active Directory.

The program creates the connection as administrator with the required permissions. It could also use any other account that has the required privileges. To make the changes visible, the program retrieves the entry from Active Directory before and after it calls the *modify()* function (*modify()* is part of the integrated scripts). Afterward, it displays the changes.

The *formatChangedEntry()* function merges the before/after entries.

LISTING 18-1 modify_ldap.php—the general program for the examples in this chapter.

```php
<?php
namespace net\xmp\phpbook;

require './HTMLPage.php';
require './LDAPConnection.php';
require './browse_ldap_types.php';
require './LDAPEntryFormatter.php';
require './AD_util.php';
// Load the script to make changes
require './_____.php';

$html = new HTMLPage('Writing in Active Directory');
// Establish connection
$ad = new LDAPConnection();
$ad->connect('doco-exch.xmp.site', 'administrator@xmp.site', 'confidential');
$ad->baseDN = 'DC=xmp,DC=site';

// Make changes
$before = $ad->getAccount($accountName, $attributes);
modify($ad, $before);
$after= $ad->getAccount($accountName, $attributes);

// and output
$table = formatChangedEntry($before, $after);
$html->addElement('h2', $before['dn']);
$html->addTable($table, array(true, true, true));
$html->printPage();
```

```
function formatChangedEntry($beforeEntry, $afterEntry)
{
    // Format entries
    $bf = new LDAPEntryFormatter($beforeEntry, 'object', 'browse_ldap.php');
    $beforeHTML = $bf->getAttributes();
    $af = new LDAPEntryFormatter($afterEntry, 'object', 'browse_ldap.php');
    $afterHTML = $af->getAttributes();
    // Merge entries
    $values = array();
    for ($i=1; $i<count($beforeHTML); $i++) {
        $values[$beforeHTML[$i][0]]['before'] = $beforeHTML[$i][1];
    }
    for ($i=1; $i<count($afterHTML); $i++) {
        $values[$afterHTML[$i][0]]['after'] = $afterHTML[$i][1];
    }
    $table = array( array('Attribute', 'Before', 'After') );
    $notset = '<i>not set</i>';
    foreach ($values as $attribute => $value) {
        $before = isset($value['before']) ? $value['before'] : $notset;
        $after = isset($value['after']) ? $value['after'] : $notset;
        $table[] = array($attribute, $before, $after);
    }
    return $table;
}
?>
```

LDAPConnection

Two methods and one attribute are added to the *LDAPConnection* class, as shown in
Listing 18-2. Because data in existing entries often need to be queried to make changes,
the *getOneEntry()* method takes over the search and error handling, and returns the attribute
either as an array or *false*. *getAccount()* is an auxiliary method that creates the filter if you
look up a Security Accounts Manager (SAM) account name (for users, groups, or computers).
If you set the *$baseDN* attribute from now on both methods, use this value as the default
value.

LISTING 18-2 Extension of the *LDAPConnection* class.

```
class LDAPConnection {

    // ...
    public $baseDN = '';
    // ...

    /**
     * Retrieving an entry with the SAM account name
     * @param string $account SAM account name
```

```php
 * @param array $attributes Wanted attribute
 * @param string $baseDN Basic DN for the search
 */
function getAccount($account, $attributes=array(), $baseDN='') {
    $filter = '(sAMAccountName=' . escapeLDAP($account) . ')';
    $account = $this->getOneEntry($filter, $attributes, $baseDN);
    if (!$account) {
        $this->exitWithError('Account not found.');
    }
    return $account;
}


/**
 * Retrieving a search entry
 * @param string $filter Filter string
 * @param array $attributes Wanted attribute
 * @param string $baseDN Basic DN for the search
 */
function getOneEntry($filter, $attributes=array(), $baseDN='') {
    if (empty($baseDN)) {
        $baseDN = $this->baseDN;
    }
    $result = ldap_search($this->handle, $baseDN, $filter, $attributes);
    if (!$result) {
        return false;
    }
    $entry = ldap_first_entry($this->handle, $result);
    if (!$entry) {
        return false;
    }
    $attr = ldap_get_attributes($this->handle, $entry);
    if (!$attr) {
        return false;
    }
    $attr['dn'] = ldap_get_dn($this->handle, $entry);
    return $attr;
}
}
```

The AD_util.php Script

The *escapeLDAP()* function from Listing 18-2 that masks critical characters in a filter string is added to the AD_util.php script shown in Listing 18-3. The asterisk placeholder is not masked.

LISTING 18-3 AD_util.php—a function to mask critical filter characters.

```php
/**
 * Mask the filter string for the search (conservative)
 * @param string $str Filter string to mask
 */
function escapeLDAP($str) {
    return preg_replace_callback('/[^-\w\s=,.*]/',
            function($m) {
                return '\\' . bin2hex($m[0]);
            },
            $str);
}
```

Writing Attributes

The first changes made to the information saved in Active Directory deal with changing, adding, and deleting attributes. With PHP, you can adapt the entry properties such as the address of a user after he has moved.

Adding Attributes

To add attributes or attribute values to an existing entry, use the *ldap_mod_add()* function. In addition to the connection resource, the distinguished name (DN) of an entry as well as an associative array containing the new attributes is passed to the function.

Listing 18-4 shows an example. In the listing, the street (*streetAddress*), postal code (*postal Code*), and location (*l*) as well as several web addresses must be added to the user. If several values are passed for an attribute, these values are included in an array.

LISTING 18-4 ldap_add_attributes.php—adding attributes to an entry.

```php
<?php
namespace net\xmp\phpbook;

$accountName = 'doris';
$attributes = array('streetAddress', 'postalCode', 'l', 'url');

function modify($ad, $entry) {
    $newattr = array();
    $newattr['streetAddress'] = 'At the Dwarfs 7';
    $newattr['postalCode'] = '12345';
```

```
    $newattr['l'] = 'Sevenmountainville';
    $newattr['url'] = array('http://snow.xmp.site/',
                            'http://dwarf.xmp.site/',
                            'http://prince.xmp.site/');
    $success = ldap_mod_add($ad->handle, $entry['dn'], $newattr);
    if (!$success) {
        $ad->exitWithError('Adding attributes failed.');
    }
    }
    ?>
```

Figure 18-3 shows the result if the function was successful: the *streetAddress*, *postalCode* and *l* attributes are now set, and new values are added to the *url* attribute that can have multiple values.

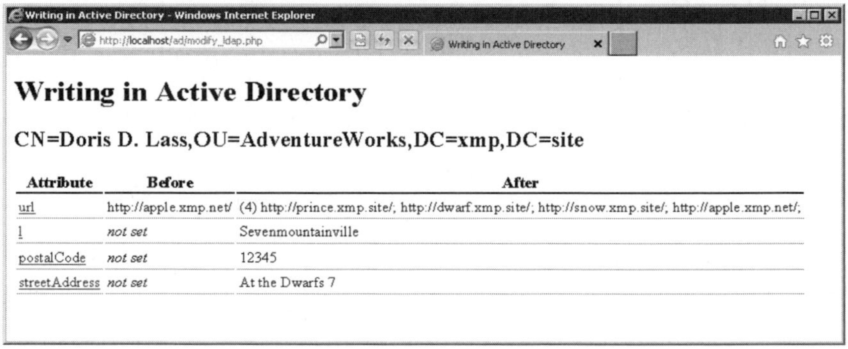

FIGURE 18-3 Adding attributes to the user.

ldap_mod_add() cannot add attributes and attribute values if:

- An attribute that can only have a single value is already set.
- The new value for an attribute with multiple values is already set.
- The new value doesn't comply with the syntax rules for the attribute.

You can check these conditions by loading and running the example script again. In the second cycle, *ldap_mod_add()* returns an error.

Deleting Attributes

To delete attributes or attribute values from an existing entry, use the *ldap_mod_del()* function. The parameters are similar to *ldap_mod_add()*: they include the connection resource and the DN of the entry as well as an associative array containing the attributes and attribute values to be deleted.

Listing 18-5 shows how to delete attributes. You must specify the value of the attribute you want to delete. If the specified value is not identical with the value in Active Directory, *ldap_mod_del()* fails. In this case, none of the attributes are deleted because the delete action is an atomic operation. If you want to delete an attribute independently of its value, specify *array()* as value.

LISTING 18-5 ldap_del_attributes.php—deleting the attributes of an entry with *ldap_mod_del()*.

```php
<?php
namespace net\xmp\phpbook;

$accountName = 'doris';
$attributes = array('streetAddress', 'postalCode', 'l', 'url');

function modify($ad, $entry) {
    $delattr = array();
    $delattr['streetAddress'] = 'At the Dwarfs 7';
    $delattr['postalCode'] = array();
    $delattr['l'] = 'Sevenmountainville';
    $delattr['url'] = array('http://snow.xmp.site/',
                            'http://dwarf.xmp.site/');
    $success = ldap_mod_del($ad->handle, $entry['dn'], $delattr);
    if (!$success) {
        $ad->exitWithError('Deleting attributes failed.');
    }
}

?>
```

Figure 18-4 shows the result if *ldap_mod_del()* were successfully completed. You can also delete a single attribute value: only two of the four values for the web address attribute (*url*) are deleted.

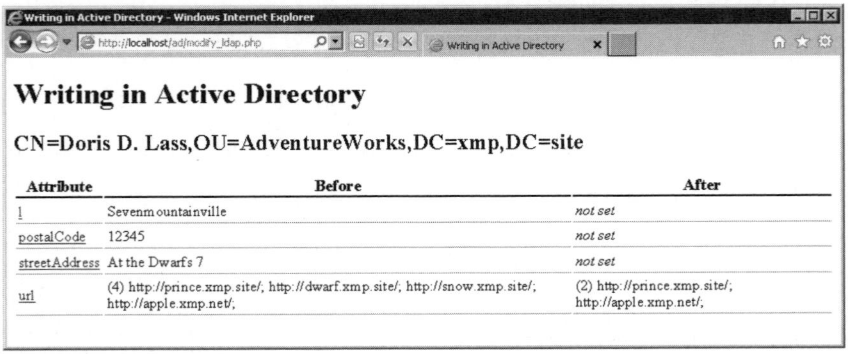

Writing in Active Directory

CN=Doris D. Lass,OU=AdventureWorks,DC=xmp,DC=site

Attribute	Before	After
l	Sevenmountainville	*not set*
postalCode	12345	*not set*
streetAddress	At the Dwarfs 7	*not set*
url	(4) http://prince.xmp.site/; http://dwarf.xmp.site/; http://snow.xmp.site/; http://apple.xmp.net/;	(2) http://prince.xmp.site/; http://apple.xmp.net/;

FIGURE 18-4 Deleting attributes.

ldap_mod_del() cannot delete attributes and attribute values if:

- An attribute is not set.
- The attribute has a different value in Active Directory than in *ldap_mod_del()*.

Run the example script again to check the conditions: in the second cycle, *ldap_mod_del()* returns the error that there are no attributes to delete.

Changing Attributes

To change the attributes or attribute values for an existing entry, use the *ldap_mod_replace()* function. The function parameters are the connection resource and the DN of the entry as well as an associative array containing the new values for the changed attributes.

> **Note** To change entries, PHP provides the alternative *ldap_modify()* function. Even though the PHP documentation suggests there is a difference, both functions are identical. In this book, we use *ldap_mod_replace()* because the function name better describes the action.

Listing 18-6 shows an example. In the listing, the new attribute values are written into an associative array, and *ldap_mod_replace()* is called with the appropriate DN.

LISTING 18-6 ldap_change_attributes.php—changing attributes with *ldap_mod_replace()*.

```php
<?php
namespace net\xmp\phpbook;

$accountName = 'doris';
$attributes = array('streetAddress', 'postalCode', 'l', 'url', 'postOfficeBox');

function modify($ad, $entry) {
    $changeattr = array();
    $changeattr['streetAddress'] = array();
    $changeattr['postOfficeBox'] = 'Palace 1';
    $changeattr['postalCode'] = '12345';
    $changeattr['l'] = 'Fairycapital';
    $changeattr['url'] = array('http://happy.xmp.site/',
                               'http://end.xmp.site/');
    $success = ldap_mod_replace($ad->handle, $entry['dn'], $changeattr);
    if (!$success) {
        $ad->exitWithError('Changing attributes failed.');
    }
}
?>
```

Figure 18-5 shows the result of this function call:

- **I**   Attributes with basic values are simply replaced with the new value.
- **postalCode**   The old and the new value can be identical; no error is generated.
- **streetAddress**   If the new value is an empty array, the attribute is deleted.
- **url**   The old values of attributes with multiple values are replaced with the new values.
- **postOfficeBox**   New attributes can be set.

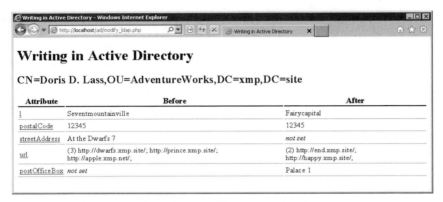

FIGURE 18-5 Changing attributes by using *ldap_mod_replace()*.

ldap_mod_replace() is the most versatile of the three attribute functions. Regardless of whether the values match or attributes already exist or need to be deleted, *ldap_mod_replace()* can perform all tasks. However, watch out for attributes with multiple values: all old values are replaced with the new values. If you only want to change a single value in the list, create a new value list by retrieving the attribute first. Alternatively, you can make the change by using *ldap_mod_add()* and *ldap_mod_del()*.

Encoding and Character Sets

Attribute functions not only expect the values in the correct syntax but also in the correct encoding (in the proper character set). Until now, the example listings ignored this fact.

The encoding is especially important for attributes that expect a string. Active Directory knows five different attribute syntaxes for common strings. Basically, all attributes that might contain characters outside the US ASCII range consist of Unicode characters (*attribute Syntax=2.5.5.12, oMSyntax=64*).

Active Directory expects that the values for Unicode strings are passed as UTF-8. However, PHP uses the ISO-8859-1 character set. To pass the values properly, you need to convert them. For this purpose, PHP provides two functions: *iconv()* and *mb_convert_encoding()*.

You can use either one of the following two calls to convert values to UTF-8, but the latter call requires the *mbstring* extension in PHP:

```
$utf8 = iconv('ISO-8859-1', 'UTF-8', $isoText);
$utf8 = mb_convert_encoding($isoText, 'UTF-8');
```

Practical Examples for Changing Attributes

Attributes must be changed for a lot of reasons when managing users. Users change their addresses, names, and phone numbers. In PHP, you can quickly make these changes if you know the corresponding attribute names. The examples in the following sections show how you can change system-relevant attributes.

The listings use the method described in the section "Writing Attributes," earlier in the chapter. The listings are not complete; they only show the most important parts. The examples don't include error handling or a preamble with the namespace declaration and the definition for the *$account* variable.

> **Note** Some examples require that the current values of certain attributes are known. The *$entry* parameter passed to *modify()* contains the information on the user or group account.

Unlocking an Account

If a user exceeds the allowed maximum number of failed logon attempts, the account can be locked automatically for security reasons. The *msDS-User-Account-Control-Computed* attribute specifies if an account is locked: if the *0x10* flag is set, the account is locked. You can unlock the account by using the *userAccountControl* attribute to delete the corresponding bit, as shown in Listing 18-7.

LISTING 18-7 Unlocking an account.

```
$attributes = array('userAccountControl', 'msDS-User-Account-Control-Computed');
function modify($ad, $entry) {
    $changeattr = array();
    $changeattr['userAccountControl'] = $entry['userAccountControl'] & ~0x10;
    ldap_mod_replace($ad->handle, $entry['dn'], $changeattr);
}
```

Activating and Deactivating Accounts

If an account is temporarily disabled, the user cannot log on. The *0x02* flag specifies the deactivation in the *userAccountControl* attribute. If you delete this flag, the account is activated, and if you set this flag the account is deactivated. Listing 18-8 shows how the account is activated.

LISTING 18-8 Activating an account.

```
$attributes = array('userAccountControl');
function modify($ad, $entry) {
    $changeattr = array();
    $changeattr['userAccountControl'] = $entry['userAccountControl'] & ~0x02;
    ldap_mod_replace($ad->handle, $entry['dn'], $changeattr);
}
```

To deactivate the account *userAccountControl* must be specified as follows:

```
$changeattr['userAccountControl'] = $entry['userAccountControl'] | 0x02;
```

Group Memberships

The group membership is controlled by the member attribute. The associated *memberOf* attribute is set automatically.

Adding a User to a Group

Use *ldap_mod_add()* to add a user to a group. Enter the DN of the user in the member attribute. In Listing 18-9, the DN of the user is added to the attribute array. To query the DN of the group necessary for the *ldap_mod_add()* function, you retrieve the group entry by using the auxiliary *getAccount()* method.

LISTING 18-9 Adding a user to a group.

```
$attributes = array('memberOf');
function modify($ad, $entry, $group='gruppenname') {
    $attr = array();
    $attr['member'] = $entry['dn'];
    $group = $ad->getAccount($group);
    ldap_mod_add($ad->handle, $group['dn'], $attr);
}
```

Note You cannot add users who are already members of the group. Therefore, you should first check if the user you want to add is already a group member.

Removing a User from a Group

To delete a user from a group, use *ldap_mod_del()*. Listing 18-10 shows how to remove a user from all groups. In the listing, the *memberOf* attribute of the user contains the DNs of the groups, and the user is removed from one group after the other.

LISTING 18-10 Removing a user from a group.

```
$attributes = array('memberOf');
function modify($ad, $entry, $group='gruppenname') {
    $attr = array();
    $attr['member'] = $entry['dn'];
    for ($i=0; $i < $entry['memberOf']['count']; $i++) {
        ldap_mod_del($ad->handle, $entry['memberOf'][$i], $attr);
    }
}
```

Note Users deleted in this manner are not deleted from the primary group (usually the domain user group) because the primary group is set with the *primaryGroupID* attribute.

Forced Password Change

To force the users to change their passwords at the next logon, use *ldap_mod_replace()* to set the *pwdLastSet* attribute to *0*, as demonstrated in Listing 18-11.

LISTING 18-11 Forcing users to change their passwords at the next logon.

```
$attributes = array('pwdLastSet');
function modify($ad, $entry) {
    $changeattr = array();
    $changeattr['pwdLastSet'] = 0;
    ldap_mod_replace($ad->handle, $entry['dn'], $changeattr);
}
```

Changing Passwords

To change the user password in PHP through LDAP, two conditions must be met: the LDAP connection must be encrypted, and the LDAP user must have permission to change the passwords for other accounts (usually a domain administrator).

> **Note** Because of the limitations of the PHP LDAP extension and the procedure required by Active Directory, users cannot change their own passwords; the LDAP connection must be delegated to a domain administrator (or a user with permission to change the passwords of other users).

Active Directory requires a server certificate so that *ldap_start_tls()* can create an encrypted connection between PHP and Active Directory. The configuration of certificates for Active Directory and PHP to accept a certificate is explained in Chapter 15, "Setting Up Active Directory."

To create an encrypted connection with the *LDAPConnection* class used in the examples, pass *true* as the fourth parameter to the *connect()* method:

```
$ad = new LDAPConnection();
$ad->connect($server, $user, $password, true);
```

Afterward, you can use *ldap_mod_replace()* for the *unicodePwd* attribute to specify the password, as shown in Listing 18-12. You need to encode the password as UTF-16 (or UCS-2) and put it in quotes. The following listing does this by using the *mb_convert_encoding()* function. You don't need to mask the quotes and other special characters in the password. However, due to a bug, you do need to call *ldap_mod_replace()* two times or both the old and the new password will be valid; you can still use the old password to log on to Active Directory, but the password cannot be used to log on to a computer.

LISTING 18-12 Changing the password for a user account.

```
$attributes = array('pwdLastSet');
function modify($ad, $entry, $password) {
    $newpwd = array();
    $newpwd['unicodePwd'] = mb_convert_encoding('"'.$password.'"', 'UCS-2LE');
    ldap_mod_replace($ad->handle, $entry['dn'], $newpwd);
    ldap_mod_replace($ad->handle, $entry['dn'], $newpwd);    // Has to be done two times!
}
```

Writing Entries

Not only can you change attributes with the LDAP interface, you can also create new entries and delete or move existing entries in the directory hierarchy.

You will need a new supporting script for these examples.

So that the supporting script can process new or deleted entries, copy modify_ldap.php (from Listing 18-1) into modify_ldap_entry.php, and then replace the following lines:

```
// Make changes
$before = $ad->getAccount($accountName, $attributes);
modify($ad, $before);
$after= $ad->getAccount($accountName, $attributes);
```

with this code:

```
// Make changes
list($before, $after) = modify($ad);
```

The *modify()* function now has full control over the entries.

Adding New Entries

To add a new entry, use the *ldap_add()* function. An associative array corresponding to the *add* and *change* functions for attributes is passed to this function. The DN passed as parameter specifies the location of the object in the directory hierarchy.

Depending on the entry type, you need to set different attributes. Independent of the entry type, you must specify the *objectClass* attribute that determines the object class for the entry.

Listing 18-13 shows how to add an organizational unit. The LDAP display name of the OU class is specified as object class *organizationalUnit*. Also, a number of additional (optional) attributes (*description, c, st*) are set. Because the DN is *OU=Hamster,OU=Test-OU,DC=xmp,DC=site*, the organizational unit is a child of the *OU=Test-OU,DC=xmp,DC=site* object in Active Directory. *ldap_add()* creates the organizational unit.

> **Note** The DN of an organizational unit has to start with *OU=* (the RDN is *ou*), or the organizational unit cannot be added. With only a few exceptions, the DN of the entries for all other object classes starts with *CN=* (the RDN is *cn*).

LISTING 18-13 ldap_add_entry.php—creating a new organizational unit.

```php
<?php
namespace net\xmp\phpbook;

function modify($ad) {
    $attr = array();
    $attr['objectClass'] = 'organizationalUnit';
    $attr['description'] = 'OU of the hamster lovers';
    $attr['c'] = 'UK';
    $attr['st'] = 'Yorkshire';
    $dn = 'OU=Hamster,OU=Test-OU,DC=xmp,DC=site';

    $success = ldap_add($ad->handle, $dn, $attr);
    if (!$success) {
        $ad->exitWithError("Couldn't create new OU");
    }
    $before = array('dn' => $dn, 'count' => 0);
    $after = $ad->getOneEntry("(distinguishedName=$dn)");
    return array($before, $after);
}
?>
```

Figure 18-6 shows the attributes of the new entry. Notice that Active Directory automatically added more attributes while the entry was created. These include the GUID (Attribute *object GUID*), structural attributes such as *ou*, *name*, and *distinguishedName*, and information on the time created and object classes.

FIGURE 18-6 Creating a new entry with *ldap_add()*.

Active Directory also created more object information. These are attributes that are not listed automatically but have to be queried (for example, *nTSecurityDescriptor, createTimeStamp, allowedAttributes, canonicalName,* and so on), and information on the creator and owner of the object as well as access rights to the object (ACLs).

Deleting Entries

You delete entries by using *ldap_delete()*, passing the DN of the entry to be deleted as a parameter. You can only delete entries that have no child entries. Therefore, you must first delete all child objects from the hierarchy before you can delete the desired entry.

Listing 18-14 shows how to recursively delete entries. The *ldap_delete_recursive()* function uses *ldap_list()* and *ldap_get_entries()* to retrieve all objects on the next level. If entries are found, the function is called recursively with the DN of the child entries in a loop. If the function reaches a directory node without child entries, it cancels the recursion and deletes the node.

LISTING 18-14 ldap_del_entry.php—deleting an entry recursively.

```php
<?php
namespace net\xmp\phpbook;

function modify($ad) {
    $dn = 'OU=test,OU=Hamster,OU=Test-OU,DC=xmp,DC=site';
    $success = ldap_delete_recursive($ad, $dn);
    if (!$success) {
        $ad->exitWithError("Couldn't delete OU");
    }
    // No output
    $before = array('dn' => "Deleted recursive: $dn", 'count' => 0);
    $after = array('count' => 0);
    return array($before, $after);
}

function ldap_delete_recursive($ad, $dn) {
    $result = ldap_list($ad->handle, $dn, '(objectClass=*)', array('name'));
    if (!$result) {
        return false;
    }
    $entries = ldap_get_entries($ad->handle, $result);
    ldap_free_result($result);
    if (!$entries) {
        return false;
    }
    for ($i = 0; $i < $entries['count']; $i++) {
        $result = ldap_delete_recursive($ad, $entries[$i]['dn']);
        if (!$result) {
            return false;
        }
    }
    return ldap_delete($ad->handle, $dn);
}
?>
```

Moving Entries

Use *ldap_rename()* to rename an entry—for example, to change its DN. Because the DN also specifies the position of the entry in the directory hierarchy, you can use *ldap_rename()* to move an entry to another position in the hierarchy. This function accepts three parameters:

- **$oldDN**   The DN of the entry to be renamed.

- **$newRDN**   The new RDN of the entry.

- **$newParentDN**   The DN of the new parent object can be zero if the entry is only renamed (but not moved) in the hierarchy.

> **Note** The *$deleteOldRDN* parameter of the function always must be *true* because Active Directory requires that the old RDN be deleted.

Listing 18-15 shows an example: the entry *OU=Relatives,OU=Hamster,OU=Test-OU,DC=xmp, DC=site* must be renamed (*OU=Relatives* changes to *OU=Relatives and friends*) and moved to a different position in the hierarchy (*OU=People,OU=Hamster,OU=Test-OU,DC=xmp,DC=site*).

LISTING 18-15 ldap_move_entry.php—moving and renaming an entry.

```php
<?php
namespace net\xmp\phpbook;

function modify($ad) {
    $attributes = array('name', 'ou', 'distinguishedName',
                        'whenChanged', 'objectGUID');
    $oldDN = 'OU=Relatives,OU=Hamster,OU=Test-OU,DC=xmp,DC=site';
    $newRDN = 'OU=Relatives and Friends';
    $newParentDN = 'OU=People,OU=Hamster,OU=Test-OU,DC=xmp,DC=site';
    $before = $ad->getOneEntry('(ou=Relatives)', $attributes);

    $success = ldap_rename($ad->handle, $oldDN, $newRDN, $newParentDN, true);
    if (!$success) {
        $ad->exitWithError("Couldn't rename OU");
    }

    $after = $ad->getOneEntry("($newRDN)", $attributes);
    return array($before, $after);
}
?>
```

> **Caution** Moving entries within the hierarchy can impact the security. An example of this would be if different group policies for entries apply on the old and the new position.

The new DN of the entry is *OU=Relatives and friends, OU=People,OU=Hamster,OU=Test-OU, DC=xmp,DC=site* (consisting of the *$newRDN* and *$parentDN*). The associated attributes *ou* and *name* also reflect the new names. The *objectGUID* indicates that the entry is still the same. Figure 18-7 shows the result.

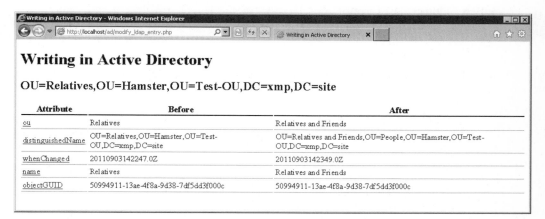

FIGURE 18-7 Moving and renaming an entry.

> **Important** Active Directory allows you to move entries even if they contain child entries. In this case, the entire tree section is moved and the DN of all child entries changes.

If an object is protected against accidental deletion, it is also protected against renaming its DN. To rename such an object, the protection against accidental deletion must first be removed.

Practical Examples

The tasks of an administrator include keeping up with staff and organization changes. Employees and guests join or leave the organization and departments as well as organizational units and groups change. The examples in the section "Writing Entries," earlier in the chapter, involve organizational units. The next sections cover four more important use cases: creating and deleting users or groups.

> **Note** The listings for these examples are not complete; they show only the most important parts. In addition, the examples don't include error handling or a preamble with the namespace declaration.

Creating a New Group

To create a new group, use the *ldap_add()* function. You should specify at least the following attributes:

- Object class (group)
- Type and scope of the group (distribution or security group, local, global, or universal group scope)
- SAM account name: the name of the group (usually identical with the RDN of the group)

Listing 18-16 shows how to create a group by calling *ldap_add()* after the array is filled. The value of the *sAMAccountName* attribute is identical to the RDN (*CN=AdventureWorks*).

LISTING 18-16 Creating a new group.

```
// Values for the groupType attribute
const GT_SECURITY_ENABLED = 0x80000000;
const GT_ACCOUNT_GROUP = 0x02;
const GT_RESOURCE_GROUP = 0x04;
const GT_UNIVERSAL_GROUP = 0x08;

function modify($ad) {
    $attr = array();
    $attr['objectClass'] = 'group';
    $attr['groupType'] = GT_ACCOUNT_GROUP | GT_SECURITY_ENABLED;
    $attr['sAMAccountName'] = 'AdventureWorks';
    $dn = 'CN=AdventureWorks,OU=Test-OU,DC=xmp,DC=site';
    ldap_add($ad->handle, $dn, $attr);
}
```

Active Directory automatically sets additional attributes, including *objectSid* (the security ID of the group).

> **Note** If you don't specify *sAMAccountName,* the SAM account name is generated automatically. If you don't specify *groupType,* a security group is created in the global scope (*groupType=0x80000002*).

Creating a New User

To use *ldap_add()* to create a new user, set *objectClass* to user. All other attributes are optional; however, you should specify the following attributes:

- User name in *givenName, initials, sn, displayName*

- Logon name in *sAMAccountName, userPrincipalName*
- The RDN (*CN=* at the beginning of the DN) should be the same as *displayName*

You can also specify the password in *unicodePwd* while creating the user. The *userAccount Control* attribute cannot be set when the user is created; it must be specified in a separate step.

> **Note** The group membership cannot be specified either, because the group membership is controlled by the member attribute of the group instead of the *memberOf* attribute of the user.

Listing 18-17 shows how to create a user. The attributes for the name and account are set and *displayName* is composed of *givenName, initials,* and *sn.* The RDN is identical to *displayName* and the slash (\), equal (=) and comma (,) characters are masked to meet the DN syntax. *ldap_add()* adds the entry.

> **Important** This listing doesn't consider the character set. Because the values for the name attributes follow the Unicode string syntax, the encoding must be in UTF-8 (see the section "Encoding and Character Sets," earlier in the chapter).

Active Directory creates the user and assigns him attributes. The *userAccountControl* attribute is set to *222hex* (normal account, no password required, account deactivated). The *primary GroupID* attribute automatically adds the user to the domain user group.

In the second step, use *ldap_mod_replace()* to set the password and *userAccountControl* to activate the account. Now the account can be used and the user can log on.

LISTING 18-17 Creating a new user.

```
// Values for the userAccountControl attribute
const UAC_ACCOUNTDISABLE = 0x0002;
const UAC_LOCKOUT = 0x0010;
const UAC_PASSWD_NOTREQD = 0x0020;
const UAC_PASSWD_CANT_CHANGE = 0x0040;
const UAC_NORMAL_ACCOUNT = 0x0200;
const UAC_INTERDOMAIN_TRUST_ACCOUNT = 0x0800;
const UAC_WORKSTATION_TRUST_ACCOUNT = 0x1000;
const UAC_SERVER_TRUST_ACCOUNT = 0x2000;
const UAC_DONT_EXPIRE_PASSWORD = 0x10000;
const UAC_PASSWORD_EXPIRED = 0x800000;

function modify($ad) {
    $attr = array();
    $attr['objectClass'] = 'user';
    $attr['sAMAccountName'] = 'doris';
```

```
    $attr['userPrincipalName'] = $attr['sAMAccountName'] . '@xmp.site';
    $attr['givenName'] = 'Doris';
    $attr['initials'] = 'D';
    $attr['sn'] = 'Lass';
    $attr['displayName'] = "$attr[givenName] $attr[initials]. $attr[sn]";
    $rdn = 'CN=' . preg_replace('/[\\\\=,]/', '\\\\$0', $attr['displayName']);
    $dn = $rdn . ',OU=Test-OU,DC=xmp,DC=site';
    ldap_add($ad->handle, $dn, $attr);

    $attr = array();
    $attr['userAccountControl'] = UAC_NORMAL_ACCOUNT;
    $attr['unicodePwd'] = mb_convert_encoding('"confidential"', 'UCS-2LE');
    ldap_mod_replace($ad->handle, $dn, $attr);
}
```

Note   The conditions that must be met before you can create or change a password are described in the section "Changing Passwords," earlier in the chapter. If no password exists, the 20_{hex} flag (no password required for account) needs be set in the *userAccountControl* attribute or the password change fails.

Deleting a User or a Group

You can delete users and groups by using *ldap_delete()* without considering any conditions. Listing 18-18 shows this function consisting of two steps:

- It reads the entry to determine the DN (the search is performed by using *sAMAccountName*)

- It deletes the user or the Group

LISTING 18-18   Deleting a user or a group.

```
function modify($ad, $accountName) {
    $account = $ad->getAccount($accountName, array('name'));
    ldap_delete($ad->handle, $account['dn']);
}
```

Note   Users and groups can have child entries (for example, *classStore* or *ms-net-ieee-80211-GroupPolicy*). For this reason, the deletion with *ldap_delete()* might fail. In this case, use the *ldap_delete_recursive()* function from Listing 18-14.

Because Active Directory automatically updates the membership status of users and groups, you don't need to set the *member* and *memberOf* attributes.

Deleting a user from Active Directory doesn't affect the user's profile data. You must delete the profile separately.

Summary

This chapter explained how you can change the information saved in Active Directory by adding, deleting, and changing attributes and entries. Some examples of things you can do include changing the group membership, creating a new user, or changing the phone number of a user.

A requirement is that the PHP user has the necessary permissions, either because he is the owner of the object to be changed, he is a member of the administrator group, or he is granted explicit rights in the ACL.

This chapter concludes the programming of Active Directory with PHP. Active Directory provides several more object and attribute types which are beyond the scope of this book. However, with the knowledge obtained here, you should be able to program most Active Directory tasks.

The next part explains how to program Exchange Server through the SOAP XML interface of Exchange Web Services.

Part IV
Exchange Server

Chapter 19
Setting Up Exchange Server

Microsoft Exchange Server 2010 is a sophisticated platform for workgroups and organizations to manage messages, task, and appointments. The user policies, the restructured rights management with Role-Based Access Control (RBAC), and the tight integration with Microsoft Active Directory simplify the administration, especially in bigger organizations. Users can access their mailboxes over the web by using Microsoft Outlook Web Access, a client for (almost) all Exchange functions. You can use the Exchange Web Services (EWS) to control Exchange with PHP applications.

The chapters in this part of the book explain, among other things, how to invite participants to conferences, how to retrieve emails, and how to search for contacts.

This chapter describes the installation of Exchange Server 2010 SP1 in a development environment. It also explains how to configure the encryption certificate and how to set up mailboxes for users.

Setting Up Required Services and Features

The installation and configuration of Exchange Server 2010 SP1 is straightforward, provided that the required services and features are installed. A typical installation takes less than an hour. The general requirements and the installation of Internet Information Services (IIS) required for web services and Outlook Web Access as well as the configuration of several other features are described in the following sections.

 Note For more information on complex installations in a production environment, consult the TechNet at *http://technet.microsoft.com/en-us/library/bb124558.aspx*.

General Requirements

To support the functionality and power of Exchange Server 2010 SP1, you need a powerful and modern infrastructure. To run Exchange, the following requirements must be met:

- **Processor:** 64 bit
- **Operating system:** At least Windows Server 2008 SP2 or R2
- **RAM:** At least 4 GB; 8 GB is recommended to install multiple roles on a computer
- **Active Directory**
  - **Forest functional level:** Windows Server 2003 or higher
  - **Domain functional level:** Windows Server 2003 or higher
  - **Schema master, global catalog, and domain controller:** Windows Server 2003 SP1 or higher; Windows Server 2008 or higher

You can continue to install the required services and features if these prerequisites are met. These requirements assume that you install all roles on a computer in a development environment.

Configuring IIS

Exchange requires the IIS web server for the Client Access role. To configure this, perform the steps described in Chapter 1, "Setting Up the Work Environment":

1. In the Server Manager, select Add Roles, and then click Web Server (IIS) role.
2. Add the role services listed in Table 19-1 to the web server.

TABLE 19-1 IIS role services

Section	Role services
Web Server	Common HTTP features	Static Content, Default Document, Directory Browsing, HTTP Errors, HTTP Redirection
Web Server	Application Development	ASP.NET, .NET Extensibility, ISAPI Extensions, ISAPI Filters
Web Server	Health and Diagnostics	HTTP Logging, Logging Tools, Request Monitor, Tracing
Web Server	Security	Basic Authentication, Windows Authentication, Digest Authentication, Client Certificate Mapping Authentication, Request Filtering
Web Server	Performance	Static Content Compression, Dynamic Content Compression
Management Tools	IIS Management Console
Management Tools	IIS 6 Management Compatibility	IIS 6 Metabase Compatibility, IIS 6 Management Console

3. Confirm to install dependent features and start the installation.

You can also run the installation from Windows PowerShell:

```
Import-Module ServerManager
Add-WindowsFeature Web-Server, Web-Net-Ext, Web-ISAPI-Ext, Web-Basic-Auth, Web-Windows-Auth,
    Web-Digest-Auth, Web-Dyn-Compression, Web-Metabase, Web-Lgcy-Mgmt-Console
```

Configuring Features

In addition to IIS, you also need to install several features.

In the Server Manager, select Features, click Add Features, and then select the features listed in Table 19-2.

Confirm the installation of dependencies.

TABLE 19-2   Features required for Exchange Server

Section	Features
.NET Framework 3.5.1 Features	.NET Framework 3.5.1, WCF Activation/HTTP Activation
Remote Server Administration Tools | Role Administration Tools	AD DS and AD LDS Tools/AD DS Tools, Web Server (IIS) Tools
	RPC over HTTP Proxy
Windows Process Activation Service	Process Model, .NET Environment, Configuration APIs

You can also run the installation from PowerShell:

```
Import-Module ServerManager
Add-WindowsFeature NET-Framework, WAS-Process-Model, RSAT-ADDS, RSAT-Web-Server,
    NET-HTTP-Activiation, RPC over HTTP Proxy
```

After the additional features are installed, you need to restart your computer.

Configuring Shared Ports

You need to enable shared ports for Exchange. To do so, start PowerShell, and then run the following command:

```
Set-Service NetTcpPortSharing -StartupType Automatic
```

After the requirements (IIS, features, port usage) for Exchange Server are met, you can install Exchange.

Installing the Office System Converter

To allow Exchange to search Microsoft Office documents, you need to install the converter that provides the filters to index these documents.

1. Download the Microsoft Office 2010 Filter Packs from *http://www.microsoft.com/ download/en/details.aspx?id=17062*.

2. Start the installer.

3. Accept the license agreement to start the installation.

Configuring DNS Entries

To configure other domain names for Exchange, add the appropriate DNS entries to the DNS servers. Usually Exchange has two names: a name within the Windows domain, and a DNS domain name for external access to the domain.

This book uses *doco-exch.xmp.site* as the internal name and *mail.phpdemo.site* as an external name for the Exchange installation. It also uses the *autodiscover.phpdemo.site* domain for the Autodiscover service.

If you use the DNS Server provided by Windows Server 2008 R2:

1. Start the DNS Manager by clicking the Windows Start button. Select Administrative Tools, and then click DNS.

2. Select the domain in *<Server>* | Forward Lookup Zones | *<Domain>*.

3. In the Action menu, click either the New Host (*A* or *AAAA*) or New Alias (CNAME) command to add the desired domain names.

Installing Exchange Server

After all preparation tasks are completed, Exchange Server can be installed and configured in just a few steps. The following installation process includes all required roles and assumes Exchange Server is the first server installed within the domain.

To install Exchange Server 2010 SP1, perform the following steps:

1. Run setup.exe from the Exchange installation media.

2. Because Steps 1 and 2 of the installation assistant should already be done, you can continue with Step 3 and select the desired languages. Select the Install Only Languages From The DVD option.

3. Click Step 4 in the setup assistant to copy the installation files and to start setup.

   The Exchange Server 2010 Setup Wizard opens.

4. On the License Agreement page, accept the license agreement.

5. On the Error Reporting page, choose if you would like to select the Error Reporting option.

6. On the Installation Type page, select Typical Exchange Server Installation, as shown in Figure 19-1.

   This installs the Hub Transport, Client Access, and Mailbox roles, as well as the Exchange Management Tools on the computer.

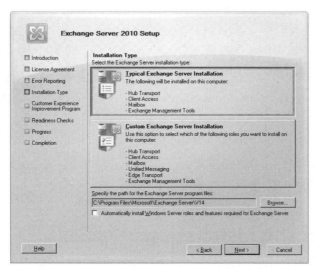

FIGURE 19-1 The Exchange Server 2010 Setup Wizard: selecting the installation type.

7. On the next page, enter the name of the Exchange organization. For the exercises in this book, use **XMP**.

8. If you still run Outlook 2003 on domain computers, select Yes on the Client Settings page.

9. If Exchange is not only accessible within the domain, but also externally, enter the domain name (**mail.phpdemo.site**) on the external domain page (the domain is *xmp.site*).

10. The Setup wizard checks the system requirements. Ignore the warning "Organization Prerequisites" (see Figure 19-2).

No errors should occur (such as missing dependencies) if your system meets the requirements described earlier in the section "Setting Up Required Services and Features." If you install Exchange Server on your domain controller, you will see additional warnings about elevated privileges, which you can ignore in a development environment.

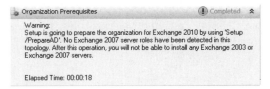

FIGURE 19-2   The wizard displays a warning regarding system requirements.

11. Click Install to start the setup.

12. After the installation has completed successfully, click Finish to exit the setup.

13. Returning to the initial setup assistant, you might want to immediately check for critical updates to Exchange Server in Step 5 of the assistant.

Exchange is now installed. You should restart your computer before you continue the configuration by using the Exchange Management Console.

Configuration After the Installation

After completing the installation, you must configure the required deployment settings by using the Exchange Management Console. The most important part is the Exchange Certificate described below. First, you need to enter the product key.

Registering Exchange

To enter the Exchange Server product key, perform the following steps:

1. Start the Exchange Management Console by clicking the Windows Start button and then clicking All Programs | Microsoft Exchange Server 2010 | Exchange Management Console.

2. In the navigation pane (on the left), select Microsoft Exchange | Microsoft Exchange On-Premises | Server Configuration, as shown in Figure 19-3.

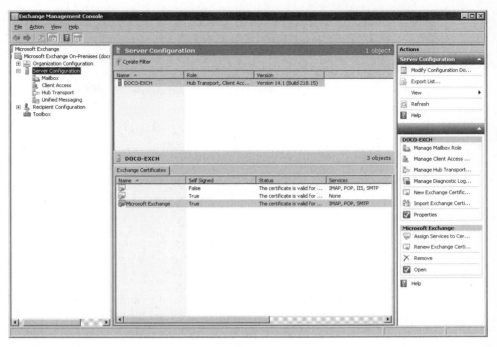

FIGURE 19-3 The Exchange Management Console.

3. In the Actions pane (on the right), click Enter Product Key.

4. In the dialog box that opens, enter the product key, and then click Enter.

In the next step, you configure the Exchange Server certificate.

Configuring the Exchange Server Certificate

Communication with Exchange Server takes place over Transport Layer Security (TLS) encrypted connections, which require a certificate for Exchange Server. During the installation of Exchange, a self-signed certificate was created and registered for the services.

You can use the self-signed certificate in a development environment, but in a production environment, you should acquire a certificate from a certification authority. Alternatively, you can use a certificate issued by your own Active Directory certification authority.

This is important for PHP programming, because it requires the associated root certificate from the certification authority. Therefore, you use the Active Directory certification authority to issue the certificate.

Requesting the Certificate

First, you need to request the certificate for Exchange by performing the following steps:

1. Start the Exchange Management Console.

2. In the navigation pane, select Microsoft Exchange | Microsoft Exchange On-Premises | Server Configuration (refer to Figure 19-3).

3. In the Actions pane, click New Exchange Certificate.

    The New Exchange Certificate Wizard opens.

4. Enter the display name for the certificate.

    You can choose any name because this name is only used for the internal Exchange administration. Click Next to confirm.

5. Exchange allows you to request certificates using placeholders. Usually you don't need a placeholder certificate; therefore, you can leave this option disabled (leave the check box cleared).

6. On the Exchange Configuration page, enter the domain names for which the certificate should be issued. You must enable at least the client access for web services and specify if the certificate is used for the intranet only or also for external access.

    - **Client Access Server (Outlook Web App)**   Select the Outlook Web App Is On The Intranet and Outlook Web App Is On The Internet check boxes, and then enter the appropriate domain names. Exchange suggests appropriate names.

    - **Client Access Server (Web Services, Outlook Anywhere, and Autodiscover)**   Select the Exchange Web Servives Is Enabled, Outlook Anywhere Is Enabled, and Autodiscover Used On The Internet check boxes. Select Long URL for Autodiscover, and then enter the external URL such as **autodiscover.phpdemo.site**.

    - **Client Access Server (POP/IMAP)**   Select these options to secure the access over POP and IMAP protocols using the certificate.

7. On the Certificate Domains page, the wizard suggests appropriate domain names, but you can enter your own names, if you like. Click the associated button to set the external domain name as common name of the certificate.

8. On the Organizations And Location page, enter the information for your organization and specify the path to the certificate request file. Click Next to confirm.

9. Before the certificate is created, the settings you selected are displayed on the New Exchange Certificate page (see Figure 19-4). Click New to generate the certificate request.

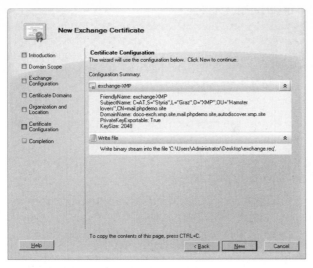

FIGURE 19-4 The Certificate Configuration page of the New Exchange Certificate Wizard.

You can also use the Exchange Management Shell to create a certificate. To do this, enter the following command:

```
New-ExchangeCertificate -GenerateRequest
        -SubjectName "c=AT, o=XMP, ou=Hamster lovers, cn=mail.phpdemo.site"
        -DomainName mail.phpdemo.site,autodiscover.phpdemo.site,doco-exch.xmp.site
        -PrivateKeyExportable $true
```

Issuing a Certificate

Send the generated certificate request to your certification authority to issue the certificate. If you run your own certification authority by using the Active Directory certificate services, copy the certificate request file to the computer on which the certification authority is installed, and then run the following PowerShell command:

```
certreq -submit -attrib "CertificateTemplate: WebServer"
```

> **Note** If you get a "Certificate not issued (Incomplete)" error message, the likely cause is that the certificate request file was saved with Unicode and not with ANSI encoding. Just open the file in Notepad, select File | Save As, set the Encoding to ANSI, and then save the file.

If the certificate registration web service is installed, you can alternatively upload the request and select web server as the certificate template.

> **Note** If you logged on as administrator and you cannot request a certificate, open the Server Manager, and then in the navigation pane, click Roles | Active Directory Certificate Services. Right-click *<name of certification authority>*, and then in the context menu that appears, select Properties. Click the Security tab, and then activate the Request Certificates permission for your administrator group.

After the certificate is issued export the new certificate by using the Server Manager as explained in Chapter 15, "Setting Up Active Directory."

Assigning Services to the Certificate

Now you need to import the issued certificate in Exchange and assign services. To do so, perform the following steps:

1. Copy the certificate to the Exchange Server computer.

2. Start the Exchange Management Console, and then in the navigation pane, click Microsoft Exchange On-Premises | Server Configuration (refer to Figure 19-3).

3. Select the pending certificate request on the Exchange Certificates tab (located toward the bottom of the center work pane), and then in the Actions pane, click Complete Pending Request.

4. Select the certificate file and assign it to the Exchange certificate.

5. After the certificate is imported, in the Actions pane, click Assign Services To Certificate. The Assign Services To Certificate Wizard opens.

6. On the first page of the wizard, select your Exchange Server, and then click Next.

7. On the Select Services page, select the services for which the certificate is used (Figure 19-5). At a minimum, you must select Internet Information Services (IIS).

FIGURE 19-5 Assigning services to the certificate.

8. Click Next and Assign to complete the assignment.

You created the certificate request, issued the certificate, imported the certificate in Exchange, and assigned services to the certificate. Next, you create mailboxes in Exchange and get started with the Exchange Web Services configuration.

Creating a Mailbox

The mailboxes for domain users are not automatically created; you create them manually. An Exchange mailbox includes emails, contacts, task, and calendar entries, all of which are organized in folders.

To create a user mailbox, perform the following steps:

1. Start the Exchange Management Console.

2. In the navigation pane, click Recipient Configuration | Mailbox. In the Actions pane, click Mailbox | New Mailbox.

   The New Mailbox Wizard opens.

3. On the Introduction page, select User Mailbox, and then click Next, as shown in Figure 19-6.

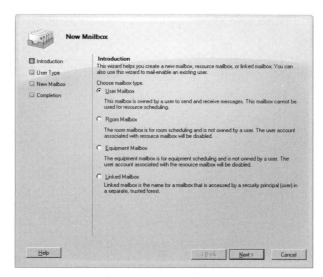

FIGURE 19-6 Selecting the mailbox type.

4. On the User Type page, specify whether to create a new user or a mailbox for an existing user. Select the Existing Users check box, and then click Add to select one or more users.

5. On the Mailbox Settings page (on the User Type page), enter the user alias used for the primary email address. Because you don't want to assign any mailbox policies at this time, click Next.

6. An overview of the configuration settings appears. Click New to create the mailbox, and then click Finish to close the wizard.

The new mailbox is created. In the result pane of the Exchange Management Console, select the new mailbox, right-click it, and select Properties from the context menu to edit its properties—for example, to add more email addresses. You can use some tabs (such as User Information, Address and Phone, or Organization) to access user data in Active Directory.

Summary

This chapter explained the typical installation of Exchange Server and the installation requirements. The configuration described installs all important server roles on the same computer.

You also learned how to install and configure a certificate for encrypted communications and how to create a new mailbox. Of course, Exchange provides many more functions. However, a detailed description of these functions is beyond the scope of this book.

The next chapter explains programming Exchange with the help of the Exchange Web Services, especially using Autodiscover to find the URL for the web services.

Chapter 20
Exchange Web Services

With the Microsoft Exchange Web Services (EWS), you can use PHP to control and program Exchange. The interface provides roughly 50 different operations to create and edit elements in Exchange (emails, calendar entries, contacts).

The EWS use Simple Object Access Protocol (SOAP), a web standard, to exchange data between programs. PHP 5 offers a SOAP extension that simplifies EWS configuration significantly. This chapter introduces the customized *SOAPClient* class for HTTPS encryption and NT LAN Manager (NTLM) authentication.

For a program to communicate with EWS, it must look up the EWS URL for the user. If the domain includes several Exchange servers, the users can be saved on different servers. Use the Autodiscover service to determine on which server a user mailbox resides.

Required PHP Extensions

The following PHP extensions are required to control the EWS from PHP:

- **SOAP** This extension handles the communication with the EWS by using SOAP messages based on a Web Services Description Language (WSDL) interface definition.

- **cURL** This extension is needed because the PHP SOAP extension cannot process the NTLM authentication required for EWS.

- **OpenSSL** Usually the communication with EWS takes place over HTTPS. The OpenSSL extension is required for cURL to work with HTTPS URLs.

Because all extensions are included in the PHP deployment, you only need to activate them in the php.ini file.

1. Open the php.ini (C:\PHP\php.ini) file in a text editor.

2. Add the following lines:

   ```
   extension=php_curl.dll
   extension=php_openssl.dll
   extension=php_soap.dll
   ```

3. Save the file.

4. Restart the associated Internet Information Services (IIS) application pool.

5. Use phpinfo() to verify that the extensions are active.

Alternatively, if you have PHP Manager installed, you can activate these extensions in the PHP Extensions section by clicking the Enable Or Disable Extensions link.

The extensions required to program EWS are now installed. However, you need to identify the appropriate EWS URL, which is described in the next section.

Autodiscover

Exchange Server provides a function to automatically retrieve user configuration data. This reduces the required administration effort, particularly for large Exchange installations. The configuration for a user is automatically retrieved.

Exchange Server 2010 includes two versions of Autodiscover: basic XML data (plain old XML [POX]), and SOAP. Because POX Autodiscover is easier to use with PHP, this book only explains this version.

How Autodiscover Searches for Configuration Data

To communicate with EWS, you need to use the Autodiscover service to perform the following:

- Retrieve the URL for Autodiscover derived from the email address
- Retrieve the configuration data
- Connect with EWS, based on the configuration URLs

The URL for Autodiscover is derived from the email address of the user. For example, the email address doris.lass@xmp.site results in the following:

> **Note** This following process actually describes the steps performed by Outlook. However, to retrieve the Autodiscover URL, you should perform the same steps as Outlook. Note that Outlook also checks in Microsoft Active Directory.

- The domain name in the email address provides the basis: xmp.site
- Possible URL 1: *https://xmp.site/Autodiscover/Autodiscover.xml*
- Possible URL 2: *https://autodiscover.xmp.site/Autodiscover/Autodiscover.xml*
- HTTP redirection: *http://autodiscover.xmp.site/Autodiscover/Autodiscover.xml* (redirects to an HTTPS URL to use Autodiscover to retrieve the configuration data)
- Service Record (SRV) DNS entries: entry for *_autodiscover._tcp.xmp.site*, including the domain name for the configuration. For example, if the entry contains the domain name extern.xmp.site, you can retrieve the configuration from *https://extern.xmp.site/Autodiscover/Autodiscover.xml*.

The method used to determine the URL depends on the Exchange server configuration.

> **Important** Because the access takes place over HTTPS, a certificate with the domain name is required. For small Exchange installations, the server must have several IP addresses to configure different certificates or the certificate needs to include several names.

Configuration Data

If you know the URL for the Autodiscover service, you can use the service to retrieve the configuration data for a user. Listing 20-1 shows part of the data. The URLs in the *ASUrl* or *EwsUrl* elements are important for using EWS with PHP. The URLs for external access (*https://mail.phpdemo.site/ews/exchange.asmx*) as well as for internal intranet access (*https://doco-exch.xmp.site/EWS/Exchange.asmx*) are listed.

You can also find the display name of the user (*DisplayName*), the email server (*Server*) and the distinguished name (DN) of the server for Active Directory (*ServerDN*) in the XML response.

LISTING 20-1 Response from the POX Autodiscover service.

```xml
<?xml version="1.0" encoding="utf-8" ?>
<Autodiscover xmlns="http://schemas.microsoft.com/exchange/autodiscover/
responseschema/2006">
<Response xmlns="http://schemas.microsoft.com/exchange/autodiscover/outlook/
responseschema/2006a">
  <User>
    <DisplayName>Doris D. Lass</DisplayName>
    <LegacyDN>/o=XMP/ou=Exchange Administrative Group (FYDIBOHF23SPDLT)
             /cn=Recipients/cn=Doris D. Lass</LegacyDN>
    <DeploymentId>2a4df4d0-8bd0-487d-abc5-1cc233d5500e</DeploymentId>
  </User>
  <Account>
    <AccountType>email</AccountType>
    <Action>settings</Action>
    <Protocol>
      <Type>EXCH</Type>
      <Server>DOCO-EXCH.xmp.site</Server>
      <ServerDN>/o=XMP/ou=Exchange Administrative Group (FYDIBOHF23SPDLT)/cn=Configuration
               /cn=Servers/cn=DOCO-EXCH</ServerDN>
      ...
      <ASUrl>https://doco-exch.xmp.site/EWS/Exchange.asmx</ASUrl>
      <EwsUrl>https://doco-exch.xmp.site/EWS/Exchange.asmx</EwsUrl>
      ...
    </Protocol>
    <Protocol>
      <Type>WEB</Type>
      <Internal>
        <OWAUrl AuthenticationMethod="Basic, Fba">https://doco-exch.xmp.site/owa/</OWAUrl>
        <Protocol>
          <Type>EXCH</Type>
          <ASUrl>https://doco-exch.xmp.site/EWS/Exchange.asmx</ASUrl>
        </Protocol>
      </Internal>
      <External>
        <OWAUrl AuthenticationMethod="Fba">https://mail.phpdemo.site/owa/</OWAUrl>
        <Protocol>
          <Type>EXPR</Type>
          <ASUrl>https://mail.phpdemo.site/ews/exchange.asmx</ASUrl>
        </Protocol>
      </External>
    </Protocol>
  </Account>
</Response>
</Autodiscover>
```

> **Note** For a description of all elements in the POX Autodiscover response, go to MSDN at
> *http://msdn.microsoft.com/en-us/library/bb204082.aspx*

Retrieving Configuration Data

The Autodiscover service requires NTLM authentication (Exchange default configuration).
You can choose any user with read access to the associated entries in Active Directory.
The searched email address is passed in an XML structure and sent over HTTP POST to the
Autodiscover URL.

The following function assumes that the URL is an HTTPS URL with NTLM authentication.
HTTP redirection or SVR entries are not considered.

Query with cURL

Listing 20-2 shows how you use the cURL PHP extension to retrieve the configuration data:

- First the XML request (*$request*) is generated.

> **Caution** The URL of the *AcceptableResponseSchema* element cannot contain spaces or
> line breaks.

- *curl_setopt_array()* configures the parameters for the connection. Important are
  CURLOPT_HTTPAUTH, *CURLOPT_USERPWD* and *CURLOPT_CAINFO*: the first two
  parameters contain the information for the NTLM authentication, and the last parameter contains information on the HTTPS certificate. The XML request is passed in
  CURLOPT_POSTFIELDS.

- *curl_exec()* sends the HTTP request and returns the response to the caller.

> **Note** This function doesn't include error queries (*curl_error()* or *curl_getinfo()*) and doesn't
> evaluate the XML, which can contain an error message. You should consider these facts in a
> production environment.

LISTING 20-2 autodiscover.php—retrieving the Autodiscover data over TLS with NTLM authentication.

```php
<?php
namespace net\xmp\phpbook;

/**
 * Retrieving the Exchange Autodiscover data
 * @param string $host Host name of the Exchange Server
 * @param string $email Email address of the user
 * @param string $login User name
 * @param string $password Password
 * @param string $CAcert Path to the CA certificate
 */
function autodiscover($host, $email, $login, $password, $CAcert) {
    $email = htmlspecialchars($email);
    $request = <<<EOF
<Autodiscover xmlns="http://schemas.microsoft.com/exchange/autodiscover/outlook/
requestschema/2006">
  <Request>
    <EMailAddress>$email</EMailAddress>
    <AcceptableResponseSchema>http://schemas.microsoft.com/exchange/autodiscover/
                        outlook/responseschema/2006a</AcceptableResponseSchema>
  </Request>
</Autodiscover>
EOF;
    $ch = curl_init("https://$host/Autodiscover/Autodiscover.xml");
    curl_setopt_array($ch, array(
        CURLOPT_HTTP_VERSION => CURL_HTTP_VERSION_1_1,
        CURLOPT_POST => true,
        CURLOPT_USERAGENT => 'PHP-cURL/NTLM',
        CURLOPT_HTTPAUTH => CURLAUTH_NTLM,
        CURLOPT_USERPWD => "$login:$password",
        CURLOPT_SSL_VERIFYPEER => true,
        CURLOPT_SSL_VERIFYHOST => 2,
        CURLOPT_CAINFO => $CAcert,
        CURLOPT_HTTPHEADER => array('Content-Type: text/xml; charset=utf-8'),
        CURLOPT_POSTFIELDS => $request,
        CURLOPT_RETURNTRANSFER => true
    ));
    $response = curl_exec($ch);
    curl_close($ch);
    return $response;
}
?>
```

The path passed with *CURLOPT_CAINFO* has to point to the base-64–encoded (PEM, CER) root certificate of the certification authority (CA) issuing the HTTPS certificate for Exchange. If the CA is a third-party CA, download the root certificate from its website and save it on a local drive.

If you use your own CA operated with the Active Directory Certificate Services, you can export the root certificate by using the Microsoft Management Console (MMC). You can also use Microsoft Internet Explorer to export the root certificate to a domain computer. To do so, click the Tools icon, and then select Internet Options. On the Content tab, click the Certificates button, and then click the Trusted Root Certification Authorities tab.

The *CURLOPT_SSL_VERIFYHOST* option specifies whether the Exchange domain name must be included in the certificate: The recommended value (*2*) checks whether the name in the certificate matches the host name.

Evaluating Configuration Data

Listing 20-3 shows how the SimpleXML PHP extension and the built-in XPath support is used to retrieve the EWS URLs. In the listing, the URLs are retrieved with two XPath expressions. The search returns an array of URLs for EWS connections because in larger Exchange installations, multiple URLs can be specified. The scripts returns only the first internal and external URL (Index 0).

LISTING 20-3 Retrieving the internal and external EWS URLs.

```php
<?php
namespace net\xmp\phpbook;
require './autodiscover.php';

$response = autodiscover('autodiscover.phpdemo.site', 'doris@xmp.site',
                         'xmp\\doris', 'confidential', './my-ca.cer');
$xml = new \SimpleXMLElement($response);
$xml->registerXPathNamespace(
      'ex', 'http://schemas.microsoft.com/exchange/autodiscover/outlook/
responseschema/2006a');
$intern = $xml->xpath('//ex:Internal//ex:ASUrl');
$extern = $xml->xpath('//ex:External//ex:ASUrl');
echo "<p>Internal EWS URL: $intern[0]\n",
     "<p>External EWS URL: $extern[0]\n";
?>
```

If you are getting errors, first try to open the Autodiscover URL with a web browser to verify that you can reach the address and that your credentials are correct. If you make it to the error message "600 Invalid Request", the URL and credentials are fine. Next, you can get additional error information from cURL by calling *curl_error()* and enabling the *CURLOPT_HEADER* and *CURLINFO_HEADER_OUT* options. Print the response of *curl_exec()*. Exchange is picky about the content type, even spaces can throw it off.

Alternative Methods for URL Queries

You can also retrieve the Autodiscovery and EWS URLs in Active Directory or by using the Exchange Management Shell.

Active Directory

Exchange saves a service connection point (SCP) in the naming context (*CN=Configuration, DC=...,DC=...*) of Active Directory.

The entries for servers providing Autodiscover functions are saved in *CN=Autodiscover, CN=Protocols,CN=<CASServer>,CN=Servers,CN=Exchange Administrative Group (<Number>), CN=Administrative Groups,CN=<Organization>,CN=Microsoft Exchange, CN=Services*. The *serviceBindingInformation* attribute contains the internal Autodiscover URL.

> **Note** The Autodiscover URL is an intranet URL, because Active Directory is only accessible from within a domain.

The entry *CN=EWS (Default Web Site),CN=HTTP,CN=Protocols,CN=<CASServer>,CN=Servers, CN=Exchange Administrative Group (<Number>),CN=Administrative Groups,CN=<Organization>, CN= Microsoft Exchange,CN=Services* contains the EWS URLs in the *msExchExternalHost Name* and *msExchInternalHostName* attributes.

Exchange Management Shell

In Exchange Management Shell (EMS), you can query the information in Active Directory by using the following cmdlets:

- **Get-clientAccessServer** The *AutoDiscoverServiceInternalUri* property contains the internal Autodiscover URL.

- **Get-WebServicesVirtualDirectory** The *InternalUrl* and *ExternalUrl* properties contain the URLs for the EWS services.

- **Get-AutodiscoverVirtualDirectory** Contains information on the IIS virtual directory used for Autodiscover.

To list the properties, use the *Format-List* cmdlet, as follows:

```
Get-clientAccessServer | fl
```

You can also set the properties by using *Set-clientAccessServer* and *Set-WebServicesVirtual Directory*. Use the parameter *-?* to get help for these functions.

SOAP and WSDL

Now that you know the URL for the EWS, you can send SOAP messages to this URL. SOAP is an XML-based protocol that ensures a structured data exchange. The WSDL definition contains information on the structure and syntax of messages.

The PHP SOAP extension parses the WSDL definitions to simplify web services programming. Instead of processing the raw XML SOAP messages, the PHP Soap extension handles the SOAP message content in the same way as PHP objects or arrays.

WSDL Structure

WSDL defines the structure and syntax for SOAP messages, based on the following:

- **Message**   A messages defines the elements of a SOAP request or a SOAP response.

- **Operation**   An operation consists of a request message (*input*) and a response message (*output*).

- **Endpoints** (*portType*)   An endpoint combines all operations available at this endpoint. EWS only uses a single endpoint.

- **Binding**   The binding specifies how the elements of a messages are transferred—for example, in the SOAP header or in the SOAP message body—as well as the SoapAction for the transfer over HTTP.

- **Service**   The service definition links an endpoint and a binding and specifies the URL for the service.

The message elements are not defined in WSDL but are included in XML Schema files. XML Schema is a syntax description language that defines the content and structure of XML elements and attributes:

- *Values* can be strings, numbers, *Boolean* expressions, data types, enumeration types, and other types.

- The *value range* can be limited; for example, you can limit the length of a string or the maximum value of a number.

- The *structure* of nested elements can be defined. To specify a sequence of elements you can use *sequence*, and *choice* to specify several elements.

- The *number* of elements can be specified by using *minOccurs* (Minimum) and *maxOcccurs* (Maximum).

- You can use *definition inheritance* to derive extended or restricted types from existing types.

EWS defines the message elements in two different files: one file for the message structure (messages.xsd), and one file for the data types (types.xsd) that comprise the message.

EWS, WSDL, and PHP

Because Exchange allows variable EWS URLs, or the URL depends on internal and external host names, the EWS WSDL definition doesn't include a service definition. This is in line with the WSDL standard but the PHP SOAP extension cannot process WSDL without service definition.

To program using WSDL support, you need to download the WSDL file and the associated XML schema files, save the files on a local drive, and then insert the service definition. Because the WSDL definition only changes if a new version of Exchange Server is installed this is a reasonable if not necessarily elegant alternative.

Adding the Service Definition

For PHP to work with EWS WSDL, perform the following steps:

1. Download the EWS WSDL file from *https://<Server>/EWS/Services.wsdl* and save the file on your local drive.

2. Download both XML schema files from *https://<Server>/EWS/Messages.xsd* and *https://<Server>/EWS/Types.xsd*.

   Save the files in the same directory as Services.wsdl.

> **Note** You can also find the three files on the Exchange Server. From the Exchange Management Shell, run the following cmdlet:
>
> ```
> Get-WebServicesVirtualDirectory | fl Path
> ```
>
> By default, the specified directory C:\Program Files\Microsoft\Exchange Server\V14\ClientAccess\exchweb\EWS) contains the files.

3. Open Services.wsdl in an editor, and then insert the following definition at the end, just before the end tag *</wsdl:definitions>* (replace *#EWS-URL#* with your EWS URL):

```
<wsdl:service name='ExchangeService'>
  <wsdl:port name='ExchangeServicePortType' binding='ExchangeServiceBinding'>
  <soap:address location='#EWS-URL#'/>
  </wsdl:port>
</wsdl:service>
```

4. Save the file.

> **Note** You can change the EWS URL at a later point in the PHP program while instantiating the *SoapClient* class (*location* parameter).

Testing the Modified EWS WSDL File

Run the test program in Listing 20-4 to confirm that your modifications were successful. For Exchange Server 2010, more than 50 functions and almost 550 data types are listed.

LISTING 20-4 test-wsdl.php—functions and data types of the EWS WSDL definition.

```php
<?php
$client = new SoapClient("./Services.wsdl", array('cache_wsdl' => WSDL_CACHE_NONE));
echo '<h1>Functions</h1><pre>';
var_dump($client->__getFunctions());
echo '</pre><h1>Typen</h1><pre>';
var_dump($client->__getTypes());
echo '</pre>';
?>
```

> **Important** Because parsing WSDL files and the associated schema files is resource-intensive, PHP caches the results. However, for the test in Listing 20-4, caching is disabled. Based on your requirements, you can also set the configuration parameters *soap.wsdl_cache_enabled* or *soap .wsdl_cache_ttl* using the php.ini file or the *ini_set()* function.
>
> In a production environment, caching should be enabled.

SOAP Messages

With the prepared WSDL file, you can start programming the Exchange Web Services. However, you cannot use the *SoapClient* class of the PHP SOAP extension because this class doesn't provide NTLM authentication for SOAP requests.

For this reason, the defined *ExchangeSoapClient* class is used. This class also uses the PHP cURL extension to send requests.

ExchangeSoapClient Class

The *ExchangeSoapClient* class is shown in Listing 20-5. This class uses cURL to send SOAP requests over HTTPS with NTLM authentication. The following information is important to understand how this class works:

- The constructor is overwritten to cache the passed options (*$options*).

- The actual work is done by the *doRequest()* method.

- Because the connection over HTTPS with NTLM authentication is time-consuming and resource-intensive, the open connection is cached in *$this->curl_handle*.

- While the first connection is created, the (fixed) parameters are set. This includes not only the user name and password but also the CA root certificate (see the section "Query with cURL," earlier in the chapter) as well as the returned response header (*CURLINFO_HEADER_OUT*) used for the tests.

- Afterward, the (variable) parameters are set: SOAPAction header, URL of the service (*$location*), and SOAP message content (*$request*).

- The metadata is retrieved by using *curl_getinfo()* and is available in the public *$this>curl_info* property for troubleshooting.

- Because the response HTTP header is provided in *$response*, the XML SOAP message is separated from the HTTP headers.

The *getLastRequestHeaders()* and *getLastResponseHeaders()* methods are overwritten to return the correct values. Both functions should only be called if the trace option for the *ExchangeSoapClient* object is set.

LISTING 20-5 *ExchangeSoapClient*—the *SoapClient* class including HTTPS and NTLM-authentication.

```php
<?php
namespace net\xmp\phpbook;

class ExchangeSoapClient extends \SoapClient {

    const TYPES_NS = "http://schemas.microsoft.com/exchange/services/2006/types";
    const MESSAGES_NS = "http://schemas.microsoft.com/exchange/services/2006/messages";

    protected $options;
    protected $curl_handle;
    public $curl_info;

    function __construct($wsdl, $options=array()) {
        $this->options = $options;
        parent::__construct($wsdl, $options);
    }
```

```php
    function __doRequest($request, $location, $action, $version, $one_way=0) {
        if (empty($this->curl_handle)) {
            $this->curl_handle = curl_init();
            curl_setopt_array($this->curl_handle, array(
                CURLOPT_HTTP_VERSION => CURL_HTTP_VERSION_1_1,
                CURLOPT_POST => true,
                CURLOPT_USERAGENT => 'PHP-cURL/NTLM-SOAP',
                CURLOPT_HTTPAUTH => CURLAUTH_NTLM,
                CURLOPT_USERPWD => $this->options['login'] . ':'
                                    .$this->options['password'],
                CURLOPT_SSL_VERIFYPEER => true,
                CURLOPT_SSL_VERIFYHOST => 2,
                CURLOPT_CAINFO => $this->options['CACert'],
                CURLOPT_RETURNTRANSFER => true,
                CURLINFO_HEADER_OUT => true,
                CURLOPT_HEADER => true));
        }
        curl_setopt_array($this->curl_handle, array(
            CURLOPT_HTTPHEADER => array("SOAPAction: \"$action\"",
                                        'Content-Type: text/xml; charset=utf-8'),
            CURLOPT_POSTFIELDS => $request,
            CURLOPT_URL => $location));
        $response = curl_exec($this->curl_handle);
        $this->curl_info = curl_getinfo($this->curl_handle);
        if ($response !== false) {
            $xml = strpos($response, '<?xml ');
            if ($xml) {
                $this->curl_info['response_header'] = substr($response, 0, $xml);
                $response = substr($response, $xml);
            } else {
                $this->curl_info['response_header'] = $response;
                $response = false;
            }
        }
        return $response;
    }

    function __getLastRequestHeaders() {
        return $this->curl_info['request_header'];
    }

    function __getLastResponseHeaders() {
        return $this->curl_info['response_header'];
    }
}
?>
```

Using the *ExchangeSoapClient* Class

Listing 20-6 shows how you use the *ExchangeSoapClient* class. It is important to set the *CACert* options, the logon name, and the password during the client instantiation. The *trace* option is necessary only for development tasks.

After the instantiation has completed successfully, the *GetFolder* operation is called. The generated SOAP message (Listing 20-7) is defined by the *$param* array. Instead of using arrays, you can also define classes with appropriate properties and pass instantiated objects of these classes. If an error occurs, an exception is triggered that is intercepted in the *try/catch* block.

For testing purposes, the request and the response, including the HTTP header as well as the response objects, are displayed.

LISTING 20-6 test-ews.php—testing the EWS with PHP.

```php
<?php
namespace net\xmp\phpbook;
require './ExchangeSoapClient.php';
require './HTMLPage.php';

$options = array('trace' => true, 'CACert' => './my-ca.cer',
                 'login' => 'doris', 'password' => 'confidential');
$client = new ExchangeSoapClient("./Services.wsdl", $options);

$param = array('FolderShape' => array('BaseShape' => 'Default'),
               'FolderIds' => array(
                   'DistinguishedFolderId' => array(array('Id' => 'inbox'),
                       array('Id' => 'drafts'))));
try {
    $response = $client->GetFolder($param);
}
catch (\Exception $e) {
    echo '<h1>Exception</h1>', $e;
    var_dump($client->curl_info);
    exit;
}
$page = new HTMLPage('EWS test');
$page->addElement('h1', 'Request');
$page->addElement('h2', 'Data');
$page->addElement('p', $client->__getLastRequest());
$page->addElement('h2', 'Header');
$page->addElement('pre', $client->__getLastRequestHeaders(), true);
$page->addElement('h1', 'Response');
$page->addElement('h2', 'Data');
$page->addElement('p', $client->__getLastResponse());
$page->addElement('h2', 'Header');
$page->addElement('pre', $client->__getLastResponseHeaders(), true);
$page->addElement('h1', 'Generated response object');
$page->addElement('pre', print_r($response, true), true);
$page->printPage();
?>
```

The output of the test program is shown in Figure 20-1.

FIGURE 20-1 Output generated by the test program test-ews.php.

Listing 20-7 shows the generated SOAP request. The relationship between the *$param* array in Listing 20-6 and the SOAP message is obvious.

> **Note** The names specified in the *$param* array must be identical to the element and attribute names in the SOAP message (the names are also case sensitive).

LISTING 20-7 A SOAP request from the *GetFolder* operation.

```xml
<?xml version="1.0" encoding="UTF-8"?>
<SOAP-ENV:Envelope xmlns:SOAP-ENV="http://schemas.xmlsoap.org/soap/envelope/"
            xmlns:ns1="http://schemas.microsoft.com/exchange/services/2006/types"
            xmlns:ns2="http://schemas.microsoft.com/exchange/services/2006/messages">
<SOAP-ENV:Body>
  <ns2:GetFolder>
    <ns2:FolderShape>
      <ns1:BaseShape>Default</ns1:BaseShape>
    </ns2:FolderShape>
    <ns2:FolderIds>
      <ns1:DistinguishedFolderId Id="inbox"/>
      <ns1:DistinguishedFolderId Id="drafts"/>
    </ns2:FolderIds>
  </ns2:GetFolder>
</SOAP-ENV:Body>
</SOAP-ENV:Envelope>
```

Information About the Following Chapters

In the following chapters, the SOAP messages are not given in full, and the PHP listings mostly show only relevant sections of the request.

Shorter SOAP Messages

The following chapters don't show full SOAP messages and use the namespace definition in Listing 20-8.

LISTING 20-8 Used XML namespaces.

```
xmlns:wsdl="http://schemas.xmlsoap.org/wsdl/"
xmlns:soap="http://schemas.xmlsoap.org/wsdl/soap"
xmlns:xs="http://www.w3.org/2001/XMLSchema"
xmlns:SOAP-ENV="http://schemas.xmlsoap.org/soap/envelope/"
xmlns:t="http://schemas.microsoft.com/exchange/services/2006/types"
xmlns:m="http://schemas.microsoft.com/exchange/services/2006/messages"
```

The request in Listing 20-7 would look like this:

```
<m:GetFolder>
  <m:FolderShape>
    <t:BaseShape>Default</t:BaseShape>
  </m:FolderShape>
  <m:FolderIds>
    <t:DistinguishedFolderId Id="inbox"/>
    <t:DistinguishedFolderId Id="drafts"/>
  </m:FolderIds>
</m:GetFolder>
```

Shorter PHP Listings

The PHP examples are also not listed in their entirety either and show only the structure of the request and the response. In addition, error-handling has been omitted. The PHP test program in Listing 20-6 would look like this:

```
$param = array('FolderShape' => array('BaseShape' => 'Default'),
               'FolderIds' => array(
                   'DistinguishedFolderId' => array(array('Id' => 'inbox'),
                                                    array('Id' => 'drafts'))));
$response = $client->GetFolder($param);
```

Object-Oriented Alternative for Parameters

The *SOAPClient* class not only accepts parameters as arrays, but also as nested objects. Thus, an object-oriented alternative for Listing 20-6 would look like Listing 20-9. Using two simple classes and the default class, the listing shows how parameters are passed.

LISTING 20-9 Objects as parameters for SOAP operations.

```
class FolderShape {
    protected $BaseShape;

    function __construct($shape) {
        $this->BaseShape = $shape;
    }
}

class FolderId {
    protected $Id;

    function __construct($id) {
        $this->Id = $id;
    }
}

$param = new \stdClass;
$param->FolderShape = new FolderShape('AllProperties');
$param->FolderIds = new \stdClass;
$param->FolderIds->DistinguishedFolderId = array(new FolderId('inbox'),
                                                 new FolderId('drafts'));
$response = $client->GetFolder($param);
```

With one exception (which is explained in Chapter 21, "Email and Exchange Web Services Basics"), you can choose any method: sometimes you need to use objects instead of arrays for EWS to work with PHP.

 Note This book primarily uses the array syntax.

Summary

This chapter explained how to use Autodiscover to retrieve the EWS URL. If the URL for the selected user is known, you can create the connection by using EWS and control it via Exchange.

For PHP to work with EWS, you need to download the WSDL definition and the schemas and modify the WSDL file locally. As shown in the next chapter, you have to make more changes on the types.xsd XML schema. However, controlling the EWS based on WSDL simplifies programming with PHP significantly.

The following chapter explains several terms of EWS and how to search, create, and delete emails in Exchange. The following chapters introduce additional aspects of the EWS, based on contacts and calendar entries.

Chapter 21

Email and Exchange Web Services Basics

This chapter explains important Microsoft Exchange Web Services (EWS) operations to find folders and elements and to create and delete elements. First, you will take a closer look at the Exchange database structure and the identification of elements.

In addition to EWS operations, important EWS schema changes are also explained to ensure a trouble-free communication between EWS and PHP.

Structure, IDs, and Views

Exchange saves all elements in an internal database. This database isn't a relational database with tables and typed columns; rather, it's a generic storage for organized data.

For each element, the element data, the element type, a unique ID, and version information are saved in the Exchange database. Because the version information changes if an element is modified, Exchange can ensure that only current data is updated, if accessed simultaneously.

Except for search functions, elements are accessed through their ID. At the same time a change key, aptly named *ChangeKey*, is passed containing the version and type information of the element. Although *ChangeKey* is optional, it should be specified to recognize simultaneous changes.

IDs of Labeled Folders

Several labeled folders have well known aliases. Table 21-1 lists several folder aliases. However, if possible, you should use the real ID of a folder instead of its alias.

TABLE 21-1 IDs for labeled folders

Name	ID	Description
Drafts	*drafts*	New messages the user hasn't sent yet; used for caching.
Deleted Items	*deleteditems*	Deleted messages not removed yet (recycle bin).
Sent Items	*sentitems*	Sent messages.
Junk E-mail	*junkemail*	Unwanted messages.
Calendar	*calendar*	Default folder for calendar entries.
Contacts	*contacts*	Default folder for contacts.
Message root folder	*msgfolderroot*	The root folder for all message folders.
Outbox	*outbox*	Messages are saved in this folder until they are sent.
Inbox	*inbox*	New messages are saved in this folder.
Root folder	*root*	The top folder in the Exchange mailbox.

Use *DistinguishedFolderId* to specify the alias IDs for operations to distinguish these IDs from the real IDs, which are specified in *FolderId*.

Viewing Elements

Elements in the Exchange database consist of properties with names and values. Properties are typed. This means syntax and limitations for values are defined.

For search results (for example, *FindFolder*) or queried elements (*GetItem*), you can use *BaseShape* to specify which properties are included in the results. *BaseShape* defines profiles for frequent use cases: *Default* for the standard properties, *IdOnly* if only the ID of an element is needed, and *AllProperties* to include all properties of an element in the results.

If you want a view to include additional properties, specify these properties with *AdditionalProperties*.

Caution A query returns only the first 256 characters (for Unicode, otherwise 512 characters) of strings and other large data types. Only a direct query, such as with *GetItem*, returns all information.

Calculated properties (properties that are dynamically generated and not saved in the database) cannot be returned as part of search queries.

Selected Properties of Elements

Table 21-2 lists selected properties of elements together with a short description.

TABLE 21-2 Selected standard properties of elements

Property	Description
Attachments	Lists all attachments of an element
Body	Text of the element
Categories	Categories assigned to the element
DateTimeCreated	Specifies when the element was created
DateTimeReceived	Specifies when the element arrived in the mailbox
DateTimeSent	Specifies when the element was sent
HasAttachments	Specifies if the element has attachments
ItemClass	Element type of email messages such as *IPM.Note*
ItemId	ID and version (*ChangeKey*) of the element
LastModifiedName	Display name of the user who changed the element last (read-only)
LastModifiedTime	Time the element was last changed (read-only)
ParentFolderId	Folder in which the element is saved
ReminderDueBy	Time of the reminder, due date
ReminderIsSet	Specifies if the reminder function is enabled
ReminderMinutesBeforeStart	Specifies the number of minutes before the due date for the reminder
Size	Size of the element in bytes
Subject	Subject of the element

Names of Properties

For some operations or parameters of operations, you must specify the property names these properties have in the Exchange database (not the position or the element names in XML of the SOAP message—although the XML element name of the property is often very similar to the name in the database). This might be necessary if you want to sort the search results by properties or to return additional properties with *AdditionalProperties*. Exchange differentiates between three property types: basic properties, property groups, and extended properties.

Basic Properties

Basic properties are properties that are only set once per element but can have several values. The display name of folders (*folder:DisplayName*) or categories for elements (*item:Categories*) are examples of basic properties.

In requests, basic properties are specified by using *FieldURI*:

```
<t:AdditionalProperties>
  <t:FieldURI FieldURI="item:Subject"/>
  <t:FieldURI FieldURI="message:IsRead"/>
</t:AdditionalProperties>
```

For a list of the basic properties, consult the MSDN article at *http://msdn.microsoft.com/ en-us/library/aa494315.aspx*. A complete list can be found in the types.xsd XML Schema of the EWS in the definition of the *UnindexedFieldURIType* data type.

Property Groups

Property groups consist of properties that can be included in an element multiple times. Typical examples are phone numbers for contacts (*contacts:PhoneNumber*) or contact information (*contacts:ImAddress*).

In requests, the entries of property groups are specified by using *IndexedFieldURI*:

```
<t:AdditionalProperties>
  <t:IndexedFieldURI FieldURI="contacts:PhoneNumber" FieldIndex="MobilePhone"/>
  <t:IndexedFieldURI FieldURI="contacts:PhysicalAddress:Street" FieldIndex="Business"/>
</t:AdditionalProperties>
```

For a list of property groups, consult the MSDN article at *http://msdn.microsoft.com/en-us/ library/aa581079.aspx*. A complete list can be found in the types.xsd XML Schema of the EWS in the definition of the *DictionaryURIType* data type.

Extended Properties

You can use extended properties (*ExtendedFieldURI* element) to specify additional MAPI properties. These properties are addressed by their types and either the predefined names, their tags, or the IDs.

```
<t:AdditionalProperties>
  <t:ExtendedFieldURI PropertyTag="0x0037" PropertyType="String"/>
  <t:ExtendedFieldURI DistinguishedPropertySetId="PublicStrings"
                      PropertyName="customerPremiumSupport" PropertyType="Boolean"/>
  <t:ExtendedFieldURI PropertySetId="00010397-0000-0200-A020-000001004088" PropertyId="3"
                      PropertyType="String"/>
</t:AdditionalProperties>
```

For a description of the syntax and the predefined names, consult the MSDN article at *http:// msdn.microsoft.com/en-us/library/aa564843.aspx*.

Finding Folders (*FindFolder*)

For the EWS to work with email, you first need to find the folders in which the emails are saved. This is done by using the *FindFolder* operation.

Selected Properties

Folders are the only objects in the Exchange database that are not derived from the generic element type. Therefore, folders have their own set of properties. The most important properties are listed in Table 21-3.

TABLE 21-3 Selected properties of folders

Property	Description
ChildFolderCount	Number of folders in the folder
DisplayName	Display name of the folder
FolderClass	Class of the folder such as *IPF.Note* for the inbox
FolderId	ID and version (*ChangeKey*) of the folder
ParentFolderId	ID of the parent folder
TotalCount	Number of elements in the folder

Request

Listing 21-1 shows an example request that uses the *FindFolder* operation.

LISTING 21-1 The *FindFolder* operation—request message.

```
<m:FindFolder Traversal="Deep">
  <m:FolderShape>
    <t:BaseShape>AllProperties</t:BaseShape>
  </m:FolderShape>
  <m:ParentFolderIds>
    <t:DistinguishedFolderId Id="msgfolderroot"/>
  </m:ParentFolderIds>
</m:FindFolder>
```

In PHP, the *ExchangeSoapClient* class generates the operation message as follows:

```
$param = array('Traversal' => 'Deep',
               'FolderShape' => array('BaseShape' => 'AllProperties'),
               'ParentFolderIds' => array(
                     'DistinguishedFolderId' => array('Id' => 'msgfolderroot')));
$response = $client->FindFolder($param);
```

The following parameters are passed to *FindFolder*:

- **Traversal**   Specifies the search area. *Deep* searches the entire hierarchy below the specified folder, and *Shallow* searches only the direct children.

- **ParentFolderIds**   Contains one or more folder IDs to be queried. *DistinguishedFolderId* specifies alias IDs, and *FolderId* specifies IDs. For example:

```
<t:FolderId Id="AQAXAEFu..." ChangeKey="CQAAABYA..."/>
```

Response

The response from the *FindFolder* operation contains the data of the folders that were found. The PHP SOAP extension converts the structure of the SOAP message into a PHP object.

XML Response

Listing 21-2 shows the response from the operation. In addition to the status information (*ResponseClass*, *ResponseCode*), the number of hits is also indicated (*TotalItemsInView*). It also shows if the last element is included in the results (*IncludesLastItemInRange*). The last information is useful if search results are paginated. *Folders* contains the actual folder information.

LISTING 21-2 The *FindFolder* operation—response message.

```
<m:FindFolderResponse>
  <m:ResponseMessages>
    <m:FindFolderResponseMessage ResponseClass="Success">
      <m:ResponseCode>NoError</m:ResponseCode>
      <m:RootFolder TotalItemsInView="18" IncludesLastItemInRange="true">
        <t:Folders>
          <t:Folder>
            <t:FolderId Id="AAAXAEFn..." ChangeKey="AQAAABYA..."/>
            <t:ParentFolderId Id="AQAXAEFn..." ChangeKey="AQAAAAsw..."/>
            <t:FolderClass>IPF.Note</t:FolderClass>
            <t:DisplayName>Inbox</t:DisplayName>
            <t:TotalCount>17</t:TotalCount>
            <t:ChildFolderCount>2</t:ChildFolderCount>
            <t:UnreadCount>0</t:UnreadCount>
          </t:Folder>
          ...
        </t:Folders>
      </m:RootFolder>
    </m:FindFolderResponseMessage>
  </m:ResponseMessages>
</m:FindFolderResponse>
```

PHP Object

The PHP SOAP extension converts the response XML to a PHP object. Nested elements correspond to nested objects.

Listing 21-3 shows how the elements are handled: *$folderlist* shows the message structure, and the folder array (*Folder* elements) is processed in a loop. Notice that with *$folder->ParentFolderId->Id*, XML elements and attributes are addressed in the same way.

> **Note**   Listing 21-3 uses HTMLPage.php (see Appendix A, "Example Scripts and Data") to display the data as a table.

LISTING 21-3 Evaluating the response message from the *FindFolder* operation.

```php
$page = new HTMLPage('Folders in Mailbox');
$folderlist = $response->ResponseMessages->FindFolderResponseMessage
                      ->RootFolder->Folders->Folder;
$folders = array();
foreach ($folderlist as $folder) {
    $folders[$folder->FolderId->Id] = $folder;
}
$table = array( array('Name', 'Folder Class', 'Parent Folder',
                      'Elements', 'Unread') );
foreach ($folders as $folder) {
    $parentId = $folder->ParentFolderId->Id;
    $parent = isset($folders[$parentId]) ? $folders[$parentId]->DisplayName
                                         : 'msgfolderroot';
    $table[] = array($folder->DisplayName, $folder->FolderClass, $parent,
                     $folder->TotalCount, $folder->UnreadCount);
}
$page->addTable($table);
$page->printPage();
```

Figure 21-1 shows the output from the sample program.

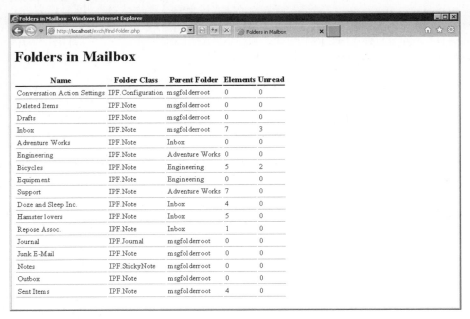

FIGURE 21-1 All folders in the mailbox.

Listing Messages (*FindItem*)

The *FindItem* operation lists the email messages. This operation works similar to *FindFolder*. Because folders can contain a large number of emails, you might want to limit the search results.

Limiting the Results (Paging)

With the EWS *IndexedPageItemView* element, you can limit the number of the search results returned by the *FindItem* operation:

```
<m:IndexedPageItemView MaxEntriesReturned="5" Offset="10" BasePoint="Beginning"/>
```

MaxEntriesReturned specifies how many hits are returned, *Offset* specifies the start position, and *Basepoint* specifies whether the offset count starts at the first element in descending order or at the last element in ascending order to simplify scrolling in both directions.

 Note Instead of *IndexedPageItemView*, you can use *FractionalPageItemView* to specify a relative (percentage) offset (numerator and denominator attributes).

In this case, the *RootFolder* element of the response contains the following attributes:

```
<m:RootFolder IndexedPagingOffset="15" TotalItemsInView="23"
              IncludesLastItemInRange="false">
```

IndexedPagingOffset contains the offset value used for the next request. This value is calculated from *Offset+MaxEntriesReturned*. *TotalItemsInView* indicates how many elements are saved in the folder, and *IncludesLastItemInRange* specifies if the search result contains the last element: if *IncludesLastItemInRange=true* and the order is descending (*BasePoint=Beginning*), it is the last element in the folder. If the order is ascending (*BasePoint=End*), the first element in the folder is included in the search results.

> **Note** You can also limit the number of results for the *FindFolder* operation by using the *IndexedPageFolderView* and *FractionalPageFolderView* elements.

Sorting

Use the *SortOrder* element presented in Listing 21-4 to sort the search results returned by *FindItem*. The properties are displayed in the specified order.

LISTING 21-4 Specifying the sort order.

```
<m:SortOrder>
  <t:FieldOrder Order="Ascending">
    <t:FieldURI FieldURI="message:Sender" />
  </t:FieldOrder>
  <t:FieldOrder Order="Descending">
    <t:FieldURI FieldURI="item:DateTimeSent" />
  </t:FieldOrder>
<m:SortOrder>
```

Exchange returns the results in the specified order. In this example, the order is ascending beginning at the sender (*message:Sender*) and descending beginning at the time sent (*item:DateTimeSent*), if the sender is the same.

> **Note** You cannot sort the results from the *FindFolder* operation.

PHP and Replacement Groups

The PHP SOAP extension cannot generate the correct XML in Listing 21-4 because in the EWS schema definition, the *FieldURI*, *IndexedFieldURI*, and *ExtendedFieldURI* elements are defined as a replacement group for the path element. Therefore, PHP returns an error message stating that the path element is missing.

There are two solutions: you can modify the EWS schema definition to not use replacement groups, or you can use type mapping to perform the XML serialization in the *SoapClient*.

Type Mapping

Type mapping cannot be used because of an error in EWS. EWS cannot process schema instances with *xsi:type*; it returns an internal server error. If you still want to use type mapping, you need to map all parent types. This is possible, but for all practical purposes, it's too much effort. Therefore, this book doesn't use type mapping; instead, it modifies the schema.

Modifying the Schema

To break the deadlock between PHP and EWS and to take advantage of the programming functionality based on WSDL, you need to modify the schema for the web services. To do this, perform the following steps:

1. Open the local copy of the types.xsd type schema in an editor.

2. Insert the following lines into the schema (at the end, before the *xs:schema* end tag):

```
<xs:group name="PathGroup">
  <xs:choice>
    <xs:element ref="t:FieldURI" />
    <xs:element ref="t:IndexedFieldURI" />
    <xs:element ref="t:ExtendedFieldURI" />
  </xs:choice>
</xs:group>
```

3. Replace all <xs:element ref="t:Path"/> instances with <xs:group ref="t:PathGroup"/>.

4. Change the definition of *NonEmptyArrayOfPathsToElementType* as follows:

```
<xs:complexType name="NonEmptyArrayOfPathsToElementType">
  <xs:choice maxOccurs="unbounded">
    <xs:element ref="t:FieldURI" />
    <xs:element ref="t:IndexedFieldURI" />
    <xs:element ref="t:ExtendedFieldURI" />
  </xs:choice>
</xs:complexType>
```

 Note You need to handle this type in a special way because PHP (currently) ignores the information relating to groups from *maxOccurs*.

5. Save the schema file.

Based on these modifications, PHP generates the correct XML for the SOAP message.

Request

After all preparations are completed, you can easily create a request that limits the results to five elements and sorts these elements by sender name and creation date.

XML Request

The XML request from the *FindItem* operation is shown in Listing 21-5. The results are limited by using *MaxEntriesReturned* and the offset and order are specified by using *BasePoint*. Use *SortOrder* to specify the sort order and *ParentFolderIds* to specify the folders to be searched.

LISTING 21-5 Message search with result limit and sorting.

```
<m:FindItem Traversal="Shallow">
  <m:ItemShape>
    <t:BaseShape>Default</t:BaseShape>
  </m:ItemShape>
  <m:IndexedPageItemView MaxEntriesReturned="5" Offset="0" BasePoint="Beginning"/>
  <m:SortOrder>
    <t:FieldOrder Order="Ascending">
      <t:FieldURI FieldURI="message:Sender"/>
    </t:FieldOrder>
    <t:FieldOrder Order="Descending">
      <t:FieldURI FieldURI="item:DateTimeCreated"/>
    </t:FieldOrder>
  </m:SortOrder>
  <m:ParentFolderIds>
    <t:DistinguishedFolderId Id="inbox"/>
  </m:ParentFolderIds>
</m:FindItem>
```

PHP

Due to the modified EWS type schema, PHP creates the request as if it would be able to handle replacement groups. This is shown in Listing 21-6.

LISTING 21-6 Creating and starting the *FindItem* operation.

```
$param = array('Traversal' => 'Shallow',
              'ItemShape' => array('BaseShape' => 'Default'),
              'ParentFolderIds' => array(
                   'DistinguishedFolderId' => array('Id'=>'inbox')),
              'IndexedPageItemView' => array(
                   'MaxEntriesReturned'=> 5,
                   'Offset' => 0,
                   'BasePoint' => "Beginning"),
                'SortOrder' => array( 'FieldOrder' => array(
                    array('Order' => 'Ascending',
                         'FieldURI' => array('FieldURI' => 'message:Sender')),
                    array('Order' => 'Descending',
                         'FieldURI' => array('FieldURI' => 'item:DateTimeCreated'))
)));
$response = $client->FindItem($param);
```

The example listing specifies an alias ID (inbox) without *ChangeKey* for the parent folder. In production environments, you should always specify the *ChangeKey*.

Response

The response message contains the searched email messages with the properties specified in the default view.

XML Response

Listing 21-7 shows the response message from the operation. The email messages found are embedded as message elements in the response, and due to the requested *Default-Item Shape*, they contain the most important properties for the listing. In this view, the sender data (*from*) doesn't include the email address but only the sender name. The content of the email (*Body*) is also not included.

LISTING 21-7 The *FindItem* operation—response message.

```
<m:FindItemResponse>
  <m:ResponseMessages>
    <m:FindItemResponseMessage ResponseClass="Success">
      <m:ResponseCode>NoError</m:ResponseCode>
      <m:RootFolder IndexedPagingOffset="5" TotalItemsInView="23"
                    IncludesLastItemInRange="false">
        <t:Items>
          <t:Message>
            <t:ItemId Id="AQAXAEFn..." ChangeKey="CQAAABYA..."/>
            <t:Subject>Furious Furrows...</</t:Subject>
            <t:Sensitivity>Normal</t:Sensitivity>
            <t:Size>1144</t:Size>
            <t:DateTimeSent>2011-07-19T13:58:28Z</t:DateTimeSent>
            <t:DateTimeCreated>2011-07-19T13:58:28Z</t:DateTimeCreated>
            <t:HasAttachments>false</t:HasAttachments>
            <t:From>
              <t:Mailbox><t:Name>Arno Hollosi</t:Name></t:Mailbox>
            </t:From>
            <t:IsRead>false</t:IsRead>
          </t:Message>
          <t:Message> ... </t:Message>
          ...
        </t:Items>
      </m:RootFolder>
    </m:FindItemResponseMessage>
  </m:ResponseMessages>
</m:FindItemResponse>
```

PHP Object

You can access messages and properties through PHP, as usual (see Listing 21-8).

LISTING 21-8 Evaluating the response message from the *FindItem* operation.

```
$page = new HTMLPage('Inbox');
$messages = $response->ResponseMessages->FindItemResponseMessage
                     ->RootFolder->Items->Message;
$table = array( array('Sender', 'Subject', 'Date', 'Read', 'Size', 'Attachments') );
foreach ($messages as $msg) {
    $read = $msg->IsRead ? 'yes' : '-';
    $attachments = $msg->HasAttachments ? 'yes' : '-';
    $table[] = array($msg->From->Mailbox->Name, $msg->Subject, $msg->DateTimeSent,
                     $read, $msg->Size, $attachments);
}
$page->addTable($table);
$page->PrintPage();
```

The output of the program is displayed in Figure 21-2. With the *Id* and *ChangeKey* values, a complete web mail script would include additional links to the detailed view of the emails.

> **Important** Direct access to *Items->Message* (Listing 21-8) only displays email messages and no appointments or other messages because these have the *MeetingRequest* or *MeetingCancellation* type. To list all elements, you must iterate through the results twice.
>
> ```
> $items = $response->ResponseMessages->FindItemResponseMessage->RootFolder->Items;
> foreach ($items as $itemType) {
>     foreach ($itemType as $singleItem) {
>         ...
>     }
> }
> ```
>
> Remember that other message types have properties different from email messages and, therefore, must be handled in a different way.

Inbox

Sender	Subject	Date	Read	Size	Attachments
Agnes B. Barstow	Re: Support ticket #4637	2011-09-04T07:44:01Z	-	1281	-
Arno Hollosi	Antediluvian anteaters (with image)	2011-09-04T07:47:51Z	-	143386	yes
Arno Hollosi	Furious Furrows...	2011-09-04T07:40:09Z	yes	1239	-
Julia A. Curtis	Support ticket #4629	2011-09-04T07:41:42Z	yes	1239	-
Tony H. Hamster	Society of Hamster Lovers	2011-09-04T07:40:40Z	-	1239	-

FIGURE 21-2 The message elements in the inbox.

Viewing a Message (*GetItem*)

To retrieve a single message, use *GetItem*. Unlike *FindItem*, *GetItem* has no 256/512 character limit for properties; it returns the full values of properties. Email attachments that must be transferred separately and the original MIME email data are excluded.

Because emails can contain HTML content, there is a risk if this content is not filtered and displayed as-is in the browser. An email can contain scripts or other dangerous HTML content. To this end, Exchange Server 2010 provides an HTML filter. However, Exchange Server 2010 mode must be requested within a SOAP header.

Requesting the Exchange 2010 Mode Within a SOAP Header

If you need the current version of Exchange Server to use new functions, you need to insert the version into the request as a SOAP header. Listing 21-9 shows the full SOAP request message: whereas the *GetItem* operation is included in the SOAP body, *RequestServerVersion* is transferred as a SOAP header.

LISTING 21-9 SOAP header *RequestServerVersion* to perform the operation in Exchange Server 2010 mode.

```xml
<?xml version="1.0" encoding="UTF-8"?>
<SOAP-ENV:Envelope xmlns:SOAP-ENV="http://schemas.xmlsoap.org/soap/envelope/"
              xmlns:t="http://schemas.microsoft.com/exchange/services/2006/types"
              xmlns:m="http://schemas.microsoft.com/exchange/services/2006/messages">
  <SOAP-ENV:Header>
    <t:RequestServerVersion Version="Exchange2010_SP1"/>
  </SOAP-ENV:Header>
  <SOAP-ENV:Body>
    <m:GetItem>
      ...
    </m:GetItem>
  </SOAP-ENV:Body>
</SOAP-ENV:Envelope>
```

In PHP, the header is generated with the *SoapHeader* class and set with *__setSoapHeaders()* (see Listing 21-10). Note that depending on your version of Exchange Server, the version string might be slightly different. To set multiple headers, the headers are passed as an array to *__setSoapHeaders()*. If *NULL* is passed, all headers are deleted.

LISTING 21-10 The PHP code to create the SOAP header.

```php
$client = new ExchangeSoapClient("./Services.wsdl", $options);
$version = array('Version' => "Exchange2010_SP1");
$header = new \SoapHeader(ExchangeSoapClient::TYPES_NS,
                     'RequestServerVersion', $version);
$client->__setSoapHeaders($header);
```

Important The IDs in Exchange 2010 are different from the those in Exchange 2007. If you want to access an element at a later time, you need to use the Exchange 2010 mode for the previous *FindItem* operation.

Because the *ExchangeSoapClient* class used in this book allows recycling, the header needs to be set only once after the instantiation.

Defining and Filtering the Message Content

Email messages contain text or HTML content. If you want to query the content, use the *BodyType* element to specify which format should be returned, as shown in the following:

```
<m:ItemShape>
  <t:BaseShape>Default</t:BaseShape>
  <t:BodyType>HTML</t:BodyType>
</m:ItemShape>
```

There are three possible values for *BodyType*: HTML, Text, and Best (which is the default, delivers HTML if available; otherwise, plain text). If the content has the wrong format, Exchange converts the content automatically into the desired format.

Because HTML messages can contain active content that might compromise security, these contents should be filtered before opened in a browser. However, it is very difficult to write a reliable HTML filter yourself. Fortunately, Exchange 2010 has a built-in HTML filter that you can specify in the *ItemShape* element:

```
<m:ItemShape>
  <t:BaseShape>Default</t:BaseShape>
  <t:FilterHtmlContent>true</t:FilterHtmlContent>
</m:ItemShape>
```

Valid values for *FilterHtmlContent* are *true* and *false*. For this function, the request has to force the processing in Exchange 2010 mode (SOAP header *RequestServerVersion*).

Requesting the Original MIME Content

The content returned in the body property is already decoded and might already be transformed or filtered. To obtain the original MIME message, specify the *IncludeMimeContent* element:

```
<m:ItemShape>
  <t:BaseShape>Default</t:BaseShape>
  <t:IncludeMimeContent>true</t:IncludeMimeContent>
</m:ItemShape>
```

Valid values for *IncludeMimeContent* are *true* and *false*.

The returned MIME message is Base-64 encoded and must be decoded for further processing. The MIME message is complete; the message contains the SMTP header, the message content, and possibly attachments.

Note Because email attachments can be large, you should consider the PHP memory requirements. Keep in mind that you might need three to four times the storage space of the email size for processing.

Request

Using the techniques from the preceding sections, you can easily create the request. Listing 21-11 shows how to retrieve two elements in a single operation.

LISTING 21-11 The *GetItem* operation—request message.

```
<m:GetItem>
  <m:ItemShape>
    <t:BaseShape>Default</t:BaseShape>
    <t:BodyType>HTML</t:BodyType>
    <t:FilterHtmlContent>true</t:FilterHtmlContent>
  </m:ItemShape>
  <m:ItemIds>
    <t:ItemId Id="AAMkADhh..." ChangeKey="CQAAABYA..."/>
    <t:ItemId Id="XBMkADh5..." ChangeKey="QACCABYg..."/>
  </m:ItemIds>
</m:GetItem>
```

The request created by using PHP has the usual pattern, as demonstrated in Listing 21-12. In the listing, *$item1* and *$item2* are result objects from a previous *FindItem* operation.

LISTING 21-12 The *GetItem* operation in PHP.

```
$param = array('ItemShape' => array('BaseShape' => 'Default',
                                    'BodyType' => 'HTML',
                                    'FilterHtmlContent' => true),
            'ItemIds' => array('ItemId' => array(
                array('Id' => $item1->ItemId->Id,
                      'ChangeKey' => $item1-> ItemId->ChangeKey),
                array('Id' => $item2->ItemId->Id,
                      'ChangeKey' => $item2-> ItemId->ChangeKey)))
);
$response = $client->GetItem($param);
```

Response

Listing 21-13 shows the response message from the *GetItem* operation in Listing 21-11. Both responses for the queried elements are saved in their own *GetItem*ResponseMessage elements instead of within items for *FindItem*. This way, you can map errors (*ResponseClass*, *ResponseCode*) at the element level.

The HTML content (*Body*) in the XML message is entity-encoded so that the HTML doesn't impact the validity of the XML message. However, the HTML in the corresponding PHP object (*$response*) is available in clear text. Keep in mind that the HTML comprises <html>, <head>, and <body> elements, not just the content of the HTML <body> element itself.

LISTING 21-13 Response message from the *GetItem* operation.

```
<m:GetItemResponse>
  <m:ResponseMessages>
    <m:GetItemResponseMessage ResponseClass="Success">
      <m:ResponseCode>NoError</m:ResponseCode>
      <m:Items>
        <t:Message>
          <t:ItemId Id="AAMkADhh..." ChangeKey="CQAAABYA..."/>
          <t:Subject>Fun at de Efteling</t:Subject>
          <t:Sensitivity>Normal</t:Sensitivity>
          <t:Body BodyType="HTML">&lt;html&gt;&#xD;
&lt;head&gt;&#xD;
&lt;meta http-equiv="Content-Type" content="text/html; charset=utf-8"&gt;&#xD;
&lt;/head&gt;&#xD;
&lt;body&gt;&#xD;
&lt;h1&gt;HTML Content&lt;/h1&gt;&#xD;
&lt;p&gt;Email with HTML content.&lt;/p&gt;&#xD;
&lt;/body&gt;&#xD;
&lt;/html&gt;&#xD;</t:Body>
          <t:Size>53200</t:Size>
          <t:DateTimeSent>2011-02-10T10:57:26Z</t:DateTimeSent>
          <t:DateTimeCreated>2011-04-19T15:46:17Z</t:DateTimeCreated>
          <t:ResponseObjects>
            <t:ReplyToItem/><t:ReplyAllToItem/><t:ForwardItem/>
          </t:ResponseObjects>
          <t:HasAttachments>false</t:HasAttachments>
          <t:IsAssociated>false</t:IsAssociated>
          <t:ToRecipients>
            <t:Mailbox>
              <t:Name>Tony H. Hamster</t:Name>
              <t:EmailAddress>tony.hamster@xmp.site</t:EmailAddress>
              <t:RoutingType>SMTP</t:RoutingType>
              <t:MailboxType>Mailbox</t:MailboxType>
            </t:Mailbox>
          </t:ToRecipients>
```

```
              <t:CcRecipients><t:Mailbox> ... </t:Mailbox></t:CcRecipients>
              <t:IsReadReceiptRequested>false</t:IsReadReceiptRequested>
              <t:From><t:Mailbox> ... </t:Mailbox></t:From>
              <t:IsRead>false</t:IsRead>
           </t:Message>
        </m:Items>
      </m:GetItemResponseMessage>
      <m:GetItemResponseMessage ResponseClass="Success">
        ...
      </m:GetItemResponseMessage>
    </m:ResponseMessages>
  </m:GetItemResponse>
```

The sender (*From*) and the recipient (*ToRecipients*, *CcRecipients*) are indicated by name and email address in *GetItem* in the *Mailbox* element. The *MailboxType* element provides more information about the address. For example, the *Mailbox* value indicates an Exchange mailbox.

> **Note** For a list and description of all values for *MailboxType*, consult the MSDN article at *http://msdn.microsoft.com/en-us/library/aa563493.aspx*.

Example

Listing 21-14 shows a full example how an email message is retrieved and displayed by using EWS. The script is created as follows:

- First, an *ExchangeSoapClient* is instantiated, and a SOAP header for Exchange 2010 is set to use the *FilterHtmlContent* function.

- The message to be displayed is specified with the *id* and *changekey GET* parameters.

> **Important** Because the request uses the Exchange 2010 mode, the previous *FindItem* operation must also be performed in Exchange 2010 mode. Otherwise, *id* and *changekey* don't match.

- The *$param* array is created and the *GetItem* operation is called.

- Afterward, certain fields of the email are written in a table (the necessary auxiliary functions are to be found at the end of the script).

This example doesn't check or solve errors, and the output of the *ToRecipients* field is simplified: the email could have several recipients.

LISTING 21-14 show-msg.php—retrieving and viewing an email.

```php
<?php
namespace net\xmp\phpbook;

require './ExchangeSoapClient.php';
require './HTMLPage.php';

$options = array('login' => 'tony', 'password' => 'confidential',
                 'CACert' => './my-ca.cer');
$client = new ExchangeSoapClient('./Services.wsdl', $options);
$header = array('Version' => 'Exchange2010_SP1');
$reqver = new \SoapHeader(ExchangeSoapClient::TYPES_NS,
                          'RequestServerVersion', $header);
$client->__setSoapHeaders($reqver);

$id = filter_input(INPUT_GET, 'id', FILTER_SANITIZE_STRING, FILTER_FLAG_STRIP_LOW);
$key = filter_input(INPUT_GET, 'changekey', FILTER_SANITIZE_STRING,
                                            FILTER_FLAG_STRIP_LOW);
$param = array('ItemShape' => array('BaseShape' => 'Default',
                                    'BodyType' => 'HTML',
                                    'FilterHtmlContent' => true),
               'ItemIds' => array('ItemId' => array('Id' => $id, 'ChangeKey' => $key))
);
$response = $client->GetItem($param);
$msg = $response->ResponseMessages->GetItemResponseMessage->Items->Message;

$page = new HTMLPage('Message');
$table = array(array('Field', 'Content'));
$table[] = addMailboxField('From', $msg->From->Mailbox);
$table[] = addMailboxField('To', $msg->ToRecipients->Mailbox);
$table[] = addStringField('Subject', $msg->Subject);
$table[] = addStringField('Sent at', $msg->DateTimeSent);
$table[] = addStringField('Size', $msg->Size);
$table[] = addBooleanField('Attachments exist', $msg->HasAttachments);
$table[] = addBooleanField('Require read receipt', $msg->IsReadReceiptRequested);
$table[] = array('content', $msg->Body->_);
$page->addTable($table, array(false, true));
$page->printPage();

function addStringField($name, $value) {
    return array($name, htmlspecialchars($value));
}

function addBooleanField($name, $value) {
    return array($name, $value ? 'yes' : 'no');
}

function addMailboxField($name, $value) {
    $value = htmlspecialchars($value->Name . ' <' . $value->EmailAddress . '>');
    return array($name, $value);
}
?>
```

Figure 21-3 shows the output of a message using the script in Listing 21-14. The HTML content was already filtered by Exchange.

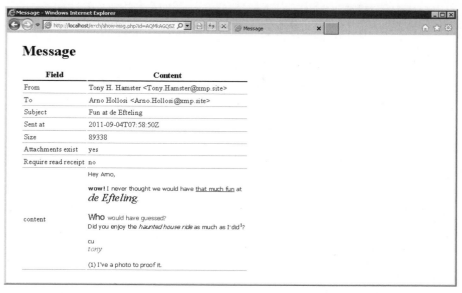

FIGURE 21-3 Output generated by the sample script msg.php.

Email Attachments (*GetAttachment*)

If an email has one or more attachments, *GetItemResponseMessage* includes the information shown in Listing 21-15, which includes file name, size and type of the attachment, and the Exchange ID of the attachment for further processing.

LISTING 21-15 Information about the attachments in the *GetItem* response message.

```
<m:GetItemResponseMessage ResponseClass="Success">
  <m:ResponseCode>NoError</m:ResponseCode>
  <m:Items>
    <t:Message>
      ...
      <t:Attachments>
        <t:FileAttachment>
          <t:AttachmentId Id="AQMkADhh..."/>
          <t:Name>CurrentPriceList.xls</t:Name>
          <t:ContentType>application/vnd.ms-excel</t:ContentType>
          <t:ContentId>dfeef8b3-e589-4c86-b463-10751e9b0906</t:ContentId>
          <t:Size>24816</t:Size>
          <t:LastModifiedTime>2011-08-19T15:46:17</t:LastModifiedTime>
          <t:IsInline>false</t:IsInline>
          <t:IsContactPhoto>false</t:IsContactPhoto>
```

```
            </t:FileAttachment>
            <t:FileAttachment> ... </t:FileAttachment>
        </t:Attachments>
        ...
        <t:HasAttachments>true</t:HasAttachments>
        ...
      </t:Message>
    </m:Items>
  </m:GetItemResponseMessage>
```

The *GetAttachment* operation is used to retrieve email attachments.

Request

Creating a request for the *GetAttachment* operation is straightforward:

```
<m:GetAttachment>
  <m:AttachmentIds>
    <t:AttachmentId Id="AQBgAEAA..."/>
  </m:AttachmentIds>
</m:GetAttachment>
```

You can specify multiple *AttachmentId* in one request. You can also use *AttachmentShape* (such as *FolderShape* and *ItemShape*) to specify properties; the *IncludeMimeContent*, *BodyType*, *FilterHtmlContent*, and *AdditionalProperties* elements are available.

The PHP code to retrieve an attachment is also short, and there is no *ChangeKey*:

```
$param = array('AttachmentIds' => array(
              'AttachmentId' => array('Id' => "AQMkADhh...")));
$response = $client->GetAttachment($param);
```

Response

Listing 21-16 shows the response. The content is essentially the same as the results returned by the *GetItem* operation. The only difference is that the content in the content element is Base-64 encoded. The content in the PHP *$response* object is already decoded.

LISTING 21-16 The *GetAttachment* operation—response message.

```
<m:GetAttachmentResponse>
  <m:ResponseMessages>
    <m:GetAttachmentResponseMessage ResponseClass="Success">
      <m:ResponseCode>NoError</m:ResponseCode>
```

```
        <m:Attachments>
          <t:FileAttachment>
            <t:AttachmentId Id="AQBgAEAA..."/>
            <t:Name>GeneralInformation.pdf</t:Name>
            <t:ContentType>application/octet-stream</t:ContentType>
            <t:ContentId>dfeef8b3-e589-4c86-b463-10751e9b0906</t:ContentId>
            <t:Content> ... </t:Content>
          </t:FileAttachment>
        </m:Attachments>
      </m:GetAttachmentResponseMessage>
    </m:ResponseMessages>
  </m:GetAttachmentResponse>
```

In PHP, you can access the content as follows:

```
$response->ResponseMessages->GetAttachmentResponseMessage->Attachments
        ->FileAttachment->Content
```

If several attachments were requested in a single *GetAttachment* operation, you access the content as follows:

```
foreach ($response->ResponseMessages->GetAttachmentResponseMessage as $msg) {
    $content = $msg->Attachments->FileAttachment->Content;
    ...
}
```

Sending a Message (*CreateItem*)

An email is sent if the *CreateItem* method creates a message element and Exchange is instructed to send this element. Exchange determines the recipient from the element and delivers the message accordingly.

If you send messages (or perform other EWS operations), EWS might not recognize the XML of the SOAP request generated by PHP because the content of the request is redundant. To avoid this problem, you need to use cloned objects instead of the array structure for parameters.

SOAP Errors Caused by References and Accessors

If a message or other elements are created, the request message might contain certain data multiple times. SOAP provides a method to reduce the size of the request: accessors (MRA, multi-reference accessor) reference data at another position. Listing 21-17 shows an example in an email message. In the listing, the sender adds herself to the *CcRecipients* element.

LISTING 21-17 The sender and Cc recipient are identical.

```
<t:From>
  <t:Mailbox>
    <t:Name>Doris D. Lass</t:Name>
    <t:EmailAddress>doris.lass@xmp.site</t:EmailAddress>
  </t:Mailbox>
</t:From>
<t:CcRecipients>
  <t:Mailbox>
    <t:Name>Doris D. Lass</t:Name>
    <t:EmailAddress>doris.lass@xmp.site</t:EmailAddress>
  </t:Mailbox>
</t:CcRecipients>
```

With the MRA method, the duplicated structure isn't necessary (see Listing 21-18). An *id* attribute is added to the first record, which is referenced by the second record by using *href*.

LISTING 21-18 Reference and accessor (MRA) reduce the size of messages.

```
<t:ToRecipients>
  <t:Mailbox id="mb1">
    <t:Name>Doris D. Lass</t:Name>
    <t:EmailAddress>doris@xmp.site</t:EmailAddress>
  </t:Mailbox>
</t:ToRecipients>
<t:ToRecipients>
  <t:Mailbox href="#mb1"/>
</t:ToRecipients>
```

Problem

PHP creates the request XML according to the described method. However, Exchange 2010 doesn't support the MRA method; instead, it returns an error (XML doesn't match schema). How can you write the PHP to create the XML in Listing 21-17?

Solution

If the operation parameters are created as objects instead of arrays in PHP and no object is used twice, PHP creates the version from Listing 21-17. Listing 21-19 shows how the solution could look. In the listing, the mailbox class is instantiated once, and for the operation parameters, the object is cloned.

LISTING 21-19 Avoiding the cloning of references and accessors.

```
class Mailbox {

    protected $EmailAddress;
    protected $Name;

    function __construct($address, $name=NULL) {
        $this->EmailAddress = $address;
        $this->Name = $name;
    }
}
$doris = new Mailbox('doris.lass@xmp.site', 'Doris D. Lass');
$param->Sender->Mailbox = $doris;
$param->CcRecipients->Mailbox = clone $doris;
```

Request

To send an email, create the email by using *CreateItem*, and then send it. You can also save the email in the Drafts folder (or in another folder).

XML Request

Listing 21-20 shows the typical properties used for this operation, which are described in the following:

- **ItemClass**   Email messages have the *IPM.Note* class

- **Subject**   Subject of the message

- **Body**   Message content

- **Sender**   Sender of the message

- **ToRecipients**, **CcRecipients**   Recipients of the message

LISTING 21-20 The *CreateItem* operation—request message to send an email.

```
<m:CreateItem MessageDisposition="SendAndSaveCopy">
  <m:Items>
    <t:Message>
      <t:ItemClass>IPM.Note</t:ItemClass>
      <t:Subject>AdventureWorks: Support ticket #45260</t:Subject>
      <t:Body BodyType="Text">Bicycle headlight is broken.</t:Body>
      <t:Sender>
        <t:Mailbox>
          <t:Name>Tony H. Hamster</t:Name>
          <t:EmailAddress>tony.hamster@xmp.site</t:EmailAddress>
```

```
          </t:Mailbox>
        </t:Sender>
        <t:ToRecipients>
          <t:Mailbox>
            <t:EmailAddress>doris.lass@xmp.site</t:EmailAddress>
          </t:Mailbox>
        </t:ToRecipients>
        <t:CcRecipients>
          <t:Mailbox>
            <t:Name>Tony H. Hamster</t:Name>
            <t:EmailAddress>tony.hamster@xmp.site</t:EmailAddress>
          </t:Mailbox>
        </t:CcRecipients>
      </t:Message>
    </m:Items>
  </m:CreateItem>
```

The *MessageDisposition* attribute determines if the email is sent or only saved. This attribute can have the following values:

- **SaveOnly**   The email is only saved (to the default folder: Drafts).
- **SendOnly**   The email is only sent and no local copy is saved.
- **SendAndSaveCopy**   The email is sent and saved (by default in the Sent Items folder).

> **Note** If you want to send a saved email at a later time, use the *SendItem* operation. You can also use *SendItem* to resend already sent emails.

If you don't want to save the email in the default folder, use *SavedItemFolderId* to specify a different folder:

```
<m:CreateItem MessageDisposition="SendAndSaveCopy">
  <m:SavedItemFolderId>
    <t:FolderId Id="fAMkAD8h..." ChangeKey="cQA3ABYA..."/>
  </m:SavedItemFolderId>
  <m:Items>
    ...
  </m:Items>
</m:CreateItem>
```

You can create and send several emails in a single *CreateItem* call. In this case, an email is saved with its own message structure within items. Therefore, ensure that the MRA method of PHP is not enabled (see the section "SOAP Errors Caused by References and Accessors," earlier in the chapter).

Creating an Email by Using PHP

Listing 21-21 shows how to use PHP to create and send an email. To do this, you use the *Mailbox* class in Listing 21-19. Instead of the array syntax, the operation parameters consist only of objects (for the request to work you need to pass *$tony* as two separate objects).

LISTING 21-21 Creating and sending an email by using *CreateItem*.

```php
<?php
namespace net\xmp\phpbook;

require './ExchangeSoapClient.php';
require './Mailbox.php';

$options = array('login' => 'tony', 'password' => 'confidential',
                 'CACert' => './my-ca.cer');
$client = new ExchangeSoapClient('./Services.wsdl', $options);

$tony = new Mailbox("tony.hamster@xmp.site");
$doris = new Mailbox("doris.lass@xmp.site");
$agnes = new Mailbox("agnes.barstow@xmp.site", "Agnes B. Barstow");

$param = new \stdClass;
$param->MessageDisposition = 'SendAndSaveCopy';
$param->Items = new \stdClass;
$param->Items->Message = new \stdClass;
$param->Items->Message->ItemClass = 'IPM.Note';
$param->Items->Message->Subject = 'AdventureWorks: Support ticket #45260';
$param->Items->Message->Body = new \stdClass;
$param->Items->Message->Body->BodyType = 'Text';
$param->Items->Message->Body->_ = 'Bicycle headlight is broken.';
$param->Items->Message->Sender = new \stdClass;
$param->Items->Message->Sender->Mailbox = $tony;
$param->Items->Message->ToRecipients = new \stdClass;
$param->Items->Message->ToRecipients->Mailbox = $doris;
$param->Items->Message->CcRecipients = new \stdClass;
$param->Items->Message->CcRecipients->Mailbox = array(clone $tony, $agnes);
$response = $client->CreateItem($param);

echo 'Email created and sent successfully.';
?>
```

Figure 21-4 shows the email created and sent in the Outlook Web App of Exchange 2010. The message content is plain text. To send the message as HTML the *Body->BodyType* in Listing 21-21 needs to be set to *HTML* and the content must be formatted as HTML.

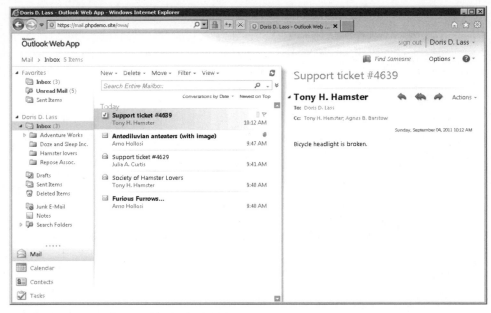

FIGURE 21-4 An email created in Outlook Web App.

Response

The response message is short and precise: the response indicates if the operation was successful or failed, but it doesn't contain any further information (see Listing 21-22).

LISTING 21-22 The *CreateItem* operation—response message.

```
<m:CreateItemResponse>
  <m:ResponseMessages>
    <m:CreateItemResponseMessage ResponseClass="Success">
      <m:ResponseCode>NoError</m:ResponseCode>
      <m:Items/>
    </m:CreateItemResponseMessage>
  </m:ResponseMessages>
</m:CreateItemResponse>
```

Deleting Messages (*DeleteItem*)

You can delete messages and other elements by using the *DeleteItem* operation. The IDs of the elements to be deleted as well as the parameter *DeleteType* that specifies which method is used are passed to the operation. Use *MoveToDeletedItems* to move the element to be deleted into the Deleted Items folder; use *HardDelete* to permanently delete the element. Use *SoftDelete* to keep the element in the folder, but mark it as deleted.

XML Messages

Listing 21-23 shows how the XML message for the request looks. The listing deletes two elements in two separate *ItemId* elements.

LISTING 21-23   The *DeleteItem* operation—XML message of the request.

```
<m:DeleteItem DeleteType="MoveToDeletedItems">
  <m:ItemIds>
    <t:ItemId Id="fAMkAD8h..." ChangeKey="cQA3ABYA..."/>
    <t:ItemId Id="CAMkAD7h..." ChangeKey="efA3ABYA..."/>
  </m:ItemsIds>
</m:DeleteItem>
```

Listing 21-24 shows the response message. For each deleted element, a separate *DeleteItem ResponseMessage* is returned.

LISTING 21-24   Response message from the *DeleteItem* operation.

```
<m:DeleteItemResponse>
  <m:ResponseMessages>
    <m:DeleteItemResponseMessage ResponseClass="Success">
      <m:ResponseCode>NoError</m:ResponseCode>
    </m:DeleteItemResponseMessage>
    <m:DeleteItemResponseMessage ResponseClass="Success">
      <m:ResponseCode>NoError</m:ResponseCode>
    </m:DeleteItemResponseMessage>
  </m:ResponseMessages>
</m:DeleteItemResponse>
```

PHP

Listing 21-25 shows the *DeleteItem* operation call in PHP.

LISTING 21-25   Deleting elements by using PHP.

```
$param = array('DeleteType' => 'MoveToDeletedItems',
    'ItemIds' => array(
        'ItemId' => array(
            array('Id' => $itemId1, 'ChangeKey' => $changeKey1),
            array('Id' => $itemId2, 'ChangeKey' => $changeKey2))));
$response = $client->DeleteItem($param);
```

The *DeleteItem* operation uses two additional parameters (*SendMeetingCancellations*, *Affected TaskOccurrences*), which you can set to delete meetings or tasks. However, meetings should be deleted with a meeting cancellation (*CancelCalendarItem*).

Summary

EWS operations provide access to the Exchange data. Use *FindFolder*, *FindItem*, and *GetItem* to query and to view folders and elements and *CreateItem* to create new elements and *DeleteItem* to delete elements. Other operations for elements are *UpdateItem*, *MoveItem*, and *CopyItem*. *UpdateItem* is introduced in the next chapter.

Elements in the Exchange database consist of properties and have an ID (*Id*) and a version (*ChangeKey*) to identify the element for operations. You indicate the properties displayed for operations by using views (*FolderShape*, *ItemShape*).

Programming EWS with PHP is basically straightforward, but because of flaws in the PHP SOAP extension and the incompatibility between EWS and PHP, the EWS schema must be modified.

The following chapter introduces contacts and explains how search expressions are used to query elements with certain properties.

Chapter 22
Contacts and Search

Microsoft Exchange provides functions to save and manage contacts. Contact elements are handled in the same manner as email messages. The *FindItem*, *GetItem*, *CreateItem*, *UpdateItem*, *DeleteItem*, *CopyItem*, and *MoveItem* operations are used in the same way for contacts.

The following sections describe the properties of contact elements in detail. The *UpdateItem* operation (which has not been described yet) is used as an example to explain how values in property groups are handled.

Afterward, you will learn how to use the *FindItem* operation to query elements with certain properties. The *Restriction* element passed as a parameter can be used to search for emails, calendar entries, or tasks.

Properties of Contacts

Contacts are elements in the Exchange database that are saved in a contact folder. These elements have the *IPM.Contact* type and are represented in SOAP messages by the *Contact* element. The *DistinguishedFolderId* for the default contact folder is contacts.

Exchange can access contacts in Microsoft Active Directory, but using Exchange Web Services (EWS), applications just have read-only access.

Standard Properties

Table 22-1 lists frequently used standard properties of a contact element. Contacts inherit the almost 40 properties of the basic element type, including: *ItemId*, *ItemClass*, *Categories*, *DateTimeCreated*, and *Subject*.

For a contact, *ItemClass* has the value *IPM.Contact*.

The *Subject* (from the basic element type) and *DisplayName* (from the contact type) properties have the same meaning, but most of the time, programs use only one of the two properties. To ensure contacts are displayed correctly in all programs, you should always use *Subject* and *DisplayName*.

TABLE 22-1 Selected properties of a contact

Property	Type	Description
Birthday	*dateTime*	Date of birth
BusinessHomePage	*anyURI*	Company website
CompanyName	*string*	Company
CompleteName	Name structure	See Table 22-2 (read-only)
ContactSource	*enumeration*	Exchange database (*Store*) or Active Directory (*ActiveDirectory*)
DisplayName	*string*	Name displayed
EmailAddresses	Sequence of email addresses	See Table 22-3
FileAs	*string*	Name for the sort or display order (Save as in Outlook)
FileAsMapping	*enumeration*	Method to automatically generate *FileAs*, for example, *LastCommaFirst*
GivenName	*string*	First name
ImAddresses	Sequence of addresses	Instant messaging addresses
Initials	*string*	Initials (first letters of middle names)
JobTitle	*string*	Position within the company
MiddleName	*string*	Middle name
PhoneNumbers	Sequence of numbers	Phone numbers
PhysicalAddresses	Sequence of addresses	See Table 22-4
Surname	*string*	Last name

Listing 22-1 shows the XML structure for a contact, including a group property (phone numbers).

LISTING 22-1 XML example for a contact.

```
<t:Contact>
  <t:ItemId Id="AQAXAEFn..." ChangeKey="EQAAABYA..." />
  <t:ItemClass>IPM.Contact</t:ItemClass>
  <t:Subject>Doris D. Lass</t:Subject>
  <t:FileAsMapping>LastCommaFirst</t:FileAsMapping>
  <t:DisplayName>Doris D. Lass</t:DisplayName>
  <t:GivenName>Doris</t:GivenName>
```

```
<t:Initials>D.</t:Initials>
<t:CompanyName>Doze and Sleep</t:CompanyName>
<t:PhoneNumbers>
  <t:Entry Key="BusinessPhone">+12 (345) 6789-0</t:Entry>
  <t:Entry Key="HomePhone">+98 (765) 43210</t:Entry>
<t:/PhoneNumbers>
<t:JobTitle>Department Manager</t:JobTitle>
<t:Surname>Lass</t:Surname>
</t:Contact>
<t:Contact>
```

Note For a complete list of the properties for a contact element, consult the MSDN article at
http://msdn.microsoft.com/en-us/library/aa581315.aspx.

Name Properties

The name properties of a contact reside in the standard properties and in the *CompleteName*
property. *CompleteName* is read-only and the values are filled in from the standard properties. Table 22-2 shows these properties and their relationship with the standard contact
properties.

If a contact is retrieved by using the *Default ItemShape* profile, only the *CompleteName*
properties are returned but not the associated name properties of the contact.

TABLE 22-2 Selected properties of *CompleteNameType* and their mapping to contact properties

Property	Contact property	Description
FirstName	*GivenName*	First name
FullName	*DisplayName*	Display name, full name in a property
Initials	*Initials*	Initials (first letters of the middle names)
LastName	*Surname*	Last name, surname
MiddleName	*MiddleName*	Middle name
Nickname	*Nickname*	Nickname
Suffix	*Generation*	Name affix, such as *Jr.* or *Sr.*
Title	*MAPI tag 0x3A45*	Salutation/title

Listing 22-2 shows an example of the XML structure for the *CompleteName* property.

LISTING 22-2 XML example for a name structure.

```
<t:Contact>
  <t:CompleteName>
    <t:FirstName>Doris</t:FirstName>
    <t:Initials>D.</t:Initials>
    <t:LastName>Lass</t:LastName>
    <t:FullName>Doris D. Lass</t:FullName>
  </t:CompleteName>
</t:Contact>
```

Properties of Email Addresses

Email addresses are a property group that can contain three saved addresses. Table 22-3 lists these properties.

TABLE 22-3 Properties of the data type email address

Property	Type	Description
_	string	Email address (content of the element "_" in PHP)
Key	enumeration	Valid values are *EmailAddress1*, *EmailAddress2*, *EmailAddress3*
MailboxType	enumeration	Type of the mailbox, such as a *Mailbox* or *OneOff*
Name	string	Name of the email account
RoutingType	string	Should always have the value SMTP

Listing 22-3 shows an example. In the listing, the email address is included in the element content, and the other properties are attributes.

LISTING 22-3 XML example of the email address structure.

```
<t:Contact>
  <t:EmailAddresses>
    <t:Entry Key="EmailAddress1">doris.lass@xmp.site</t:Entry>
    <t:Entry Key="EmailAddress2" Name="Dr. Aboba">dr.aboba@phpdemo.site</t:Entry>
  </t:EmailAddresses>
</t:Contact>
```

Address Properties

You can save three different addresses for a contact: the business address (*Business*), the home address (*Home*), and an additional address (*Other*). Use the *PostalAddressIndex* contact property to indicate which of the three addresses is used as the postal address. Table 22-4 lists the properties of an address entry.

TABLE 22-4 Properties of addresses

Property	Type	Description
City	string	City
CountryOrRegion	string	Country
Key	enumeration	Valid values are *Business*, *Home*, *Other*
PostalCode	string	Postal code
State	string	State
Street	string	Street, including street number and other details

Listing 22-4 shows how to specify the home address.

LISTING 22-4 XML example of an address.

```
<t:Contact>
  <t:PhysicalAddresses>
    <t:Entry Key="Home">
      <t:Street>Dwarfs 7</t:Street>
      <t:City>Sevenmountainville</t:City>
      <t:CountryOrRegion>Far Away Land</t:CountryOrRegion>
      <t:PostalCode>12345</t:PostalCode>
    </t:Entry>
  </t:PhysicalAddresses>
  <t:PostalAddressIndex>Home</t:PostalAddressIndex>
</t:Contact>
```

Changing a Contact (*UpdateItem*)

To change the contact data, use the *UpdateItem* operation. *UpdateItem* offers three functions to change properties:

- **SetItemField**   Sets (and overwrites) the properties of an element.

- **DeleteItemField**   Deletes a property.

- **AppendToItemField**   Adds data to an existing property. This function is allowed only for certain properties. For example, for contacts, it's allowed only for the *note* property represented by the body element.

Request

The *UpdateItem* operation can change several elements—and in each element, several properties—at the same time. Use *ItemChange* to specify elements and *Updates* for the properties that you want to change. The three change functions have the same format: the property to be changed is defined by an identifier, and the new or added data are indicated in the same structure as the elements. (You don't have to specify this data if you delete a property.) The property that is changed is declared twice: once by its name, and then by the structure. However, EWS expects both declarations, which must correspond.

> **Note** A list of the property names can be found in the types.xsd XML schema (*UnindexedField URIType* and *DictionaryURIType*) and in the MSDN article at *http://msdn.microsoft.com/en-us/ library/aa581022.aspx* (click the link to the desired sub type).

The operation also expects information regarding conflicts if the *ChangeKey* is not current, as a result of a change that occurred in the meantime. There are three possible modes (through *ConflictResolution*):

- **NeverOverwrite**   If a conflict occurs, the process is terminated with an error.
- **AlwaysOverwrite**   The current change overwrites all previous changes.
- **AutoResolve**   Exchange tries to resolve the conflict. If the conflict can be solved, the change is applied. Otherwise, Exchange returns an error.

Which mode you use depends on your requirements. Because the functionality of *AutoResolve* is quite limited, it almost always behaves like *NeverOverwrite*.

XML Request

Listing 22-5 shows the XML of an example request. The following changes are made to the properties:

- The nickname is set to a new value.

> **Note** The nickname is not displayed in Outlook Web App.

- The state is set for the home address (property group). It is apparent that the property is set twice. The key is located in the *FieldIndex* and in the *Key* attribute.

- Text is added to the note (body).

- The *Manager* property is deleted.

LISTING 22-5 *UpdateItem* operation—XML request to change a contact.

```xml
<m:UpdateItem ConflictResolution="AutoResolve">
  <m:ItemChanges>
    <t:ItemChange>
      <t:ItemId Id="AQAXAEFn..." ChangeKey="EQAAABYA..."/>
      <t:Updates>
        <t:SetItemField>
          <t:FieldURI FieldURI="contacts:Nickname"/>
          <t:Contact>
            <t:Nickname>Doribori</t:Nickname>
          </t:Contact>
        </t:SetItemField>
        <t:SetItemField>
          <t:IndexedFieldURI FieldURI="contacts:PhysicalAddress:State" FieldIndex="Business"/>
          <t:Contact>
            <t:PhysicalAddresses>
              <t:Entry Key="Business">
                <t:State>Manymountains</t:State>
              </t:Entry>
            </t:PhysicalAddresses>
          </t:Contact>
        </t:SetItemField>
        <t:AppendToItemField>
          <t:FieldURI FieldURI="item:Body"/>
          <t:Contact>
            <t:Body BodyType="Text">Expert in time travel.</t:Body>
          </t:Contact>
        </t:AppendToItemField>
        <t:DeleteItemField>
          <t:FieldURI FieldURI="contacts:Manager"/>
        </t:DeleteItemField>
      </t:Updates>
    </t:ItemChange>
  </m:ItemChanges>
</m:UpdateItem>
```

Creating the Request in PHP

Listing 22-6 shows how the *UpdateItem* operation is created in PHP and the XML structure is reflected in the array nesting of *$param*.

LISTING 22-6 Creating and starting the *UpdateItem* operation in PHP.

```php
// $itemId contains the contact's ID information
$param = array('ConflictResolution' => 'AutoResolve',
    'ItemChanges' => array(
        'ItemChange' => array(
            'ItemId' => array('Id' => $itemId->Id,
                              'ChangeKey' => $itemId->ChangeKey),
            'Updates' => array(
                'SetItemField' => array(
                    array(
                        'FieldURI' => array('FieldURI' => 'contacts:Nickname'),
                        'Contact' => array('Nickname' => 'Doribori')),
                    array(
                        'IndexedFieldURI' => array(
                            'FieldURI' => 'contacts:PhysicalAddress:State',
                            'FieldIndex' => 'Home'),
                        'Contact' => array(
                            'PhysicalAddresses' => array(
                                'Entry' => array(
                                    'Key' => 'Home',
                                    'State' => 'Manymountains'))))),
                'AppendToItemField' => array(
                    'FieldURI' => array('FieldURI' => 'item:Body'),
                    'Contact' => array(
                        'Body' => array('_' => "\nExpert in time travel.",
                                        'BodyType' => 'Text'))),
                'DeleteItemField' => array(
                    'FieldURI' => array('FieldURI' => 'contacts:Manager'))
))));
$response = $client->UpdateItem($param);
```

Figure 22-1 shows the contact before and after the *UpdateItem* operation; in Outlook Web App in the figure, the field Manager is deleted, the State is new, and Note contains an additional row. Because *AppendToItemField* adds the new text directly, the line break has to be inserted with \n, as shown in Listing 22-6.

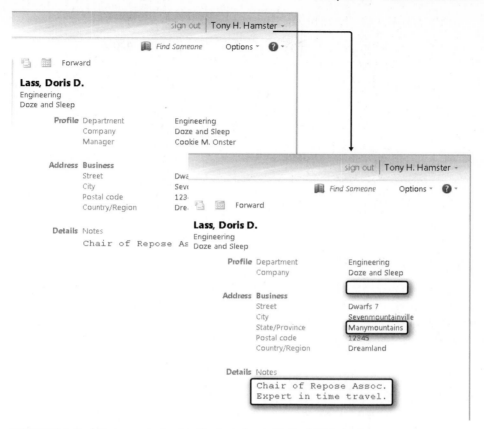

FIGURE 22-1 Updating a contact entry (Contact view in Outlook Web App).

Response

Listing 22-7 shows the response from the *UpdateItem* operation. For each element, the *ItemId* is returned with the new *ChangeKey*.

LISTING 22-7 The *UpdateItem* operation—XML response message.

```
<m:UpdateItemResponse>
  <m:ResponseMessages>
    <m:UpdateItemResponseMessage ResponseClass="Success">
      <m:ResponseCode>NoError</m:ResponseCode>
      <m:Items>
        <t:Contact>
          <t:ItemId Id="AQAXAEFn..." ChangeKey="EQAAABYB..."/>
        </t:Contact>
      </m:Items>
    </m:UpdateItemResponseMessage>
  </m:ResponseMessages>
</m:UpdateItemResponse>
```

Finding Certain Properties

Until now, we used the *FindItem* operation only to find and list the content of folders. Chapter 21, "Email and Exchange Web Services Basics," described paging and sorting search results. But if a folder (for example, the contact folder or the inbox) contains a large number of elements, it makes sense to only return elements that meet certain criteria.

In Exchange, you can do this by using search limits (restriction parameter). Using search expressions, you can create complex queries to check if properties have certain values.

Because replacement groups are used, you need to modify the XML schema for PHP to communicate with EWS.

Expressions

EWS provides different search expressions for queries:

- *Boolean* expressions to link other expressions
- Comparison expressions to compare the property values with a given value or with other properties
- Additional expressions to compare names or to check if a property exists

The combination of these expressions allows you to create almost any query. All expressions refer to the element being checked. Therefore, the combination with other elements in the query is not possible (for instance, a search similar to a *JOIN* in a relational database).

Boolean Expressions

Three *Boolean* expressions are implemented in EWS (see Table 22-5).

TABLE 22-5   Boolean expressions

Expression	Description
And	*Boolean AND* operator to combine expressions
Or	*Boolean OR* operator to combine expressions
Not	Negates the included expression

Comparison Expressions

To compare properties, use the expressions listed in Table 22-6. The first operator indicates the property that is compared, and the second operator can be a fixed value or another property.

TABLE 22-6   Expressions with two operators

Expression	Description
IsEqualTo	*True*, if the property is equal to the second operator
IsGreaterThan	*True*, if the property is greater than the second operator
IsGreaterThanOrEqualTo	*True*, if the property is greater than or equal to the second operator
IsLessThan	*True*, if the property is less than the second operator
IsLessThanOrEqualTo	*True*, if the property is less than or equal to the second operator
IsNotEqualTo	*True*, if the property is not equal to the second operator

The second operator is embedded in the *FieldURIOrConstant* element (see Listing 22-8). When comparing with a second property, use *FieldURI, IndexedFieldURI,* or *ExtendendFieldURI* instead of Constant.

LISTING 22-8   Example of the *IsGreaterThan* expression.

```
<t:IsGreaterThan>
  <t:FieldURI FieldURI="item:DateTimeCreated"/>
  <t:FieldURIOrConstant>
    <t:Constant>2011-01-01T00:00:00Z</t:Constant>
  </t:FieldURIOrConstant>
</t:IsGreaterThan>
```

Additional Expressions

Of the additional expressions provided by EWS, *Contains* (for searching and comparing strings) is the most commonly used. Table 22-7 lists the additional query expressions.

TABLE 22-7   Additional expressions

Expression	Description
Contains	Comparison of strings
Excludes	*True*, if the bitwise *AND* operator of the bit mask and the property amount to Zero
Exists	*True*, if the element has the specified property

Listing 22-9 shows an example of the *Contains* expression to find all elements whose first name begins with "A". The search mode is specified with *ContainmentMode*: full match (*FullString*), property starts with search text (*Prefixed*), or the search text is included in the property value (*Substring*). Use *ContainmentComparison* to specify how the comparison is performed: exact comparison (*Exact*), case insensitive (*IgnoreCase*), ignore diacritical markers (*IgnoreNonSpacingCharacters*) or a combination of the last two (*IgnoreCaseAndNonSpacing Characters*).

LISTING 22-9   Example of the *Contains* expression.

```
<t:Contains ContainmentMode="Prefixed" ContainmentComparison="IgnoreCase">
  <t:FieldURI FieldURI="contacts:GivenName"/>
  <t:Constant>A</t:Constant>
</t:Contains>
```

Preparation: Modifying the Schema

In EWS, Web Services Description Language (WSDL) search expressions are used with replacement groups. To solve the problems that might occur when PHP and EWS interact, you need to modify the web services schema. To do this, perform the following steps:

1. Open the local copy of the types.xsd type schema in an editor.

2. Insert the following lines into the schema (near the end, before the *xs:schema* end tag).

```
<xs:group name="SearchExpressionGroup">
  <xs:choice>
    <xs:element ref="t:Exists"/>
    <xs:element ref="t:Excludes"/>
    <xs:element ref="t:IsEqualTo"/>
    <xs:element ref="t:IsNotEqualTo"/>
    <xs:element ref="t:IsGreaterThan"/>
    <xs:element ref="t:IsGreaterThanOrEqualTo"/>
    <xs:element ref="t:IsLessThan"/>
    <xs:element ref="t:IsLessThanOrEqualTo"/>
    <xs:element ref="t:Contains"/>
    <xs:element ref="t:Not"/>
    <xs:element ref="t:And"/>
    <xs:element ref="t:Or"/>
  </xs:choice>
</xs:group>
```

3. Replace all `<xs:element ref="t:SearchExpression"/>` instances with `<xs:group ref="t:SearchExpressionGroup"/>`.

4. Change the definition of *MultipleOperandBooleanExpressionType*, as follows:

```
<xs:complexType name="MultipleOperandBooleanExpressionType" abstract="true">
  <xs:complexContent>
    <xs:extension base="t:SearchExpressionType">
      <xs:sequence>
        <xs:choice minOccurs="1" maxOccurs="unbounded">
          <xs:element ref="t:Exists"/>
          <xs:element ref="t:Excludes"/>
          <xs:element ref="t:IsEqualTo"/>
          <xs:element ref="t:IsNotEqualTo"/>
          <xs:element ref="t:IsGreaterThan"/>
          <xs:element ref="t:IsGreaterThanOrEqualTo"/>
          <xs:element ref="t:IsLessThan"/>
          <xs:element ref="t:IsLessThanOrEqualTo"/>
          <xs:element ref="t:Contains"/>
          <xs:element ref="t:Not"/>
          <xs:element ref="t:And"/>
          <xs:element ref="t:Or"/>
        </xs:choice>
      </xs:sequence>
    </xs:extension>
  </xs:complexContent>
</xs:complexType>
```

Note You need to handle this type in a special way because PHP (currently) ignores the information from *maxOccurs* relating to groups.

5. Save the schema file.

Based on these modifications, PHP generates the correct XML for search expressions in SOAP messages.

Defining the Search in a Request

You specify search expressions for the *FindItem* and *FindFolder* operations in the *Restriction* element. The example shows how to find contacts by using *FindItem*.

Listing 22-10 shows a search for contacts created in 2011 and living in Dreamsville, for which the assistant name property is not set.

LISTING 22-10 The *FindItem* operation with search limits.

```
<m:FindItem Traversal="Shallow">
  <m:ItemShape>
    <t:BaseShape>IdOnly</t:BaseShape>
  </m:ItemShape>
  <m:Restriction>
    <t:And>
      <t:IsGreaterThan>
        <t:FieldURI FieldURI="item:DateTimeCreated" />
        <t:FieldURIOrConstant>
          <t:Constant Value="2011-01-01T00:00:00Z" />
        </t:FieldURIOrConstant>
      </t:IsGreaterThan>
      <t:Contains ContainmentMode="FullString" ContainmentComparison="Exact">
        <t:IndexedFieldURI FieldURI="contacts:PhysicalAddress:City" FieldIndex="Home" />
        <t:Constant Value="Dreamsville" />
      </t:Contains>
      <t:Not>
        <t:Exists>
          <t:FieldURI FieldURI="contacts:AssistantName" />
        </t:Exists>
      </t:Not>
    </t:And>
  </m:Restriction>
  <m:ParentFolderIds>
    <t:DistinguishedFolderId Id="contacts" />
  </m:ParentFolderIds>
</m:FindItem>
```

Complete PHP Example

Using the following PHP example, you can search for contacts that fall within certain limitations. The example consists of three scripts: the search form, the search parameters for the *FindItem* operation, and the search and output of the results.

The Search Form

The search form in Listing 22-11 uses the *HTMLPage* class (see Appendix A, "Example Scripts and Data") to create the page and contains the search fields for city, postal code, country, creation date, as well as non-existing fields.

LISTING 22-11 find-contact-form.php—search form for contacts.

```php
<?php
namespace net\xmp\phpbook;
require './HTMLPage.php';

$page = new HTMLPage('Search contacts');
$page->addHTML('<form method="post" action="find-contact.php">');
$table = array(array('Field', 'Input'));
$table[] = array('Case-sensitive',
                 '<input type="checkbox" name="case" value="1">');
$table[] = array('Search mode', '<select name="mode">
   <option value="exact">Exact</option>
   <option value="prefix">Starts with</option>
   <option value="substr">Contains</option></select>');
$table[] = array('City', '<input name="City"  size="40">');
$table[] = array('Postal code', '<input name="PostalCode" size="8">');
$table[] = array('Country', '<input name="CountryOrRegion" size="40">');
$table[] = array('Created after', '<input name="created" size="12">');
$table[] = array('Field not included', '<select name="field">
    <option value="-">-</option>
    <option value="assistant">Assistant</option>
    <option value="manager">Manager</option>
    <option value="jobtitle">Position</option></select>');
$page->addTable($table, array(false, true));
$page->addHTML('<input type="submit" value="Search"/>');
$page->addHTML('</form>');
$page->printPage();
?>
```

Figure 22-2 shows the search form. Note that the content of the fields corresponds to the query in Listing 22-10.

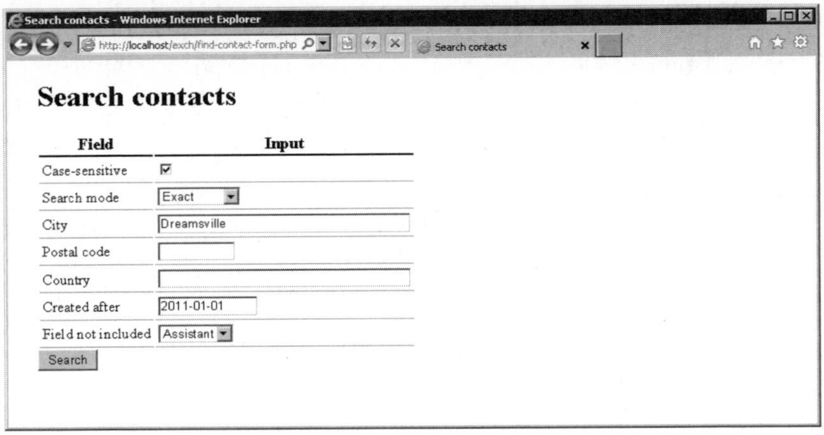

FIGURE 22-2 Completed search form for contacts.

Creating the Search Parameters

The *SearchParameters* class, including auxiliary functions to create the search parameters, is shown in Listing 22-12. This class contains the following methods:

- **getSearchParameters()** Compiles the complete parameter array. The array structure is for the most part identical to the query in Listing 22-10.

- **addHomeAddressContains()** Adds a search limit for the home address.

- **addCreatedAfter()** Adds a search limit for the creation date.

- **addNoField()** Adds a search limit for missing property fields.

- **getValue()** and **getWhiteListValue()** Auxiliary methods to retrieve data from the passed form parameters.

LISTING 22-12 SearchParameters.php—auxiliary class to create the search parameter array.

```php
<?php
namespace net\xmp\phpbook;

class SearchParameters {

    protected $values;
    protected $restrictions;
    protected $mode;
    protected $comparison;

    function __construct($values) {
        $this->values = $values;
    }
```

```php
function getParams() {
    $this->restrictions = array();
    $this->mode = $this->getWhiteListValue('mode', array('exact' => 'FullString',
                                     'prefix' => 'Prefixed',
                                     'substr' => 'Substring'), 'substr');
    $this->comparison = empty($this->values['case']) ? 'IgnoreCase' : 'Exact';
    $this->addHomeAddressContains('City');
    $this->addHomeAddressContains('PostalCode');
    $this->addHomeAddressContains('CountryOrRegion');
    $this->addCreatedAfter();
    $this->addNoField();
    $param = array('Traversal' => 'Shallow',
        'ItemShape' => array('BaseShape' => 'Default'),
        'ParentFolderIds' => array('DistinguishedFolderId' => array(
                                'Id' => 'contacts')));
    if (!empty($this->restrictions)) {
        $param['Restriction'] = array('And' => $this->restrictions);
    }
    return $param;
}


protected function addHomeAddressContains($field) {
    $value = $this->getValue($field);
    if (empty($value)) {
        return;
    }
    $contains =  array('ContainmentMode' => $this->mode,
                    'ContainmentComparison' => $this->comparison,
                    'IndexedFieldURI' => array(
                        'FieldURI' => "contacts:PhysicalAddress:$field",
                        'FieldIndex' => "Home"),
                    'Constant' => array('Value' => $value));
    if (!isset($this->restrictions['Contains'])) {
        $this->restrictions['Contains'] = array($contains);
    }
    else {
        $this->restrictions['Contains'][] = $contains;
    }
}


protected function addCreatedAfter() {
    $date = $this->getValue('created');
    if (!empty($date)) {
        $timestamp = $date . 'T00:00:00Z';
        $this->restrictions['IsGreaterThan'] = array(
            'FieldURI' => array('FieldURI' => "item:DateTimeCreated"),
            'FieldURIOrConstant' => array('Constant' => array(
                                'Value' => $timestamp)));
    }
}
```

```php
    protected function addNoField() {
        $noField = $this->getWhiteListValue('field', array('-' => false,
                                   'manager' => 'contacts:Manager',
                                   'assistant' => 'contacts:AssistantName',
                                   'jobtitle' => 'contacts:JobTitle'), '-');
        if ($noField !== false) {
            $this->restrictions['Not'] = array('Exists' => array('FieldURI' => array(
                                   'FieldURI' => $noField)));
        }
    }

    function getValue($name) {
        if (!isset($this->values[$name])) {
            return false;
        }
        return trim(filter_var($this->values[$name], FILTER_UNSAFE_RAW,
                                   FILTER_FLAG_STRIP_LOW));
    }

    function getWhiteListValue($name, $list, $default) {
        $value = $this->getValue($name);
        return isset($list[$value]) ? $list[$value] : $list[$default];
    }
  }
}
?>
```

Contact Search

The script in Listing 22-13 searches for contacts. The *FindItem* operation call is straight-forward because the *SearchParameters* class creates the required parameters. The result is returned using the *HTMLPage* class (Appendix A). The *getEntry()* function searches in the results for the home address entry.

ExchangeSoapClient is called with the *SOAP_SINGLE_ELEMENT_ARRAYS* option so that no distinction between a single hit or several hits must be made.

LISTING 22-13 find-contact.php—searching for contacts.

```php
<?php
namespace net\xmp\phpbook;
require './ExchangeSoapClient.php';
require './HTMLPage.php';
require './SearchParameters.php';

$options = array('login' => 'arno', 'password' => 'confidential',
              'CACert' => './my-ca.cer', 'features' => SOAP_SINGLE_ELEMENT_ARRAYS);
$client = new ExchangeSoapClient('./Services.wsdl', $options);
```

```
$sp = new SearchParameters($_POST);
$param = $sp->getParams();
$response = $client->FindItem($param);

$page = new HTMLPage('Contacts found');
$table = array( array('Name', 'Position', 'Company', 'City', 'Postal code', 'Country') );
$items = $response->ResponseMessages->FindItemResponseMessage[0]->RootFolder->Items;
if (isset($items->Contact)) {
    foreach ($items->Contact as $item) {
        $home = getEntry($item->PhysicalAddresses->Entry, 'Home');
        $table[] = array($item->CompleteName->FullName,
                         $item->JobTitle, $item->CompanyName,
                         $home->City, $home->PostalCode, $home->CountryOrRegion);
    }
    $page->addTable($table);
}
else {
    $page->addElement('p', 'No contacts meet the criteria.');
}
$page->printPage();

function getEntry($entries, $key) {
    foreach ($entries as $entry) {
        if ($entry->Key == $key) {
            return $entry;
        }
    }
    return null;
}
```

Figure 22-3 depicts the result of the contact search. The figure demonstrates how entries that are found are listed in a table.

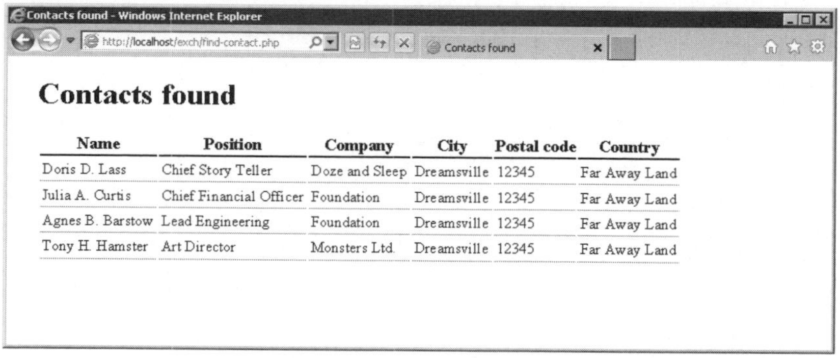

Name	Position	Company	City	Postal code	Country
Doris D. Lass	Chief Story Teller	Doze and Sleep	Dreamsville	12345	Far Away Land
Julia A. Curtis	Chief Financial Officer	Foundation	Dreamsville	12345	Far Away Land
Agnes B. Barstow	Lead Engineering	Foundation	Dreamsville	12345	Far Away Land
Tony H. Hamster	Art Director	Monsters Ltd.	Dreamsville	12345	Far Away Land

FIGURE 22-3 The result of a contact search.

Summary

Managing contacts and searching for contact information are daily tasks of professional life. Exchange provides all the necessary functions for these tasks via EWS element operations. You can also save contacts in different folders to organize the contacts.

With the *Restriction* element in the *FindItem* operation, you can query elements with certain properties. You can also combine search expressions by using *Boolean* expressions to create complex queries.

The next chapter describes the Exchange calendar function in detail and shows how a user (such as the PHP user) can impersonate another user in an EWS operation.

Chapter 23
Calendar and Impersonation

The calendar in Microsoft Exchange provides a full-fledged system to manage individual and organization-wide appointments. In addition to common calendar entries and recurring appointments with flexible intervals, Exchange also manages attendees and resources.

This chapter introduces important properties of calendar entries as well as meeting procedures and messages. You also learn about the impersonation of other users, which is important for PHP applications. The impersonation allows you to specify an application user who handles user requests to enable a continuous single sign-on.

Calendar Entries

The calendar is a folder in Exchange in which the individual appointments are saved as elements. This folder has the *DistinguishedFolderId* calendar. To query and create the elements saved in this folder, use the *FindItem*, *GetItem*, and *CreateItem* operations.

Exchange provides three calendar entry types:

- Common calendar entries intended only for the management of individual appointments

- Meetings with invited attendees and booked resources

- Recurring appointments in selectable intervals, based on a recurring master

All three types have a universal set of properties. Exchange provides additional attributes to manage attendees and specify recurring appointments. This book only describes common calendar entries and meetings.

Standard Properties

Each calendar entry (independent of its type) has a universal set of properties. The most important properties are listed in Table 23-1. Several of these properties (for example, *duration*) are read-only because they are calculated from other data.

TABLE 23-1   Selected properties of a calendar entry

Property	Type	Description
AdjacentMeetingCount	*xs:int*	Number of the events occurring close to the time of this event (read-only)
Body	String	Description
CalendarItemType	Enumeration	Event type: *Single*, *Occurrence* (appointment, part of a recurring series), *Exception* (appointment, part of a recurring series but with different properties), and *RecurringMaster* (base entry for recurring series)
ConflictingMeetingCount	*xs:int*	Number of the events coinciding with this event (read-only)
Duration	*xs:duration*	Length of the event (read-only)
End	*xs:dateTime*	End time of the event
IsAllDayEvent	*xs:boolean*	Indicates if it is an all-day event
IsRecurring	*xs:boolean*	Indicates if the appointment belongs to a series of recurring appointments (read-only); the recurring master has a value of *false*
ItemClass	String	Has the value *IPM.Appointment*
LegacyFreeBusyStatus	Enumeration	Status: *Free*, *Tentative*, *Busy*, *OOF* (out of office), *NoData*
Location	*xs:string*	Location
MeetingTimeZone	Time zone type	Writable property indicating the time zone for the event
ReminderDueBy	*xs:dateTime*	Time of the reminder
ReminderIsSet	*xs:boolean*	Indicates if the reminder function is enabled
ReminderMinutesBeforeStart	Integer	Indicates the number of minutes before the event that the reminder is sent
Start	*xs:dateTime*	Start time
Subject	*xs:string*	Subject
TimeZone	*xs:string*	Text presentation of the time zone (read-only)

Meetings

Meetings and calendar entries are different because meetings have attendees and resources. Exchange sends invitations automatically and evaluates the responses from the attendees. Table 23-2 lists several meeting properties.

TABLE 23-2 Selected meeting properties

Property	Type	Description
AllowNewTimeProposal	xs:boolean	Indicates if an attendee can suggest a new appointment
AppointmentReplyTime	xs:dateTime	The time at which the response was sent
AppointmentSequenceNumber	xs:int	Version of the calendar entry
AppointmentState	xs:int	Bit mask of the meeting status
IsCancelled	xs:boolean	Indicates if the meeting is canceled
IsMeeting	xs:boolean	Indicates if it is a meeting
IsResponseRequested	xs:boolean	Specifies if a response is required
MeetingRequestWasSent	xs:boolean	Indicates if invitations were sent to the attendees
MyResponseType	Response type	Own response to the meeting invitation
OptionalAttendees	Attendee structure	Optional attendees
Organizer	Recipients structure	Organizer of the meeting
RequiredAttendees	Attendee structure	Required attendees
Resources	Attendee structure	Resources for the meeting (room, and so on)

Recurring Appointments

Recurring appointments are appointments with the same properties occurring in specified intervals. Recurring appointments are specified in the recurring master, and although the occurrences can be handled like normal calendar entries, they are not saved in the calendar folder; instead, they're managed as attachments to the recurring master. Table 23-3 lists additional properties for a recurring master.

TABLE 23-3 Additional properties of the recurring master

Property	Type	Description
DeletedOccurrences	Array	Start time array of all deleted recurring appointments
FirstOccurrence	*OccurrenceInfoType*	ID and time of the first recurring appointment
LastOccurrence	*OccurrenceInfoType*	ID and time of the last recurring appointment
ModifiedOccurrences	Array	Array of all modified recurring appointments with ID and time
Recurrence	*RecurrenceType*	Contains all information about intervals and the time of the last recurring appointments

If an occurrence changes, it is an exception. Also, individual occurrences can be deleted. Each occurrence has an index specifying which recurring appointment corresponds to this occurrence. Exchange Web Services (EWS) provides parameters (for example, for *GetItem*) to retrieve the ID of the recurring master from an occurrence or from the index of the occurrence.

Time and Time Zones

For calendar applications, the exact time is required because the different time zones as well as the standard and summer time (Daylight Savings Time) need to be considered. The coordinated universal time (UTC) is the basis used by Exchange for internal time information.

Time Format

The time has the *xs:dateTime* format of the W3C XML schema specification—for example, *2011-09-13T10:30:00Z* (format: *year-month-day "T" hours:minutes:seconds "Z"*). The *Z* stands for the UTC time zone.

Use the *gmdate()* function to create a compliant time string in PHP:

```
$dateTime = gmdate('Y-m-d\TH:i:s\Z', $timestamp);
```

To parse such a time string and to create a timestamp (since PHP 5.3), use the *DateTime* class:

```
$time = DateTime::createFromFormat('Y-m-d\TH:i:s\Z', $dateTime, new DateTimeZone('UTC'));
$timestamp = $time->getTimestamp();
```

Specifying the Time for Requests

Because Exchange responses use the UTC time, you can specify the time for requests in EWS operations by using a UTC offset.

Use *+/-Offset* to specify the offset directly in *xs:dateTime*; for example, *2011-09-13T10 :30:00+02:00* indicates the same time as *2011-09-13T08:30:00Z*, because the suffix *+02:00* means it is two hours later than the UTC time.

You can also use the *MeetingTimeZone*, *StartTimeZone*, or *EndTimeZone* properties to specify the offset or the time zone. For a detailed description of these elements and the complex dependencies, consult the MSDN articles at *http://msdn.microsoft.com/en-us/library/ dd633701.aspx* and *http://msdn.microsoft.com/en-us/library/dd633689.aspx*.

If you use none of these elements and specify a time without offset, the local time zone of Exchange Server (Exchange 2010) is used. If you use Exchange Server 2007, you should specify the time always as UTC or with an offset.

Creating a Common Calendar Entry

A common calendar entry is created by using *CreateItem*, which is different from a meeting because no additional attendees are invited and no invitations are sent.

The Request Message

Listing 23-1 shows how to create a common calendar entry. Because this isn't a meeting with attendees, *SendMeetingInvitations* is set to *SendToNone*. Also, because the time zone is not specified for the start and end time, the local time zone of Exchange Server is used.

LISTING 23-1 Creating a new calendar entry by using *CreateItem*.

```
<m:CreateItem SendMeetingInvitations="SendToNone">
  <m:Items>
    <t:CalendarItem>
      <t:Subject>Afternoon nap</t:Subject>
      <t:Start>2011-09-13T12:00:00</t:Start>
      <t:End>2011-09-13T12:20:00</t:End>
      <t:Location>Office</t:Location>
    </t:CalendarItem>
  </m:Items>
</m:CreateItem>
```

In PHP, a calendar entry is created as shown in Listing 23-2.

LISTING 23-2 Creating a calendar entry in PHP.

```php
$param = array('SendMeetingInvitations' => 'SendToNone',
    'Items' => array('CalendarItem' => array(
        'Subject' => 'Afternoon nap',
        'Start' => '2011-09-13T12:00:00',
        'End' => '2011-09-13T12:20:00',
        'Location' => 'Office')));
$response = $client->CreateItem($param);
```

The Response Message

Listing 23-3 shows the response from the *CreateItem* operation. If the operation is successful, the *ItemId* of the created element (ID with *ChangeKey*) is returned.

LISTING 23-3 *CreateItem* operation: response message.

```xml
<m:CreateItemResponse>
  <m:ResponseMessages>
    <m:CreateItemResponseMessage ResponseClass="Success">
      <m:ResponseCode>NoError</m:ResponseCode>
      <m:Items>
        <t:CalendarItem>
          <t:ItemId Id="AQAXAEFn..." ChangeKey="DwAAABYA..."/>
        </t:CalendarItem>
      </m:Items>
    </m:CreateItemResponseMessage>
  </m:ResponseMessages>
</m:CreateItemResponse>
```

Created Entry

Listing 23-4 shows how the created calendar entry is retrieved. *$itemId* and *$changeKey* are set according to the response message. Default is used for *ItemShape*, and three additional properties are specified with *AdditionalProperties*.

LISTING 23-4 Retrieving the calendar entry.

```
$param = array('ItemShape' => array('BaseShape' => 'Default',
    'AdditionalProperties' => array(
        'FieldURI' => array(
            array('FieldURI' => 'item:ReminderDueBy'),
            array('FieldURI' => 'item:ReminderIsSet'),
            array('FieldURI' => 'item:ReminderMinutesBeforeStart')))),
    'ItemIds' => array('ItemId' => array('Id' => $itemId, 'ChangeKey' => $changeKey)));
$response = $client->GetItem($param);
```

Listing 23-5 shows the created calendar entry. Exchange automatically completes several properties; for example, *LegacyFreeBusyStatus* is set to *Busy* or the reminder (*ReminderIsSet*) is set to 15 minutes before the appointment starts (*ReminderMinutesBeforeStart*). The start and end times are returned in UTC.

LISTING 23-5 Calendar entry created.

```
<t:CalendarItem>
    <t:ItemId Id="AQAXAEFn..." ChangeKey="DwAAABYA..." />
    <t:Subject>Afternoon nap</t:Subject>
    <t:ResponseObjects><t:ForwardItem/></t:ResponseObjects>
    <t:ReminderDueBy>2011-09-13T10:00:00Z</t:ReminderDueBy>
    <t:ReminderIsSet>true</t:ReminderIsSet>
    <t:ReminderMinutesBeforeStart>15</t:ReminderMinutesBeforeStart>
    <t:HasAttachments>false</t:HasAttachments>
    <t:Start>2011-09-13T10:00:00Z</t:Start>
    <t:End>2011-09-13T10:20:00Z</t:End>
    <t:LegacyFreeBusyStatus>Busy</t:LegacyFreeBusyStatus>
    <t:Location>Office</t:Location>
    <t:CalendarItemType>Single</t:CalendarItemType>
    <t:Organizer>
       <t:Mailbox>
          <t:Name>Doris D. Lass</t:Name>
          <t:EmailAddress>doris.lass@xmp.site</t:EmailAddress>
          <t:RoutingType>SMTP</t:RoutingType>
       </t:Mailbox>
    </t:Organizer>
</t:CalendarItem>
```

Meetings

A meeting differs from a simple calendar entry because attendees are invited to the meeting, and Exchange evaluates the attendees' responses and adds the responses to the calendar entry.

Creating a Meeting

When you create a meeting, Exchange adds a calendar entry to the calendar of the organizer and the free/busy status (*LegacyFreeBusyStatus*) is set to *Busy*. Next, Exchange sends the invitations to the attendees; the invitation is saved in the inboxes of the attendees, a calendar entry is created in the attendees' calendars and their free/busy status is set to *Tentative*.

You can use *CreateItem* to create a meeting directly or *UpdateItem* to change a calendar entry into a meeting by adding attendees.

The XML Request Message

Listing 23-6 shows how to create a meeting by using the *CreateItem* operation. You specify required attendees via *RequiredAttendees*, optional attendees with *OptionalAttendees*, and resources (for example, a room) with *Resources*.

LISTING 23-6 Creating a meeting by using *CreateItem*.

```
<m:CreateItem SendMeetingInvitations="SendOnlyToAll">
  <m:Items>
    <t:CalendarItem>
      <t:Subject>Creativity meeting</t:Subject>
      <t:Start>2011-09-13T12:21:00</t:Start>
      <t:End>2011-09-13T13:00:00</t:End>
      <t:RequiredAttendees>
        <t:Attendee>
          <t:Mailbox><t:EmailAddress>tony.hamster@xmp.site</t:EmailAddress></t:Mailbox>
        </t:Attendee>
        <t:Attendee>
          <t:Mailbox><t:EmailAddress>doris.lass@xmp.site</t:EmailAddress></t:Mailbox>
        </t:Attendee>
      </t:RequiredAttendees>
      <t:OptionalAttendees>
        <t:Attendee>
          <t:Mailbox><t:EmailAddress>arno.hollosi@xmp.site</t:EmailAddress></t:Mailbox>
        </t:Attendee>
      </t:OptionalAttendees>
      <t:Resources>
        <t:Attendee>
          <t:Mailbox><t:EmailAddress>sun.porch@xmp.site</t:EmailAddress></t:Mailbox>
        </t:Attendee>
      </t:Resources>
    </t:CalendarItem>
  </m:Items>
</m:CreateItem>
```

The *SendMeetingInvitations* attribute indicates if invitations are sent:

- **SendToNone**   No invitation is sent.

- **SendOnlyToAll**   Invitations are sent to all attendees and resources.

- **SendToAllAndSaveCopy**   Invitations are sent to all attendees and a copy of the invitation is saved in the Sent Items folder.

If you change a meeting by using the *UpdateItem* operation (for example, to add or remove attendees) the following two options are available:

- **SendOnlyToChanged**   Sends messages only to added or removed attendees.

- **SendToChangedAndSaveCopy**   Same as *SendOnlyToChanged*; in addition, a copy of the message is saved in the Sent Items folder.

A Complete PHP Example

Listings 23-7 and 23-8 show how to create a meeting in PHP. Listing 23-7 creates the input form used to create a meeting. The form includes text boxes for subject, location, start, end, attendees, and resources.

LISTING 23-7 Generating an HTML form to create a meeting (add-meeting.php).

```php
<?php
namespace net\xmp\phpbook;
require './HTMLPage.php';

$page = new HTMLPage('Create meeting');
$page->addHTML('<form method="post" action="create-meeting.php">');
$table = array(array('Field', 'Input'));
$table[] = array('Subject', '<input name="subject" size="40">');
$table[] = array('Location', '<input name="location" size="40">');
$table[] = array('Start time', '<input name="start" size="9"> <input name="startT"
size="4">');
$table[] = array('End time', '<input name="end" size="9"> <input name="endT"
size="4">');
$table[] = array('Attendees', '<input name="required[]" size="30"><br />'
            . '<input name="required[]" size="30"><br />'
            . '<input name="required[]" size="30">');
$table[] = array('Optional attendees', '<input name="optional[]" size="30"><br />'
            . '<input name="optional[]" size="30">');
$table[] = array('Resources', '<input name="resource[]" size="30"><br />'
            . '<input name="resource[]" size="30">');
$page->addTable($table, array(false, true));
$page->addHTML('<input type="submit" value="Create"/>');
$page->addHTML('</form>');
$page->printPage();
?>
```

Figure 23-1 shows the completed form. Notice that the date is entered in the ISO format and the attendees are identified by their email addresses.

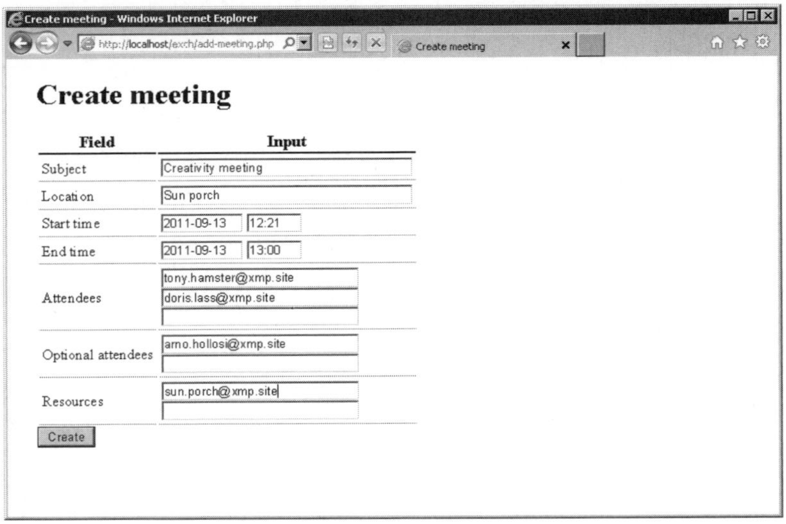

FIGURE 23-1 The completed form to create a meeting.

In Listing 23-8, the form data is evaluated and the *CreateItem* operation is called. The *get MeetingParameters()* function creates the parameters for the operation but doesn't check for errors such as the syntax of date and time. The *getValue()* function retrieves a form value and *getAttendees()* creates the array for the attendees by using the *mailbox* class (see Chapter 21, "Email and Exchange Web Services Basics").

LISTING 23-8 Creating a meeting by using the *CreateItem* operation (create-meeting.php).

```php
<?php
namespace net\xmp\phpbook;

require './ExchangeSoapClient.php';
require './HTMLPage.php';
require './Mailbox.php';

$page = new HTMLPage('Create meeting');
try {
    $param = getMeetingParameters();
    $options = array('login' => 'agnes', 'password' => 'confidential',
                     'CACert' => './my-ca.cer');
    $client = new ExchangeSoapClient('./Services.wsdl', $options);
    $client->CreateItem($param);
    $page->addElement('p', 'Meeting was created.');
```

```php
} catch (\Exception $e) {
    $page->addElement('h2', 'Error (Exception)');
    $page->addElement('p', $e);
}
$page->printPage();

function getMeetingParameters() {
    $param = array('SendMeetingInvitations' => 'SendOnlyToAll',
        'Items' => array('CalendarItem' => array(
            'Subject' => getValue('subject'),
            'Start' => getValue('start') . 'T' . getValue('startT') . ':00',
            'End' => getValue('end') . 'T' . getValue('endT') . ':00',
            'Location' => getValue('location'),
            'RequiredAttendees' => getAttendees('required'),
            'OptionalAttendees' => getAttendees('optional'),
            'Resources' => getAttendees('resource'))));
    return $param;
}

function getValue($name) {
    if (!isset($_POST[$name])) {
        throw new \Exception('Text field "$name" not specified.');
    }
    return filter_input(INPUT_POST, $name, FILTER_UNSAFE_RAW, FILTER_FLAG_STRIP_LOW);
}

function getAttendees($name) {
    if (!isset($_POST[$name]) || !is_array($_POST[$name])) {
        throw new \Exception('Text field "$name" not specified.');
    }
    $attendee = array();
    foreach ($_POST[$name] as $mail) {
        $email = trim(filter_var($mail, FILTER_SANITIZE_EMAIL));
        if (!empty($email)) {
            $attendee[] = array('Mailbox' => new Mailbox($email));
        }
    }
    if (!count($attendee)) {
        return null;
    }
    return array('Attendee' => $attendee);
}
?>
```

Figure 23-2 shows the meeting invitation in Outlook Web App. The next section explains the structure and design of a meeting invitation.

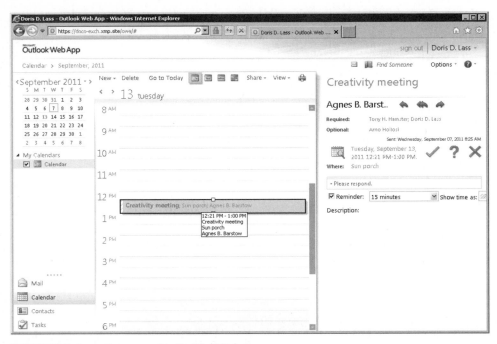

FIGURE 23-2 A meeting request in Outlook Web App.

Creating the Meeting Invitation

After the organizer creates a meeting, the meeting invitations are sent to the attendees and saved in their inboxes, and the associated calendar entries are added. The invitation (*MeetingRequest*) is explained in more detail in the following subsection.

The XML Structure

Listing 23-9 shows the structure of a meeting invitation saved in the inboxes of the attendees. The listing contains only selected properties and the complete mailbox structure is only shown for the organizer. Tony and Doris received the invitation directly (*ToRecipients*), and Arno, an optional attendee, was added to Cc (*CcRecipients*).

LISTING 23-9 Meeting invitation structure (*MeetingRequest*).

```
<t:MeetingRequest>
  <t:ItemId Id="AAMkAGM0..." ChangeKey="CwAAABYA..."/>
  <t:ItemClass>IPM.Schedule.Meeting.Request</t:ItemClass>
  <t:Subject>Creativity meeting</t:Subject>
  <t:ToRecipients>
    <t:Mailbox> ... Tony ... </t:Mailbox>
    <t:Mailbox> ... Doris ... </t:Mailbox>
  </t:ToRecipients>
  <t:CcRecipients>
    <t:Mailbox> ... Arno ... </t:Mailbox>
  </t:CcRecipients>
  <t:AssociatedCalendarItemId Id="AAMkAGM0..." ChangeKey="DwAAABYA..."/>
  <t:IsDelegated>false</t:IsDelegated>
  <t:IsOutOfDate>false</t:IsOutOfDate>
  <t:HasBeenProcessed>true</t:HasBeenProcessed>
  <t:MeetingRequestType>NewMeetingRequest</t:MeetingRequestType>
  <t:IntendedFreeBusyStatus>Busy</t:IntendedFreeBusyStatus>
  <t:Start>2011-09-13T10:21:00Z</t:Start>
  <t:End>2011-09-13T11:00:00Z</t:End>
  <t:LegacyFreeBusyStatus>Tentative</t:LegacyFreeBusyStatus>
  <t:IsMeeting>true</t:IsMeeting>
  <t:IsCancelled>false</t:IsCancelled>
  <t:MeetingRequestWasSent>true</t:MeetingRequestWasSent>
  <t:Organizer>
    <t:Mailbox>
      <t:Name>Agnes B. Barstow</t:Name>
      <t:EmailAddress>agnes.barstow@xmp.site</t:EmailAddress>
      <t:RoutingType>SMTP</t:RoutingType>
      <t:MailboxType>Mailbox</t:MailboxType>
    </t:Mailbox>
  </t:Organizer>
  <t:RequiredAttendees>
    <t:Attendee>
      <t:Mailbox> ... Agnes ... </t:Mailbox>
      <t:ResponseType>Unknown</t:ResponseType>
    </t:Attendee>
    <t:Attendee>
      <t:Mailbox> ... Tony ... </t:Mailbox>
      <t:ResponseType>Unknown</t:ResponseType>
    </t:Attendee>
    <t:Attendee>
      <t:Mailbox> ... Doris ... </t:Mailbox>
      <t:ResponseType>Unknown</t:ResponseType>
    </t:Attendee>
  </t:RequiredAttendees>
  <t:OptionalAttendees>
    <t:Attendee>
      <t:Mailbox> ... Arno ... </t:Mailbox>
      <t:ResponseType>Unknown</t:ResponseType>
    </t:Attendee>
  </t:OptionalAttendees>
</t:MeetingRequest>
```

Selected Properties

Table 23-4 lists several selected properties of the meeting invitation.

TABLE 23-4 Selected properties of a meeting invitation

Property	Description
AssociatedCalendarItemId	Points to the associated calendar entry.
HasBeenProcessed	Indicates if Exchange processed the invitation and created the associated calendar entry.
IntendedFreeBusyStatus	Status set by the organizer of the meeting. If the status is *Busy,* the status is applied if the attendee accepts the invitation.
IsOutOfDate	Indicates if the invitation is still current. If not, the invitation data might not be valid and the meeting properties should be retrieved from the calendar entry.
MeetingRequestType	Invitation message type: *NewMeetingRequest*: the message is an invitation to a new meeting. *FullUpdate, InformationalUpdate*: the message indicates that an existing invitation was changed. *Outdated*: the message is no longer current.

Responding to a Meeting Invitation

An attendee can respond to a meeting invitation in three different ways: accept, accept tentatively, or decline. Each of the three responses has a different element in the response message created by the *CreateItem* operation.

The response can refer to two different IDs: the invitation ID, or the ID of the associated calendar entry. If an attendee responds to the invitation, the invitation is automatically deleted. If an attendee responds to the calendar entry, the invitation doesn't change.

If the invitation is accepted or tentatively accepted, the calendar entry is deleted and a new calendar entry is created (*LegacyFreeBusyStatus, MyResponseType, AppointmentReplyTime*). If the invitation is declined, the calendar entry is deleted and no new entry is created.

The response is sent as *MeetingResponse* to the organizer of the meeting and saved in the organizer's inbox. The calendar entry is automatically updated. The *MeetingResponse* structure is similar to *MeetingRequest* that is presented in Listing 23-9, and the *ResponseType* element contains the response.

Accepting an Invitation

To accept an invitation, use the *CreateItem* operation to create an *AcceptItem*. Listing 23-10 shows the XML of the request. With the *MessageDisposition* attribute, you can specify if the response is only sent (*SendOnly*) or also saved (*SendAndSaveCopy*). The *SaveOnly* option should not be used for an invitation response.

LISTING 23-10 Accepting a meeting or a meeting invitation.

```
<m:CreateItem MessageDisposition="SendOnly">
  <m:Items>
    <t:AcceptItem>
      <t:ReferenceItemId Id="AAMkAGM0..." ChangeKey="CwAAABYA..."/>
    </t:AcceptItem>
  </m:Items>
</m:CreateItem>
```

Listing 23-11 shows how to accept a meeting in PHP. *$itemId* and *$changeKey* reference the meeting invitation or the associated calendar entry that is automatically created.

LISTING 23-11 Accepting a meeting in PHP.

```
$param = array('MessageDisposition' => 'SendOnly',
    'Items' => array(
        'AcceptItem' => array(
            'ReferenceItemId' => array('Id' => $itemId, 'ChangeKey' => $changeKey))));
$response = $client->CreateItem($param);
```

Listing 23-12 shows the XML response to the meeting acceptance, containing the new IDs for the calendar entry and for the (deleted) meeting request.

LISTING 23-12 XML response to the *CreateItem* operation to accept a meeting.

```
<m:CreateItemResponse003E
  <m:ResponseMessages>
    <m:CreateItemResponseMessage ResponseClass="Success">
      <m:ResponseCode>NoError</m:ResponseCode>
      <m:Items>
        <t:CalendarItem>
          <t:ItemId Id="AAAWAEp1..." ChangeKey="DwAAABYA..."/>
        </t:CalendarItem>
        <t:MeetingRequest>
          <t:ItemId Id="AAAWAEp1..." ChangeKey="CwAAABYA..."/>
        </t:MeetingRequest>
      </m:Items>
    </m:CreateItemResponseMessage>
  </m:ResponseMessages>
</m:CreateItemResponse003E
```

Tentatively Accepting an Invitation

To accept an invitation tentatively, use the *CreateItem* operation to create a *Tentatively AcceptItem*. Listing 23-13 shows the XML request that has the same structure as *AcceptItem*.

LISTING 23-13 XML request to tentatively accept a meeting.

```
<m:CreateItem MessageDisposition="SendOnly">
  <m:Items>
    <t:TentativelyAcceptItem>
      <t:ReferenceItemId Id="AAMkAGM0..." ChangeKey="CwAAABYA..."/>
    </t:TentativelyAcceptItem>
  </m:Items>
</m:CreateItem>
```

Declining an Invitation

To decline a meeting invitation, send a *DeclineItem* message that has the same structure as the other two response types. For all three types, you can set additional message properties. Listing 23-14 shows how an additional message is added in the message sent to the organizer.

LISTING 23-14 Declining a meeting and sending a message to the organizer.

```
<m:CreateItem MessageDisposition="SendOnly">
  <m:Items>
    <t:DeclineItem>
      <t:Body BodyType="Text">I have to feed my hamsters.</t:Body>
      <t:ReferenceItemId Id="AAMkAGM0..." ChangeKey="CwAAABYA..."/>
    </t:DeclineItem>
  </m:Items>
</m:CreateItem>
```

The generated rejection for the meeting invitation is shown in Figure 23-3. The text is part of the message.

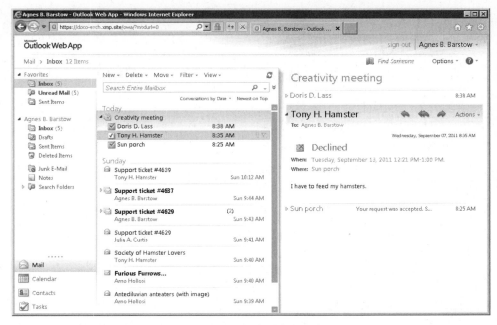

FIGURE 23-3 Declining a meeting invitation (Outlook Web App view).

A Complete PHP Example

Listing 23-15 shows a complete example of a declined meeting invitation.

First *Items->MeetingRequest* searches the inbox for meeting invitations. Then, in the listing, the first invitation is selected (*$items[0]*).

Next, the meeting invitation is retrieved and the data is displayed. The invitation is declined with a *DeclineItem* message.

And finally, the SOAP response (IDs of the invitation and the calendar entry) is displayed.

LISTING 23-15 Declining a meeting invitation (answer-meeting-request.php).

```php
<?php
namespace net\xmp\phpbook;
require './ExchangeSoapClient.php';
require './HTMLPage.php';

$page = new HTMLPage('Decline meeting request');
$options = array('login' => 'tony', 'password' => 'confidential',
                 'CACert' => './my-ca.cer');
$client = new ExchangeSoapClient('./Services.wsdl', $options);
```

```php
// Search inbox
$param = array('Traversal' => 'Shallow',
    'ItemShape' => array('BaseShape' => 'IdOnly'),
    'ParentFolderIds' => array('DistinguishedFolderId' => array('Id' => 'inbox')));
$response = $client->FindItem($param);

// Select the first meeting invitation
$item = $response->ResponseMessages->FindItemResponseMessage->RootFolder
                ->Items->MeetingRequest;
$item = $item[0];

// Retrieve selected meeting invitation
$param = array('ItemShape' => array('BaseShape' => 'Default'),
    'ItemIds' => array('ItemId' => array('Id' => $item->ItemId->Id,
                                    'ChangeKey' => $item->ItemId->ChangeKey)));
$response = $client->GetItem($param);
$item = $response->ResponseMessages->GetItemResponseMessage->Items->MeetingRequest;

// Display meeting invitation
$table = array(array('Field', 'value'));
$table[] = array('Subject', $item->Subject);
$table[] = array('Start time', $item->Start);
$table[] = array('End time', $item->End);
$table[] = array('Location', $item->Location);
$table[] = array('Organizer', $item->Organizer->Mailbox->Name);
$table[] = array('ItemID (before): ', splitString($item->ItemId->Id));
$table[] = array('CalendarItemID (before): ', splitString($item-
>AssociatedCalendarItemId->Id));
$page->addTable($table);

// Send decline message
$param = array('MessageDisposition' => 'SendOnly',
    'Items' => array('DeclineItem' => array(
            'ReferenceItemId' => array('Id' => $item->ItemId->Id,
                                    'ChangeKey' => $item->ItemId->ChangeKey),
            'Body' => array('BodyType' => 'Text',
                            '_' => 'I have to feed my hamsters.'))));
$response = $client->CreateItem($param);

// Display response
$page->addElement('h2', 'SOAP response message');
$items = $response->ResponseMessages->CreateItemResponseMessage->Items;
$table = array(array('Field', 'Value'));
$table[] = array('ItemID (after): ', splitString($items->MeetingRequest->ItemId->Id));
$table[] = array('CalendarItemID (after): ',
                splitString($items->CalendarItem->ItemId->Id));
$page->addTable($table);
$page->printPage();

// Auxiliary function: Insert space to allow line break
function splitString($str) {
    return preg_replace('/(.{33})/', '$1 ', $str);
}
?>
```

Figure 23-4 shows the output of the scripts and the arrow points to the different IDs of the meeting invitation before and after the function call. Because the meeting is declined, the ID of the associated calendar entry doesn't change.

However, you can accept the invitation by replacing *DeclineItem* with *AcceptItem* or *TentativelyAcceptItem* in the script.

Note The start and end time are displayed in UTC, although the local time was used (see the section "Time and Time Zones," earlier in the chapter).

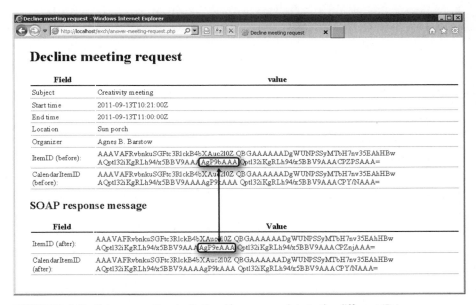

FIGURE 23-4 Declining a meeting invitation (the arrow points to the different IDs).

Canceling a Meeting

You can cancel a meeting by simply deleting the associated entry from the calendar by using *DeleteItem*. You can also create a message canceling the meeting by using *CancelCalendarItem*.

The Request Message

Use the *CreateItem* operation to cancel the meeting. Like email messages, this message has a *MessageDisposition* attribute. *ReferenceItemId* contains the ID of the meeting to be deleted, and *NewBodyContent* (not *Body*!) adds text to the message. Listing 23-16 shows the XML message of the request.

LISTING 23-16 Declining a meeting—the XML message of the request.

```
<m:CreateItem MessageDisposition="SendAndSaveCopy">
  <m:Items>
    <t:CancelCalendarItem>
      <t:Subject>Creativity meeting canceled</t:Subject>
      <t:IsReadReceiptRequested>true</t:IsReadReceiptRequested>
      <t:ReferenceItemId Id="AQAXAEFn..." ChangeKey="DwAAABYA..."/>
      <t:NewBodyContent BodyType="Text">We've run out of ideas.</t:NewBodyContent>
    </t:CancelCalendarItem>
  </m:Items>
</m:CreateItem>
```

Listing 23-17 shows how to use PHP to create and send the decline message.

LISTING 23-17 Declining a meeting in PHP.

```
$param = array('MessageDisposition' => 'SendAndSaveCopy',
    'Items' => array(
        'CancelCalendarItem' => array(
            'Subject' => 'Creativity meeting canceled',
            'IsReadReceiptRequested' => true,
            'ReferenceItemId' => array('Id'=>$itemId, 'ChangeKey'=>$changeKey),
            'NewBodyContent' => array('BodyType' => 'Text',
                                      '_' => "We've run out of ideas."),
)));
$response = $client->CreateItem($param);
```

Figure 23-5 shows the declined meeting in Outlook Web App. Notice that the content of *NewBodyContent* is the message body.

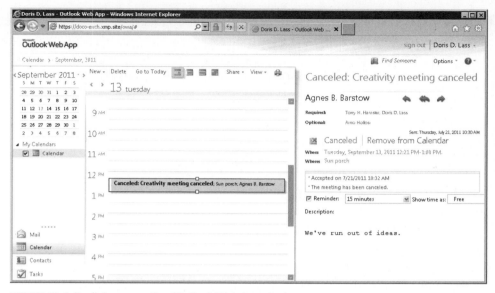

FIGURE 23-5 Declining a meeting (Outlook Web App view).

The Response Message

The response is a common *CreateItemResponse*, containing the ID of the deleted calendar entry, as shown in Listing 23-18.

LISTING 23-18 Declining a meeting—the XML response message.

```xml
<m:CreateItemResponse>
  <m:ResponseMessages>
    <m:CreateItemResponseMessage ResponseClass="Success">
      <m:ResponseCode>NoError</m:ResponseCode>
      <m:Items>
        <t:CalendarItem>
          <t:ItemId Id="AQAXAEFn..." ChangeKey="DwAAABYA..."/>
        </t:CalendarItem>
      </m:Items>
    </m:CreateItemResponseMessage>
  </m:ResponseMessages>
</m:CreateItemResponse>
```

Appointment Conflicts

To determine if other entries are adjacent to or conflict with a calendar entry, query the *ConflictingMeetingCount* and *AdjacentMeetingCount* properties. You can query information to the adjacent or conflicting entries by using the *ConflictingMeetings* and *AdjacentMeetings* properties.

The Request Message

Because the properties for adjacent or conflicting appointments are calculated, you can query them only for a *GetItem* operation but not for a *FindItem* operation.

The XML Request Message

Listing 23-19 shows the XML request. In the listing, you use *GetItem* to retrieve the information on adjacent or conflicting appointments. For the *ItemShape Default*, you have to specify the properties with *AdditionalProperties* or set *ItemShape* to *AllProperties*.

LISTING 23-19 An XML request to identify adjacent and conflicting calendar entries.

```
<m:GetItem>
  <m:ItemShape>
    <t:BaseShape>Default</t:BaseShape>
    <t:AdditionalProperties>
      <t:FieldURI FieldURI="calendar:ConflictingMeetingCount" />
      <t:FieldURI FieldURI="calendar:AdjacentMeetingCount" />
      <t:FieldURI FieldURI="calendar:ConflictingMeetings" />
      <t:FieldURI FieldURI="calendar:AdjacentMeetings" />
    </t:AdditionalProperties>
  </m:ItemShape>
  <m:ItemIds>
    <t:ItemId Id="AQAXAEFn..." ChangeKey="DwAAABYA..." />
  </m:ItemIds>
</m:GetItem>
```

Using PHP to Identify Calendar Conflicts

Listing 23-20 shows the PHP section to create and call the operation.

LISTING 23-20 Identifying adjacent and conflicting calendar entries in PHP.

```php
$param = array('ItemShape' => array('BaseShape' => 'Default',
    'AdditionalProperties' => array(
        'FieldURI' => array(
            array('FieldURI' => 'calendar:ConflictingMeetingCount'),
            array('FieldURI' => 'calendar:AdjacentMeetingCount'),
            array('FieldURI' => 'calendar:ConflictingMeetings'),
            array('FieldURI' => 'calendar:AdjacentMeetings')))),
    'ItemIds' => array(
        'ItemId' => array('Id'=> $itemId, 'ChangeKey' => $changeKey)));
$response = $client->GetItem($param);
```

The Response Message

For each appointment, the ID (*ItemId*), subject (*Subject*), start time (*Start*), end time (*End*), free/busy data (*LegacyFreeBusyStatus*), and location (*Location*) are returned.

The *GetItemResponse* contains the required information about the adjacent or conflicting entries, as presented in Listing 23-21.

LISTING 23-21 The search operation response (short version).

```xml
<m:GetItemResponse>
  <m:ResponseMessages>
    <m:GetItemResponseMessage ResponseClass="Success">
      <m:ResponseCode>NoError</m:ResponseCode>
      <m:Items>
        <t:CalendarItem>
          <t:ItemId Id="AQAXAEFn..." ChangeKey="DwAAABYA..." />
          <t:Subject>Creativity meeting</t:Subject>
          <t:Start>2011-09-13T10:21:00Z</t:Start>
          <t:End>2011-09-13T11:00:00Z</t:End>
          <t:ConflictingMeetingCount>1</t:ConflictingMeetingCount>
          <t:AdjacentMeetingCount>1</t:AdjacentMeetingCount>
          <t:ConflictingMeetings>
            <t:CalendarItem>
              <t:ItemId Id="AQAXAEFn..." ChangeKey="DwAAABYA..." />
              <t:Subject>Design meeting</t:Subject>
              <t:Start>2011-09-13T09:30:00Z</t:Start>
              <t:End>2011-09-13T10:30:00Z</t:End>
              <t:LegacyFreeBusyStatus>Busy</t:LegacyFreeBusyStatus>
              <t:Location>Office Doris</t:Location>
            </t:CalendarItem>
          </t:ConflictingMeetings>
          <t:AdjacentMeetings>
            <t:CalendarItem>
              <t:ItemId Id="AQAXAEFn..." ChangeKey="DwAAABYA..." />
              <t:Subject>Customer presentation</t:Subject>
              <t:Start>2011-09-13T11:00:00Z</t:Start>
```

```
                    <t:End>2011-09-13T12:00:00Z</t:End>
                    <t:LegacyFreeBusyStatus>Busy</t:LegacyFreeBusyStatus>
                    <t:Location />
                  </t:CalendarItem>
                </t:AdjacentMeetings>
              </t:CalendarItem>
            </m:Items>
          </m:GetItemResponseMessage>
        </m:ResponseMessages>
      </m:GetItemResponse>
```

Listing 23-24 shows an evaluation example for this response in PHP.

Searching the Calendar

Even though you can query entries in the calendar folder with the *FindItem* operation, this search is not efficient: for recurring appointments only, the master entry is displayed, but not all consecutive appointments based on the master entry. In Exchange, these appointments are managed as attachments to the recurring master. To determine if there are recurring appointments within a certain time period, you would need to search for the recurring masters, request the attachments, and derive the time for the recurring appointments.

Fortunately, Exchange provides a function that performs this complex task. In a *FindItem* operation, *CalendarView* displays all appointments (even recurring appointments) within a certain time period.

The Request Message

Listing 23-22 shows the XML request. *CalendarView* has two attributes: *StartDate* and *EndDate*. In the listing, the time is specified with a two-hour UTC offset and *IdOnly* is used for *ItemShape*.

LISTING 23-22 An XML request from the *FindItem* operation with *CalendarView*.

```
<m:FindItem Traversal="Shallow">
  <m:ItemShape>
    <t:BaseShape>IdOnly</t:BaseShape>
  </m:ItemShape>
  <m:CalendarView StartDate="2011-09-12T00:00:00+02:00"
                  EndDate="2011-09-16T23:59:59+02:00" />
  <m:ParentFolderIds>
    <t:DistinguishedFolderId Id="calendar" />
  </m:ParentFolderIds>
</m:FindItem>
```

The Response Message

The response from the search operation with *CalendarView* is identical to the response messages from a *FindItem* operation (see Listing 23-23).

LISTING 23-23 *FindItem* operation with *CalendarView*: response message (short version).

```
<m:FindItemResponse>
  <m:ResponseMessages>
    <m:FindItemResponseMessage ResponseClass="Success">
      <m:ResponseCode>NoError</m:ResponseCode>
      <m:RootFolder TotalItemsInView="5" IncludesLastItemInRange="true">
        <t:Items>
          <t:CalendarItem>
            <t:ItemId Id="AQAXAEFn..." ChangeKey="DwAAABYA..." />
          </t:CalendarItem>
          <t:CalendarItem>
            <t:ItemId Id="cQAXAEF3..." ChangeKey="DwAxxBYv..." />
          </t:CalendarItem>
          ...
        </t:Items>
      </m:RootFolder>
    </m:FindItemResponseMessage>
  </m:ResponseMessages>
</m:FindItemResponse>
```

A Complete PHP Example

The following example uses the calendar shown in Figure 23-6. The week of September 12th through the 16th contains the recurring creative meeting with one changed appointment on Wednesday and two individual appointments on Tuesday.

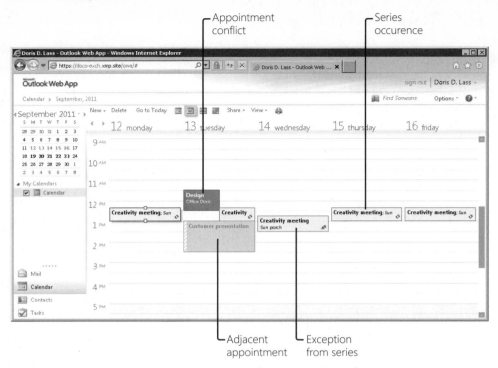

FIGURE 23-6 Appointments between September 12th and September 16th.

In Listing 23-24, the appointments within this time period are queried, and for the third entry (creative meeting on Tuesday), adjacent appointments and appointment conflicts are displayed. Appointments are queried with the *CalendarView* parameter to also show recurring appointments.

To view conflicts and adjacent appointments, *AdditionalProperties* adds additional properties to the Default-*Baseshape* of *GetItem*.

Note that in Listing 23-24, the *ExchangeSoapClient* is used with the SOAP_SINGLE_ELEMENT_ ARRAYS option. For this reason, the *FindItemResponseMessage* must be accessed with *$response-> ResponseMessages->FindItemResponseMessage[0]*.

LISTING 23-24 view-calendar.php—displaying appointments in the calendar with *CalendarView*.

```php
<?php
namespace net\xmp\phpbook;
require './ExchangeSoapClient.php';
require './HTMLPage.php';
```

```php
$options = array('login' => 'doris', 'password' => 'confidential',
                 'CACert' => './my-ca.cer',
                 'features' => SOAP_SINGLE_ELEMENT_ARRAYS);
$client = new ExchangeSoapClient('./Services.wsdl', $options);

// Search for appointments within the given time frame
$param = array('Traversal' => 'Shallow',
    'ItemShape' => array('BaseShape' => 'Default',),
    'CalendarView' => array(
        'StartDate' => '2011-09-12T00:00:00',
        'EndDate' => '2011-09-16T23:59:59'),
    'ParentFolderIds' => array(
        'DistinguishedFolderId' => array('Id' => 'calendar')));
$response = $client->FindItem($param);

$page = new HTMLPage('Calendar search');
$items = $response->ResponseMessages->FindItemResponseMessage[0]
                ->RootFolder->Items->CalendarItem;
showMeetings('Appointments in the given time frame', $items, $page);

// Select any appointment and show adjacent appointments and conflicts
$item = $items[2];
$param = array('ItemShape' => array(
                    'BaseShape' => 'Default',
                    'AdditionalProperties' => array(
                        'FieldURI' => array(
                            array('FieldURI' => 'calendar:ConflictingMeetingCount'),
                            array('FieldURI' => 'calendar:AdjacentMeetingCount'),
                            array('FieldURI' => 'calendar:ConflictingMeetings'),
                            array('FieldURI' => 'calendar:AdjacentMeetings')))),
                'ItemIds' => array(
                    'ItemId' => array('Id' => $item->ItemId->Id,
                                      'ChangeKey' => $item->ItemId->ChangeKey)));
$response = $client->GetItem($param);

$item = $response->ResponseMessages->GetItemResponseMessage[0]
                ->Items->CalendarItem[0];
if ($item->ConflictingMeetingCount) {
    showMeetings('Conflicting meetings',
                $item->ConflictingMeetings->CalendarItem, $page, false);
}
if ($item->AdjacentMeetingCount) {
    showMeetings('Adjacent appointments',
                $item->AdjacentMeetings->CalendarItem, $page, false);
}
$page->printPage();

function showMeetings($name, $items, $page, $showType=true) {
```

```
    $page->addElement('h2', $name);
    $table = array(array('Subject', 'Start', 'End', 'Status'));
    if ($showType) {
        $table[0][] = 'Type';
    }
    foreach ($items as $item) {
        $data = array($item->Subject, $item->Start, $item->End,
                      $item->LegacyFreeBusyStatus);
        if ($showType) {
            $data[] = $item->CalendarItemType;
        }
        $table[] = $data;
    }
    $page->addTable($table);
}
?>
```

Figure 23-7 shows the result of the calendar search.

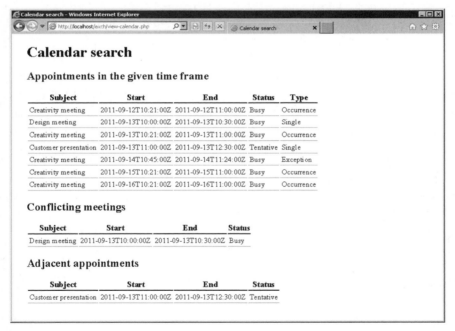

FIGURE 23-7 The result of the calendar search.

In the figure, all seven appointments are listed and the individual appointments have the type *Single*, recurring appointments have the type *Occurrence*, and the exception on Wednesday has the type *Exception*. The start and end times are specified in UTC and should be converted into the appropriate time zone.

Impersonation

Until now the user whose mailbox was accessed was used for NT LAN Manager (NTLM) authentication to connect to the EWS. The drawback of this method is that you need to know the password of the user, because you must specify the password while instantiating *ExchangeSoapClient*.

Especially for Internet applications in your own organization, this means that you cannot use a significant advantage: although users are already logged on to the domain and the PHP application can process the Windows single sign-on authentication, the password must be reentered to access the mailbox.

With impersonation, EWS offers a simple solution: you can grant a user the right to impersonate other users. This means that you can grant the PHP application user the right to impersonate mailbox users.

Granting Impersonation Rights

To grant a user the right to impersonate other users, use the *New-ManagementRole Assignment* cmdlet of the Exchange Management Shell.

```
New-ManagementRoleAssignment -Name:<Name> -Role:ApplicationImpersonation -User:<User>
```

The *<Name>* is freely selectable and serves as ID for the right added to the Role-Based Access Control (RBAC) database. As a user, you must specify a domain user because Exchange Server (or the server with the Exchange Client Access server role) doesn't recognize local web server users (for example, application pool users).

The command grants the user the right to impersonate all other users. You can specify restrictions while granting the right: you can limit the right to only impersonate the users within a certain organizational unit.

```
New-ManagementRoleAssignment -Name:<Name> -Role:ApplicationImpersonation
   -User:<User> -RecipientOrganizationalUnitScope:<Name of the OU>
```

With definable managements scopes (*ManagementScope*), you can grant granular rights. To grant the user *PHPWebUser* the right to impersonate only the user Tony (principal tony@xmp.site), use the following script:

```
New-ManagementScope -Name:exchPHPTony
   -RecipientRestrictionFilter "UserPrincipalName -eq 'tony@xmp.site'"
New-ManagementRoleAssignment -Name:exchImpersPHPWeb -Role:ApplicationImpersonation
   -User:PHPWebUser -CustomRecipientWriteScope:exchPHPTony
```

> **Note** This description applies only to Exchange Server 2010. For more information about grant-ing rights in Exchange Server 2007 consult the article on MSDN at *http://msdn.microsoft.com/en-us/library/bb204095%28v=EXCHG.80%29.aspx*.

Impersonation in EWS Operations

The impersonation is specified in the SOAP *ExchangeImpersonation* header of the request message, as shown in the *FindItem* operation in Listing 23-25.

LISTING 23-25 Impersonation of other users using the SOAP *ExchangeImpersonation* header.

```
<SOAP-ENV:Envelope xmlns:SOAP-ENV="http://schemas.xmlsoap.org/soap/envelope/"
                   xmlns:t="http://schemas.microsoft.com/exchange/services/2006/types"
                   xmlns:m="http://schemas.microsoft.com/exchange/services/2006/messages">
<SOAP-ENV:Header>
  <t:ExchangeImpersonation>
    <t:ConnectingSID>
      <t:PrincipalName>doris@xmp.site</t:PrincipalName>
    </t:ConnectingSID>
  </t:ExchangeImpersonation>
</SOAP-ENV:Header>
<SOAP-ENV:Body>
  <m:FindItem Traversal="Shallow">
    <m:ItemShape>
      <t:BaseShape>IdOnly</t:BaseShape>
    </m:ItemShape>
    <m:CalendarView StartDate="2011-09-12T00:00:00" EndDate="2011-09-16T23:59:59" />
    <m:ParentFolderIds>
      <t:DistinguishedFolderId Id="calendar" />
    </m:ParentFolderIds>
  </m:FindItem>
</SOAP-ENV:Body>
</SOAP-ENV:Envelope>
```

Three methods are available to specify an impersonated user: principal name, SID, and email address.

Impersonation by Using Principal Names

Listing 23-26 shows the SOAP header structure if you specify the principal name by using *PrincipalName*. Although the principal name is written like an email address, it does not nec-essarily have to be identical to the user's primary email address. For example, Doris, who has the logon name *doris* in the domain *xmp.site*, has a principal name of *doris@xmp.site*, but a primary email address of *doris.lass@xmp.site*. It is good practice though that the user's princi-pal name and the primary email address are the same.

LISTING 23-26 Impersonation using the principal.

```
<t:ExchangeImpersonation>
  <t:ConnectingSID>
    <t:PrincipalName>doris@xmp.site</t:PrincipalName>
  </t:ConnectingSID>
</t:ExchangeImpersonation>
```

Listing 23-27 shows how to specify the SOAP header in PHP.

LISTING 23-27 Specifying the SOAP header for impersonation by using the principal in PHP.

```
$header = array('ConnectingSID' => array('PrincipalName' => 'doris@xmp.site'));
$impersonate = new \SoapHeader(ExchangeSoapClient::TYPES_NS,
                              'ExchangeImpersonation', $header);
$client->__setSoapHeaders($impersonate);
```

Caution If you want to indicate additional SOAP headers (for example, for the EWS version), you need to specify all headers in a single *__setSoapHeaders()* call.

Impersonation by Using Email Addresses

You also can define the impersonated user by using his primary email address, as illustrated in Listing 23-28.

LISTING 23-28 Impersonation using the primary email address.

```
<t:ExchangeImpersonation>
  <t:ConnectingSID>
    <t:PrimarySmtpAddress>doris.lass@xmp.site</t:PrimarySmtpAddress>
  </t:ConnectingSID>
</t:ExchangeImpersonation>
```

Listing 23-29 shows how to specify the SOAP header in PHP.

LISTING 23-29 Impersonation using the primary email address in PHP.

```
$header = array('ConnectingSID' => array('PrimarySmtpAddress' => 'doris.lass@xmp.site'));
$impersonate = new \SoapHeader(ExchangeSoapClient::TYPES_NS,
                              'ExchangeImpersonation', $header);
$client->__setSoapHeaders($impersonate);
```

Impersonation by Using Security IDs (SID)

The third method for specifying the impersonated user is to use the SID of the user, as demonstrated in Listing 23-30.

LISTING 23-30 Impersonation using the SID.

```
<t:ExchangeImpersonation>
  <t:ConnectingSID>
    <t:SID>S-1-5-21-1465576585-1264251571-1973391373-1108</t:SID>
  </t:ConnectingSID>
</t:ExchangeImpersonation>
```

Listing 23-31 shows how to specify the SOAP header in PHP.

LISTING 23-31 Impersonation using the SID in PHP.

```
$header = array('ConnectingSID' => array(
                'SID' => 'S-1-5-21-1465576585-1264251571-1973391373-1108'));
$impersonate = new \SoapHeader(ExchangeSoapClient::TYPES_NS,
                              'ExchangeImpersonation', $header);
$client->__setSoapHeaders($impersonate);
```

Additional Steps

The EWS provides many more operations that are beyond the scope of this book. If you approach the task of EWS programming, you will repeatedly encounter communication problems between PHP and EWS.

Be sure to disable Web Services Description Language caching for the PHP page in php.ini or with the *cache_wsdl=WSDL_CACHE_NONE* option during the instantiation of *ExchangeSoapClient*.

The *__getLastRequest()* and *__getLastResponse()* functions are helpful to check which XML messages were sent and received.

Pay attention to the encoding: all requests and data must be UTF-8 encoded. If PHP complains about missing parameters while creating request messages, the parameters are either incorrectly embedded in the array or, because of an error in the PHP SOAP extension, PHP erroneously interprets an instruction as mandatory. In the latter case, you must modify the schema (for example, you have to set *minOccurs* for single elements instead of for *xs:sequence* or *xs:choice*).

The same applies if the request created with PHP is missing parameters: the cause usually is inaccurate interpretation of the schema or wrong array parameter embedding.

The developer documentation on MSDN includes many examples and additional explanations. You can find the documentation at *http://msdn.microsoft.com/en-us/library/dd877012%28EXCHG.140%29.aspx*.

Summary

This chapter explained the basics of working with calendar entries, how to invite attendees to a meeting, and how to accept or decline a meeting invitation. The *CalendarView* is a search method with which you can easily find all appointments and recurring appointments in a certain time period.

With the impersonation of other users, you can realize a consistent single sign-on in PHP because the connection is authenticated on the NTLM level with the PHP application user, and the mailbox of the end-user can be accessed.

Because the PHP SOAP extension cannot process WSDL correctly, you need to modify the EWS schema (usually types.xsd). But don't be discouraged: as you can see in the PHP code examples, the programming of EWS is straightforward after you have mastered the initial obstacles.

On that note: Happy Coding!

Appendix A
Example Scripts and Data

This appendix contains listings that are used in different example programs throughout this book to create an HTML page or to establish a connection to a database as well as a database chart of the example database.

The *HTMLPage* Class

The *HTMLPage* class (Listing A-1) creates the HTML content and ensures that the content is properly encoded to avoid security gaps such as cross-site scripting. *HTMLPage* provides the following methods:

- **__construct($title, $template)**   Title of the page and the file name (optional) of the HTML template is passed to the constructor.

- **printPage()**   Loads the template and creates the HTML page. The content created up to now is displayed with the template.

- **get($name, $escape)**   Method to retrieve properties of the class. *$escape* indicates if the returned value is masked for the HTML view.

- **addElement($name, $content)**   The HTML element *$name* containing *$content* is added to the HTML page.

- **addHTML($html)**   Adds unfiltered content to the HTML page.

- **addTable($content)**   Adds a table to the output. *$content* is a two-dimensional array containing the table data. The first line of the array contains table headings (HTML element <th>).

- **addList($items)** Adds a list to the output. *$items* is an one-dimensional array containing the list entries or a two-dimensional array if the first part should be highlighted.

- **escape($txt)** Masks a passed value to secure the HTML output.

LISTING A-1 HTMLPage.php—using the *HTMLPage* class to create HTML pages.

```php
<?php
namespace net\xmp\phpbook;

class HTMLPage {

    protected $title;
    protected $content;
    protected $template;

    function __construct($title, $template='./template.html') {
        $this->title = $title;
        $this->content = '';
        $this->template = $template;
    }

    /**
     * Displays the created HTML page.
     */
    function printPage() {
        global $page;
        $page = $this;
        require $this->template;
    }

    /**
     * Returns single data fields of HTMLPage.
     *
     * @param string $name Name of the data field
     * @param boolean $escape Indicates if the value for HTML output is masked
     */
    function get($name, $escape=true) {
        if ($escape) {
            return $this->escape($this->$name);
        } else {
            return $this->$name;
        }
    }

    /**
     * Adds a HTML element with text to the page.
     *
     * @param string $name Name of the HTML element
     * @param string $content Content of the element
     * @param boolean $keepWhiteSpace Leave white space as is
```

```
 */
function addElement($name, $content, $keepWhiteSpace=false) {
    $this->content .= "<$name>" . $this->escape($content, $keepWhiteSpace)
                      . "</$name>";
}


/**
 * Adds unfiltered HTML to the page.
 *
 * @param string $html HTML to be added
 */
function addHTML($html) {
    $this->content .= $html;
}


/**
 * Adds a table to the page.
 *
 * @param array $content Two-dimensional array:
 *                       First line contains headings  (<th>)
 *                       The following lines contain data (<td>)
 * @param array $rawHTML Indicates which columns are added as unfiltered HTML
 */
function addTable($content, $rawHTML=array()) {
    $this->content .= "<table>\n";
    // Adds a header
    $this->content .= "<thead><tr>\n";
    foreach ($content[0] as $cell) {
        $this->addElement('th', $cell);
    }
    $this->content .= "</tr></thead>\n";
    // Adds data
    $this->content .= '<tbody>';
    for ($i = 1; $i < count($content); $i++) {
        $this->content .= '<tr>';
        for ($j = 0; $j < count($content[$i]); $j++) {
            if (empty($rawHTML[$j])) {
                $this->addElement('td', $content[$i][$j]);
            } else {
                $this->addHTML('<td>' . $content[$i][$j] . '</td>');
            }
        }
        $this->content .= "</tr>\n";
    }
    $this->content .= "</tbody></table>\n";
}


/**
 * Adds a list to the page.
 *
 * @param array $items List entries. If the entry is an array the first part is
 *                     highlighted and the second part is displayed normally
 * @param boolean $rawHTML Indicates if the entries are added unfiltered.
```

```php
    */
    function addList($items, $rawHTML=false) {
        $this->content .= "<ul>\n";
        foreach ($items as $item) {
            if (!is_array($item)) {
                $rawHTML ? $this->addHTML('<li>' . $item . '</li>')
                         : $this->addElement('li', $item);
            } else {
                $this->content .= '<li>';
                $this->addElement('b', $item[0] . ': ');
                $this->content .= $rawHTML ? $item[1] : $this->escape($item[1]);
                $this->content .= '</li>';
            }
        }
        $this->content .= "</ul>\n";
    }

    /**
     * Masks the text displayed on the HTML page
     * Replaces critical characters with entities and
     * deletes all characters less than chr(32) depending on white space option
     *
     * @param string $txt Text
     * @param boolean $keepWhiteSpace Leave white space as is
     */
    function escape($txt, $keepWhiteSpace=false) {
        if ($keepWhiteSpace) {
            $txt = preg_replace('/[\\x00-\\x08\\x0b-\\x1f]/', '', $txt);
            return filter_var($txt, FILTER_SANITIZE_SPECIAL_CHARS);
        } else {
            $txt = preg_replace('/\s+/', ' ', $txt);
            return filter_var($txt, FILTER_SANITIZE_SPECIAL_CHARS,
                              FILTER_FLAG_STRIP_LOW);
        }
    }
}
```

The HTML Template

The HTML template (Listing A-2) provides the frame for the HTML page output. The template expects an *HTMLPage* object in the *$page* variable to display the title and content (using *$page->get()*).

LISTING A-2 template.html—HTML template for the example application.

```html
<!DOCTYPE  html>
<html>
<head>
    <meta charset="UTF-8"  />
    <title><?php echo $page->get('title') ?></title>
    <style  type="text/css">
        th { font-size: 110%; border-bottom: 2px solid  black }
        td { padding: 3px; border-bottom: 1px solid  #aaa }
    </style>
</head>
<body>
    <h1><?php echo $page->get('title') ?></h1>
    <?php echo $page->get('content', false) ?>
</body>
</html>
```

Note The scripts use PHP 5.3 namespaces. Because no other special features of PHP 5.3 are used, you can run the scripts in PHP 5.2 after you remove all lines containing the namespace definition.

The *DatabaseConnection* Class

The *DatabaseConnection* class (Listing A-3) provides three methods:

- **connect()**   Establishes the connection with SQL Server using predefined parameters.

- **close()**   Disconnects the SQL Server connection.

- **exitWithError()**   Displays SQL Server error messages and exits the program.

If your application requires other connection parameters for the *connect()* method, modify the *$serverName* and *$connectionInfo* class properties accordingly.

LISTING A-3 DatabaseConnection.php—database connection to SQL Server.

```php
<?php
namespace net\xmp\phpbook;

class DatabaseConnection {

    public $handle = null;
    protected $serverName = '(local)';
    protected $connectionInfo = array(
        'Database' => 'AdventureworksLT2008',
        'CharacterSet' => 'UTF-8'
    );

    /**
     * Establishes a connection with SQL.
     * Uses predefined connection parameters.
     */
    function connect() {
        $this->handle = sqlsrv_connect($this->serverName, $this->connectionInfo);
        if ($this->handle === false) {
            $this->exitWithError('database connection failed');
        }
    }

    /**
     * Disconnects the SQL Server connection.
     */
    function close() {
        if ($this->handle) {
            sqlsrv_close($this->handle);
            $this->handle = null;
        }
    }

    /**
     * Closes the program, returns error messages from SQL Server
     *
     * @param string $txt Error description
     */
    function exitWithError($txt) {
        $errors = sqlsrv_errors();
        $html = new HTMLPage('Database error');
        $html->addElement('p', $txt);
        $table = array(array('SQL status', 'Code', 'Message'));
```

```
        foreach ($errors as $error) {
            // Error messages have the ISO-8859-1 format
            $msg = iconv('ISO-8859-1', 'UTF-8', $error['message']);
            $table[] = array($error['SQLSTATE'], $error['code'], $msg);
        }
        $html->addTable($table);
        $html->printPage();
        $this->close();
        exit;
    }
}
?>
```

Example Database: *AdventureWorksLT2008*

The example database *AdventureWorksLT2008* consists of 11 tables in the *SalesLT* schema. The tables are:

- **Customer**   Information about the customer (name, company, email address, …)
- **CustomerAddress**   Connection table between customer and address
- **Address**   Address (street, city, postal code, …)
- **SalesOrderHeader**   Order (order date, customer, weight, total, …)
- **SalesOrderDetail**   Single article in the order (product, price, amount, …)
- **Product**   Product information (name, size, color, photo, price, …)
- **ProductCategory**   Product categories, hierarchy possible
- **ProductModel**   Model of a product
- **ProductDescription**   Product description in a certain language
- **ProductModelProductDescription**   Connection table between product model and product description
- **ErrorLog**   Error log table

In Figure A-1, you can see the database diagram as produced by SQL Server's Database Diagram Designer. Column names are shown for each table, and the tables' primary keys are marked with small key symbols. The lines between the tables depict the one-to-many relationships based on foreign keys.

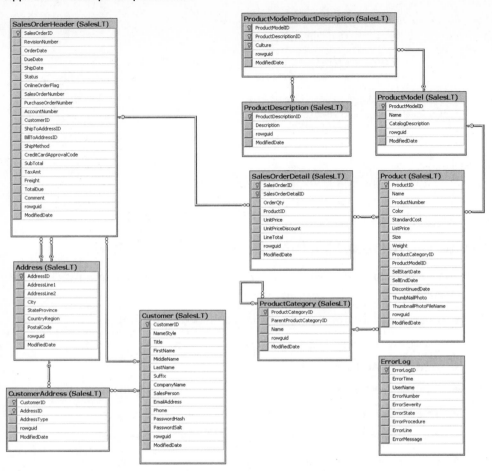

FIGURE A-1 Chart of the example database *AdventureWorksLT2008*.

Index

Symbols

$_ENV global variable, 141
$_SERVER
  variables, 140–143
    CGI, 140
    of an HTTP request, 141
$_SERVER["AUTH_USER"]
  variable, 95
$_SERVER['HTTPS'] variable, 24
$_SERVER['LOCAL_ADDR']
  variable, 24
$_SERVER["LOGON_USER"]
  variable, 95
$_SERVER["REMOTE_USER"]
  variable, 95
$_SERVER['SERVER_ADDR']
  variable, 24
$_SERVER variables
  for client certificate, 113
  for retrieving connection
    and server certificate
    information, 113
__DIR__ constant, 141
__FILE__ constant, 141
[HOST=...] (php.ini file), 65
@@IDENTITY, 241
[PATH=...] (php.ini file), 65
@@ROWCOUNT, 358

A

Abort Request action type (URL
  Rewrite), 144, 152
access
  access control list (ACL), 452
  access rights in Active
    Directory, 451–453
    access control list (ACL), 452
    administrator groups, 452
  identity and access rights, 96–98
    anonymous authentication, 97
    application pool identity, 96
    path logon information, 97
    securing PHP application, 98
  impersonation, 360, 587–590
    by using email address, 589
    by using PrincipalName, 588
    by using SID, 590
    granting rights, 587
    required permissions, 360
    (see also stored procedures)

permissions (SQL Server), 353–355
  common, 353
  database principals, 344
  database roles, 345
  effective permission for
    object, 354
  impersonation, 360
  managing using SSMS, 355–356
  managing using T-SQL, 356–358
  ownership chain, 354
  server roles, 344
  stored procedures and, 358–359
user authentication, 92–95
  authentication against AD, 95
  authorization rules, 98–100
  basic, 92
  digest, 92
  installing required role
    services, 93
  retrieving authentication in
    PHP, 95
  setting up using command
    line, 94
  setting up using IIS
    Manager, 93–94
  Windows, 92
accessing data in SQL Server from
  PHP, 279–318
AdventureWorksLT2008 sample
  database, 279
approach and process, 279
closing database
  connection, 280–282, 284
database connections, 285–291
  authentication, 287–288
  connection pooling, 289–290
  more connection options, 290
  server names, 286
database queries, 291–303
  filtering and masking data,
    292–293
  parameterizing statements, 291,
    293–294
  PDO and, 311–313
  search_products.php sample
    program, 294–297
  SQL Injection, 291–292
data types, 304–316
  converting from PHP to SQL
    Server, 304
  converting from SQL Server to
    PHP, 304–305

  streams, 306–309
  opening database
    connection, 280–282, 283
  PDO driver, 310–316
  preparations, 279–280
  prepared statements, 299–303
    PDO and, 311–313
  product_list.php sample
    program, 280–282
    overview of individual
      steps, 282–284
  retrieving results, 280–282, 284,
    297–299
    as objects, 297–298
    individual fields, 299
  sending query, 280–282, 283
  valid login, 280
accountExpires attribute (domain
  objects), 434
account operators in AD, 452
accounts in AD
  activating and deactivating, 464
  finding users with locked or
    deactivated accounts, 445
  unlocking, 463
<action> configuration
  element, 170
Active Directory (AD), 365, 368,
  372, 385
  access rights, 451–453
    access control list (ACL), 452
    administrator groups, 452
    account operators, 452
  accounts
    activating and deactivating, 464
    unlocking, 463
  administrators, 452
  attribute classes, 426–430
    attributes for, 427
    finding and viewing, 428
    syntax, 428–430
    syntax, adding additional
      information to, 430
    userPrincipalName, 426
  attributes, 458–463
    adding, 458–459
    changing, 461–462
    changing, practical examples
      for, 463
    deleting, 459–461
  authentication against, 95
  Autodiscover and EWS URLs, 498

C

About the Author

Arno Hollosi works as coordinator in the University Department for Information Technologies and Business Informatics at CAMPUS 02, Graz, Austria. After studying telematics, he worked at the Institute for Applied Data Processing, where he focused on cryptography, PKI, and XML. Later, he worked as the technical lead of a special task force at the Federal Chancellery of the Republic of Austria, where he was responsible for the IT strategy, and later as a systems architect and quality manager for Siemens international projects.

What do you think of this book?

We want to hear from you!
To participate in a brief online survey, please visit:

microsoft.com/learning/booksurvey

Tell us how well this book meets your needs—what works effectively, and what we can do better. Your feedback will help us continually improve our books and learning resources for you.

Thank you in advance for your input!